The Future of U.S. Capitalism

U.S. capitalism is slowly changing. The direction of future changes in the institutions and organizations that make up the economic system can best be understood by examining trends of the last half century, by exploring their major determinants and whether these causal forces will continue to influence the future, and by determining what new factors will play a major role in the years to come. Frederic L. Pryor rigorously uses such an approach to present a synthesis of the future path of the economic system. He divides his analysis into three parts.

The first section looks at changes within the economy that will influence the development of the economic system. Among these are the aging of the population and its adverse impact on saving and economic growth, the widening disparities in income, globalization, and, in some ways, the increasing fragility of the financial system.

The second section examines external factors influencing the evolution of U.S. capitalism. These include rising costs of natural resources, certain types of environmental degradation, the nation's declining social capital, and political changes arising not just from internal factors, such as the growing distrust of government, but also from an evolving world political situation.

The third section focuses on institutions and organizations in the economy. In the private sector, the evolving nature of the corporation and the growing concentration of individual markets receive particular attention. In the public sector, particular emphasis is given to the changing roles of government regulation and of public expenditures.

The author has written this study in nontechnical language for those concerned with how the U.S. economic system is evolving. For specialists, he analyzes a variety of technical issues underlying these forecasts in a series of appendices.

Frederic L. Pryor is Emeritus Professor of Economics at Swarthmore College and one of the world's leading specialists in the comparative study of economic systems. His career has spanned both academia and consulting. In addition to teaching at Swarthmore, he has been affiliated with Lincoln University, the University of California at Berkeley, Yale University, the University of Michigan, and several universities in Switzerland and France. His academic work also includes the authorship of 11 books and more than 90 articles in professional journals, primarily on the comparative study of different economic systems.

As an economic consultant and researcher, Professor Pryor has worked at a variety of positions for the World Bank, the commonwealth of Pennsylvania, the Danish government, several departments of the U.S. government, the Soros International Economic Advisory Group, the Hoover Institution, the Brookings Institution, the University of Indiana, and the Wissenschaftszentrum Berlin. He continues to work as a consultant and researcher. Living in Swarthmore, Pennsylvania, he also serves on the boards of several nonprofit institutions.

The Future of U.S. Capitalism

FREDERIC L. PRYOR
Swarthmore College

CAMBRIDGE
UNIVERSITY PRESS

PUBLISHED BY THE PRESS SYNDICATE OF THE UNIVERSITY OF CAMBRIDGE
The Pitt Building, Trumpington Street, Cambridge, United Kingdom

CAMBRIDGE UNIVERSITY PRESS
The Edinburgh Building, Cambridge CB2 2RU, UK
40 West 20th Street, New York, NY 10011-4211, USA
477 Williamstown Road, Port Melbourne, VIC 3207, Australia
Ruiz de Alarcón 13, 28014 Madrid, Spain
Dock House, The Waterfront, Cape Town 8001, South Africa

http://www.cambridge.org

First published 2002

Printed in the United States of America

Typeface Times 10/12 pt.   *System* QuarkXPress [AU]

A catalog record for this book is available from the British Library.

Library of Congress Cataloging in Publication Data available.

ISBN 0 521 81358 1 hardback

To the memory of my parents

Contents

List of Tables in Text   viii
List of Charts in Text   ix
List of Appendices and Accompanying Tables and Charts   ix
List of External Appendices and Accompanying Tables and Charts   xi
Acknowledgments   xiii

Introduction
  1 Setting the Stage   1

Internal Influences on the Economic System
  2 Saving and Economic Growth   26
  3 Economic Fluctuations and Financial Crises   54
  4 Economic Inequality   82
  5 Globalization   112

External Influences on the Economic System
  6 Natural Resources and the Environment   146
  7 Social Factors   175
  8 Political Factors   207

Changes in Crucial Economic Institutions and Organizations
  9 Evolution of Business Enterprises   238
 10 Evolution of Market Competition   261
 11 Evolution of Government Regulation and Ownership   292
 12 Evolution of Government Spending   322

Summary
 13 Whither U.S. Capitalism?   352

Appendices   368
Bibliography   401
Name Index   431
Subject Index   441

List of Tables in Text

1.1:	Types of Capitalist Systems in Early 1990s	12
2.1:	Average Annual Saving and Investment as a Percent of GDP	29
2.2:	Estimates of Future Population Growth and Elderly–Dependency–Ratios	32
2.3:	Initial Simulation	38
2.4:	Different Scenarios of Changes in the Ratio of Net Annual Saving to GDP	40
3.1:	Trends in Financial Fragility and Distress	61
6.1:	Direct and Indirect Consumption of Natural Resources and Agricultural Products by Households with Different Incomes	159
7.1:	Relationship of Social Trend Variables with Other Variables Relevant to the Economy of Key OECD Nations, Mid 1990s	186
9.1:	Ratios of Establishments to Enterprises of Different Size Firms, 1954–1997	246
9.2:	Measures of the Size of Enterprises by the Number of Employees, 1958–1997	253
9.3:	Measures of the Size of Non-Agricultural Private Establishments by the Number of Employees, 1953–1997	255
10.1:	Global Data on the Share of Recent Mergers Within the Same Narrowly Defined Industry (Horizontal Mergers)	263
10.2:	Weighted Four-Digit Concentration Ratios in the U.S., 1963–1992	267
11.1:	Indices of Laissez Faire Micro-Economic Policies for OECD Nations in the Late 1990s	294
11.2:	Trends in Federal Governmental Expenditures on Regulation	303
11.3:	Employment in State Owned Enterprises in Key OECD Nations in 1995	314
11.4:	Composition of the Wealth Portfolios of Private Individuals and the Nonprofit Sector	317
12.1:	The Economic Status of Elderly Families	327
12.2:	Government Expenditures in Leading OECD Nations in 1995 as Percentage of GDP	328
12.3:	Current Public Expenditures (Federal, State, Local as a Percentage of GDP)	332

13.1:   A Classification of the Role of Government in Leading
        OECD Nations in the 1990s   357

Lists of Charts in Text

1.1   Economic Systems of Industrialized Economies   9
3.1:   Financial Volatility Indicators   56
3.2:   Average Daily Foreign Exchange Turnover in U.S.   63
4.1a: Real Family Money Income Levels at Various
        Percentiles in the U.S   85
4.1b: Ratio of Family Money Income Levels to Median Family
        Income in the U.S.   85
4.2:   Certain Factors Underlying Changes in the
        U.S. Income Distribution   99
5.1:   Index of Per Capita U.S. International Communications   129
8.1:   Voter Participation and Trust in Government   213
8.2:   Percent of People Believing Federal Income
        Taxes are "Too High"   217
8.3:   Crime and Punishment   219
9.1:   Estimated Value of Business Mergers   248

List of Appendices and Accompanying Tables and Charts

Appendices

2.1:   Economic Growth Rates, 1950–2000   368
2.2:   Details about the Simulation Model   368
2.3:   The Impact of the Interest Rate on the Saving Rate   371
2.4:   Notes on the Consumption Replacement Ratio   372
3.1:   Sources of Data for Tables and Charts in Chapter 3   373
4.1:   Data Sources for Charts in Chapter 4   375
5.1:   Quantitative Indicators of Globalization   375
5.2:   Sources of Data on Globalization   379
6.1:   Trends: Resource and Environmental Indicators   382
6.2:   Notes and Data Sources for Charts and Tables   387
7.1:   Sources of Data Used in Regressions in Table 7.1   389
8.1:   Data Sources for Chapter 8   389
8.2:   Two Possible Political Outcomes of Declining
        Social Solidarity   391
11.1:   A Formal View of Changes in Governmental Regulation   393

11.2:   Changes in Patterns of U.S. Governmental Ownership   397
12.1:   Gross Investment by the Public Sector   398
12.2:   Two Islands: A Parable about Welfare Expenditures   398

Tables in Appendices
A2.1:   Average Annual Growth Rates of GDP, GDP per
               Capita, and Productivity   369
A2.2:   Changes in the Saving Rate When Other
               Parameter Values are Changed   371
A2.3:   Changes in Net Saving Between 2000 and 2050
               with Different Consumption Replacement Ratios
               and Changes in Population and Income Growth Rates   372
A7.1:   Sources of Data for Social Indicators   390
A11.1:   Selected Federal Actions Directly Affecting
               the Regulation of Markets   394
A11.2:   Trends in the Size of the U.S. Governmental and
               Nonprofit Sectors   396
A11.3:   The Size of the Different Levels of Government:
               Capital Stock and Employment Measures   397
A12.1:   Gross Investment by the Public Sector   399

Charts in Appendices
A5.1a: U.S. Exports and Imports as a Percentage of GDP   376
A5.1b: U.S. Exports and Imports of Goods and Services
               as a Ratio of Exportable Goods and Services   376
A5.2a: Annual Flow of Legal Immigrants
               as a Percent of the Total U.S. Population   378
A5.2b: Percent of Foreign Born in the U.S.   378
A5.3a: International Capital Flows as Percent of GDP   380
A5.3b: Long-Term Foreign Investment of a
               Percent of GDP   380
A6.1a: Food Prices Deflated by the Cost of Living   383
A6.1b: Food Prices Deflated by a Wage Index   383
A6.2a: Raw Material Prices Deflated by the Cost of Living   385
A6.2b: Raw Material Prices Deflated by a Wage Index   385
A6.3a: Air Pollution Indicators   386
A6.3b: Water Pollution Indicators   386
A6.4:   Annual Deviations from Average Temperature
               over the 20th Century   388

List of External Appendices
and Accompanying Tables and Charts*

External Appendices

X-1.1:	Shifts in the Composition of the Labor Force	X-1-1
X-1.2:	Three Popular Views about Systemic Change	X-1-8
X-I.3:	Notes on Systemic Collapse in General and on the Soviet Case in Particular	X-1-15
X-2.1:	Other Population Forecasts	X-2-1
X-2.2:	Some Mathematical Properties of the Simulation Model: Four Notes	X-2-2
X-4.1:	Income Distribution Regressions	X-4-1
X-4.2:	Income Shares	X-4-15
X-4.3:	Income Inequality and Economic Growth	X-4-17
X-5.1:	U.S. Public Opinion about Free Trade and Protectionism	X-5-1
X-5.2:	General Economic Objections to Globalization	X-5-3
X-6.1:	Natural Resource and Agricultural Composition of GDP Aggregates	X-6-1
X-7.1:	More Detailed Data on Social Trends	X-7-1
X-7.2:	Data on Charity and Volunteering	X-7-14
X-7.3:	Sources of Data on "Disconnected Labor"	X-7-18
X-7.4:	Data on Governmental Effectiveness	X-7-19
X-9.1:	Methods of Data Adjustment	X-9-1
X-9.2:	Establishment Size	X-9-2
X-9.3:	Measures of Competitive Dynamics	X-9-4
X-9.4:	Employment Size of Very Large Enterprises	X-9-6
X-10.1	Mergers in "New Economy Industries"	X-10-1
X-10.2:	Changes in Industrial Concentration between 1992 and 1997	X-10-3
X-11.1:	Changes in the Patterns of Private Ownership	X-11-1
X-12.1:	Hidden Expenditures in the Federal Budget	X-12-1

Tables in External Appendices

X-1.1:	Distribution of Full-Time Equivalent Workers by Industry in the U.S.	X-1-2

---

* These can be viewed at my website. http://www.swarthmore.edu/socsci/economics/fpryor1/. A compact disk with these appendices is also in the collection of the McCabe Library of Swarthmore College.

X-1.2:   Distribution of the Labor Force in Various Occupations   X-1-5
X-2.1:   Governmental Forecasts of Future Population
          Growth and Elderly-Dependency-Ratios   X-2-1
X-4.1:   Two Stage Least Squares Regressions
          Explaining Relative Income Levels, 1948–1997   X-4-5
X-4.2:   Augmented Dickey-Fuller (ADF) Tests   X-4-7
X-4.3:   DOLS Cointegrating Vectors and Tests for Cointegration   X-4-9
X-4.4:   Error Correction Model for Changes in Relative
          Income Levels, 1948–1997   X-4-11
X-4.5:   Shares of Different Types of Income
          in the National Income   X-4-16
X-6.1:   Resource Composition of Macroeconomic Aggregates   X-6-1
X-7.1:   Annual Indicators of Personal Charity
          and Volunteering   X-7-15
X-7.2:   Government Effectiveness Index, 1999   X-7-20
X-7.3:   Components of Government Effectiveness Index   X-7-22
X-9.1:   Pareto Coefficients for the Size Distribution
          of Enterprises   X-9-3
X-9.2:   Various Measurements of Establishment
          Size Holding Employment Structure Constant   X-9-5
X-9.3:   Some Data on Large Enterprises from an
          International Perspective   X-9-8
X-10.1   Mergers and the New Economy Industries (NEI)
          in the U.S. Private Sector   X-10-2
X-10.2:   Industrial Concentration Ratios
          (SIC Classification), 1992 and 1997   X-10-4
X-11.1:   Trends in the Size of Nonprofit and
          Cooperative Sectors, Wealth Indicators   X-11-4
X-12.1:   Federal Government: Trends in Off-Budget
          Spending and Tax-Expenditures   X-12-2
X-12.2:   Transfers from the Federal Government
          to State and Local Governments   X-12-6

Chart in External Appendices
X-7.1:   Some Social Indicators   X-7-2

Acknowledgments

Few books are the product of a single person working in an intellectual vacuum, and for this study I needed all the help I could get.

I am especially indebted to those who willingly gave me their time and counsel. For readings the entire manuscript and making many helpful suggestions, I am grateful to Richard duBoff, Dan Pryor, Mil Pryor, and Zora Pryor. For commenting on individual chapters, I greatly appreciate the help of my Swarthmore colleagues: Tom Dee, Robinson Hollister, Philip Jefferson, Mark Kuperberg, James Kurth, Ellen Magenheim, Steven O'Connell, Bernard Saffran, David Smith, Robin Wagner-Pacifici, and Larry Westphal. From other universities I gratefully received similar assistance from Robert Putnam, F. M. Scherer, and Jon van Til.

For other assistance including the supplying of manuscripts, data, or advice, I would like to thank Aaron Catlin, Trey Cole, Philip Everson, James Gwartney, Ted Gurr, Thorvaldur Gylfason, Ross McKitrick, Bjorn Matthiasson, Michael Novak, Martin Paldam, Bruce D. Phillips, Jeffrey Sachs, Kenneth Simonson, Mark Vendamia, Andrew Warner, and Murray Weitzman. I am also indebted to Victoria Wilson-Schwartz, my editor, who tried to turned a sprawling manuscript into readable English; to Audree Penner who set up the book in type; and to Edward Fuller, Diane Modes, and Zora Pryor, who helped with the proofreading. Finally, I would like to thank Swarthmore College for the use of its research and computer facilities.

CHAPTER 1

Setting the Stage

It is difficult to make predictions, especially about the future.

— *Nobel laureate in physics, Neils Bohr[1]*

A half century hence, will it be the best of times, the worst of times—or both? Have we reached the point where our economic system will no longer change—in effect, the end of history? Or is change accelerating at such a pace that our economic system in 2050 will be unrecognizable to most of us today? In the years immediately preceding the beginning of the 21st century, the acerbic dictum of Neils Bohr in the chapter's epigraph was ignored and we suffered a plethora of predictions, most based on little more than a few random anecdotes and what the predictor had for breakfast. This book is quite different—before sketching my views about the future course of the economic system, I want to look systematically at the most relevant evidence.

The usual platitude to justify studying the future is that it will help us make plans. More important, however, such an exercise is useful for understanding what is happening in the present, because it forces us to distinguish transient from more permanent changes. Thus, in this book I explore such questions as: What have been the key trends in the U.S. economic system in the second half of the 20th century and what causes underlay them? If current trends will not continue, what will replace them, and why? At what points do we lack sufficient knowledge, either theoretical or factual, to make responsible predictions about the future?

This is not an exercise in prophecy, but rather an attempt to understand the implications of today's complicated economic reality. Of course, we can make forecasts with considerable accuracy in those cases where a well-understood cause underlies particular systemic changes and where other causal forces do not intervene. However, we reach the limit of responsible prediction in other

---

[1] Cited by Laura Lee, *Bad Predictions: 2000 Years of the Best Minds Making the Worst Forecasts* (2000).

cases where several different causal forces impinge on the economic system and pull it in opposite directions, unless we have good reasons to believe that one set of causal forces is sufficiently strong to prevail over the others. In still other cases, all we can do is speak of tendencies.

An example of such an approach is found in my discussion in Chapter 10 of the implications of the merger wave of the 1980s and 1990s on market competition in the future. I present data showing that such mergers have led to a considerable increase in market concentration over the period. Before predicting that market competition will decline, however, other questions require answers: How much influence will other relevant factors, such as increased foreign trade or the rise of buying and selling over the internet, exercise on the future state of competition? How long will this merger wave continue? Will these merged enterprises prove successful or will they later fall apart into their constituent parts? Both the data and the theories presented in this chapter allow considerable clarification of many of these issues, and I argue that there will be a strong tendency toward a decrease in market competition. Nevertheless, a firm prediction about the future of market competition is not possible from merger considerations alone. In brief, we can discuss the future of the economic system in a methodical fashion and set up direction signs for turning points, even though much of what will actually happen will depend on certain policy decisions that are difficult to predict.

In this chapter I address the following issues in turn: alternative approaches for analyzing the future; some ways in which alternative forms of capitalism can be defined; methods by which causes of change in economic systems can be systematically examined and forecast errors can be minimized; and finally, a very brief preview of the rest of the book.

At this point, I must also point out that this book comes in three quite separate parts: the discussion in the text; the brief discussion of particular points and the listing of certain source materials in the appendices contained in this book; and the more extended analysis of certain ideas and assertions that are contained in the "external appendices," which can be found at my specially created website: www.swarthmore.edu/SocSci/Economics/fpryor1/. The contents of the various external appendices are listed in the table of contents of this book.

A. Approaching the Topic[2]

Let me start by saying what this book is not about. It is not about the economy *per se*, that is, the way we will live and work and what technology has in store for

---

[2]   In this section I refer to the following sources: U.S. Commission on National Security (1999),

us. Rather, it is about the institutions and organizations through which economic activity is channeled. This distinction receives greater attention below. It also does not concern itself with how the economic system should evolve or how the economic aspirations of U.S. citizens can best be realized. Rather, it focuses on changes most likely to occur, regardless of whether they are desirable or not. In brief, it is an exercise in positive, not normative, economics.

During most of the second half of the 20th century, the changing U.S. economic system was viewed from the perspective of "capitalism versus communism." But after the collapse of the Soviet economy, the question has become more subtle and more interesting: What kind of capitalism will we have?

Some seem to believe that we have reached the most efficient and stable economic system possible, that any future change will be relatively unimportant, and that the subject does not deserve further consideration. But to suppose that economic history will suddenly cease to be interesting once it has reached the beginning of the 21st century defies our experience of systemic change in the 20th century. In part, such a view springs from a failure of imagination and an aversion to change.

Some seem to believe that the future is so unknowable that prediction is worthless. We can only wring our hands in utter frustration and lament along with the historian Immanuel Wallerstein[3]:

> We have entered a time of troubles. The outcome is uncertain. We cannot be sure what kind of historical system will replace the one in which we find ourselves. What we can know with certainty is that the very peculiar system in which we live, and in which the states have played a crucial role in supporting the processes of the endless accumulation of capital, can no longer continue to function.

Such overarching fatalism is inappropriate. Many aspects of economic reality are not subject to random change; they are cumulative and influenced by causal forces which, to a certain extent, can be analyzed. Moreover, the economic system—which is the focus of this analysis—usually changes relatively slowly.

Finally, some seem to believe that the next half-century will bring dramatic changes to the economic system, so that it will barely be recognizable to those

---

Gallopin, *et al.* (1997), Halal (1986), Kahn (1979), Rifkin (2000), and Wallerstein (1999, p. 75.)

[3]   The intellectual justification for such a position can be quite fancy, resting, for instance, on complexity theory that emphasizes the existence of "points of bifurcation" or "qualitative leaps" when the system veers far from equilibrium. This means that we can neither predict when such changes will occur nor what the outcome will be and can only rely on airy abstractions such as "small events can have large effects" while "large events have only small effects."

of us who live long enough to see its new incarnation. According to Jeremy Rifkin, markets will give way to networks and ownership will become less important. Others foresee that work will become more flexible; organizations will become more decentralized and organic; and economic scarcity will become less severe. Moreover, bandwidth will be unlimited; the information revolution will make us more knowledgeable and perhaps wiser; society will coalesce again; and the government sphere will drastically shrink. By way of contrast, I believe that power and wealth will continue to be important in coming decades; that economic scarcities will persist and, therefore, so will conflicts of interest in the allocation of goods and services; and that the dead hands of history and custom limit possible changes in the economic system.

Because so many past predictions of the future have proven so spectacularly wrong, in recent years many futurists have turned away from making simple forecasts. One increasingly common approach is scenario analysis, in which the future is imagined on the basis of alternative assumptions. What would happen in the coming decades if population continues to grow exponentially and raw material scarcities become acute? Or if population stopped growing and material scarcities become less acute? What would happen if the pace of globalization accelerates, but in a way such that developments are structured by a series of *ad hoc* arrangements between governments, rather than the decisive interventions of some type of future world government? How would these scenarios of the future be different if human nature were more or less adaptable to particular forces of change? Some take this approach one step further and envision alternative future worlds. For instance, in 1986 William Halal foresaw only three main possibilities of the U.S. economic system in 2000: greater corporate domination, more control over the economy by government bureaucracies, or "democratic free enterprise." From an equally broad perspective, the U.S. Commission on National Security/21st Century foresees the world economy in terms of four possibilities: globalism triumphant; a democratic peace of cooperating but sovereign nations; nationalist protectionism; or division and mayhem.

Such scenario exercises are extremely useful for contingency planning (by individuals, business firms, and governments) and for exploring the implications of certain crucial decisions or changes of a set of crucial parameters of the economy. Some, such as Herman Kahn or Gilberto Gallopin, have provided imaginative and insightful analyses. Nevertheless, scenarios are not predictions unless supplemented by additional analysis. That is, we have no assurance about the probabilities of the various scenarios or whether all of the most likely possible outcomes are explored. Although such an approach permits a limited number of concrete possibilities to be taken into account in a vivid and stimulating fashion, it can obscure underlying (and impersonal) causal forces by placing too much weight on our ability to change the course of history.

My approach is different. Because I stress analysis of the causes underlying various changes, I generally focus on the most likely outcomes. In cases where counteracting forces are at work, such as an acute scarcity of raw materials (Chapter 6) or a variety of possible changes in demographic variables (Chapter 2), alternative scenarios must, of course, be specified. Although I often try to indicate when policy interventions might be helpful, in many cases it does not seem likely that such measures will be taken, because of the relative strength of contending political interests. Moreover, in certain cases, such as the slowdown I predict in future economic growth (Chapter 2), governmental intervention to ameliorate the problem is limited because the major cause cannot be greatly influenced by policy, namely a demographic shift resulting in a change in the ratio of active workers who save and retired people who draw down their savings.

B. Possibilities of Capitalism[4]

Most studies of the future dealing with economic matters focus on the economy; I focus instead on the economic system. After briefly distinguishing between the two concepts, I examine a variety of different types of capitalist systems to show the possible directions that the U.S. economic system might take.

1. The Economy

The economy consists of the myriad activities involved in production, consumption, and the distribution of goods and income. Production involves the use of technology, natural resources, land, labor, and capital, both physical and human (such as education). Distribution occurs not only through the market but through gifts, grants, non-market trades and various governmental measures such as transfers, subsidies, or tax breaks.

Much has been written about the future of the economy. Leaving aside forecasts about technology ("in 2050, every home will have robots carrying out the major share of the housework"), several crucial arguments play an important role in such analyses and it is worthwhile to review briefly three of the most important and credible propositions (see External Appendix X-1.1 for more detailed supporting evidence).

---

[4]   In the text of this section I refer to studies by Bell (1973), Esping-Andersen (1990), Pryor (1996), and Soskice (1999).

One prediction is called Petty's "law": Over the course of economic development, the labor force shifts away from agriculture toward manufacturing and thence to services, an hypothesis that receives ample empirical support. Two serious problems with this approach arise: First, since services are carried out in all sectors, the share of the labor force in the formal "service sector" depends upon the degree to which such services are spun off into separate entities. Second, "services"are undifferentiated and, since various services currently employ more than three quarters of the labor force, this law is not too helpful for discussing the future.[5]

Another important prediction, amply supported by evidence for past years, is that the share of the labor force producing information will increase, while the share of workers producing goods or homemaking services will decline. In short, the knowledge industries are gaining in relative importance, a phenomenon obvious to anyone at the end of the 20th century, but not to many a generation ago when pioneering social scientists such as Daniel Bell originally pointed out this development.

Yet another hypothesis is that the economy will develop a more complex structure. In this context structural complexity refers to three phenomena: the information requirements for the system to function; the heterogeneity of decision-making units (for instance, individuals or firms); and the extensiveness of the interrelations between different sectors of the economy. Elsewhere I develop a series of quantitative indicators to demonstrate increasing structural complexity of many aspects—but not all—of the economy.

Many other interesting hypotheses have been offered about long-term trends in the economy. It is, however, not my intention to review them here, because few have great relevance to the economic system *per se*. That is, these trends, like those summarized by Petty's law or the shift in occupational structure or the increasing complexity of the economy, have occurred in industrial economies, regardless of system. They are neither system-determining nor system-deter-

---

[5]   Many have tried to repair this second failing. Daniel Bell (1973) suggested dividing services into three groups: industrial services (transportation and utilities), business services (trade, finance, insurance, and real estate) and human services (health, education, research and development, recreation and entertainment, government). A much different approach is to divide the various industries in the economy according to whether they deal primarily with other businesses (either providing goods or services) or, instead, with consumers (providing goods or services), either in a business or a non-commercial relationship. This exercise is carried out in External Appendix X-1.1 and shows that in the U.S., the share of the labor force producing and moving goods at a distance has considerably declined, while the share of those providing services to other businesses or consumers has increased, and, finally, the share of those providing collective services (education, social services, and government) increased up to 1975 and then leveled off for the next quarter century.

mined, but, instead, are a function of economic development and technological change.

It is, of course, necessary to give attention to changes in the economy to show the context of the future economic system. But this is not my primary concern.

2. The Economic System

According to a common formulation, an economic system consists of institutions and organizations. Institutions consist of the rules, laws, and customs that constrain and guide economic activities. Organizations are groups of individuals working together for at least one common purpose and whose joint actions have an impact on the allocation of goods and services, for instance, a corporation or a cooperative. The interaction of institutions and organizations generates mechanisms that lead to production, distribution, and consumption of goods and services, for instance, particular kinds of markets or governmental allocations.

While such an abstract approach does not take us very far in predicting the fate of U.S. capitalism, it does help us frame the topic at hand. It means, for instance, that in discussing the economic system, we must take into account not only strictly economic factors but also political and social factors, at least in so far as they influence economic outcomes.

Capitalism is commonly considered to be an economic system with three major features: (i) markets serve as the primary means by which goods, services, and factors of production (land, labor, and capital) are allocated; (ii) the rights of private property are crucial and the owners' prospect of receiving profits serves as a primary incentive for their engaging in economic activities; and (iii) the direct roles in the economy of collective organizations such as the government, the church, or charitable foundations are relatively small. Unfortunately, this kind of definition is so general that it obscures the differences between various kinds of capitalism.

I can illustrate contrasting forms of capitalism by presenting two other ways of looking at economic systems of industrial nations. The first is a broad approach, taking into account various combinations of political, social, and economic factors; the second is a narrower approach that focuses on certain microstructural aspects of the system. In later chapters, I look briefly at still other major differences in the institutions and organizations of capitalist systems.

3. Capitalist Systems: A Broad Approach

From this perspective economic systems can be defined in terms of three dimensions:

One dimension is primarily political—the relative importance of governmental participation in the economy through expenditures, regulation, or ownership of the means of production. Government expenditures include not only the financing of such traditional functions as diplomacy, internal or external security, or education but also investment to provide the physical and human infrastructure of the economy, subsidies to encourage particular types of production, and transfers of resources from one group to another. Governmental regulation includes not just micro-economic rules that constrain and guide particular economic activities, but also monetary and fiscal policies that are designed to stabilize the economy either through the governmental budget or the central bank.

The second dimension is almost exclusively economic—the extent to which open and competitive markets influence the economy, in contrast to markets characterized by oligopoly or monopoly or markets heavily influenced or modified by social or religious constraints.

The third dimension is primarily social—the degree of social solidarity. This designates not just the extent to which people agree on the basic ground rules regulating their economic interactions and are able and willing to work cooperatively on projects of mutual interest, but also the isolation of particular social groups from each other on the basis of income, race, or some other characteristic. The economic implications of social solidarity are manifold and include the relative importance of charitable giving; the willingness of the population to tax itself in order to equalize income and life chances; the honesty and efficiency of the government; and the readiness to resolve economic differences through negotiation and other social mechanisms that submerge individual interests in the interests of the entire society. In the following chapters I focus particular attention on social trust, "social capital," and inequality, which are three measurable manifestations of social solidarity.

These three dimensions of capitalism can be combined, as shown in Chart 1.1. Such an exercise yields eight different types of economic systems, and it is relevant for the rest of my argument to focus brief attention on those in the lower part of the diagram where the government influence is relatively low.

Americans are most familiar with the liberal market economy, where social solidarity is sufficient to insure general agreement on a set of ground rules for carrying out economic activities, and a generally accepted mechanism is available to enforce them. Although American individualism may seem antithetical to social solidarity, this social bond is sufficiently strong to allow market transactions to occur with a minimum of friction.

If both social solidarity and governmental influence are low, we have anarchy of the type described by Thomas Hobbes as a war of one against all. Examples of such a system are seen in various types of chaotic economies in the past or, to a certain extent, in the Russian economy of the 1990s. The existence of such economic systems puts in sharp relief the key role social solidarity plays in liberal capitalism.

In an economic system composed primarily of large corporations with little competition and with a subservient or accommodating government, we have oligarchic capitalism. The society and economy are dominated by a relatively small number of corporate executives with a high degree of political and economic power. In the following chapters I pay considerable attention to the possibility that the U.S. economic system is moving in this direction.

If social solidarity is high but open economic competition is low, disputes can be settled through negotiations of capital, labor, and consumer (or governmental) interests on an industrial or national level. I designate such an economic system as decentralized corporatism. In the first years after World War II, the economic systems of both Austria and the Netherlands began to move toward such a system. In more recent years, however, such national negotiations have given way to negotiated agreements on the industry level, a phenomenon receiving attention in the next typological exercise.

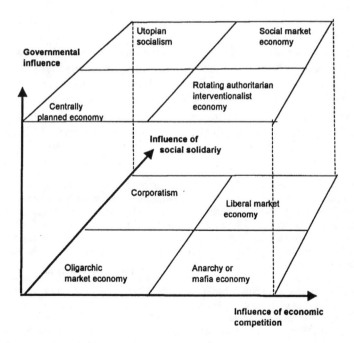

Chart 1.1. Economic Systems of Industrialized Economies

In the following chapters I specify particular economic roles of the U.S. government that will increase and decrease in importance. Nevertheless, I argue that the overall governmental influence on the U.S. economy will probably not greatly increase. For the purposes of this discussion, therefore, it is not relevant to consider the other four economic systems in the diagram.[6]

What is important is to determine the direction along each of these axes that U.S. capitalism has been traveling and whether it is likely to change course. In the second half of the 20th century the U.S. economic system moved toward increased governmental influence and, in the last quarter of the century (as argued in Chapter 7), decreased social solidarity. Key themes of this book are that, in the coming decades, social solidarity will continue to decline, as well as market competition, and, as a result, the U.S. economic system will move from a liberal market economy toward an oligarchic market economy.

While Chart 1.1 provides a useful organizing device, it does not begin to cover all the different dimensions of capitalism and does not capture certain key social and political dimensions. For instance, the chart says nothing about the type of government, so that two types of liberal (in an economic sense) capitalist systems can be found in the same part of the chart, one with a democratic government, the other with an authoritarian government that does not greatly intervene in the economy (for example, the economic system in Chile under General Augusto Pinochet).

Because of the qualitative nature of the three dimensions, such an approach also does not readily allow quantitative comparisons between, let us say, different OECD nations. Nevertheless, it does permit us to organize a qualitative discussion of some major directions in which the U.S. economic systems might change. Since multiple causal forces are acting on most economic systems, such a schema also permits us at the end of the book to line up the various forces dis-

---

6   A situation where both social solidarity and economic competition are low, and where the government allocates resources, represents a centrally planned economy. Such an economic system has both communist and fascist versions, depending on whether property is owned (and profits are taken) by the government or by private interests.

An economic system where both open economic competition and social solidarity are high, but where the government plays a major role in redistributing income is the welfare state or a social market economy.

Two less familiar economic systems can also be specified. A rotating authoritarian, interventionist economy occurs in a police state where strong governmental intervention is necessary to keep certain aspects of the economy functioning and yet open economic competition occurs in many parts of the economy and the authoritarian leaders are often changed (even, perhaps, by some type of election), so that different economic interests take control from time to time.

Utopian socialism occurs when both the government influence and social solidarity play key roles and little open economic competition occurs. This system appears unstable.

cussed in each chapter in a systematic manner, so that possible directions of overall change can be established. For instance, if the social glue holding the economy together dissolves (see Chapter 7), liberal capitalism might be slowly replaced by Hobbesian anarchy or mafia capitalism. But if other causal forces are working in other directions and if industrial consolidation continues unabated (Chapters 9 and 10), the U.S. might arrive at oligarchic capitalism. If income inequalities continue to increase (Chapter 4), the U.S. might be pushed toward a rotating authoritarian, interventionist economy, if only to maintain domestic political order. Or a serious ecological crisis that cannot be mastered by market incentives (Chapter 6) might move the U.S. economic system toward a centrally planned economy.

In brief, the chart although incomplete provides a useful way of structuring the discussion so that we can separate and relate the consequences of a large number of possible causes.

4. Capitalist Systems: A Narrower Economic Perspective

Other ways of looking at various capitalist systems allow more quantitative comparison. The typology discussed below focuses on more strictly economic phenomena and uses two dimensions that have been explored by a number of European economists. Such an approach reveals some major differences between U.S. capitalism and that of most other OECD nations.

One crucial distinction in the production sphere is the degree to which economic activities such as labor negotiations, apprentice programs, the setting of standards, allocation of credit, or even research are carried out either at the company level, the industrial level (for instance, by trade associations) or at the national level (by various types of joint committees of representatives from industry, labor, and government). If the government plays primarily a coordinating role, such supra-enterprise activities represent a type of corporatism (in Chart 1.1) David Soskice presents evidence that such supra-enterprise coordination also has an important impact on those lines of production in which the nation has a comparative advantage.

A second crucial distinction is the type of governmental participation in the economy. In a particularly insightful analysis of the relation between citizen and state, Gøsta Esping-Andersen distinguishes two contrasting approaches toward governmental welfare expenditures. Some governments base their welfare transfers on the principle that all individuals have an entitlement to the same monetary amount, a system I label "universal welfare system." For instance, all might receive roughly the same old age pension, independent on what they had previously contributed to the pension system. Other nations tailor such transfers to

Table 1.1. *Types of Capitalist Systems in Early 1990s*

	Universal welfare systems	Particularistic welfare systems
High coordination of productive activities above the enterprise level	Austria, Australia, Belgium, Denmark, Finland, France, Germany, Netherlands, Norway, Sweden	Italy, Japan, Switzerland
Low coordination of production activities above the enterprise level	New Zealand, U.K.	Canada, U.S.

Note: For the distribution of nations according to their welfare system I use the evaluations of Esping-Andersen (1990), who defines this ranking in terms of "decommodification of labor." For coordination I use an unweighted average of scales of "centralization" and "coordination" by the OECD (1997-a, p. 71), scaling the pluses or minuses as an eighth of a point. The OECD shows (p.73) that their rankings are quite similar to those of nine other studies. The rankings by Soskice (1999), which are based on the degree of interlocking directorates of large enterprises in the various countries, are also quite similar.

individuals on the basis of either their economic need (defined by some governmentally established standards) or their previous work; I label this approach a "particularistic welfare system."

Table 1.1 combines these criteria and places various OECD nations in the appropriate quadrants. The results show that the institutions and organizations of U.S. and Canadian economic systems are quite different from those of other OECD nations. While this kind of typology is highly suggestive, we must avoid two possible errors of interpretation.

• No simple one-to-one relationship exists between the types of capitalist system shown in Table 1.1 and various indicators of economic performance. For instance, the type of welfare system and the coordination above the level of the enterprise are not significantly related to the growth of per capita GDP, other possible causal factors held constant.[7] Contrary to expectations, the inequality of family income is not significantly related to the type of welfare system, although it is inversely related to coordination of production above the enterprise level, other factors held constant. Such results do *not* mean that the eco-

---

[7]   In these regression experiments the explanatory variables were the per capita GDP, the ratio of

nomic system defined according to these criteria has little influence on economic performance, but rather that we must proceed with caution.

Given that no single type of capitalist system clearly outperforms the others, there is also little reason to believe that various types of capitalist systems will converge toward a common model along these characteristics.[8] This result also means that U.S. capitalism is not necessarily superior or inferior to these other economic systems.

• The placement of economies along the two dimensions of the typology cannot be easily tied to other features of their society. For instance, my experiments to use results from the World Value Study to determine if such data would predict the placement of various nations in Table 1.1 were totally unsuccessful.[9] That should come as no surprise because the economic system of a particular nation is the outcome of a complex mix of historical, economic, political, and social factors that do not easily lend themselves to such a simplistic approach.

Of course, many other typologies of capitalism can be constructed, depending on the purpose of the discussion. For instance, I draw on quantitative analyses of the relative importance of government expenditures, regulation, and ownership from industrialized OECD nations to construct Table 13.1. This analysis shows—not unexpectedly—that the U.S., the U.K., Japan, and Switzerland are the nations where the government plays the smallest role in economic life along all three dimensions.

To provide perspective on U.S. capitalism, I carry out in this book a number of comparisons between various industrialized OECD nations. In almost all cases the U.S. appears almost alone at one extreme, and the results in Table 1.1 preview these findings. Such exercises provide evidence from the economic sphere of "American exceptionalism," a theme that intellectuals and scholars from various disciplines have been exploring for the last several centuries.[10]

---

trade to GDP, the logarithm of the population, and the system variable, all for 1995. The variables to be explained included were per capita GDP growth from 1985 to 1995 and a measure (Gini coefficient) of family income inequality, corrected for size of family.

8   Freeman (2000) carried out a useful empirical analysis of such lack of convergence in the area of labor-market institutions.

9   Using national data from Inglehart, Basañez and Moreno (1998), I carried out several statistical experiments using factor analysis. None of the derived dimensions revealed any correlation of rankings with the countries in Table 1.1. Simple correlation of various value scales did, however, yield some surprising results. For instance, scales for three values composing the alleged "protestant ethic" namely thrift (Variable 232), hard work (V-228), and entrepreneurship (V-323), yielded quite different rankings of the various OECD nations.

10   Almost three hundred years ago travelers and scholars began to remark on the difference

Given that the U.S. economic system has had a much different past than that of most other industrialized nations, and that its present configuration of institutions and organizations is also special, it seems likely that the future U.S. economic system should also be unique. Even the economic systems of Canada and the U.S., which appear in the same quadrant in Table 1.1, operate quite differently in other ways, so that their future economic systems will probably diverge as well.

As a result of American exceptionalism, we cannot learn about the future of U.S. capitalism by looking at the future of capitalism in general. Obviously, changes in other capitalist nations will influence developments in the U.S. Nevertheless, for better or worse, the fate of the U.S. economic system will be special, a function of its unique past and present.

C. Change in Advanced Capitalist Systems[11]

As noted above, I reject the view that U.S. capitalism will not greatly change. I also reject the hypothesis that change in the U.S. economy and economic system is accelerating and will continue on this rising path in the coming decades. The arguments underlying these assertions are presented in External Appendix X-1.2.

In analyzing how economic systems change, neoclassical economists would argue that we should follow the great Victorian economist Alfred Marshall, whose watchword was the Latin aphorism "nature does not take leaps." As a result, he focused on incremental or marginal changes in institutions, economic organizations, and economic variables. But according to the recent theory of punctuated equilibrium, we must employ a slightly different watchword, namely "nature only occasionally take leaps." I might also add that from a long historical perspective some of these leaps in economic institutions and systems

---

between the old and new worlds. By the 19th century remarks about "American exceptionalism" usually included the key notion of the lack of a feudal tradition in the new world, for instance, a poem by Goethe (1988 (1825?)) ("America, you have it better than this old continent, You have no crumbling castles and fallen battlements. And in these present times you have no blight, of useless memories or senseless fights...."). The most careful and lengthy assessment is by deTocqueville (1969 (1835)). In the 20th century this intellectual tradition continued with the useful studies by Louis Harzt (1955) and Seymour Martin Lipset (1996). In the narrower field of economics, books by Michel Albert (1993) or Charles Hampden-Turner and Alfons Trompenaars (1993) provide interesting insights. Contrary to the impression gained from Table 1.1, there are also significant differences in the economic system of Canada and the U.S., as argued by Lipset (1996, Chapter 3; and Card and Freeman (1993)

[11]   In this section I refer to my research published in Pryor (2000-c).

appear to be only short hops or pirouettes; witness, the rapid rise and similarly speedy fall of fascism in the 1930s and 1940s or of centrally planned socialist systems in Eastern Europe from the late 1940s to 1990.

Because economic systems usually change more by evolution than by revolution, structural discontinuities do not often occur and, moreover, they are notoriously difficult to predict. Sometimes such structural changes result from the outcome of political struggle. In other cases the underlying cause is technological change, and in the future, the advances in biotechnology, genetics, or in nano-technology might have such an impact. In the coming decades, climatic change or acute scarcities of key raw materials such as oil might also result in a structural leap of the economic system. Finally, for certain institutions and organizations, changes in government economic policies might also have such an effect.

In some cases in later chapters, I try to indicate where such structural discontinuities might arise, even though they may be impossible to foresee or, in many cases (for instance, where technology is involved), to imagine. Nevertheless, both to avoid taking too many flights of speculative fancy based merely on subjective hunches and to stay close to the available empirical evidence, I base my argument on the assumption that such structural wildcards will not have an enormous influence on the future evolution of American capitalism in the next half century.

Further discussion of my analytic techniques for studying the future of U.S. capitalism does not seem necessary at this point. Nevertheless, it is worthwhile to mention briefly certain techniques that I avoid. For the most part I eschew systematic scenario analysis, because the number of permutations and combinations are endless and tax both the patience and the memory of the reader. I also avoid placing too much emphasis on single causes—a favorite device of those writing science fiction or sketching utopias and dystopias, because, in most cases, many causal factors influence outcomes (often in opposite directions). Finally, I do not find it necessary to employ highly technical econometric forecasting techniques, primarily because the critical parameters underlying institutional and systemic change do not easily lend themselves to such an analysis.

In brief, I am trying to analyze the most probable future of the economic system on the basis of the best information currently available, not on the entire range of possible changes that the economic system might experience. I focus more on the *petits pas*, rather than any possible and unpredictable *grand jeté*, that the economic system might take. To keep the analysis orderly, I also separate the immediate causes of systemic change into two basic sets: internal and external.

Internal forces are immediately related to the economy and include globalization, gradual changes in technology such as the relative fall in communication costs), shifts in the demographic structure, or policy blunders by the government. I argue in External Appendix X-1.3 that the latter were a major cause of the collapse of the Soviet economic system. Dysfunctional operations of major economic institutions or organizations also serve as an important impetus for change. For instance, the relatively poor economic performance of the U.K. from 1950 through 1980 played an important role in encouraging new political forces to move the economic system from one of the most statist economies in Western Europe in the early 1960s to one of the least by the end of the century (see Chapter 13). Economic events which are politically intolerable represent another internal cause of change. For instance, in the U.S. many governmental regulations on banks in the 1990s originated in the 1930s as a direct response to the bank failures during the Great Depression.

External forces include changes in the ecological, social, and political circumstances, trends discussed in Chapters 6 through 8. Ecological changes include raw material scarcities or increasing pollution and global warming. Changes in the political environment not closely related to the economy include those attributable to wars, shifting ideologies and attitudes toward government, and evolving configurations of civil society. Some of these external causes of systemic change are difficult to predict, while others lend themselves to systematic analysis. A major purpose of my discussion is to sort through the possible external forces acting upon the system to determine which permit responsible forecasting.

Such a focus on immediate causes of change to the economic system should not, of course, blind us to the fact that the ultimate causes may be different. For instance, the ultimate cause of a change in the external environment, such as pollution or global warming, might be unregulated economic activities; and the ultimate cause of a change in the income distribution might be political or social. Nevertheless, the distinction between immediate external and internal causes of change allows us to go about the analysis of specific causes in a relatively simple fashion, without having to solve the deep problems of ultimate causation.

Although economic systems can mutate into quite different forms in a slow and evolutionary fashion, few people are conscious of these major structural changes. This lack of awareness stems in part from the complexity of the system, especially since it is difficult to measure and understand these structural elements. Indeed, many of these changes represent abstractions far removed from most aspects of normal daily life. This lack of awareness is also due to the passage of time and the isolation of one generation from the experience of another—grandchildren usually have little knowledge of the concrete circumstances of how their grandparents lived. My purpose is to increase awareness of such systemic changes.

D. Approaches toward Prediction[12]

My approach toward prediction—and, more modestly, the specification of tendencies—is influenced by the dismal track record of futurology. I then draw certain brief lessons from these shortcomings.

1. Lessons from the Past

At the 1892/93 World's Fair in Chicago, some eminent Americans were asked to make their predictions about the U.S. a century hence. These short essays, published in a book by Dave Walter, make amusing reading. A series of radio broadcasts in the late 1960s asked another select group to make their predictions about what the U.S. would be like in 2000. These broadcasts, published in a book by Irving A. Falk, evoke a similar reaction. How could the forecasts have been so mistaken?

Some of the errors are elemental. Many forecasters confused the world as it should be with the world as it actually will be. Many confused a "possibility" with a "high probability," and let their fantasies run amok, paying little attention to the close connection between past and future. Finally, many disregarded Talleyrand's ardent exhortation that we must, above all, avoid enthusiasm. Thus, we have intelligent public personalities like Hubert H. Humphery predicting in the late 1960s that by 2000 we will be living on the floor of the ocean, utilizing tides as energy sources; scientists will have virtually eliminated bacterial and viral diseases; robots will be used for everyday work; we will speak a universal language; we will control the weather; and commercial transport will be carried out by ballistic missiles.

The record of prophecies concerned with technology and science is similarly disappointing. In a fascinating book Steven Schnaars presents a catalogue of prediction errors made in the 20th century by alleged experts.[13] He examines, for instance, a well-known set of forecasts made by two highly regarded futurists, Herman Kahn and Anthony J. Wiener, for the year 2000 and shows that only about 25 percent of their predictions were realized. Even when more people are drawn into these exercises in prediction, the record of success is not much better. For instance, when *Industrial Research* surveyed 1,433 scientists and engineers in 1968 about the predictions in the Kahn-Wiener list, they proved grossly

---

[12] In this section I refer to studies by Anon. (1920), Anon (1968), Bell (1973), (1976), Gordon and Helmer (1964), Humphrey (in Falk (1970)), Kahn and Wiener (1967), Schnaars (1989), and Walter (1992), and Wise (1976).

[13] George Wise's (1976) study of predictive success is also useful, even though it is much less

optimistic: slightly less than one third of the major technological breakthroughs that they expected to occur between 1975 and 2000 actually came about.

The margin of forecast error depends, of course, on the subject of the predictions and the period for which the predictions are made. From an interesting set of predictions made in 1920 in *Scientific American*, I calculate that roughly 65 percent were actually realized by 1950. But most of these predictions are banal—for instance, that a bridge would be built where the Golden Gate bridge now stands in San Francisco. In 1958 the RAND Corporation carried out a more ambitious study, utilizing a Delphi technique (a structured interaction between the predictors) and an all-star cast of scientists. According to my calculations, only about 25 percent of the predictions made about advances in the pure sciences or in space exploration by the year 2000 were actually realized.[14] One unnamed participant noted in the Appendix of this study: "I believe that one overwhelming breakthrough ... is imminent in the field of behavioral sciences. It will be a realization that we cannot successfully predict the [technological] future because its nature depends on discoveries as yet unmade and inventions as yet uninvented."

Accurately forecasting the *impact* of such technological changes is no easier. George Wise looked at the predicted social, political, or economic effects of particular technological changes and found incredible blunders, for instance, the forecast in 1900 that automobile usage would never take hold. Only 25 percent of all these predictions of effects came true, a result to give pause to those confidently discussing the impact of e-commerce (see Chapter 10) on competition.

In the political and economic field such prediction errors are, of course, legion. Before World War II, few predicted the fall of the colonial system. After the war, few foresaw the rise of militant Islam. In the economic field, few foresaw the energy crisis, the dramatic economic success of South Korea and Taiwan, or the rise and fall (and rise again?) of Japanese industry. Accurate prediction of the long-term behavior of certain economic variables such as population or GDP has also proven elusive. For instance, writing in 1967 Kahn and Wiener predicted that in the year 2000, the U.S. population would be 318.4

---

plete than Schnaar's. I find it depressing that it is outsiders, rather than those in the forecasting mainstream, who carry out research on prediction errors. For instance, the various contributors to the anniversary issue of *Technological Forecasting and Social Change*, 62, No. 1 and 2 (August/September/1999) were so busy congratulating themselves that none worried about whether the enterprise in which they were engaged had any validity.

[14] If any additional proof is needed about the weaknesses of the Delphi technique for forecasting, it can be found in an essay by Tashakori, *et al.* (1988). They used this methodology to predict that between 1988 and 2000 there would be a significant decline in individualism in America!

million, when it actually turned out to be closer to 275 million. It is noteworthy that about half of the U.S. population in 2000 was alive in 1967, which means that their prediction error appears even worse than at first sight.

Perhaps the worst record of prediction is in the social realm, particularly by those who have the strongest faith in "progress" of the perfectability of humankind. But many of these "forecasts" are too casual to deserve analysis.

Many false prophecies are, of course, random guesses based on little evidence other than hunches and anecdotes. In this regard we must keep in mind the observation attributed to Cato the Elder, "I wonder that a soothsayer doesn't laugh when he sees another soothsayer."[15] Cicero adds, "For how many things predicted by them really come true? If any do come true, then what reasons can be advanced why the agreement of the events with the prophecy may not be due to chance."

Other wrong predictions are due to an insufficient appreciation of the randomness of events and margins for error. In making their population forecast Kahn and Wiener were surely aware of the considerable fluctuations over time in birth rates and the fact that birth rates in the middle 1960s, when they made their forecast, were relatively high. They chose, for reasons unknown, to believe that the situation in the 1960s would last at least for the next three decades.

An even deeper and more subtle forecasting error in these studies arises because the predictor focuses attention on causal relationships that are true only if all other causal factors are held constant and, as a result, does not examine the behavior of these other causal factors. For instance, many have argued that the retirement age will fall without taking into account that our longer life expectancy means that more accumulated savings are needed to finance retirement.

Fortunately, the future of social and economic structures appears easier to predict than particular events or variables, in large part because structures usually change only slowly and, in many cases, the causal variables are clearer. A well-known example is the work of Daniel Bell on changes in contemporary capitalism and the coming post-industrial society. Starting with ideas about the shift of the labor force to services and to knowledge-intensive occupations, he argues a number of propositions that have subsequently become commonplace, for instance, that post-industrial society will be organized around knowledge (of which a central element is theoretical knowledge), that education will more and more be the key to social mobility and economic advancement, and that power will be defined increasingly in terms of institutional position, rather than just personal wealth. He also argued that as the economy shifts more to services, labor unions will lose power and membership. From such an approach he made

---

[15] Cited by Cicero (1926, p. 429).

a number of startling and insightful predictions which I draw upon in later chapters.

Nevertheless, events have shown Bell to be overly optimistic about the pace of change and totally wrong about major aspects of the economic system. For instance, he argued:

> A post-industrial society ... is increasingly a communal society wherein public mechanisms rather than the market become the allocators of goods, and public choice, rather than individual demand, becomes the arbiter of services. A communal society by its very nature multiplies the definition or rights—the rights of children, of students, of the poor, of minorities—and translates them into claims of the community. The rise of externalities ... turns clean air, clean water, and mass transit into public issues and increases the need for social regulation and controls. The demand for higher education and better health expands greatly the role of government as funder and setter of standards. The need for amenities, the cry for a better quality of life, brings government into the areas of environment, recreation, and culture.

Perhaps Bell confused what ought to occur, losing sight of political and economic feasibility.[16] Or perhaps people are less rational than Bell had assumed. Or perhaps Bell was simply extrapolating from a few decades in the past and did not realize that around the middle 1970s, trends in both government regulations and expenditures would sharply change.

2. My Approach

From the mistakes of others, I draw five short but important lessons:

First, I make a conscious effort not to confuse how I want the economy to evolve with how it actually *will* evolve. I find disheartening many of the changes I foresee.

Second, forecasting the future requires a careful study of the past and present. For this reason I spend considerable effort not just trying to unearth current trends but also to determine their causes and to ask whether these causal forces can be expected to operate in the future.

---

[16]   In a recent book Robert J. Samuelson (1995) develops these points made by Bell and then argues that we can't afford the taxes to pay for such entitlements, so that a cutback in governmental expenditures is necessary. For my own views on trends in public expenditures, see Chapter 12.

Third, I rely much more on statistics than on anecdotes. Much of the analysis of the economic system and its evolution must, by necessity, be statistical, because this is the only way in which the aggregative impact of many different events can be evaluated. I try, however, to present the data in a fashion that they can be readily understood and to illustrate what they mean through relatively concrete examples. For the specialists or those wishing further proof, I place the technical details of these calculations and most of the sources in a series of appendices.

Fourth, I try from the very beginning of the analysis to take into account the uncertainties surrounding any forecasts. Sometimes this means presenting a range of estimates or heavily qualifying my conclusions to take particular contingencies into account.

Fifth, at a certain point in all speculations about the future, it becomes impossible to make any kind of responsible forecast. We may not understand exactly what is happening in the present; the underlying data for making the forecasts may not be very good; or too many causal factors may enter the picture and it may not be clear which is strongest. Some phenomena which could greatly influence the future of capitalism, for instance, the rise of the internet, might be still too new to understand all of their implications. Or, the government, churches, or other agencies might step in to solve certain problems if key people come to recognize the difficulty and believe they can help to solve it. In brief, because we are not all-knowing nor passive witnesses to our fate, the future is, to a certain extent, indeterminate. In many instances in the following discussion, I simply note that we have reached the limits of responsible prediction and move to another topic.

E. Plan of Attack[17]

In Chapters 2 through 5, I look at four of the most important internal causes of change of the economic system. These include slower economic growth, because of the adverse impact of demographic changes on saving; increasing fragility of the economy particularly in the financial sphere; adverse changes in the inequality of income; and trends toward international economic integration (globalization) and a possible future backlash against this trend. In some major respects my evaluation of these factors differs considerably from the majority view of the economics profession, at least as recorded in the recent "Millennium Survey."

[17] In this section the Millennium Survey among economists is by Pryor (2000-b) and reference is also made to public opinion studies of the Pew Research Center (Pew, 1999).

In Chapters 6 through 8, I examine some important external forces of change of U.S. capitalism. These include the impact of changes in the physical environment, as well as social, and political changes. In contrast with many well-known futurists, I argue that a deteriorating physical environment or raw material scarcities will probably have a minor impact on the economic system (even though it may have a major effect on the economy), while, by way of contrast, declining social cohesiveness will play a crucial role in the future economic system. The discussion of political factors focuses not just on wars and revolutions, but on more subtle phenomena, such as declining trust toward government, which will, in turn, influence the future economic role of the government.

The next four chapters focus directly on the emerging new economic institutions and organizations. Chapters 9 and 10 deal with changes in the structure of the private sector, particularly regarding the size of enterprises and the degree of industrial concentration in individual markets. In contrast to the conventional wisdom, I present evidence that the new information technologies are leading to larger, not smaller, enterprises and that market competition is decreasing as well. In Chapters 11 and 12, I discuss changes in governmental intervention in the economy, particularly regarding public regulation of production, the extent of public ownership, and public expenditures. Despite the weakening of certain governmental policy making tools and a decline in government regulation, in part due to globalization, I argue that the role of government in other aspects of the economy, particularly public expenditures, will increase in importance.

Although I focus most analytic attention on the government and the private profit-making sectors, the U.S. economic system has a number of other institutional and organizational complexes that require attention if we are to gain a fuller view of how the entire system will evolve. These complexes include home production, the underground economy, and the nonprofit and cooperative sectors. These receive brief attention in Chapters 7, 8, and 11 respectively.

Chapter 13 provides an overview. In certain instances, the analyses in particular chapters point to changes in the opposite direction, so it is necessary to assess which set of forces is stronger. I also turn back to the diagram in this chapter and argue that it is most likely that U.S. capitalism will move toward an oligarchic market economy, rather than remaining as it currently is, or moving either toward corporatism or a social market economy. Undoubtedly, my own subjective biases influence how much I weigh the various forces in play, but readers can, if they wish, make their own estimates from the raw materials that I present.

To keep the book readable, I try to minimize footnotes and bunch the references at the beginning of each section by author and date. Those wishing fuller citations can then consult the bibliography. The appendices contain notes on the statistical sources and methods of estimation. They also present short essays on specialized topics mentioned in the text that some may feel deserve further elucidation but that are not of direct relevance to the main discussion.

In brief, I try to provide a guidebook to understand the changes that might befall U.S. capitalism, to specify the indicators by which they can be observed, and to assess some of their major economic impacts. Three warnings are, however, necessary: If you are looking for a set of easy-to-read, airy speculations about our economic future that are stated with absolute certainty and are based on a set of piquant anecdotes, my advice is to turn either to astrologers or to social science fiction. If you are looking for policy prescriptions, either to hasten the advent of a particular new economic system or to preserve the old, you will likewise be disappointed: my primary purpose is to diagnose, not to prescribe. In economics as in medicine, however, diagnosis is necessary before the proper remedies can be considered. Finally, if you wish confirmation or positive feedback to the hyper-optimism about the future of U.S. capitalism revealed in surveys of general public opinion surveys, this book is not for you. Although it is not my intention to make pessimism fashionable among economists again, I show that the U.S. economic system faces some very serious problems in the coming decades.

INTERNAL
INFLUENCES
ON THE
ECONOMIC
SYSTEM

CHAPTER 2

Saving and Economic Growth

At A.D. 2000 one can retire with a comfortable income
at the age of 50; and retirement will be compulsory
at 60, except for those with skills in scant supply.

— *Author R.G. Ruste, 1967*[1]

    A thousand years ago at the dawn of the second millennium, the prevailing opinion in Europe was deep pessimism—most felt that the end of the world was at hand. At the dawn of the third millennium, hyper-optimism reigned, at least in the United States. According to a large segment of the business media and many leading economic commentators, the U.S. had finally achieved the "new economy": the business cycle had been tamed; growth of productivity had taken a quantum leap upward; and prosperity lay ahead as far as the eye could see. Such enthusiasm arose from two sources. Performance of the U.S. economy during the second half of the 1990s had been remarkable—unemployment and inflation were down, and GDP and productivity growth were up. According to a new and fervent secular faith, as we entered the post-industrial world, information technology, combined with the infinite business possibilities offered by the internet, would usher in a new era. By the time these lines are read, such optimism might appear as naive as the apocalyptic predictions appearing a millennium ago.

    A majority of economists, however, were not so sanguine as the population as a whole, according to a survey of the profession presented in the Millennium Survey. The economists foresaw a rate of productivity growth in the coming decades only slightly higher than in the past. Moreover, in the background contrary voices—my own included—were muttering that the recent decline in the national saving rate (saving/GDP) would continue, as the ratio of retired workers drawing down their savings to active workers building up their savings would rise. This, in turn, would lead to a lower investment rate and, under believable circumstances, to a lower per capita growth rate of the GDP.

---

[1]   Cited by Laura Lee, *Bad Predictions: 2000 Years of the Best Minds Making the Worst Forecasts* (2000). Richard Erdos (1988) discusses the European state of mind in 1000 A.D. The results of the Millennium survey appear in Pryor (2000-b).

I begin by discussing the building blocks for such a pessimistic analysis, namely, productivity growth, saving, and demographic change in the recent past. The next two sections present a simple simulation model that shows how the saving rate falls as life expectancy increases and the baby boomers begin to retire. The fourth section examines some critical implications of the decline in the saving rate on the economy, particularly slower economic growth and a deflation of the price of financial assets. The final section outlines some important impacts of these developments on the economic system.

A. The Building Blocks: Productivity, Saving, and the Age Structure[2]

1. The Alleged "New Economy": Growth of Production and Productivity

Economic performance in the U.S. slowly deteriorated in the second half of the 20th century until the last five years of the 1990s. Nevertheless, the economic successes of the last five years of the century gave rise to the notion that we are entering the "new economy." I present more precise data on these matters in Appendix 2.1.

Determination of the causes of this productivity surge is a knotty problem. According to popular belief, the impact of the revolution in information technology, the increased use of computers, and the rise of the internet underlay this quantum leap. Dark-horse candidates include the increasing use of new management techniques[3] and the introduction of a new generation of computer-guided machine tools that result in greater precision, less use of energy and materials, and higher quality (and fewer repairs) of the finished product. The exact impact of computers and information technology deserves examination.

Dale Jorgenson and Kevin Stroh argue that the fall in computer prices, which averaged 28 percent a year from 1995 through 1999, underlay the enormous increase in investment in computing and telecommunication equipment during this period. And productivity allegedly increased accordingly. The key question is the degree to which the acceleration in productivity can be traced to technological advances in the computer, telecommunication and associated industries

---

2 In the text of this section I refer to studies by Bosworth, Burtless, and Sabelhaus (1991), Gokhale, Kotlikoff, and Sabelhaus (1996), Gordon (2000), Jorgenson and Stiroh (2000), Lee and Tuljalpukar (1994), Nordhaus (2001), Oliner and Sichel (2000), Parker (1999), Quinn, (1999), and Tobin and Sommers (2000).

3 The use of "lean production techniques" is of particular importance. These techniques include just-in-time inventory systems, elimination of batch processing, and a new perspective in the production of goods and services, all described by Womack and Jones (1996).

(hereafter, "the new economy industries") or to a general advance in productivity across the entire economy.

At the turn of the millennium the general consensus of economists was that productivity changes in the new economy industries, which accounted for a small share of GDP, were responsible for one half or more of the productivity changes in the entire economy. Robert J. Gordon points out that productivity always rises in the upswing of the business cycle (when capital and labor are utilized more efficiently) and takes the dramatic position that when this effect is factored out, the productivity changes in the economy as a whole were entirely due to the productivity advances in the new economy industries. This means that the information technology revolution did not have a measurable impact on productivity in the economy except in the narrow group of new economy industries. Two other studies, by Oliner and Sichel and by William Nordhaus, dispute Gordon's calculations and, using quite different methods, estimate that roughly half of the productivity changes for the economy as a whole can be traced to the rise in productivity in the new economy industries (Nordhaus, however, focuses only on labor rather than total factor productivity). This means that the remaining industries also experienced an acceleration in productivity during the second half of the 1990s, although not to the extent of the new economy industries. Finally Jorgenson and Stiroh, utilizing still other statistical methods and a more massive data set than the others, arrive at results somewhere between those of Gordon and the other two studies. They also reach another interesting conclusion. "There is no evidence of spillovers from production of information technology to the industries that use this technology ... the empirical record provides little support for the 'new economy' picture of spillovers cascading from information technology producers onto users of this technology."

Jorgenson and Stiroh also find few grounds for believing that the blinding pace of technological change in the computer and telecommunications industry in the late 1990s will continue forever, a conclusion I find highly plausible. They argue further that if such technological change should diminish, economic growth would "be hit with a double whammy—slower total factor productivity growth in important industries that produce high-tech equipment and slower capital accumulation in other sectors that invest in and use the high-tech equipment."

In brief, in the last five years of the 1990s. the fall in computer prices led to an increase in the capital used by workers, so that an important share of the productivity increase can be traced to more capital per worker. All of the studies find that at least half—and perhaps more—of the total increase in productivity of the economy as a whole can be traced to changing productivity in a small group of industries, a conclusion considerably different from the conventional wisdom. If, as argued below, saving will dramatically decline, forecasts of economic growth in the future becomes even more bleak.

Table 2.1. *Average Annual Saving and Investment as a Percent of GDP*

Line number	1950s	1960s	1970s	1980s	1990s
Domestic saving: NIPA estimates based on flows of income and expenditures					
1. Total gross domestic saving	21.1%	21.0%	19.7%	18.5%	17.0%
2. Private	15.8	17.1	18.4	19.2	17.2
3. Personal	5.2	5.7	6.8	6.7	4.6
4. Business	10.6	11.4	11.6	12.6	12.5
5. Governmental	5.3	4.0	1.3	-0.8	-0.1
Domestic saving: Federal Reserve estimates based on flows of income and expenditures					
6. Personal saving	7.3	7.3	8.0	8.5	4.3
Domestic saving: Federal Reserve estimates based on asset data (balance sheet data)					
7. Change in net worth (tangible and financial assets)	18.8	18.9	25.5	26.9	26.6
Investment: NIPA data					
8. Total gross investment (private + government)	21.2	20.7	20.4	20.5	18.6
9. Depreciation	10.5	10.2	11.1	12.5	12.3
10. Foreign investment (- = net capital outflow)	- 0.1	-0.6	-0.2	1.5	1.2
11. U.S. financed investment (line 8—line 10)	21.3	21.3	20.6	19.0	17.4
12. Net domestic investment (line 8—line 9)	10.6	9.9	9.1	9.5	7.5

Note: Both the saving and investment series omit expenditures on consumer durables. All personal saving series include non-profit organizations along with households and exclude consumer durables. The sum of various parts may not add up to the totals because of rounding. Total domestic saving (line 1) and investment (line 11) are slightly different because of statistical discrepancies in the underlying data.

The official NIPA data (national income and product accounts) for the 1950s are not completely compatible with the data from 1960 onward. The data come from the U.S. Department of Commerce, Bureau of Economic Analysis (1998-b) and website: (http://www.bea.doc.gov/bea/dn1.htm), Tables 5.1 and 5.2.

The flow of funds data come from the website of the Board of Governors of the Federal Reserve: (http://www.bog.frb.fed.us/releases/z1/Current/data.htm), Table F-9. The asset data come from Table B-100.

2. Saving and Investment Rates

In the last few decades of the 20th century, saving and investment rates were falling. Because a greater fall of the domestic saving rate in the next half century is a key to my argument about declining investment and economic growth in the future, some historical perspective of the behavior of these variables is necessary.

Table 2.1 shows how rates of saving and investment were falling over the second half of the 20th century. Because my focus is on economic growth, I omit expenditures for consumer durables (for instance, refrigerators and cars) both from the saving and investment data (which usually include them.) Two sets of such statistics are available, the official national income and product accounts (NIPA) produced by the Department of Commerce and the flow of funds accounts produced by the Federal Reserve Bank, which are based on different statistics and use a somewhat different definition of saving from the NIPA estimates.[4]

The flow data reveal several noteworthy trends. The domestic saving rate, shown in line 1 of Table 2.1, slowly declined over the entire period. The fall was particularly dramatic in the 1990s when personal saving (line 3) fell considerably and was not offset by an increase in business saving (line 4). Although the investment rate (line 8) in the 1980s and 1990s was buoyed by a large inflow of foreign funds (line 10), it was not enough to offset the fall of domestic saving in the 1990s. As a consequence, the investment rate fell as well, since investment must equal the saving to finance it—you can't spend what you don't have.

Various arguments are offered to explain this fall of the saving rate during the 1990s. Some analysts such as Berry Bosworth, Gary Burtless, and John Sabelhaus or Jonathan Parker argue that this fall in the saving rate occurred in all age groups.[5] Others, such as Jagadeesh Gokhale, Laurence Kotlikoff, and John Sabelhaus argue that the fall came from a redistribution of income from the young to the old and also from a fall in the saving rate especially of the elderly, due to a declining need for saving both for bequest and precautionary purposes.[6] Still others stress the fact that since most saving in the U.S. in recent years

---

4   Gale and Sabelhaus (1999) carefully dissect and analyze the various official definitions of personal savings.

5   Using SIPP (Survey of Income and Program Participation) data, Venti and Wise (1996) argue the reverse, namely that in recent years personal saving has increased, particularly as a result of governmental tax measures to encourage saving for retirement. These calculations are highly controversial.

6   Saving for precautionary purposes has declined because of the expansion of various types of government insurance programs (disability insurance, unemployment insurance, life-span

has been through unrealized capital gains, much of the lower rate of saving, at least measured in traditional ways, is due to the definitions employed by national income accountants. The exact impact on the flow of saving of this increase of wealth is, however, hotly disputed.[7] While these various microeconomic effects are important in the short-run, I show in the analysis below that long-term shifts in the age structure of the population will prove to have a more lasting impact.

The estimations of saving in Line 7 of Table 2.1 are based on balance sheet information of individuals (saving = change in net worth valued in current year prices) and include the unrealized capital gains. They reveal a much higher saving rate than the flow data and indicate no noticeable decline in the 1990s. Part of this "saving" merely represents the increase in the value of assets that arose when the general price level (including prices of assets) increased. Another part of this higher saving represents the unrealized capital gains occurring when the price of assets rose faster than other goods and services, so that their owners would receive additional purchasing power upon sale. In the case of corporate securities, this reflects a general rise in Tobin's q ratio (measured by James Tobin and Dan Sommers), which is the price of a company's equities in comparison to the replacement value of that company's plant and equipment.[8] In the last years of the 1990s this was particularly manifest in the enormous (but temporary) stock market valuations of new dot.com companies which had low sales, few physical assets, and no record of profits. Their value is also volatile, a matter discussed in more detail later and also in Chapter 3, where I discuss financial crises.

---

insurance through Social Security, etc.) that help families reduce risk. Moreover, the rising share of wealth held in annuities such as Social Security and private pensions eliminates the precautionary savings needed to prevent outliving one's assets. Some argue convincingly that the savings for bequest purposes declined because of the deterioration in family solidarity, as shown by the declining share of the elderly living with their children and the rising fraction of marriages ending in divorce (Chapter 7).

[7]   Parker (1999, p. 26) presents evidence that the effect of unrealized capital gains accounts for no more than a small share of the fall of the saving rate as conventionally measured by flows. I argue below, however, that this wealth effect may become considerably more important in the future. Auerbach and Kotlikoff (1990) provide evidence that in the 1980s, certain other factors, such as the increasing ratio of government expenditures to the GDP, the high deficits of the federal government at that time, various saving disincentives, and the behavior of stock prices can explain only a very small fraction of the change in the saving rate. They also dismiss another set of hypothesized causes such as business cycle conditions, changes in income equality, and an increase in female labor force participation.

[8]   The rise in unrealized capital gains can also be seen in the ratio of financial to total assets held by individuals. From the 1950s through the 1980s, this ratio slowly fell; in the 1990s, however, it suddenly rose about 9 percent.

Table 2.2. *Estimates of Future Population Growth and Elderly-Dependency-Ratios*

	Average annual population growth	Elderly-Dependency Ratios		
		1960	1980	1995
	1960–1995			
Actual data	1.08%	17.6%	19.8%	21.9%
Forecasts:	1995–2050	2010	2030	2050
Low population growth	0.03	22.3	40.9	51.5
Median population growth	0.63	22.3	36.4	39.1
High population growth	1.23	22.6	33.1	30.6

Note: In this table the elderly-dependency-ratio is defined as the ratio of the population 65 and older to those in the working ages from 20 up to 65. Low and high estimates are defined in terms of the 95 percent confidence limits around the median population growth. As noted in the text, the margin of error is large.

The current data come from U.S. Council of Economic Advisers (annual, 2000). The forecasts are by Lee and Tuljalpukar (1994). They offer a more lucid explanation of their stochastic estimating procedures in Lee and Tuljalpukar (1998). Their estimates are slightly different from those presented above, due to the log normal distribution used in their projections. I estimate the elderly-dependency-ratio directly from their population estimates, rather than from their direct calculations of this ratio, in order to achieve consistency with the other estimates in this chapter.

External Appendix X-2.1 presents other forecasts of the U.S. population in 2050.

Given these conflicting interpretations of the fall in the saving rate in the last two decades of the 20th century, no definite conclusions can be drawn. My argument below, however, is grounded on quite different factors than have received attention so far.

3. Demographic and Labor Force Changes

As everyone knows, in the future the U.S. population will become older. This aspect of the population structure I will call the *elderly-dependency-ratio*, which is the ratio of the elderly (those 65 and older) to those in the working ages (those from 20 up to 65). Demographic projections of the age structure vary considerably from source to source, in major part because of different methods used for estimating birth, death, and immigration rates, all of which influence the age structure. In the rest of this chapter I employ estimates by Ronald Lee and Shripad Tuljalpukar (hereafter L-T), since they are based on the most sophisticated methodology available at the time of writing, namely probabilistic estimates of mortality and fertility. This permit estimation of the margins of error of the forecasts.

From the population projections presented in Table 2.2, we can draw two simple conclusions. First, the nation is facing a dramatic rise in the elderly-dependency-ratio in the next half century. Second, it is hard to predict exactly how high the rise will be. For instance, the L-T calculations give a 95 percent probability that in 2050 the elderly-dependency-ratio will lie somewhere between 30.6 and 51.5 percent, which is an enormous margin of error. This means that in the analysis of future saving, we must consider a number of possible demographic scenarios.

The elderly-dependency-ratio is one of the key determinants of the *retirement-ratio*, which is the ratio of retired to active workers. The two ratios differ because some elderly remain in the labor force, while others less than 65 are retired. As argued below, the retirement-ratio is a critical factor for the determination of the national saving rate because it focuses on the relative number of retired workers who are drawing down their savings (very few of the elderly live exclusively on asset income) and the number of active workers who are building up their savings. Several other factors must, however, also be taken into account in determining the retirement-ratio:

• *Life expectancy is increasing.* In 2000 a person of 65 could expect to live 15 more years; by 2050 this will be much closer to 20 years. Moreover, due to advances in medicine, the group of "young-old" (those between 65 and 75) will be healthier than a generation before.

• *Older workers.* Causal forces determining the number of workers more than 64 in the labor force differ somewhat for men and women. Joseph Quinn shows that from the mid-1960s to the mid-1980s, the share of men from 60 to 69 in the labor force declined. Since then, however, this percent has leveled off. For women in the same age cohort and in the same period, the pattern was more irregular. In general, however, their percentage participation in the labor force remained roughly the same until the mid 1980s, but thereafter it began to increase slowly. The number of elderly workers also depends on economic circumstances. In the 1990s many of those who, in an earlier era, would have retired were taking either bridge jobs or postponing retirement. A variety of factors underlay this development: improved health status of the elderly; evolving patterns of home ownership and of the availability of private pensions; changes in mandatory retirement laws; Social Security payments to the working elderly; and the degree to which inflation eroded the real value of savings.

These demographic considerations have two important implications for the estimates of future rates of saving. First, it is necessary to take both the rising life expectancy and the possible postponement of retirement explicitly into account. Some argue that the retirement age will decrease, despite longer life expectancy. Given the large portion of the population with few assets at age 65 (discussed in Chapter 12), a further decline in the average retirement age seems unlikely and, throughout this discussion, I investigate two scenarios: that the retirement age will remain the same and that it will rise. Second, if the customary retirement age remains the same, future cohorts will have to have a higher annual saving rate to finance the longer retirement period brought about by the longer life span. If, by way of contrast, future cohorts extend their working years so that their total length of retirement remains the same, then they will need to save less each year while they work because they will be able to accumulate retirement funds over a longer lifetime in the labor force.

B. The Impact of Demography on Saving [9]

The major tool for analyzing the impact of demography on saving is a simple simulation model that allows us to consider the impact of a number of possibilities in a coherent fashion. The model combines some insights from recent studies on the relation between demographic structure and saving[10] with the power of the recent vintage of generational accounting models, especially by Alan Auerbach and Laurence Kotlikoff and by Hans Fehr and Laurence Kotlikoff. I start off with a very stylized situation which is far from the real world, namely hyper-rational active and retired workers making decisions to build up or draw down their savings. Once, however, the mechanics of the model and the major results are clear, I relax these assumptions and bring the analysis closer to reality to show that the insights gained from the stylized model generally hold in situations that we are more likely to encounter in the coming decades. Although other factors also influence personal saving, many can be easily brought into the analysis in a qualitative fashion.

1. The Model

I first divide the L-T population estimates (Table 2.2) into workers and retirees, with workers including all those from 25 up to some prespecified retire-

---

[9]   In the text of this section I refer to studies by Auerbach and Kotlikoff (1990), Fehr and Kotlikoff (1994), and Gokhale et al. (1996).

[10]   Recent empirical studies on population structure and saving include those of Mason (1990), Paxson (1996), and Bloom and Sachs (1996). Recent demographic-economic simulation models employing this type of data include those of Lee, Mason, and Miller (forthcoming-a,b) and Cutler, Poterba, Sheiner, and Summers (1990). Most of this type of simulation work is carried out for the developing nations in order to analyze the effect of the demographic transition on growth.

ment age.[11] In the real world, of course, only a fraction of those between 25 and the retirement age participate in the labor force and the number of retirees must be multiplied by a similar fraction in order to determine the retired workers. The value of this fraction, however, has no impact on the simulation results which focus on changes in the net saving rate for the nation.

Workers are assumed to have labor income increasing at a fixed percent each year for their working lifetime. With full knowledge of how their incomes will change up to their retirement, the active workers save (or draw down their savings) so as to have during retirement a certain fraction of their average consumption during their working lifetime (the *consumption-replacement-ratio*). More specifically, they will borrow when they begin their working life, pay off their debts and save during middle age, and then draw down their savings when they retire so that they will smooth out their consumption stream over their entire lifetime. I discuss what this consumption-replacement-ratio might be later in the chapter, as well as in greater detail in Appendix 2.4.

After making a guess about the future growth and interest rates when they enter the labor force, the workers simultaneously decide their consumption-replacement-ratio and their saving ratio during their working years; if one of these ratios is known, the other can be easily determined. Moreover, in the lifetime income approach toward saving that is used in this discussion, both depend on the degree to which savers value a dollar's worth of consumption now and during their retirement. Nevertheless, as I show below, it is simpler to look at the saving decision in terms of the consumption-replacement-ratio, rather than the annual saving ratio and the relative value of present and future consumption. Moreover, my approach also allows us to see connections between many other economic phenomena which, up to now, have been considered unrelated.

At the time of death, which is assumed to be known, all individuals will have exhausted their savings and leave no inheritance. Although the model features complete certainty about the age at death, this is not essential to the calculations.[12] To simplify calculations, I assume four age groups: one cohort of active workers and three cohorts of retired workers (65–69, 70–84, and over 84). Within each cohort, I also assume that the population at each age within the separate cohorts is numerically the same. This has little impact on the results and simplifies the calculations by allowing the calculations for one worker to be easily

---

[11] In starting the simulation, I assume that in 2000, people begin working at 25 and retire at 65, so that their working life of 40 years is roughly similar to that occurring around 2000. This means that the L-T population estimates of the 20–64 cohort in Table 2.2 have to be modified accordingly. In various simulations, however, I change this assumption about the length of the working life.

[12] Alternatively, the date of death is not known but all retirees purchase an annuity from an insurance company that knows exactly the average age of death and has no administrative costs.

aggregated for the entire population in the cohort and, at the same time, simplifies interpretation of the results. The initial model assumes an equilibrium situation, with the only sources of change coming from shifts in the age structure, the life expectancy, and the retirement age.

Finally, as noted above, I assume the workers to be hyper-rational. The future growth and interest rate that they use in their saving decision are the same as the actual growth and interest rate in the years to come. Later I look at more realistic situations.

In brief, these are the rules of the initial simulation game. Given these assumptions, the actual choice of the saving rate depends on the consumption-replacement-ratio, the interest rate, and the annual growth of labor income. A concrete example is in order: If the initial income of all workers is $100, if their desired consumption-replacement-ratio is 1.0, if they work 45 years and retire for 15, if their income growth is 1.8 percent a year, if the annual interest rate on savings is 3 percent, then they would plan to consume $122.50 each year during their work life. As a result, they would borrow in their early working years, pay off these debts later, and save enough during the last two decades of their working life so that their total savings (plus interest on this account) would be sufficient to finance an annual consumption at $122.50 during their 15 years of retirement. From the same data we can calculate that the ratio of their accumulated savings at retirement to their total income (work income plus net interest income) over their working lifetime will be about 21.8 percent. This simple numerical example shows what is happening to particular individuals; the aggregation of the saving (or dissaving) of individuals at various ages allows calculation of the national saving rate.

The assumption that workers exhaust their savings by time of death means, of course, that they have no bequest motive for saving. This simplification may not be totally unrealistic at the beginning of the new millennium. That is, I follow the argument of Jagadeesh Gokhale and his colleagues that the high U.S. divorce rate and the high mobility of both children and their parents (either divorced or still married) mean that contact between family members is decreasing and the urge to leave large sums to descendants is ebbing. This is reflected in the writings of personal advice columnists in the late 20th century, such as Ann Landers, who continually emphasized that parents owe their children nothing after raising them and paying for their education. A flippant example of this attitude is provided by the sight of white-haired drivers crouched behind the steering wheels of expensive cars with bumper-stickers reading "I'm spending my kid's inheritance."

One implication of this model is that the average consumption of retirees is usually a fraction of the consumption of current workers, unless the consumption-replacement-ratio is considerably above unity. This is because the income of retired workers, when making their consumption and saving decisions, is less than those currently in the labor force. For instance, in the above numerical example, retirees between 70 and 84 will consume only about 60 percent of what a current worker is consuming.[13] Moreover, if the rate of the growth of average income increases, the average consumption of retirees becomes an even lower fraction of the average consumption of workers because the gap between the annual income during the working years of the two groups becomes greater.

There are several small strings to be tied up so that the model can be viewed as a whole. To make my simulations consistent with the L-T population forecasts, I assume that between 2000 and 2050, the life expectancy will annually rise by 0.1 years so that in 2050 it will be 85. I also assume that interest income (or borrowing costs) consist of transactions with an "external financial sector," which is simply a bookkeeping device to keep the financial flows balanced within the model. Net income flows from this external sector are not, however, very great. I further assume that in 2000, workers start working at 25 and plan to retire at 65 so that they can have 15 years of retirement.

Nevertheless, the model allows the planned retirement age to be raised as life expectancy increases. The presence of dependents under 25 does not appear explicitly in the model, but, as shown below, changes in the consumption-replacement-ratio can take changing family size into account. Details of the simulation model, as well as other assumptions to simplify the calculations, are outlined in Appendix 2.2.

In brief, the core of the model combines the annual calculation of the saving of workers and the dissaving of retirees, using projections of the U.S. demographic structure to derive the number of workers and retirees. I have not specified the institutional context of saving, for instance, whether it occurs through the Social Security system or through withheld business profits which are used for investment purposes. The hyper-rationality assumption means that individuals who have the Social Security accounts or who own the businesses take fully into account the saving carried out by these institutions in their name when they make their decisions about how much of their personal income they will personally save. Certain aspects of the model can also be described mathematically, an exercise carried out in External Appendix X-2.2.

---

[13] In actuality, per capita consumption of those over 65 is about 79 percent of those between 25 and 65, most likely because Social Security benefits have been raised in a fashion to narrow the consumption gap between generations. My model does not take this phenomenon directly into account but, as argued in greater detail below, raising these benefits has the same effect as raising the consumption-replacement-ratio because it lowers the current consumption of active workers and raises the consumption of retired workers.

Table 2.3. *Initial Simulation*

Parameters			
Population growth	0.63% (median L-T estimate for entire population)		
Consumption-replacement-ratio	1.0		
Participation rate	1.0		
Interest rate	3.0%		
Annual per capita growth of labor income	1.8%		
Retirement and age of death			
2000	65 and 80 years		
2050	70 and 85 years		
Statistics on annual saving		2000	2050
Ratio of saving of workers to total production		25.1%	22.5%
Ratio of dissaving of retirees to total production		11.7	13.8
Net saving (gross saving minus gross dissaving)		13.4	8.7
Change in net saving (percentage points)		-4.8%	

Note: Totals may not add because of rounding. Prices are assumed to be stable.

2. The Main Simulation Results

The model is now ready for a trial run. Let's assume that the real interest rate is 3 percent, that there is no inflation, and that per capita incomes are growing at 1.8 percent. If the age of retirement rises to 70 by 2050 and if, at the same time, the life expectancy increases to 85, the ratio of net saving of the nation (that is, the saving of the workers minus the saving drawn down by retirees) to total income will fall 4.8 percentage points. These initial simulation results, presented in more detail in Table 2.3, represent my judgement of the likely outcome in 2050 and will serve as the baseline for other simulation experiments.

Several features deserve particular attention. The workers in this model have an impressive annual saving rate in 2000, but it is offset in part by considerable dissaving on the part of retirees. As a result, net saving for the country as a whole in 2000 is 13.4 percent. This is roughly 1.3 percentage points below actual net private domestic saving in the U.S. in 1999. In the model I also implicitly assume (at least, in the initial discussion) that the saving of businesses (and Social Security) are fully transparent so that individuals take them fully into account when making their own saving decisions. This, of course, is unrealistic. Part of the difference between my results and actual saving around 2000 is due to the influence of other factors that are not included in this discussion.

The decline in the saving rate of active workers over the next half-century is due to the fact that although they still have 15 years of retirement, the retirement age rises from 65 in 2000 to 70 in 2050. Thus, workers at the end of the period have 45 years of working life, rather than 40, to accumulate their retirement savings and, therefore, their annual saving rate does not need to be as great. This change in the net saving rate is the focus of the rest of the analysis.

Since a number of parameters can change, we must consider a number of scenarios generated by the simulation model. These simulations, however, generate a great many numbers, and to avoid clutter in further discussion, I report only three critical statistics for each scenario: the initial and final net saving rates and the change in the net saving ratio. Table 2.4 reports the results when the major parameters are changed, while all other parameters of the initial simulation are held constant.

Panel A of Table 2.4 depicts the effect of population growth on the level and changes in net saving. Since a faster growth means a lower elderly-dependency-ratio (Table 2.2), the ratio of retired to active workers will also be lower. As a result, the relative dissaving by retired workers falls; and the overall decline in the net saving ratio is also less. Clearly, the fall in the saving ratio between 2000 and 2050 is quite sensitive to a change in the age structure of the population which, as previously argued, is uncertain.

Panel B of Table 2.4 shows that a faster growth of labor income leads to a smaller decline in the net saving rate. This comes about because, as pointed out above, the faster the growth of worker income, the smaller is the ratio of a retired worker's consumption to that of an active worker. As a result, the higher growth rates of labor income are associated with a lower rate of dissaving (in relation to the current GDP) of retired workers, and the net saving rate does not fall as rapidly. It is important to realize, however, that this effect is relatively small. For instance, a doubling of the annual growth rate of worker income from 1.2 to 2.4 percent is associated with a decline in the net saving rate of only 1.3 percentage points.

Panel C of Table 2.4 displays the results of varying the consumption-replacement-ratio (ρ). The basic insight is that a rising ρ raises the saving rate in the short-term because workers are saving more. After they retire, however, they will be spending more and, since the ratio of retireees (dissavers) to workers (savers) is rising, net saving will fall in the long-term. But this argument has a number of exceptions and we must proceed with caution.

As noted above, a person entering the labor force decides on ρ and the annual saving rate at the same time and both decisions reflect the degree to which a saver values a dollar of current and future consumption. Unfortunately, some complicated interactions are occurring in the simulation at this point and it is

Table 2.4. *Different Scenarios of Changes in the Ratio of Net Annual Saving to GDP*

	2000	2050	Change
Panel A: Using different L-T population projections			
Low	13.4%	5.0%	-8.4%
Medium	13.4	8.7	-4.8
High	13.4	11.3	-2.0
Panel B: Using different annual growth rates of average worker income			
0.9%	10.3%	4.3%	-6.0%
1.2%	11.5	6.0	-5.5
1.5%	12.5	7.4	-5.1
1.8%	13.4	8.7	-4.8
2.1%	14.2	9.7	-4.5
2.4%	14.8	10.6	-4.2
Panel C: Using different consumption-replacement-ratios			
0.8	11.1%	11.4%	+0.4%
1.0	13.4	8.7	-4.8
1.2	15.7	5.9	-9.8
Panel D: Using different retirement ages			
65	13.4%	10.5%	-3.0%
70	13.4	8.7	-4.8
Panel E: Using different interest rates			
3%	13.4%	8.7%	-4.8%
5%	10.2	5.6	-4.6
7%	7.4	3.1	-4.3

Note: These results are derived from the simulation model discussed in the text and in Appendix 2.2. All parameters are the same as in the initial simulation shown in Table 2.3 except those under examination.

important to focus on changes in net saving with a variety of parameter values.[14] The conclusions drawn from these simulation experiments of changes in ρ in a variety of configurations of other parameter values can be quickly summarized. In Table 2.4, two out of the three simulations result in a decline in net saving ratio by 2050. Of the 36 simulation results reported in Appendix Table 2.3, 30

---

14 When this model is described mathematically (External Appendix X-2.2), r is combined in the algebraic expression determining the net saving rate and also with a number of other parameters of the model. This means that a number of complex interaction effects are occurring and it is sometimes difficult to understand exactly what is happening. For instance, in Table 2.4 an increasing consumption-replacement-ratio is associated with greater net saving in 2000, but with less net saving in 2050.

reveal a decrease in the net saving ratio. The exceptions occur only in cases which are unlikely to occur in the coming decades so that, in all probability, the net saving rate will decline considerably by 2050.[15]

Panel D of Table 2.4 shows the effects of a change in the retirement age (more details are presented in Appendix Tables A2.2 and A2.3). If the retirement age remains at 65, rather than rising to 70, the impact on net saving is quite mixed. When other parameters are varied, keeping the retirement age at 65 results in a relatively more favorable change in the net saving situation (e.g., a smaller decline) than when it is raised to 70 in 10 out of 18 simulations. Several offsetting factors are at work. On the one hand, when the retirement age remains at 65, gross saving increases considerably, since workers must save for a much longer retirement (which rises from 15 to 20 years by 2050). As a result, more net saving occurs, other factors remaining constant. Moreover, the level of consumption on which retirees base their spending (dissaving) is relatively lower, because consumption during the working years is less, due to their higher saving. On the other hand, the relative number of retired workers is much greater than when the retirement age is 70, so that net saving should decline more. The exact assumptions for other parameter values of the model determine which of these offsetting factors dominates the results.[16]

Finally, as shown in Panel E of Table 2.4, the impact of the interest rate is not strong. A complex interaction of several variables determines the simulation results, since the interest rate has an impact on three factors: the lifetime income, the accumulated savings needed for retirement, and the ratio of the consumption of retired to current workers. Table A2.2 in the Appendices presents the results of an additional set of simulations showing the changes in net saving

[15] One case occurs with a high population growth rate combined with a retirement age at 65 (but not 70), the other with a low consumption-replacement-ratio. Two counteracting mechanisms seem to offset the general trend toward a drop in the net saving rate with a rising consumption ratio. In the first case, a high population growth (that is, internal growth—immigration is not taken into account) results in a smaller share of retired people, so that total dissaving of retirees declines in comparison to total saving of workers. As for the second case, it is important to note that when the consumption-replacement-ratio decreases, the net saving rate decreases more slowly. This is because in 2050 the assumed working years (45) in which a worker's saving takes place is much longer than his assumed retirement years (15), so that the change in saving in each year of the working life is relatively small. This is shown mathematically in External Appendix X-2.2. In some cases this effect is enough to offset the general trend toward a decline in net saving between 2000 and 2050. This offset also gives rise to what might be called the "paradox of profligacy," namely, that a low annual saving for future retirement is associated with a smaller decline (or even an increase) of net saving in the future.

[16] From the equations in External Appendix X-2.2, it can be readily demonstrated that the relative values of the saving rate and the relative percentage of an adult's lifespan spent working determine which effect dominates.

when the change in interest rate is accompanied by changes in other parameters as well. The results are mixed, but, generally speaking, the savings ratio is relatively insensitive to changes in the interest rate under a variety of conditions. If, however, the interest rate is not held constant but is changing over time, this conclusion may have to be modified. Before such a complication can be discussed, several additional factors require attention.

The results up to now show that the most probable values of the parameters (Table 2.3) lead to a declining rate of net saving in the first half of the 21st century. A variety of other simulations in which the parameters are varied reveal that in the overwhelming number of cases, similar results are obtained. It is now time to determine whether more realistic assumptions about saving behavior lead to the same conclusion.

C. Variations on the Theme [17]

1. Changing the Rationality Assumptions

Of course, savers are not as rational as I have assumed up to now. For instance, individual savers cannot accurately predict the future growth and interest rates and, moreover, the assumption that the growth rate remains constant as the saving rate declines stretches credulity even more. It is, therefore, important to see what happens when these assumptions are relaxed.

The key to such an analysis is to interpret deviations from rationality in terms of different values for the consumption-replacement-ratio. For instance, the consumption-replacement-ratio ρ represents not just the degree to which savers value a dollar of consumption in the present and the future, but also their best guesses about what economic growth will be. In this respect it can be said to depend on how pessimistic or optimistic they are about the economy and their own place in it.

Accurately predicting the future growth rate for the purpose of drawing up a lifetime plan for saving is, of course, extremely difficult, especially since (as I discuss below), the saving rate and the growth rate have a reciprocal influence on each other. What happens, for example, if the growth rate of labor income is actually less that what they initially foresee? Hyper-rational workers will save more in absolute terms if they believe that their rate of income growth will be high, rather than low, so that in this case of overoptimism, they will end up with more accumulated savings than they need to in order to meet their goals of a

---

[17]   In the text in this section I refer to analysis by Cutler and Meara (1999).

specified consumption-replacement-ratio.[18] If, for instance, actual growth turns out to be 1.2 percent a year, but the savers initially believe it will be 1.8 (and never realize throughout their working life what is really happening), a quick simulation shows that the net saving rate does not fall 4.8 percentage points between 2000 and 2050, as predicted by the original model (Table 2.4), but only 1.8 percentage points. Thus unrealistic optimism about the growth rate (in this case, lasting a half century!) acts in the same manner as an increase in the consumption-replacement-ratio and, in most cases, slows down the decline in net saving. By way of contrast, extreme pessimism about the future growth rate, if it turns out to be unwarranted, leads to a greater fall in the saving rate.

Suppose, however, workers are not sufficiently rational to save according to the lifetime income approach. One simplistic alternative assumption about saving behavior is that workers save a constant proportion of their income each year. Simulation experiments along these lines, however, show that the conclusions about a decline in the net saving rate are little different. This is because the change in the age structure of the population dominates any results due to this change in saving behavior.[19]

It is possible, of course, to abandon any belief in the rationality of savers and assume, in the manner of Auerbach and Kotlikoff, that the saving rate of people at each specific age level (the age-specific saving rates) will remain constant. Such an approach predicts still greater declines in the saving rate than shown in my simulations.[20] Unfortunately, the further we move from any theory of rational behavior, the less able we are to determine the effects of different parameters, such as the rates of growth or interest, on the final saving rate.

The consumption-replacement-ratio incorporates both rational and irrational elements. Since this ratio depends, in part, on the value of a dollar of consumption today and in the future, the saving rate can fall if workers become more present-oriented. Such a phenomenon reflects a change in taste and not of irrationality, at least if the savers are willing to live with the consequences of lower consumption during their retirement years.

[18] At this point I am still assuming that workers save according to their predictions of their life time income. More irrational workers who believe that good times will last forever might squander everything. Whether deliberately encouraging optimism in order to increase the saving rate so that saving and investment will be higher is, however, problematic, because optimism may lead to irrationality. That is, in such a situation, people may consume more and save less, because they delude themselves into thinking that their retirement consumption will be magically financed!

[19] In the experiments I maintained the same consumption-replacement-ratio. Thus a Keynesian approach toward saving does not change the major conclusions.

[20] Their results and mine are, however, difficult to compare because they calculate saving as a ratio of net national product and, moreover, use different demographic assumptions than I do. For instance, their saving model of constant age-specific saving rates does not take into account either changes in life expectancy or the retirement age.

It is, however, irrational for individual savers not to take into account the saving carried out in their name either through withheld earnings of the corporations in which they own stock or through the Social Security withholding taxes. In such a case, this "unaccounted saving" can be considered as an unintended increase in the consumption-replacement-ratio, because savers will have more assets to liquidate during their retirement years than they had originally planned. In brief, such unaccounted saving raises the net saving ratio of the nation, even while it is unintended.

These considerations raise, however, the question of what are the most realistic values to set for the consumption-replacement-ratio in an analysis of this kind. Unfortunately, considerable disagreement exists in the economic literature about what the real-life value of the consumption-replacement-ratio is or "should" be in terms of some model of rational behavior.[21] The values I have chosen for the scenario analysis reflect the range of ratios I have found in my reading. My own intuition, however, is that this ratio is considerably closer to 1.2 than 0.8, a figure often bandied about in the literature, because of medical expenditures made for individuals by the government. Although the short term decline in the net saving rate in the late 1980s and 1990s suggests that the consumption-replacement-ratio is falling, the decline in average family size (see below) and the rising costs of medical care for the elderly act in the opposite direction, that is, to encourage saving.

One last aspect of rationality deserves note. If savers were as hyper-rational as I have assumed, they would not only make their saving decisions when they start work, but also decide on their retirement age. In this case, however, I have denied them this opportunity and, instead, have imposed a mandatory retirement age. But in a free-choice situation, retirement and saving decisions depend, in part, on the changing life expectancy, Given relatively reasonable assumptions about the nature of work, it seems likely that with rising life expectancy in the future, workers will postpone their retirement so that they will need to save less during any given year of their working life. Comparisons of the scenarios with an initial retirement age of 65 and a final mandatory retirement age of either 65 or 70 show the impact if workers face only two possible retirement ages. Nevertheless, a more exact modeling of a simultaneous decision about retirement and saving would not markedly change the major conclusions drawn from the various scenarios in Table 2.4.

---

[21]   Three main approaches to this problem can be found in the literature. Some such as Engen *et al.* (1999) derive this ratio using a dynamic stochastic optimization model; others use the advice of personal finance gurus; and still others use information derived from consumption budgets of households headed by people of different ages. The derived rates range generally from 0.8 to 1.2. For further discussion of this matter, see Appendix 2.4.

2. Relation of the Model to Other Factors Influencing Saving

What other factors beside those taken into account by the model might influence the saving rate? In this respect, the most important impacts are on the consumption-replacement-ratio ρ.

- *Family size.* In part, ρ reflects the number of children in a family. If a family has a large number of children, the personal consumption of the parents is generally less than in a smaller family (I assume that parents do not set aside a fixed amount of consumption to be divided among their children, no matter how many they have). Their saving rate to replace a given fraction of their personal consumption during their working years for their retirement period is, therefore, lower, even while the national net saving rate in the middle of 21st century is higher because these retirees are dissaving less. But there is another impact of a larger family size as well, since more children lead to a more rapidly growing population. As a result, the slower decline in the long-term of net saving arising from a lower r due to a large family reinforces slower decline in the long term of net saving arising from a faster population growth (Panel A, Table 2.4, which does not, however, take this factor of the number of children into account). In brief, larger families dampen the long-term decline in the net saving rate in two respects.

- *Changing medical needs of the elderly.* An important part of consumption expenditures of the elderly is medical care and, according to the research of David Cutler and Ellen Meara, medical costs are rising faster for the elderly than for any other segment of the population. If workers—the elderly of the future—wish to maintain other parts of their consumption when they are retired and also to cover these rising medical costs, they must raise their saving during their working lifetime. In the vocabulary of the model, they must adopt a higher consumption-replacement-ratio. Of course, most of the saving for medical expenditures of the elderly is carried out through Medicare taxes during the working years (which lowers current consumption and raises forced saving), and most of the expenditures for medical purposes after retirement are drawn from the Medicare trust fund. But the institutional forms through which such saving and expenditures take place are not important. Rather, it is the ratio of total expenditures of retired workers (including medical care) to their total expenditures (income minus saving and taxes) during their working years that is the key.

- *Political clout of the elderly.* Up to now I have assumed that Social Security payouts are based on what a worker puts into the system. But the current system features intergenerational transfers from the workers to the retired that occur when the elderly are able to use their political muscle to raise the Social Security payouts over and above what they would have received on the basis of their own contributions. This means, in effect, that the consumption-replacement-ratio increases—consumption of active workers is lowered, while consumption of retired workers is raised.

• *Precautionary saving and saving for bequests*. The model assumes that the age of death is known so that the people aren't worried about running out of income in old age. In fact, with the increasing annuitization of income during retirement through pensions and Social Security, the precautionary motive for saving has, indeed, become less important. In this respect, the model appears realistic and no reinterpretations of the results are necessary. I have also assumed, however, that workers are not motivated by a desire to leave their accumulated wealth to someone else. This raises some analytic problems because bequests break the one-to-one relation between annual saving and the consumption-replacement-ratio. That is, the bequest motive either raises saving during the working years or lowers consumption during the retirement years. Moreover, bequests also change the saving and consumption behavior of those receiving them. Unfortunately, we cannot take these various factors properly into account simply by reinterpreting the results of the simulations or changing certain parameters, Thus, an analysis of the impact of bequests on the saving ratio must be left for other economists. In any case, the bequest motive is of great importance primarily for the wealthier segment of the population, not for the population as a whole.

3. A Very Brief Comment on Changes in the Labor Supply

What is the impact of a change in the labor force participation rate on net saving? Simulation experiments along these lines show that the net saving results are not affected, at least when the participation ratios change in even increments over the 50 year period.

D. Some Implications for the Economy[22]

1. Aggregate Saving

Although these simulation results suggest a fall in the personal saving rate in the future, this does not necessarily mean that the total saving rate will decline. Since the model focuses only on voluntary personal saving, it is important to take into account other types of saving in the economy before generalizing about the overall saving rate. Three other sources of saving deserve attention: foreign capital inflows, business saving, and government saving.

---

[22] In the text in this section I refer to studies by Auerbach and Hassett (1991), Baker and Weisbrot (2000), Bosworth and Burtless (1998), Lee and Tuljapukar (1998), and Schieber and Shoven (1997).

Barry Bosworth and Gary Burtless show that aging of the population is occurring in almost all industrialized countries. Thus, sooner or later these nations will also face a declining personal saving rate. As a result, they will have less capital to export and, therefore, these foreign capital flows do not seem a promising source for offsetting the fall in personal saving in the U.S.

When businesses retain their profits, rather than distributing them in the form of dividends, saving increases. Such decisions act, among other things, to raise the value of a company's common stock. Alan Auerbach and Kevin Hassett argue that because such a linkage is clear, those in the labor force wishing to save are easily able to "pierce the veil of corporate saving." This means that, at least in part, these workers/savers take such corporate saving into account in making their personal saving decisions. If the substitution between these two forms of saving is not one-to-one, then some of this business saving represents a type of involuntary personal saving. As noted above, such involuntary saving acts to increase the consumption-replacement-ratio; and, as the elderly cash in their assets to finance their retirement, their consumption will be higher than planned. In the economic literature, however, I have found no very convincing arguments to suggest any change in the degree to which businesses will retain their profits and increase their saving. If business saving does increase and is not taken into account in the saving decisions of the share holders, the short-run saving ratio rises. But in the long-term, the net saving ratio will fall more in the future when the retirees cash in their assets (Table 2.4, panel C). Thus, the hope for a higher rate of business saving is hardly the answer to the long-term saving drought.

Involuntary personal saving might occur through the government sector as well. If it comes about through higher Social Security taxes, then it can be argued that individuals will "pierce the governmental veil" as they do the corporate veil and will take this "forced saving" into account in their voluntary saving decisions. Again, if the substitution is not one-to-one, net personal saving might fall less than it otherwise would have, and a higher consumption replacement rate will result.

But this has a paradoxical impact. As the government tries to "save" Social Security, either by increasing taxes to this fund or by raising the retirement age, such measures may be offset by a decline in personal saving so that the net saving rate of the nation will not be greatly changed.

Although the various types of saving that complement personal saving do not seem very promising as solutions to the decline in the net saving ratio, one other possibility suggests itself. As the net saving rate from the combined sources of saving falls, the interest rate will rise (unless offset by other changes in the economy that will reduce the demand for investment funds). This can have an impact on saving, but, as I indicated, the impact seems modest. A more important factor—the impact of the falling saving rate on asset prices—needs to be taken into account.

2. Asset Prices and Future Recessions

One peculiarity of saving in the 1990s, as shown in Table 2.2 (line 7), is that when it is measured in terms of changes in the net worth of individuals, no decline in the saving rate occurred. As discussed above, this was due in large measure to the rise in unrealized capital gains. These values are, however, highly dependent on the price of these assets, which can be volatile.

The decline in the rate of saving, as measured by flows and analyzed in the simulation model, will bring about, of course, a fall in the demand for assets serving as a vehicle for saving. This, in turn, will cause prices of physical, and even financial assets, to fall. Such a fall in asset price is reinforced if the decline in saving is accompanied by a rise in interest rates resulting from a decline in the relative availability of loanable funds. The situation becomes even worse if foreign lenders lose confidence in the U.S. dollar. The dollar will fall in value against other currencies, foreign investors will repatriate their investment funds, and the downward pressure on asset prices will be reinforced.

As a result, much of the extraordinary growth in "saving" due to unrealized capital gains will disappear. Or, to view the matter from a more personal perspective, the value of pension funds established on a defined contribution basis will fall, so that when workers cash in their pension claims, they will receive much less than they expected. Without government assistance, pension plans with defined benefits may even face bankruptcy as a result of the fall in asset prices and, as a result, those holding claims on them may also receive much less than they planned. In both cases, enormous pressures will be placed on the government to provide more financial assistance to the elderly.

Up to now I have taken full employment for granted, but at this point, the realism of such an assumption also needs to be examined. Unfortunately, a determinate conclusion is difficult to draw because the relative strength of counteracting forces cannot be easily assessed.

The decline in asset prices could lead to a fall in aggregate demand and a rise in unemployment for two reasons: (a) The loss of wealth arising from the fall in asset prices might lead to a decline in consumption as people attempt (unsuccessfully, if we draw out the implications of a simple Keynesian model) to rebuild their assets. (b) The fall in asset prices might increase risk and discourage new investment. As a result, the economy could end up in a situation similar to that of the early 1930s when saving and new investment were almost zero. Nevertheless, the recession might be longer lasting since the shift in the demographic balance between savers and non-savers that would bring about the fall in asset prices would take place over a period of two decades.

But four offsetting forces can also be specified: (a) The results from Table 2.4 and Appendix Table A2.2 suggest that any effect of a higher interest rate should be small.

(b) Given that the U.S. personal saving rate, when capital gains are included in the definition of saving, is considerably higher than what a lifetime saving model would predict, under certain assumptions, a fall in asset values might have very little impact at all on saving. It does not seem promising, however, to place much weight on this effect. (c) Aggregate consumption would rise as the demographic balance shifted from savers to dissavers. (d) The government might try to offset the fall in aggregate demand with traditional remedies, such as lower taxes or higher public expenditures.

While it would be interesting to speculate about this situation in greater detail, we must postpone further discussion of the stability of the U.S. economic system to the next chapter when a set of additional considerations are taken into account. For my immediate purposes, it is more important to turn directly to the impact on economic growth.

3. Economic Growth

To simplify this part of the discussion, I assume again the economy will operate at full employment and conclude that the economic growth rate will decline. Obviously, if the fall in asset prices or other events discussed above cause an economic slowdown, growth of income and GDP will be even lower than what I foresee.

In the first part of this chapter I assume a constant economic growth rate that is somehow given from the outside. More attention, however, needs to be paid to the determinants of growth resulting from a change in the saving rate. The situation is complicated because, at full employment, the impact of a falling saving rate on economic growth depends on our view of technological change. Assume for the moment that the introduction of new technology is unrelated to a change in the capital stock. Those economists analyzing such a situation (employing, for instance, a Solow-type neoclassical growth model) predict that in the short run, a decline in the saving rate will lead to a more slowly growing GDP; but that in the long-run, the growth rate will be the same as before, although the per capita GDP would be lower than if the saving rate had not fallen.[23]

It seems more realistic to assume, however, that technological change depends on what is happening within the system. In particular, since new technology is embodied in new equipment, then a decline in the saving rate will lead

---

[23] This counter-intuitive long-term result occurs because, with greater investment, the productivity of additional units of capital investment declines as diminishing returns become stronger. When the capital stock is sufficiently large, the growth induced by additional investment will be quite low. If saving and investment are lower, the capital stock will also be lower so that the impact of diminishing returns will be much less. In this latter case, however, the capital stock per worker is lower so that the level of per capita GDP is lower than if the saving and investment rates had not declined.

to slower growth in both the short and long runs, a conclusion that accords more with common sense.

A rigorous forecast of the future growth rate of the U.S. requires investigation of changes in such key variables as the rate of technological change, the rate of depreciation, the rate of saving, and the ratio of capital to output. Table 2.2 shows that in the 1990s, gross private domestic saving and investment (line 2) and depreciation (consumption of fixed capital, line 9) were respectively 17.2 and 12.3 percent of the GDP. Other things being equal, if the private saving rate falls more than 4.9 percentage points, it will no longer cover depreciation and the net capital stock would start to shrink. At this point, GDP growth could only be maintained if (i) governmental saving and foreign capital inflows offset the decline of private saving, or (ii) if technological change affecting the entire capital stock (more exactly, disembodied technological change) is sufficiently high to offset the negative impact on output of the declining net capital stock. Neither seems very likely.

In the initial simulation, where I tried to assign the most realistic values to the different parameters, the saving rate falls 4.8 percentage points between 2000 and 2050. Most of the other scenarios reported in this discussion show declines of the saving rate between 4 and 6 percent. This suggests that capital accumulation will be much slower, and, under the most plausible assumptions, the rate of growth of the U.S. economy will be slower as well. A slower growth of income reinforces the decline in the saving rate (Table 2.4, Panel B) which, in turn, will lead to an even slower rate of growth. In brief, under the most plausible assumptions, growth of the economy will be considerably slower in the middle of the 21st century than in the last decade of the previous century.

4. Other Considerations and a Brief Summary

For the most part, this discussion of a future decline in the net saving rate is detached from any institutional context. As such, my argument about the saving drought is much broader than the current discussion about crises in particular types of saving. For instance, in recent years various Cassandras have expressed considerable concern about the future bankruptcy of the Social Security system, although recently Dean Baker and Mark Weisbrod expressed skepticism about the likelihood of this trend because of some of the unrealistic assumptions underlying the pessimistic projections. Others, such as Sylvester Schieber and John Shoven, provide evidence that some decades from now the solvency of private pension funds is also questionable. Their argument rests on many of the same demographic circumstances that I discuss above, but does not include the impact of the decline in asset prices. But these two types of crises are only particular manifestations of a more general decline in net saving that I have shown as highly probable.

A key policy issue also deserves mention, since it concerns Social Security. In their simulations of the Social Security system, Ronald Lee and Shripad Tuljapurkar argue that the results for 2050 are particularly sensitive to changes in GDP. In their model they do not, however, take into account the decline in the growth rate that is brought about by a fall in the national saving rate. If such considerations are factored into their simulations, then the future financial health of Social Security becomes even more precarious than currently believed.

The government faces several basic policy options to offset the deceleration in per capita growth. It can direct more funds into research and development in order to stimulate technological change, although such a policy strategy has limits. It can introduce measures to boost population growth, either by encouraging larger families or by allowing more immigration of young workers. It can also increase its own saving and recycle these funds to investors. Or it can try to encourage private saving by tax incentives while, at the same time, manipulating other parameters (such as not allowing the retirement age to rise) so that the net saving rate would not greatly change by 2050. This last approach is dangerous, however, because if the entire policy package is not implemented, the situation may actually become worse. This is because, in most cases, the fall in the saving rate is greater in the long-run when the consumption-replacement-ratio rises (Table 2.4, Panel C).

To summarize, when we focus primarily on the relative consumption of active and retired workers, and the relative population size of these two groups, the personal saving rate will most probably decline considerably over the next half-century and this will lead to slower economic growth. The various scenarios provide some idea of the magnitudes of the fall in saving under different sets of circumstances. Alternative sources of saving are unlikely to compensate as an avenue of escape. We must squarely face the unsettling implications: the growth of the economy will decline, the interest rate will rise, and asset prices will decline.

E. Some Implications for the Economic System

A major ideological justification of capitalism is that it leads to high economic growth rates and "a rising tide lifts all boats," that is, in the long-run everyone wins. With low economic growth, struggles over the proper distribution of income become more intense because the fight more closely approximates a zero-sum game—if I win, you lose. The outline of such a situation can be vaguely discerned by examination of political squabbles during the late 1970s and 1980s when the growth rate of the GDP and of productivity took a distinct downturn. This means, in turn, that governmental policies are more difficult to formulate and implement because the distributive implications of such policies become more important. Welfare measures to aid the poor become particularly contentious because the financing comes out of the customary consumption of higher income groups, rather than out of the additional growth of income, a situation culminating in the dramatic change in the welfare program in the middle 1990s before the economy began to take off again. Other governmental policies are also affected because these battles over the distribution of income and the impacts of particular governmental policies on particular income groups increase general social distrust, phenomena discussed in greater detail in Chapters 7 and 8.

If the lower saving rate is accompanied by higher interest rates, the difficulties of young entrepreneurs in obtaining adequate financing become more serious. This, in turn, means that the competition facing existing firms comes less from new firms and more from other existing firms who have coexisted in the same markets for a long time. Such a situation provides a greater incentive to merge or to engage in collusive behavior, so that prices to consumers rise. Under plausible circumstances, technical change may also be adversely affected. As documented in Chapters 10 and 11, mergers were dramatically on the rise in the 1990s, so that current trends toward market concentration would be accelerated.

Finally, the drop in asset prices accompanying a fall in the saving rate could also have a number of impacts on the economic system. As noted above, the income obtained from cashing in pension claims might fall below that which the savers expect, so that political pressures will increase for more governmental pension aid to the elderly. A decline in asset prices might also trigger a serious economic downturn and this, in turn, could have an important impact on the architecture of U.S. capitalism, witness the institutional and organizational changes enacted during the Great Depression in the 1930s. The possibilities of a serious economic downturn in the coming decades receive greater attention in the next chapter.

In brief, the declining net saving rate will have three serious economic impacts—a falling economic growth rate, a rising interest rate, and falling asset prices. These consequences, in turn, can have a considerable impact on the distribution of income and globalization, two facets of the economy discussed respectively in Chapters 4 and 5. They also have considerable influence on the social and political system, discussed in Chapters 7 and 8. And finally, they will induce considerable changes to economic institutions and organizations in both the public and private sectors, themes discussed in Chapters 9 through 12.

All these changes in the economic system stem from the simple fact that the balance between active workers who build up their savings and retired workers who draw down their savings will begin to shift dramatically in the decades ahead. Other factors that I discuss in later chapters will also have an impact on the future of U.S. capitalism, but the ramifications of the fall in saving number among the most serious.

CHAPTER 3

Economic Fluctuations and Financial Crises

1930 will be a splendid employment year.

—*U.S. Department of Labor, early October 1929*[1]

At the beginning of the 21st century, certain storm clouds appeared on America's economic horizon—a high deficit in the balance of trade, overvalued stock prices, and high internal indebtedness. This chapter, however, focuses on long-term problems of economic stability, rather than short-run difficulties that the economy may encounter in the near future.

Unfortunately, no theory of the business cycle or financial crises commands general support among economists. Older theories (for instance, by Karl Marx) that predict ever wider swings of production and unemployment have been discredited by events in the past century. Very recent theories of the decreasing severity (or death) of the business cycle rest on quite dubious assumptions as Victor Zarnowitz has demonstrated, and, as shown below, receive little support from the evidence. So what's really going to happen to production fluctuations in the future?

A majority of U.S. economists have a rather humdrum view of the future of economic fluctuations and financial crises. As revealed in the Millennium Survey, they believe that the severity of production fluctuations will not greatly change in the first half of the 21st century. On the other hand, a majority also believes that volatility on the financial side of the economy will "somewhat" increase.

To gain perspective on these issues, I look carefully at the behavior of the business cycle and key financial variables over the last half century. The spotlight turns first on the financial side of the economy since many believe, on the basis of events in 1929, that financial crises can trigger production volatility

---

[1] Cited by Laura Lee, *Bad Predictions: 2000 Years of the Best Minds Making the Worst Forecasts* (2000). In this introduction I also draw upon Zarnowitz (1999) and the results of the Millennium Survey, presented in (Pryor, 2000-b).

and recessions. (Of course, it is also possible for fluctuations in production to cause financial crises). This discussion is followed by a similar examination of fluctuations of production. For both financial and production fluctuations I first study some long-term indicators of volatility, then investigate various measures of the fragility of the economy (its ability to withstand shocks), and finally explore whether such shocks will become more severe in the coming decades.

Both my investigations lead to the seemingly contradictory result that, over the last half century, most volatility indicators show little change, but that fragility has considerably increased. In the last section I attempt to show how these conclusions can be reconciled, and in such a way as to be able to make some tentative predictions about the future.

A. Financial Fluctuations and Crises[2]

As explicated by a number of monetary economists, such as Martin H. Wolfson or Hyman Minsky, financial fragility has increased and, as a result, this will lead both to greater financial volatility and distress in the future. These analysts generally measure fragility in terms of financial leverage, for instance, the ratio of debt to income. To explore this argument, it is useful to start by briefly reviewing certain indicators of financial volatility and fragility. Then I examine a series of measures of rising financial distress in the U.S. that seems to be the result of the increasing financial fragility.

1. Indications of Financial Volatility

Financial volatility certainly rose from the 1950s through the 1980s, as shown in an analysis of 59 monthly series from 1950 through 1990 of financial variables, such as interest rates, stock prices, and the volume of bank loans, which Elliott Sulcove and I have presented elsewhere. Although the ups and downs seemed to have increased up to 1990, since then such volatility appears to have leveled off, so that we cannot speak comfortably about a half-century trend. To illustrate this point, Chart 3.1 presents several series of financial data showing the monthly deviations of prices from a five-year moving average.

---

[2] The text in this section refers to studies by: Campbell *et al.* (2000), Epstein and Schor (1991), Malkiel and Xu (1995), Minsky (1982), Pryor and Sulcove (1995), Schwert (1989), Sobol (1998), and Wolfson (1986, 1990).

Panel A: Interest Rates of 3 year Government Bonds

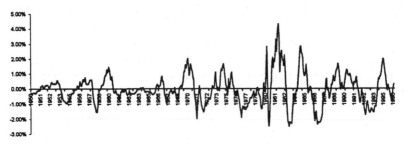

Panel B: Percentage Deviations of S & P 500 Stock Index

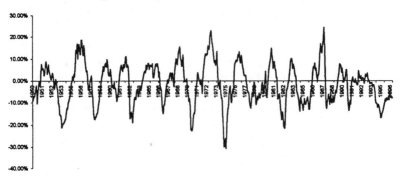

Panel C: Percentage Deviations of Foreign Exchange Rate Index, G-10 Nations

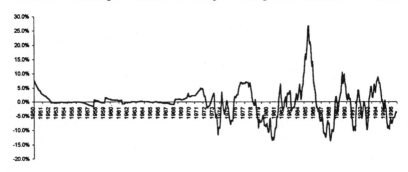

Chart 3.1. Financial volatility: Deviations from a 5-year moving average

Note: Sources are presented in Appendix 3.1.

Panel A shows deviations of three year Treasury bond yields from a five-year running average of these yields.[3] Until the 1970s, these interest rates followed closely the trend, but thereafter the series seems to go wild for a while, before settling down and following the trend more closely in the 1990s. Examining how monthly yields vary from the trend (more exactly, the variance of monthly yields) in different decades reveals nothing of importance that cannot be seen from a visual examination.[4] Since yields depend on the expected price increase over the life of the bond, I also investigated the "real yield" of these Treasury bonds, by subtracting the rise in the GDP deflator over the next three years. Although the fluctuations in this new series are much smaller, no important new information about bond yield volatility is gained.

Panel B of Chart 3.1 shows deviations from a trend (a five-year rolling average) of the prices of the S & P index of 500 leading stocks. The series ends before the price run-up in the late 1990s. No apparent increase in the volatility of this stock index can be discerned. Close analyses of the variance of monthly stock price indices by William Schwert or by John Campbell and his colleagues also reveal no long-term increase in volatility, although, of course, noticeable spikes in this index are apparent in the late 1920s and 1930s, as well as in the mid 1970s and in 1987. Some interpretative problems, however, arise.

In contrast to the market as a whole, price volatility of individual stocks reveals an upward trend from 1962 through 1997, a trend that does not reflect merely a random drift. Nevertheless, such rising volatility on the level of individual stocks does not appear either in stock indices for particular industries or on the level of the market as a whole, according to the results of John Campbell. Moreover, certain, but not all, parts of the securities market also reveal increased volatility over time. For instance, from the middle to the late 1990s, the volatility index (VIX) of the Chicago Board of Option Exchange showed a rising volatility which was not paralleled by a similar movement in the stock index.[5]

Campbell and his colleagues offer several possible explanations for this increasing volatility of the stock prices of individual companies: (a) The break up of large conglomerates in previous decades meant that firms became more specialized in particular markets, so that poor performance in one industry in

---

[3]   These average yields rose from the 1950s to the middle 1960s; thereafter no trend value is apparent.

[4]   Analysis of the variances of the deviations from the five-year rolling averages reveal that in the 1950s and 1960s they were considerably lower than in the last three decades of the century. For both this and the series discussed in the text, the 1980s showed the greatest variances of the yields. For calculating the "real yield," I used the GDP deflator from the U.S. Department of Commerce, Bureau of Economic Analysis website: (http://www.bea.doc.gov/bea/dn1.htm).

[5]   These data on the VIX were obtained from the Chicago Board of Option Exchange. Unfortunately, the index does not go further back in time than the mid 1980s.

which the company was engaged was not offset by good performance in another. (b) In later years companies began issuing stock earlier in their life cycle (witness the increasing number of initial public offerings) and these "young" stocks are more volatile. (c) A greater share of stocks began to be owned by institutional investors and the transactions of any of these large funds for any particular stock had a considerably greater impact on stocks prices than those of individual investors. Moreover, portfolio managers have a certain herd mentality and, in this regard, Campbell and his colleagues cite a finding by Burton G. Malkiel and Yexiao Xu that prices of individual stocks are generally more volatile when institutional investors own a higher proportion. This unexpected empirical result cannot, however, be taken completely at face value because institutional investors may deliberately select stocks with more volatile prices. As a result, the direction of causation of this relationship between institutional ownership and stock volatility is unclear. Unfortunately, the relative validity— if any—of these three explanatory factors has not been empirically established.

It is sometimes argued that because of the falling cost of communication, timely information about the firm's performance is more rapidly disseminated; and this might cause greater stock price volatility as more investors rush to take advantage of the latest tidbit of news. The study by John Campbell points out that a greater information flow might actually lower the volatility of stock returns of the various companies. This is because investors would have more accurate information about the future profits of the company and the stock price would more accurately reflect the actual performance of the company.

With various types of financial institutions holding an ever increasing share of corporate stocks (see Chapter 11), the decision-making procedures of such institutions become an ever greater factor in stock market volatility. Whether or not money managers are, in the words of Paul Krugman, "an extremely dangerous flock of financial sheep" has yet to be proven. The degree to which automatic trading programs contribute to greater stock market volatility also remains an open question, although they seem to have played an important role during one phase of the stock price plunge of October 1987.

Panel C of Chart 3.1 shows deviations from the trend of the exchange rate of the dollar with the foreign currencies of major industrial nations (combined into an index). The dramatic increase in currency volatility in the mid-1970s came after the introduction of floating exchange rates and the gradual loosening of capital controls between industrial nations in the 1970s and 1980s.[6] In the last

---

6   Epstein and Schor (1991, p. 142) present an extremely useful aggregated index of these developments in capital controls from 1968 through 1987; it includes 16 countries. Between 1975

quarter of the century, no apparent time trend in volatility is discernible. Nevertheless, as in the case of stock prices, the exchange rate of the dollar with the currency of particular countries shows considerable volatility in the 1990s, especially with the Japanese yen. Fluctuations in these yen/dollar exchange rates also have little relation with changes in the relative price levels of tradable goods in the two countries.[7]

	Yen per dollar
January 1, 1990	146.25
April 29, 1990	158.90
April 19. 1995	81.12
August 11, 1998	147.14
November 2, 1998	114.52
May 20, 1999	124.45
January 3, 2000	101.70
April 2, 2001	126.75

In brief, although some key aggregative indicators show increased financial volatility for the first few decades after 1950, no trend of increasing volatility over the entire second half of the 20th century is apparent. This conclusion, however, should not hide the fact that volatility on a more microeconomic level appears to be increasing for certain indicators, such as individual stock prices. In addition, certain securities markets, such as particular option exchanges, also reveal increasing volatility. Thus, we cannot rest smugly in the belief that financial volatility has been mastered and, at this point must look more closely at other parts of the financial picture.

2. Financial Fragility and Distress

Financial fragility measures the potential difficulty in meeting financial obligations. Most commonly, such fragility is measured in terms of financial leverage, that is, some ratio of financial liabilities either to physical or financial assets or to income. Because of the necessity to pay both interest and principal on loans, a financial shock may reduce the value of particular assets, and this event, in turn, may make it difficult to meet financial obligations. The resulting illiquidity or bankruptcy may cascade through the system because creditors who

---

and 1985 this index declined from 14 to 7 (where 32 represents tight controls in all countries and 0 represents no controls).

[7] These data are drawn from the Board of Governors of the Federal Reserve web site: www.http://www.federalreserve.gov/.

are dependent on these payments to meet their obligations then experience a loss of liquidity or bankruptcy.

Panel A in Table 3.1 presents some series measuring financial fragility. The first three lines of the table provide indicators for the economy as a whole. Line 1 shows the increasing leverage in the economy, as measured by a ratio of debt to GDP. Line 2 reveals the same phenomenon in a different way, namely, the rising ratio of financial to tangible assets. And line 3 calls attention to the increasing share of such financial assets held by banks, financial intermediaries, and other institutions of the financial sector, rather than individuals or non-financial companies.

Lines 4 through 6 of the table show how this increasing leverage is reflected in particular sectors. Line 4 reveals the rising indebtedness of the household sector. Since the ratio of debt to income of households has doubled and the interest rate has more than doubled, households are using a considerably larger share of their disposable income to service their debts. Lines 5 and 6 provide evidence that financial leverage in the non-financial corporate sector has almost doubled and that interest payments, as a share of the total value added (wages and profits), have more than quadrupled.

The following two lines of the table focus on the increasing leverage of commercial banks. Line 7 of the table shows that in the commercial banking sector, liquid assets to meet emergencies are a declining share of total assets. Nevertheless, as revealed in line 8, the share of such liquid assets to their illiquid liabilities has increased; in this respect, the commercial banking sector is in a better position to meet immediate demands for liquidity than it was in previous decades.

From such data on increasing leverage, however, we cannot immediately conclude that the system is more fragile, and, therefore, more vulnerable to financial shocks. This is because various new methods of financial control may have been developed to contain incipient financial and banking crises. For example, the capacity for almost instant communication and the possibility of quick infusions of liquidity by the Federal Reserve to banks in distress, combined with various types of deposit insurance arrangements, can offset certain financial shocks, as dramatically illustrated in the stock market crash in 1987. Certainly, the evidence of financial volatility cited above does not suggest that the rising financial fragility shown in Table 3.1 has led to increased financial fluctuations during the last half of the 20th century, at least on a macro-economic level.

On a micro-economic level, however, the increasing financial leverage appears to have led to the expected increase in financial distress, as revealed in lines 9 through 14. Line 9 shows (at least up to the 1990s) an increasing number of major banking and/or financial crises, as classified by Martin Wolfson.

Table 3.1. *Trends in Financial Fragility and Distress*

	1950s	1960s	1970s	1980s	1990s
Panel A. Financial Fragility Indicators					
General indicators:					
1. Ratio: total credit market debt to GDP	1.358	1.469	1.521	1.917	2.415
2. Ratio: financial assets to tangible assets in private, non-financial sector (financial interrelations ratio)	1.477	1.719	1.545	1.602	2.236
3. Ratio: financial assets held by financial sector to total financial assets (financial intermediation ratio)	0.316	0.351	0.431	0.488	0.501
Household and corporate indicators					
4. Ratio: household liabilities (debts) to disposable income	44.5%	65.1%	67.6%	75.2%	88.6%
5. Ratio: total liabilities to total assets, non-financial corporate enterprises	28.1%	33.2%	36.7%	42.8%	51.1%
6. Ratio: total interest payments of non-financial corporate sector to GDP originating from total corporate sector	1.9%	3.1%	5.7%	9.2%	8.3%
Bank indicators					
7. Ratio: commercial banks, liquid assets to total assets	48.4%	29.5%	18.6%	15.3%	18.4%
8. Ratio: commercial banks, liquid assets to liquid liabilities	76.1%	60.2%	62.4%	83.1%	97.9%
Panel B. Financial Distress Indicators					
9. Number of major banking/financial crises	0	1	2	6	n.a.
10. Failure rate of businesses per 1000 listed firms	40.3	50.1	34.2	89.7	92.0
11. Ratio: liabilities of failed businesses to total credit (borrowing) of non-financial businesses	0.59%	0.74%	0.58%	1.19%	1.36%
12. Ratio: deposits of failed banks to total deposits insured by FDIC	0.005%	0.007%	0.058%	0.445%	0.569%
13. Personal bankruptcies per 10,000 people over 19 years old	4.7	12.3	12.7	21.9	47.8
14. Mortgages with delinquent payments	2.32%	3.20%	4.32%	5.32%	4.44%

Note: For fragility indicators, data for 1990s cover 1990 through 1998; for distress indicators, 1990 through 1997. n.a. = not available.

Lines 10 and 11 in the table reveal an increasing rate of business failures and, moreover, a rising importance of such bankruptcies in the credit picture, at least when the unmet debts are measured against the total credit extended to the total non-financial business sector. Line 12 of the table reveals that people are putting more of their savings into shaky banks, as measured by the ratio of deposits in failed banks to total bank deposits insured by the Federal Deposit Insurance Corporation. Finally, lines 13 and 14 show increasing personal bankruptcies and, up to the 1990s, delinquent mortgages. Although this trend was, in part, abetted by a loosening of bankruptcy laws, it also appears to reflect a significant rise in serious financial distress of individuals in the second half of the 20th century.

The increasing fragility of the financial system shown in Panel A of Table 3.1 seems to have caused in part the rising level of financial distress shown in Panel B. We have no credible theory to help us predict how such fragility will change in the future, but a simple extrapolation of current trends suggests that it will increase. If so, the financial volatility on the macro-level depends on the nature of shocks to the system.

3. Future Financial Shocks

A fragile system may not experience significant volatility if the shocks to the system are light, so that their adverse impact can be contained. But heavy shocks may set the system on a downward spiral, especially if the financial distress is sufficiently great that bankruptcies and liquidity shortages cascade through the system. It is useful, therefore, to examine briefly both the external and internal shocks that might bring about such a deteriorating situation.

a. *Shocks from abroad:* A critical shock to the financial system emanating from the outside world could occur if a large share of foreign assets in the U.S. are liquidated and withdrawn.

This might happen, for instance, if the Euro appears a more promising investment medium than at the beginning of the 21st century. One important aspect of the increasing globalization of the capital market, discussed in greater detail in Chapter 5, is the ever larger volume (in gross terms) of foreign exchange entering U.S. markets. Chart 3.2 shows that, as a percent of the monetary base, the total daily foreign exchange turnover (transactions) rose from less than 5 percent in 1977 to almost 70 percent by 1998. As a percent of the annual GDP, this daily turnover rose from 0.2 percent to 4.0 percent in the same period (or almost 15 times the GDP each day). The turnover of foreign exchange also dwarfed the sales of domestic securities, as shown by the comparison between the daily foreign exchange turnover and the monthly sales of stocks on all U.S. stock exchanges. In brief, financial transactions between U.S. and foreign businesses

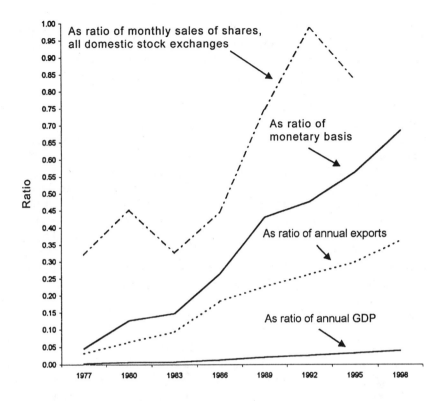

Chart 3.2. Average Daily Foreign Exchange Turnover in U.S.

Note: Sources of data are given in Appendix 3.1.

have soared; and foreign purchases and holding of U.S. dollars and dollar assets have amounted to an ever larger part of the U.S. economy.

A major part of the short-term capital flow has been between the United States and a relatively small number of industrialized nations. One part of this stream appeared to have had little direct effect on the U.S. economy, namely currency swaps and various transactions between those residing abroad that occur because much of the exchange of goods, services, and securities between foreign nations has been denominated in U.S. dollars.[8] But a significant part of

---

8 A German buys a good denominated in dollars from a Japanese. The German exchanges Euros into dollars, which are sent to the Japanese, who converts the dollars into yen. The amount of dollars held abroad does not change, although their distribution in Germany and Japan is different. Sometime along this financial path, the good in question is also sent from Japan to Germany.

these currency flows could have a potentially serious impact on U.S. financial conditions, for example, the flows of short-term speculative funds or the capital flows for investment purposes, much of which come from foreign financial institutions attempting to spread their financial risks. The purchases by foreign governments of U.S. securities as part of their international reserves are included among these capital flows as well. In certain circumstances, many of these foreign-held funds could be quickly withdrawn.

Some idea of the rising importance to the U.S. economy of such foreign governmental portfolio investment can be seen from data presented by Dorothy Sobol on the holders of Treasury securities. It can be argued that these are much more important to the financial health of the U.S. economy than the volume of currency crossing the border. In 1970 the share held by non-U.S. citizens amounted to somewhat less than 9 percent; but by the end of 1997 it had risen to almost 38 percent. Indeed, from 1995 through 1997, the amount of new bonds purchased by foreigners exceeded those purchased by U.S. citizens. By the end of the century two nations, the U.K. and Japan, owned almost half of U.S. governmental bonds held abroad. Thus, in June 1997, when Japanese Prime Minister Hashimoto publicly mused that his government might have to sell some of its large holding in these bonds, the Dow-Jones stock index fell 192 points the next day because investors feared a rapid fall in the price of bonds and soaring interest rates as a result of the future Japanese sell-off.

The actions of foreign governments aside, the most serious threat posed by the increasing flow of foreign exchange is the possibility that many private foreign holders of U.S. dollars or securities might decide to withdraw these funds at the same time. This could occur, not just for the classical reason that foreigners "lose confidence" in the dollar,[9] but for other reasons as well. For instance, a burst of new investment opportunities in other nations might draw investment funds out of the U.S. Moreover, the U.S. may lose its standing as the world's premier safe harbor for currency as memories of the financial difficulties in Asia in the late 1990s fade or if confidence in the Euro finally increases and its strength against the dollar begins to rise.

    b. *A potentially devastating domestic shock:* Under some circumstances, a decline in domestic asset prices and the resulting evaporation of significant amounts of unrealized capital gain might cause a serious internal shock to the financial system. The U.S. had a taste of this possibility, at least in the

---

[9] Some argue that such a loss of confidence might occur as the U.S. continues to run large trade or current account deficits. Others offer two counter-arguments. First, foreigners place many of their funds in the United States in investments with high yields, so that a massive outflow of funds is unlikely. Second, the U.S. governmental statisticians overstate the trade deficit because of their difficulties in measuring exports and imports.

short-run, with the crash of dot-com equities in 2000-2001. In the previous chapter I examine this possibility for the long-term. More specifically, I argue that as the population ages and the number of retired workers drawing down their savings increases in comparison to active workers building up their savings, the ratio of net saving to GDP will decrease. Among other things this means that at a given price, the quantity demanded of financial and real assets will fall, and such a decline in demand will, in turn, bring about a fall in asset prices. Moreover, as shown in the discussion about Table 2.1, unrealized capital gains account for a significant share of saving when saving is measured in terms of a change in net worth, rather than in terms of the flows in the national account statistics. The impact of a long-term fall in asset values would, therefore, have a major impact on the economy as a whole.

It is certainly possible for investors to fully anticipate this future decline in relative asset prices and the evaporation of unrealized capital gains. Or this process might occur at a sufficiently slow pace so that financial markets experience no serious repercussions, other than a gradual rise in interest rates. Nevertheless, the demographic shifts of workers to retirees is considerable and occurs primarily in the two decades between 2010 and 2030. More specifically, from the population projection used in the simulations in Chapter 2 we find that the ratio of the people over 64 to those between 25 and 65 rises from 25 percent in 2010 to 32 percent in 2020, and to 44 percent in 2030. Under certain conditions, the change in relative asset prices induced by these changes in the age distribution might be sufficiently abrupt to cause serious difficulties in financial markets and the possibility of a monetary crisis.

B. Production Fluctuations[10]

We cannot analyze volatility in the "real" or productive side of the economy in quite the same way as financial volatility, because two important performance indicators are involved: the degree to which production fluctuates within a desirable range and the degree to which the economy falls short of full employment. After discussing the relevant performance indicators, I then argue that fiscal and monetary policy are becoming less effective tools for stabilizing production and, moreover, that the production sphere will be subject to increasing shocks. Both of these developments will, of course, adversely affect the macroeconomic performance of the U.S. economy in the future.

---

[10]   In this section I draw upon studies by: Bordo et al. (1999), Cohen (1998), Jefferson (1998), Mayer (2001), McConnell and Quiros (1997), Pryor and Schaffer (2000), and Pryor and Sulcove (1995).

1. Performance Indicators

Indicators of aggregate production, such as the GDP, reveal a declining volatility over the post-World War II period. One measure of such fluctuations is the percentage deviation of actual production from some standard of full employment, which is often determined on a time-series graph of the GDP by connecting the production peaks in the business cycle.[11] Between 1950 and 1974, the average annual deviation of this full-employment standard was 4.0 percent; between 1975 and 1997, 2.7 percent. In the last quarter of the 20th century, annual GDP clearly manifested lower fluctuations.

Production fluctuations can also be measured by differences in the unemployment rate from its long-term trend, and this also reveals a decline in production volatility. Elliott Sulcove and I use yet another approach by measuring deviations of 29 different time-series of physical production and unemployment and measuring their deviations from trends determined from a five-year moving average. Almost all calculations show a decrease in volatility between the 1950s and the 1990s.

Other studies confirm these empirical results.[12] Margaret McConnell and Gabriel Quiros perform a much more detailed statistical test of changing volatility, looking at the quarterly growth rates of the GDP from the early 1950s to the middle 1990s. Employing a sophisticated statistical technique, they show that the U.S. economy experienced a structural break in the first quarter of 1964 that resulted in significantly less volatility in GDP. Further, such a break did not occur in any of the other large industrialized nations comprising the G-7.[13] In brief, the Marxian hypothesis of ever more violent business cycles receives no support from the U.S. data, at least in the second half of the 20th century.

---

[11]   I used an exponential curve to connect the two peaks of the business cycle on the time- series graph. The problem, however, is which business cycle peak to select. On the graph I looked at 15 year intervals and calculated all of the "production potential" lines. I then selected that peak whose "potential production" line lay above the lines from other peaks within the interval.

[12]   For instance, Christine Romer (1999) calculated a standard deviation of percentage changes and finds a decline in volatility in GNP, industrial production, and the unemployment rate between 1948 and 1984 and between 1985 and 1997. Moreover, for the entire 1948-1997 period she finds a decline in volatility of these indicators in comparison to the period between 1886 and 1916 and also between 1920 and 1940.

[13]   Unfortunately, the authors do not explain what caused this structural break. They do explore the matter statistically, by decomposing the GDP time-series, and find that some of the break emanated from a fall in the volatility of durable goods production. The timing of this break also corresponded to a reduction in the proportion of durables accounted for by inventories, a change due, in part, to utilization of new computer methods of inventory control. The various causal mechanisms underlying the structure break still remain, however, unclear.

From the perspective of the maintenance of full employment, however, the performance of the U.S. economy in the second half of the 20th century does not appear so successful. Two series are of particular interest: the rate of unemployment measured in the standard manner and the rate of joblessness of prime-age males (men between 25 and 50), who, according to conventional bourgeois expectations, ought to be employed. This latter measure includes both the unemployed in a traditional sense and those who have dropped out of the labor force for reasons such as discouragement about finding work. It provides a particularly sensitive indicator of the strength of the labor market and is used in the next chapter to analyze changes in the income distribution. From 1950 through 1998, the annual rate of increase (not percentage points of increase) of the unemployment rate was 1.0 percent; and of the joblessness rate, 1.6 percent.[14]

Although both indicators suggest that the U.S. was slowly deviating from a full-employment economy in the second half of the 20th century, two counter-arguments to this interpretation can be offered. First, as the complexity of the U.S. economy increases and jobs become more specialized, frictional unemployment (the unemployment of people between jobs) has increased, because of greater difficulties in matching jobs to people with the requisite skills. Second, part of the rising joblessness among prime-age males was "voluntary," either because they did not want to work or because they chose work in the underground economy or in the home and, as a result, were not counted as part of the labor force. A closer examination of the rising joblessness rate, however, does not offer much support for this second argument, as shown in the evidence David Schaffer and I have presented elsewhere.

In contrast to macro-financial volatility, which increased and then leveled off over the second half of the 20th century, production volatility decreased. Nevertheless, in terms of the increasing rates of unemployment or joblessness of prime-age males, the production performance over the last half century does not appear an unalloyed success.

2. The Tradeoff Between Less Volatility and Greater Effectiveness of Fiscal Policy

In this subsection I argue that in the next few decades, fiscal policy will probably be less effective than hitherto in stabilizing the economy. The analysis is

---

[14] Both these rates were calculated by fitting an exponential curve to the series and are statistically significant. The unemployment data come from the Bureau of Labor Statistics website: BLS Web site: http://stats.bls.gov/datahome.htm. The sources of data on joblessness rate are found in Appendix 4.1.

complicated by the fact that we must take account of a tradeoff between the effectiveness of fiscal policy and short-term volatility of the economy, because both depend on the value of the Keynesian multiplier.

A tax cut or an increase in government spending raises the GDP a specified amount, namely, the amount of purchasing power injected into the economy times the multiplier.[15] Although a higher multiplier indicates that a given tax cut or spending increase has a greater positive impact, it also means that the economy is more volatile in the short-run and more sensitive to random shocks such as changes in exports or investment or autonomous shifts in consumption. By way of contrast, if the multiplier is low, the economy is less sensitive to these shocks, manifests less short-term volatility; but, in a serious recession, fiscal policy is also a less effective tool for regaining full employment.

In any discussion of this tradeoff between effectiveness of fiscal policy and production volatility, the key question is the magnitude of the Keynesian multiplier and how it will evolve in the future. Standard Keynesian analysis tells us that the fiscal multiplier is inversely related to both the marginal propensity to save and import. These are respectively the additional amounts saved (in contrast to consumed) or imported (in contrast to being spent on domestic goods and services) from an additional dollar of income. Both saving and imports represent purchasing power not spent on domestic goods and services, and, in an important sense, they represent leakages of expenditures away from domestic production. Any injection of purchasing power into the economy by the government (fiscal policy) to raise the aggregate demand for domestic production thus has a lower effectiveness because of such offsets. The multiplier is also related to certain automatic injections of governmental funds (for instance, payments to the unemployed) into the economy during times of recession.

In brief, if the multiplier is low, the economy is less likely to experience short-term volatility, such as a short recession; but if such a recession lasts, the effectiveness of discretionary fiscal policy to restore full employment is less. If the multiplier is high, the economy is likely to experience greater volatility, but the effectiveness of discretionary fiscal policy is also greater. To determine the changing value of the multiplier, it is necessary to take into account offsetting trends in the marginal propensities to save and to import. I discuss the various factors in turn, assuming a fixed exchange rate (since fiscal policy is most effective under these conditions).

---

[15] Part of the purchasing power injected into the economy by the government for, let us say, building a dam, is used by the construction workers to purchase consumption goods. And part of these dollars are spent by others. Thus, a dollar injected into the economy may, in the end, raise GDP by $1.40 . The ratio of the final increase in GDP to the initial amount of purchasing power injected is the multiplier. Actually, there are several different multipliers depending upon the type of expenditure or tax cut; but for purposes of this argument, such a refinement is not necessary.

• *The marginal propensity to save (MPS):* As argued in Chapter 2, personal saving as a share of income will probably decline considerably in the future, when the baby boom generation starts retiring after 2010. In the long term, this decline in the saving rate will undoubtedly be accompanied by a fall in the MPS. That is, retirees not only draw down their accumulated savings but usually spend all of the new income they receive. Thus, an injection by the government of additional funds into the economy should have a greater effect in a recession because the multiplier is greater; or, to put the matter differently, less purchasing power will leak out into saving during the various rounds of additional income and spending that result from this injection. By way of contrast, if the MPS is high, the fiscal impact of government intervention is low, because most of the injected funds will be saved rather than spent, so that this extra purchasing power will not cycle very far through the economy.

• *The marginal propensity to import (MPM):* To understand the impact of the MPM, consider for a moment why state and local governments do not engage in fiscal policy. Even if these governments were permitted to employ such policy tools,[16] such efforts would be ineffective to raise the income of citizens under their jurisdiction. This is because, at this level of the national economy, statistical studies show that consumers have a high marginal propensity to import from other areas. That is, they would spend a great deal of this additional purchasing power on goods produced in other cities and states. In brief, cities and states within the U.S. have high MPMs because they are heavily involved in the national economy. Thus, fiscal policy at the local level would be ineffective (unless the local government buys only locally produced goods and services and requires all others to follow its example, which is impossible).

In like manner, globalization of the U.S. economy raises the national MPM because consumers are more aware of foreign goods than they used to be and foreign competition in U.S. domestic markets increases. And this is exactly what we find empirically.[17] More specifically, in the U.S. the MPM in the 1950s was .07; in the 1960s, .09; in the 1970s, .10; in the 1980s, .18; and, in the 1990s, .34. As a result, the fiscal multiplier fell and the effectiveness of fiscal policy decreased, especially in the 1980s and beyond. At the same time, however, the lower multiplier means that the economy became less sensitive to small shocks

---

[16] All U.S. state governments, with the exception of Vermont, have some type of constitutional or legal requirement for a balanced state governmental budget (Eichengreen, 1990).

[17] Let imports (M) be a linear function of GDP (Y), so that $M = a + bY$. In this formula "b" is the MPM. I simply fitted constant price data to this formula using standard regression techniques and report the "b" coefficient. The data come from the website of the Department of Commerce, Bureau of Economic Analysis: www.bea.doc.gov/bea/dn1.htm.

and, over the period, no sufficiently large shock came along to push the economy into a serious depression, which would require serious fiscal injections to counteract.

• *Automatic stabilizers:* During most of the second half of the 20th century, various entitlement programs for different types of welfare led to automatic counter-cyclical changes in federal governmental expenditures. For instance, if economic times were bad, more women were eligible for funds from the Aid for Dependent Children program. A series of reforms of the federal welfare system in the middle 1990s, however, diminished the impact of these fiscal stabilizers. More specifically, many types of welfare payments were transformed from automatic entitlements for individuals to a system of fixed block grants to the states, which could change the rules by which they were distributed, constrained only by various rules mandated by the federal government.

Under the earlier welfare regime, if a recession brought on an increased demand for welfare payments, the federal government would finance them by either selling bonds or printing more money. This increase in welfare expenditures has become less automatic in the reformed welfare regime because none of the states can print money or run large budget deficits (see footnote 16). Thus, during a serious recession when state revenues are falling, this constraint might force a state to reduce the amount of welfare funds distributed even as the number of welfare applicants increased, at least if it did not have sufficient cash reserves to meet this increased demand for welfare payments. Since the welfare recipients would have less to spend, the aggregate demand for goods and services in the new system would be less than under the previous system. In brief, the new welfare regime acts to intensify the volatility of the economy.

Lining up these various offsetting trends, we see that two of them, a falling marginal propensity to save and the change in the welfare system, are leading to a higher multiplier, while one, the rising marginal propensity to import, will lead to a falling fiscal multiplier. If the former two factors are stronger, the U.S. will experience greater short-term production volatility in the future, but the impact of discretionary fiscal policy will also be greater. If the latter is stronger, the U.S. will experience less short-term production volatility, but the impact of discretionary fiscal policy will also be smaller.

In the immediate future, before net saving begin to decline because of the changing age distribution, it seems likely that the MPM effect will be stronger. Thus, in the coming years we will experience less short-term volatility combined with less effective fiscal policy. If, as in the 1990s, the economy does not experience any large negative shock, prosperity will continue. If, however, the economy experiences a severe negative shock and spirals into a serious recession, governmental fiscal policy will be less able to halt the downward movement and bring the economy back to full employment. After the demographic shift has begun and the saving rate declines, this situation might be the reverse, so that we will experience more production volatility but, at the same time, the government will be more able to keep the nation from falling into a deep recession. Unfortunately, the relative strengths of these offsetting effects have not been calculated, as far as I can determine, so any prediction on these matters is subject to considerable uncertainty.

3. Other Factors Influencing the Effectiveness of Fiscal Policy in the Coming Decades

Up to now I have assumed that discretionary fiscal policy can be an effective policy tool for smoothing the business cycle. Many types of changes in taxes and government expenditures that make up fiscal policy require Congressional approval and, as I argue in later chapters from a variety of perspectives, it seems likely that a workable consensus in Congress will become increasingly difficult to achieve. As a result, Congress will take much longer to implement such policies. Three other lags—in recognizing that an economic downturn has occurred, in implementing the policy, and in the policy actually having a marked impact, seem likely to become greater as the complexity of the economy increases. As a result of these four lags, fiscal policy might stimulate or dampen the economy at the wrong time so that the business cycle would be accentuated, rather than smoothed.

The impact of fiscal policy on the exchange rate and the balance of payments also affects policy effectiveness. In a fixed rate regime with a constant money supply, an expansionary fiscal policy influences the balance of payments in two offsetting ways. Such policy would tend to raise the interest rate, an outcome that would attract foreign funds from abroad and give rise to a surplus in the balance of payments. But the greater domestic purchasing power would lead to more imports, which would give rise to a deficit in the balance of payments. Whichever of these two forces acting on the balance of payments is stronger, the Federal Reserve could offset by means of the proper monetary policy so that, in the end, the foreign exchange account would remain in balance so that the exchange rate would remain the same. In such a situation, however, there is no guarantee that the final equilibrium of the domestic economy would be at a state of full employment.

If the foreign exchange rate is floating according to supply-and-demand forces, as it was during the 1990s, the argument has one more step. Under usual circumstances,[18] a depreciation is expansionary since it encourages exports (since they are now less expensive) and discourages imports (since they are now

---

[18]   More technically, if the Marshall-Lerner conditions are met.

more expensive). The impact of expansionary fiscal policy is thus enhanced if the currency depreciates, because the inflow of foreign funds stimulated by the rise in interest is greater than the outflow of foreign funds resulting from more domestic purchasing power. In the reverse situation when the currency appreciates, the impact of fiscal policy is reduced. Since changing foreign exchange rates also give rise to flows of certain speculative funds, an unambiguous determination of the impact of fiscal policy becomes even more difficult, thereby reducing the government's willingness to employ this policy tool to stabilize production.

Since the floating exchange regime in place at the turn of the millennium seems likely to endure for at least the next decade, the near-term future use of discretionary fiscal policy seems limited. In the far future, much greater economic integration with the rest of the world is likely to reduce the effectiveness of such policy tool even more.[19]

4. The Decreasing Effectiveness of Monetary Policy to Stabilize Production

The Federal Reserve uses monetary policy not just to stabilize production, interest rates, and foreign exchange rates, but also to fight inflation. Using monetary policy to achieve full employment is constrained because the Fed sometimes faces a tradeoff with the competing goal of restraining prices. Moreover, the influence of changes in the interest rate on investment and thereby on aggregate production is weak and uncertain. Further, in a globalized economy, additional constraints are placed on the monetary policy goal of stabilizing production at full employment. In the discussion below I focus particularly on the

---

[19] If, in the far future, the U.S. joins with the EU nations to form an Economic Union of Atlantic Nations, this will lower the effectiveness of discretionary fiscal policy even more. In such an event, the exchange rate would be fixed, but the marginal propensity to import would undoubtedly rise considerably, so that the federal government would be in the same position as U.S. states and cities today. Moreover, as a part of this supranational union, the U.S. would not have the benefits that U.S. states and cities now draw from current automatic fiscal stabilizers. Some idea of the magnitudes involved can be gained from estimates by Sachs and Sala-i-Martín (1992), who look at the nine census regions within the U.S. According to their estimates, in the 1980s the automatic fiscal offset by the federal government to any fall in relative regional income amounted to roughly 40 cents per dollar of income decline. Given the changes in the federal welfare system in the mid 1990s, however, this fiscal offset by the federal government is now smaller. In any kind of Economic Union of Atlantic Nations, such a fiscal offset from the supranational government would probably be quite weak. This is because the political willingness to transfer domestic tax revenues to other ("foreign") nations within any such Union would be more feeble than to transfer funds from one U.S. state to another through the federal budget.

impact of globalization in reducing the effectiveness of monetary policy in stabilizing production and achieving full employment.

• *Control over the money supply.* City and state governments do not engage in monetary policy to stabilize their local economies because they have no control over their money supply. In the past, this has not been the case for the federal government, which could issue its own currency. Nevertheless, the degree to which the federal government can control the money supply becomes increasingly problematic in a globalized economy. This can be seen in a recent book by Benjamin Cohen, who disputes the long held notion that all currencies are national ("One nation/one money"), since in many countries, several different currencies (for instance, U.S. dollars and the national currency) are used. One dramatic indicator is the foreign holdings of U.S. dollars, which Philip Jefferson has shown to represent at the end of 1995 more than half of the total currency issued by the U.S. government. It is, of course, difficult for U.S. monetary authorities to control the domestic money supply through such traditional tools of monetary policy as open market operations if a huge share of dollars and U.S. bonds are held abroad and if large amounts of foreign exchange and dollars flow in and out of the economy every day, as shown in Chart 3.2.[20] The problem of the effectiveness of monetary policy is compounded by the introduction of electronic money and of "money" created through credit card debt.

• *Control over the interest rate:* In an integrated national financial market, interest rates vary little from locality to locality. If, for some reason, interest rates are higher in one region than another, lenders from other regions would try to do business there to take advantage of these higher interest rates. Such market responses (technically, "interest arbitrage") would eventually lead to similar interest rates in all regions again because the supply of available credit in the high interest region would increase. Or if a municipal government buys bonds (that is, supplies credit) within its city limits in order to lower the interest rate (and raise the price of bonds), other suppliers of credit within the city would sell the bonds in their portfolios to the city at this higher price and then

---

[20]   The impact of electronic money (e-money) on monetary policy is a controversial issue. Some argue that with the advent of e-money, central bank control over interest rates also becomes weaker, especially as the demand for traditional money declines. Moreover, if physical cash disappears, so might traditional banks: people would store their monetary assets with an electronic custodian who would neither issue liabilities nor extend credit, but would merely transfer (as directed) the ownership over such stored assets, for instance, in making loans. Others argue that specialized financial intermediaries will always be necessary as purveyors of information, for instance, to help people and firms distinguish between good and bad credit risks. Further, central banks can borrow or lend e-money so as to influence interest rates. Without knowing how e-money will be institutionalized in the future, it is difficult to make any forecast about its impact on monetary policy.

use these funds to buy bonds in other regions at lower prices (and higher interest rates). So the city government's monetary policy would have little stimulus to the municipal economy.

If financial markets on a global level become fully integrated, the same situation would arise, so that interest rates around the world would be roughly equal, plus or minus various types of risk factors. As a result, domestic monetary authorities will have less and less influence on the (global) interest rate in the future, just as cities and states have little influence on the national interest rate now. With these two developments in mind, we can now focus more directly on the changing effectiveness of monetary policy for stabilizing the economy when the exchange rate is either fixed or floating.

The increasing economic integration of industrial nations (see Chapter 5) has led to fewer controls on international capital flows and an ever-climbing volume of investment flows crossing national borders. Under a fixed exchange rate system, policy makers face, however, the "impossible trinity," namely a country's ability to have a fixed exchange rate, capital mobility, and an independent monetary policy all at the same time. This is because, with a fixed exchange rate, the monetary authorities must focus their full efforts on maintaining an interest rate such that the free flows of investment or speculative funds in and out of the economy will not imbalance the foreign exchange accounts and put pressure on the exchange rate. As a result, monetary policy cannot be easily used for stabilizing production at the full employment level. Thus, for a variety of reasons—the declining control of the monetary authorities over the money supply and interest rates, the impact of the "impossible trinity," and the uncertain impact of interest rates on investment—monetary policy in a fixed exchange rate regime will not be an effective tool of stabilization policy.

In a floating exchange rate regime, the monetary authorities no longer need to worry about maintaining a fixed exchange rate. To the contrary, they can appreciate or depreciate the dollar directly by selling or buying foreign exchange for dollars; or they can indirectly influence the exchange rate by open market operations which would change the interest rate and stimulate or discourage a flow of investment funds into the U.S. and, correspondingly, appreciate or depreciate the dollar.

Of course, the direct manipulation of exchange rates by the monetary authorities to influence aggregate demand is a blatant type of beggar-thy-neighbor policy and is discouraged by international norms except in cases where it is used to stabilize short-term currency fluctuations or where it is necessary to correct a "fundamental disequilibrium." But the indirect manipulation of exchange rates by open market operations to lower the domestic interest rate, which would induce certain investors to move their investments abroad, has a similar effect of cheapening the dollar in terms of foreign currencies and stimulating the domestic economy.

Although monetary policy in a floating exchange rate regime can have an important stabilizing role, its use by the U.S. government is constrained because, as the global superpower, any type of beggar-thy-neighbor policy might have disastrous global effects. Moreover, this stabilizing role is likely to diminish in the future for two reasons. First, as argued above, the ability to influence domestic interest rates becomes attenuated as world capital markets become more integrated. Second, international agreements will undoubtedly constrain domestic monetary authorities from using this tool as freely as now because of its adverse impact on other countries.

In brief, because of weakening control over the money supply and interest rates brought about by globalization, monetary policy is likely to become a less effective policy to stabilize production. Such a result obtains, whether or not the exchange rates are fixed or floating.

• *The influence of increased financial complexity.* In the last decades of the 20th century, various new financial instruments, such as specialized options and derivatives, have proliferated. Moreover, non-bank financial institutions, such as insurance companies, pension funds, and specialized security dealers, began to exercise a greater influence in financial markets. At the same time, the Federal Reserve Bank's control over bank activities began to have a smaller influence in the operation of domestic credit markets. Although the Fed was given an increased regulatory role over some non-bank institutions and transactions in the Gramm-Leach-Bliley Act of 1999, the stabilizing effect of this change has been questioned. Based on an assessment of the growing complexity of the financial system and the ways in which the Federal Reserve Bank makes its decision, some experts, such as Martin Mayer, argue that it seems unlikely these increased regulatory powers will be exercised effectively and that the Feds influence on financial markets will continue to decline.

5. Future Production Shocks

It seems likely that shocks to the production system, like those to the financial system, will increase in magnitude.

a. *External Shocks:* Given the rising share of exports in the GDP (discussed in detail in Chapter 5), the U.S. economy will be more subject to production shocks from abroad. This could include, for instance, a significant fall in exports as a result of an economic recession experienced by its major trade partners. This would, in turn, result in a fall in the total demand for goods and services produced in the U.S. and a rise in domestic unemployment. It is, of course, true that in 1997-98, the U.S. weathered the severe financial crises and recessions in a number of developing nations, such as Thailand, Indonesia,

Korea, Russia, and Brazil, which resulted in a decline in their demand for U.S. exports. But this fortunate outcome for the U.S. occurred because U.S. exports to these nations were a relatively small share of total foreign trade. Moreover, in those years the U.S. economy was in exceptionally good shape and investment returned to Asia relatively quickly. As a result, aggregate U.S. production did not decline. But more serious difficulties to more important trade partners might have graver repercussions. Moreover, some analysts such as Michael Bordo and his colleagues present evidence that the impact on the GDP of these exchange-rate crises in developing nations have become more severe than in the past, so that foreign shocks of this nature to the U.S. economy may increase in magnitude.

On the import side, external shocks could include sudden increases in raw material prices, such as the rapid rise in oil prices in the 1970s or in 2000. It should be noted, however, that because of the shift in the U.S. toward a service economy, many consider the country less vulnerable to sudden price changes in raw materials. Because the information economy is so energy intensive, however, such confidence may be misplaced, at least regarding oil prices.

b. *Internal Shocks:* I believe that internal shocks pose a much greater threat to the U.S. economy than those originating from abroad, especially a spillover from a crisis in the financial sector. If financial volatility on a microeconomic level becomes greater as a result of the growing fragility of the financial system, this may trigger fluctuations in production as well. The linkage between financial and production fluctuations is loose—witness the minuscule effect of the 1987 stock market crash on the GDP. Nevertheless, a really severe financial crisis, as in 1929, could spillover to the production side with disastrous effects.

The dramatic fall in asset prices discussed in the previous chapter seems the most important threat because it could have three potentially adverse impacts on aggregate demand: The fall in the value of wealth holdings might result in lower personal consumption. The fall in asset prices might result in less new investment. And the bankruptcies occurring as a result of the financial problems might lower the confidence of both consumers and investors even more.

Another type of spillover occurs when the buying behavior of consumers is affected by their financial balances. For instance, the 1990-91 slowdown in the U.S. economy seemed due in large measure to a retrenchment on the part of consumers in response to their over-indebtedness in the late 1980s. There was little that the monetary or fiscal authorities could have done to stimulate production in these circumstances.

6. A Brief Summary

Volatility of aggregate production decreased in the second half of the 20th century, even while the economy appeared to move further from its full employment potential until the last few years of the century. In the next few decades, fiscal policy will probably become a less effective stabilization tool, because of the rising marginal propensity to import accompanying globalization. Moreover, because of globalization and the increasing integration of world capital markets, monetary authorities will be less able to control the money supply and interest rates, so that monetary policy will also become a less effective stabilization tool.

If the U.S. experiences a major economic depression in the future, the major cause will most likely be a spillover from a financial crisis, itself resulting from a growing fragility of the financial system. But to make this claim with any certainty, we must ask why no such event occurred in the second half of the 20th century.

C. Resolving a Paradox [21]

The discussion above contains an apparent contradiction. The analysis of financial fragility suggests that the U.S. economy is becoming ever more vulnerable to shocks, and the analysis of the production side of the economy suggests that governmental stabilization tools are becoming less effective. Why aren't these developments reflected in the performance indicators of the financial sector, which show a leveling off of financial volatility after an increase up to the 1980s? And why do we find a reduction, not an increase, in the volatility of aggregate production in the second half of the 20th century? These apparent inconsistencies can be resolved in several ways:

• *Better macroeconomic policies:* According to this argument, economic science has reached a point of such sophistication and accuracy that policy makers know when and how to intervene strategically to avoid a cumulative downturn and, in particular, how to avoid the policy mistakes that exacerbated recessions and financial panics in the past.

As regards fiscal policy I find this argument dubious. Although policy makers may know what to do, effective fiscal policy depends, not just on timely decisions by both the federal administration and Congress, but also on rapid implementation, as noted above. Since governmental tax and expenditure policies have an impact, not only on aggregate demand but also on the distribution of income, additional problems of policy formulation and implementation arise, especially in an era when economic growth is much slower than before. In later chapters I argue that it will become more and more difficult to reach a political

---

[21] In the text of this section I refer to a study by Zarnowitz (1999).

consensus necessary to implement effective policies for stabilizing the economy. In other words, the political deadlock in Congress in the late 1990s will continue, thereby reducing the possibility of pursuing effective fiscal measures, whatever happens to the magnitude of the fiscal multiplier. As noted above, fiscal policy becomes even weaker in the current system of floating exchange rates, a currency regime which should continue for many years.

Despite increasing globalization, monetary policy seemed to be playing an important stabilizing role and, in the last years of the 20th century, the Federal Reserve appeared to be getting more adept. For instance, its intervention in the stock market crash of October 1987 prevented not just a long-term fall in stock prices but also a recession resulting from a fall of investment. Or its skillful handling of the September 1998 collapse of Long Term Capital Management, the world's largest hedge fund, which likewise could have resulted in a severe liquidity crisis and a serious cascade of bankruptcies.

Nevertheless, it is widely recognized that monetary policy has its limits, even in a floating exchange rate regime. It is, for instance, doubtful that monetary policy could offset certain severe shocks, such as a rapid decline in asset prices or the impact of a major decline in aggregate demand. Certainly, the monetary policies implemented in Japan that led to an extremely low interest rate and an undervalued exchange rate have not proven successful in markedly improving that country economic performance. And, as argued above, the ability of the Federal Reserve to control either the money supply or interest rates will become weaker.

• *Counteracting structural changes:* According to this argument, while many indicators discussed above point to greater fragility of the economy and vulnerability to shocks, other structural changes counteract the impact of these developments. One can cite numerous examples of ways in which the economy is better able to manage financial risks. Certainly commercial banks have tools that allow them to operate with much less liquidity. Various types of futures markets, derivative instruments, and insurance arrangements have also been devised that allow financial risks of default to be more widely spread or placed in the hands of those more able to bear them.

On the production side, other changes counteract trends toward greater volatility. For instance, annuitization of pensions (discussed in Chapter 2) has made the spending of the elderly much less sensitive to business cycle conditions. New methods of inventory control apparently reduce fluctuations originating from the production side of the economy. The shift into services, which historically have shown less volatility than the production of goods, may also moderate the business cycle although, as Victor Zarnowitz points out, services are themselves exhibiting more cyclical behavior, so that their past performance does not necessarily presage the future.

It is possible that these changes have helped to reduce production and financial volatility in the last few decades of the 20th century. Unfortunately, the strength of these and other structural changes to counteract the growing financial fragility in the coming decades is not known, and it is reasonable to harbor doubts about their effectiveness.

It is also possible—although not probable, at least in the current political climate—that the U.S. will take certain policy steps that might further offset the impact of external and internal shocks. For instance, certain limitations could be placed on the indebtedness of financial institutions not currently regulated.[22] Or switchgate policies could be set up to insure that transfer payments to the state and local governments would be automatically increased if unemployment passes a certain point. We certainly have no dearth of suggestions for improving either the domestic or the international financial architecture. It remains to be seen whether these or other measures would be strong enough to offset the increasing fragility of the economy.

• *The "big one" is yet to come:* According to this argument, in the last few decades of the 20th century a series of adventitious events offset the impact of adverse financial or production shocks, so that the U.S. economy did not face a serious recession or downward financial spiral. Nevertheless, the country cannot expect such good fortune to continue forever, and when any serious shock does occur, its overall effect will be extremely severe because of the increased fragility of the economic system. Although I find considerable merit in this argument, it will be convincing to many only after the economy has experienced severe difficulties.

In brief, the paradox of increasing fragility coexisting with little recent change in financial volatility and decreasing fluctuations in production cannot be convincingly resolved. We lack credible data to support any of the explanations offered above. In other words, at this point we have reached the limit of responsible prediction.

---

22 For instance, the Long Term Capital Management company managed to leverage roughly $5 billion in assets to obtain securities worth about $125 billion and derivatives contracts with a notional value of considerably more.

 One measure for limiting volatility that has received considerable support is a limitation on margin requirements. Although margin debt as a percentage of total value of corporate securities rose considerably over the second half of the 20th century and, on January 1, 2000, was higher than at any point during the period, it was still slightly less than 3 percent of the total market value of these securities. As a result, this proposal would have little impact on stock market volatility. The calculation is based on margin debt data from the Financial Market Center (http://www.fmcenter.org/front.asp) and the Federal Reserve's flow of funds data (Table B100) on the value of corporate securities.

D. Some Impacts on the Economy and the Economic System of Greater Volatility

In the previous chapter I could speak with more certainty about the future than in this chapter, because demographic changes are more certain than changes in the Keynesian multiplier and the effectiveness of monetary and fiscal policy to dampen production fluctuations. In looking at the impact on such volatility, I can only speak conditionally: If the growing financial fragility leads to greater volatility of production, the effects both on U.S. economic performance and the economic system would be serious.

As noted in the previous chapter, deepening recessions will lower investment and, of course, the growth rate. This would reinforce the tendency toward a declining growth of GDP brought about by the falling saving rate due to a changing age-distribution. Although such production fluctuations always bring about increased joblessness and a fall in income, in these circumstances the low-income population is always hurt the most; I discuss this and other issues of income inequality in greater detail in the next chapter.

Serious recessions, just like other national emergencies such as war, usually have an important influence on economic institutions and organizations—witness the changes in the economic system occurring as a result of the great depression in the 1930s and World War II in the 1940s. At this point three possible impacts of adverse macroeconomic developments on the economic system should be briefly noted:

• *Backlash against globalization.* The political forces opposing current trends toward greater integration of the world economy would be greatly strengthened. As a result, it would be likely that the U.S. government would provide more protection of domestic production from international competition and, in addition, would reintroduce controls on international capital movements. It is also possible that the share of the national economy represented by exports and imports which has been rising for several decades, would begin to decline. I analyze these issues at greater length Chapter 5.

• *Rising governmental expenditures:* If involuntary unemployment would increase, public programs to provide employment and governmental expenditures to aid the unemployed would also undoubtedly increase. Such policy responses, fueled by domestic political pressures, would increase governmental expenditures in the economy.

• *Reversal of the deregulation trend:* Steps would probably be taken to give the government greater control over the economy and, as a result, the current trend toward deregulation, described in detail in Chapter 11, would be reversed. It took a half century to get rid of many of the measures instituted under the New Deal to address economic problems caused by the economic depression in the 1930s. The measures taken to combat the ill effects of another economic depression may prove just as durable.

In brief, the impact on the U.S. economic system of a severe financial crisis or an adverse production shock would be great. Like a major war, however, such events cannot be easily predicted. Nevertheless, I believe that the possibilities of a major economic depression in the coming decades are sufficiently high to worry about because of the increasing fragility of the financial system, the possibility of a significant fall in asset prices, and the diminished effectiveness of monetary and fiscal policy.

If such a depression occurs, its impact would probably outweigh most of the other factors discussed in this book. In order to analyze systematically these other factors impinging on the future of U.S. capitalism, I assume in the remaining chapters that an extremely serious downturn will not occur. I keep my fingers crossed in the hope that the U.S. will really have such a lucky break.

CHAPTER 4

Income Inequality

[Long before 1993], America will have no very rich or very poor.[1]
—*Editor/Politician T.V. Powderly, 1893*

During the 1950s and 1960s family incomes became considerably more equal. Thereafter, the trend was reversed, so that, by the dawn of the new millennium, percentage income differentials between the rich and the poor were much greater than in 1950. According to the Millennium Survey, professional economists expect such inequality to become even greater in the future and, moreover, to have a significant impact on the economic system. In exploring the causes of growing inequality, we face some serious issues about how the U.S. economic system will function in the future.

In the following analysis I first outline the major income trends in the second half of the 20th century, and then try to disentangle their underlying determinants. Of particular interest are trends in "relative income ratios," a measure focusing on the incomes of the poor and the rich as ratios of the median income. I argue that these relative income ratios moved in opposite directions in the second half of the 20th century; that this relationship was causal, not fortuitous; and that this trend is likely to continue in the future. Finally, I explore how increasing inequality of income might affect both the structure and the functioning of the future economic system.

A. Increasing Economic Inequality [2]

1. An International Perspective

In comparison to other industrialized nations, the distribution of income in the United States is highly unequal. The most rigorous empirical analyses of this

---

[1]   Cited in Dave Walter, *Today Then: America's Best Minds Look 100 Years into the Future on the Occasion of the 1893 World's Columbian Exposition* (1992). Results of the Millennium Survey are presented in Pryor (2000-b).

[2]   In the text in this section, I refer to studies by Atkinson (1999), Feldstein (1999), Gottschalk and

phenomenon have come from the Luxembourg Income Study, a multinational cooperative study of income inequality that employs a roughly similar methodology for each country. Peter Gottschalk and Timothy Smeeding look at "adjusted personal income," which takes account of both the total household income and the number of household members when calculating the income for each member. They compare relative income ratios of these adjusted personal incomes in OECD nations (the major industrial nations in the world) at particular points in the income distribution and obtain startling results. For those in the 10th percentile of the income distribution (the low-income end), these ratios in the United States were lower than in the other 18 nations; and for those in the 90th percentile (the high-income end), the U.S. relative income ratios were second highest (a shade less than Ireland). In brief, in relation to the median income, the poor were poorer and the rich were generally richer in the U.S. than in these other industrial nations.

From a comparison in which individual incomes were converted to dollars in a manner to take account of the relative purchasing power of the various currencies, an even more dramatic contrast emerges. Although the U.S. has the highest average per capita income in a sample of fourteen industrial nations, the absolute level of income of those in the 10th percentile in the U.S. was lower than in any of the other nations. In brief, the poor in the U.S. are not only poorer on a relative scale but on an absolute scale as well. Not unexpectedly, at the other end of the income distribution the rich in the U.S. had higher incomes on an absolute scale.

Trends in inequality are quite different in various industrial nations. Recent studies, for instance, by Anthony Atkinson, Lawrence Katz, or Horst Siebert, show that in the 20 years following 1975, income inequality increased in the U.K., U.S., West Germany, and Japan, while remaining roughly constant in Canada, and decreasing in France, Italy, and Norway. Trends in the dispersion of earnings have also varied considerably.

2. Current Trends in the U.S.

In the discussion below, I focus on the total monetary income of families and exclude non-related household members. While this income measure is less satisfactory than adjusted personal income of all household members, both measures reveal the same pattern over time and the choice of family monetary income allows the discussion to cover a longer time period and also to be comparable to the results of many others.

Danziger (1998), Gottschalk and Smeeding (1997), Katz (1999), and Siebert (1999).

Chart 4.1a shows the changes over a half century of family income at different points of the income distribution, all adjusted for price changes. Average family incomes at the top of the income distribution in the 80th and 95th percentiles increased at average annual rates respectively of 2.0 and 2.1 percent. At the same time family incomes of those in the bottom of the income distribution in the 10th and 20th percentiles rose at average annual rates respectively of 1.6 and 1.4 percent. Even more important, the real money income of those in both the 10th and 20th percentiles did not essentially change from 1970 to the end of the century, while those in the 80th and 95th percentiles increased at average annual rates of 1.0 and 1.4 percent.

The ratios of family income at various points in the income distribution to the median income (relative income ratios), as shown in Chart 4.1b, reveal other aspects of the picture. Among those in the 10th percentiles of the income distribution, for instance, the relative income ratio rose slightly from the early 1950s to the mid 1960s; but from the mid-1960s to the end of the century, the ratio declined about 10 percent (3.2 percentage points). For those in the 20th percentile, the relative income ratio remained roughly constant until the mid-1960s and then declined 8 percent (4.1 percentage points) to the end of the century. By way of contrast, the relative income ratios of those in the 80th and 95th percentiles declined until the mid 1960s and then increased 15 and 27 percent respectively by 2000. In brief, at both ends of the income distribution inequality decreased from the late 1940s to the mid- 1960s and thereafter began to increase. Particularly noteworthy, the picture did not seem to change greatly in the prosperous years of the 1990s.

2. Interpretations

At their face value, these data seem to confirm both Marxist and populist rhetoric about the class struggle and the long-term trends of the rich getting richer at the expense of the poor. Nevertheless, three counter-arguments are raised by those who believe that trends toward widening inequality are not worth worrying about:

a. Definition of income: Some argue that the data presented in the two charts refer to family money income before taxes and that once taxes and transfers are taken into account, the picture is much less grim. The facts, however, do not bear this out, at least since 1979, when the Census Bureau began to calculate more complete measures of income to supplement the series on family money income. At any point in time, inclusion of capital gains and non-salary benefits, such as health insurance supplements, reveal greater income inequality, while inclusion of various types of taxes and governmental transfers such as

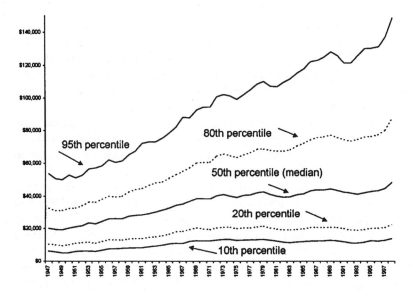

Chart 4.1a. Real Family Money Income Levels at Various Percentiles in the United States: 1997 dollars.

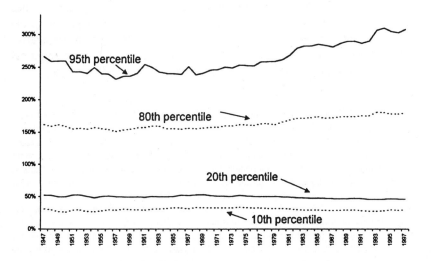

Chart 4.1b. Ratio of Family Money Income Levels to Median Family Income in the United States.

Note: Sources and methods are presented in Appendix 4.1.

Medicaid and free school lunches reveal less inequality. Of course, these more complete measures of income more closely approximate the "welfare" of the family units as most people would define it. It is significant, however, that the time-trends of inequality, as measured by these improved methods, move in a very similar way to my data on family money incomes for the period the various series overlap.[3]

   b. Income mobility: The data in the charts reflect a family's income only for a single year. Some might emphasize that the U.S. labor market is highly dynamic, and that those in the lowest percentile of the income distribution do not necessarily remain there very long.

   Results from most of the available studies on income mobility do not lend themselves to so sanguine a view. For instance, Peter Gottschalk and Sheldon Danziger show that from year to year, roughly three-quarters of the families in the lowest income quintile (that is, with the lowest 20 percent of incomes) remain there. Overall income stability, as measured by the percent of people staying in the same income quintiles two years in a row, actually increased between the mid-1970s and the early 1990s (for those in the lowest income quintile, this fraction remained roughly the same). For a much longer time interval, namely the 21 years between 1969 and 1990, similar data show that slightly less than a third of the families remained in the lowest income quintile, a result due in part to the fact that over the course of time, many young families manage to pull themselves out of poverty.[4] A more revealing approach to the question of income mobility, however, is to examine changes in the relative income of individual families over five or ten year periods. Several empirical studies show a slight decrease in long-term income mobility in the U.S.[5]

---

[3]   Measures of income inequality, using various definitions of income, are presented at the Census Bureau web site cited in Appendix 4.1. Many studies focus on those aspects of governmental policy that influence these various elements of income, in particular taxes and transfers. For instance, Mishel et al. (1999, p. 99), show that between 1977 and 1992, the burden of federal taxes on the bottom four-fifths of the income distribution remained roughly the same, while it decreased among those in the top fifth, particularly for the top 1 percent. Although the impact of the tax changes specified by the Omnibus Budget Reconciliation Act of 1993 should have begun to reverse these trends, the Bush tax bill signed into law in 2001 will place a relatively greater tax burden on those with middle and low incomes. Moreover, it is noteworthy that a rising share of total taxes are collected by state and local governments, where the shares of income paid in taxes by the rich and the poor are less graduated than federal taxes. This means that the overall tax structure is becoming less progressive, even without taking into account changes in the tax laws.

[4]   This phenomenon occurs, of course, in other countries as well and comparative studies of income mobility suggest that in this respect, the United States falls roughly in the middle of industrial nations, despite its more dynamic labor market.

[5]   This evidence is reviewed by Pryor (1996), p. 31. The same source cites other studies showing an increasing inequality of consumption.

c. *Irrelevance*: Martin Feldstein and other neoclassical economists argue that increasing overall income inequality does not matter if it is the result of rising incomes at the top, since the rich are not taking away income from those at the bottom. That is, if one segment of the income distribution is gaining while the others are not losing, then overall welfare is increasing, if other factors remain the same (the Pareto criterion of welfare improvement).

This neoclassical argument deserves to be taken seriously. In the next section I demonstrate, contrary to Feldstein, that a causal relationship appears to exist between high and low incomes and that they move in opposite directions. I argue further that other economic performance criteria do not remain constant when the income distribution becomes more unequal. Chapter 7 addresses some additional and knotty issues about social cohesiveness that accompany increasing income inequality, even if incomes of the poor are increasing in some absolute sense. Finally, at the end of this chapter and in Chapter 8, I present evidence that effectiveness of governmental economic policy making appears to decline with increasing income inequality.

B. What Is Causing the Income Distribution to Become More Unequal?[6]

Because economists use several quite different analytic techniques to disentangle the causal elements, it is difficult to compare directly the various conclusions drawn from such studies. Therefore, I divide this brief review according to the particular analytical or statistical technique that is employed by researchers.

1. Regression Analysis[7]

This statistical technique permits us to calculate a formula showing the independent impact of various postulated causes on changes in relative income ratios. Because such formulae are calculated separately for the rich and poor, we

---

[6] In the text of this section I draw upon studies by: Abowd and Bognanno (1995), Anderton and Brenton (1998), Atkinson (2000), Burtless (1998), Devroye and Freeman (2000), Ellwood and Summers (1986), Feenstra and Hanson (1995, 1996-a, 1996-b), Howell and Huebler (2001), Hyclak (2000), Karoly and Burtless (1995), Katz (1999), Katz *et al.* (1995), Lawrence and Slaughter (1993), Pryor (1999), Pryor and Schaffer (2000), Rodrik (1997), Slaughter and Swagel (1997), and Wood (1994).

[7] This discussion draws heavily on Jefferson and Pryor (2001). The technical aspects of this analysis are presented in External Appendix X-4.1.

can also isolate causal factors that influence incomes of one group, but not the other.

At the bottom of the income distribution, it is generally believed that the relative income ratios of families in the 10th percentile increase as the share of female-headed households decreases and as government transfer payments increase. It also seems likely that such relative income should decline with weakening labor market conditions and a fall in available jobs. As noted briefly in Chapter 3, this can be measured by the percentage of prime-age males (men 25 to 50) who are without employment. In the calculations reported below, most of these conjectures receive support.

Explaining relative income ratios at the top end is more difficult. Some might argue that since the dramatic rise in salaries and bonuses of high corporate officials is tied to company performance, the relative income ratios of those in the 95th percentile are related to measures of corporate success such as profit rates, the share of property income, or stock market performance. Such variables, however, do not prove successful predictors for three possible reasons: (a) property income (profits, interest, and rents), which constitute a considerable portion of total income of the affluent, did not greatly change as a share of total personal income over the second half of the 20th century (as shown in External Appendix X-4.2); (b) the empirical link between enterprise performance and executive salaries has been quite loose; and (c) the extremely high salaries of corporate executives were generally limited to the CEO and a small number of others, while the salaries of other managers were not out of line, at least with international standards as analyzed by John Abowd and Michael Bognanno.

Another hypothesis about the relative income ratio of families at the top of the income distribution focuses on the impact of female participation in the labor force. The greatest rise in female participation in the labor force came from educated women, who were generally married to educated men with high incomes (see below). Therefore, relative family income ratios of the rich should be positively related to female labor force participation.[8]

In the initial specification, both sets of regressions (External Appendix X-4.1) reveal a statistically significant and negative relationship between the relative incomes at the high and low ends of the income distribution. That is, as the relative income ratio at the top increased, this ratio at the bottom end of the

---

[8] A few technical details deserve note. To both the equations explaining relative income at the top and the bottom, a time trend, a lagged dependent variable, and the relative income level ratio at the other end of the income distribution were added. In addition, two sets of data were explored: the relative income ratios of those in the bottom 10th and the top 95th percentile, and the relative income of those in the bottom 20th and the top 80th percentiles. The regressions for each set were calculated as a simultaneous equation system using a two-stage least squares technique.

income distribution decreased, and vice versa. In other words, populist and Marxist claims about the rich getting richer at the expense of the poor appear to have some foundation and the neoclassical arguments deprecating the significance of increasing income inequality appear in error.

Although I agree with this conclusion, at this point the evidence is far from conclusive because of several technical difficulties. Most important, these calculations use contemporaneous variables, and such an approach does not necessarily indicate causation since both high and low incomes may be influenced by certain underlying causes which are not included in the calculations. Some high-power econometric techniques are necessary to investigate these issues. I describe in excruciating detail the technical details in Appendix X-4.1.[9]

The final specifications of the regressions yield some important results. The *levels* of the relative incomes of rich and poor significantly remain inversely related to each other (External Appendix X-4.1). Moreover, such regressions results for the relative income ratio at the 10th percentile confirm several of our conjectures: the ratio falls if the percentage of female-headed families increases, and it rises if government transfers increase. At the top end of the income distribution, it is harder to isolate the underlying causal factors. Nevertheless, the inverse relationship between relative income ratios of rich and poor is still found. In looking at the determinants of *changes* in relative incomes ratios, the inverse relationship between the relative incomes of rich and poor is still found (External Appendix X-4.1), at least in the equation for at the top end of the income distribution. Nevertheless, this is sufficient to support the more general results about the inverse relation between the relative income levels at both ends of the distribution.[10]

In brief, although these statistical experiments provide powerful evidence that the poor are getting poorer because the rich are getting richer (and *vice versa*), the underlying reasons for such a relationship are not clear. Such calcu-

---

[9]   The key question is whether the inverse correlation between relative income ratios of rich and poor appears because both relative income variables wander away from a determinate trend in the opposite direction. An augmented Dickey-Fuller test shows that at conventional significance levels, this explanation cannot be rejected. A more powerful test using the Stock and Watson dynamic estimator for the cointegrating vector shows, however, that this inverse relationship between income at the two ends of the income distribution is not spurious, at least between the relative income ratios for the 10th and 95th percentiles. To explore these causal relations from a different perspective, the equations were reestimated to examine more carefully the dynamic stochastic processes by using a dynamic error correction specification, which yielded the same general conclusions.

[10] The regression results when using the relative income levels at the 20th and 80th percentiles do not reach the same levels of statistical significance as those achieved in the regressions at the 10th and 95th percentiles. This is because the other explanatory variables are more appropriate for those with very low or high income levels.

lations also do not show whether the relative gap between the incomes of rich and poor will continue to widen or to close. All we know at this point is that they move over time in opposite directions and that some causal mechanism lies behind such trends. Nevertheless, with some additional information these calculations can be employed to make some predictions about the future (see below).

2. Decomposition Techniques

This statistical technique looks at income inequality of particular groups and then asks what happens if the overall mix of the various groups changes, all other causal factors remaining constant. For instance, because we know the income distribution for various age groups, we can determine what would happen to the overall income distribution of the population if the age composition changes, other things remaining the same. Similarly, we can determine how the overall distribution of income would be different if changes occurred in the racial composition, educational levels of workers, unemployment, work status of women, or the structure of industry. For instance, Lynn Karoly and Gary Burtless (hereafter K-B) employ this technique in a particularly fruitful manner.[11]

K-B focus on the inequality of adjusted personal incomes (that is, incomes taking the number of household members into account) and investigate the impact of the increasing share of female-headed households and the decreasing share of men who are employed. To carry out this analysis they employ an interesting conceptual device, namely to define each household as consisting of a husband and a wife, but to consider the husband's income in a female-headed (i.e., fatherless) household to be zero (and do not include him in the calculation of adjusted personal incomes). Using this technique, Gary Burtless shows that between 1969 and 1994 the share of income contributed by male adults in this

---

[11]   Other useful studies along these lines are by Ryscavage *et al.* (1995), Cancian and Reed (1999), Burtless (1998), and Mishel, Burnstein, and Schmitt (1999). Ryscavage et al., for instance, find that for the period 1969 - 1989, the most important demographic and economic changes reducing the income share of the lowest fifth were a shift in household type (from married couples toward non-married couples, single-parent families, and non-family households), a change in the work experience of the household head toward less-than-full-time work, increase in labor force participation of wives, and a shift in employment away from manufacturing. Furthermore, the key changes along these dimensions occurred in the 1970s, rather than the 1980s when inequality worsened. None of these demographic and economic variables had much influence on the income share of the highest fifth of the income distribution. While such an exercise is useful, it does not easily allow the interaction of several effects to be taken into account together.

artificially defined family declined, partly because the percentage of male adults earning income fell, partly because per capita male earnings shrank slightly over the period, and partly because an increasing number of families were fatherless.

K-B also emphasize that the income distribution became more unequal because of the impact of other changes in the economy. Of particular interest, those with high incomes in 1993 were more likely to receive non-labor income (property income, pensions, government transfers) than in 1959. Two factors underlay this change: a relative decline in governmental transfer payments going to the poorest families and a widening inequality of wealth, which meant that a greater share of property income went to a smaller number of high income people. Burtless also argues that between 1969 and 1979 and between 1979 and 1993, this changing distribution of non-labor income accounted for roughly 50 and 30 percent respectively of the widening income inequality.

K-B also find an increasingly important impact on the distribution of adjusted family income of the income of wives participating in the labor force. Two factors also underlay this change: the rise in female-headed households (as already noted) and the changing earning pattern of women, particularly those with considerable education.[12] More specifically, increases in labor force participation of women between the mid-1960s and the mid-1990s were directly related to their education. Moreover, from 1979 through the mid 1990s, hourly wages of women were greater for families where the husband earned a high income, and, in addition, wages of these wives in higher-income families increased faster than those in lower-income families. As a result, total earnings of married women, which were barely related to their husbands earnings in the early 1970s, became positively related by the mid 1990s.

At the end of the 1990s, debate about the exact impact of female earnings on the changing distribution of income was heated, and a number of technical factors prevented unanimity on the issue. Nevertheless, the explanation that makes the most sense to me is by Gary Burtless, who emphasizes three key factors at work: The change in the proportion of female earnings in total family earnings and the increasingly positive relation between female earnings and total earnings acted to increase inequality of adjusted personal income between 1979 and 1993. The slightly increasing equality of women's wages acted, however, to decrease it. He argues, nevertheless, that the overall effect of female earnings worked strongly in the direction of increasing income inequality.[13] In the earlier

12   The three following factual statements are respectively supported by data from Pryor and Schaffer (2000, p. 8); Mishel, Bernstein and Schmitt (1999, pp. 75-6); and Levy (1998, p. 155).

13   Cancian and Reed (1999 look at the question differently and reach much different results. They pose a hypothetical question: What happens to the income distribution when women's earnings are set at zero. They show that the distribution of income becomes more unequal and, over time

period from 1969 to 1979, by way of contrast, the impact of women's wages on the widening income inequality was much less important, as was the correlation between the earnings of women and total adjusted personal income.

3. Trends in Wage Differentials

From 1950 to the early 1970s the distribution of labor earnings was relatively stable. Since then, the dispersion of earnings rapidly increased, with the relative wages of those with more education and experience rising the most, as shown by Lawrence Katz and collaborators. David L. Schaffer and I show that although the educational differential increased from the early 1970s through the mid 1990s, the economic returns to cognitive skills (holding formal education constant) also increased and that it is important to keep these two factors separate. We also provide evidence in the same period for prime-age males that for occupations requiring a university education, real earnings in that subset of occupations requiring particularly high cognitive skills increased considerably, while real wages in the remaining university-level occupations stagnated. Between the mid 1990s and the end of the century, however, wage differentials began to narrow somewhat, reflecting the dramatic upswing of the business cycle in that period.[14]

But wage differentials alone cannot, however, account for the gap between rich and poor, and here's why:

• *Partial nature*: The focus on individual earnings does not take into account the contribution of other family members, particularly spouses, to the income enjoyed by a family. Moreover, wages are only one part of total income

income differentials would widen less than they actually did. This result occurs partly because female-headed households, which have become relatively more numerous, would have no income. Another contributing factor to these results is the changing inequality of women's wages.

Mishel, Bernstein, and Schmidt (1999, p. 81) show that for prime-age married couples the elimination of women's wages would make the income distribution somewhat more equal, which parallels the findings of K-B. They also provide evidence (p. 47), that since the early 1970s only married couples with a wife in the paid labor force have experienced an increase in median income. Married couples where the wife is not in the paid labor force or families headed by a single adult have experienced stagnating or falling wages.

[14] Greenwood (1999) argues the widening of wage differentials up to the mid 1990s reflected, in part, the dramatic introduction of new information technologies requiring skills held by only a small number of workers. In the past new technologies have had a similar effect and he notes that as these new skills become more widespread, such wage differentials shrink. The quantitative importance of this technological factor in the current changes in wage differentials is unclear.

and widening wage differentials may be offset by other income flows.[15] Gary Burtless's decomposition of the various factors underlying changes in income inequality shows that the combined effect of increases in earnings differentials accounted for only about a quarter of the rising inequality in adjusted personal income from 1969 through 1993 and in the prosperous years of the late 1990s, any equalizing of wages should have had a similarly small impact on the overall distribution of income. It might also be added that increasing differences in wages between groups (defined in terms of race, gender, education, and occupation) accounted for a relatively small part of the changes in the overall income distribution.[16]

   • *Omission of institutional and organizational influences:* Thomas Hyclak presents econometric evidence showing that institutional and organization factors accounted for roughly half of the increasing wage inequalities in the 1980s.[17] More specifically, the lower the minimum wage in comparison to the average wage and the lower the percentage of the labor force covered by union wage contracts, the greater the wage inequalities. It is often argued, however, that a low minimum wage reduces unemployment (and increases labor market "flexibility"), which raises income of those previously without work. This, in turn, reduces overall income inequalities, even while wage inequalities are increasing. Such an argument, however, seems dubious in light of an interesting comparison between industrial nations by David Howell and Friedrich Huebler who find no tradeoff between unemployment and earnings inequality.

   These institutional and organizational factors appear to have led to greater wage inequality in the second half of the 20th century. For instance, over the

---

[15] A technical problem also arises: which wages should be used in the analysis. Karoly (1993) shows that wage inequalities appear to be rising much less dramatically when wages are measured on an annual, rather than on a weekly, basis.

[16] Pryor and Schaffer (2000, Chapter 6) divided the population into 96 groups by gender, race, education, and occupational class, and looked at the changes in relative wages between these groups. The wage differentials between these groups are changing more slowly than overall wage differentials. For instance, between 1970-71 and 1994-95, less than 20 percent of the increasing inequality of hourly wages can be explained by rising inequalities between average wages of the different educational groups. The major cause of the widening of overall earnings differentials was the increasing wage differences within the various groups. It proved difficult to determine exactly what was happening because we did not have comparable data to separate the impact of changing distributions of education, cognitive skills, and experience in particular occupations.

[17] Other studies investigating the impact of these institutional and organizational factors, for instance, Freeman (1993), Freeman (1998-b), and Horrigan and Mincy (1999), find a smaller impact than Hyclak.

period the ratio of the federal minimum wage to the average hourly earnings of production workers slowly declined from about 50 percent to 40 percent.[18] At the same time, the share of the nonagricultural labor force enrolled in labor unions declined from 30 percent in the early 1950s to 13.5 percent by the middle 1990s.[19] Some economists, such as Anthony Atkinson, also point to another factor in the growing wage inequalities, namely, the breakdown of the unacknowledged social norm within business enterprises that led to more equal wages than strict market norms might suggest. Allegedly the greater heterogeneity of the labor force and the greater weight placed by corporate executives on short-term profits contributed to this change in corporate values. Federal tax policies also provided incentives for firms to offer non-taxed fringe benefits, particularly to high wage workers and employees, a phenomenon which Thomas Hyclak shows led to widening real compensation differences.

4. Four Popular but Incorrect Theories about Wage and Income Inequalities

At this point it is worthwhile to mention briefly four factors I do *not* believe to have been important in the increasing inequality of wages and salaries in the second half of the 20th century.

a. The role of the welfare system: Some argue that the system of welfare payments in the U.S. has created poverty, namely by encouraging illegitimacy, single-parent families, welfare dependency, and high unemployment of black youth. The literature on these issues is vast and, at this point, I rely on a review of the empirical evidence by David Ellwood and Lawrence Summers, who show that such institutional factors have had only a minor impact on the changing inequalities of wages or income.

b. The impact of imports from developing nations: Many observers argue that increasing foreign trade with low-wage nations has lowered the real wages of less-educated American workers in the last quarter of the 20th century. At first sight this appears unlikely—after all, during the period imports from low-wage nations (excluding the OPEC nations) amounted to less than 2 percent of

---

[18]   The federal minimum data come from *Statistical Abstract 1999,* Table 705. The data on average hourly earnings of production workers come from series EEU0050006, obtained from the U.S. Department of Labor website: www.dol.gov .

[19]   The earlier unionization data come from Pryor (1996, p. 88). The later data come from *Income and Earnings* 46, No. 1 (January 1999), p. 9 and *Statistical Abstract 1998,* Table 712. Although this decline in unionization contributed to a widening of wage differentials in the middle range of wages, I do not believe it affected the extremes, where the role of labor unions has never been important.

the GDP.[20] But the argument has impeccable theoretical credentials, namely, the Heckscher-Ohlin and Stolper-Samuelson theorems. It is claimed that because the U.S. has a higher proportion of well-educated than less-educated workers in comparison to developing nations, the relative wages of poorly-educated workers in comparison to well-educated workers in the U.S. are higher. As a result, the U.S. has a comparative disadvantage in selling goods that embody the labor of these less-educated workers because of relatively higher labor costs. Imports, especially from developing nations, are more likely to embody the labor of less-educated workers, and these imports will, in turn, lower the relative prices of such goods on the U.S. markets. As a result of competition from such imported goods, less-educated workers either lose their jobs or must accept lower wages.

Various empirical studies yield mixed results. Adrian Wood provides supporting evidence that this theoretical possibility has actually happened in the U.S. and other industrialized nations. Dani Rodrik presents an interesting variant of the same argument, namely that globalization has made the demand for less-educated U.S. workers more sensitive to wages abroad because producers can more easily shift their jobs to plants in low-wage nations. This means, of course, that less-educated workers in the U.S. cannot bargain as effectively as before to obtain higher wages. Still another variant, argued by Bob Anderton and Paul Brenton and by Robert Feenstra and Gordon Hanson, is that outsourcing of intermediate products that are primarily made by less-educated workers is placing a downward pressure on the wages of the less educated in the U.S., a matter discussed in more detail in Chapter 5.

But some important counter-evidence deserves to be taken into account. Import penetration of foreign-made goods has not occurred especially in those branches of U.S. manufacturing employing a high proportion of less-educated workers, as I show elsewhere. Although such a comparison does not take account of foreign outsourcing of part of the production chain, such trade with developing nations was still too small to have, I believe, a macro impact on the wages or employment of less-educated American workers in the 1980s and 1990s.[21] In the coming decades, however, this situation may change. Robert Lawrence and Matthew Slaughter also analyze data on U.S. manufacturing prices and find no evidence of falling prices (relative to the general price level)

---

[20] These low-wage nations include all Latin American nations plus all non-OPEC nations of Africa and Asia except Israel, Japan, and South Africa. In the middle 1990s, for instance, such imports amounted to about 1.8 percent of the GDP.

[21] Outsourcing of production of goods and services to sources of cheap labor in developing countries not only affects low-skilled U.S. workers, but also those with high skills as well. For instance, U.S. companies have been increasing their use of computer programmers from Bangalore in India.

of goods produced by less-educated workers. Subsequent studies, summarized by Matthew Slaughter and Phillip Swagel, refine this approach and have obtained mixed results, for instance, such conclusions hold for the 1960s and 1980s, but not for the 1970s. Gary Burtless also points out that those economic sectors producing both traded and non-traded goods and services have been shifting their employment structure toward more educated workers, so foreign trade does not appear to have been a major factor underlying a loss of employment by less-educated workers. Finally, the gap between wages in the U.S. and in its major trade partners is narrowing, so that over time this gap has exerted an ever smaller influence on U.S. wages.

Surveying this welter of conflicting results, I find the evidence linking increased imports from developing nations to falling wages and disappearing jobs among less-educated U.S. workers to be unconvincing, especially given the relatively small share of the U.S. GDP that is involved. Although it is certainly possible that, under certain conditions, imports from developing nations might reduce the relative wages of less-educated or less-skilled workers in the U.S. Nevertheless, it seems unlikely to happen in the near future.

c. A widening of the gap in cognitive skills among workers: If differences in cognitive skills among workers have widened, as some assert (see below), this might have contributed to the growing earnings gap. Unfortunately, I have been unable to find any useful measures of this growing gap in cognitive skills, but if it actually occurred in the U.S., its impact on the wage distribution was probably minor. This conclusion is based on cross-country evidence provided by Dan Devroye and Richard Freeman, who draw on data from the International Adult Literacy Survey to show that only about 7 percent of the differences in earnings inequalities can be attributed to differences in such skill differentials among the nations in the sample.

d. Skill-biased technical change: Many claim that a particular type of technological change favoring more-educated workers over less-educated ones is responsible for the widening wage gap between the two groups. This claim seems highly exaggerated. As David L. Schaffer and I argue at length in an empirical analysis of employment and wages in 500 different occupations from the mid-1960s to the mid-1990s, the number of workers in those occupations requiring a university education actually rose more slowly than the number of workers with a university degree. Moreover, those jobs requiring little education increased faster than the number of workers with 12 or fewer years of schooling. As a result, a rising share of university-educated workers took "high-school jobs," a rising share of high-school graduates accepted "drop-out jobs," and a rising share of high-school dropouts were bumped completely out of the labor force. The downward mobility of more-educated workers to occupations where their educational credentials are not as necessary had a twofold impact: it depressed wages in those already in these occupations while, at the same time, it widened the wage spread within each of these occupations.

As noted above, wages in the subset of occupations requiring both a university education and high cognitive skills soared while wages of university-educated workers in other occupations stagnated in the latter part of the century. In the short run, certain computer skills have also commanded a wage premium. Only in these relatively narrow ways did technological advances contribute to income inequality, especially at the high end of the income distribution.

5. A Brief Summary

The regression analysis of relative income ratios shows that a certain causal mechanism linked incomes at the two ends of the income distribution so that they moved in opposite directions. Unfortunately, the nature of this mechanism remains unclear. For low-income families, the rising share of female-headed households and the strength of the labor market also influenced the relative income ratio. The analysis using a decomposition technique focuses special attention on the distribution of wealth and government transfers, and on the increasing importance of female labor force participation as contributing factor to widening income differentials. The analysis of wage differentials shows that although they are widening, they contributed only slightly to the increasing income inequality. Finally, the increased wage inequality does not appear to be caused to a major extent either by import competition, widening differences in cognitive skills among workers, or skill-biased technical change. Given these causal factors underlying increasing income inequality in the last quarter of the 20th century, to what extent can we expect such trends to continue for the next 25 or 50 years?

C. Future Changes in Income Inequalities [22]

Prediction of the future of the income distribution requires us to forecast the direction that some of the underlying causal forces will take in the coming decades. Such an exercise raises many obvious problems and, therefore, it seems most useful to focus on only a few of the many factors mentioned

---

[22]   In the text of this section I refer to studies by: Abramson *et al.* (1995), Durlauf (1996), Dyson (1997), Federman *et al.* (1996), Jargowsky (1997), Jäntti and Danziger (2000), Lindert (2000), Pryor (2000-b), Pryor and Schaffer (2000), U.S. Department of Commerce, Census Bureau (1999), and Wattenberg (1991).

above. I also consider several other factors which might not have been very important in the 20th century but may play a more influential role on changes in the future.

1. A Review of Some Familiar Causal Forces

Trends in the ratio of incomes at a particular percentile of the income distribution to the median income reveal considerable inertia.[23] In the near term, therefore, we can expect a continuation of past trends. For the further future, it is useful to look at relative income ratios of the rich and the poor separately.

    *a. Income at the High End of the Income Distribution.*The influence of the concentration of wealth is a crucial factor, because, as noted above, property income provides an important share of total income of high-income groups. For purposes of this discussion, I focus on augmented wealth, a broad measure which includes not just net holdings of financial and real assets but also claims on Social Security and private pensions.

In the 75 years following the end of World War I, the share of income accounted for by the wealthiest 5 percent of the population and the share of augmented wealth held by the wealthiest 1 percent moved together in the same direction.[24] As shown by the dotted line in Chart 4.2, the share of augmented wealth held by the wealthiest 1 percent fell considerably from the 1950s to the 1970s, especially because of the rise in Social Security wealth of the rest of the population. Thereafter, however, wealth began to become more concentrated and, by the end of the century, was approaching its 1950 level.[25] The run-up in

---

[23]   This can be seen by the importance of the calculated coefficients in the regressions reported in External Appendix X-4.1.

[24]   Data on wealth held by the top 1 percent come from Wolff (1995, 1996). Data on the income of the top 5 percent come from Department of Commerce, Bureau of the Census (1975), Series G319-G324 and G342. I extend Wolff's series using data from Kennickell (2000-a, 2000-b).

[25]   Kennickell, (2000-a, 2000-b) presents evidence from *Survey of Consumer Finances* in different years that the distribution of wealth became more unequal between 1989 and 1998. As a percentage of the total, the net worth of the wealthiest 400 families rose from 1.5 percent in 1989 to 2.6 percent in 1998; and the same percentage of the wealthiest 1 percent of families (excluding the top 400) rose from 30.2 percent in 1989 to 34.0 percent in 1998. It must be noted, however, that these data are based on sample surveys and, for the wealthiest, the margin of error (more technically, the 95 percent confidence level) is large. For instance, using the same underlying data but making different adjustments, Wolff (1999-b) finds a less dramatic increase in wealth concentration for the same period and shows that between 1995 and 1998, wealth concentration decreased very slightly.

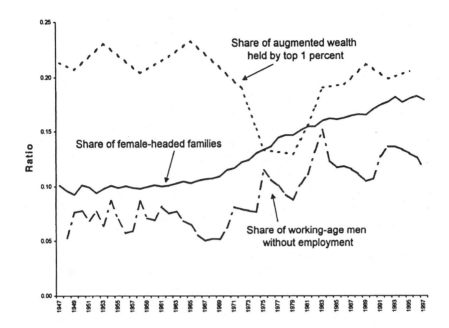

Chart 4.2. Certain Factors Underlying Changes in the U.S. Income Distribution

Note: Augmented wealth includes cash and bank deposits, real estate, bonds, and mutual funds, net equity in unincorporated businesses, trust funds, consumer durables, cash surrender value of life insurance, pension claims, IRAs, Keogh plans, and the discounted value of Social Security benefits minus the current value of debts and other obligations.

Sources and estimation methods are presented in Appendix 4.1.

stock prices in the 1990s played a considerable role in this rise in wealth inequality in the 1990s and, undoubtedly, the fall in stock prices in the early years of the millennium will have the opposite force.

Nevertheless, the rise in the concentration of wealth suggests that income inequality will continue to rise, at least in the near future. If high income families continue to save a larger share of their income than low income families and if the temporary elimination of the inheritance tax that passed into law in 2001 becomes permanent, wealth will become even more concentrated in the future, and it seems likely that the relative income of those in the 95th percentile will continue to rise, other things equal.

An important change in the organization of industry can also contribute to this rising concentration of income and wealth. I argue in Chapter 10 that industrial concentration will increase in the first half of the 21st century. If I am correct, we can reasonably assume that this will lead to a rising share of property income (especially profits), a greater concentration of wealth, and higher relative income ratios for the rich who own this wealth. The rise in interest rates discussed in Chapter 2 will have the same income effect, since the rich are net creditors.

It also seems likely that trends in technological change, which have been an important factor underlying the rising wage premium for the cognitive skills of the most highly educated, will continue. This means that the relative earnings of those in occupations requiring both a high education and high cognitive skills will continue to rise.[26]

As noted above, the increasing labor force participation of women contributed to the rising inequality of income. This is because the fastest growing share of the female labor force in the second half of the 20th century were well-educated and these women were also more likely to be married to high-earning men. As David Schaffer and I show elsewhere, by the end of the century this rise in the labor force participation of women was tapering off and, in the coming decades, should have relatively little impact on a future widening of income levels. Indeed, some public opinion data presented by Ben Wattenberg suggests the rising labor force participation rate of women should level off in the future.

In brief, most of the factors noted above point toward a rise in the relative income ratios of those with high incomes and it is difficult to imagine offsets to those forces. Regardless of what happens at the bottom end of the income distribution, the relative income ratios of those at the top will probably continue to grow and the line in Chart 4.1b indicating the income of the rich as a percent of the median income seems likely to climb even more in the decades ahead.

   b. Income at the Low End of the Income Distribution. In 1998 those living with incomes below the poverty limit amounted to 12.7 percent of the population, which was little different from the percentage in 1989 or, for that matter, in 1968 according to data from the Census Bureau. The prosperity of the late

---

[26]   At the very top of the income distribution, the increase in CEO compensation in major companies showed no sign of abating in the 1990s. According to Mishel, *et al,* (1999, p.211) the ratio of total compensation of CEOs of the largest firms (unfortunately, they do not specify the number of firms in their sample) to the average worker rose from 20.3 in 1965, to 28.5 in 1979, to 56.1 in 1989 and to 115.7 in 1995. Another analysis (*Business Week,* 4/20/1998) showed that the total earnings of an average boss in the largest 365 U.S. firms was 326 times the wage income of an average factory worker in 1997. As noted above, only a small number of executives receive such salaries.

1990s had little impact on this poverty rate.[27] Even when income is calculated in the broadest possible manner, the results are roughly the same.

Nevertheless, some factors in the declining relative income ratios of the low-income population in the past seem likely to weaken in the future. As shown by the solid line in Chart 4.2, the share of female-headed families, who generally have much lower family incomes than traditional two-parent families, began to increase in the mid 1960s, rising steadily in the next three decades from about 10 percent of all families to about 18 percent. This trend appears to some to be leveling off. Although many commentators are not shy to "explain" such a slow-down in the growth of female-headed families, little credible evidence is offered. Although the underlying causes of this slight leveling off of the share of female-headed families remain obscure, it should not increase as fast in the future, if only because of the increasing constraints on welfare payments to single mothers and the continued availability of abortions. In Chapter 7 I take up these matters in greater detail.

The dash-and-dotted line in Chart 4.2 shows the share of prime-age men without employment. This includes those men officially counted as unemployed as well as those not even considered to be in the labor force, either because they are too discouraged to look for work or because they are engaged in other activities that are not officially counted as work, for instance, the underground economy or crime. The series deals only with males between 25 and 50 who have generally completed their education and who are not yet old enough either to retire or to collect supplemental social insurance, at least without difficulty.

As mentioned in Chapter 3, the rate of joblessness among prime-age males increased at an average annual rate of 1.6 percent a year (not percentage points) during the second half of the 20th century and, as discussed in External Appendix X-4.1, it was inversely related (although short of statistical significance in our calculation) to the relative income ratios of low income families. Marxists might interpret such a trend in joblessness as pointing toward a rising "industrial reserve army of the unemployed." As noted in the previous chapter, however, this increase may be partly due to a more benign trend, namely, greater frictional unemployment due to mounting difficulties of matching workers to jobs in an increasingly complex economy. Nevertheless, such a long-term development is disturbing.

Elsewhere, David Schaffer and I argue at length that it is quite possible this upward trend in male joblessness may not continue in the future. Much of the increase of male joblessness has, at the same time, been accompanied by a ris-

---

[27]   For certain subgroups, by way of contrast, the situation was different. For African-Americans those living in poverty amounted to 26.1 percent in 1998, falling more than three percentage points since 1995 and reaching its lowest level since such statistics began to be published.

ing labor force participation of women; and, as noted above, this latter trend might level off. If the rate at which labor is absorbed into the U.S. economy continues at anywhere near its previous rate and if the conjecture about a slowing down of the growth of female labor force participation is correct, then employers will begin to focus more attention on hiring and training some of the men who are currently jobless. Although these "ifs" are shaky, it does not seem likely that in the future the rising joblessness of men will play as strong a role in lowering the relative income of those families in the lowest 10th percentile of income. If this optimistic scenario is incorrect, then relative income ratios, as well as certain social trends discussed in Chapter 7, may worsen.

2. (Relatively) New Influences on the Income Distribution

Several other factors, which did not play an important role in the past, might influence the distribution of income in the future. They include changes in raw material prices, a low-income poverty-trap, and the changing role of government.

a. Raw material and food prices: As discussed in Chapter 6, it is possible that the prices of raw material and food will rise in the future, relative to the general price index, because of resource shortages and/or the impact of pollution and global warming. I show in that chapter that if this occurs, low income families will be the hardest hit because a larger share of their consumption expenditures is spent on food and goods with a large raw material and food component. In this case, the real income of those in the low-income population will fall, even while their monetary income remains the same.

b. Education and the poverty-trap: The poverty-trap describes a situation where those in poverty cannot escape. An international comparison of nine OECD nations by Markus Jäntti and Sheldon Danziger shows that those nations with the highest percentage of poverty (defined in terms of those with incomes less than half of the median) also have the smallest percentage of poor people able to achieve higher incomes in the next period. According to these calculations, the U.S. had the highest rate of poverty and the second lowest rate of those able to escape from poverty. What lies behind such poor U.S. performance?

In the latter part of the 20th century the low-income population in the U.S. was increasingly concentrated in the urban core of large metropolitan areas. For instance, between 1969 and 1989 the percentage of poor living in the inner cities rose from 34 to 43 percent.[28] Moreover, within the inner city of metropolitan

---

[28]   In the same period the percentage of poor in the non-metropolitan areas fell from 44 to 28 percent, while in the suburbs it rose from 22 to 29 percent (Massey, 1996). The latter figure is some-

areas, the poor were increasingly concentrated in particular neighborhoods. For instance, Alan Abramson and his colleagues show that between 1970 and 1990 for the 100 largest metropolitan areas, the poor were less and less evenly distributed over census tracts and more and more isolated in their own enclaves, exposed only to members of their own group.[29] As a result, schools were increasingly segregated by income.

Paul A. Jargowsky's assertion that "schools in poor inner-city neighborhoods, with some notable exceptions, are.dangerous, overcrowded, and ineffective" is accepted by most observers and lies behind the assertion about a rising gap in cognitive skills discussed above. Without doubt, during the latter part of the 20th century the quality of primary and secondary schooling in these poverty neighborhoods was considerably inferior to that found in the suburbs or, to a certain extent, rural areas, a problem exacerbated by the fiscal constraints of inner-city school districts.

The problem of inferior schooling in low-income areas has been compounded by social factors as well. Because of the values learned at home, children from poor families tend to be less receptive toward education than children in the suburbs. Moreover, home conditions are less conducive to systematic studying. As a result, according to Maya Federman and her colleagues, the children of the poor tend to experience more problems in school than their more affluent counterparts, for example, repeating a grade, being expelled, or not graduating.

Given the importance of education as a determinant of income and occupation, the children of the poor also have lower chances for success in life than children from families with higher incomes. While this problem can be solved in part by the infusion of federal and state funds into the schools of poor areas, I argue below that this is unlikely to occur, at least in the near future, so that such an inter-generational poverty-trap (interestingly modeled by Steven Durlauf) may be self perpetuating. If so, then there is only a small chance that the relative income ratios of the poor—or their children—will rise.

A particular facet of this inequality in both family income and educational opportunities is the so-called digital divide, the uneven penetration of computer

what misleading since it does not take into account that suburbs are becoming increasingly differentiated into poor and rich suburbs. The increasing concentration of low income people in high-poverty neighborhoods is shown in different ways by Blank (1997, p. 29) and Jargowsky (1997, pp. 34–41).

[29] One measure of these phenomena is a "dissimilarity index," which shows the percentage of the poor who would have to move from one census tract to another to achieve an even distribution of poor people throughout a metropolitan area. Between 1970 and 1990, this dissimilarity index for the 100 largest metropolitan areas rose from 32.9 to 36.4 percent. Another measure is an "isolation index," which indicates the degree to which designated "census tracts of the poor" are populated with the poor. In the same period this index increased from 19.5 to 21.3 percent.

ownership and access to the internet.[30] Some, such as Nobel laureate Freeman Dyson, view the situation with alarm and note: "The child of computer-owning parents grows up computer-literate and is showered with opportunities to enter the world of high-tech education and industry. The child without access ... is left behind." It is difficult to judge whether the situation on the ground is so grim, but in 1997, for instance, computer ownership among those with household incomes of more than $50,000 was more than five times that of households with incomes of less than $15,000. More than twice the percentage of non-Hispanic whites owned computers than Hispanics or non-Hispanic Blacks. Differential access to the internet was even more dramatic. Although both computer ownership and on-line access rates increased between 1994 and 1997, the percentage point differences between groups actually widened. In the coming years these differences may narrow, but around the turn of the millennium they contributed to the poverty-trap and stagnating relative incomes of the poor.

The poverty-trap effect is likely to become stronger in the coming decades arising from the trend, documented above and in Chapter 7, that low-income families are being increasingly concentrated in poverty neighborhoods. Some social implications of this trend are revealed by a massive experiment of the U.S. Department of Housing and Urban Development which, in five cities, took a random sample of low-income families from poor neighborhoods and resettled them in middle-class neighborhoods. Analysis of the early results by Jens Ludwig and his colleagues show that children in families experiencing such a move have higher educational achievement and lower arrest rates for violent crimes than those children remaining in the low-income neighborhoods. [31] The adverse neighborhood effects, combined with the increasing concentration of the poor, makes it likely that the poverty trap will become an ever stronger force underlying the decline of the income of those in the lowest income decile, relative to the median income.

    c. The role of government: The changing roles of government have complex influences on the distribution of income which I discuss in other chapters.[32] For instance, as noted in Chapter 3, a number of federal entitlement programs

[30] All data in this paragraph come from McConnaughey and Lader (1999).

[31] Such analyses have been made by Jens Ludwig and his colleagues (2001-a), (2000-b). The Moving to Opportunity Program (MTO) in Baltimore, Boston, Chicago, Los Angeles, and New York, as well as early precursor experiments such as the Gautreaux Program in Chicago, are described at the MTO website: www.motresearch.org.

[32] For instance, Gokhale *et al.* (1999) use a simulation model to argue that the Social Security system acts to widen the inequality of wealth. This is because low income parents tend to rely on annuitized wealth (particularly Social Security) to finance their old age and such wealth, of course, is not passed on to their children. By way of contrast, high income parents are likely to

that automatically increased payments to the poor during periods of recession were turned over to the states. These state governments, however, are constrained by requirements to maintain balanced budgets and, therefore, can do less than the federal government to assist low-income groups during hard economic times.

One possible governmental response to growing income inequality is to increase income transfers to the poor, so that they will be able to buy more than their earnings would otherwise permit. Although such a policy would narrow differentials of real consumption, the experience of the last half century does not provide much optimism that such a policy would ever be implemented on any scale. Expenditures at all levels of government for welfare and social services and payment to the unemployed and disabled, as a percent of GDP, increased between 1950 and 1975 when income inequalities were decreasing. But from 1975 through 2000, when income inequalities were increasing, this ratio of such governmental transfers to GDP decreased at an average annual rate of 0.5 percent.[33] Of major industrial countries, the U.S. numbers among those least willing to redistribute income in this fashion,[34] and there is little evidence that U.S. policies in this regard will change.

Although this matter is discussed in greater detail below and in Chapter 12, it is also worthwhile to note at this point that in certain respects, the government serves to reinforce existing trends toward greater income equality or inequality. That is, the greater the social (and income) distance between groups of people, the more politically contentious income redistribution programs become; correspondingly, the less the social distance, the greater the empathy of the members of the privileged group for the others and the easier income redistribution programs become to set up and implement.

The government can also influence the income distribution by mandated minimum wage legislation and the like. It is, however, difficult to foresee what political forces might reverse the decline in the inflation-adjusted minimum wage that occurred in the last third of the 20th century.

finance a higher percentage of their retirement from accumulated wealth which, if they die early, is passed on to their children. Liebman (forthcoming) argues that with the increasing labor force participation of women, particularly those with higher education, Social Security payments are becoming more progressive because a smaller percentage are distributed as widow payments to wealthy women who never contributed to the system.

[33] This annual rate of decline is statistically significant. The sources for these data on government expenditures are described in Appendix 4.1.

[34] Evidence from a number of countries {Smeeding (1998)} shows that the ratio of income of those in the 10th percentile to the median income is relatively strongly related to total social transfers as a percentage of GDP. In this respect, the United States ranks very low.

3. A Very Brief Summary

Future changes in the distribution of income are difficult to predict with confidence, especially because these changes depend to a certain extent upon political will. Nevertheless, from the evidence of the last half century and from foreseeable factors influencing incomes in the future, several developments seem probable. The real incomes of the rich, as well as their income relative to the median, will probably rise. Although changes in the real incomes of the poor are unclear, their income relative to the median will probably fall. Thus the movement of the relative income ratios of the rich and poor will probably continue to diverge in the same manner as in the last quarter of the 20th century and, as a result, the income gap between the rich and the poor will continue to widen. Although income inequality in the U.S. at the end of the 20th century was still less than it was in the 1920s, as Peter Lindert has demonstrated, it may well exceed the 1920s level during the decades to come.

This is not a novel conclusion. According to the Millennium Survey, an overwhelming majority of U.S. economists believe that income inequalities will not narrow in the next half century and a considerable proportion believe that such inequalities will widen, especially in the first quarter of the 21st century.

D. Some Impacts of Increasing Income Inequality[35]

In this section I touch only briefly on some of the most important implications of increasing income inequality on the economy and economic system. In later chapters I discuss many of these issues at greater length.

1. Influences of Income Inequality on the Economy

a. Microeconomic impacts: Large differentials in income between the rich and the poor lead to many obvious differences in their way of life. Various economists, such as Timothy Smeeding or Maya Federman, present the evidence showing that the poor, for instance, die earlier and have a higher incidence of illness. As discussed above, the increasing concentration of the low-income population into particular neighborhoods has led to a breakdown in many urban

---

[35]   In the text of this section I draw on the research of: Berg and Sachs (1998), Bowles, Gordon, and Weisskoff (1990), Duncan and Brooks-Gunn (1997), Federman *et al.* (1996), Furman and Stiglitz (1999), Laband and Sophocleus (1992), Rodrik (1998), Smeeding (1998), and Wolff (1999-a).

amenities in these areas that were formerly available to those with meager means. These poor neighborhoods have a higher proportion of vacant, older, and decaying housing. When income gaps are large, low-income people are viewed as worse credit risks. As a result, they have more difficulty in borrowing from financial institutions to even out their consumption patterns and, thus, are more likely to experience such problems as eviction or inability to obtain a mortgage, as shown by Jason Furman and Joseph Stiglitz or by Maya Federman. Among the social ills associated with large income differentials, the poor are much more likely to be crime victims than the rich. Greg Duncan and Jeanne Brooks-Gunn argue that the children of the poor are also placed at risk intellectually, emotionally, and physically.

Considerable research is currently being carried out on the impact of income inequality on the ability of small groups to cooperate on projects of common interest. Although primarily focused on the rural sector—for instance, the maintenance of an irrigation system, the implementation of conservation measures, or the supply of local public goods—such results have relevance for urban areas as well. I discuss many other aspects of the impact of income inequality and the creation of social capital in Chapter 7.

b. Macroeconomic impacts: Will greater income inequality influence future economic growth in the U.S.? Economists have sharply conflicting views on the relationship between economic inequality and economic growth.

Many economic theorists argue that income inequality leads to higher economic growth, not just because saving is higher but because the disincentive effect of redistribution programs is reduced. Others argue the reverse, that income equality leads to higher economic growth because the political climate is more stable and also because a wider number of people can participate in the investment process. These arguments are reviewed in greater detail in External Appendix X-4.3. To put it mildly, however, the theoretical evidence is mixed.

At first glance, the empirical evidence may seem less ambiguous. Unfortunately, the straightforward regression investigations of the two variables in many countries, holding a variety of other variables constant, raise some serious problems of interpretation. The evidence is fragile and robust conclusions cannot be drawn. Furthermore, technical problems arise in most of the statistical investigations of this relationship because they do not take into account the multiplicity of causal factors that influence both inequality and growth or the fact that growth and inequality may also have mutual influences on each other. These problems can, however, be circumvented in several different ways and two studies with particular relevance to the arguments in later chapters deserve to be briefly reviewed.

These analyses look at changes in economic growth in periods when income inequality could not have greatly changed. Dani Rodrik investigates why per capita economic growth in a cross-section of nations differed markedly in the 1975–89 period from what it had been in 1960–75. He argues that critical factors underlying the ability of a nation to adjust to the oil shocks of the 1970s were: the magnitude of the external events on the economy, the latent social conflicts within the society, and the institutions in place to manage these conflicts and to produce effective policy responses. The oil price increases required such policies as devaluation and fiscal retrenchment to avoid inflation and rising debt, but such policies have very different distributional impacts and require delicate negotiations if they are not to upset the prevailing social bargains and trigger a distributional conflict. He uses several proxy variables to indicate latent social conflict to substantiate his theory, of which one of the most successful is a measure of the inequality of income.[36]

A related study is by Andrew Berg and Jeffrey Sachs, who investigate the underlying causes of success of a nation in recovering from balance of payments crises and resuming its economic growth. They show that a more equal distribution of income leads to a more rapid recovery and faster growth and argue that such equality facilitates the compromises needed to respond appropriately to external shocks.

Although both the Rodrik and the Berg-Sachs studies suggest a direct linkage between income inequality and policy effectiveness for achieving economic growth, an indirect causal connection is also possible. That is, the linkage between the two variables may be mediated by social trust, which in turn might be a function of income equality. These relationships are examined more systematically in Chapter 7.[37]

Studies like these suggest that the U.S. may experience greater political stalemate in the coming years because of increasing income inequality and of an associated breakdown in trust between social groups so that no group is willing to bear adverse distributional impacts of particular economic policy measures. That is, income inequality leads to difficulties in setting up and implementing effective economic policies to respond to various economic shocks

---

[36] The proxies for conflict-management institutions also include a variable indicating the quality of governmental institutions, with the data coming from the International Country Risk Guide, and a variable indicating the degree of democracy in the nation.

[37] The relationship between income inequality and social trust depends partly on how inequality is measured. Of particular interest, the relationship appears strongest when the ratio of the 90th decile to the 50th decile of income is used. Neither the ratio of the 50th decile to the 10th decile or the ratio of the 90th decile to the 10th decile reveal a significant relation to social trust. Similar results are obtained when an Atkinson measure of equality is used. Thus it appears that greater inequality at the top of the income distribution is the critical factor underlying social trust, rather than overall income inequality.

because the possible distribution impacts on particular groups are more than the political structure can absorb. As a result, economic growth will be slower than if income differentials were smaller.

The relationships between income inequality and other macroeconomic variables have also received attention in recent years. I briefly discuss two such studies in External Appendix X-4.3; but, unfortunately, the evidence to support their conclusions is fragile.

2. Influences of Income Inequality on the Economic System

Potentially, the two greatest impacts of increasing income inequality on the economic system are changes in the role of government and changes in the social structure underlying the system. Although a thorough discussion about the social impact must be postponed until Chapter 7, several aspects deserve brief attention now.

As I have suggested above, it does not seem likely that the U.S. will respond to growing income inequality by increasing transfers to low-income members of the population. Of course, such income transfers to the poor might come about as a result of private charity. Nevertheless, as I argue in Chapter 7 (and show in External Appendix X-7.2), the ratio of such expenditures to GDP appears to be declining and this trend does not seem likely to change. Edward N. Wolff draws a similar conclusion from his statistical analysis of charity expenditures: "As the fortunes of the poor decline, there is little indication that the rich become more generous or that charitable giving increases."[38] But given the uncertainties in the underlying data, such conclusions are tentative.

In part, the government's lack of response to increasing income inequality can be traced to population shifts. As noted above, an increasing share of the poor is concentrated in the central part of large metropolitan areas. In the last few decades of the 20th century, however, a majority of voters have lived in the suburbs where such poverty is removed from their immediate view—and political understanding. Given this change in the geographical distribution of voters, the possibility of governmental income transfers from the suburbs to the cities appears less likely and, as a result, the ill-effects of urban poverty seem unlikely to be ameliorated by governmental action in the future. In Chapter 8 I review other evidence that leads to similar conclusions.

[38] He does note an exception, namely donations specifically targeted for human services, which are associated with poverty. These amounted, however, to roughly one tenth of total charity expenditures. A major problem of this analysis is that the data used are from the AAFRC, a series which, as noted in External Appendix X-7.2, may not accurately portray total charitable giving by individuals.

As Samuel Bowles and his colleagues argue at length, increased income inequalities lead to more social tensions. In turn, this could lead to greater emphasis on internal security and it seems likely that the wealthier will devote more resources to protect their property from harm by others. For instance, between 1952 and 1997, current governmental expenditures for police, prisons, and administration of justice by all levels of government as a share of GDP increased from 0.6 percent in the early 1950s to 1.7 percent in the mid 1990s, with a sharp increase starting in the 1970s when two changes took place: income inequality began to increase and, because of the postwar baby boom, the share of the population in the age groups most likely to commit crimes increased.[39] Other aspects of this problem receive attention in Chapter 12.

Of course, part of this proportionate increase in government expenditures on internal security was due to a faster rise in the cost of these services as compared to the cost of production of goods. But part also represented an increasing share of the real GDP devoted to civilian safety and protection of property. The share of police, detectives, civilian and governmental guards, prison workers and the like to the total civilian labor force almost doubled from 0.9 percent in 1950 to 1.7 percent in 1995.[40] If we include judges, lawyers, and paralegals in this total, the shares rise from 1.3 to 2.6 percent of total civilian labor force. Recent scholarly estimates by David Laband and John Sophocleus place the combined public and private costs (including various safety measures) of fighting crime in the U.S. at roughly 5.3 percent of the GDP in the late 1980s and early 1990s.

Although increasing income inequalities and security expenditures have moved together, this does not, of course, prove a causal link. In Chapter 8 I analyze changes in the crime rate in considerable detail, but at this point it is worth noting that only a part of these costs in fighting crime were due to the social tensions arising from an ever increasing inequality of income. Nevertheless, rising income disparities play an important contributing role.

In isolation, increasing governmental expenditures for the protection of people and property will not lead to a significant change in the economic system. But increasing inequality of income can lead to a decline in the relative number of those with middle incomes. If it is true that a functioning and stable democ-

---

[39] The data on civilian safety expenditures come from Tables 3.16 and 3.17 of the national account statistics.

[40] Data for 1971 through 1995 come from the calculations of Pryor and Schaffer (2000) using the occupational nomenclature employed in the early 1990s. Data for 1950, 1960, and 1970 come from the censuses of population for these years and were adjusted to achieve comparability. For certain occupations such as supervisory personnel, prison guards, paralegals, and others, I had to assume that the rate of increase between 1950 and 1971 was the same as between 1971 and 1995.

racy depends upon a large and politically powerful middle class, then such a hollowing-out of the middle-income group could cause a significant disturbance in the political equilibrium of the U.S. Under certain circumstances, a rise in the political power of high-income groups, combined with ever increasing internal security expenditures, could lead to a shift toward what is described in Chapter 1 as an oligarchic economy, an authoritarian system in which governmental interventions primarily serve the economic interests of whatever elite has power. Serious consideration of this possibility, however, must be postponed to Chapters 7 and 8, when other relevant political and social factors can be taken more systematically into account.

This brief review surveys a number of important impacts of increasing economic inequality on both microeconomic and macroeconomic performance, as well as on the institutions and organizations comprising the economic system. One major conclusion should be clear: Although the real incomes of the poor may increase in the future, income inequality *per se* has important economic ramifications that cannot be ignored.

E. A Brief Final Word

Although incomes became more equal in the third quarter of the 20th century, the trend reversed in the final quarter and inequality dramatically increased. Analysis of the underlying causes, as well as consideration of some new factors that will influence income differentials in the future, suggest that in the coming decades both income and wealth will continue to become more unequally distributed. It seems likely that a widening income gap between rich and poor will lead to a decline in the effectiveness of government in responding to adverse shocks to the economy, which, in turn, may reinforce the lower economic growth resulting from a decline in the saving rate. Increasing income inequality, combined with a concentration of the poor in the inner city, may also lead to a weakening of the political consensus for transferring income from the rich to the poor. The social impacts of widening income differences between rich and poor are, I believe, more important to the economic system than the economic impacts and later chapters will repeatedly return to new aspects of this theme.

CHAPTER 5

Globalization

[In 2000], technology will eliminate scarcity and nations and classes will disappear as the new era of awareness creates a race of World Men whose allegiance is universal.

—*Engineer R. Buckminster Fuller*[1]

Although globalization has different economic, political, social and cultural meanings, in this chapter I use the term to characterize a process leading toward worldwide economic integration, that is, the creating of a unified world market for goods, capital, and labor. In modern times the first great wave of globalization occurred from 1840 to 1914. Looking back over this period John Maynard Keynes remarked:

The inhabitant of London could order by telephone, sipping his morning tea in bed, the various products of the whole earth, in such quantity as he might see fit, and could reasonably expect their early delivery upon his doorstep; he could at the same moment and by the same means adventure his wealth in the natural resources and new enterprises of any quarter of the world, and share, without exertion or even trouble, in their prospective fruits and advantages; or he could decide to couple the security of his fortunes with the good faith of the townspeople of any substantial municipality in any continent that fancy or information might recommend. He could secure forthwith, if he wished it, cheap and comfortable means of transit to any country or climate without passport or other formality, could despatch his servant to the neighbouring office of a bank for such supply of the precious metals as might seem convenient, and could then proceed abroad to foreign quarters, without knowledge of their religion, language, or customs.

---

[1]   Cited by Laura Lee, *Bad Predictions: 2000 Years of the Best Minds Making the Worst Forecasts* (2000). The quotation comes from Keynes (1971 (1919)). The Millenium Survey mentioned in the introduction below is presented by Pryor (2000-b).

Some economists have provided quantitative evidence showing that the current level of globalization is not greatly different from that described by Keynes. Although distinctly a minority view, in particular respects it is reasonable, as I discuss below. Nevertheless, the falling costs of transportation and communications in the current wave of globalization, combined with the much deeper changes in national institutions and organizations to accommodate this increasing global integration, suggest that the earlier and current waves of globalization are both quantitatively and qualitatively different. Moreover, a majority of U.S. economists, according to the Millennium Survey expect the new globalization to accelerate and to be one of the three greatest influences in shaping the future economic system—a view that may be overly sanguine, as I argue below.

The first step is to determine how far globalization has actually proceeded, the forces propelling it, and whether these forces will persist or abate. This requires examination of institutional/organizational evidence, as well as more quantitative macroeconomic indicators, tasks that take up the first two sections of this chapter.

The second step is to explore how globalization affects different aspects of the economy and the economic system. The analysis below focuses particularly on the impact of globalization on various performance indicators, as well as on the ability of the government to carry out its economic policies.

The final step is to assess the strength of a possible backlash against further globalization, since the first great wave of globalization in the 19th century ended with rising barriers to the free flow of goods, labor, and capital. This reaction lasted for three decades, and a similar retreat might mark the end of the current wave of globalization, which started in the second half of the 20th century.

A. Some Institutional/Organizational Aspects of U.S. Globalization[2]

For private business organizations, the new globalism implies a growing integration of markets and a greater necessity to take into account in their decision making the economic situation in foreign nations, the state of worldwide markets, and the activities of foreign enterprises. For other types of organization such as governments or nonprofit groups, it implies a growing cooperation and consultation in the economic sphere. The increasing globalization reflects a greater structural complexity of the economy, which requires not only new institutions but also new types of organizations.

---

[2]   Sources mentioned or cited in the text of this section are: Anon (2000.-b), Cantwell (1995), Doremus (1998), La Porta (1998), Mahoney (1999), Perkins (1997), Sasson (1996), Sykes (1995), and Union of International Associations (1998).

1. Private Sector Institutions/Organizations

An obvious example of a global economic organization in the private sector is, of course, the multinational enterprise (MNE), those firms with significant production facilities and offices in two or more nations. Despite the publicity they have received, by the end of the 20th century the economic role of those firms defined as MNEs by statistical agencies of the U.S. government was limited.

The labor force employed abroad in MNEs has been relatively small. For instance, the U.S. affiliates of foreign companies employed 5.2 million workers in 1997, which was about 3.8 percent of the U.S. employed civilian labor force. This percentage had, nevertheless, risen from 2.5 percent in 1982. In the same year foreign affiliates of U.S. companies employed 8.0 million workers, which amounted to 5.9 percent of the U.S. employed civilian labor force. This had fallen from 6.6 percent in 1982.[3]

Despite their relatively small share of total employment, MNEs have played a crucial role in U.S. foreign trade. In 1997, for instance, trade of U.S. affiliates of foreign MNEs was 20.4 percent of U.S. exports of goods and 30.0 percent of U.S. imports. In the same year U.S. multinationals accounted for 63.0 percent of U.S. exports of goods and 40.2 percent of imports. Combining these data, we see that U.S. and foreign multinationals together carried out roughly three quarters of the U.S. foreign trade turnover of goods. This percentage began to decline—about 4 percentage points between 1989 and 1997—but the long-term implications of this interesting short-term development are unclear.

A particularly important change in the private sector has been the creation of a network of international commercial arbitration courts dealing with issues related to this trade. By 1993, according to Saskia Sasson, such courts existed in 127 countries, and they have been slowly developing international legal standards for dispute resolution.

Nevertheless, most U.S. MNEs are not "world companies" and they still carry out most of their business in the U.S. In 1997, for instance, the foreign affiliates in which they owned a majority share produced only 25 percent of their gross product, accounted for only 23 percent of their profits and employed only 25 percent of their labor force. Moreover, although large firms are more likely to have foreign affiliates than small, Richard J. Mahoney points out that only half of the 100 largest U.S. firms had any non-U.S. nationals on their

---

[3]   The data in this and the next paragraph come from Mataloni (1999) and Zeile (1999). The foreign affiliates of U.S. companies include not only majority-owned affiliates but also "other" affiliates. Both the data sets on U.S. and foreign MNEs exclude banking enterprises. The exports of multinationals include exports to their affiliates not just by the parent company, but other companies as well. The same holds for imports to the U.S. as well.

Boards of Directors in the late 1990s and, moreover, such foreign directors comprised less than 10 percent of the outside directors (directors who had no daily employment with the firm) of these 100 firms. As Paul Doremus and Rafael La Porta forcefully argue, U.S. and foreign MNEs are also not converging toward a single type of global managerial system. Because MNEs are closely tied to a single territorial base, the national political and economic structures and the type of capitalist system in which they are embedded continue to shape the ownership structure, operations, internal governance, long-term financing, research and development, direct investment, intra-firm trading strategies, and other aspects of their business.

Other important developments point toward greater world economic integration. The older model of MNE featured roughly similar plants in many countries, each relatively autonomous and serving national markets. Except for a certain standardization of products and determination of which factory should service which countries, such an arrangement required relatively little international communication and coordination from the home office. A pioneering exception was the Singer Company in the early 20th century, which divided production among its foreign subsidiaries, which would ship their products all over the world.

By way of contrast, the newer model of MNE requires much more coordination, since factories in different nations of a given company specialize in different parts of production or in different functions of management.[4] Indeed, the share of R and D of the world's largest firms that is carried on outside the home country increased considerably from the early 1970s to the mid 1980s (some useful data are presented by John Cantwell) and it seems likely that this trend will continue. Both the parent MNE and the foreign affiliates can participate in the design or manufacturing of a given product, and facilities in both countries can draw upon the marketing experience of each other. It seems clear that these international interactions are the critical changes affecting the firm, rather than the rising share of facilities or sales in one country or another. This is, in part, reflected in the soaring volume of international communications discussed below.

Three particular aspects of the MNEs deserve brief note: Cross-border mergers or acquisitions have considerably increased in dollar volume, as shown in

[4]   For instance, Hewlett-Packard manages certain parts of its product lines from France, rather than the U.S.; and IBM has research laboratories in a number of countries (China, India, Israel, Japan, and Switzerland), supplying their results to IBM affiliates in other nations. Such cooperation also occurs in marketing and design. For instance, Levi Strauss and Häagen-Dazs have introduced into the U.S. market new products first designed respectively for the Japanese and Argentinian markets. (*Business Week,* September 7, 1998, pp. 56–8).

detail in Chapter 9. Moreover, a critical problem arising from such cross-border mergers and purchases is the increasing potential for the global monopolization of certain industries, a prospect discussed in great detail in Chapter 10. Finally, multinational firms are appearing in all branches of production, including services. For instance, the two law firms (Baker and McKenzie; and White and Case) with the most extensive network of foreign offices have branches, respectively, in 35 and 24 nations; and, on a different side of the justice system, some MNEs run prisons in several different nations.

Globalization in the private sector is not, of course, confined to profit-seeking enterprises; the number of nonprofit private organizations with branches in several nations is soaring. One list by the Union of International Associations (UIA) of organizations with branches in three or more nations includes almost 16,600 international, non-governmental (and non-business) organizations for 1998. Only 832 such organizations existed in 1951 and their number has been growing at an annual rate of 6.6 percent. This listing does not include various national groups with an international focus, such as local groups focusing on issues of foreign relations. The activities of these international non-governmental groups which are included in the UIA list cover the spectrum of human endeavors. Their political clout can be seen, for instance, in their key role in the defeat of the Multilateral Agreement on Investment (MAI) in 1997/98, their disruption of the Seattle World Trade Organization (WTO) meeting in 1999, or in their bringing forceful international attention to the necessity of debt relief for the most highly indebted poor countries (the HIPC initiative) in 2000 at the International Monetary Fund meeting in Prague.

2. Governmental Institutions/Organizations

The most obvious example of globalization in the field of government is the growth of inter-governmental organizations, many of which deal with economic problems. In 1900 only a few such organizations existed, for instance, the International Telecommunications Union, the International Institute of Agriculture (predecessor to the U.N. Food and Agriculture Organization), or the International Rail Congress Committee, and these focused primarily on technical issues. In the 1920s the creation of the League of Nations brought into existence several other new international organizations. By the end of the 20th century the United Nations included 18 affiliated international organs such as the ILO, UNESCO, the International Fund for Agricultural Development, and so forth, not to mention 5 regional commissions, 68 information offices, more than 120 centers, institutions, and other bodies.

The U.S. government is enmeshed in a dense network of bilateral and multilateral treaties, and more accumulate every year. For instance, from 1955 to 1997, the U.S. State Department's annual publication *Treaties in Force* has more than doubled in pages, and, it should be added, in later years the pages are bigger and the type is smaller. Of particular interest is the creation of inter-governmental agencies that have the potential for evolving into global economic regulators. In the financial sector, for instance, these include the Basle Committee on Banking Supervision, the Committee on the Global Financial System, the Committee on Payments and Settlement Systems, the International Association of Insurance Supervisors, and the International Organization of Securities Commission. In the area of trade, the U.S. has entered into a number of international treaties and organizations encouraging economic integration through the reduction of trade barriers. These range from agreements with particular countries (Israel) to regional and worldwide organizations such as NAFTA or the WTO.[5]

3. Hidden Globalism

It is sometimes argued by those on the political left that globalized production requires global regulation. In one sense this proposition has been validated, not through the aegis of any central international organization, but rather through a series of treaties and/or independent international organizations outside the U.N. system. Certain inter-governmental agreements to regulate various types of economic activities in all countries have received publicity, for instance the International Court of Justice (2000), the Montreal Protocol of 1987 for reduction of emissions of chlorofluorocarbons or the Law of the Sea Convention of 1982.

These are, however, only the most visible aspects of a broad movement toward economic cooperation among nations that is resulting in the coordination of a vast spectrum of governmental policies: environmental, banking regulation, product standards, trade rules, labor regulations, antitrust policies, taxation and subsidy measures, and so on. In certain cases these cooperative arrangements have been incorporated in the law of various nations, but more often they have been embodied either in the regulatory practices followed by governmental agencies or in the regulations of national trade organizations that are binding on its members. The United States has participated in many such

---

[5] Regional agreements are proliferating as well, although many have fallen into desuetude. In 1994 the IMF listed 68 preferential economic agreements, running from the ASEAN sponsored Free Trade Area (AFTA) and the Andean Pact (ANCOM) to the West African Economic and Monetary Union (WAEMU) (Lawrence, 1996).

globalizing arrangements, but often their international origins are hidden, dropping from sight because the agreements are enforced by national agencies, and not by some international institution. Some examples are in order.

The Basle Accord of 1988 between various industrial nations and the subsequent proposals developed by the Basel Committee on Banking Supervision has set common minimum standards of capital adequacy for major banks doing business across national borders, which national governments have agreed to enforce. The International Organization of Securities Commissions (IOSCO) is trying to work out common principles of security regulations, and an OECD subcommittee is at work formulating standards for corporate governance. Private organizations, which have been delegated quasi-governmental power, are also participating in this movement. For instance, the International Bar Association is creating a model bankruptcy code, and, in January 2001, the International Accounting Standards Committee received new powers to propose various accounting rules for adoption by the different national accounting boards for facilitating the listing of securities from one nation on the stock exchanges of other countries.

Even less visible cases of institutionalized globalization are the organizations for common product standards for quality, safety, labeling, or technical specifications. The International Organization for Standardization, founded in 1947, and the Codex Alimentarius Commission, created by the World Health Organization in 1962, are well-known international standardization groups. John Sykes analyzes the activities of many other such organizations which operate away from the glare of publicity, for example, the International Telecommunications Union, the International Conference on Weights and Measures, the International Bureau for the Standardization of Man-Made Fibres, the International Commission on Illumination, the International Air Transport Association, the International Institute of Refrigeration, and the International Institute of Welding. Although some *de facto* international standards arise because of the global dominance of the products of a few companies, in other cases private trade organizations in various nations have come together to set standards as well. From a broader perspective, these organizational innovations exemplify a broader movement in international law, which, according John A. Perkins, "has extended into areas once thought to be exclusively of internal concern.... [Some] developments become binding on states without their consent, contrary to the premise once thought to be fundamental."

In brief, the rules by which the production of goods and services is carried out are converging internationally, organizations crossing national boundaries are growing in number and influence, and inter-governmental organizations are playing an expanding role in the international political economy. In these respects we are witnessing growing world economic integration. Moreover, even if many aspects of globalization, such as falling barriers to world trade, are reversed in the future, most of the institutional/organizational changes discussed above seem likely to remain.

B. Indicators of Globalization [6]

Now let's look at four key globalizing trends and see what's causing them. The first three trends concern flows of foreign trade, labor, and capital and have sometimes been classified as aspects of "internationalization"; the last trend concerns the international flow of information, which has skyrocketed in recent years. The extensive data on which I base my generalizations are presented in Appendix 5.1.

1. The Growing Importance of Foreign Trade

Globalization defined in terms of the relative volume of foreign trade and domestic production of goods and services reveals an accelerating growth of trade. The ratios of exports or imports to the GDP, which are common measurements of the external orientation of the economy, were roughly the same in the early 1970s as they were in the first decade of the century. Since that time, however, the ratio have approximately doubled.

Many claim, however, that these ratios must really be calculated only in terms of the production of goods and services that are traded on world markets, so as to take into account the declining importance of tradable goods and services as a share of the total GDP over the century. A recalculation of these trade ratios for just the production of tradable goods shows, however, roughly the same picture, but with the upsurge taking place in the middle and late 1960s and at a faster rate until the end of the century. For services the picture is somewhat different. Although the ratio of exports of tradable services to total production of such services began to rise in the early 1970s, little change in a similar ratio for imports occurred during the second half of the 20th century, so that up to the end of the century, globalization took place primarily on the export side.

---

[6] For discussion in the text of this section, I draw upon: Anderton and Wincoop (2001-b), Baier and Bergstrand (1998), Bordo *et al.* (1999), Ceglowski (1994), Cooper (1985), Crockett (1997), Engel and Rogers (1998), Herring and Litan (1995), Jones, (1997), Kaplan, (1998), Obstfeld (1988), Pritchett (1997), Wei (1996), and Zevin (1992). Results from the Millennium Survey come from Pryor (2000-b).

Several other new features of the foreign trade picture, with implications for the economic system, deserve brief mention:

• By the end of World War II the U.S. changed from a net exporter to a net importer of raw materials, which suggests that in this important respect the U.S. became more economically dependent on foreign countries.

• Since the mid 1970s the vertical chain of domestic production has to some degree been disintegrating. More concretely, foreign outsourcing of intermediate goods used in domestic production, for instance, certain electronic components, has become more important. Although such outsourcing still makes up a relatively small share of total foreign trade, as discussed in Appendix 5.1, its share in the total value of imported goods roughly doubled between 1972 and 1990. This, of course, provides yet another example that the U.S. economy is becoming more interdependent with the rest of the world.

• The share of trade within the same industries, in contrast to trade between different industries, has risen dramatically, which suggests that competition in many individual domestic markets has become greater. As discussed in Chapter 10, however, the competitive impact of foreign trade may not be so great in the future as in the past, due to the increasing volume of cross-border mergers between enterprises in the same line of production, combined with a high volume of foreign trade between multinationals and their foreign affiliates.

• Companies engaged in foreign trade have changed. Such activities are no longer centered in small and medium-size trading firms located in large cities along the coasts; instead, foreign trade is predominantly being carried out by large—often multinational—corporations more broadly spread out across the nation.

These trends, combined with other information, give us some important clues about why the trade/GDP ratio has risen since the 1970s and what might happen to it in the future. Using a gravity model and bilateral trade data of OECD nations from 1958 to 1988, Scott Baier and Jeffrey Bergstrand estimate that roughly one third of the growth of the trade/GDP ratio occurred as a result of the combined effect of falling tariffs and transport costs, the former being roughly twice as important as the latter. Assuming that all of the growth of outsourcing (vertical specialization) represents new foreign trade, such a development probably accounted for roughly 5 to 8 percent of the rise in the trade/GDP ratio. If one third of the exports of multinational enterprises across borders represents trade that otherwise would not have taken place without the growth of affiliates abroad, this means that such trade by MNEs would account for 5 percent of the growth of export/trade ratio and 13 percent of the growth of the import/GDP ratio. Combined, all these factors account for roughly half of the growth of the trade/GDP ratio. Although it is difficult to isolate the causal factors underlying the remaining growth of this ratio, it seems likely that the rise of trade within particular industries, which made available a greater variety of goods to consumers, played a particularly important role, a conjecture that remains to be proven.

On the microeconomic side of foreign trade, the most common test of market integration is simple: Are the prices at all locations the same, once the costs of transporting the goods from one location to another and the special taxes levied on the goods in question in some locations are taken into account. This, of course, is the famous "law of one price."

For some important raw materials and agricultural products which sell on world markets, such as oil or wheat, the law of one price appears to hold on the wholesale level. By way of contrast, the situation for manufactured goods is quite different and suggests that world markets are from from integrated. A number of careful empirical studies have dealt with the question, either directly or in the context of testing the purchasing-power-parity theory of exchange rates (whether exchange rates reflect the relative purchasing power of various currencies). For instance, Janet Ceglowski uses quarterly data from 1974 through 1990 to examine ratios of U.S. export prices to German and Japanese export prices (expressed in dollars) for a number of highly comparable product groups. She finds that these ratios are not stable in the long-run and, moreover, show little tendency of heading toward a mean value. A more recent study by Charles Engel and John Rogers, which uses more countries but also broader product categories, shows long-lasting and large divergences in prices for the same goods in different market economies.[7] In brief, the law of one price does not hold for many manufactured goods.

World market integration has not yet been achieved for a number of reasons. Goods produced in various countries have not become complete substitutes for each other, as discussed in greater detail below. Moreover, importers or exporters do not like to change prices each time exchange rates change; for a variety of reasons they often prefer instead to "price to market." Given current exchange rates fluctuations, a phenomenon discussed in more detail in Chapter 3, this business policy has many advantages.

Further, many barriers to trade remain. Some are "natural," for instance, the cost of transportation. Certainly the costs of transportation relative to the cost of goods in foreign trade have fallen considerably in the second half of the 20th century, but it does not seem likely that further declines will have a significant effect on foreign trade.[8] As discussed in greater detail below, the falling costs of

[7] We would expect the prices of particular goods in various U.S. cities to converge as transportation costs fall. Nevertheless, my own research (Pryor, 1995-a) suggests that this does not seem to be happening.

[8] For individuals, average air transportation revenues per passenger mile fell from 30 cents to 11

communications and the increasing use of the internet to convey information about different products and services available for foreign trade should prove much more important in encouraging ever-increasing openness.

Artificial barriers to trade include tariffs, trade quotas, or constraints on particular specifications of the imported goods. By the mid 1990s U.S. tariffs had fallen to less than 2.5 percent of the value of total imports, and it seems doubtful that any further fall in tariff rates would result in a significant increase in trade. Non-tariff barriers such as special "quality regulations"are, however, a different story and, at least in the 1980s, added as a whole somewhere between 13 and 38 percent of the cost of imported goods, according to several different estimates.[9]

The private sector also throws up barriers to foreign trade. One example is the "home bias" of consumers. In this regard it is worth noting that without any official trade barriers at all, national borders still make some differences because foreign goods or services are not completely substitutable for their domestically produced counterparts: unfamiliarity, differences in taste, and inconveniences all play a role. But these barriers are not only economic, because any differences due to language, legal system, or culture also raise barriers. The degree of home-bias, or as some have phrased it, the "impact of a border," is difficult to estimate. According to Shang-Jin Wei, the degree of "home bias" in U.S. trade is roughly 5 percent and does not seem likely to present a major impediment for increasing openness. By way of contrast, James Anderson and Eric van Wincoop estimate that borders amount to a tariff equivalent of U.S. borders of roughly 50 percent.[10]

Producers and sellers can also raise trade barriers. For instance, Levi's jeans or Ford Escorts cost twice as much in London as in New York, and only a small part of the difference can be explained by higher consumption taxes, shipping

cents (1990 prices) between 1950 and 1990; for freight, shipment and port costs per ton of sea freight fell from $34 to $29 in the same period. These data come from UNDP (1999, p. 30) and Herring and Litan (1995, p. 14). From 1960 to 1998, transportation costs as a percent of exports and imports declined from about 7.2 percent to 3.2 percent. Part of this latter decline was due to a fall in real transportation costs; part was due to a rise in the trade of goods with a high ratio of value to weight. These data come from official balance of payment statistics (www.bea.doc.gov/bea/di1.htm).

[9]   The lower estimate is by Harrigan (1993); the higher estimate is by Lee and Swagel (1997). A third estimate by Laird and Yates (1990) lies closer to Harrigan's.

[10] Wei's estimates of the home bias do not appear much different from average tariff levels. McCallum's estimate (1996) of the U.S. home-bias amounting to a tariff equivalent 16.8 percent lies between the estimates of Wei and Anderson and Wincoop (2001-a). Janet Ceglowski (1998) and Anderson and Wincoop (2001-b) have useful discussions of the problems involved in such estimates.

costs, or customs duties. International organizations have also created artificial barriers to trade.[11]

How far are we from a truly integrated world market? One way to approach the problem is to ask how high the ratio of trade to GDP in the U.S. can reach. In 1980 the United States produced about one sixth of all goods and services in the world.[12] In a totally integrated world market the ratio of exports or imports to GDP in the United States would be about 83 percent—if national boundaries made no difference, if transportation and communication costs were zero, if all goods and services could be traded, and if several more esoteric conditions are also met.[13] Obviously none of these assumptions will ever be true, but they present the theoretical limit of economic openness. Since the ratios of manufactured exports or imports to production were respectively 40 and 50 percent in the mid 1990s,[14] it does not seem likely that these ratios can continue to rise at the same rate as they have in the last third of the 20th century. Moreover, certain changes such as the introduction of "lean production" and just-in-time inventory methods make it important for supplying firms to be located within quick transportation to the purchasing firm. On the other hand the ratios of service exports and imports to service production were respectively 9 and 6 percent, so trade in services still has considerable potential to grow.

We can draw several conclusions from this statistical discussion. First, the rise in the ratio of exports or imports to the GDP has limits. Second, the current trade/GDP ratios in the U.S. are probably some distance from these limits. Several factors underlying the rapid increase of trade in the second half of the 20th century will become less important as a stimulus for trade, for instance, falling tariffs and transportation costs or a rising level of intra-industry trade. On the other hand, raw material imports, vertical specialization, and intra-firm trade of MNEs are likely to play larger roles in trade expansion. All-in-all, it seems likely that the relative importance of trade in the U.S. economy should continue to rise (at a decreasing rate) over at least the next few decades, key political

---

[11] For instance, the European Court upheld the right of an Austrian eyeglass maker to sell at a lower price outside the EU and to sue anyone reimporting the discounted glasses for resale in any EU member country (Economist, August 22, 1998, p. 17). (The same situation exists with reimporting of pharmaceuticals produced in the U.S. which sell for a lower price abroad.) The introduction of the Euro will make price comparisons easier within Europe and many of these price discrepancies will undoubtedly narrow, although a home bias may exist for other reasons.

[12] The basic data for this estimate come from Summers and Heston (1988) and are calculated using a purchasing-power-parity rate of exchange. I have supplemented their data with estimates for countries they did not include.

[13] This ratio of 83 percent is roughly that of Luxembourg, a country accounting for 0.03 percent of the world domestic product.

[14] All data in this paragraphs come from Appendix 5.1.

and economic conditions remaining the same. This proviso, I must stress, is crucial, since any major war or depression could radically alter the picture. Although globalization is likely to increase, I can find no credible evidence that this rate will accelerate, unlike the majority of economists replying to the Millennium Survey.

2. *Flow of Labor*

World barriers to flows of labor, as manifested by immigration quotas, were much higher at the end of the 20th century than the beginning. Moreover, in contrast to the flow of goods, the data on immigration into the U.S. reveal a decline, not an increase, of globalization.

The most useful indicators to analyze this phenomenon focus either on yearly immigrants or the total foreign-born population in the U.S. As a percent of the population, the flow of immigrants to the U.S. was quite high until the late 1920s. Immediately thereafter, the ratio fell precipitously and then slowly but steadily rose in the years following World War II. Nevertheless, by the end of the century this ratio was still far below what it was in the first two decades of the century.

The percentage of foreign-born in the U.S. population reveals a somewhat different pattern, hitting a peak in 1910, falling steadily until 1970, and then rising thereafter. Nevertheless, by the end of the century the percentage of foreign-born in the U.S. was also far below what it was in the opening decades of the century.

Several economic factors increase the attractiveness of immigration to the U.S. The most obvious, of course, relate to relative wages in the U.S. and other nations. Charles Jones notes that in 1988, half of the world's population lived in countries where the GDP per worker was less than 11.8 percent of production per worker in the United States, which gives some indications of the difference in wages between the U.S. and these nations. Lant Pritchett points out, moreover, that this income gap between advanced industrial and economically less developed nations widened from 1960 to the mid 1990s.[15] Many argue that the income gap should begin to close as foreign investment and technologies reach these poor countries. On this premise and employing a sophisticated estimating technique, Charles Jones concludes that the number of nations with a per capita GDP of 10 percent or less of the U.S. average will fall from 45 in 1988 to 29

---

[15] This conclusion is not accepted by all economists because of certain measurement problems (Wade, 2001).

in 2050. Nevertheless, for a much larger group of nations, the differences in average GDP in absolute terms should widen, even as the relative differences decrease. This means that the economic incentives for workers to emigrate to the United States (or other economically advanced nations) should remain strong in the next half century. Other studies on the widening dispersion of world income (reviewed in External Appendix X-5.2) suggest that this incentive for international migration will become stronger for a number of decades, reinforced by the falling costs of movement from one country to another.

Whatever the strength of the incentives, the immigrant flow to the U.S. is determined in part by immigration quotas and by the ease or difficulty in stopping illegal immigration. It is difficult to predict how immigration laws will change. As indicated below, a certain political backlash against immigration appears to be growing. Nevertheless, according to Robert Kaplan, business people argue that "... it is far more cost-efficient to import [labor] from the rest of the world's talent [pool] than to train citizens at home, especially as weak or nonexistent national education standards and insufficient tax revenues make a mockery of many local American schools."

If world labor markets were as integrated as those within the United States, labor could migrate freely from location to location, and wages would be roughly similar in most areas (the law of one price in labor markets). Obviously this is not the situation at the cusp of the new millennium nor is it likely to be in the foreseeable future. Nevertheless, with the more widespread knowledge of English, job mobility of educated labor has been significantly rising. Mobility for less-educated workers may also increase, given the growing economic incentives for migration and the relative ease of illegal entry.

3. Flow of Capital

As a percent of GDP, *gross* flows of short and long-term international capital to and from the U.S. were considerably greater at the end of the 20th century than at the beginning. Such capital flows were also directed at a much wider group of industries than formerly, according to the research of Michael Bordo and his colleagues. In this respect, globalization is increasing. Andrew Crockett points out another aspect of this phenomenon, namely that the dollar value of sales of bonds and equities across the U.S. borders rose from 4.1 percent of the U.S. GDP in 1975 to 151.5 percent in 1996. Such capital flows are part of the rising flood of foreign exchange that crosses U.S. borders, a phenomenon discussed in Chapter 3 and pictured in Chart 3.2.

To make this picture more complicated, Maurice Obstfeld points out that *net* capital flows (gross outflows minus gross inflows of capital) declined as a share of GDP, a phenomenon occurring in many other industrial nations as well. This means that a person in one country may be lending capital abroad, while his neighbor is borrowing capital from another foreign nation. Some argue that this signals declining globalization since, among other things, it means that the national investment rate has become more dependent on the domestic national saving rate than in a previous era. In most respects, however, it seems to me that the gross flows of capital, rather than the net flows, are the more telling indicator of globalization because they reflect individual decisions made on the ground.

The upturn in these gross flows of capital was particularly evident by the early 1970s and reflects a perception that foreign investment had become safer. This, in turn, can be traced in part to greater flows of information, the rise of international accounting standards, and greater financial disclosure requirements—all aspects of the institutional/organizational processes discussed above. These changing institutional factors should encourage even more international capital flows in the future, other things being equal. Furthermore, foreign investment of all types was more protected against discriminatory treatment and/or confiscation at the end of the century than in the early years following World War II.[16] As a result, this has encouraged many domestic enterprises to build production facilities abroad, rather than servicing these foreign markets by exports from home.

How true are the repeated assertions that capital markets are more integrated than goods markets, that financial market integration has been rapidly increasing in the last half of the 20th century, and that such financial integration is much greater now than before World War I? The evidence is mixed and, despite the greater international flow of capital, we should be wary of drawing facile generalizations about changes in capital market integration.

Certainly the number of industrial countries with governmental controls on cross-border financial flows, such as limits on capital movements, multiple exchange rates, or requirements to surrender export proceeds, has fallen dramatically since the mid 1970s. But this does not indicate increasing globalization over the century since, in the years immediately preceding World War I, such restrictions did not exist at all.

If we define integration of world financial markets in terms of equality of interest rates in various industrial nations, then the relevant data suggest that such integration was far from realized by the end of the 20th century. More

---

[16]   This should not be interpreted to mean that foreign direct investment has assumed a larger share of total gross capital flows, in contrast to investments in foreign securities. Over the 20th century the share of portfolio investment slightly increased.

specifically, although interest rates (both nominal and real) of different countries followed roughly parallel tracks in the second half of the 20th century, there is little indication that these rates in different nations became more closely correlated, as economists approaching the topic from quite different perspective, such Maurice Bordo, Richard Cooper, or Robert Zevin, have emphasized.

I tried to look at this changing integration of world financial markets in a different and simpler way by investigating whether the dispersion of interest rates had narrowed in the last half of the 20th century. Maurice Obstfeld shows that although differences in interest rates between the U.S. and Britain declined markedly between the late 1960s and the mid 1990s, this gap was still somewhat higher than at the beginning of the century. With perfect capital mobility, the interest rate differential should be zero. Looking at ten industrial nations (including the U.S.) over the post World War II years, I also could not find any narrowing of interest rate differences between nations (a statistical experiment described in Appendix 5.2, Section E). More sophisticated statistical tests of increasing financial market integration show that only in a very narrow sense could such a development be observed, but further investigation of such issues at this point requires consideration of some ferocious technical details which would take us too far from our major themes.[17] Other approaches toward measuring integration of financial markets lead to ambiguous results.[18]

The creation of certain new organizations will undoubtedly serve to advance international financial integration. For the world as a whole, an important step in this direction was taken when the Basil Committee on Banking Supervision undertook in 1988 to set up uniform banking standards for the world economy in order to harmonize, at least in part, banking regulations in the major industrial countries. In Europe, of course, the new European

---

[17] Frankel (1985) has a useful summary of the very large literature on these issues. These more sensitive tests of financial integration require comparisons of interest rates with particular types of corrections. One correction reflects the forward rates of the currencies and such "covered interest parity" do indeed show a considerable convergence since the end of the 1970s Thus in this narrow sense financial markets are becoming integrated. If interest rates are corrected to take into account other risks (uncovered interest parity), less financial integration is found. If interest rates are corrected to take into account expected inflation (real interest parity), no change in financial integration is found. It should be clear that for all three criteria to be met, the economies of the world must be integrated along many different dimensions

[18] For instance, one possible measure of increasing financial integration is a rising share of foreign assets or foreign liabilities to domestic assets. Golub (1990) shows in a comparison of the 1970s and the 1980s of twelve industrial nations that the unweighted average of these ratios for most of the nations in the sample rose. Nevertheless, the experiences in the individual nations are so different that it is hazardous to draw an overall conclusion.

Central Bank created at the end of the 1990s in Frankfurt will act to unify European interest rates and banking regulations.

In brief, the evidence on the global integration of financial markets is contradictory. The data on gross flows of capital to and from the U.S. suggest a rising integration during the second half of the 20th century. The rising volume of money flows between the U.S. and foreign nations, which I discuss in Chapter 3, points in the same direction. Nevertheless, the data on convergence of interest rates in different industrial nations yields a far less certain picture.

4. Information Flows

A key dimension of the "new globalization" is increased international communications. Although I focus primarily on the economic implication, the political, social, and cultural impact of this change is, as many have correctly emphasized, very important as well.

Chart 5.1 presents a rough index of per capita international communications and suggests a dramatic change in the orientation of the economic system. The index contains four components of communications flowing over national borders, each given equal weight: letters, telephone calls, foreign travel, and an estimate of fax/e-mail messages. The underlying data (described in Appendix 5.2) do not, however, permit a separation of commercial and business matters from social, political, and cultural communications and, as a result, this index is crude. I stop calculation of the index in the early 1990s, because estimates of the volume of e-mail become increasingly uncertain. Despite its flaws, the index provides a useful orientation to an important aspect of globalization.

The relative rates of growth of communications, production of goods and services, and foreign trade have differed considerably over time. In the period between 1921 and 1970, per capita communications between the U.S. and the rest of the world rose at roughly 0.7 percent a year. By way of comparison, both real per capita GDP and foreign trade were experiencing an average annual increase of roughly 2.7 percent a year. From 1970 to 1994, such communications rose at roughly 5.8 percent a year, while real per capita GDP and foreign trade grew at respective rates of 1.8 percent and 4.9 percent a year. In brief, globalization of the U.S., defined in terms of per capita international communications flows, lagged other indicator of the economy before 1970 and led them thereafter.

Falling costs of communications due to the application of the new information technologies were, of course, a major impetus for the dramatic rise of the index. For instance, between 1950 and 1990 the real cost of a 3 minute phone call from London to New York fell from $53.20 to $3.32, as noted by Richard

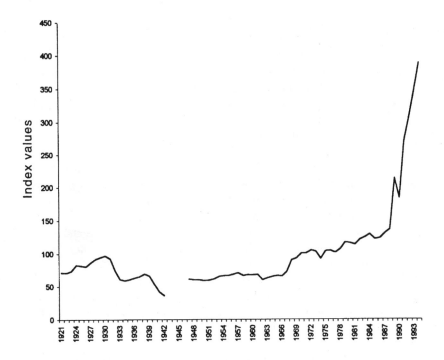

Chart 5.1. Index of Per Capita U.S. International Communications

Note: 1970 = 100. The sources and methods of calculating this index are presented in Appendix 5.2.

Herring and Robert Litan. By the end of the 20th century the cost of a long e-mail including the same information as the telephone conversation was practically zero.

The falling costs of communications have a considerable impact on the economy. Coordination of business activities within MNEs becomes easier, more information is available about goods and services that could enter foreign trade, and the costs of international financial flows fall dramatically. Other things equal, this should encourage greater flows of trade and finance in the future. In particular, such falling costs should encourage both further vertical specialization (global sourcing) and greater intra-industry trade, two phenomena discussed above. The greater economic interconnectedness of the world reflected in this rising volume of international communications also increases the need for greater coordination of economic policies among nations.

5. A Brief Summary

In the latter half of the 20th century the globalization of the U.S. economy was not a unidimensional process. Indeed, in certain respects such as immigration or net capital flows, the country did not move beyond the level of globalization achieved at the beginning of the century. Examination of degree to which the law of one price applies to various markets for goods, labor, or financial instruments shows that the U.S. is far from being fully integrated into world markets. Nevertheless, in some important respects—trade/production ratios, gross flows of capital, communications with those in other countries—the macro-economic indicators show a rising degree of globalization starting in the 1960s and 1970s. The fall in the costs of international communications offers the possibility of much closer world economic integration in future years. Such a prediction assumes, however, that political factors remain constant, and, as I show below, a backlash against globalization is possible that could reverse this seemingly inexorable trend.[19]

C. Some Impacts of Increased Globalization on U.S. Economic Policy Making [20]

In the preceding chapters I try to puncture several myths about globalization. For instance, in Chapter 4 I show that, contrary to popular belief, increased foreign trade was not a major causal factor underlying the widening income gap between rich and poor; and in Chapter 3 I argue that more openness to world trade can lead to increased instability of domestic production, especially when abetted by financial instabilities arising for internal causes. At this point it is useful to review from a broad perspective the impact of globalization on the effectiveness of the U.S. government's economic policy making. This serves as a prelude to subsequent discussion of a possible U.S. backlash against globalization that could reverse current trends toward greater world economic integration.

---

[19] It would require too great a digression to discuss in detail why globalization of the economy seemed to increase most dramatically in the 1960s and 1970s. Certainly an ideological change occurred: This was reflected by the dismantling of controls over both domestic economic activities and the international flow of capital, as well as the increasing market-orientation of other governmental policies in the domestic regulation of production. The two oil shocks in the 1970s also contributed to the feeling that the established policies were not suitable to the new era. It might be added that the 1970s were also the years in which the dominance of U.S. multinational enterprises began to be seriously contested by foreign MNEs.

[20] In this section of the text I refer to studies by Cooper (1985), Macrae (1984), and Rodrik (1997).

The rising share of foreign trade in the U.S. economy in the last quarter of the 20th century, as shown in Chapter 3, was accompanied by a declining effectiveness of fiscal policy because of greater leakages out of the economy of any governmental injections of purchasing power. In the same chapter I also argue that the increasing integration of international financial markets lessens the ability of the Federal Reserve to influence interest rates. In brief, these signs point toward a future in which a more integrated world market will weaken the federal government's ability to carry out macroeconomic policies to stabilize the economy, just as state and local governments levels cannot effectively use monetary and fiscal policy measures to influence aggregate economic activity within their jurisdictions in the integrated U.S. domestic economy.

Globalization has also limited the powers of government to implement microeconomic policies. In cases where the U.S. gains when all other nations follow the same rules, this limitation has been voluntarily accepted. For instance, by joining the World Trade Organization and signing various multilateral tariff reduction agreements, the U.S. limited its possibilities of instituting certain types of trade barriers to protect particular industries. But the other signatory nations are also bound by the same rules so that the U.S. gains. Or in signing the 1997 Global Telecommunications Agreement, the U.S. agreed to drop a number of domestic regulations for telecommunications such as requirements that such utilities be domestically owned, in return for similar agreements by other nations, which would allow U.S. companies to enter these markets. The net benefits of this paticular agreement to the U.S., however, can be challenged when we investigate which segments in the U.S. are the net gainers.

In other spheres of governmental policy making, globalization limits microeconomic policy making arising from the greater mobility of capital and labor. For instance, nations now face the same dilemma that local governments do when it comes to taxing companies within their jurisdiction, although not to such an extent. Certain multinational enterprises with sales and factory sites all over the world have relocated—or have threatened to relocate—their headquarters to obtain tax concessions. For instance, in 1998 the Swedish company Ericsson moved its headquarters to London, in part to avoid high Swedish taxes, and a similar move was announced the next year by the Swedish-Swiss firm ABB. The impact of such corporation tactics was shown in 1999, when Allianz, a giant German insurance company, and three other large German firms threatened to move their headquarters to another country unless certain tax regulations were changed, a power-play that forced the Social Democratic government to capitulate. Of course, relocation has many human and economic costs, and mobility of businesses and labor between nations is less sensitive to small differences in tax rates, than their mobility within a single nation.

Globalization and the rising importance of the internet multiply the complications and costs of collecting corporate taxes, as well as enforcing particular laws and regulations in other ways. The sheer volume of business carried on in cyberspace makes it more and more difficult to determine where taxes should be paid. For instance, if units in different nations collaborate on a particular project, it is often problematic to determine the contribution (value-added) of the different national teams. For some types of activities in cyberspace, such as pay-for-view movies, advising services, or "live experiences," it is difficult to determine in which country such weightless transactions take place or how they could be taxed. This topic receives further attention in Chapter 8 in the discussion about enforcement of U.S. laws against gambling and pornography, where such services are routed through the internet from a server located in some Caribbean island, but which may originate elsewhere. Electronic money transfers, which are increasingly common, also make income easier to hide from tax authorities.

Since capital is more mobile than labor, it can be easily demonstrated that globalization will eventually lead to a falling share of taxes paid by capital and a rising share paid by labor. Dani Rodrik's cross-country evidence shows that the tax rate on capital income is inversely related to trade openness. His time-series data also reveal that in major OECD nations (including the U.S.) from the early 1980s to the mid 1990s, tax rates on capital income fell, while tax rates on labor income rose.

Some argue that the mobility of labor will also begin to place similar constraints on personal taxation. At the present time individual migration to escape high taxes is relatively limited, but visionaries, such as Norman Macrae, foresee much greater labor mobility in the future, aided by telecommuting, so that a particular U.S. job (for instance, computer programming) could be carried out on the beach of some tax haven in a Pacific island. In this way onerous personal taxes can also be more easily avoided, and personal tax rates throughout the world will gradually converge. This fascinating forecast seems to me, however, to lie in the realm of social science fiction.[21]

Like taxation, globalization also reduces governmental regulatory powers. Threats to relocate unless certain regulations are changed may become more common. Enforcement of certain antitrust regulations also becomes more difficult, particularly when a proposed merger is justified to the authorities by the domestic companies involved as "the only way to meet foreign competition." I discuss this problem in greater detail in Chapter 10. Strange complications also

---

[21] Macrae also argues that formal organizations lose their importance when people can connect through the world wide web, rather than through personal contact. Since so many telecommuting workers will be independent agents, the influence of labor unions will also decline.

arise when, in an international merger, the antitrust authorities of particular nations involved reach different conclusions. Given the logic of globalization, one way to neutralize such corporate power plays is to internationalize certain kinds of business regulations or antitrust enforcement. In Chapter 9 I discuss other issues arising from obscure nations providing havens which allow U.S. companies to evade domestic laws and regulations.

Finally, globalization actually creates many new microeconomic problems for governmental policy makers to solve. One obvious difficulty arises from increasing U.S. dependency on other economies. For instance, the greater net imports of raw materials, as Richard Cooper has emphasized, make the U.S. markets more vulnerable to raw material shocks originating from abroad and more sensitive to other types of external economic influences as well.[22]

Although I focus on particular ways in which globalization weakens governmental policy making in the U.S. economy, this does not mean that the economic powers of the government are diminishing in *all* dimensions or that the rise of neoliberalism is inevitable. To arrive at a more balanced view of the future of the state, many more aspects of the government sector need to be analyzed and are taken up in later chapters.

D. The Backlash Against Further Globalization[23]

Although in 1870 the first great wave of globalization seemed unstoppable, Kevin O'Rourke and Jeffrey Williamson show in an interesting fashion how it engendered a backlash that led to higher tariffs in Europe to protect agricultural incomes, and the beginning of immigration quotas in the U.S. to protect industrial wages. Although globalization appears unstoppable at the dawn of the new millennium, extrapolations are dangerous, especially because the process of the U.S. integration into the world economy during the 1980s and 1990s was abetted by a particular set of political and economic circumstances that may not last in the years to come. Even though, according to such authorities as Ralph

---

[22] A number of economists, for instance, Kuszczak and Murray (1985), have used sophisticated statistical technique to show how domestic U.S. prices and interest rates respond to various types of shocks in other industrial nations. The degree to which such sensitivity has changed over time, however, is a subject for future research.

[23] In this section of the text I draw on studies by Brimlow (1995), Bryant (forthcoming), Ehrenberg (1994), Feenstra (1998), Gilpin (2000), Gray (1998), James (2001), O'Rourke and Williamson (1999), Pfaller, Gough, and Therborn (1991), Polanyi (1944), Rhodes (1998), Rodrik (1997), Schiff (2000), and Williamson (1996, 1998).

Bryant, problems with ramifications spilling across national borders are grow-ing in importance relative to problems of strictly domestic governance, this does not mean that the U.S. will meet these challenges through greater integration into the world economy.

Nevertheless, parallels between the first and second large waves of global-ization cannot be taken too far. Architects of the current international economic system have attempted to insure that the new institutions and organizations will endure, and that the rules of the new economic game will be enforced. Nevertheless, the permanence—or malleability—of such institutions and organ-izations depends very much on the international environment in which they are functioning. It is, therefore, important to review the emerging sources of back-lash, classified somewhat arbitrarily into economic, political, and social sources of discontent.

1. Economic

The maintenance of domestic prosperity is crucial to continued globalization, because in times of economic hardship, political support for free trade declines. In Chapter 3 I argue that the U.S. will become increasingly vulnerable to finan-cial crises and, if these ever lead to a serious and long-term recession, the forces of protectionism would become more powerful. If, during a period of rising U.S. unemployment, large trading partners such as Japan and China continue to fol-low their traditional practices of achieving domestic prosperity by maintaining large trade surpluses with the U.S., then a backlash may become particularly acute.

Free trade is also targeted when low-skilled workers or industries employing such workers are seen as hurt by imports from low-wage nations and workers who are laid off are slow to be rehired in other industries. Although Chapter 3 presents evidence that in the second half of the 20th century, this was not an important factor underlying U.S. unemployment, common perceptions are polit-ically much stronger than any econometric results.

Another familiar worry is that immigration of low-skilled workers into the U.S. also lowers the wages of all domestic low-skilled workers and results in a more unequal distribution of income. Given simple supply and demand consid-erations, such an argument has merit and in certain years in the past, immigra-tion seems to have played this role. For instance, Jeffrey Williamson shows that heavy immigration in the 19th century created greater wage inequalities in cap-ital- and land-rich nations such as the U.S., which, in turn, led to rising immi-gration barriers. In more recent times we heard H. Ross Perot claim that freer flows of capital will result in the "great sucking sound" of U.S. investment capital leaving (or neglecting) labor intensive industries in the U.S. to finance the same industries in low wage nations, leading to more unemployment and a decline in the wages of unskilled workers in the U.S.

Although the arguments about the impact of immigration on wages have theoretical merit, comparisons of wages or unemployment between areas with and without large immigrant workers raise serious doubts about their importance.[24] Although Ross Perot is correct that some U.S. jobs have decamped for Mexico, up to the end of the 20th century, this movement was offset by new jobs opening up in the U.S. so that high domestic employment could be maintained.

The economic arguments for protectionism ultimately rest on public opinion defined in a particular sense, but this is difficult to gauge. Polling results on support for free trade or protectionism show that minor changes in wording have considerable influence on the outcomes.

Looking at the responses to the same question about free trade posed in different years, I find a considerable increase in protectionism from the early 1950s to the early 1980s and, thereafter, a slight decrease (see External Appendix X-5.1 for details). Nevertheless, at the end of the millennium during a period of great prosperity, more than half of the U.S. adults seemed to hold protectionist sentiments. But the importance of the opinions of the general public about trade policy—except in extreme situations—can be questioned, especially given the enormous differences in opinions between the leaders who make the decisions and the general public. For instance, in November 1982 a Gallup poll asked whether tariffs were necessary to protect jobs or should be eliminated to lower the cost of goods. Only 23 percent of the general public believed tariffs should be eliminated, while 67 percent of the sample of opinion leaders held such a belief.

It seems, therefore, that the crucial public opinion refers to only a select number of politically influential Americans. Robert Gilpin argues that after the 1960s, protectionist sentiment among U.S. policy makers increased. As examples of such protectionist sentiments, he points to the Multi-Fiber Arrangement of 1973, the rise of voluntary export restraints and the increasing abuse of antidumping rules, as well as the aggressive use of section 301 in the 1974 trade law and the super-301 section in the 1988 trade law, which allow U.S. trade officials to take punitive action against countries found to be engaging in "unfair" trading practices. He decries the Japanese-U.S. semiconductor agreement of 1986 and the automobile agreement of 1994 as "hidden protectionism" and equivalent to "voluntary import expansion" concessions by Japan. Moreover, he

---

[24] The evidence is reviewed in Pryor and Schaffer (2000). Most cross-section studies show very little wage impact.

views the NAFTA agreement as a Pyrrhic victory, since later trade liberalization measures faced fierce battles. These include the 1997 defeat of fast-track legislation to accelerate tariff reduction negotiations between the U.S. and other nations, the declining support for expanding NAFTA to include other nations in Latin America, and the bitter fight in Congress in 2000 over a bill to normalize trade relations with China, which eventually passed.

Gilpin's argument seems overdrawn. Some U.S. trading partners have been violating certain generally accepted norms of international trade (or trade norms recognized by the U.S.), and, at a certain point, redress became necessary. The U.S. certainly has not had an obligation to be the world's importer of last resort, especially in view of the rising prosperity of many of its trading partners and the decline of the Cold War, which reduced the necessity to make unilateral trade concessions to keep the anti-Soviet bloc together. Nevertheless, Gilpin's argument about rising protectionist sentiments among U.S. policy makers has merit and the U.S. backlash against further trade liberalization in the late 1990s during a period of prosperity does not augur well for the cause of free trade in the immediate future.

John Gray, however, counters that "America will not retreat into isolationism and protectionism. Too many corporate interests [FLP: of both exporters and importers] would be harmed by such a retreat." If, however, the U.S. enters a severe recession, members of Congress, who are ultimately dependent on voter support, may not be able to resist protectionist pressures.[25]

For many decades the U.S. foreign economic policy has generally supported the international institutions fostering freer trade and the reduction of barriers to international trade. Any important weakening of American support for freer trade and unilateral retreat into protectionism might well lead to the ultimate collapse of the current international trade system, despite alleged U.S. corporate interests in maintaining it.

In the circus surrounding the WTO meeting in Seattle in 1999, the IMF meeting in Washington in 2000, or the gathering of Western Hemisphere leaders in Quebec City in 2001, a series of other reactions against globalization were aired. These included the claim that globalization impedes the economic growth of developing nations, widens the inequality of world income, promotes greater environmental destruction, and tends to destabilize the world economy. In the waning years of the 20th century environmentalists were also seriously alarmed

---

[25]   In January 1988 the Gallup poll asked U.S. adults how it would affect their likelihood of voting for a particular candidate, who favored an increase in taxes on foreign imports to protect American jobs in certain industries. 70 percent replied that they would be more likely to vote for such a person. I review in External Appendix X-5.2 the major arguments against globalization that seem to be most convincing to the public.

about the impact of certain international organizations on domestic policies. Much publicity was given to the overturning by the GATT/WTO of the U.S.´s import ban on shrimp and tuna harvested with nets that killed, respectively, dolphins and turtles, as well as of a provision in the Clean Air Act regarding the imports of gasoline with certain types of impurities (because the provision was more strictly enforced against importers than domestic producers). In more general terms, many fear that globalization would lead to a general race-to-the-bottom among nations, lowering their environmental (not to mention labor and health) standards in order to become more competitive. Although I do not believe that these arguments have much merit (see External Appendix X-5.3), they resonate among a considerable portion of the U.S. population.[26]

2. Political

The "impossible trinity" of trade policies discussed in the previous chapter has a more general analogue for the analyses of goals of globalization:[27] It is impossible to pursue at the same time greater world economic integration, proper governmental management of its domestic economic affairs to solve current problems, and national sovereignty. The last of the three refers particularly to the ability of domestic political groups to influence governmental economic policies.

In an era of relatively free capital flows between nations, the first and the third goals can be simultaneously met, but the government is weakened in solving key macroeconomic and microeconomic problems, as I argue above. The second and third goals can be simultaneously met, but at the expense of the first, since certain national economic problems may require policy solutions that act against expanded flows of goods, labor, or capital. The first and second goals can be simultaneously met by close coordination of governmental economic policies with those of other nations, but this cannot easily occur through domestic political mobilization; it often occurs at the expense of the economic interests of domestic groups. Such a process seems to reflect the integration process among the members of the European Union.

The problem of maintaining national sovereignty in the global village is particularly acute, and it is a commonplace among politicians of the various indus-

---

[26] It might also be noted that high international standards can be set through various international organizations or, as previously noted, through treaties. Many of the arguments about globalization having an adverse impact on high national standards are the same as those used to argue that globalization has an adverse impact on the welfare state, an issue discussed below.

[27] Several economists analyze this conflict of goals, among them Lawrence Summers (1999) and Dani Rodrik (2000).

trial powers to declare that world markets should not dominate domestic politics. In the U.S., for instance, former Presidential candidate Patrick Buchanan drew upon an obscure book to define the problem in this way:[28]

> The question ... that is presented to every American is whether the United States will take the opportunity which is offered to shape her own life in her own way and in accord with her own ideals, or whether this opportunity will be thrust aside for an elusive and delusive old-world concept of sordid international shopkeeping.

In less strident language other American populists decry the nation's dependence on foreign imports, export markets, and capital flows, which limits the sphere of U.S. governmental policies and allegedly brings unemployment, trade deficits, loss of government revenue, income inequality, environmental degradation, and other ills. Other concerns about high immigration, the dangers of unfettered liberalism, and the special importance of particular groups threatened by a fall in tariffs add spice to the anti-globalization stew. Some combination of these views resonates more strongly among voters than my dryer arguments about the decreasing effectiveness of monetary and fiscal policy.[29] Although the case against globalization may lack a certain internal coherence, Harold James documents how such views proved politically effective in the past and could, in particular circumstances, become more powerful in the U.S. in the future.

---

[28]   Buchanan is citing from *America Self-Contained* by Samuel Crowther (1933). It does not seem accidental that such a book was published in the depths of the depression.

[29]   In the discussion below I leave aside the political problems of eroding sovereignty. The principle of sovereignty, established in the Treaty of Westphalia in 1648, underlies the modern state system and incorporates the idea that a nation's actions toward its own citizens are not the concern of other governments. The rapid obsolescence of this principle can be readily seen. Examples include the establishment of an International Criminal Court; the international actions taken in 1999 such as the war in Kosovo; and the ruling by a London high court that Augusto Pinochet could be extradited to Spain for crimes against Chileans. A formal and frank recognition of this decline of the notion of sovereignty can be found in a statement by the UN Secretary General, Kofi Annan, on the day that UN forces landed in East Timor to stop the slaughter there: "Nothing in the [UN] charter precludes a recognition that there are rights beyond borders." (*New York Times,* September 21, 1999).

   Technology is also changing the meaning of national sovereignty. For instance, who has criminal jurisdiction over the 1999 case of a Portuguese computer hacker living in Australia who page-jacked web-sites of companies in the U.S. to his pornographic site and then mousetrapped the unwary surfers so they couldn't get out of his site without going to other pornographic web-sites, probably set up in a number of other countries, which paid him a fee for delivering them potential customers? (*New York Times,* September 23, 1999).

The notion that globalization will emasculate all domestic institutions does not warrant serious discussion. Nevertheless, a number of Europeans, as surveyed by Martin Rhodes, have expressed a more plausible concern, namely that globalization is seriously damaging their welfare states, which will soon be drowned in a wave of global neoliberalism. Two brief rebuttals are in order. First, as shown by Alfred Pfaller and his colleagues, there is little empirical evidence that "lagging international competitiveness" is related to high welfare state spending.[30] Second, as argued by Ronald Ehrenberg, devaluating the exchange rate can compensate for the higher prices of exports brought about by increased taxes used to finance welfare state expenditures. Such a policy action would bring total wages (money wages plus welfare benefits) into line again with national productivity levels, although the money wage portion (defined in terms of a foreign currency) of total wages would be lower if the welfare benefits increase. In other words, if taxes to support a welfare state make a nation's exports too high-priced to be competitive on world markets, a devaluation of the exchange rate would change the relative values of money wages and welfare benefits so that, on the whole, total real wages including both types of income would remain roughly the same. If the exchange rate cannot be changed, then other mechanisms can bring about an eventual equilibration of the nation's economy again, but the transition would take longer and be more painful (for instance, more unemployment). The key point is that the price effect of higher taxes to support a welfare state can be offset by lower monetary wages measured in terms of a foreign currency. Similar considerations can be raised to show that globalization need not lead to lower environmental, labor, or health standards. Nevertheless, these are difficult arguments for politicians wishing to be reelected to sell to their constituents.

Another source of backlash arises from increasing citizen distrust of various international and intergovernmental organizations. In part, this arises from their lack of transparency, for instance, the secrecy by which decisions are made by the WTO or World Bank. In part, it arises from lack of confidence in the quality of these decisions, for instance, the evidence that IMF conditionality agreements to countries such as Indonesia in the late 1990s seemed to have made economic conditions worse, not better. And, in part, it arises from the cumbersomeness of the decision-making and resentment that in many international organizations, such as the UN General Assembly or the WTO, even the smallest nation in the world has the same number of votes as the U.S.

---

[30] Sweden, which allegedly illustrates the trade-off between economic growth and a welfare state, had a very respectable growth rate in the years immediately preceding the new millennium as the structure problems limiting its growth in the 1980s and early 1990s were gradually resolved.

The polemic about the loss of sovereignty is almost always tied to crude arguments against free trade.[31] Another popular claim about U.S. multinational enterprises is that they have forgotten how to "salute the flag" and have become companies without a country, menacing the economic security of their U.S. workers in an unprincipled search for higher profits. Although these complaints are coupled with concerns about sovereignty, it seems most useful to focus attention on the more general sovereignty argument against globalization because, in a limited sense, it is correct. A brief cost/benefit approach is in order.

Any contact with others brings a loss of personal autonomy, since we must take into account the impact of our actions on others. Similarly any law—let us say, a ban on murder—limits our personal sovereignty. Nevertheless, contact with others has benefits, and a ban against murder provides increased personal security. It is obvious, for instance, that the rules of the World Trade Organization limit U.S. sovereignty by restricting the government's ability to impose certain trade restrictions; at the same time, however, the rules limit the ability of U.S. trading partners to restrict imports from the U.S. A basic idea underlying the WTO's existence is that once trade retaliation begins, it is difficult to stop and, as a result, all nations lose. Clearly globalization limits sovereignty, but we should not overlook the benefits of such a loss.

Unfortunately, this kind of argument about tradeoffs between costs and benefits is difficult to make in a politically acceptable manner, given the absolute sense in which many people understand the concept of sovereignty. Such an absolute approach toward sovereignty appears to be increasing and is manifested in various ways. At the turn of the millennium examples include the hesitation of the U.S. to sign the Comprehensive Test Ban Treaty or the treaty to found an International Criminal Court, its reluctance to pay in full its contributions to the United Nations and other international organizations, and its propensity toward unilateralism. Under Presdient George W. Bush this included his policy steps to scrap the Anti-Ballistic Missile Test Ban Treaty with Russia, or his abrupt withdrawing from particular multilateral agreements, for instance, the Kyoto Agreement on global warming or the joint OECD efforts to crack down on international tax havens.

It should also be clear that the present trend of globalization cannot continue if armed conflict—either civil wars or international aggression—occurring in third world nations should spread to industrialized nations. Detailed discussion of this topic must be postponed until Chapter 7.

---

[31] Few popular authors worried about the loss of sovereignty or opposed to tariff reduction and free trade fail to cite Abraham Lincoln's famous remark: "I don't know much about the tariff. But I know this much. When we buy manufactured goods abroad, we get the goods and the foreigner gets the money. When we buy the manufactured goods at home, we get both the goods and the money."

3. Social

Many years ago Karl Polanyi forcefully reminded us that markets can only exist within a web of social relations; and if the market moves outside certain social parameters, the results can be tragic. We do not need to accept his interpretations of politics in the period between the two world wars to realize that social considerations set some important constraints on globalization. Some economists, such as Dani Rodrik or Robert Feenstra, argue that globalization heightens economic insecurity of workers because domestic firms who employ them face greater competition on domestic and world markets. If national social welfare systems are not strengthened in a manner to counteract such fears, social unrest inimical to further globalization may well become stronger. The two economicsts also make another important point—social assistance and various types of temporary "escape clauses" in trade agreements are much more focused alternatives to specific social problems caused by imports than trade barriers.

Globalization can also bring about results that are viewed as seriously unfair. For instance, serious political problems can arise if U.S. workers perceive that some of the jobs exported by U.S. corporations to low-wage nations are being held by 12 year old children working 14 hour days. Even though domestic job displacement caused by imports of such goods may be temporary, serious social and moral issues are involved. Fairness issues also arise if U.S. trading partners prefer to carry out business in ways to discriminate against U.S. exports and when attempts fail to "level the playing field" by imposing outside standards.[32]

Although the 1990s were generally a decade of prosperity in the U.S., a backlash for lowering the immigration quotas and enforcing them more strictly seemed to be developing and the reason was cultural: the traditional ethos of the U.S. was feared to be diluted because of the presence of a large group who did not participate in normal civic life, in part because of an inability to speak English.[33] Another

---

[32] An oft-cited example is the Kodak-Fuji dispute, whereby Fuji's tactics (aided by business blunders by Kodak) shut Kodak out of Japanese domestic markets.

[33] For instance, in 1990 about 6.4 percent of the population between 18 and 64 were reported in the U.S. census as unable to speak English "very well." More alarmingly, about a quarter of these had been born in the U.S. and, presumably, had attended U.S. schools. About half of those unable to speak English "very well" lived in what the Census Bureau classifies as linguistically isolated households, those household in which no person over 13 speaks English "very well." Of course, these data raise many problems of interpretation because the level of speaking English is self-reported and, therefore, subjective. Nevertheless, such data suggest that a growing number of Americans are living in ethnic enclaves and not mastering the dominant language and culture. These data come from comparisons of Table 15 in Department of Commerce, Census

facet of this perceived problem was the presence of "transmigrants," those immigrants who, because of low-cost communication and transportation costs, maintain their primary emotional orientation and political allegiance toward their home country, even while living decades in the United States.[34]

Particular aspects of the globalization process reduce what has been called "social capital," an aspect of social solidarity discussed in detail in Chapter 7. For instance, the growth of the multinational enterprises often leads to less attention being focused on stakeholders such as the workers employed in individual countries or on the communities in which their plants are located. Some, such as Maurice Schiff or Peter Brimlow, argue that increased international migration can also lead to a decline in social capital in the receiving country because of the attendant social disruptions and conflicts, as well as adverse impacts on the national ethos. In certain countries other cultural issues are associated with globalization, where the process is equated to U.S. economic, political, or cultural hegemony, but these need not detain us.[35]

E. Concluding Remarks

Some powerful forces are pushing globalization forward: an ever-widening network of international institutions and organizations, falling transportation and communications costs that encourage more international trade, increasing economic incentives for international migration, and falling barriers to international capital movements.

But these processes do not yield unalloyed advantages. To some extent globalization has impaired the ability of the U.S. government's to carry out effective macroeconomic policies for stabilizing the economy and particular micro-

---

Bureau (1993-b) and Table 3 in Department of Commerce, Census Bureau (1993-a).

[34]   The term "transmigrant" comes from Schiller (1999). The degree to which current immigrants to the U.S. are more or less assimilated than immigrants of a previous generation is a matter of considerable debate and uncertainty, as seen in various contributions to Hirschman et al. (1999). A graphic example of transmigrant phenomenon was the reaction of Cuban-Americans to the U.S. government's attempt in 2000 to send six year old Elián Gonzales back to his father in Cuba—displaying the American flag upside down and violent demonstrations against U.S. court actions. Such reactions led many Americans to believe that these immigrants were still playing politics by (pre-Castro) Cuban rules.

[35]   In many countries the increasing visibility of McDonalds or Coca Cola or the dominance of American movies and magazines are held to be dangerous to the nation's culture. The same might be said of the appearance in the U.S. of such cultural imports as Pokémon, Nintendo, or Teletubbies.

economic policies for achieving other goals as well. Further, globalization is associated with ever greater flows of foreign exchange and securities across national borders, which, in turn, makes the economy more fragile and susceptible to financial crises.

Sources of backlash against globalization are manifold. Some are economic and concern the impact of free trade and immigration on wages and employment of low-skilled workers. Some are political and concern the loss of national sovereignty and the declining ability of government to solve current economic problems. Some are social and cultural and raise issues of fairness and societal cohesiveness. Such a backlash becomes politically much more important in periods of recession or war, adverse events that could begin the unraveling of the present world system, as each nation adopts domestic policies to solve its own economic problems at the expense of its neighbors.

It seems a distinct possibility that if the United States—economically the most powerful nation in the world—were to reduce its commitment to free trade and other aspects of globalization, other industrial nations would also follow suit. The various international organizations dealing with trade problems, such as the World Trade Organization, have limited capacities for enforcement of regulations and their powers can rapidly become overwhelmed.

Global economic integration greatly declined in the 1930s and 1940s as a result of economic depression, the Smoot-Hawley tariff of 1930, and World War II. After the war, it took more than a quarter century to achieve the degree of globalization prevailing in 1900. Despite the denser network of international institutions and organizations, despite the increased trade and capital flows, and despite the much lower costs of communication and transportation, I can find no convincing reason why such a retreat from globalization could not occur again if the political forces of protectionism gathered strength, especially if triggered either by war or depression. The key factor is whether future governments of the U.S., whose economic support for globalization is vital for its continuance, will have the wisdom and the political will to implement policies that will maintain current political and economic conditions. At this point we reach the limits of responsible prediction.

F. Important Internal Factors Influencing the Future of U.S. Capitalism: A Wrap-up

The last four chapters focus on causal factors internal to the U.S. economy that will have an important influence on the future of U.S. capitalism. I make the following major arguments:

• Other things equal, a shift in the age distribution will lead to a fall in the net saving ratio and, as a consequence, the rate of economic growth will most likely decline as well (Chapter 2).

• Other things equal, the increasing financial fragility of the U.S. economy is likely to lead to more severe financial crises which, in turn, are likely to have a serious and adverse effect on production (Chapter 3).

• Other things equal, income and wealth are likely to become increasingly unequal in the years ahead (Chapter 4).

• Other things equal, world economic integration is likely to continue, although possibly at a slower rate than in the latter quarter of the 20th century. The backlash against globalization may eventually become sufficiently strong to reverse the process (Chapter 5).

The combination of slower growth and recession is likely to exacerbate social tensions, and income redistribution by the government will become more contentious. The widening income differentials will also make the necessary consensus for effective governmental policy more difficult to achieve. Finally, increasing globalization will weaken the ability of the federal government to use monetary and fiscal policy to relieve unemployment in times of recession.

In the next three chapters I turn from internal to external influences on the economic system and focus particular attention on ecological, social, and political forces.

EXTERNAL
INFLUENCES
ON THE
ECONOMIC
SYSTEM

CHAPTER 6

Natural Resources and the Environment

In the 1970s the world will undergo famines—hundreds of millions of people are going to starve to death in spite of the crash programs embarked upon now.

—*Biologist Paul Ehrlich, 1968*

History warns us that a number of economies have collapsed, either because they exhausted their raw materials or polluted their environment. For example, Edward Hyams has documented how deforestation and soil erosion eventually led to the destruction and abandonment of the formerly rich Sind area in the Indus Valley around 1500 B.C. and destruction of soil fertility on the Euphrates in the region south of Hit led to the collapse of Assyrian civilization. Although examples of collapse caused by pollution are more difficult to find because the historical record is so sparse, some have speculated that abandonment of many large cities in the Mesoamerican forests was tied, at least in part, to the difficulty in maintaining a source of pure water that would not be contaminated by the urban sewage.

Such cases raise some uncomfortable questions about contemporary U.S. capitalism. To render these issues tractable, we must first investigate briefly the degree to which overpopulation, mineral exhaustion, and environmental difficulties such as pollution and global warming have overtaken us. I then present two scenarios of the future because of the uncertainties involved in determining exactly what will happen to the environment in the future. The first draws on the assumptions of many environmentalists, analyzing what will happen to the economy if raw material prices rise steeply and ecological conditions considerably deteriorate. The second draws on the assumptions of many economists, examining what will happen to the economy if environmental conditions change only slowly in the coming decades. Finally, I attempt to assess the relative probability of each scenario and their impacts. Although the effects of the two sce-

---

[1] Cited by Laura Lee, *Bad Predictions: 2000 Years of the Best Minds Making the Worst Forecasts* (2000). In the text of this introduction I mention work by Hyams (1952).

narios on the U.S. economy are quite dissimilar, their effects on the economic system are not greatly different, except in certain extreme cases which I outline.

A. Current Trends[2]

World population has been increasing at an unprecedented rate, rising from slightly less than a billion in 1800 to 2.5 billion in 1950 and about 6.1 billion in 2000 (an average annual increase of 1.8 percent since 1950). Recent estimates by the United Nations foresee an annual population growth of roughly 1.0 percent a year from 1995 to 2050, when the earth will house about 9.8 billion people. For the United States the population has increased from 5.3 million in 1800 to 151.7 million in 1950 to about 275 million in 2000 (an average annual increase of 1.2 percent since 1950).[3] The estimates of Ronald Lee and Shripad-Tuljalpukar discussed in Chapter 2 reveal a considerable range of uncertainty of annual growth rates of the U.S. population in the coming decades. More specifically, within a 95 percent limit of confidence, their estimated annual average rates of increase between 2000 and 2050 vary between 0.03 and 1.20 percent.

We cannot, however, automatically conclude that this population increase has been or will be accompanied by an increasing relative scarcity of natural resources and foodstuffs. Productivity growth could offset diminishing returns in agriculture and mineral extraction; moreover, our actual reserves of resources can be much larger than we now estimate.

In 1980 Paul Ehrlich, a biologist and one of the nation's leading Malthusians (doomsters) and Julian Simon, an economist and one of the profession's leading optimists (boomsters) made a famous $1000 bet. After talking past each other for years about the seriousness of a future shortage of raw materials and foodstuffs, they chose a unique way to resolve their differences. The specific wager centered on what the inflation-adjusted price of five metals might be 10 years in the future. This bet attracted considerable attention; and, according to John Tierney, "at stake was much more [FLP than the money]—a view of the planet's ultimate limits, a vision of humanity's destiny. It was a bet between the Cassandra and the Dr. Pangloss of our era."[4] In 1990 each of the five metals had a

---

[2]   In the text in this section I draw upon studies by: Balling (1992), Crosson (1983), Darnay (1992), Goklany (2000), Karl et al. (1993), Lee and Tuljalpukar (1994), Michaels and Balling (1997), National Research Council (1986), Simon (1996), Singer (1997, Tierney (1990), United Nations (1995), U.S. CEQ (1998), and U. S. Department of Agriculture, annual (1999).

[3]   These data and the population forecasts come from U.S. Department of Commerce, Census Bureau (annual 1997), pp. 8-9.

[4]   Or, in the dryer language of economics, will the carrying capacity of the earth, as manifested by

lower inflation-adjusted price than ten years before, and Ehrlich paid off without public comment. He noted later, however, that this bet had no lesson for the future of the planet: "Simon is like the guy who jumps off the Empire State Building and says how great things are going so far as he passes the 10th floor."

For an informed discussion about the impact of possible future shortages of foodstuffs and raw material or of environmental degradation, it is necessary to look at some century-long trends. The data on which I base many of my generalizations are presented in much greater detail in Appendix 6.1 .

1. Changes in the Real Price of Food

Thomas Malthus forcefully argued that increasing population leads to rising food prices, a critical indicator of relative scarcity in an economic system based on the market allocation of goods and services. Assuming that capital and land are fixed and technology does not improve, he hypothesized that an increasing population will eventually lead to diminishing returns in agricultural production. That is, over time each additional farmer will have a smaller piece of land to work and the production of each additional farmer will be ever smaller. In a market economy this also means that both the price of food compared with the cost of living and the rent received by land owners will rise.

The conditions underlying the Malthusian prediction are highly restrictive. The diminishing returns on the land can be offset either by a rapid growth of productive inputs, such as capital equipment and fertilizer, or by technological advances, which allow a farmer to produce more food with the same inputs. Unfortunately, we cannot easily tell the strength of these two factors offsetting diminishing returns. Nevertheless, we can easily detect any rising scarcity of foodstuffs as reflected by rising food prices.

Over the 20th century, the general price of food has declined when compared to the consumer price index (as shown in Charts A6.1a and A6.1b in Appendix 6.1). In similar comparisons, the prices of wheat and beef have declined or remained roughly the same over the same period. When compared to the average hourly wage of manufacturing production workers (to see how long they must work in order to pay for a given quantity of food), all three series show an unambiguous decline of food prices over the 20th century. In brief, the Malthusian prediction does not hold for the United States in the 20th century. More

ever more acute shortages, set limits on production and/or population? Or will this carrying capacity actually increase as a result of technological change?

technically, during this century, technology and additional productive inputs more than offset the diminishing returns to the finite resources of U.S. land, as reflected crudely by the decline in the share of farmers in the labor force from 40 percent in 1900 to 2.5 percent a century later.

Such past trends in agriculture do not, of course, secure the future, a matter discussed later in this chapter. Such trends also do not eliminate particular policy dilemmas, for instance, reaching the limit of the potential for improving agricultural productivity using customary methods. Such a situation would require us either to turn toward biotechnology to improve production or to face much lower increases in agricultural yields. Moreover, even if the general food supply remains ample, diminishing returns can set in for particular foodstuffs, so that the pattern of food consumption might greatly change. In such a case, however, a properly constructed price index of foodstuffs would not show a significant rise.

2. Changes in the Real Price of Natural Resources

The Ehrlich-Simon bet focused on the price of raw materials and these can be analyzed in the same manner as the prices of foodstuffs. Over the 20th century the price indices of fuels and related products and also of metals and metal products, as well individual prices of crude petroleum and copper, were relatively unchanging when compared to an index of prices paid for consumer goods and services (see Charts A6.2a and A6.2b in Appendix 6.1). When compared to the average hourly wage of production workers in manufacturing, all four series showed dramatically declining trends over the same period. Again, diminishing returns in the extraction of raw materials appear to be offset by other factors and the Malthusian nightmare did not overtake the U.S.

The raw material series show more extreme variations than the food prices, especially in the second half of the 20th century. Among other things, this means that determining long-term scarcities of raw materials by looking at price behavior in a single decade is not a very meaningful exercise. It would have made more economic sense if Ehrlich and Simon had bet about raw material prices over the course of a century. Unfortunately, neither of the contestants would have been living to collect the money and gloat over the results.

Of course, unlike most raw materials, food is a renewable resource, at least as long as measures are taken to maintain the fertility of the land. By way of contrast, conservation measures are more feasible for raw materials since food is a biological necessity and conservation of food has its limits. The two oil shocks in the 1970s, for example, led first to a dramatic short-term rise in the price of oil-based fuels and then to the introduction of more fuel saving engines and the greater use of insulation in buildings. Home owners gradually switched from oil to natural gas as their home heating fuel. Ceramics also began to replace metal parts in certain internal combustion engines, not only saving metal but also allowing more efficient fuel consumption.

3. Environmental Quality

Environmental degradation has occurred under all economic systems and the pollution problems in the centrally planned systems in Eastern Europe have received considerable scholarly attention.[5] In all economic systems, the extent of such environmental degradation is determined largely by the direct and indirect incentives the system offers to producers and consumers to limit the environmental pollution they create. Since measures to reduce such pollution are costly, many people will bypass them unless sanctioned in some manner—political, moral, religious, or economic—by an outside authority. Can liberal capitalism actually control pollution? The relevant data are complex and it is useful to discuss air, water, and land degradation separately before turning to global warming.

a. *Air quality:* It is well known that the concentration in the air of some important pollutants has been increasing, such as greenhouse gases. Air pollution, as revealed by chemical analysis of rainfall over the entire country, shows that certain pollutants, for instance, ammonium ions, also increased in the air between 1988 and 1995.

Nevertheless, measures of other types of air pollution reveal a much more favorable picture. In the last quarter of the 20th century, the levels of three major air pollutants—sulfur dioxide, carbon monoxide, and particulate matter—declined.[6] Concentrations of nitrogen dioxide, ozone, and lead also decreased over the same period, according to data of the U.S. Council on Environmental Quality. Further, an aggregate air pollution index, which measures the number of days when different pollutants were over a specified level at various monitoring sites, also fell. The acidity of rain and its sulfate ion concentration decreased; and, according to Arsen Darnay, the amount of atmospheric radioactivity arising from strontium 90 and cesium 137 fell markedly from the mid 1960s to 1990.

---

[5]   Much has been written about pollution in centrally planned economies. Two books focusing on the Soviet Union are: Murray Feshbach and Albert Friendly, Jr. (1992) and Goldman (1972).

[6]   This is shown in Chart A6.3a in Appendix 6.1. Although estimates of various types of emissions into the air can be found for many years, few nationwide data series on the actual concentration of various pollutants are available until the middle 1970s.

Complicating the analysis of the underlying causes, pollution depends not just on emission rates, which vary considerably depending on the type of impurity, but also upon the degree to which the atmosphere can dissipate them. Emission rates, in turn, depend not just on technology but also on shifts in the production pattern and, of course, environmental regulations.

Moreover, several caveats deserve note. The science of air pollution contains many uncertainties. For instance, in 2001 a study showed a dramatic decline in the atmosphere since 1990 of hydroxyl radicals, which purge the air of many types of contaminants and methane (a powerful heat-trapping greenhouse gas). If this finding is validated and the decline continues, projections of air pollution and atmospheric warming must be revised upward. Furthermore, measures taken to reduce one kind of pollution may intensify another. For instance, the gasoline additive MTBE reduced air pollution from automobiles but found its way into drinking water, thus posing a threat to health since it may be carcinogenic.

b. Water quality and quantity: Three common series measuring water pollution—DDT residues in fish, the concentration of fecal coliform, and dissolved phosphorus—all show a statistically significant decline in the last quarter of the 20th century (Appendix 6.1). Other readily available series from the U. S. Council on Environmental Quality show that dissolved cadmium or lead in the nation's water also show downward trends. Farming practices in the last quarter of the 20th century exhibited a decreasing use of pesticides. As a result, the percentage of water runoff containing such chemicals, not to mention food samples with pesticide residues, has decreased since the late 1970s. Farm use of commercial fertilizer has also leveled off, which means that this source of water pollution has not increased.

Although water pollution (like air pollution) appears to be decreasing, we cannot be entirely sure. Most importantly, such readily available data cover only a few of the hundreds of pollutants that lead to degradation. Moreover, even in the same river, trends in different pollutants can be quite different.[7]

The quantity of water is as important as its quality, and many have sounded the alarm that we are using water resources in the U.S. faster than such resources are being replenished. Wet-land reserves in many parts of the nation are also declining, according to the U.S. Council on Environmental Quality.

---

[7]   A nice example of such mixed results is found in Meadows, et al. (1992), p. 91, who show that in the Rhine River in Germany, proper sewage treatment has led to disolved oxygen increasing to nearly normal levels since the 1970s and to cadmium levels falling about a quarter since their 1970 peak. Nevertheless, in the same river chloride from mining wastes and nitrogen from fertilizer runoff have been rising steadily since the 1940s, which, among other things, reduce the available usages of such water.

Unfortunately, it is difficult to gain an overall view of changes in water levels of the nation's aquifers and the impact of such changes on agriculture. In the early 1990s about one sixth of total crop land was irrigated, much from underground sources.[8] Unfortunately, aggregate estimates for all of the relevant underground water aquifers for such irrigation in the U.S. do not seem to have been made. Nevertheless, water levels in the Great Plains aquifer, which is the nation's largest, have been declining at a considerable rate, and, as a result, irrigation farming had to be abandoned in certain areas, such as parts of Texas.[9] Average rates of decline are deceptive, however, because in some restricted areas fed by this aquifer (for instance, Nebraska), the underground water level rose.

The situation is not totally grim from the demand side. Although total national water usage increased considerably between 1940 and 1980, both total and per capita usage, as well as water use in irrigation, has been declining since then. Part of this decline can be attributed to more efficient use of water for agricultural and industrial purposes.

If we try to measure the scarcity of water in terms of changes in its relative price, we run into the unfortunate fact that the price of water does not accurately reflect the interaction of supply and demand because it is highly influenced by governmental policy. For the consumer, the inflation adjusted cost of water appears to have risen slightly over 1 percent a year between 1953 and 1998.[10] This reflects rising costs due to (a) more rigorous standards of treatment imposed by the government; and (b) transport of water to urban areas that have outgrown nearby sources of water. As far as I can determine, the U.S. government does not collect the data to allow calculation of a nationwide price index for irrigation water.

[8]   This was calculated from data on total irrigated land (*Statistical Abstract of the United States 1997*, Table 1087) and data on crop land harvested (Ibid., Table 1080). To the extent that some irrigated land is not used for crops, the datum in the text overestimates the dependency on irrigation. Data on water usage presented later in the text come from Ibid., Table 375.

[9]   According to U.S. Geological Service reports (U.S. Geological Service 1994) and (www.ne.cr.usgs.gov/highplains/hp96_web_report/hp96_factsheet.htm}, the water level in the Great Plains aquifer, which supplies water for about 20 percent of all irrigated land in the U.S. and 30 percent of the groundwater used for irrigation, fell on the average of 9.9 feet between 1940, when extensive irrigation began, and 1980 (and fell an additional 2.8 feet between 1980 and 1996). In some places the water level fell as much as 100 feet from 1940 through 1980.

[10]   This datum is drawn from components of the consumer price index, divided by the overall consumer price index. Unfortunately, the cost of water to the consumer is combined with sewage service as well, but since sewage processing requires considerable water, it seems likely that both water and sewage costs moved in tandem. The source of data is the Bureau of Labor Statistics web-site, http://stats.bls.gov/sahome.html.

c. Land quality: Data from the U.S. Department of Agriculture show that, contrary to myth, the total acreage of crop land has declined only slightly since 1940. Between 1952 and 1992, timberlands in the United States declined slightly less than 4 percent, but the annual net growth of timber (measured in billion cubic feet) was considerably higher than removals. Thus, timber resources, according to one measure, actually increased in the second half of the 20th century.

Measuring changes in the quality of its soil, however, raises difficulties. Although the National Resources Inventory (and its successor, the Conservation Needs Inventory) collects data on soil quality, the data do not seem comparable from year to year. We can, however, get a clearer picture about changes in soil erosion: In 1982 the National Research Council presented evidence that about 75 percent of crop land was eroding at a slower rate than new top soil was being created. Moreover, between 1982 and 1992, both water and air erosion of U.S. crop land declined.[11] Certain data cited by Julian Simon also suggest that the share of crop land experiencing a net loss of soil due to erosion has declined dramatically since the 1950s; but problems of data comparability arise, so that we cannot be sure. These imperfect data also suggest that in 25 percent of crop land, the annual average loss of soil due to various types of erosion is much higher than the average replenishment rate, so that these areas are suffering a net soil loss.

What is the impact of this erosion on production? Pierre Crosson estimates that in 50 years average land yields will be 8 percent less, if 1977 levels of both erosion and technology continue. But many factors, including farming practices, are changing. For instance, from the late 1980s to the mid 1990s, a noticeable percentage of farmers has moved away from conventional tillage methods toward those urged by conservationists. By 1998 only 38 percent of planted acres were cultivated by conventional tillage methods leaving a large residue of subsoil.[12] Such a responsible adoption of better farming methods shows that American farmers have a long time horizon.

In other respects, the outlook for land quality reveals offsetting trends. Relatively little effort has been given to reducing the annual flow of solid wastes.

---

11 U.S. Council on Environmental Quality (1998), Table 7.6 . This table, taken from the National Resources Inventory conducted by the U.S. Department of Agriculture, does not include data from the 1971 inventory (cited by Crosson (1983)) indicating that total erosion was lower in 1971 (6.8 tons per acre) than in 1982 (7.4 tons per acre). The datum on net top soil creation comes from the National Research Council, Committee on Conservation Needs and Opportunities (1986), p. 9.

12 U.S. Council on Environmental Quality (1998), Table 7.5. Other data in this paragraph come from the same source, Tables 7.1 and 8.10 .

Measured in terms of pounds per capita, the trend since 1960 has been quite flat. A major influence on the annual flow of solid wastes is the distribution of production among industries; and the movement into a service economy has presumably been a factor in keeping the trend from rising.

In the biosphere, the loss of plant and animal diversity continues. The causes are quite varied: in the forests, for instance, the rapid replanting-harvesting of forests has an important adverse impact on biodiversity. Up to now, however, it has proven difficult to determine the rate of decline in diversity or to measure its economic impact.[13]

In brief, while degradation of the air, water, and land in the U.S. has been considerable, the trends in recent years have been favorable, at least for the most readily available indicators. With per capita income rising, the nation appears willing to invest in measures to reduce such degradation. To a noticeable extent, such efforts seem to be paying off, at least in the short-run.

4. Global Warming as a Special Type of Environmental Degradation

The average daily temperatures in the U.S. reveal a statistically significant upward trend with an increase in the 20th century between 0.5 and 0.6 degrees Celsius (about 1.0 degree Fahrenheit). The pattern of increase (shown in Chart A6.4 in Appendix 6.1) is highly irregular, with a rise up to 1940, a fall between 1940 and 1980, and a rise from 1980 to the end of the century. Data for the average global temperature are less reliable than for the United States, but three recent estimates show roughly the same worldwide rise over the century as in the U.S.[14] The meaning and interpretation of these observations, however, are subject to fierce debate. Moreover, weather satellite data on air temperatures in

---

[13] Determining the economic value of biodiversity raises enormous problems. According to Wilson (1988), we do not know the true number of plant and animal species on Earth, even to the nearest order of magnitude; current guesses range between 5 and 30 million. We also do not know the annual rate of species extinction, and I have seen estimates ranging from 17,500 to 40,000 per year, the larger part of which are attributed to human activities. Finally, the economic value of particular species ranges enormously. For instance, a recently discovered Mexican wild grass, a perennial related to corn, has been estimated to have an annual value of $6.8 billion through its potential to create a perennial hybrid of corn (Norton, 1988), while other plant species may have a zero or even a negative value. As a result, estimations of the seriousness of the problem of extinction vary widely. Some biologists ignore the problem as unimportant while others are greatly alarmed. For instance, Paul Ehrlich (1988) ominously declares: "Extrapolation of current trends in the reduction of diversity implies a denouement for civilization within the next 100 years comparable to a nuclear winter."

[14] The three global studies referred to are by: P. D. Jones, *et al.*; H. Wilson and J. Hansen; and K.

the troposphere (up to 7 km.) generally shows no warming, despite predictions to the contrary from most climate models; and the stratosphere (above 7 km.) appears to be cooling.[15] This unexpected widening gap in temperature between the troposphere and the earth's surface increases difficulties in interpretating the temperature data.

The leading candidate for the increase in surface temperatures on the earth is the emission of greenhouse gases, of which carbon dioxide (CO_2) has received the most attention. World CO_2 emissions rose from 1900 to the early 1990s at about 1.6 percent a year, and the actual carbon dioxide in the air rose in the same period at an average annual rate of about 0.2 percent.[16] Moreover, this CO_2 concentration in the air has been accelerating: between 1953 and 1975 it rose at an annual rate of 0.33 percent; and from 1975 through 1992, 0.43 percent. Other greenhouse gases, such as atmospheric methane, nitrous oxides, and chlorofluorocarbons (CFCs), have also been accumulating in the atmosphere.

Although the linkage between greenhouse gases and temperature is a well-established in physics, some climatologists, such as Robert Balling or S. Fred Singer have challenged the major role of these gases in the present trend toward global warming. Some note that the earth's temperature rose faster in the period from 1900 to 1940 than it did from 1940 to the end of the century, when emission of greenhouse gases was climbing much more rapidly (and absorption of carbon dioxide by tropical rain forests at the same time was declining more rapidly). Obviously, the relationship between changes in atmospheric CO_2 and the surface temperature of the earth is far from tight. Others point out that both temperature and greenhouse gases have fluctuated quite strongly over the past several hundred thousand years and that we are currently not close to the historic highs.

Ya. Vinnikov, *et al.* All three studies are presented in Boden (1994). Problems arise in correcting the temperature series for an upward bias independent of the CO_2 content that originates from increasing urbanization.

[15] Studies by R. W. Spencer and J. R. Christy (1994) and by J. K. Angel (1994) present data on temperatures in the troposphere and stratosphere. The former study uses satellite data, covers only 1979–1993, and shows no statistically significant trend. The latter study uses radiosonde records for the period from 1958 to 1992 and reveals an apparent cooling in the stratosphere below a pressure of 300 millibars. From a different data base Singer (1998) shows a high correlation between balloon and satellite based temperatures, with the latter also showing a cooling between 1978 and 1996. I am grateful to Ross McKitrick for helping me through the thicket of climatological data.

[16] Data on carbon dioxide emissions come from Keeling (1994) and C. Marland (1994). The two data series are spliced. Data on actual carbon dioxide in the air come from the Siple Station in Antarctica and Mauna Loa in Hawaii and are cited by Neftel (1994) and Keeling and Whorf (1994).

Underlying such changes in global temperatures in the past are changes in solar activity, changes in the length of the solar magnetic cycles, astronomical cycles, regular changes in the eccentricity of earth's orbit, movement in the tilt and precession of the axis of rotation (which shift our orientation toward the sun), variation in the tide-raising forces of the moon, and changing water vapor and cloud density in the atmosphere. Such natural causes, not greenhouse gases, probably underlay previous temperature changes, such as the "little ice-age" (roughly 1300 to 1850).[17] If any of these natural phenomena has played an important role in the 20th century, then little can be done to modify the current trend toward global warming.

Whatever are the exact causes of global warming, we know that the surface temperature of the earth can change suddenly. Climatological history records episodes when surface temperatures abruptly and massively rose to a new plateau.[18] The non-linear mechanisms underlying climatic change are, as yet, poorly understood and many key parameters are unknown.

The weather impacts of global warming that are important to agriculture are also far from clear. Certain models of the climatic changes suggest that global warming will be associated with increased volatility of the weather, which means not only greater variation in rain and temperature but also more severe storms, hurricanes, and other destructive weather phenomena. Nevertheless, the available evidence for the 20th century reveals no such trends.[19] The data of Indur Goklany, who has also estimated the long-term economic impact of floods and hurricanes, reveal no upward long-term trends in such damage, measured as a percent of national wealth.

Whatever the causes, the surface temperature of the earth has been rising and, lacking counterevidence, it seems likely that such a trend will continue. Nevertheless, the impact of such a change is open to interpretation. For instance,

---

[17] Estimated temperatures for this period can be found in Lamb (1982). A fascinating reconstruction of this climatic anomaly from both historical and climatological sources is by Ladurie (1971).

[18] According to Stevens (1999) the earth's temperature abruptly shifted upward, apparently caused by a release of methane locked in the ocean floor that might have been touched off by the previous, more gradual warming. More recently, the transition out of the last ice age took place within a human lifetime or less. Calvin (2000) argues that the melting polar cap, combined with the increasing high-latitude rainfall, could put enough fresh water into the seas to suppress an important salt-flushing mechanism. This, in turn, would lead to a rearrangement of ocean currents and a sudden and long-lasting change (fall) in temperature. Bright (2000) discusses other environmental "surprises."

[19] Of course, the impact of global warming on tropical or subtropical nations, especially those with considerable land area close to sea level, will be severe. This is not, however, of great relevance to the U.S. economic system, except insofar as immigration pressures increase.

Patrick Michaels and Robert Balling, Jr. note that global warming has not led to much change in summer temperatures, but, instead, has lengthened the growing season. Moreover, Thomas Karl and his colleagues provide evidence that in the United States the decrease in the daily temperature range (between day and night) was roughly equal to the increase in the mean temperature. This means that global warming merely reduces diurnal temperatures differences. Both studies suggest that economic consequences of global warming will not be as serious as commonly believed.

5. A Final Note

Although the macro-indicators discussed above paint a relatively optimistic picture for the U.S. (with the exception of global warming), I do not cover many critical issues: overfishing, desertification; eutrophication of lakes or invasion by non-native and predatory flora and fauna; new pests and diseases, the growing immunity of micro-organisms to standard preventive treatments; and adverse changes in geomorphology, to name a few. I also do not discuss the incentives for governments to reduce pollution, especially in cases where the costs of pollution by domestic producers can be placed on other countries, for instance, the emission of greenhouse gases.

B. A Pessimistic Scenario for the Future: The Environmental Nightmare [20]

The 21st century can be quite different from the 20th. Technology may not advance fast enough to offset the diminishing returns in raw material extraction and agriculture. For instance, Charles Mann points out that in the last decades of the 20th century the growth of agricultural R and D funds began to decline throughout the world and that funds for the 16 large international agricultural research laboratories stagnated or declined in the 1990s.[21] If cutbacks to agricultural research continue, agricultural productivity may not grow at the pace required to meet the world's expanding population. Further, particular political or ideological factors could prevent the government or other economic organizations from employing effective policy tools to reduce pollution and environ-

---

[20] In the text of this section I refer to studies by: Brown, Gardner and Halweil, (1998), Ehrlich (1988), Mann (1999), and Strong (2001).

[21] Some of this decline in governmental R and D funds has, however, been made up by large biotech firms, which have for some time been able to patent genetically modified seeds.

mental degradation.[22] As noted above, the relation between greenhouse gases and global temperatures may not be as linear as many believe so that sudden temperature and climatic changes could occur.

In this section I assume the worst: that raw materials and foodstuffs will become increasingly costly and the environment will become more degraded. I follow a macro-approach and do not deal with such crucial micro-economic issues as possible changes in our way of life because of such changes.

1. The Impact of Moderate Scarcities of Natural Resources and Foodstuffs

   a. The effect of price changes on consumption: What would happen if the prices of raw materials and foodstuffs doubled or tripled in relation to other prices? As commonly believed, low-income consumers spend a larger share of their income on goods and a smaller share on services, than do those with higher incomes. Since the production of most services embodies fewer natural resources and agricultural products than does the production of goods, any inflation-adjusted rise in the price of natural resources and agricultural products would fall more heavily on those with lower incomes. Table 6.1 shows the shares of total consumption of raw materials of household units with different incomes, taking account of both their direct consumption of these natural resources (for example, purchase of gasoline) and the natural resources embodied in the goods they buy (for instance, not just the iron in a purchased automobile, but also the iron in the machines used to make the automobiles).

Such calculations show clearly that raw materials and agricultural products generally account for a higher share of total consumption expenditures of low-income than high-income households.

The only exceptions are metals and nonmetallic ores, neither of which constitutes an important share of total consumption of the various income classes. Of course, the exact impact depends on the degrees to which prices change: Other things equal, if raw material and agricultural product prices instantaneously tripled, households with an income between $5000 and $9999 would

---

[22] Those who believe in the imminent second coming of Christ would most likely hold that long-term efforts for environmental protection and clean up are futile. As a result, it should not be surprising that committed evangelical Protestants view expenditures on the environment much less favorably than other groups in the population, according to an index calculated from public opinion data by Kohut *et al.* (2000, p. 48). A telling example is provided by James Watt, a former Secretary of the Interior and a member of a Pentecostal denomination, who argued against large expenditures on the environment and noted that we do not know "how many future generations we can count on before the Lord returns" (cited by Kohut, p. 49).

Table 6.1. *Direct and Indirect Consumption of Natural Resources and Agricultural Products by Households with Different Incomes*

Percentage of Total Consumption Expenditures, 1992

Annual income of expenditure units	Average	$5000 -9999	$10000 -14999	$15000 -19999	$20000 -29999	$30000 -39999	$40000 -49999	$50000 -69999	$70000 and over
Specific natural resources and agricultural products product groups									
Livestock and products	1.9%	2.5%	2.3%	2.4%	2.1%	1.9%	1.8%	1.7%	1.4%
Other agricultural products	1.9	2.5	2.3	2.3	2.0	1.9	1.8	1.7	1.4
Forestry, fishery products	0.3	0.3	0.3	0.3	0.3	0.2	0.2	0.2	0.2
Metallic ores mining	0.1	0.1	0.1	0.1	0.1	0.1	0.1	0.1	0.1
Coal mining	0.5	0.7	0.6	0.6	0.5	0.5	0.5	0.5	0.4
Crude petroleum, natural gas	3.2	4.1	3.7	3.7	3.5	3.3	3.1	3.0	2.5
Non-metallic mineral mining	0.1	0.1	0.1	0.1	0.1	0.1	0.1	0.1	0.1
Total	7.9	10.2	9.4	9.5	8.6	8.0	7.7	7.4	6.2

Notes: These estimates are made from the detailed worksheets of the *1992 Consumer Expenditure Survey* (U.S. Department of Labor, Bureau of Labor Statistics, 1995), employing a commodity by commodity input-output matrix (Department of Commerce, Bureau of Economic Analysis, 1998-a) to determine the indirect consumption. I present in External Appendix X-6.1 similar calculations for major end-use components of the GDP.

experience a fall in real income of 30.6%, while such a unit with an income of $70,000 or more would experience only an 18.6% income fall.

In this other-things-equal scenario, the impact of a shortage of raw material and agricultural products would be greater on the poor than the rich. This, in turn, would reinforce the trends discussed in Chapter 4 toward greater inequality. The exact impact on welfare depends, however, on the degree to which consumers can substitute other products for raw material-intensive goods. Of course, in the case of basic foods consumed by low-income families, such possibilities are more limited.

The key assumption underlying this prediction can be challenged on two grounds. The money income of the poor could rise faster than that of the rich and, as a result, offset—at least in part—the fall in real income calculated from the table. But, as discussed in Chapter 4, money income differentials are more likely to widen, not narrow. Or this differential decline in real income of the poor occasioned by a rise in raw material prices could be offset by increased governmental transfers to them. As I argue in Chapters 7 and 12, such increased transfers also do not seem likely. Thus, if raw material and foodstuff prices doubled or tripled, a considerable segment of the low-income population would probably fall below the poverty line.

   b. The effect of price changes on other GDP aggregates: For analyzing the changes in the composition of the GDP that would accompany a steep price increase of raw materials and agricultural products, we can draw upon a set of estimates similar to those in Table 6.1, which are presented in External Appendix X-6.1. Except for the impact of price increases of fuels and natural gas, the impact of such price changes would be small for gross private investment and government expenditures. For exports and imports, however, the situation is different.

As noted in Chapter 5, the U.S. has increasingly become a net importer of raw materials. As a result, a rise in raw material prices would have an adverse impact on the balance of payments. Since oil imports are so large, aggregate imports would be particularly hard hit. Some idea of the impact can be gained if we assume that exports and imports are balanced in the initial year and then the price of all natural resources and agricultural products doubles. Other things equal, the trade deficit would amount to 6.8 percent of the new monetary value of exports.[23]

It is highly possible that higher prices of natural resources and agricultural materials would also reduce the growth rate, at least in the short run. Consider-

---

[23]   Of course, as a net exporter of agricultural products the U.S. would gain if only these prices rise and the trade surplus would be 0.5 percent of the new value of exports. By way of contrast, if only the price of crude petroleum and natural gas double, the overall trade deficit would be 7.7 percent of the new value of exports because the U.S. is a large net importer of oil.

able funds would have to be invested in equipment for new resource-saving methods of production, rather than for raising labor productivity, so the growth rate of GDP would decline. The oil shocks in the 1970s had, to a certain extent, a similar impact on the economy.

c. *Effects on rental income in the raw material and agricultural sectors:* Any rise in prices of natural resources or foodstuffs would raise the rental income of those who own mines, oil wells, and agricultural lands. While particular individuals might gain considerably, the overall impact on the distribution of income should be small. In the mid 1990s, for instance, profits in the mining sector generally amounted to 1 percent or less of total corporate profits, so that even a tripling of these profits would not have a major economic impact.

A rise in agricultural prices would, of course, shift income toward the owners of land. What magnitudes are at stake? At present, roughly 40 to 50 percent of all U.S. farm land is rented, and rents paid to absentee landowners amount to roughly 0.4 percent of national income.[24] Thus, total rent on land (including the implicit rent that farm owners pay to themselves if they work their own land) amounts to roughly 1 percent of the national income. A tripling of these rents would have only a small influence on the economy as a whole.

d. *Adjustment costs:* Any dramatic change in raw material and agricultural prices would force a change in the composition of production and consumption, and this can be costly. Furthermore, the faster or greater the price changes, the higher such adjustment costs would be. Surely the tenfold rise in price of crude petroleum between 1970 and 1981 was a major factor in the slowdown of U.S. economic growth during the period, not to mention the price inflation and rise in unemployment during the 1970s.[25] By way of contrast, if the price changes are slow or if they can be properly anticipated, the situation is different: Policy changes can be carried out with greater deliberation and understanding to meet the challenge and, moreover, the necessary re-equipping of many production processes to respond to this relative price change can be carried out more systematically. But don't bet on it. Given the lax attitudes of the

[24] Data on farm tenure in the early 1990s come from *Statistical Abstract 1995,* p. 67; the estimate in the text is rough since about 56 percent of all farm land is farmed by a part-owner, and the percentages held by the farmer and the absentee owner are not specified. The rents paid by farmers to absentee landlords come from U.S. Department of Commerce, Bureau of Economic Analysis (1998-b), Table 8.8.

[25] In comparison to the cost of crude oil, the price of motor fuel increased only fourfold during the same period because the costs of refining this fuel into gasoline did not greatly change. Further, the real price of crude oil decreased from this high in 1981, so that in 1995, for instance, it was only 31 percent above the 1970 level (*Statistical Abstract 1997,* Table 933).

U.S. governmental and private sectors toward fuel efficiency in the 1990s, such farsightedness regarding oil price increases seems unlikely.

In brief, if raw material and agricultural prices rise sharply, the economy will be hurt—real consumption differentials between rich and poor increase, economic growth will decline, resource owners become wealthier at the expense of the rest of the population, the economy must adjust to greater deficits in the balance of payments, and high short-run costs will be incurred. Most of these difficulties can, in part, be ameliorated by the policy tools currently available to the U.S. government. As a result, none of these problems seem of sufficient importance to lead to major changes in the economic system.

2. Shortages and Prices—The Scarier Version

It is important at this point to consider more extreme scenarios, which point to troubling transformations of the economic, political, and social systems. Assume, for a moment, that absolute limits exist for certain natural resources, such as irrigation water, or that diminishing returns will become extremely severe in the extraction of raw materials for energy production. Regarding water, for instance, Lester Brown and his colleagues argue that present worldwide water usage will, in coming decades, result in falling water tables throughout most of the world, depletion of underground aquifers, and a global decline of 75 percent in the amount of fresh water per person.[26] If they are right, we will experience a global decline in irrigated acreage per person; a fall in world agricultural production; and a dramatic rise in food prices worldwide (because foreign trade would keep food prices in all nations roughly equal unless governments imposed export bans). A decline of food production, particularly among the developing nations, might also result from a falling oceanic fish catch due to over-fishing or a decline in the available arable land, due either to soil erosion or to an increasingly adverse impact of various types of pollution including pesticides.

Dramatically rising prices of foodstuffs and raw materials would push a greater share of the world's population below the poverty line and malnutrition

---

[26] In its survey of global trends until 2015, the U.S. National Intelligence Council (www.cia.gov/publications/globaltrends2015) argues that by 2015 half of the world's population will live in countries—mostly in Africa, the Middle East, South Asia, and northern China—that have less than 1,700 cubic meters of water per capita per year and must be considered "water-stressed. In India, for instance, the NIC predicts that per capita water availability will fall by 50 to 75 percent. The major culprits are, of course, population growth and overutilization of water for irrigation. In India the water table is currently falling between 3 and 10 feet a year, and in the northern grain-growing areas of China, the water level is falling at five feet per year.

and starvation would spread. Governments could respond in various ways and if, as suggested above, ameliorating measures such as a direct income redistribution program are not politically feasible in the U.S., three radical alterations in the U.S. economic and political system can be envisioned.

• *Political centralization*: Political unrest occasioned by the much higher price of foodstuffs and raw materials could be contained by tightened governmental controls on the population, to dampen social disorders. This would, of course, involve a strengthening of the external and internal security forces and move the U.S. political system more toward despotism or oligarchy, a possibility discussed at greater length in Chapter 8.

• *Centralization of the economic system*: The nation might redistribute income by indirect means, but this would contravene the free-market ideology prevailing up to that point. Such measures might include price controls; a ration system for particularly crucial goods; and nationalization of certain key raw material sources, so as to prevent excessive profits (and political power) accruing to a small group of owners. These kinds of measures might lead to central governmental direction of the economy to allocate important raw materials and agricultural goods, especially if domestic prices were maintained at lower levels than world market prices.

• *Anarchy and disintegration*. If the government is either unwilling or unable to take ameliorating measures discussed above, then another outcome is imaginable. Ownership of highly scarce natural resources would lead both to extreme wealth and a change in those holding political power. These resource owners might engage private security companies to protect these natural resources, which might eventually lead to the creation of permanent private armies. Property rights formerly protected by the law of the state would crumble in the face of such unprecedented concentration of private power. Normal markets would cease to function and private force would play a more important role in the allocation of resources.

Extreme shortages of foodstuffs and raw materials would probably trigger some combination of these systemic changes discussed above. The government would take certain compensatory measures, while strengthening the security system. Nevertheless, the market system would to some extent disintegrate, and private economic and political power would play a role hitherto unknown in our history.

The international implications of dramatically higher prices for foodstuffs and raw materials appear even more depressing. The problem might be ameliorated by massive transfers from wealthy to poor countries. Such a solution, nevertheless, seems even more improbable than a corresponding transfer between the rich and the poor within the U.S., especially since even the richer segment of the U.S. population would experience a fall in real income. More likely, U.S.

defense expenditures would increase, not just to contain political unrest in the developing world from reaching U.S. borders, but also to prevent the massive and illegal immigration from resource-poor nations with falling real incomes to the U.S. that would be stimulated by the growing income gaps between nations. Furthermore, small nations possessing scarce resources would become more inviting targets for military actions by larger powers lacking such resources, witness the 1991 Persian Gulf War.

4. Gloomy News about Environmental Degradation and Global Warming

From the discussion above, it should be clear that predicting the economic impact of environmental degradation and global warming is a risky endeavor. Non-linear effects are particularly difficult to predict. For instance, the gradual loss of a wetland area may have little economic impact until a particular threshhold is reached when both the wildlife and the plants might rapidly begin to disappear. Lacking any testable forecasting model, dramatic predictions can be made. For instance, relying on such non-linear effects the physicist John Holdren (quoted approvingly by Paul Ehrlich) estimates that a carbon dioxide-induced climatic change before 2020 could lead to deaths by famine of as many as a billion people.

Looking at the problem in a more humdrum fashion, the impacts of environmental degradation and global warming in the U.S. can be quite similar to those of resource scarcities, namely, higher costs of production and lower real incomes. For instance, environmental degradation means higher costs of purifying polluted water for industrial use and greater use of fertilizers to restore exhausted land. In other cases, pollution directly impedes production. For instance, the discharge of organic wastes into lakes and rivers reduces its dissolved oxygen level, which is needed to support aquatic life, so that fishing costs rise. The improper disposal of radioactive wastes can reduce available land for agriculture (as in the area around Chernobyl), so that less fertile land must be farmed. The heat and dryness due to global warming can promote desertification and also reduce the available farm land. In these cases, economic growth would fall as production costs rise. From the same considerations as those discussed in the case of resource scarcities, it seems almost inevitable that these costs of environmental degradation and global warming would fall disproportionately on those with low incomes.

Some economic effects of environmental degradation, however, are quite different from those of resource scarcity. For instance, heavier pollution can lead to higher levels of sickness and reduced life expectancy. Possible sources of disease include mercury or lead contamination of air and water, toxic agricultural pesticides in our food, and higher ultraviolet radiation due to the expanding ozone hole. Consumer welfare in the form of amenities, such as enjoyment of unspoiled nature, pure air, and the presence of wildlife, would decline. Certain types of pollution arising from radioactive wastes, pesticides, and industrial chemicals can also affect the human genetic and reproductive systems. In these cases, the impact on the distribution of real income would be less apparent since they would fall more evenly on the entire population.

Some analysts of the impact of global warming, such as Maurice Strong, foresee other dramatic impacts if surface temperatures continue to rise. The polar icecaps would melt so that much of Florida would be under water; seven year droughts in the Great Plains could occur that would devastate domestic agricultural production if underground waters were unequal to the task of providing irrigation; and the insect and rodent population might explode. Such scenarios are based on assumptions, however, which I believe have a low probability.

C. An Optimistic Scenario: The Conventional Wisdom Among Economists[27]

According to the Millennium Survey, most professional economists express little concern about environmental problems affecting the U.S. economy or the U.S. economic system. An important exception: most respondents believed that global warming is indeed happening and that it will have an important impact on the economic system, but only after half a century. On what is this optimism based?

1. Foodstuffs

It is possible that technological progress offsetting diminishing returns in agriculture, such as the green revolution, will slow down; but up to the end of the 20th century few signs of such a deceleration were visible. For instance, between 1948 and 1994, growth of total factor productivity in agriculture (that is, taking labor, land, capital, and all other inputs into account so that technological change can be isolated) reveals a slight, but statistically significant, acceleration.[28]

---

[27]   In the text of this section I mention studies by: Cline (1992), Darmstadter and Toman (1993), Mendelsohn and Newman (1999), Nordhaus (2000), and Council on Environmental Quality (1998). The results of the Millennium Study are presented in Pryor (2000-b).

[28]   Data for farm productivity for 1948 through 1994 come from U.S. Council of Economic Advisors (annual, 1997, p. 410). I calculated quadratic trends for both farm output per unit of total

Of course, several factors could slow down this growth of agricultural production and/or productivity, especially the decline in usable farm land. This
could occur either by land degradation (for instance, by overuse of pesticides
and artificial fertilizers that poison the land), or by farming practices that cause
either loss of fertility or the actual loss of the soil itself through wind or water
erosion.[29] As noted above, such degradation did not occur during the last third
of the 20th century. A more likely danger is the increasing scarcity of irrigation
water as underground aquifers are exhausted, but this problem is difficult to
assess because of lack of relevant data for the nation as a whole. Nevertheless,
from 1980 to the end of the century the daily use of water for all purposes
declined, according to data of the Council on Environmental Quality. Similar
trends can also be found for particular usages of water, such as for irrigation.
The quantity of water drawn from underground sources also dropped. Although
water scarcity is a crucial factor limiting agricultural production in many
nations, particularly in the third world, it does not seem to be an insurmountable
problem in the United States. The rise in the international price of foodstuffs
occasioned by a water scarcity in other nations, particularly the developing
nations, does not worry many in the U.S., in large measure because those
nations needing imported food will be unable to finance such purchases. In
other words, because food consumption in those nations with water shortages
may rise more slowly than the actual need for food, starvation may occur, but if
nations with sufficient water do not respond with food aid, the world market
price for food will not greatly rise. This is, of course, a terrible situation for
humanity as a whole.

2. Natural Resources

Three offsets to the diminishing returns to labor in the extraction of raw
materials are often cited. First, greater labor productivity can be gained by
greater mechanization. Second, advances in technology have reduced the cost
both of extracting and of refining raw materials. New methods, for instance,
allow us to capture much more gas and oil in an oil field than previously. Third,
new discoveries of mineral deposits shift production away from high-cost and
exhausted deposits to new and more rewarding sites. As the Mesabi range was

---

factor inputs and farm outputs per unit of farm labor; the generalizations in the text are based
on the calculated coefficient for the squared term in the regression calculation. In the same period,
however, labor productivity growth reveals a small, but statistically significant, deceleration .

[29]   Urban sprawl is insignificant as a cause of decline in arable land, as shown by Simon (1996),
pp. 138-9.

gradually exhausted and the cost of extracting iron ore rose, American producers simply turned to other sources, such as scrap metal or imports from foreign countries.

Although the data reveal no increasing scarcity in raw materials (Tables A6.2a and A6.2b in Appendix 6.1), the great unknown is whether this is due mainly to technical change or to new discoveries. A standard way of isolating the rate of technical change (namely the calculation of production functions) raises many serious econometric problems. For what they are worth, my own experiments along these lines showed little evidence of diminishing returns either for the U.S. mining industry as a whole or for the extraction of individual minerals (with the exception of petroleum) for the second half of the 20th century. But I put no great faith in these results and believe that the question is still open.

Buying on the world market is an obvious alternative to searching for new domestic sources of supply of raw materials in the U.S. As noted in the previous chapter, the U.S. has become a net raw material importer. In 1929, U.S. net exports (exports minus imports) of raw materials (including petroleum, coal products, and all primary products) amounted to about 6.5 percent of the GDP originating in the mining sector.[30] By 1950, however, the U.S. was a net importer of raw materials and, by 1991, such net imports amounted to about 30 percent of the GDP originating in the domestic mining sector.

Such a development focuses our vision on a broader question: Will the world gradually exhaust its supply of raw materials so that their price will rise? Conventionally, many analysts start with estimates of world reserves of various minerals, but these estimates are extremely misleading and change dramatically over time.[31] The falling inflation-adjusted price of raw materials suggests that technological innovation in extraction and use of such resources combined in some unknown proportion with the discovery of new deposits has more than offset diminishing returns. If new discoveries of raw materials slow down in the 21st century, which seems likely, then only new techniques for extracting, refining, and using of raw materials can offset the rising costs of obtaining these gifts from the earth. Few economists see much credible empirical evidence, however,

---

[30] Data on the share of raw material exports to GDP originating in the raw material sector come from Pryor (1996), p. 189.

[31] Kahn, Brown, and Martel (1976, p. 92) document how, over a period of two decades (1950 to 1970), the estimated world reserves of many raw materials soared. For instance, in this period, estimated iron deposits rose 1221 percent; estimated oil reserves, 507 percent; and so forth. Clearly estimating known reserves is an inexact science and projecting mineral scarcities in the future by looking at current estimated reserves has yielded many dubious predictions, seldom validated by subsequent events.

that most raw material prices, after falling throughout the second half of the 20th century, will begin to rise sharply in the decades to come. Oil may prove an exception to this generalization.

3. Environmental Degradation and Global Warming

Part of the conventional optimism of economists about pollution—at least pollution whose impact is primarily local—rests on the assumption that it can be controlled by regulations compatible with a market.[32] These include particular types of effluent taxes (taxes on the amount of pollutants emitted) or markets for pollution rights (pollution is only permitted by those with a license, but such licenses—which are limited—can be privately bought and sold). Such market-compatible regulations have become increasingly widespread and the improving indicators of environmental health in the U.S. provide evidence for the efficacy of such regulation.

On the international level, profitable economic activities in one country may increase pollution in other nations and the problem becomes more difficult to solve. The optimism expressed in the Millennium Survey seems to spring from the faith that self-interested nations can come together and create common rules to constrain such activities. Indeed, since 1950 more than 130 multilateral treaties and convention have been signed that set up international environmental standards.[33] To overcome difficulties of voluntary enforcement of these agreements, several options are open: forming special international courts to impose penalties, exercising unilateral sanctions or political pressure, or, if a common pool of resources is involved, establishing property rights. Still other solutions may evolve.[34]

Finding international methods to contain global warming appears more intractable. As noted above, many respectable climatologists are still unsure about the exact causes of the current global warming. Given the infant state of climate modeling, it is foolish for me to attempt to resolve these scientific questions or, because of non-linearities, to extrapolate historic trends into the future.

---

[32] As shown in the case of the Soviet Union, governmental planning and administration of the economy is not necessarily effective for controlling the emission of greenhouse gases. Direct, in contrast to market-compatible, controls on pollution have proven ineffective or uneconomic in many countries.

[33] These are listed in OECD (1999-c), 304-13 and cover atmospheric pollution, inland water pollution, fisheries, nuclear damages, marine pollution, transportation, and so forth.

[34] For instance, using a game-theoretic model, Alpay (2000) points out that non-cooperative solutions are also possible if shifts in the terms-of-trade occur when pollution abatement measures are taken.

For the sake of argument, however, let us assume that a slow global warming will continue over the foreseeable future and that, to a certain extent, it is related to the accumulating CO_2 in the atmosphere from human activity. Let us also adopt the assumptions of William R. Cline that governments will do little to control the problem. In this business-as-usual scenario, he estimates the surface temperature of the earth should rise about 2.5 degrees Celsius by 2050; about 5.7 Celsius by 2100; and about 10 degrees Celsius by 2275. (These temperature changes amount respectively to 4.5, 10.2, and 18.0 degrees Fahrenheit).

To measure the economic costs of such global warming is an even more heroic exercise. In some cases a limited global warming fueled by rising CO_2 levels yields certain agricultural benefits (through enhanced capacity for photosynthesis); in other cases, presumed negative effects, such as rising sea levels, have been disputed.[35] Joel Darmstadter and Michael Toman point out additional difficulties of analysis, namely the numerous disputes about various feedback mechanisms within the climate and non-linear impacts on agriculture and other human activities.

William R. Cline examines over 15 different types of cost impacts of global warming in the U.S., for instance, on costs in various branches of production or on leisure activities and amenities, such as air conditioning. The four highest costs stem from higher food prices because of a decline in agricultural production, greater fuel usage, most expensive water (because of lower rainfall), and higher mortality and morbidity. From this analysis he estimates an overall annual cost of 61.6 billion dollars in 2050 and 335.7 billion dollars in 2275. If we make the conservative estimate that GDP will rise at an annual rate of 1 percent between 1990 and 2050 and 0.5 percent thereafter, these costs amount respectively to 0.6 and 1.0 percent of the GDP in the corresponding years, which makes the economic impact of global warming in the U.S. less frightening. Most serious studies, for instance, those cited by William Nordhaus, estimate that a temperature increase of 2.5 degrees Celsius would have a direct impact on the U.S. GDP from 1 to 2.5 percent, although one study by Robert Mendelsohn and Jaime Newman concludes that the net economic impacts will be slightly positive, not negative!

---

[35] Singer (1998, p. 18) argues that although the melting of glaciers and the thermal expansion of ocean water will lead naturally to a rise in the sea level, increased evaporation from the ocean will lead to greater precipitation and accumulation of ice in the polar regions that would, in turn, lower the sea level. Although the ocean level has been rising over the 20th century, he provides time-series evidence (p. 18-9) of an inverse relation between sea-level rise and average global temperature. From this evidence he claims that global warming will slow down, rather than accelerate, the ongoing rise in sea levels.

Of course, this kind of calculation is fraught with uncertainty. Nagging doubts remain whether these estimates have taken all additional costs into account. For instance, higher air temperatures led to higher water temperatures and the destruction of a large share of the coral reef in the Indian Ocean at the end of the 1990s and, on a broader scale, could lead to a significant decline of fishing yields which, in turn, could result not just in a rise in price of fish, but also of substitute foods providing alternate sources of proteins. Costs can also mount significantly if non-linearities and threshold effects are encountered.

A benefit/cost analysis of measures to reduce the emission of greenhouse gases to slow global warming faces formidable obstacles, because both the benefits and the abatement costs are difficult to estimate. Moreover, for making such an analysis, we must take a long time-period under consideration and our tradeoffs between the value of a dollar of present and future consumption (the social discount ratio) plays a crucial role in the results obtained.

These difficulties have, however, not deterred several notable attempts. Depending on various assumptions, William Cline's estimates of the ratio of the global benefits of pollution abatement to the global costs run from 0.24 to 8.24, so that the net benefits of abatement measures are unclear; for local areas the range of these ratios could be even wider. If Cline's estimates (higher than most) of total costs of global warming are anywhere close to the mark, the economic problems occasioned by global warming for the nation as a whole do not appear serious, even if he underestimates costs by an order of magnitude.

In brief, the most accepted estimates of the costs of global warming suggest that, at least for the next half century, they will not be sufficiently great to provide the necessary incentive for costly measures to reduce greenhouse gases. When and how global warming will become politically more salient in the U.S. is difficult to judge, because it depends in part on whether global warming accelerates and if improved economic estimates point to much higher costs.

D. Which Scenario is Most Probable and What are the Implications for the Economic System?[36]

The various scenarios rest on contrasting assumptions: (a) The level of technology can/cannot advance sufficiently fast to offset the diminishing returns in raw material and agricultural production. (b) Effective policy tools to reduce pollution and environmental degradation can/cannot be successfully implemented in the market economies of the U.S. and other nations. (c) The relation

---

[36]   In the text in this section I mention a book by Meadows, *et al.* (1972).

between greenhouse gases and global temperatures are/are not predictable and linear. On a more concrete level the scenarios considered in the discussion above differ about the predicted severity of future raw material and agricultural shortages and about the extent to which these shortages will have an impact on the economic system. These various arguments need to be confronted.

1. Raw Materials and Foodstuffs

For the United States the diminishing return scenario for foodstuffs does not appear credible. The country's good fortune in the past to have sufficient arable land for its population seems likely to continue in the future, both because of a slowly growing population and the availability of large amounts of land. Of course, many local problems, such as the declining water level of the Great Plains aquifer, must still be addressed. And despite sufficient arable land and water, other problems might emerge: a combination of crop disease and the loss of plant diversity could reduce productivity, as could adverse weather conditions arising from global warming.

Problems arising from the demand side are much more probable. The world as a whole may experience a shortage of foodstuffs because of agricultural crises in the developing nations arising from a high population growth combined with an increasing scarcity of water and a growing shortage of arable land due to farming practices. Two outcomes are possible: Such shortages in developing nations could lead to a higher volume of food exports from the U.S. (and other food exporting nations) and rising world prices for foodstuffs. Or else mass starvation in the Third World could lead to international political unrest, which would divert investment funds in the industrial nations to defense purposes and, ironically, possibly slow the growth of technological improvements in agriculture.

Although relative prices of foodstuffs may rise in the United States because of world conditions, at the cusp of the new millennium it does not seem likely that such price increases will be sufficiently steep to cause major changes in the economic system. Within the U.S. agricultural system, we should expect some important institutional and organizational changes, especially due to the growing dominance of large farms. These changes, however, should have little impact on U.S. capitalism as a whole.

For nonrenewable raw materials predictions are more uncertain. Recycling can considerably extend the available supply of certain raw materials such as aluminum. More generally, however, the rate of technology advance is the key, and this is difficult to predict. Part of the problem lies in our inability to disentangle statistically the separate contributions of technological change and of newly discovered supply sources in reducing raw material prices over the 20th century.

Forecasting models of raw material prices are in a primitive state, since they need to take into account a variety of resources and their possibilities of substitutions, technical change, and interactions of resource extraction with environmental degradation. The best known example to construct such a model is a book by Donella Meadows and her colleagues, *Limits to Growth*, which was the first of several books on the topic financed by the Club of Rome.[37] These attempted to consider together the various types of interactions between population, capital, labor, production, natural resources, food output, and pollution. Although these models are complex and take into account many different factors, they are basically Malthusian in spirit (as its authors readily admit). That is, they do not allow either for advancing technology to offset diminishing returns or for normal governmental policies and institutions to reduce environmental degradation.

In short, these models lead us back to the same crucial assumptions that separated the optimistic and pessimistic scenarios sketched above. Nevertheless, from such models we can draw one important conclusion—the economic collapse that they envision would not happen suddenly but would be the result of a long process of price increases in raw materials and foodstuffs.

Even though the economic growth of the planet is expected to continue, a dramatic increase in the prices of most raw materials seems unlikely for the first half of the 21st century, given the experience of the 20th century. Nevertheless, shortages and ensuing price increases could certainly affect particular natural resources. Nevertheless, as in the case of foodstuffs, it seems unlikely that price increases of natural resources would have a significant impact on U.S. capitalism. Certainly the U.S. economy was able to absorb a dramatic rise in the price

---

[37] A more technical description of this project is by Meadows, *et al.* (1974). In 1974 the Club of Rome published a kinder, gentler version of this model (Mesarovic and Pestel, 1974). Unfortunately, this latter book only made predictions out to 2025, which was before the economic collapse foreseen by Meadow et al. set in.

Meadows and her colleagues argued that the carrying capacity of the earth is declining, due to resource depletion and increased pollution. Their computer simulations showed that without mitigating measures, within the lifetime of those living in 1970 overall production, especially of food, would begin to decrease and economic collapse would be imminent. .

This kind of world-system model has been heatedly attacked. For instance, various authors in Cole, *et al.* (1973) strongly criticize the data, the arbitrary assumptions, and the sensitivity of the results to arbitrary choices of unknown parameters. Nevertheless, given its most basic assumptions, the logic of the Club of Rome is correct: If growth of population is exponential, if there are limits on the availability of raw materials and foodstuffs, and if technological advance is slow, then sooner or later the system bumps against these fixed constraints and collapse occurs.

of oil in the 1970s without sweeping changes in the institutions or organizations of the economy.[38]

The effects on the system of environmental degradation are also uncertain. The growing scientific knowledge of the environmental impact of particular chemicals and industrial byproducts will most likely lead to greater governmental regulation, especially since those adversely affected appear more and more willing and able to organize politically to press for reform. Increasing demand for unspoiled recreation space may likewise lead to added political support for conservation.

In many of these cases, especially those requiring international agreements, new organizations will have to be devised for enforcement purposes. For instance, over-fishing is difficult to police. To limit fishing in the world's oceans, unusual enforcement mechanisms, handled by special international and domestic agencies, combined with special licensing procedures for fishers, may be required. Protection of fragile coral reefs may require even more complicated enforcement measures.

Sometimes, problems of environmental degradation can be overcome by new technologies. Air pollution through emission of CFC gases in refrigerators was reduced by new methods of refrigeration; lead used as an anti-knocking agent in gasoline was lowered by changes in the design of automobile engines, combined with alternate, less harmful additives to gasoline. But in many cases such technological fixes are less likely.[39]

In brief, I expect relative scarcities of foodstuffs and raw materials, as manifested by price increases, to have some impact on the economy. Their impact, nevertheless, will probably not be great enough to lead to significant changes in the economic system.

2. Global Warming

The most uncertain part of the analysis is the discussion about the future impacts of global warming, since we face a thicket of scientific, technological,

---

[38]   As Mesarovic and Pestel (1974) point out, in any type of extreme shortages of raw materials and foodstuffs, the poorer countries in the world will suffer the most, just as I argue that it is the poor that would suffer the most in the domestic economy.

[39]   For instance, a major contributor to the rising level of greenhouse gases (particularly CO_2) in the atmosphere is energy production. In the United States, total energy consumption per capita has been rising at an average annual rate of about 0.6 percent a year over the last half century. Technology has certainly resulted in more efficient energy production and usage, and this, combined with a shift toward the production of services, has led to a significant decline in energy consumption per dollar of GDP. These factors have not, however, been sufficiently

and economic difficulties in making predictions. Although I present the results of several serious studies showing the economic costs of global warming as a negligible ratio of the GDP for the next 50 or 100 years, these results are subject to a considerable margin of error. Political uncertainties also obscure our view. As indicated above, I doubt that the leading industrial nations will have sufficient economic incentive or political will to forge in the near future an effective agreement to limit production of greenhouse gases in the near future, especially with the collapse of international talks in 2000 to implement certain parts of the 1997 Kyoto Agreement and the U.S. repudiation of the entire agreement in 2001.

3. Coda

After reviewing the available evidence and several scenarios, I can quickly state the most general conclusion. Future shortages in natural resources or agricultural products and adverse changes in the environment caused by pollution or global warming may have noticeable impacts on the U.S. economy. But they will probably not be great enough to lead to significant changes in the U.S. economic system. Nevertheless, these outcomes are subject to considerable uncertainty.

strong to reduce the total output of energy and the accompanying rising level of emission of greenhouse gases. The Cheney energy plan of 2001 suggests little to improve matters.

CHAPTER 7

General Social Factors

All Americans will have happy homes [in the 20th century].Vice and immorality will have largely, if not altogether ceased to exist. There will be not only great intellectual advancement, but also very great moral advancement.

— *Politician Sidney G. Brock, 1893* [1]

In a sweeping survey of world history, the French historian Fernand Braudel makes a pertinent observation:

"The worst error of all is to suppose that capitalism is simply 'an economic system,' whereas in fact it lives off the social order, standing almost on a footing with the state .... Capitalism also benefits from all the support that culture provides for the stability of the social edifice, for culture—though unequally distributed and shot through with contradictory currents—does in the end contribute the best of itself to propping up the existing order ... And lastly capitalism can count on the dominant classes, who, when they defend it, are defending themselves. Of the various social hierarchies—the hierarchies of wealth, of state power or of culture, that oppose yet support each other—which is the most important. The answer ... is that it may depend on the time, the place, and who is speaking."

The purpose of this chapter is to explore the concrete implications of this argument and to determine how particular cultural and social factors might influence the economic system and its direction of change. In the first three sections of this chapter I try to specify some economically relevant social trends in the U.S. and then to examine their impact. In the last two sections I use a similar approach for the analysis of cultural trends.

---

[1]   Cited by Laura Lee, *Bad Predictions: 2000 Years of the Best Minds Making the Worst Forecasts* (2000). The quotation in the text comes from Braudel (1982), p. 623.

A. Some Relevant Social Trends[2]

Three social trends are particularly relevant to the future of U.S. capitalism: the breakup of the traditional family, the decline in social capital, and the fading social trust. Each of these three trends receives brief attention below; a more extensive analysis with the supporting data for the various generalizations is in External Appendix X-7.1. Two other crucial social trends, widening economic inequality and the rise in lawlessness, receive attention in Chapters 4 and 8 respectively.

1. The Breakup of the Traditional Family

In the second half of the 20th century, the traditional family began to dissolve. From 1950 to the mid 1990s, the percentage of illegitimate to total births rose almost tenfold, to about 32 percent; and the percentage of children living within single parent-families more than tripled, to about 25 percent. Both series rose steadily throughout the period and showed no sign of slowing down. In the same period the annual number of divorces per 1000 married women roughly doubled, to 19.8; about one half of the annual number of marriages ended in divorce, which was more than double the rate in 1950. The divorce rate, however, hit a peak in the early 1980s and fell slightly in the following two decades. (All time-series are graphed in External Appendix X-7.1). The percentage of people declaring their marriages as "very happy" declined, and the percentage of unwed adult women entering marriage fell by a third. Partly, though not solely because of divorce and falling marriage rates, an increasing share of the adult population was living alone.

The increasing percentage of children in single-parent families is, of course, a function of both the higher divorce rate and the rising rate of illegitimacy. In contrast to many countries, cohabitation relationships in the U.S. do not seem to last long. Thus, many children of single mothers in the U.S. had no long-term day-to-day contact with an adult male, and, if an adult male did live with the family for a short period, his relation with the children was often shallow—or even dangerous.[3] Some serious economic implications of this trend receive attention below.

---

[2]   In the text of this section I mention studies by: Alesina and La Ferrara (2000), Costa and Kahn (2001), Fuchs and Klingemann (2000), Inglehart (1997), Klingemann (1999), Putnam (2000), Riesman (1950), Robinson and Godbey (1997), and de Tocqueville (1969 (1835)).

[3]   According to data cited by Miringoff and Miringoff (1999), p. 75, the children reported as maltreated rose from 1.01 percent in 1976 to 4.70 percent in 1996. Although part of this increase was

2. The Decline of Social Capital

The social orientation of people has two important dimensions.[4] The first concerns the guideposts of a personal values, duties, and actions; and whether these emerge primarily from within the person (either as inculcated during childhood or developed later in life) or from without, that is, from other persons. Sociologist David Riesman defines these poles as "inner-directed" and "other-directed." The inner-directed person is self-reliant, self-directed, and consistent; the other-directed person is more attuned to the opinions, ideas, and initiative of others.

A second dimension concerns the degree to which individuals act alone or in groups to achieve their goals for changing their social and political environment. Cooperative work, however, requires a set of shared norms and experiences, which some, such as Robert Putnam designate as "social capital."[5] It is an important aspect of our social solidarity.

In various nations and times, these traits have come together in different combinations. Other-directedness and high social capital characterize many traditional societies. Inner-directedness and high social capital occurred together in the American frontier in the early 19th century, where Alexis de Tocqueville marveled over these self-directed individuals, who joined with their fellow citizens in all sorts of projects for the improvement of their own lot and their joint benefit as a community. By way of contrast, the Japanese in the late 20th century are said to be other-directed and have little social capital, at least as measured by the data of Ronald Inglehart showing the percentage of adults participating in voluntary organizations for various purposes. At the turn of the millennium the U.S. seems to combine inner-direction with low social capital, a combination that is characterized by considerable entrepreneurial activity and, at the same time, wide social cleavages—a capitalism with a very hard edge. Hans-Dieter Klingemann and his coauthors use data from the World Value Study to show that among the 27 nations in their sample, the Americans rank among the highest of those placing importance on self responsibility (believing

---

undoubtedly due to more frequent reporting of abusive incidents, part was also due to the rising frequency of such family arrangements and tensions between the mother's temporary live-in boy friend and her children.

4 As commonly used, the term "individualism" often confounds these dimensions and, in addition, has a number of other meanings as well. Therefore, I do not use the term in this analysis.

5 The word "capital" in this phrase is somewhat misleading because economists usually assume that more capital is always good. By way of contrast, too much social capital can lead to an entirely static and conformist society. Furthermore, some types of social capital with a narrow radius, for instance, the informal norms shared by members of a criminal gang, cannot be considered beneficial to society at all.

that people should provide for themselves and not rely on the government) and among the lowest in their solidarity with the disadvantaged (believing that people are poor because of laziness and can escape their poverty by hard work).

Putnam's approach toward social capital, which I follow, is particularly valuable because he does not rely on anecdotes and subjective impressions, but, instead, buttresses his analysis with a series of quantitative indicators. He measures social capital in terms of membership and participation in a variety of group activities and shows that in the last third of the 20th century, social capital in the U.S. was declining. For instance, civic engagement, as evidenced in such activities as attending a public meeting on town or school affairs, serving on a committee or as an officer of some local organization, writing a member of Congress on some issue, joining one of various national chapter-based voluntary associations, or attending meetings of some social club, all declined in this period. In the religious sphere, Putnam presents data showing a decline in rates of church membership and attendance.[6] In the work place it is well known that union membership as a percent of the non-agricultural labor force has been steadily declining since the mid 1950s (see below), but Putnam also shows that average membership in eight national professional associations also began to decline a decade later. As discussed in the next chapter, direct political participation, measured in terms of voting or an active knowledge of public affairs, has waned. Economists have begun to explore these issues as well and, using other data sets, Dora Costa and Matthew Kahn also find a decline in most types of social capital. As explored in Chapters 5 and 9, the growing size of enterprises and the increasing importance of multi-plant enterprises (both foreign and domestically owned) mean that employers are becoming less bound to specific communities and their top executives are less likely to play important community roles.[7]

One implication of the declining social capital is that Americans are spending more time in relatively solitary pursuits such as watching television, casino gambling, or surfing the internet and less time in activities allowing a significant social interaction. For instance, from time-budget data John Robinson and Geoffrey Godbey conclude that time spent in religious and organizational work fell from 2.3 hours a week to 1.7 hours a week between 1965 and 1985, a

---

[6] Kohut et al. (2000) and Bennett (1999, p. 175) have similar data on religion. As noted below, declining church membership is not a good indicator of the role of particular religious groups in political activities, witness the role of fundamentalist groups in school board decisions not to teach about evolution or in their influence in the 1999 defeat of a state-wide lottery to help finance college scholarships in Alabama.

[7] Although some such as Everett Ladd (1999) have challenged these conclusions about declining social capital (see External Appendix X-7.1), I find this counter-evidence unconvincing.

decline of 26 percent. Further, the time spent socializing with others declined from 6.8 to 5.7 hours a week between 1965 and 1985, a fall of 16 percent. On the social level Putnam presents data showing a decline in the number of times people entertain at home, attend dinner parties, eat together with their entire family, attend a social evening with neighbors, or engage in other types of informal socializing.

A valuable but imperfect measure of social capital—or social solidarity—is charitable gifts and volunteer work. In the second half of the 20th century, charitable donations by individuals rose as a share of disposable income in the 1950s and then appeared to fall in the 1960s and beyond, as shown in the somewhat uncertain data presented in External Appendix X-7.2. In the same period volunteer work rose from the 1970s to the late 1980s and then began to fall, as measured either as a percentage of either the labor force (so as to compare the relative amounts of unpaid and paid work) or the population from 15 through 64 (also External Appendix X-7.2). Moreover, the emphasis in volunteer work seemed to change from community projects to personal, one-to-one services (for instance, helping the sick and the elderly).

The causes of this decline in social capital in the second half of the 20th century are controversial. Putnam, however, provides evidence that the change occurred primarily between, rather than within, generations: those of a given age have less social capital than those of the same age in previous years. Further, his data suggest that the primary culprit is television. Although time spent working for a living declined and leisure time increased, watching television took up almost all of the additional leisure; and the time used for social activities, clubs or civic engagement, as noted above, actually fell.[8] Using a different type of statistical analysis Costa and Kahn argue that for social capital outside the home (for instance, membership in groups or volunteerism), the major culprit is rising community heterogeneity, particularly income inequality. For the fall of social capital within the home (for instance, entertaining others or eating together as a family), they point toward rising rates of women's labor force participation.

---

[8] From a careful analysis of time-budget data over a period from 1965 through 1985, Robinson and Godbey (1997) show that free time (p, 126) increased 4.8 hours for American adults, while time spent watching TV (p. 145), 4.7 hours. TV watching by children was considerably greater; Bennett (1994) notes that data collected by the Carnegie Council on Adolescent Development show teenagers spending more than 20 hours a week watching TV, 5 hours on homework, and less than 2 hours on reading.

Robinson and Godbey's evidence on working time goes against the conventional belief, as expressed by Schor (1991), that leisure time has actually decreased. The methods used by Robinson and Godbey are defended in their book and also in Robinson (1994).

3. Two Related Trends: Declining Social Trust and Deepening Social Cleavages

Social trust, an important aspect of social solidarity, is conceptually different from social capital. It has been measured in the General Social Survey (GSS), which poses a question of the following type: "Generally speaking, would you say that most people can be trusted or that you can't be too careful in dealing with people." Those respondents choosing the first alternative declined from 55 percent in 1960 to 38 percent in 1998 (see External Appendix X-7.1). Despite the crudeness of this indicator, it reflects an important social phenomenon that, as I show below, appears to explain some changes in the economy.[9] The decline in social trust also parallels the decline of trust in the government that I document in the next chapter.

We would expect to find a high level of social distrust where social cleavages are great. Such social fissures are manifested, for instance, by ethnic heterogeneity and separation, linguistic diversity, or income inequalities. When looking at a sample of individuals, these conjectures receive impressive support in a study by Alberto Alesina and Eliana La Ferrara. On a more macro level in the U.S., a number of phenomena reflect these increasing social cleavages (and are documented in External Appendix X-7.1). These include:

- The growing importance of gated communities, in which, by the end of the 20th century, 3 percent of American families lived.
- The high degree of housing segregation by race and income.
- The increasing segregation by race in public schools and the rising percentage of children educated at home or in private schools.
- The development of various "narrow-band" media channels directed solely at very specific subgroups in society—in analyses of the internet this phenomenon is called cyber-balkanization.
- The rising percentage of adults living alone.
- The increasing share of workers in temporary or contingent jobs.
- Growing ideological extremism, as manifested by hate groups, armed "patriot" groups, and religious cults.

---

[9]   Various studies explore the determinants of trust on an individual level and find it related to the level of education, the region of residence, ethnicity, the ethnic diversity of their city, and membership in civic organizations (social capital). Such results would suggest, for instance, that the increased immigration into the United States (see Chapter 5) would reduce social trust, as argued by Schiff (2000). Cross-national comparisons also show the average level of social trust to be related to the average level of per capita GDP and membership in various organizations (social capital). As noted below, Knack and Keefer (1997) divide civic organizations into "Putnam groups," which have cultural, educational, and social purposes and "Olson groups," which focus on economic and political self-betterment. It is only membership in "Putnam groups" that is significantly correlated with social trust.

- The reconfiguration of U.S. cities and residential architecture to guard against intrusion by outsiders and to avoid face-to-face interaction with others.[10]

4. A Cautionary Note

Social trends are notoriously difficult to predict. For instance, few foresaw the social unrest and revolution in values that occurred in the late 1960s and 1970s in the U.S. or, more recently, the upsurge social activism in the waning years of the 20th century, most noticeably directed against organizations putatively tied to globalization such as the World Trade Organization and the World Bank.

The decline in the traditional family, social capital, and social trust should not mask the fact that other social trends, especially those which have much less impact on the economic system, are improving, for instance, the rates of drug misuse, rates of teen-age smoking or pregnancies, the rate of industrial accidents, and indicators of poor health all show a downturn at the end of the 20th century. For purposes of this discussion, the best that can be done is to ask what changes in U.S. capitalism might occur if the three social trends discussed above—a disintegrating traditional family, a fall in social capital, and declining social trust—continue their current course in the following decades.

B. Possible Impacts of Social Trends on the Economy and Economic System[11]

Determining the specific impact that the social trends discussed above might have on either the economy or economic system raises some obvious difficulties, but one way to attack the problem is to look at these relationships using evi-

---

[10] This is the theme of a fascinating book on the "architecture of fear" that is edited by Nan Ellin (1997). One essay by Steven Flusty (1997) notes that "Public open space has come under assault as privatization has reacted opportunistically to public sector penury.... [I]t becomes apparent that the sites in which daily life and face-to-facer interaction take place—the streets, parks, bazaars, and plazas—are being sacrificed to redundant zones of oversight and proprietary control. This threatens the free exchange of ideas engendering a progressive society. It creates an impediment to the cross-cultural communications necessary to knit together diverse groups. It is a rejection of the individual's right to space in which to be."

[11] In the text of this section I draw on: Berg and Sachs (1988), Easterly and Levine (1997), Knack and Keefer (1997), LaPorta *et al.,* (1999), Lipset and Lenz (2000), Mauro (1995), Olson (1982), Poterba (1996), Rodrik (1998), and Sennett (1998).

dence from many countries at a single point in time. I first discuss some of the work by others and then turn to my own calculations.

1. What Others Argue

Many social commentators have linked social trends to particular economic consequences. For instance, the decline in the traditional family is resulting in an increasing number of children who are likely to have difficulties in school and in pursuing productive careers as adults. This development, reinforced by the decline in social capital, the decline in social trust, and the growing isolation and cleavages in society, makes it probable that the underclass (the brutal Marxist term is Lumpenproletariat) will continue to grow. In turn, this trend is linked to greater income inequality and its attendant problems. Unless countermeasures are taken, it also seems likely that both the growing homeless and prison population (discussed in the next chapter) will continue in the future.

Turning more directly to the economy, many argue that high income inequality, low social capital, and low social trust (or more serious social cleavages) will have four negative impacts on the economy and economic system.

• *Markets and other economic and social institutions experience more internal conflicts and, as a result, higher transaction costs and more inefficiencies.* This proposition is generally argued from theoretical considerations (such as game theory) or particular historical cases, rather than from formal quantitative analysis.[12] Various studies of organizations have tried to show a quantitative link between social capital or trust and performance, for instance, a firm's record of innovation or likelihood to go bankrupt. Nevertheless, the conclusions of such studies are limited and counterexamples are readily at hand. For instance, although the United States has higher social capital (as measured by higher participation in voluntary organizations) than most other industrial economies, transaction costs in the U.S., reflected in the number of lawyers per capita, are higher. In Chapter 11 I explore other aspects of this problem, especially the high level of adversarial legalism in the U.S. Although this proposition linking the social trends to greater inefficiencies and high transactions costs has theoretical appeal, its empirical confirmation has been weak.

• *Governmental economic activities are less effective.* Some argue that the social trends discussed above will not lead to the "proper" level of production

---

[12]   Two quite different but useful examples are studies by Jean-Philippe Platteau (1994-a, 1994-b) and Janet Tai Landa (1994). Management specialists have focused attention on the relation between trust and performance for individual organizations, but many of these articles suffer from problems in obtaining measures both of trust and of performance.

of "public goods" or goods and services with externalities. These are goods and services that would not be adequately supplied in the marketplace, because all or some of the benefits are costlessly extended to others who, moreover, cannot be excluded from their enjoyment and cannot easily be charged for them. Examples include the services of a lighthouse or of an ICBM missile defense, or inoculations against a communicable disease. The linkage between the social trends and the supply of such goods and services receives empirical support from variety of studies. For instance, from a worldwide sample William Easterly and Ross Levine show that social cleavages (defined in terms of ethno-linguistic diversity) are associated with less investment in education. Rafael LaPorta and his colleagues find that social trust at a national level leads to increased judicial efficiency, tax compliance, and the adequacy of the economic infrastructure supplied by the government; and, moreover, corruption among governmental officials in such nations is lower. Paolo Mauro also shows not only that corruption is positively related to social cleavages (measured in terms of ethno-linguistic diversity) but that per capita economic growth is higher when corruption is lower.[13] Seymour Martin Lipset and Gabriel Lenz tie higher governmental corruption to greater income inequality. James Poterba compares education expenditures across U.S. state and local governments and finds that, other things being equal, age cleavages (manifested by a large fraction of elderly in a jurisdiction) lead to lower public spending on education; moreover, spending is even less when the youth are predominantly from a different racial group than the elderly—a situation where age and ethnicity cleavages reinforce each other.

• *Governments are less able to deal effectively with problems arising from external or internal shocks and to pursue policies more conducive to economic growth.* Evidence on the influence of low social capital, social trust, and wide income differentials on the effectiveness of government policy comes from a variety of studies. For instance, using a worldwide sample Easterly and Levine show that ethnic diversity is associated with exchange rates more likely to be out of equilibrium (in particular, when the black market and official exchange rates are greatly different), other determinants held constant. As noted in Chapter 4, Andrew Berg and Jeffrey Sachs argue that social cleavages, measured in terms of income inequality, not only lead to greater political instability but make it more difficult to adopt appropriate economic policies. For example, they use a cross-national empirical analysis to show that nations with large income inequalities are more likely to engage in excessive foreign borrowing and are

---

[13] Measuring social cleavages by ethno-linguistic diversity raises many problems. On such a count Rwanda, which consists primarily of Hutu and Tutsi, would be considered to have fewer social cleavages than a country like Madagascar, which has 50 or so ethnic groups; but the inter-group hostilities in the respective countries indicate otherwise.

less able to pay off these debts so that rescheduling is necessary. Dani Rodrik uses another cross-national sample to demonstrate that recovery from shocks to the balance of payment is less successful when social trust is lower. A different kind of evidence for the relation between governmental effectiveness and social trust is more impressionistic and comes from the statements of politicians responsible for making such economic policy in crisis conditions. For instance, a former Dutch Prime Minister, Rund Lubbers (cited by Richard Sennett), claimed that the Dutch trust in their government made possible painful economic adjustments which a more adversarial citizenry would not have accepted.

• *Economic growth is slower and investment risks are higher because property is less secure, justice is less assured, and transaction costs are greater.* Empirical evidence about the relationship of income inequality, social trust, or social capital to economic growth is much more mixed so that no firm conclusions can be drawn. For instance, Steven Knack and Phillip Keefer point out some possible implications of the argument developed by Mancur Olson: In situations with low social capital, enterprises are more likely to focus strictly on productive activities than in situations where social capital is high and firms can use their connections to obtain economic advantages through manipulation of governmental taxes, subsidies, and regulations (in economic jargon, engage in "rent-seeking"). This suggests that the economy should grow faster, not slower, in a situation with low social capital. This hypothesis is too delicious to let sit, but when Knack and Keefer test it with a worldwide sample, they find that social capital (measured by participation in organizations) has no significant impact on growth. Unwilling to let go, they then divide organizational membership measuring social capital into two groups, "Putnam groups" (such as sport and cultural organizations) that are not rent-seeking organizations and "Olson groups" (such as labor unions and political clubs) which serve as coalitions to redistribute income (and thereby lower economic growth). Unfortunately, they find no relation between either type of social capital and economic growth. Finally, they use their worldwide sample to show, however, that economic growth is positively related to social trust and also to an index of civic norms (the degree to which individuals follow laws and other rules of civic behavior), other factors held constant. This is the strongest evidence I have seen that it is trust, rather than social capital, that has the critical impact on the economy.[14]

We must, however, not be over-hasty in drawing any conclusions about social influences on economic growth or governmental effectiveness, or on the optimal

---

[14] Some contrary evidence, which I do not find convincing, is by La Porta *et al.* (1999), who carry out a similar exercise in a somewhat different way, but fail to find a statistically significant relation between trust and economic growth.

level of governmental expenditures from these studies. As noted in Chapter 4 when discussing the relationship between economic growth and the inequality of income, fitting a simple formula to these two variables is inadequate to determine accurately all of the statistical relationships because of mutual influences of the different variables on each other (two-way causation). For example, although high social trust may lead to a higher per capita income, a high per capita income can also enhance social trust, so that separating their different impacts becomes more difficult. Finally, the relevance to the future of the U.S. economy of such results drawn from worldwide samples is questionable. A much more homogeneous sample (for instance, the key industrialized nations of the OECD) would provide a more appropriate basis of comparison.

2. The Impact of Social Variables on the Economy of Key OECD Nations

In the discussion below I report the result of a series of statistical experiments examining the linkage of three social variables—income equality, social capital, and social trust—on different indicators of the performance and other features of the economy and the government.[15] I calculate relationships measuring the impact of each of the social variables on the economy twice, once for descriptive purposes without holding any other possible causal factor constant, once for analytic purposes, holding per capita income, the logarithm of the population, and the ratio of trade to the GDP constant since these may account for some of the relationship between the social variables and the indicators to be explained.

The 20 different economic variables to be explained measure many different aspects of the economy and are explained in detail in Appendix 7.1. The variable of government effectiveness, which is particularly important for this analysis, is discussed in detail in External Appendix X-7.4; it is based on the replies of about one hundred business executives in each OECD nation to fifty questions posed by the World Economic Forum and the International Institute for Managerial Development. Although this group would have an obvious ide-

---

[15]   To measure income equality, I start with the "gini coefficient," a statistic indicating the percentage of income that must be redistributed so that everyone has the same income. By subtracting this statistic from 1, I have an indicator of income equality, where income is measured in terms of adjusted monetary family income, taking account of the number of family members. The measure of social capital is the share of the adult population belonging to a variety of voluntary organizations for social and cultural purposes. And the measure of social trust reflects the answers to a question about trusting others that was used in the discussion about U.S. trends. The latter two sets of data come from the World Value Study, More exact information about the three variables and their sources can be found in Appendix 7.1.

Table 7.1. *Relationship of Social Trend Variables with Other Variables Relevant to the Economy of OECD Nations. Mid 1990s*

Panel A: Statistically significant correlations: Social trend variables with each other

	Simple correlations		Correlations, key factors held constant	
	Social trust	Social capital	Social trust	Social capital
Income equality	**Positive**	No	No	No
Social capital	**Positive**		**Positive**	

Panel B: Statistically significant correlations: Social trend variables with other variables

	Income equality		Social trust		Social capital	
	Simple correlations	Key factors constant	Simple correlations	Key factors constant	Simple correlations	Key factors constant
Economic system variables						
Public expenditures/GDP	No	No	No	No	No	No
Governmental transfers/ GDP	**Positive**	**Positive**	No	No	No	No
Public regulation	No	**Positive**	No	No	No	No
Public ownership	**Positive**	No	No	No	No	No
Economic success variables						
Per capita growth, 1985-95	No	No	**Positive**	No	Negative*	Negative
Governmental effectiveness	No	No	No	No	Positive*	Positive'
Other variables: objective						
Rate of serious crime	No	No	No	No	No	No
Strike days per employee	No	No	No	No	No	No

Other variables: Survey of business executives

A. Government and society

Social cohesion a government priority	No	No	No	No	No	No
Lack of governmental corruption	No	Positive	Positive	Positive	Positive	Positive
Discrimination is not a handicap	No	No	No	No	No	No
Social values support competition	No	No	No	No	No	No

B. Management

Managers don't neglect societal responsibilities	**Positive**	No	**Positive**	**Positive**	**Positive**	**Positive**
Managers have sense of entrepreneurship	No	No	No	No	**Positive**	**Positive**
Globalization not threatening	No	No	**Positive**	**Positive**	**Positive**	**Positive**
Technological cooperation common	No	No	**Positive**	**Positive**	**Positive**	No

C. Labor

People flexible to new challenges	No	No	No	**Positive**	No	No*
Productive labor relations	No	No	**Positive**	No	No	No
Work ethic	No	No	No	No	No	No
Problems at work:						
Alcohol, drug abuse not serious	**Positive**	No	No	No	No	No
Harassment, violence not serious	**Positive**	No	No	No	No	No

Note: The key factors held constant are: per capita GDP (PPP estimate), logarithm of the population, and the ratio of trade to GDP. Boldface = regression coefficient meets the test of 0.05 level of significance. * = coefficient is within the 0.06 level of statistical significance. No = no significant relationships. Data on total government expenditures and transfer expenditures come from Tables 11.1 and 11.4. More information and the sources for the other data are presented in Appendix 7.1. For almost all regressions the sample includes 18 most relevant OECD nations: Iceland, Luxembourg, Mexico, Turkey, and the three Central or East European nations are not included. Data gaps also prevent some of the remaining 21 countries from being included.

ological bias, it should not greatly affect differences between countries and it has the advantage of sampling a subgroup with firsthand knowledge about the functioning of the entire economy.[16]

Given the nature of the data, the results of the statistical experiments presented in Table 7.1 should be considered only as suggestive, rather than definitive. If the relationship is statistically significant, I report whether the relationship is positive or negative; to avoid clutter, other results are not reported.

Panel A shows the relation of the three social variables with each other. Although social trust and social capital are significantly related to each other, unexpectedly, neither is significantly related to income inequality when other factors are held constant.[17]

The first four rows of Panel B show the relation of the social trend variables to various indicators of the economic system. The results indicate that income equality is related both to the degree of government regulation of the economy and governmental transfers (such as Social Security or welfare expenditures). The first of these relationships receives extended discussion in Chapter 12; the second relationship cannot be easily interpreted because both could be the cause of the other variable. Neither social trust nor social capital is related to any of the four indicators of the economic system.

My results linking the social variables to various indicators of economic success are quite different from those of others, who use a worldwide sample. I find, for instance, that per capita economic growth is higher where the average level of social capital is lower, a result providing support for Olson's hypothesis mentioned above. This inverse relationship, however, does not permit us to determine whether lower levels of social capital cause, or are a result of, higher economic growth. I also find no significant relation of economic growth with the other social variables. If we are willing to accept results with a less rigorous criterion of statistical significance, then we find that high levels of social capi-

---

[16]   Further, it is highly related to a similar index calculated by Kaufmann *et al.* (2000) that draws from a broader data base and is discussed in Appendix 11.2.

[17]   In a personal letter Robert Putnam expressed skepticism because, in contrast to other studies, I did not find a significant relationship between social capital or trust with income equality. To examine the matter further, I recalculated the regressions after removing several countries that were far different from the others and that might unduly influence my conclusions. This did not, however, change my results in Panel A. Part of the difference between my results and those of others may lie in the manner in which the social capital indicator is calculated. My method, discussed in Appendix 7.1, tries to focus on membership in just those organizations where the social capital element is strongest..

Some claim that the social trust variable for the U.S. for 1990 is too high in comparison to the level found in other studies. Arbitrarily lowering the value by 30 percent and recalculating the regressions with inequality does not change the results reported in Panel A of Table 7.1.

tal are positively related to governmental effectiveness, a result that seems reasonable in light of the previous discussion. Surprisingly, however, neither social trust or income equality reveal such a relationship.

When we turn to other features of the economy, the statistical results are also important. Both social trust and social capital have significant and positive relationships with the lack of governmental corruption, managerial attention to social considerations, technological cooperation, and confidence in the face of the challenges of globalization. Given my previous discussion, such results seem reasonable. More unexpectedly, as the equality of income increases, labor force disciplinary problems—shown by such indicators as alcohol and drug abuse or harassment and violence in the work place—begin to diminish. Income equality is, however, unrelated to most other indicators.

C. Implications for the Future [18]

1. Direct Economic Impacts of the Social Trends

From these international comparisons between industrialized nations we can, if proper precautions are taken, draw some conclusions about changes in the U.S. economy and economic system in the coming decades.

If the cross-section results reported above have any validity for changes in the U.S. over time, then several conclusions can be derived about the role of government: The decline in social capital, social trust, and the rising income inequality will reduce the effectiveness of the government in carrying out its economic policies, for instance, measures that might increase economic growth.[19] Furthermore, increasing inequality of income seems likely to push the economic system toward a smaller governmental role, in terms both of regulation and income transfers, two changes discussed in greater detail in Chapters 11 and 12. Moreover, if social trust is one of the determinants of "confidence in the government," then declining social trust will also undermine the legitimacy of government. Both the decline in social trust and social capital also point toward an increase in governmental corruption, that would further reduce such legitimacy. Finally, the combination of widening income differentials, lower levels of social capital, and of inner-directed and self-absorbed citizens points

[18]   In the text of this section I refer to studies by: Case, *et al.* (2000), Case and Paxton (2000), Eisner (1989), Gruber (2000), and Wallerstein (2000).

[19]   A correlation between these variables can be found using data from Knack and Keefer (1997) and I conjecture that the causation runs from social trust to confidence in government, rather than the reverse.

toward a merciless economy—where the needy are cloaked with social invisibility and largely abandoned to their fate, assisted primarily by private charities, which do not have sufficient funds to properly carry out their work.

Turning toward the management of enterprises, results from Table 7.1 suggest that the declining levels of social trust and social capital will lead toward a greater neglect by the managers of their societal responsibilities, as well as a decline in both entrepreneurship and technological cooperation. Managers' readiness to meet the challenges of globalization might also ebb, which could contribute to the backlash against increasing global economic integration discussed in Chapter 5. The prevailing positive attitudes of managers toward globalization might also decline. On the side of labor, widening income differentials might lead to greater disciplinary problems in the work place.[20]

The other social trends documented above, also have important implications. The breakdown of the family has both direct and indirect impacts on other social variables and the economy. Most directly, female-headed families are characterized by low average incomes, so that as such households proliferate, the distribution of income will become more unequal. As a consequence, a higher share of the nation's children are likely to experience malnutrition and inadequate medical care, and to have difficulties in school and later life.

These conclusions are based on empirical studies of children from single-parent families showing that they are more likely to experience academic difficulties in school (especially those with divorced parents); not to participate in extracurricular activities; to manifest increased levels of depression, stress, anxiety, and aggression; and to drop out of high school. In addition, girls from such families have been shown to be more likely to bear illegitimate children.[21] Of course, the statistical problems in separating the contributing causal factors to these social problems are formidable.[22] Nevertheless, recent and sophisticated econometric evidence by Anne Case and her colleagues or by Jonathan Gruber

---

[20] The evidence for the last quarter of the 20th century does not, however, point toward any increase in strikes.

[21] These generalizations are based on the studies cited by Popenoe (1996, Chapter 2) and Fields and Smith (1999).

[22] As Fields and Smith (1998) show in their empirical work on predictors of academic difficulties (measured by whether children are in the grade in school corresponding to their age), variables indicating family structure are not always significant when a variety of other causal variables are held constant. The statistical problems of untangling such relationships are immense, especially since causality goes in both directions (poverty is one of the causes of broken marriages and illegitimacy, and these, in turn, are important causes of poverty) and because of the correlation of causes (low education of parents leads to poor school performance of children, but low education of parents is also correlated with illegitimacy and broken marriages). Studies of these issues need to move away from the use of single equation models toward statistical models allowing the analysis of two-way causation.

show that children raised by step-, adoptive-, or foster-mothers receive significantly less education than do birth children of the same women. Children living with step mothers, who do not have their own children, also receive less health care. Some researchers also present evidence that having a divorced parent serves as a predictor for: long-term unemployment; receipt of governmental welfare payments; engaging in crime, spending time in prison; or, according to Judith Wallerstein, experiencing difficulties in forming satisfying, long term relationships. All of these, of course, have an impact on social trust and social capital.

Most of these conclusions have intuitive plausibility, despite the statistical difficulties encountered in isolating the exact causal mechanisms involved. Of greatest importance for this discussion, these results suggest mechanisms underlying an inter-generational perpetuation of low incomes, ever widening income inequalities, and the creation of a permanent underclass.

It must also be noted that particular social changes might have important impacts that are neither direct nor immediately visible. For instance, the replacement of active civic participation with passive television viewing may have no apparent noticeable effects in the short-run; but in the end might prove devastating to the nation.[23]

2. A Digression on Home Production

Family structure is related to home production which, as briefly noted in Chapter 1, constitutes one of the five major institutional complexes of any economic system. At this point a brief digression is useful to explore another relationship between changing family structure and the future of the economic system.

If we measure home production—which includes cooking and cleaning—either by the cost of hiring someone to carry out such work or by the market value of time spent in home production, the magnitudes of this nonmarket pro-

---

[23] Television might be the equivalent of "soma," a drug taken in Aldous Huxley's *Brave New World* that made its users less concerned with outside events. "One dram is worth two damns." In a later essay, Huxley (1958) focuses more on barbiturates and tranquilizers as playing the same role. Nevertheless, he also noted that many of the "well-fed young television-watchers are completely indifferent to the idea of self-government." If he were writing in the 1990s, he might have focused even more on television which, as he noted in 1958, communicates messages that are neither true nor false but unreal and "totally irrelevant" to important societal concerns. Putnam (2000) provides data showing that an increasing number of television watchers in the U.S. turn on the set, not for a particular program or purpose, but simply to pass the time. He also notes an inverse relation between television watching and a person's social trust, a relationship also shown in experimental evidence by Glaeser, *et al.* (1999).

duction are high. Unfortunately, home production has not, for the most part, been recorded in the official national account statistics, and we must turn to alternative calculations.

According to the estimates of Robert Eisner, in the late 1940s, home production amounted to about 61 percent of officially recorded personal consumption expenditures.[24] In the following decades, however, this ratio fell so that it was 52 percent in the 1970s, the last decade for which his estimates are available.

Clearly part of the falling share of nonmarket home production was due to a decline in the share of adults who spent their time primarily at home. Specifically, the share of the non-institutionalized population from 20 through 64 who were employed outside the home steadily rose from 68.4 percent in the late 1940s to 76.3 percent in the 1970s to 81.7 percent in the 1990s.[25] Underlying such an increase in labor force participation were the changing attitudes toward women working outside the home and the weakening of the family structure, manifested by both the decline in the marriage rate, and the rise in the number of single-parent families. In addition, the rapid introduction of household equipment, for instance, automatic dishwashers, led to increased labor productivity of household production, so that fewer hours needed to be spent in such nonmarket activities.

It seems likely that nonmarket home production as a share of total consumption should continue to decline in the coming decades. Important contributing factors to this trend include the high divorce rate, the rising share of single-parent households, and the dramatic decrease in average family size from 1970 to the end of the century.[26]

D. Trends in Values and Culture[27]

Are values and the culture changing in a way to strongly influence changes in the economy and the economic system? I look first at several trends of the

[24]   The data on home produced services for consumption (which exclude home produced investment goods and services such as home improvements) come from Eisner (1989),Table 6, line 59; the total non-market production from the household sector comes from Table 6, line 47. For consistency I use the data on personal consumption expenditures and GNP presented in his book.

[25]   The time-series data on employed civilians, as well as the total population from 20 through 64. come from U.S. Council of Economic Advisers (annual, 1999). To the civilian labor force I added the resident armed forces and from the population I subtracted the number of adults in prisons. The latter data were gathered from U.S. Department of Justice, Bureau of Justice Statistics (1998) and U. S. Department of Commerce, Bureau of the Census (annual, various years).

[26]   Average family size decreased from 3.41 in 1970 to 2.62 in 1998. The data come from the U.S. Department of Commerce, Bureau of the Census (annual, 1999), p. 60.

[27]   In this section I cite studies by: Bell (1976), Bok (1997), Bowman (1996), Colimore (1998),

"spirit of capitalism" particularly relevant to what Max Weber called the "Protestant ethic," namely the value of hard work, saving, and entrepreneurship.[28] Then I look briefly at materialist and post-materialist values, before turning to an examination of the revolt against rationalism.

1. The Decline of the "Protestant Ethic" and the Rise of Hedonism

In 1976 the sociologist Daniel Bell argued that the cultural prerequisites of capitalism are being undercut by modernism and hedonism. More specifically, the older "bourgeois values" favoring self-control over self-expression; hard work over sensual enjoyment; saving, investment, and entrepreneurship over consumption; rationality over unreflective spontaneity; and planning for tomorrow over instant gratification were losing their primacy. With only a touch of exaggeration he declared: "The greatest single engine in the destruction of the Protestant ethic was the invention of the installment plan. Previously one had to save in order to buy. But with credit cards one could indulge in instant gratification." He claimed that modernism aimed at the death of the traditional bourgeois world-view, which was rationalistic, matter-of-fact, and pragmatic, first, by denying its values in art, then by denigrating its lifestyle. "Today's culture is prodigal, promiscuous, dominated by an anti-rational, anti-intellectual temper in which the self is taken as the touchstone of all cultural judgement, and the effect on the self is the measure of the aesthetic worth of experience."[29]

This theme has been picked up by numerous social commentators from all over the political spectrum and, in addition, is found in a variety of apocalyptic strains (for instance, Eric Hobsbawm). Some claim, for instance, that rage—the reverse of bourgeois prudence—has gained prestige in certain social circles and

Dean (1998), Fogel (2000), Ger and Belk (1996), Hobsbawm (1976), Inglehart (1990), Kohut et al., (2000), Kurth (1999), Lipset (1996), Myers (2000), Orren (1997), Schumpeter (1950), Social Security Administration (2000), and Weber (1958 (1904)).

[28] As noted in Chapter 1, results from the World Value Study suggest that the so-called Protestant ethic is not a single dimension since the rank ordering of OECD nations regarding hard work, saving, and entrepreneurship are quite different. I use this term, therefore, simply as a shorthand expression for the three values.

[29] In an afterword written 20 years later, Daniel Bell (1996) cites two subversive books to illustrate these points: Bryan Burrough's 1990 book *Barbarians at the Gate, the Decline of RJR Nabisco*, which shows the total disregard of any social and human values in attempts to make money from mega-mergers; and David Stockman's 1986 book *Triumph of Politics*, which reports how he cooked the government's books in order to push through Reagan's tax policies, which led to a tripling of the federal debt in the next decade.

in finding ever new loci for expression. One political scientist, James Kurth, has argued: "Expressive individualism—with its contempt for and protest against all hierarchies, communities, traditions, and customs—represents the logical conclusion and the ultimate extreme of secularization," an analysis with its roots in Nietzsche and other critics of Western rationalism.

Although Bell's basic arguments were not new (Pitirim Sorokin, for instance, had raised them several decades before), his elegant style and his definition of the problem as a "cultural contradiction" made it particularly cogent to an America engaged in the Cold War. His arguments were also readily accessible to the general public, since they were primarily based on a qualitative analysis of cultural conditions (as manifested both in values held by individuals and in art, literature, or other goods and services produced for non-utilitarian consumption), rather than from a dry statistical analysis of quantitative information.

At the end of the century some social scientists, such as Nobel laureate Robert Fogel, raised an argument almost opposite to that of Bell's, namely, that the U.S. has recently been experiencing a wave of religious fervor, as it has periodically throughout its history, and this has a certain polarizing aspect. According to this line of thought, the new emphasis on personal, rather than governmental, responsibilities might have a considerable social and political impact, that may lead, perhaps, to a realignment of political parties or a reduced role of government. In their analysis of survey data Andrew Kohut and his coauthors point out, for instance, that between 1987 and 1996, the representation of white evangelical Protestants among registered voters rose from 19 to 24 percent. Nevertheless, they also note (p. 18) that the total share in the adult population of those belonging to all religious traditions in the U.S. barely changed between 1965 and 1996; that those belonging to various Protestant evangelical groups rose only from 23.9 to 25.4 percent; and that the largest percentage increase was registered among atheists, agnostics, or those expressing no religious preference (from 9.7 to 16.3 percent). They also present data showing that the percentage of Americans who go to church more than once or twice a month, who pray frequently, or declare religion to be "very important" in their life has declined (p. 24).

What has risen is not religious belief *per se*, but the heightened political activism of committed Protestant evangelicals and their shift toward a more conservative political stance. By this I refer not just to attitudes toward social issues but, to a lesser degree, toward the scope of government, for instance, environmental protection (see footnote 22, Chapter 6). I do not see any "great religious awakening" and a resulting change in economic behavior, governmental economic policies, or the economic system. More likely, the growing heterogeneity in religious belief points toward a greater potential for domestic strife, particularly over social issues. Exit polls in the 2000 Presidential election provide some supporting evidence.[30]

2. The Rise of Post-Materialist Values

The sociologist Max Weber did not stress materialism in his investigation of the spirit of capitalism, but economists have always highlighted the analytic importance of human desires for greater wealth and consumption. Analyses focusing on economic concerns, a manifestation of "materialist values," have defined the right-left spectrum that dominated political discourse for most of the 20th century. Recently, a number of sociologists and political scientists, such as Ronald Inglehart, have begun to argue against this economic approach, claiming that "materialist values" are being supplanted by "post-materialist values." In particular, political discourse based on post-materialist values place less emphasis on economic security and a satisfactory standard of living and more weight to ecological, political, social, and quality-of-life concerns.[31] Inglehart also presents evidence that such post-materialist values exclude many traditional leftist goals, such as nationalization of the means of production. He buttresses his case about a shift in values on quantitative analyses of public opinion data—in massive amounts—from many countries, rather than the traditional type of cultural analysis.

[30] An MSN/NBC exit poll revealed that of the 14 percent of American adults who identify with the religious right, 80 percent voted for Bush; of the 83 percent who do not, 54 percent voted for Gore (www.msnbc.com/m/d2k/g/polls/asp?office=P&state=N1). According to the same poll, of the 42 percent of Americans claiming to attend a religious service once a week or more, the Gore-Bush vote was respectively 39 and 59 percent; of those claiming to attend a religious service less often or never, the Gore-Bush vote was respectively 55 and 41 percent. If African-Americans and Jews had been factored out of these results, the differences would have been greater. Some political observers, such as Michael Novak, argue that the impact of religious belief in Presidential elections has been steadily increasing in the last few decades.

[31] Inglehart's analysis about the direction in which American values are shifting is not universally shared; others view this shift in terms of moral decay. For instance, Daniel Yankelovich (1984) draws upon public opinion data to show that Americans now place less value on what they owe to others as a matter of moral obligation on observing society's rules, or sacrifice as a moral good, replacing these former virtues by more pragmatic rules of behavior. He notes, however, that Americans still place a high (verbal) value on concern for others such as family or ethnic group, neighborliness, and caring for the community. (It is, of course, a quite different issue whether such concerns are translated into action.) Unfortunately, in neither this nor other essays on American values does he ever present his empirical evidence, claiming that the underlying public opinion data are "proprietary."

Although a shift in political value has undoubtedly taken place, it might better be called "post-modern," rather than "post-materialist," since "materialism" in its old-fashioned sense seems to be increasing in strength. For instance, as cited by Karlyn Bowman, Roper polls in 1975 and 1994 show that the percentage of Americans seeing "a lot of money" as part of "the good life" increased from 38 to 63 percent. The percent of entering university students believing that it is "very important or essential" to become "very well off financially" rose from 39 percent in 1970 to 74 percent in 1978, as David Myers notes. Of course, when respondents to such polls are given a number of goals to select, they give less verbal support to those they perceive as "materialistic." For example, a survey by the Harwood Group revealed that 66 percent of Americans would be more satisfied with their lives if they were able to spend more time with their families and friends, while placing less importance on "a nicer car," a "bigger house," and more "nice things" to satisfy their wishes for a good life. Nevertheless, the time-budget data cited earlier showing that Americans are spending more time before the TV screen and less time socializing suggest that their alleged "non-materialist values" are not reflected by actual deeds.

Studies by Güliz Ger and Russel Belk show that Americans rank quite high in materialist values—defined along several different dimensions—in international comparisons that include economically less developed nations (which allegedly have not entered the "post-materialist" stage). In brief, by the end of the 20th century the U.S. population had sufficiently low social capital and high inner-directedness to continue focusing on money making and competitive consumption, even at the cost of quality-of-life and social goals.

3. The Revolt Against Rationalism

A cultural trend that has not received much attention but may ultimately have an important impact on the economic system in the coming decades is the growing "revolt against rationalism," a trend noted by Daniel Bell. Numerous social commentators, such as Seymour Martin Lipset, have noted a growing lack of respect for authority, anti-elitism, and populism, arguing that they contribute to higher crime rates, school indiscipline, and low electoral turnouts. The most important consequence, however, may be the loss of respect for scientific enquiry and reasoned debate.

With the decline in social trust and trust in authority, irrational beliefs have flourished and anti-intellectualism seemed in ascendance at the end of the 20th century. Indicators of this trend are readily available.[32] In the late 1990s the

---

[32]   Part of the revolt against rationalism may be due to a loss of certainty, even in the hard sciences.

movement by creationists to eliminate from the public school curriculum both the teaching of biological evolution and cosmographic theories placing the origins of the universe many billions of years ago reached a fever pitch.[33] The anti-evolutionist movement, I might add, had wide public support. For instance, a 1999 Gallup poll reveals that 44 percent of American adults believe in creationism and 64 percent believe that it should be taught in schools.[34]

Several other examples of the revolt against rationalism deserve brief mention. According to a survey cited by Edward Colemore, which compares changes in American beliefs between 1976 and 1996, the percentage believing in spiritualism rose from 12 to 52 percent; in faith healing, from 10 to 45 percent; in UFOs from 24 to 30 percent; in astrology, from 17 to 37 percent. Moreover, according to another national poll in 1994, 21 percent believed the world would come to an end within a few decades; indeed, 15 percent of adults thought that the Persian Gulf War fulfilled a biblical prophecy and that Armageddon was at hand. None of these beliefs seem conducive to investment and long-range economic planning.[35]

For instance, Nobel Prize laureate Ilya Prigogine (1997), who made his reputation studying disequilibrium thermodynamics, argues that the omnipresence of repetition, stability, and equilibrium which served as the basis of classical science is being replaced by both a more probabilistic approach and by concepts drawn from chaos and complexity theory, which reflect the instability, evolution, and fluctuation found everywhere in the natural world.

[33] The Board of Education of Kansas took a major step in this direction by eliminating questions about evolution or cosmography from the state examinations required of all high school biology students. After an election for the Board, this decision was reversed. Other states have banned the use of the word "evolution," replacing it with euphemisms, or have demanded that textbooks have disclaimers pointing out that evolution is a mere "theory" that does not disprove the story of God's creation of the world.

[34] According to a Gallup poll, only 10 percent of Americans say they hold a secular evolutionist view of the world, while 44 percent declared they believe in strict biblical creationism, which, among other things, means that God created man sometime within the last 10,000 years. Other polls show roughly similar results. (*Economist*, September 4, 1999, p. 36; and Benen (1999)).

American politicians are also pandering to such views. In 1999 in the runup to the presidential election, the various candidates were asked to comment on the Kansas Board of Education decision. Steve Forbes called the teaching of evolution of life on earth "a massive fraud," and Gary Bauer declared that he rejected the basic tenet of evolutionism. Other candidates were somewhat less categorical. Al Gore declared that localities should be free to teach creationism as well as the theory of evolution. George W. Bush said that the children should be exposed to different theories about how the world started including creationism.

[35] The poll indicating the end of the world would come within several decades was commissioned by the *U.S. News and World Report* and cited by Diamond (1997). Wojcik (1997, Chapter 1) cites the poll on Armageddon and, moreover, notes that one third of U.S. teen-agers believe that the world will end within their lifetime.

Some of these beliefs might, in part, be tied to the calendrical accident of the looming change in the millennium. Other aspects of the revolt against rationalism reflect what is designated above as "expressive individualism." For instance, Jodi Dean argues that the strong belief in "alien abductions" and the wide popularity of various conspiracy theories reflect the total mistrust of all authority—governmental, scientific, or mainstream religion—which has characterized an ever larger portion of the U.S. population.

Such a revolt against rationalism can also influence political and economic views through an unwillingness to sift carefully empirical evidence on particular issues. For instance, Derek Bok points out public opinion data showing that most people think 50 percent of Social Security payments go for overhead (according to the Social Security Administration, it is roughly 1 percent). Such a belief could lead to a loss of public backing for the system and increasing support for privatization of the system. In the next chapter I document the abysmally low political knowledge of U.S. adults. As Gary Orren argues, such unwillingness for serious investigation of political issues, combined with distrust of government, invites quick fixes to complex problems, for instance, term limits, tax revolts, third-party panaceas, or extremist appeals, while, at the same time, discouraging steady and pragmatic solutions.

In these few pages I cannot present a full analysis of the revolt against rationalism, of the characteristics of those who takes this approach, or of the exact influence they might have on political and economic change. But the shards of evidence I have presented on changing attitudes toward science or government certainly do not seem to bode well for the continued economic growth of the nation.

4. Three Non-Trends

In the discussion above I focus on trends that seem most likely to have an impact on U.S. capitalism. It is useful, however, to note briefly three predicted influences that have not appeared, namely a diminishing value placed on greater consumption, a crumbling of the entrepreneurial spirit, and a loss of individualism.

Classical economists believed that the utility of each additional dollar of income is less than the previous one. Among other things, this should mean that with the rising standard of living, many characteristics of early capitalism should slowly decline in importance, for instance, the fierce struggle among producers, or the jockeying for social position, especially through competitive consumption. Instead, we should have greater leisure for the self-development of our human potential. Obviously, this has not occurred, nor are there any credible signs that it will occur in the coming decades, since the material standards of the "good life" seem to be continually raised. As noted above, greed and obsession for money making remain important aspects of the culture.

Joseph A. Schumpeter also argued that the civilization of capitalism is crumbling: the entrepreneurial function is being bureaucratized; economic progress is becoming automatized; and the social strata defending capitalism are becoming weaker while the non-proprietied critics of capitalism—especially intellectuals—are becoming stronger. As a result, the ideological structure supporting the economic system is eroded. At the end of the 20th century this prophecy was still unrealized, the "new class" that was supposed to demolish capitalism has not appeared, and few credible signs point toward a validation of Schumpeter's gloomy forecast in the decades to come.

Finally, the fear that we are becoming a nation of other-directed sheep has also not yet received confirmation. From the evidence presented by Karlyn Bowman, it appears that public opinion data points toward an upsurge in self-reliance.

E. The Impact of Cultural Trends[36]

The various cultural trends discussed above—or others—could be pursued in much greater depth, but already, two important questions arise: How much do these trends influence the economic system? And what kind of predictive value do they have for its future? In hindsight, we can convincingly argue that "culture matters to an economy" and, following the approach of Lawrence Harrison and Samuel Huntington, point to many historical examples. Unfortunately, as I argue below, the analysis of current culture and values may tell us little about the future.

Let us begin by trying to link actual economic behavior to the cultural trends that seem most relevant to our concerns. It is particularly important to consider on which areas of life these cultural trends have an influence.[37] Can we be hard-driving, rational, capitalist workers by day, but hedonists at night, wallowing in sensuousness—in brief, work hard, play hard?[38] Can we operate highly success-

---

[36] In the text of this section, I refer to studies by: Albert (1993), Brooks (2000), Harrison and Huntington (2000), Pryor (1983), (1996), Reynolds, Hay, and Camp (1999), Robinson and Godbey (1997), Tilgher (1930), and Yankelovitch (1994).

[37] Such an approach contrasts with Inglehart's (1990, Chapter 1), who holds it self-evident that a shift toward post-materialist values, as he measures them, will be reflected in slower economic growth. His graphs charting the relationship between materialist values and growth rates hold no other variables constant and, in addition, do not indicate which is acting as the causal variable. Inglehart's basic assumption may be right, but the causal linkage has not been established empirically in any kind of rigorous fashion.

[38] The World Value Study (Inglehart, et al., 1998, V-121) asked respondents if they concurred with the following statement about work: "I enjoy working but I don't let it interfere with the rest of

fully in the ugly, materialistic, dog-eat-dog world in which we live, while having lofty post-materialist thoughts about the way the world should be when talking to public opinion pollsters? After all, history records many examples of groups with seemingly strange religious beliefs and otherworldly values who have been able to operate extremely successfully in a market economy—the Quakers in post Elizabethan England, for example, or the Old Believers in czarist Russia or the Amish in the U.S. To this end it is useful to look briefly at three behavioral characteristics cited by Weber as representing "the spirit of capitalism," that made the American economy so successful—saving, hard work, and entrepreneurship—to see how they have been affected by these cultural trends discussed above.

1. Personal Saving

If we judge from the number of personal bankruptcies and the rising amount of credit card debt, Americans are apparently saving less and less. Nevertheless, the actual statistics on saving are much more ambiguous. As discussed in detail in Chapter 2, trends in personal saving raise problems of interpretation. Nevertheless, the most cited series on personal saving that are presented in Table 2.1 show that the rate of personal saving, measured in terms of flows of money, declined in the U.S. in the last few decades of the 20th century, even while the extent of decline is disputed. By way of contrast, the saving rate measured in terms of changes in assets (which includes unrealized capital gains) shows an increase.

From such mixed evidence we must reach a Scottish verdict of "not proven" for any proposition about the decline of saving over the last quarter of the 20th century. Although other causal factors may be offsetting the cultural factors leading to less saving, it is difficult to demonstrate what these might be, so the cultural explanation must be viewed with considerable skepticism. The long-term decline in the saving rate that I foresee in Chapter 2 has little to do with cultural values and much more to do with demography.

2. The Work Ethic

In the last third of the 20th century the work week in the U.S. was slowly declining, as shown in the time budget studies of John Robinson and Geoffrey

---

my life." The percentage of Americans agreeing was tied for 7th highest out of 16 OECD nations.

Godbey. This may tell us less, however, about the work ethic than about the trade-off between work and leisure as per capita income rises. Participation in the formal work force has also increased. Measuring the work ethic—particularly how hard people work—raises some obvious problems, and we must proceed cautiously.[39]

The rate of absenteeism provides an interesting indicator of the work ethic. Since 1957 the *Current Population Survey* (CPS) began to include questions about work absences due to sickness and to "other" reasons. Although these series reveal a number of inconsistencies over time, as I have pointed out elsewhere, we can draw one major conclusion: From 1957 to the mid 1980s, the rate of absenteeism remained relatively flat, and since then it has fallen.

Attempts to collect data on absenteeism, as well as other aspects of the work ethic, directly from enterprises raises a curious difficulty. My own sample survey work reveals that most managers have the subjective impression that absenteeism increased in the 1970s. Given the empirical results from the Current Population Survey (based on enterprise records) that absenteeism was relatively constant during this period, such a survey result seems to reflect "nostalgia bias" by the managers, rather than reality. As the Italian sociologist Adriano Tilgher laconically noted, "Every country resounds to the lament that the work-fever does not burn in the younger generation." The managers also expressed the opinion that people are working less hard and with less attention to quality. When corrected for the nostalgia bias discovered in the absenteeism data, no changes in these two indicators are apparent.[40]

---

[39]   One approach is to look at surveys of business people in various countries to see how they rate their workers. The World Economic Forum asked business people in various countries the degree of their agreement with the statement "The average worker (in my country) is among the world's most hard working." (This variable is also used in Table 7.1). Out of 21 major OECD countries American managers placed their workers 11th from the top. Nevertheless I could find no correlation of this indicator with any other important measure of economic success, such as per capita growth of GDP or governmental effectiveness, either in simple regressions or holding other causal factors constant.

[40]   Daniel S. Hammermesh (2000) reaches opposite conclusions about changes in the work ethic, which he defined in terms of commitment to one's job, in an interesting fashion. He provides evidence that, holding all relevant factors constant, the share of hourly (in contrast to salaried) workers has increased in the U.S. He argues that employers tend to offer salaried positions to workers, who have a high commitment toward their work and do not require monitoring, while they offer hourly paid positions to those who are less dedicated to the goals of the enterprise and who are less willing to work intensively without supervision. Noting the decline of social trust and regression results showing that a salaried position is related to one's work satisfaction in the past, he argues that the unexpected rise in hourly work is related to a declining work commitment. While ingenious, this argument provides little evidence that social trust and work commitment are directly related and, moreover, assumes certain directions of causality between work attitudes and the type of work situation that can be questioned (perhaps intensive work monitoring increases social distrust). Furthermore, as shown in the text, employer perceptions

Ideas about the relative importance of hard work and luck in getting ahead are also another aspect of the work ethic. From the General Social Survey[41] we find that the percentage of people believing that hard work was the more important factor explaining success increased from 62 percent in the 1972—82 period to 67 percent in the 1988—94 period. At the same time, those believing that luck was more important increased from 10.6 to 12.3 percent. Both groups increased at the expense of those believing that luck and labor were equally important. Internationally, the U.S. is in that group of nations whose citizens are most likely to believe in the importance of hard work as a key to success.[42]

Other aspects of the work ethic include employee loyalty to a firm and work satisfaction. Michel Albert argues that "a diligent and devoted management of a stable work force is one of the decisive ingredients for achieving a competitive edge." In this respect many claim that the downsizing experienced of many large firms in America has destroyed this trust. But sample survey data reveal a different picture.[43] A Roper Poll asked how satisfied people were with their work, and from 1973 through 1992, there was little change—about 85 percent claimed they were satisfied. In 1992, 82 percent of those queried said they felt loyal to their place of employment, 88 percent said other people usually notice when a job is done well; and 89 percent were proud to be working for their employer. Other sample survey data reveal little change over the last few decades.

about commitment to work may not correspond to reality. Although Hammermesh's various indicators are consistent with each other and, for this reason, his analysis deserves serious consideration, a causal linkage between social trust and the work ethic can only be established when direct indicators of work commitment, such as my measure of absenteeism, can be used.

[41]   These data are found on the web site of the Inter-University Consortium for Political and Social Research at: www.icpsr.umich.edu/gss/codebook/getahead.htm)

[42]   From the World Value Study results (Inglehart *et al.*, 1998) for the early 1990s, the United States was one of the few countries in the world where a higher percentage of those between 19 and 29 believed their work to be "very important" in their lives than older cohorts (V-4 and p. 6) and numbered among the top of those believing that hard work, rather than luck and connections, brings success (V-255). The U.S. also ranked high in the percentage of those taking pride in their work (V-115), those deriving a great deal of satisfaction from their work (V-116), those believing that work is the most important thing in their life (V-122), and those believing that it is fair to pay efficient workers more salary (V-125). Among respondents from industrialized nations, the U.S. scored toward the top of those nations believing in the importance of children being taught the value of hard work (V-228). With all this emphasis on hard work overcoming all obstacles, some may find it curious that the U.S. numbered among the top nations in the percentage of its citizens believing that job security is an important aspect of a job (V-102), but the two are not really related since people may work hard out of fear of losing their job (the "whip of hunger").

[43]   The sources of these data are cited in Pryor and Schaffer, 1998, p. 212.

In a witty analysis David Brooks provides a possible explanation for some of theses ideas about work satisfaction:

> " ...the Berkeley-style baby boomers have become the hard-working capitalists, oriented toward the long term. The hedonism of Woodstock mythology has been domesticated and now serves as a management tool for the Fortune 500 ... Countercultural capitalists are not restrained by the old puritanical or Protestant code. Instead, they have constructed their own ethos that creates a similar and perhaps more rigorous system of restraint. They have transformed work into a spiritual and intellectual vocation, so they approach their labor with the fervor of artists and missionaries."

I might add that the boomers' disdain for traditional or bourgeois ideas has proved quite useful when harnessing the new information technologies for business success and the accumulation of wealth.

Although some pollsters, such as Daniel Yankelovotch, claim public opinion data show "a shift from the Protestant ethic valuation of work as having intrinsic moral value to work as a source of personal satisfaction, and therefore less tolerance for work that does not provide personal satisfaction." I find no such evidence confirming a shift away from the belief in hard work.[44]

3. Entrepreneurship

The notion that entrepreneurship may be declining is generally based on the well-known observation (documented in Appendix table A2.1) that GDP, labor productivity, and total factor productivity growth rates all declined from the 1960s up to the mid 1990s. Such evidence; however, is indirect and ambiguous since other causal factors may be at work.

Two more direct indicators of entrepreneurship reveal a much different picture. In the second half of the 20th century, the ratio of new patents issued to U.S. individuals and corporations to the population between 20 and 65 have fluctuated irregularly, but, over the half century, no long-term upward or downward trend is apparent. Although the 1980s and 1990s witnessed an upturn in this ratio, the level in the 1950s was not surpassed. A more telling indicator of

---

[44] Although some social observers also argue that it becomes absurd to work long and hard for an employer who thinks only of selling out and moving on (Sennett 1998), it is far from clear that American workers have come to the same conclusion.

entrepreneurship is new businesses formed each year. The annual number of such new businesses, measured as a percent of the population between 20 and 65 (those people who might start them), rose steadily in the second half of the 20th century, from around 0.1 percent in 1950 to 0.5 percent in the late 1990s.[45]

It might seem that general cultural trends are quite irrelevant to entrepreneurship. According to this argument, the economy only needs a few individuals with such instincts who are relatively immune to cultural trends. If we do not hamper them too much, the economy will flourish.

But evidence suggests that entrepreneurship is by no means immune to the climate of the times. In a ten nation empirical comparison, Paul Reynolds and his co-workers show that the level of entrepreneurship, as measured by business startups per 100 people, depends on favorable governmental policies, the availability of infrastructure including finance and other help for new enterprises, the general level of education, and social and cultural values that legitimize and encourage such activity. They also show that economic growth is faster with a higher number of start-ups.

Determining whether the number of business startups will continue to rise in the U.S. requires a forecast of changes in government policy, the availability of finance for new enterprises, and the entrepreneurial climate, which includes the general level of optimism and the respect for entrepreneurial activity. All of these are difficult to predict. On a higher level of abstraction, Reynolds shows that business startups are directly related to a nation's educational level and inversely related to its inequality of income. From the evidence presented above, the impact of these two factors in the U.S. may mostly cancel each other out. In brief, future trends of entrepreneurship in the U.S. cannot be easily foreseen, but storm clouds do not appear on the horizon.

4. A Final Word on Cultural Trends

The U.S. experienced important cultural changes in the second half of the 20th century. Nevertheless, the argument that this portends ill news for the economy or the economic system, seems questionable. One would think that the shift toward hedonism, the revolt against rationalism, and other traits would be socially and economically dysfunctional. But, in fact, such a shift cannot be eas-

---

[45] Data on patents include not just inventions but designs, new botanical species, and reissues. These data come from Department of Commerce, Bureau of the Census (annual, various years; and 1975), series W-96 to W-108. The data on business startups come from the Council of Economic Advisers (annual) and Department of Commerce, Bureau of the Census (1975), Series V-21.

ily tied to changes in saving behavior, hard work, entrepreneurship, or, for that matter, a decline in economic growth or efficiency.

We also have little reason to think that this disconnect between the values Americans express to public opinion polls and their actual behavior will not continue in the coming decades. After all, given present labor laws in the U.S., workers with records of absenteeism and idleness can be fired, so that in order to support their putative hedonism, irrationalism, and post-materialist goals during their nights and weekends, they still have to work diligently and rationally during the day. At the end we are still left with a puzzle: In the long run, will these cultural shifts have a profoundly detrimental effect on the functioning of the U.S. economy? Or will Americans continue to compartmentalize their lives, behaving according to one set of cultural values by day and another by night?

It must also be emphasized that cultural values can change rapidly—witness the changes in U.S. attitudes before and after the early 1930s or before and after the late 1960s and early 1970s. The value shift occasioned by the Great Depression led to dramatic changes in the economic system and a more expansive role for government. Other crises of equal magnitude might hit the economy in the future, as argued in Chapter 3, and might also have a profound effect. The Vietnam War and the shift in values occurring around 1970 had a much smaller impact, although they unexpectedly accelerated a rightward shift in U.S. politics in the following decades.

F. A Brief Summary

Returning for a moment to the three-dimensional diagram of economic systems which is presented in Chapter 1, we can see that along the dimension of social solidarity, the evidence presented in this chapter suggests a definite decline. The disintegration of the traditional family, the decline in social capital, and the erosion in social trust all point in this direction.

Although the social and cultural systems have an impact on both economic performance and the economic systems in a general sense, it proves difficult to disentangle their exact causal linkages. In part, this is because the data are not very satisfactory; in part, because the causal relationships are subtle and cannot be easily disentangled.

Of the three quantitative indicators of social trends—income inequality, social trust, and social capital—only income inequality seems to have a direct impact on the economic system, more specifically, on the role of the government. I defer further discussion of these matters to Chapters 11 and 12.

The key message of this chapter is that the decline of social capital and social trust can have important indirect effects on the economy and economic system, since, as noted in Chapter 1, a successful capitalist system is based on trust. Under certain political and economic circumstances, explored in later chapters, a capitalist system without such trust can degenerate into a gangster economy or, alternatively, an oligarchy. Furthermore, social trust and social capital are positively related to a number of varied features of the economy, for instance, entrepreneurship, technological cooperation, and managers fulfilling their social responsibilities. Greater income equality and social trust also seem to improve the functioning of the labor market.

This chapter also presents evidence that a decline of social capital and social trust can have an adverse impact on the operations of both governments and markets. Among the more startling findings is the correlation between diminished social cohesion and greater governmental corruption. More subtle impacts may also be felt, such as a decline in entrepreneurship or in the social responsibility of business leaders. Furthermore, the combination of inner-directedness, the decline of social capital, and greater income inequalities, would make for a capitalism with much less mercy, much more envy, and with a much greater potential for social conflict in the future.

Cultural shifts and their influence on the economy are difficult to forecast. Certainly the three major cultural shifts discussed above—the decline of the "Protestant ethic" (including the rise of hedonism), the rise of post-materialist values, and the revolt against rationalism, have not had their expected impact on saving, hard work, or entrepreneurship. In brief, U.S. capitalism will probably remain resolutely acquisitive, individualistic, and hard-working.

When even the present is murky, I cannot go beyond these tentative conjectures. In brief, we have reached the limits of responsible prediction.

CHAPTER 8

General Political Factors

*By 2000, politics will simply fade away. We will
not see any political parties.*

—Engineer R. Buckminster Fuller, circa 1971[1]

How might political factors actually influence the economic system, both now and in the future? To attack these questions, it is important to
distinguish between the government's strength and its degree of economic
intervention. By governmental strength I mean its ability to make and to
implement effectively various economic policies, to enforce contracts and
property rights, to provide effective internal security, and to prevent certain
regions of the country (generally the wealthiest, those that are experiencing a
net outflow of resources to subsidize poorer regions) from seceding and forming independent nations. By economic intervention I mean its expenditures for
various goods and services, governmental allocation of resources (either
directly through state-owned enterprises or indirectly through regulation of
production and distribution), and its stabilization of the economy.

These two dimensions of governmental influence on the economy vary
considerably among nominally capitalist nations. For instance, as Carmelo
Mesa-Lago documents, the Pinochet government in Chile in the 1970s and
1980s was strong, but its interventions into the economy were limited. By way
of contrast, the Yeltsin government in Russia in the 1990s was weak, but inter-
vened considerably into the economy, usually without achieving its stated
intentions.

This distinction guides the first part of the discussion of this chapter, but
already some major problems of prediction loom. Certain unforeseen and dramatic political changes, either gradual or sudden, can profoundly affect the
government's strength and economic intervention. These include:

---

[1] Cited by Laura Lee, *Bad Predictions: 2000 Years of the Best Minds Making the Worst Forecasts*
(2000). The study mentioned in this introduction is by Mesa-Lago (2000).

• *Major wars.* In contrast to minor armed interventions, such as the Persian Gulf War in 1990 or the Kosovo War in 1999, these usually lead to much greater governmental intervention into the economy, because modern warfare requires an all-out mobilization of resources. This mobilization might take the form, for instance, of rationing consumer goods, directly allocating key raw materials, price controls, or reducing trade openness in order to limit economic vulnerability. The impact of war on the subsequent strength of a government or its economic intervention is, however, much harder to predict. Governments can be strengthened or weakened by war, depending on how the war is fought and whether it is won or lost. Moreover, even during a minor war government strength can be weakened if it makes economic policy blunders, for instance, the U.S. inflation during and after the Vietnam War. The degree of intervention a government retains at the conclusion of a war is also contingent on many different factors.

• *Serious economic downturns.* These and other economic crises can lead to greater intervention by the government in the economy. Nevertheless, it is unclear whether such events strengthen or weaken the government thereafter. This depends, in part, on the economic and social resources at the government's disposal (including coercion) and the effectiveness of its measures to meet the challenges occasioned by these crises.

• *Violent replacement of the current political elites.* This is another extraordinary political event that might lead to dramatic changes in the role of the government in the economic system. These changes can occur either by some type of domestic revolution, such as in China in the late 1940s, or by defeat and occupation, for instance, the occupation of the southern states in the U.S. after the Civil War, which led to the dissolution of their slave-holding system. But such spectacular political events are relatively rare, they are difficult to predict, and their impact on the economic system is indeterminate. Less dramatically, a change in political elites can occur through the electoral process, but again their impact on either the strength or the economic interventions of the government cannot be easily predicted far in advance.

If we focus only on such highly visible political changes, we would quickly reach the limits of responsible prediction about changes in the economic system. But subtle trends that attract little attention might be more important than dramatic changes. For instance, if the population becomes increasingly distrustful of the national government or indifferent to political issues, or if the nation faces a long-term political stalemate, governmental powers could gradually shift to a wealthy economic elite that does have the power to get things done. Or a series of incremental but cumulative changes, such as additional welfare measures for particular population groups or a gradual deregulation of industry, can lead in the long term to a profound alteration of the economic system.

This chapter begins with an analysis of the various types of political events that could influence the government's strength to make and implement economic policies and argues that the most predictable trends point toward a significant weakening of its ability to carry out some current functions of the state. Discussion then turns to some ways the functions of the government are changing, particularly in response to the growing need for internal security. Then I examine some of the forces that might alter the government's present role in the economy, noting that a weakening of the government eventually leads to a reduction in governmental economic intervention. Finally, I explore some of the ways an oligarchic form of government could emerge, formed by the fusion of economic and political elites.

A. Long-term Forces Influencing the Strength of the Government[2]

A number of economic trends that point toward reduced effectiveness of economic policy making by the central government receive discussion in other chapters. For instance, in Chapter 3 I argue that increased globalization eventually leads to a weakening of the government's ability to use monetary and fiscal policy to stabilize the macro-economy. Moreover, the adoption of international rules and standards for trade facilitates international economic flows, but reduces the federal government's capacity to pursue independent micro-economic policies, for instance, special subsidies to enterprises in the "sunrise industries" that will become important in future foreign trade. In Chapter 5 I note that heavier reliance on foreign trade, especially in raw materials, leads to greater vulnerability and sensitivity to economic shocks abroad and to reduced ability of the government to stabilize the economy. Chapter 7 documents the decline of social capital and social trust, and the widening of income differentials, three trends that also influence the government's ability to formulate and implement effectively its economic policies. Finally, Chapter 12 discusses how certain domestic changes have also led to a weakening of the federal government, for instance, the welfare reforms in the mid-1990s which reduced the federal government's automatic fiscal stabilizer, not to mention its direct decision-making powers in welfare policy.

[2]   In the text of this section, I draw on studies by: Anderson (1999), Bell (1987), Bennett (1999), Bernstein and Houston (2000), Blumstein (2000), Delli-Carpini and Keeter (1996), Derlugian (1998), Dionne (1991), Donohue and Levitt (2001), Fox (2000), Freeman and Rodgers (1999), Friman and Andreas (1999), Inglehart, et. al.(1998), Ingraham and Rosenbloom (2000), Joyce (2001), Kaplan (1998), Kappell (2000), Ladd (1999), Levine and Kleeman {1992), Nye, Zelikow, and King (1997), Omae (1995), Park (1998), Pithart, 1996), Putnam (2000), Raphael and Winter-Ebmer (2001), Rosenfeld (2000), Spellman (2000), and Verba, Schlozman, and Brady (1997).

Focusing on more general political factors influencing the strength of the government, three interrelated issues deserve attention: the centrifugal forces at work in modern industrial states, the decline in trust in the government and in political participation, and increasing lawlessness.

1. Centrifugal Political Forces

In the 1990s many nations experienced strong centrifugal forces. Separatist movements gained considerable strength in Scotland, Corsica, Brittany, Lombardy, Wallonia, Catalonia, and the Basque region. Czechoslovakia, the Soviet Union, and Yugoslavia dissolved, creating many new independent nations. This is not all—the historian Georgi Derlugian claims that 60 states around the world face grave and immediate dangers from separatist movements. These centrifugal forces are aided by the falling barriers to international trade: large domestic markets are no longer necessary to achieve economies of large scale production, since large markets can now be obtained more easily through foreign trade. As a result, the economic viability of smaller states is enhanced.[3]

Focusing on the United States, some political observers, such as Ken'ichi Ohmae or Robert Kaplan, argue that regions, not nations, are the key economic units of the future. Kaplan foresees a regional breakup with certain parts of Canada uniting with adjoining parts of the U.S. to create more "natural" economic units, for instance, Cascadia, which would combine British Columbia with the states of Washington and Oregon.

Jonathan Kappell offers an interesting counter-argument. The expansion of the internet makes it increasingly difficult for individual states either to collect sales taxes on goods or services sold over the internet or to enforce other state laws and regulations. This arises because of the difficulties in finding out where the goods and services are actually produced. As a result, the federal government, which has a larger range of power, will be increasingly pressed by the individual states to take over these taxation and enforcement functions, a situation acting to counter centrifugal forces. Chapter 9 analyzes some of the challenges of regulating business in an ever more wired planet.

---

[3]   Even if the U.S. were to break up into regions, this would not necessarily mean the end of liberal capitalism in any of the separate entities. Globalization, measured by such indicators as the ratio of trade to GDP, would increase because these smaller nations would be less self-sufficient. It should be noted, however, that making or maintaining cooperative agreements between nations to structure the world economy might be considerably more difficult. That is, it is easier for international organizations to oversee such agreements in 150 states, of which five are overwhelmingly dominant, than in 500 small states, where such a structural centralization is not found.

I find it difficult to take seriously conjectures about a U.S. political breakup, or, for that matter, to bring systematic social scientific analysis to the subject.[4] Nevertheless, it is important to note that separatist movements usually spring up in the presence of large and distinct areas of ethnic or linguistic segregation. Such segregation can be found in the United States, but only on a micro-scale. The high mobility of the U.S. population precludes the kind of macro-scale segregation that would encourage separatism.

In brief, I do not believe that centrifugal forces pose a significant threat to the economic role of the U.S. government in general, even though many of the powers of the federal government may devolve to the state and local governments. Along these lines, Daniel Bell has argued that currently there is a mismatch in the scale of various political units and the new economic and political problems that they are asked to handle. More specifically, the federal government is too small to solve the emerging big problems of economic life, for instance, those which are international in scope and require a transfer of state sovereignty to some type of international organization. At the same time, the federal government is becoming too big to solve the small problems of economic life, especially those requiring detailed local knowledge, so that in certain areas federal sovereignty must be transferred to the state and local governments.

2. A Decline in Political Participation and Trust in Government

A government can be democratic in form, but its strength depends upon its political legitimacy. This, in turn, requires that the citizens have a certain respect for, and trust in, their government and its laws. No government can easily administer all of its laws, and any decline in voluntary compliance places a heavier economic burden on the private sector to enforce contracts, agreements, and informal understandings with suppliers, customers, and workers. Trust in government is a keystone of a liberal, market system. Moreover, without the trust of its citizens, certain vital governmental functions, such as the collection of taxes, are imperiled.

---

4   One reason is the lack of credible empirical evidence. Although the economic literature has a number of rigorous analyses of the breakup of nations (see, for instance, Alesina and Spolaore (1997) or Bolton and Roland (1997)), these are strictly theoretical. As far as I can determine, no attempt has been made to calculate the parameter values that make so much difference in the outcomes. Although others, such as Bookman (1994) have carried out empirical studies of national breakups, these are ex post case studies and give little attention to the specifics of the U.S. situation. Arguing against the possible breakup of the U.S. are studies like those of Hall and Lindholm (1999), but they basically assume that U.S. political unity is everlasting and provide little persuasive evidence, other than anecdotes, that their assumption is correct.

Václav Havel (cited by Petr Pithart) has pointed to another consequence of this loss of trust in government:

> Civil society encourages ordinary people to participate in government, thereby strengthening relations between citizens and their state.... In a stable democracy it is possible for people to work for the public benefit by doing what the state would normally do, they take on some responsibility of their own.... When citizens detect in politicians a lenient attitude toward improper things or simply evil, they automatically and often subconsciously are encouraged to imitate this.... [Moreover] if one implies that it does not matter whether a certain institution in the constitution should or should not exist, one indirectly encourages citizens to conclude that it does not matter whether or not they pay taxes.

In brief, declining political participation and greater mistrust of government can give rise to two unfortunate outcomes. They can push a vibrant liberal capitalism closer toward the stagnant, gangster capitalism characterizing post-communist Russia in the 1990s; or they can lead to the centralization of power in an oligarchy, so that the economy would be managed for the benefit of a privileged political and economic elite. The latter possibility receives more attention later in this chapter.

Related to these issues is the degree of political participation of the citizenry. A low degree of participation can indicate either indifference or a feeling of helplessness. Neither of these seems consistent either with a vibrant democracy or very successful governmental intervention into the economy. This is because citizen possess local knowledge, which is necessary for the government to utilize if such policies are to be implemented effectively.

Critical questions are, therefore, whether political participation is falling in the United States, and distrust of government is rising. One measure of political participation is the percentage of eligible voters who actually exercise their voting privileges. Voter turnout has varied over U.S. history, ranging from more than 70 percent between 1840 and 1900 to a low of slightly below 50 percent in 1920 and 1924. Chart 8.1 shows that in the second half of the 20th century, a peak in voting participation of 63 percent was achieved in 1960. Thereafter, the voting turnout decreased on an average of 1.4 percentage points each presidential election.

Of course, the percentage of voter participation is partly a function of actual access to the polls, and until the passage of the Voting Rights Act of 1965, African-Americans were systematically barred or discouraged from voting in some southern states. If we add these disenfranchised voters to the total number

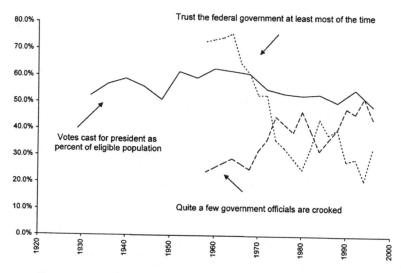

Chart 8.1. Voter Participation and Trust in the Government

Note: Chart 8.1. Trust in the federal government: How much of the time do you think you can trust the government in Washington to do what is right?" The graph combines "most of the time" and "just about always." Are governement officials honest: "Do you think that quite a few of the people running the governemtn are crooked?" The graph refers to those answering "quite a few." The questions are asked in even years and the data are smoothed for the years in between. Sources are listed in Appendix 8.1.

of voters before 1965, the subsequent decline of voter participation would appear even steeper. Although the ebbing voter participation might be interpreted as increasing satisfaction with the current state of political affairs, this would imply a high level of trust in the government. But, as I show below, a majority of Americans do not trust their government.

Political participation, of course, takes many other forms than voting and can involve contribution of time, skills, and money. In a recent book Robert Putnam documents the decline since the early 1960s in citizen interest or knowledge of public affairs, their party identification, their participation in campaign activities, and their civic engagement in political life in a variety of other forms.[5]

An intelligent participation in public affairs requires a knowledge of political issues. By the end of the 20th century, such a grasp of the key issues appeared

---

[5] The National Commission on Civic Renewal employs a similar but less nuanced approach than Putnam in calculating their "index of civic health," which combines 22 indicators. The index

abysmally low—both in absolute terms and in comparison with that in other industrialized nations, as documented by Michael Delli-Carpini and Scott Keeter. For instance, William Bennett documents the depressing fact that in 1999 more Americans could identify which TV show featured Homer, Bart, and Maggie (*The Simpsons*) than could name the Vice President of the United States (Al Gore). Such a lack of necessary knowledge extended even to political elites: for instance, at an early stage in the election campaign for U.S. president in 2000, the winning candidate, George W. Bush, was unable to name the political leaders of Pakistan and India, to distinguish between Slovakia and Slovenia, and to know the correct names of the people living in particular localities such as Greece and Kosovo. Such indifference or intellectual laziness reflects one facet of the rising revolt against rationalism discussed in the previous chapter—a knowledge of political facts is no longer considered essential in politics because only the raw exercise of power is considered important.

Participation in the political campaigns has also changed. Financial contributions to political campaigns have risen but, as Sydney Verba and his coauthors have noted:

> Class matters profoundly for American politics ... [and] as long as citizens increasingly donate money rather than time to politics, the voices heard through the medium of citizen participation will be loud, clear, and far from equal.... When money replaces time as the principal form of political currency, as it is doing in this age where political campaigns are conducted primarily through television, the playing field is no longer level.

What are the causes of this downward trend in political participation? The literature offers various explanations ranging from geopolitical considerations—a

---

shows a 27 percent fall between 1972 and 1994, and then a rapid upturn so that by 1997 it was only 13 percent below the 1972 level (www.pual.umd.edu/civicrenewal/). Data on other types of political participation come from Verba, Schlozman, and Brady (1995), pp. 51 and 72. In this discussion I also draw heavily upon their 1997 article.

Using two different surveys, one in 1967 and the other in 1987, Ladd (1999), p. 102, provides some counter evidence. Unfortunately, the comparability of these two surveys is not clear, and, since Putnam uses consistent series, his evidence seems more credible. On some criteria, such as contacting a member of congress on some issue, Ladd (p. 104) and Putnam (Chapter 5) report such different data and trends that it is difficult to believe they are writing about the same country. Again, however, the polling results cited by Ladd do not seem comparable, in contrast to Putnam's treatment of the data. For yet other indicators of political involvement where Putnam and Ladd show quite opposite trends, both use the same Roper poll data, but Ladd (p. 105) examines a period from 1981 to 1997, while Putnam (Table 1) looks at a longer period, from 1973-74 to 1993-94.

waning sense of national struggle against an external enemy (the USSR)—to personal factors, such as the impact of television and a growing sense of isolation in an increasingly complicated world. To me, however, a key factor is the trust they place in government. If citizens do not believe that election outcomes are important because they place little trust in the government to improve their situation, then they will not bother to vote or to take part in other citizen activities to influence political outcomes of importance to the entire nation. Instead, they might confine their political activities to less public methods to influence policies that have a direct impact on their narrow interests.

Chart 8.1 provides some public opinion data collected by the National Election Studies (NES) on two indicators of public trust toward government. Every four-year period between 1958 and the middle 1990s showed an average decline of 5.5 percentage points in the trust exhibited toward the federal government. In the same time intervals, doubts about the honesty of government officials showed an average rise of 2.4 percentage points in these four-year intervals. The NES also calculates a general index of trust in the government that includes these two questions plus a question asking whether the government is run by a few big interests looking out for themselves (or for all the people) and another question about whether the government wastes much tax revenue. This index of trust in government, running from 0 to 100 percent, decreased an average of 2.5 percentage points during every four-year interval. Equally important, these trends are manifested across all education, income, occupation, and age groups. And, it must be added, long-term trends in trust in other institutions, such as the press, the military, academe, and the medical system were also downward during the second half of the 20th century.[6]

Political scientists and journalists have focused considerable attention on these matters, writing books with such titles as: *Why Americans Hate Politics* (by E. J. Dionne) or *Why People Don't Trust Government* (by Joseph Nye and coauthors). It does not seem accidental that the decline in trust in government was particularly apparent in the decade from the mid 1960s to the mid 1970s, when the Vietnam War and the Watergate scandal took place. An explanation for the failure of such trust to return to its previous levels after 1975 can only be speculative. Possible causes include the increasing partisanship in politics and the gridlock in the federal government. Charles Levine and Rosslyn Kleeman add to this list the declining effectiveness of the federal civil service, as manifested by the high turnover of experienced civil servants. Patricia Ingraham and David Rosenbloom also emphasize that competent administrative practices are not aided by the uncertain rewards for merit for federal employees.

---

[6] Data on trust in other institutions comes from Blendon, *et al.* (1997).

Everett Ladd argues that trust in local government or its departments has been higher than in the federal government. In 1997, for instance, 78 percent of respondents trusted their local fire department "a lot". But that datum becomes less impressive when we notice that, according to the same poll, less than one half extend such trust to their local police department, less than one third to their local schools, and less than one tenth to their state government.

The declining trust in government is an aspect of the more general decline in social trust which, as noted in the previous chapter, leads to a declining effectiveness in government policy making. Some political commentators argue that a growing belief in democratic values and an increasing awareness of the gap between these norms and political reality underlies the declining trust in government. If this smiley-face interpretation is correct, however, it would suggest that participation in political life would be increasing, not decreasing.[7]

The diminished trust in government and the declining levels of political participation have been accompanied by an ever-louder rhetoric of extreme economic individualism. Examples include the increasingly common declarations that the government should have no significant role in the economy, the prominence of identity politics and other single-issue candidates, and the rise of private armies of "patriot groups." Another manifestation of such discontent comes from the World Value Study by Ronald Inglehart and his colleagues, in which 7 percent of Americans told pollsters that significant political change can only come through revolution, a figure unmatched among the OECD countries except in Italy. These political matters receive further discussion in Appendix 8.2.

Given the waning trust in government, certain adverse consequences of this trend deserve some brief documentation, particularly regarding the payment of taxes. Cheating on taxes, which could be one manifestation of distrust toward government, has apparently remained roughly constant. For instance, some estimates suggest that the difference between what citizens declare as their income for tax purposes and what they actually earn remained roughly constant from 1947 through 1996—fluctuating between 9 and 14 percent, but showing little trend over time, accord to the research of Thae Park.[8] Further, no rising tide of

---

[7]   Other counter-arguments to my interpretation about the causal relation between decreasing trust and political participation can be offered. For instance, Citrin (1974) presents cross-tabulations drawn from three presidential elections showing that no linear relation exists between trust in government on the one hand and voting, participation in campaign activities, or attitudes toward various types of political protest on the other. Although the relevance of such cross-section evidence to the long time-series is not entirely clear, such an apparent contradiction points toward the necessity of much greater research on this topic.

[8]   The Park data represent the best estimates of deliberate under-reporting of income that are made by the Bureau of Economic Analysis of the U.S. Department of Commerce. Andreoni,

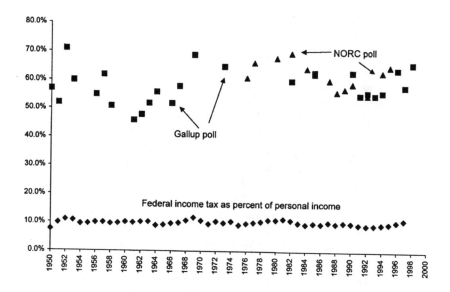

Chart 8.2. Percent of Public Believing Federal Income Taxes are "Too High"

Note: Chart 8.2. "How do you consider the amount of income tax you (or your husband) pay?" The chart records those believing this percent is "too high." The data generally refer to those actually paying the tax and are usually asked in the first three months of the year.

Sources are presented in Appendix 8.1.

discontent about the level of taxes can be observed. For instance, Chart 8.2 shows that the percentage of those believing that federal income taxes are "too high" has remained roughly constant. Changing tax rates do not contaminate these results since the ratio of taxes to income remained roughly constant throughout the period.[9]

Erard and Feinstein (1998) report data based on IRS estimates for the period from 1973 through 1992 that also show a rough constancy, although the level is around 17 percent. Feige (1996) points out, however, that the IRS estimates rest on some fragile assumptions. It is also likely that tax chiseling may increase during the early decades of the 21st century because in the late 1990s the Congress passed legislation making it more difficult for the Internal Revenue Service to pursue tax delinquents as vigorously as in the past.

9   For the Gallup Poll numbers, the trend is upward but the slope coefficient is small and not statistically significant. For the NORC numbers, the time-series is much shorter and shows a downward trend; similarly, the slope is small and not statistically significant.

3. Lawlessness

As noted in Chapter 1, the criminal sector comprises one of the five basic institutional structures defining an economic system. An important indicator of the government's strength is its ability to suppress this sector of the economy.

Measuring the size of the criminal sector raises some obvious difficulties, since much of its activity is deliberately secret. Moreover, other analytic problems arise in deciding what to include in such an estimate and how to assess the economic consequences of criminality. For instance, in addition to the direct costs of crime (e.g., costs of police protection, legal and judicial costs), we must also take into account both the cost to crime victims (e.g., medical bills and lost productivity), the costs of deterrence (e.g., locks, alarm systems), and certain implicit costs (e.g., lost opportunities for constructive activities). One recent estimate by David Anderson places the resource cost in the middle 1990s at more than 13 percent of the GDP. To this must be added illegal transfers (e.g., stolen goods) which he estimated as amounting to more than 7 percent of the GDP in the same year (a figure that does not include income tax evasion). Although we may cavil at the exactness of these calculations, especially the resource cost, its order of magnitude is the crucial feature to note.[10] Clearly the criminal sector has an important impact on both the economy and the economic system.

Has crime been increasing in the past few decades, and how will it change in the future? Chart 8.3 shows that the crime rate, as measured by crimes reported to the police and assembled by the FBI, roughly adjusted for relevant demographic shifts, rose dramatically until the mid 1970s; it then leveled off until 1990, and thereafter began to decline. Furthermore, even the rise in the crime rate in the first part of the period may be less than it appears since the series probably started from an artificially low base.[11] Many questions can be raised about the accuracy of the FBI numbers; and victim statistics are, generally speaking, a more accurate measure of actual crimes committed, since they

---

[10] Anderson cites a number of previous studies which are narrower and consequently yield lower estimates of the costs of crime. One previous study that also takes a broad perspective is that of Laband and Sophocleus (1992). We can extract data from their various calculations to yield a ratio of illegal transfers as a ratio of GDP that has the same order of magnitude as Anderson's.

[11] In the 1950s and 1960s homicides in the U.S. were considerably lower than in many previous decades, especially the 1920s (Graham, 1969), and this may be true for other crimes as well. Unfortunately, the U.S. government did not collect national crime statistics until the 1930s. Nevertheless, Graham estimates that, contrary to expectations, property crimes declined in the early 1930s. Combined with homicide data, this suggests that the overall crime rate was higher in the 1920s than in the early 1950s.

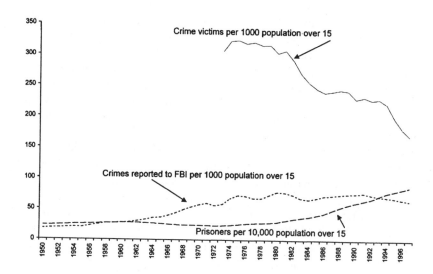

Chart 8.3. Crime and Punishment

Note: Sources and mthods are presented in Appendix 8.1.

reflect the crimes people tell pollsters that were committed against them. Chart 8.3 shows that these crime victimization rates began a significant descent in the late 1970s that continued to the end of the century.

If crime is due to the lack of social capital or social trust or if it reflects economic cleavages, then the trends in crime are puzzling in the light of the trends analyzed in Chapter 7. Has the repressive strength of the government increased sufficiently to offset any such social or economic causes of increased crime?

To gain perspective, it is necessary to begin with the well-known fact that because young men commit a disproportionate number of crimes, the population structure plays a crucial role in the crime rate. If, for instance, the crime rate is calculated as a percentage of the population between 16 through 24, then the FBI crime rate reveals only a small downturn commencing after 1990; and the victimization rates remains relatively level until 1993, when they begin a significant decline. Alfred Blumstein shows that arrest rates for violent crimes of those under 25, who played a crucial role in the run-up of the crime rate in the 1980s, began a dramatic decline after 1993. So the downward trends in Chart 8.3 only partly reflect demographic factors.

It is also critically important to note that a higher rate of incarceration reduces the crime rate, since potential criminals are removed from the streets. At the end of 1999, for instance, slightly more than 2.0 million people (mostly young men) were incarcerated.[12] If the incarceration rate had remained at its 1980 level, so that many more potential criminals were at large and committing one crime a month, then both the FBI and the victimization rates would have risen steadily from 1980 onward. William Spellman estimates the prison expansion in the last quarter of the 20th century reduced the crime rate by about 35 percent.

Other factors have also been advanced to explain the drop in crime, for instance, more police officers and improved policing strategies, decline in the trade of crack cocaine after the late 1980s, and increasing expenditures on crime prevention, such as security guards and alarms.[13] Recently John Donohue and Steven Levitt presented some interesting but controversial evidence that the decline in the published crime rate is also causally related to the legalization of abortion roughly twenty years earlier. They offer three major arguments: the cohort of young men (who commit the most crimes) was smaller; given the characteristics of the women who had abortions, a disproportionate number of this cohort who were most likely to commit crimes were not born; and finally, women were better able to time their childbearing and thus could provide a more nurturing environment for the children that they did bear. If this fascinating hypothesis is correct (some counterevidence is offered by Ted Joyce) such a one-time change in the law reduced the overall level of crime, but the underlying trend would assert itself again and crime would begin to rise from this lower base.

Finally, it should be noted that the availability of employment, especially for young men, can have an effect on crime. Although the relationships between crime and unemployment are difficult to disentangle using time-series data, cross-section studies yield less ambiguous results. In the last quarter of the 20th

---

[12] This datum comes from Department of Justice, Bureau of Justice Statistics (www.ojp.usdoj.gov/bjs/welcome.htm). It can be compared to certain segments of the labor force in the same year. Prisoners numbered more than all independent farmers and farm managers or the combined number of members of the armed forces and state and local police. According to the U.S. Department of Justice, by the end of 1999, 6.3 million people were either in prison or on probation or parole—3.1 percent of all U.S. adults.

[13] My own attempts to use evidence from the various OECD nations to link crime rates with different measures of social capital, trust, and income inequality, while holding constant per capita GDP, the economic size of the nation, and the importance of the trade sector constant, did not prove successful. I suspect that an important reason for this failure lay in my inability to include variables in these regression experiments that reflected police expenditures and incarceration rates.

century, Steven Raphael and Rudolf Winter-Ebmer find that crime rates across states rose as unemployment rates increased, and they attribute about 40 percent of the decline in property crime rates in the 1990s to the fall in unemployment rates. In the last two decades of the 20th century, Richard Freeman and William Rodgers find that across various metropolitan areas at a given point in time, crime per youth (those between 16 and 24) also drop significantly as unemployment fell and from these results estimate that the decline in unemployment between 1992 and 1997 resulted in a 3.9 percent decline in crimes committed by youth. Jared Bernstein and Ellen Houston supply supporting evidence for this conclusion.[14]

In short, the declining trends in crime and victimization in the last decade of the 20th century were, in part, an artifact of a changing population structure, higher rates of incarceration, a fall in unemployment, a one-time change in the number of police and policing practices, and possibly an increase in the number of abortions two decades before.

Predicting future trends in the crime rate is hazardous. Moreover, as Alan Fox shows, two different crime patterns can be found in the U.S.—one for the young and one for the mature—and these have moved in somewhat different directions. Some, such as Richard Rosenfeld, also point to another factor—the decline in intra-family homicides is evidence that the U.S. is becoming more "civilized." This factor, combined with the aging of the population, suggests that we should expect a continued decline in the crime rate. Nevertheless, the continual decline in social capital and social trust, the widening economic cleavages, and the one-time nature of many of the factors underlying the decline in the crime rate in the 1990s suggest that in the future, the crime rate may turn up again.

Several other approaches toward determining trends in criminal activity deserve brief mention. Some economists have tried to estimate the changing size of the underground economy, using a variety of ingenious and indirect measures, primarily related to monetary indicators. Most estimates of this untaxed and unregulated sector of the economy show a slow increase in the share of such illegal activities in the total economy, although the evidence for such a trend is a bit shaky.[15] Activities of international crime syndicates seem to be on

---

[14] Grogger (1998) presents some contrary econometric evidence, showing that criminal activity of young men is not significantly related to unemployment but, instead, is inversely related to wages that they receive or could receive in the marketplace.

Both the studies by Raphael and Winter-Ebmer and by Freeman and Rodgers also find that the crime rate declines as the incarceration rate rises and confirm the results of Spellman cited above.

[15] For instance, data presented by Dixon (1999), Feige (1989-a and 1994), Matera (1985, p. 45) and Porter and Bayer (1989) suggest that the relative share of the underground economy in the

the rise, according to the studies presented by H. Richard Friman and Peter Andreas. Furthermore, as discussed in greater detail in Chapter 12, the spread of the internet has made certain types of shady business practices much easier, including international money laundering, use of offshore tax havens, and setting up private bank accounts in obscure countries to avoid legal and tax liabilities. At the turn of the millennium, very rough estimates of money hidden from legal and tax liabilities in these offshore activities ran into trillions of dollars for the world as a whole.

Yet another approach to track crime trends is to look at indicators of illegal behavior that are less cosmic and easier to measure. For instance, Robert Putnam presents data showing that the share of Americans observing traffic laws decreased in the second half of the 20th century. I also present evidence below showing that governmental corruption appears to have increased in the U.S. in the last few decades of the 20th century. Moreover, incidents of large-scale defiance of legal norms appear in the daily press with increasing frequency, although such anecdotal evidence must be taken cautiously. In 2000, examples of such lawlessness included the noisy and illegal activities of the Cuban-American community in Miami during the imbroglio over the six-year-old Cuban refugee Elián Gonzales and the encouragement by Republican Senators of citizens to break the law requiring them to answer questions for the Census (a law which they themselves had previously voted to enact). One important counterexample of increased lawlessness—the relatively constant rate of income-tax evasion noted above—may be less a manifestation of a respect for laws than a fear of the IRS, at least until the late 1990s when that agency's enforcement powers were reduced.

4. A Brief Summary

Centrifugal political forces are not, in my opinion, a cause for alarm in the U.S. But the ebbing trust in government and the declining personal participation in the political process point toward a weakening of the government's ability to make and implement new laws and policies. Although certain repressive forces of the government have undoubtedly increased, especially its ability to incarcerate lawbreakers, this seems to be primarily a response to a mounting disrespect for the nation's laws and not indicative of the government's ability to formulate and implement effective economic policies.

United States was growing in recent decades. Contrary evidence, however, is provided by Frey and Pommerehne (1982) and Paglin (1994).

In the long run the diminishing trust in government and declining participation citizen participation in political affairs, combined with increased lawlessness and a burgeoning role of money in campaign financing, point to several different outcomes. At best, U.S. capitalism will evolve toward a set of economic institutions presupposing strong distrust between citizens and their government and toward economic policies highly skewed toward maintaining or increasing the advantages of the wealthy. At worst, such social and political trends will lead to decreasing governmental effectiveness, to a decline in democracy, and to a further increase in the political power of a wealthy elite. More evidence is required before a judgement can be made about the possibilities of these or other outcomes, but these possibilities must be seriously considered.

B. Shifting Functions of the State[16]

In some ways the strength of the government has been waning; in other respects it is waxing. But which functions fall into these two categories?

As noted in previous chapters, the government's ability to carry out monetary and fiscal policy to stabilize the macro-economy is weakening, and the combined impact of decreasing social trust and increasing globalization is also impairing the government's effectiveness in micro-economic policy making. As I argue in Chapter 11, government regulation of business has also been diminishing.

On the other hand, as I contend in Chapter 12, public expenditures as a ratio of GDP will probably rise. One segment of such mounting expenditures is for the maintenance of internal security and of the domestic tranquility necessary to allow the nation to compete successfully in the world marketplace. In this brief discussion I focus on two special topics dealing with these latter issues, namely the emerging challenges to ensure internal security and to maintain the government's monopoly of force. Both are crucial factors for determining the oligarchic tendencies in the political and economic system.

1. The Greater Political Salience of Internal Security

As noted above, although the crime rate was falling in the last years of the 20th century, this tendency may be only temporary. Moreover, certain other indi-

---

[16] In this section of the text I mention studies by: Andreas (1999), van Creveld (1991), and the U.S. National Intelligence Council (wwww.cia/gov/cia/publications).

cators of lawlessness were rising. To gain greater perspective, other facets of internal security in the U.S. require attention.

Globalization has brought new problems of enforcing domestic laws. Illegal behavior on an international level, especially through the activities of multinational crime syndicates, appeared to be on the upswing in the 1990s and, in the future, could have an adverse impact on internal security of the U.S. As noted bluntly in the U.S. National Intelligence Council's survey of trends until 2015, in the future "governments will have less and less control over flows of information, technology, diseases, migrants, arms, and financial transactions across ... their borders." To this list we can add endangered species, body parts, babies, prostitutes, pornography, untaxed cigarettes and other goods, antiques, toxic wastes, biological weapons such as anthrax germs, and nuclear materials.

One immediate consequence of these trends is the rising importance of governmental expenditures on law enforcement. As shown in Table 12.2, the share of internal security expenditures in the GDP rose from 0.6 percent in the 1950s to 1.4 percent from 1990 through 1997. Unless some dramatic and unlikely social changes occur, it seems likely that both the size of the criminal sector and the share of total resources devoted to internal security will continue to rise in the coming decades.

Peter Andreas argues that another consequence is that protection of U.S. borders has become a more salient political issue. In important respects the defense of national borders is becoming a police rather than a military function and, according to an oft-quoted aphorism among political scholars, police and criminal justice matters may be regarded as the last bastion of the doctrine of sovereignty. What is important to note is that although the government may be playing a smaller direct role in the economy, this does not necessarily imply a state that is less punitive or has a weaker police. This proposition reflects the distinction between state strength and state functions.

2. A Loss of the Government's Monopoly of Power?

As pointed out in Chapter 4, the number of persons engaged in occupations focusing on the protection of life and property has increased significantly as a percentage of the labor force since the 1960s. Of particular relevance to this discussion, by the mid 1990s the guards and watchmen in the private sector were about equal in number to all police and detectives in the public sector. In the last quarter of the 20th century, these two occupational groups were annually increasing at 4.9 and 1.7 percent respectively. If this trend continues into the 21st century, this private police force would greatly outnumber those in the public sector.[17]

---

[17]   These estimates come from the occupational data base assembled by Pryor and Schaffer (2000).

This prospect, paralleled by the rising power of organized crime and by the types of social breakdown discussed above and in previous chapters, has led some political scientists, such as Martin van Creveld, to a radical conclusion: Governments in the 21st century may lose their monopoly of the use of organized violence and, in consequence, the major threat of warfare for the U.S. will be internal, not external. In particular, the rise of private security groups, paralleled by the considerable power of organized crime and the increasing stridency of particular religious or racial sects, might possibly be accompanied by an increased capability for waging internal warfare, either against each other or the government.

If the government loses its domestic monopoly of power, the economic system might evolve into some type of gangster capitalism of the type witnessed in Russia in the 1990s. This possibility, which I hope is remote, would be accompanied by rising risks to investment, high costs of contract enforcement, and economic stagnation, not to mention much greater inequality of income and wealth.

C. Long-term Political Forces Underlying Governmental Intervention into the Economy[18]

In this overview of political factors affecting the future of U.S. capitalism, it is important to take account not just of the general strength of the government to make and implement policy but also some of the forces that shape these policies, especially with regard to economic activities.

After looking briefly at public opinion data, I consider the possibility that wars and other types of political conflicts might lead to greater governmental intervention into the economy. I focus particularly upon the ideological climate, leaving discussion of more economic concerns to Chapters 11 and 12.

1. Public Opinion Data for Economic Ideologies

As in many economically advanced nations, traditional ideological fervor about the desirability of governmental intervention in the economy has dampened in the U.S. For instance, using public opinion data from eleven countries,

---

[18] In this section of the text, I refer to studies by: Alexander (1999), Bracken (1999), Gurr and Harff (1994), Huntington (1996), Inglehart (1990), Kurth (1994), Mandelbaum (1998-99) Pew Research Center (1998), (1999), Raspail (1975), Sadowski (1998), Sivard (1996), Sunstein (2001), and Wallensteen and Sollenberg (1999).

Ronald Inglehart shows that support for an extensive state role in the economy—redistribution regulation, and ownership of the means of production—is inversely related to the per capita GDP of the nation, with the support for such policies by U.S. respondents scoring particularly low. He attributes this inverse relationship to the emergence of new values (misleadingly called "post-materialist") accompanying economic growth that place less emphasis on economics and more stress on other concerns, such as quality of life. He also shows a considerable decline in "social class voting patterns" from the end of World War II up to 1990 in the U.S. and four other industrialized nations, associated with the rising importance of non-economic political issues that correspond to these new values.

Curiously, even the mounting environmental concerns have not led to greater public support of broad governmental regulation (as opposed to narrowly targeted governmental interventions) in this area. For instance, a Pew Research Center study shows that belief in the general responsibility of government for broad areas of concern in the economy, such as conserving natural resources, actually fell between the early 1960s and the mid 1990s. Indeed, according to a later study by the same group, in the late 1980s anti-state ideologies were sufficiently widespread that more than two fifths of all Americans told survey takers that they consider the U.S. government to be a major threat to the nation's well-being in future decades (with another third believing it a minor threat). In contrast to previous decades, during the 1990s much greater public discussion focused on privatization of services such as road repairs, schools, and parks, which would then be financed by user fees. Such (currently free) services constitute a larger percentage of personal consumption of the poor than the rich and, as a result, they represent an important income transfer to low income families. Any such privatization, if carried out to an extreme, would have a highly regressive impact on the distribution of real income, not to mention a corrosive effect on social solidarity.

The rising importance of anti-state ideologies, however, was not reflected in views about taxation. As shown in Chart 8.2, the level of dissatisfaction expressed about federal taxation by the U.S. public in the second half of the 20th century did not greatly change. In Chapter 12, I discuss in some detail opinion polls focusing on various types of government expenditures, showing that the public was generally satisfied with their current level as well. Further, a considerable body of other public opinion data indicates that Americans generally accept the status quo regarding particular types of governmental intervention into the economy.

From such contradictory data we might conclude that much of the overt anti-state ideology does not mean very much, other than a reflection of the revolt against rationalism and against the necessity of holding consistent political opinions. Furthermore, a strong argument can be made that public opinion does not appear to be an important factor in governmental policy guidelines concerning general economic interventions—in contrast to specific interventions that benefit particular economic interests. For instance, as noted in Chapter 11, no ground swell of public opinion forced the important steps taken in the late 1970s and early 1980s to deregulate the airline or trucking industries.

2. Macro-Political Events Influencing Governmental Intervention into the Economy

Although certain macro-political events such as revolutions are difficult to predict, history teaches some lessons about their consequences. For instance, the combined impact of the Depression in the 1930s and World War II in the first half of the 1940s led not just to an immediate increase in the government's direct role in the allocation of strategic materials and the rationing of civilian goods, but also to price controls and other regulation of industries and to higher federal taxes to help finance the added functions of government.[19] After World War II the U.S. took many decades to reduce much of this increased governmental participation in the economy. The ratio of taxes and government expenditures to the GDP never returned to the level of the 1930s. And the economic system moved, instead, to a higher plateau of government involvement. It seems likely that any serious downturn in the economy would again bring an escalation of governmental intervention in the economy.

Wars and their economic impact are harder to predict, but the subject is too important to be passed over, even if firm answers cannot be given. It is useful to begin by reviewing briefly some statistics of armed conflict in the second half of the 20th century.

Traditional wars, where one country invades another for such a straightforward goal as gaining territory (often historically disputed between them), became relatively infrequent. For instance, Ruth Sivard lists 142 wars occurring from 1950 through 1995, of which, only about 15 percent might be so classified as "traditional." The remaining conflicts in her list were civil wars (with or without foreign intervention), wars of independence, bloody civic repressions, or various types of ethnic or political armed struggles. A more inclusive counting of armed struggles by Peter Wallensteen and Margareta Sollenberg for the period from 1989 through 1998 includes 92 intra-state armed conflicts with no foreign intervention, nine intra-state armed conflicts with foreign intervention, but

---

[19] This thesis about public expenditures and taxes, originally propounded by Peacock and Wiseman (1961), admits of some exceptions and, furthermore, is incorrect in a number of details (as argued in Pryor (1968)). Nevertheless, it provides an important clue in understanding the rise in the ratio of government expenditures to the GDP after World War II in many countries.

only seven inter-state armed conflicts. Of growing significance in the 20th century annals of war were inter-ethnic conflicts. Ted Gurr and Barbara Harff show that from 1950 through the mid 1990s, the number of such conflicts, as manifested by armed rebellions, quadrupled. Nevertheless, from about 1994 to the end of the century, ethnic protests (both peaceful and violent) and armed rebellions declined. This apparent turning point in 1994 admits, at least at this early stage, of quite varying interpretations.[20]

Contrary to the cliché, dating at least as far back as Immanuel Kant, world trade does not necessarily bring about world peace.[21] For instance, Germany invaded or fought against its largest trade partners in both world wars. I doubt that the presence of multinational enterprises in potentially belligerent countries can do much to head off future conflicts. If the experience during World War II is any indication (for instance, the German division of IT&T actively aided the Nazi war effort), the branches of multinational enterprises located in enemy countries generally cooperate fully with the jurisdiction in which they are located in order to protect the ownership interests of their stockholders.

Michael Mandelbaum argues that the international political situation in the 21st century, nevertheless, appears qualitatively different from that in previous centuries for several reasons. He lists the rapidly increasing globalization in the last quarter of the 20th century; the rising costs of a major war in terms of casualties and property destruction, and the smaller rewards in victory as particularly important. To this list should be added the deliberate attempt by the architects

---

[20] Information about the frequency of armed conflicts before and after 1994 was supplied by Ted Gurr (personal communication). The three most plausible interpretations are themselves contradictory: First, the late 1990s represent merely a breathing spell in the quest for ethnic self-determination. The analysis of Brzezinski (1993) lends considerable support to this view. Second, various domestic groups are beginning to realize that they can no longer play off the U.S. and the U.S.S.R. against each other to leverage their own (weak) political power and quest for independence. Or third, the world has reached some sort of equilibrium in which minorities are coming to appreciate the advantages of not taking the route of complete independence; witness, the Scottish nationalists who talk about an independent Scotland within a European Union. This latter phenomenon may, however, be limited only to industrialized nations.

[21] According to Kant (1967 (1795), First Supplement): "Nations ... united because of mutual interest. The spirit of commerce, which is incompatible with war, sooner or later gains the upper hand in every state. As the power of money is perhaps the most dependable of all the power ... states see themselves forced, without any moral urge, to promote honorable peace and by mediation to prevent war wherever it threatens to break out." Several years later the Napoleonic wars broke out! Kant's proposition has been repeated often thereafter, only to be dashed by the cold fact that wars have winners and losers and for the winners, the net benefits may be considerable, even though the benefits to the entire system are negative. Kant's doctrine was updated in the latter part of the 20th century—no two nations with McDonald's franchises would go to war. Unfortunately, the troubles in Yugoslavia in the 1990s belied this optimism.

of many international organizations and the diplomats negotiating agreements between nations to create unbreakable bonds. This was, for instance, explicitly stated in the formation of the European Union (EU). In creating this thickening web of political, economic, and social connections between industrialized nations, the negotiators of the new international institutions have paid great attention to dispute resolution mechanisms to avoid armed conflicts. Although the ultimate success of these efforts remains to be seen, I can find no credible evidence suggesting that disagreements between the U.S. and other industrialized nations would lead to armed conflict between them.[22] Insofar as peace encourages trade and other economic interchanges, globalization—at least between industrialized nations—will continue.

But the potential for armed conflict between industrial nations (the "North") and the poorer nations (the "South") is greater, and this issue deserves attention. Some commentators, such as Samuel Huntington, have hypothesized a titanic North-South armed conflict between Christian industrialized nations and some sort of grand alliance of nations representing Confucian and Islamic civilizations. This hypothesis has been sharply criticized, for instance, by James Kurth; and I myself find the scenario improbable.[23] Some also argue that globalization increases the possibility of inter-ethnic war as dissonant cultures come into closer contact or as the wave of democratization (in part, independent of globalization) in the 1970s and 1980s reduced many of the restraints that authoritarian regimes had previously imposed to suppress inter-ethnic strife. Although some examples of the latter can be cited, for instance, the inter-ethnic conflicts in Yugoslavia in the 1990s that had previously been suppressed by President Tito, Yahya Sadowski uses cross-national data to show that the evidence supporting such propositions is weak.

The problem for the U.S. lies elsewhere. The most likely armed conflicts involving the U.S. are interventions to achieve particular political goals. From

---

[22] Mandelbaum (1998-9) also emphasizes that democracies are less likely to wage war against each other than other nations, and democratic political arrangements are spreading throughout the planet. But some dark clouds are on the horizon, and armed conflicts are certainly possible in the coming decades, for instance, between Greece and Turkey over Cyprus, between India and Pakistan over Kashmir, between any number of countries in the Middle East, or even between the U.S. and a resurgent and highly nationalistic Russia (or China). Certainly the American public is not optimistic about peace. According to a Pew Research Center survey (1999), 37 percent of Americans believed that in the next fifty years a nuclear war involving the U.S. will definitely or will probably happen.

[23] Indeed, the reverse may be more likely: that some governments in the developing world may not want much contact with the West, because of its secular influences. It is possible that a two-tiered international system may evolve, with ever increasing internationalization and globalization between the industrialized nations and relatively fragile bonds between developing countries, who may often be at war.

1950 through 1989 the U.S. fought two medium-scale wars (Korea and Vietnam) and, in addition, about once a year sent troops or military assistance to foreign conflicts.[24] From 1990 through 1995, such military actions increased to about three a year. At least in the early stages of the unipolar world arising from the collapse of the Soviet Union, U.S. military interventions in the third world increased in the 1990s. Whether the new presidential administration in 2001 will implement its stated intention to halt this trend remains to be seen. In brief, U.S. involvement in various military actions in the second half of the 20th century has been a deliberate, not defensive, political act. The key question for the 21st century is whether the U.S. wishes to continue this role as global policeman, especially for humanitarian purposes against genocide in "faraway countries about which we know nothing."

These medium-scale wars may have only medium-term effects on the U.S. economy—witness the inflation and ballooning of U.S. governmental debt as a result of the Vietnam war, which, however, were halted by the end of the 1970s. In fact, no armed conflict since World War II has had any significant and long-lasting impact on the U.S. economic system *per se*. At the beginning of the new millennium, no developing nation is likely to start a war against an industrialized nation, if only because of the superior firepower of the latter, unless such military action can be carried out by terroritst tactics that make it impossible to determine the perpetrator (such as poisoning a water reservoir).[25]

But nagging qualms remain. John Alexander argues that in the future, the military balance in the world may tip away from the United States, not only because of nuclear proliferation but also because relatively poor states may acquire relatively inexpensive biological and chemical weapons. As a result, future international conflicts between any states, rich or poor, may result in greater loss of life and property damage than in the 20th century. For instance, in 1998 during political disputes between Taiwan and China, a handful of computer hackers from the former country are said to have crippled 360,000 computers in the latter country in a few days, inflicting an estimated $120 million in damages.[26] And the future of cyber-terrorism looks worse—for instance, Cass Sunstein notes that the love-bug virus caused an estimated $10 billion damages worldwide.

---

[24] In many cases such intervention was to assist the evacuation of civilians, but in other cases more direct combat was involved. The data in the text are drawn from a list by Grimmett (1996). I have counted as "one military action" several military efforts occurring in the same country in the same year,

[25] The nightmare scenario conjured up by Jean Raspail (1976), I believe, a low probablility, namely millions of third world immigrants simply arriving by sea and inundating any industrial nation unable to ship some of them back and too morally scrupulous to massacre them.

[26] *The Economist,* October 30, 1999, p. 46.

In analyzing the growing war-making potential of 21st century Asian nations, Paul Bracken points out that in the early 1990s Iraq, normally considered a ninth-rate military power, accumulated at least 157 germ bombs for delivery by aircraft, artillery and short range rockets. Of the 25 germ warfare missiles, 16 contained botulinum toxin; 5, anthrax; and 4, aflatoxin, which causes long-term liver cancer. Such a potential for warfare means that nations like Iraq will be less vulnerable to Western influences and more assertive of their own national aims.

It should also be noted that international crime syndicates, which, as noted above, appear to be growing in importance, would have considerable incentive to divert attention from their own activities by helping to supply domestic terrorists with some of these non-conventional weapons. Leaving aside possible apocalyptic results, such warfare, either against an external or internal enemy, would obviously increase investment risks and, very likely decrease economic growth. Various aspects of globalization—particularly foreign trade and international flows of capital or labor—would be adversely affected as well.

In cases of considerable property damage or loss of life in the U.S., governmental expenditures—particularly for security—would undoubtedly increase. Nevertheless, it is difficult to see any compelling mechanisms that would link these impacts to any other major change in the economic system *per se*. In most such cases of domestic terrorism, it seems more likely that the increasing central governmental powers would be augmented in the political, not economic, sphere. As previously noted, it is quite possible to have a police state coexisting with a liberal capitalist economic system.

By way of contrast, wars between non-industrial nations or civil strife within them seem highly likely to continue for many decades in the future. This is because struggles over fertile land, raw materials and other environmental concerns have high political salience, especially since most in these nations are dependent upon agriculture and natural resource production.[27] For instance, because water usage is growing considerably faster than the population in these developing nations, serious conflicts over water rights are clearly looming on the horizon; witness, the current difficulties between Syria and Turkey over waters from the Euphrates, between Israel and her neighbors over control of the headwaters of the Jordan River, or between Namibia and

---

[27] Those analyzing the relation between environmental pressures and war include Gleick (1993) and Homer-Dixon (1991). Kaplan (1994) has a more lurid version of the same argument. For a useful small-scale case study, see Durham (1979), who analyzes the "soccer war" between El Salvador (one of the most densely populated nations in the world), and Honduras. He emphasizes, however, that much of the land scarcity underlying this brief conflict was the result of an increasing inequality of land distribution and not overpopulation per se.

Botswana over the Okavango River.[28] Pressures on farm land can arise either from overpopulation or from destruction of previously used land through environmental neglect, such as flooding or soil erosion due to deforestation. Uncontrollable emigration from land-scarce nations can also lead to international conflict; one such flashpoint in the future might be Assam, because of Bangladeshi migration to India. Other sources of armed conflict, either inter- or intra-state, arise from the breakdown of fragile governments in the third world, for instance, in the late 1990s, the situation in the Angola, Congo, Liberia, and Sierra Leone.

At first sight it is difficult to imagine that any major conflicts in the Third World would have a significant impact on the U.S. economic system. But could the U.S. government allow itself to be sucked into these disputes in a manner that eventually required the commitment of massive resources? This could occur in cases of states closely allied to the U.S., such as Israel, Saudi Arabia, South Korea, Taiwan, or Turkey, were attacked; or if U.S. foreign bases were threatened; or if some raw materials vital to the U.S. strength, such as oil, were at stake. Unfortunately, too many possibilities are open to make any kind of useful prediction.

3. A Brief Summary and an Hypothesis

At the end of the 20th century U.S. citizens seemed to be discontented in a general way with their government, manifested by such symptoms as a loss of trust in government, lower political participation, and strident expression of anti-state beliefs. Nevertheless, public opinion data concerning specific measures show little support for a dramatic political overhaul. Other things being equal, it does not seem likely that the degree of governmental intervention into the economy will radically alter in the coming decades, short of an unexpected economic crisis or a major war, neither of which can be responsibly predicted. Nevertheless, one important proposition deserves consideration because certain other things do not remain equal.

In the previous chapter I present evidence that the effectiveness of governmental action will decline because it depends, in part, on social capital, which itself is on the wane. As the government's strength—its ability to make and implement policy—diminishes in the economic sphere, its interventions will become less effective. The government will also become less able to coordinate

---

[28] The current international disputes over water are discussed in various publications of the Green Cross International (http://www.gci.ch/).

its various interventions and to enforce the measures it will undertake. As the interventions prove less and less effective, the political forces supporting them also tend to weaken. As a result the government will experience a downward spiral of increasing impotence and decreasing legitimacy.

In brief, it seems likely that the incremental but cumulative changes discussed above point toward a diminution of the role of the government in the economy. Such hidden and gradual change will probably have a more important long-term impact on U.S. capitalism than any specific event or dramatic change in public opinion.

D. The Rise of Oligarchy?[29]

It is useful to consider briefly some extreme political outcomes that would undoubtedly change the economic system. In Appendix 8.2 I briefly discuss two possibilities, tyranny and social revolution, neither of which I consider very likely. In this section, however, I consider a more likely possibility, namely the rise of a political-economic oligarchy.

As suggested above, the declining public interest in public affairs and the swelling influence of money in political campaigns can strengthen the political power of an economic elite. Such a development can also exacerbate governmental corruption (see below), especially when combined with a diminished respect for government and its laws, declining social capital, and ebbing social trust. If governmental regulations and laws can be molded to the advantage of the ruling elite and its allies, considerable incentives are given to gaining wealth through political influence (called "rent seeking" by economists), rather than productive economic activity.

Rent seeking is aided by greater contact between business and governmental elites, and the boundary between these spheres is becoming more porous. Special forums are being established for the elite of both spheres to mingle with each other, away from the glare of publicity (for instance, at the annual World Economic Forum in Davos, Switzerland). Corporations are also stepping beyond their customary lobbying for tax or licensing privileges. For instance, when the Microsoft Corporation was facing an antitrust suit from the Department of Justice in early 1999, Thomas Friedman reports that the company hired several firms to lobby the Congress to reduce by 7.9 percent the funding of the Department's Antitrust Division in fiscal 2000, in order to hobble its enforcement efforts. This

---

[29] This section of the text refers to studies by: Friedman (2000), Goel and Nelson (1998), and Gramsci (1977 (1916)).

is, of course, a type of "clean-hand corruption," where no money overtly flows from the corporation to government officials.

We cannot tell if clean-hand corruption became more common in the last part of the 20th century, but it certainly appears that dirty-hand corruption was. More specifically, according to the statistics of Rajeene Goel and Michael Nelson, successful prosecution of corruption cases rose steadily from 1975 through 1991 on all levels of government, but especially on the federal level. Assuming that actual corrupt practices parallels the frequency of such prosecution (or the willingness of juries to convict), then economic policy making was, in fact, becoming dirtier.

Is the U.S. any more corrupt than other nations? In an international "Perception of Corruption Index," which covers 85 nations and is derived from opinion polls of business people dealing with governments, in 1998 the U.S. ranked as having the 17th most honest government. This seems relatively reassuring—until we note that the U.S. scored 7.5 on a scale running from zero (highly corrupt) to ten (highly honest).[30]

Although the economic impact of clean-hand corruption has not yet been measured,[31] dirty-hand corruption can have some serious consequences for the economic performance of a nation, since it diverts resources from productive investment in fixed capital, research and development, and worker training into other pockets. Various cross-country comparisons suggest that corruption leads to lower investment rates, lower GDP growth rates, lower governmental expenditures on health and education, and reduced productivity of public investment.[32]

For the government to change from informal oligarchic control and corruption to a more formalized (and authoritarian) structure, certain political, economic, and social conditions must be fulfilled. In particular, the political side of such a systemic change requires an intensification of the trend toward the withdrawal of active citizen participation from political life. As Antonio Gramsci has noted:

---

[30] The web site of Transparency International (http://www.transparency.de/) provides more information. Tanzi (1998) presents data on country rankings for the four years that the index has been calculated. The U.S. rating did not greatly change over this short period.

[31] There are, of course, thousands of anecdotes about such practices. For instance, the U.S. Congress created the Foreign Sales Corporation (later declared by the WTO to represent an illegal income tax subsidy for exports) to provide a countermeasure for the practice by various European nations of not collecting value-added tax on exports. The FSCs allowed domestic U.S. firms to avoid roughly $4 billion in taxes, with the Boeing Corporation, which has lobbied hard to retain the program, being one of the largest beneficiaries (Mannusson, 2000). In the discussion in Chapter 12 about the so-called tax-expenditures, I try to quantify the magnitude of some of these special tax favors.

[32] Mauro (1995) has a particularly interesting empirical study of this issue. Tanzi (1998) summarizes the literature linking corruption to various economic performance indicators.

Indifference is actually the mainspring of history. But in a negative sense. What comes to pass, either the evil that afflicts everyone or the possible good brought about by an act of general valor, is due not so much to the initiative of the active few as to the indifference, the absenteeism of the many. What comes to pass does so not so much because a few people want it to happen, as because the mass of citizens abdicate their responsibility and let things be.... The destinies of an epoch are manipulated in the interests of ... the immediate ends of small groups of activists.

The economic requirements for greater oligarchic control include an increasing dominance of production by a small number of very large firms and increasing monopolization of individual markets. These structural changes in the economy appear to be happening and are the focus of empirical investigation in Chapters 9 and 10. Under an oligarchy the government would serve primarily as a handmaiden to elite groups, it would spend lavishly on measures to maintain domestic order. And it would dole out only sufficient social welfare funds to the rest of the population that would be needed to prevent popular discontent from reaching dangerous levels.

E. A Final Word

From general political considerations discussed above, it seems likely that both the government's ability to make and implement policy and its specific interventions into most aspects of the economy are likely to decrease in the first half of the 21st century. Under certain circumstances declining trust in government and reduced political participation could lead either to the government's loss of its monopoly of power, anarchy, and a type of gangster capitalism *à la russe*, or to the replacement of democracy by some type of oligarchy, where a small economic elite will manipulate the levers of power behind the facade of a formal democratic structure.

To attach probabilities to these possibilities, we need to look more carefully at the changing institutions and organizations of both the private and public sectors. These are the focus of the analysis in the next four chapters.

F. Important External Factors Influencing the Future of U.S. Capitalism: A Wrap-up

The last three chapters focus on causal factors external to the U.S. economy that will have an important influence of the future of U.S. capitalism. I make the following major arguments:

• Other things equal, it does not seem likely that either rising agricultural and raw material prices or increasing pollution will have a major effect on the future economic system, even though economic performance may be adversely affected (Chapter 6).

• Other things equal, social trust and social capital will continue to decline and have an important and adverse impact on the future effectiveness of economic institutions and organizations. Cultural factors, however, will have less impact on the functioning of the economy or economic system (Chapter 7).

• Other things equal, the declining trust in government and decreasing political participation will lead to less effectiveness of governmental economic policy making (Chapter 8).

Any adverse shock to the economy from environmental, raw material, or agricultural factors will have a particularly heavy impact on the real income of those with the lowest income. The decline of social capital and trust will raise transactions costs and expenditures for domestic security, and, moreover, will increase difficulties in reaching a political consensus necessary for effective governmental economic policies. The attitudes toward government, combined with its declining effectiveness, will strengthen those forces pushing our political system toward an economic-political oligarchy. Large scale wars and/or economic crises will lead to greater governmental participation in the economy.

CHANGES IN CRUCIAL
ECONOMIC INSTITUTIONS
AND ORGANIZATIONS

CHAPTER 9

Evolution of Business Enterprises

[In the 20th century] capital may fight shy ... of [investing in] vast corporations and business aggregations ... [as] top heavy and cumbersome.[1]

—*Journalist Bill Nye 1893*

We find no dearth of predictions about the future of the corporation, or, more generally, the business enterprise. Many such forecasts, either of changes in its internal structure or its place within the entire economic system, are based on considerations of technology and the alleged economies of large scale production. Some futurists, influenced by such works as Aldous Huxley's *Brave New World* or George Orwell's *1984*, foresee that technology will push the economic system toward a radical centralization: A handful of very large enterprises will operate on a worldwide scale and will dominate both the economy and the government. Others, such as Norman Macrae foresee that technology will have the reverse impact: The importance of scale of production will decline so that small firms will be more than able to compete successfully against the mega-corporations. Still others, such as Peter F. Drucker, approach the future of the business enterprise from the standpoint of management: Since the effectiveness of knowledge workers will be the key to future business success, they will have to be given more power in corporate decision-making to keep them motivated, corporate hierarchies will become flatter and more decentralized, and enterprises may, perhaps, become smaller as dissatisfied specialists leave to start their own firms.[2] Some, such as John Bryne, even go so far as to

---

[1] Cited in Dave Walter, *Today Then: America's Best Minds Look 100 Years into the Future on the Occasion of the 1893 World's Columbian Exposition* (1992). In the text of this section I mention studies by Bryne (1999), Drucker (1999-b), Macrae (1984), (1994), and Scholes (1998).

[2] A survey I conducted of American corporate executives (1996, pp. 128–36) showed a curious result: Although 40 to 50 percent of their corporations had carried out decentralizing measures in the previous decade, such as creating more profit centers (so that individual executives have more decision-making power and are held responsible for the profits and losses of their units),

speak of leaderless corporations, with management tasks carried out by teams of equals.

Still others, using corporate finance as the predictive key, foresee the possible demise of the traditional corporation. For instance, in his Nobel Prize acceptance speech, Myron S. Scholes argued that, in the future, corporations will not need to raise capital by issuing stock to the general public, since they will be able to obtain these funds more easily by employing new risk management instruments, such as specialized derivatives, that do not involve an ownership interest. By such techniques, the managers can leverage their original ownership stake and corporate ownership will become more concentrated. These new "synthetic entities" will replace the current corporate form.[3] Others argue that improved cash management and inventory management techniques will also reduce the capital needs of large corporations.

Of the various issues surrounding the future of business enterprise, I focus in this chapter on the average size (defined in terms of labor force) and the size distribution of business enterprises. This provides the most direct picture of the organizational framework in which other problems, such as management, corporate governance, finance, and ownership, will play themselves out. Further, it also allows both economic theory and data to be applied to the problem in a systematic fashion.

A focus on enterprise size, moreover, also allows us to discuss some important impacts of size on the functioning of the organization. For instance, research over the last few decades suggests that both patented inventions and innovations generally increase less than proportionately to firm size, so that larger firm size may result in a slowdown in technological advance.[4] Work satisfaction, measured both by surveys and also by behavioral measures (such as

---

only about 20 percent expected that more such measures would be taken in the next decade. In contrast to the futurists, the executives believed that they had, by and large, already met the organizational challenges of the future.

[3] Scholes' approach toward corporate finance assumes a degree of financial skill which few managers seem to possess, witness, the spectacular failures of some hedge funds that have followed his approach. The most notable instance was the Long-Term Capital Management which, in September 1998, was about to default on its margin calls. The company had been able to leverage its original capital of roughly $5 billion to purchase securities valued at roughly $125 billion and, reportedly, had entered into derivatives contracts with notional value which was far greater. It was bailed out by an injection of about $3.6 billion from various creditor banks. Myron Scholes, was a principal and co-founder of the firm.

[4] Such studies include those of Acs and Audretsch (1991-a), (1991-b), and Scherer (1965). In the rest of this paragraph I draw on research by Davis and Haltiwanger (1995), Dunn (1982), Lang and Johnson (1994); Scherer (1976), Schmidt and Zimmermann (1991), and Shepard and Hougland (1982).

rates of absenteeism), appears greater in both small plants (establishments) and firms than in larger production units. Wage differentials are also smaller than in large establishments and enterprises, so that the size distribution of enterprises has an impact on the size distribution of income. Giant corporations may also be "too large to fail," which, for instance, suggests that governments may have to bail out some of them, which they would never do for smaller firms. Some also argue that the employment of an ever larger share of the labor force by a small number of giant firms concentrates political power and increases the likelihood of special interest legislation, a conjecture which, however, is difficult to test.[5]

Unfortunately, the basic data on the changing size distribution of business enterprises are not very satisfactory. In the past, the necessary facts for informed discussion were lacking, which may explain why speculations about the future size of business enterprise have varied so widely. After developing some comparable data series, I show, for instance, that enterprise size, measured in terms of labor force, is likely to increase in the future.[6]

After briefly reviewing some conflicting forecasts about the distribution and average size of enterprises by some leading economic theorists, I look at the merger boom in the last decade and a half of the 20th century, a phenomenon which seems to confound all of these theories. Then, I present measures of enterprise (firm) and establishment (plant) size to determine which other aspects of the leading theories of firm size provide insight into the underlying causal forces. From the factual basis of this historical analysis, I turn to predictions about the changing size of enterprises. The next chapter examines developments in industrial structure and market competition. Together, the two chapters provide crucial evidence about the possible evolution in the U.S. to an oligarchic economic system.

---

[5]   Much of the evidence comes from case studies of particular types of legislation (e.g., Vogel's (1982) study of air pollution legislation), and considerable disagreements arise about how the results should be interpreted. Clearly the impact of enterprise size on legislation depends to a large degree upon the type of laws under consideration, so that the general proposition needs to be qualified.

[6]   Throughout this discussion, I do not distinguish between enterprises with different legal forms since, for my purposes, the distinction is not important. At the end of the 20th century the privately-owned corporation was the dominant organization for production of goods and services. According to national account statistics (Table 1.15), from 1950 to 1998, the corporate share of the total national income rose from 56 to about 61 percent. The national income originating from sole proprietorships, partnerships, and other business forms declined correspondingly.

A. Some Current Theories about Evolving Enterprise Size[7]

Although a number of theories help us understand why the size distribution of enterprises differs from one industry than another, few focus on the size distribution for the economy as a whole. Most economic theories focus primarily on either economies of large scale production or the impact of technology, two related approaches that lead to quite different predictions.

1. Are Marx and Schumpeter Right about Economies of Scale?

Economists in the Marxist tradition hold that enterprises are becoming ever larger and, moreover, the largest enterprises are accounting for an ever larger share of production. The argument is based on the assumption that, at any point in time, economies of large scale production are very large and that, over time, these become increasingly important because of technological change. Thus, large firms always have lower average costs and higher profits than smaller firms. As Karl Marx stated in vivid terms, "One capitalist always kills many ... [and] along with the constantly diminishing number of the magnates of capital ... grows the mass of misery, oppression, slavery, degradation, exploitation."

Joseph Schumpeter added credibility to this assertion by arguing that enterprise administration, particularly for research and development, featured particularly important economies of scale. More specifically, only the large, oligopolistic firms can finance a satisfactory R and D program leading to new technological discoveries to maintain or increase market share. (As noted above and discussed below, the evidence for this proposition is weak). From such a standpoint he argued that large enterprises tend to become ever larger over time, both in absolute terms and as a share of total production (relative terms).

Empirical evidence on the relative and absolute size of productive units over time provides some support for this proposition about large economies of scale. For instance, as I have documented elsewhere[8], the share of total manufacturing assets owned by the 100 largest manufacturing firms in the U.S. did not greatly change from 1909 to the late 1940s. Thereafter, according to the evidence pre-

---

[7]   In the text in this section I cite studies by: Acs and Audretsch (1990), (1991-a), (1991-b), Audretsch (forthcoming), Brynjolfsson *et al.* (1994), Carlsson, *et al.* (1994), Davis, Haltiwanger, and Schuh (1996), Dosi (1988), DuBoff (1989), Ijiri and Simon (1977), Marx (1912), Pryor (1973), Pryor (2001-a), Quandt (1966), Scherer (1965), (1991), and Sutton (1997), (1998).

[8]   Pryor (1973).

sented by Richard DuBoff, this percentage rose rapidly from 40 to 50 percent by the end of the 1960s and continued slowly upward for the next several decades thereafter. The percentage of the labor force in manufacturing establishments (plants) over 1000 employees also doubled between 1909 and the early 1960s and, presumably, the average absolute size of manufacturing enterprises (firms) increased even faster.[9]

Nevertheless, evidence to demonstrate a relation between research and development expenditures and enterprise size seems weak. Various economists, such as F. M. Scherer or Zoltan Acs and David Audretsch, show that in most industries, the ratio of R and D expenditures to sales is roughly constant among firms over most of the size range. Acs and Audretsch also present evidence that in recent decades innovative activity per employee has actually been greater in small firms than in large.

It should be added that Marx and Schumpeter could be right about the growing importance of large firms, but for reasons quite different from economies of large scale production or administration. For instance, globalization and the increasing importance of exports in the U.S. economy provide an important impetus for the growth of large firms, since they are more able to produce and sell in an expanding world market. This proposition receives statistical support by Erik Brynjolfsson and his coauthors. To increase the size of a firm, mergers appear to offer the fastest and often safest possibility, especially when foreign production facilities are involved. This is because the purchasing company can presumably take advantage of the expertise and business contacts of the acquired company, rather than going through a painful learning process, although in reality (for instance, the Daimler-Chrysler merger) this is not always the case. Top corporate executives have yet another incentive to merge their firm with others since their total compensation, not to mention their personal power, is strongly correlated with the size and growth of their companies. Thus, these managers have special incentives to expand their firms and fulfill Marx's predictions, even though shareholders do not necessarily gain by these actions.

---

[9] Generalizing about the average size of manufacturing establishments is tricky because the size distribution is so skewed. In recent years the average size of establishments with more than 19 workers barely changed. Averages which place greater statistical weight on larger establishments have increased. Further, changes in the sectoral composition of production within manufacturing also markedly affect the results. These matters are discussed in detail by Pryor (1973, Chapter 5).

I have been unable to locate comparable statistics of enterprise size over the first half of the century that are suitable for my purpose. However, it seems likely that their average size increased faster than that of establishments since falling costs of communication, especially as a result of the spread of the new information technology of the period (for instance, the telephone) lowered the expenses of managing a multi-establishment firm.

2. Is Gibrat Right about Dynamic Random Processes?

In the 1930s Robert Gibrat, a French engineer, analyzed the size distribution of firms in terms of a dynamic process whereby the percentage growth of any firm is random and is also independent of its original size so that economies of scale play no role. This approach has given rise to an extensive literature reviewed by John Sutton. When played out over time, this process of random change yields an increasingly skewed distribution of firm sizes. According to simulations using this approach, the median enterprise size remains the same, but a rising share of the labor force is employed by the largest firms, as Marx predicted.

Unfortunately, such a simple theoretical result is complicated by several facts. First, Gibrat's basic assumption about the independence of growth and firm size has been fiercely attacked, for instance, by Steven Davis and his coauthors. In particular, it is more difficult for large firms to maintain the same percentage growth than small firms. Furthermore, new firms are born and old firms die, which complicates any time-series analysis. Although some economists such as Yuji Iriri and Herbert Simon or John Sutton have built various dynamic effects into the model, this makes the final conclusions more problematic because with the proper assumptions, almost any result about changes in the size distribution of firms can be obtained. Furthermore, as Richard Quandt has forcefully pointed out, it is very difficult to test any of these hypotheses, even with data for individual firms, because determining which type of distribution is reflected best by the data requires very fine statistical distinctions that seldom can be made. Such a task becomes impossible when the enterprises are grouped into a small number of size categories, the usual form in which the government presents such raw data. Finally, some of Gibrat's conclusions for the long-term have been challenged, for instance, that a rising share of the labor force will be working for the 100 or 1000 largest enterprises.

3. Will Information Technology Reduce Firm Size?

Some economists analyzing the impact of information technology argue that changes of firm size should be approached in terms of the falling cost of collecting, processing, and analyzing information. Starting from the notion that enterprises are essentially information-processing entities, enthusiasts foresee the "coming of the new organization" or the "second industrial divide."[10] The

---

[10] In the popular business media this kind of discussion has a particularly lyrical tone. For instance, *Business Week* (August 28, 2000, p. 87) informs us that the 21st century corporation,

key to their argument is the hypothesis (or assertion) that the lower information costs decrease the minimum efficient size that enterprises need to be competitive and, as a result, average firm size in the nation will fall. If large firms are more likely to introduce this new technology, then the share of the labor force working in these large firms should decrease.

At this point of the discussion we need to proceed carefully because lower information costs can have offsetting impacts on the overall economies of scale of a firm. The most convincing argument supporting the hypothesis that falling information costs will lead to a smaller average size of production units refer to establishments (plants):

• The new information technology has reduced the specificity of capital, which means that the same machine can be used for multiple purposes in the production process. In other words, capital equipment has become more flexible. As Giovanni Dosi notes:

> As compared to 'classical' (electromechanical) automation of mass production, numerically controlled machine tools, flexible manufacturing systems, and robots allow a much greater flexibility of production in terms of ... minimum scale of production.

Empirical studies, summarized by David Audretsch or Bo Carlsson and his collaborators, also show how industries adopting such flexible production have been able to reduce their average plant size more than other industries. Falling information costs reduce the minimum efficient size in other ways as well. For instance, firms producing their own intermediate products can now more easily subcontract such production without fear of being at the mercy of opportunistic behavior of a large supplier.[11] That is, as the minimum efficient size of potential

---

in contrast to that in the 20th century, will be organized as a network, not as a pyramid; it will have an external, not internal, focus and will aim for interdependencies, not self-sufficiency; its style will be flexible, not structured; its source of strength will be change, not stability; its major resources will be intangible, not physical; its operations will feature virtual, not vertical, integration; its production methods will employ mass customization, not mass production; its reach will be global, not local; its financials will be posted in real-time, not quarterly; its inventory will be measured in hours, not months; its strategy will be bottom-up, not top-down; its leadership will be inspirational, not dogmatic; its job expectations for workers will be their personal growth, not their security; its corporate motivation will be to build, not to compete; its improvements will be revolutionary, not incremental; its quality standards will be the absolute best, not just the affordable best.

[11]   The literature on information technology also features references to other types of economies of scale, but I have been unable to find any serious empirical analysis of them. For instance, falling information costs might yield economies of scope, or reduce costs of producing multiple

subcontractors falls from use of the new information technology, competition among them becomes more intense and the subcontracting industry is no longer dominated by a few large producers with the necessary complement of large machines.

• The new information technology lowers the cost of transacting with the outside world: gathering information, searching for partners, and negotiating and supervising contracts. The extreme exemplar is the "virtual corporation," which has almost no labor force because it subcontracts all aspects of design, production, and sales. Such firms are primarily built around an idea and the effort to build a profitable business process around it, subcontracting all other functions such as production or sales.

• The new information technology raises labor productivity and, thus, allows fewer workers to produce a given amount of output. Other things being equal (including the size of markets), firm size as measured by labor force should shrink because of the substitution of capital for labor.[12]

While these arguments seem quite plausible, other arguments that focus more on the enterprise (firm) rather than the establishment level point exactly in the opposite direction, namely that information technology will lead to larger, not smaller, enterprises. Two of these reasons need to be taken especially into account:

• The new technology can lower the costs of organizing and utilizing hierarchies, for example, long-run planning, coordination, supervision, evaluation of in-house employees, or quality controls. As a result, an enterprise can consist of more establishments than previously and enterprise size can become larger, even while its individual establishments are smaller.

• The new technology also makes it easier for individual managers to specialize in particular functional areas, such as foreign trade, so that these do not need to be subcontracted to outside firms. With the substitution of in-house labor for tasks previously subcontracted, the workforce of the enterprise becomes larger.

Since various economic theories yield contradictory conclusions, it is best to stop at this point and look at some of the empirical work on these issues. Unfortunately, few studies are available and they do not focus directly on the issue under consideration.[13] It is, however, possible to evaluate the claim that infor-

---

products or of distribution, or reduce expenditures for branding. Few data on these possible impacts are available.

[12] This argument, which is often found in the popular press, is not well developed and serious doubts about its validity can be raised when account is taken of the results of econometric studies, such as those by Morrison and Berndt (1991), (1992).

[13] Several recent empirical studies of the manufacturing sector, particularly by Brynjolfson, Ma-

Table 9.1. *Ratios of Establishments to Enterprises of Different Size Firms, 1954–1997*

Year	All firms with at least 1 employee	Firms with >19 employees	Firms with >99 employees	Firms with >999 employees	Firms with >9999 employees
1954	1.1	—	—	—	—
1958	1.3	3.0	9.8	71.1	306.8
1963	1.2	3.0	10.8	84.8	355.1
1967	1.2	3.1	11.6	97.7	406.4
1972	1.3	3.4	14.1	124.2	498.4
1977	1.3	3.5	14.3	122.5	488.3
1982	1.3	3.6	15.3	134.9	577.1
1987	1.3	3.5	14.1	128.4	574.6
1992	1.3	3.4	13.7	121.5	543.1
1997	1.3	3.3	12.5	99.5	547.3

Note: The estimates of the number of firms are based on data published by the Department of Commerce, Census Bureau, *Enterprise Statistics,* various years, adjusted for comparability to cover the entire private sector excluding agriculture. The estimation methods are described in External Appendix X-9.1 The data for 1997 were obtained from a special tabulation of the Census Bureau made by Trey Cole, whom I would like to thank. For the early years of this table, the estimates are rough approximations.

mation technology promotes economies of coordination that allows an enterprise to oversee a larger number of establishments where actual production or sales are carried out.[14] To clarify a key definition used in the data on this issue, an establishment is a geographically separate unit of the firm such as a factory, sales office, or other specialized branch, which can interact either with the parent enterprise or with outside firms.

Table 9.1 presents some data on the changing ratio of establishments to enterprises and covers not just the manufacturing sector, which is usually the primary focus, but the entire private sector except for agriculture, forestry, and fishing.

lone, Gurbaxani, and Kambil (1994) and by Komninos (1994), show that enterprises with greater investment in information technology have tended to be smaller in size, other things being equal. Their results do not mean, however, that the size of an average manufacturing firm has declined, but rather that enterprise size has increased less rapidly than it would have in the absence of investment in new information technology.

[14]   For the moment, I leave aside the possibility that average establishment size can fall faster than the average number of establishments supervised by one enterprise, so that the overall size of the enterprise declines.

It also covers only enterprises and establishments located within the borders of the U.S. As foreign subsidiaries, owned primarily by the largest firms, became more important, establishment/enterprise ratios are understated, especially for large multinationals.

Several conclusions can be quickly drawn from these estimates. The estimated establishment/enterprise ratio for the larger firms rose dramatically from 1954 to about 1982. Thereafter, it leveled off or slightly declined. As expected, the ratio rises with the size of the firm so that in 1992, firms with 10,000 or more workers averaged more than 500 subordinate establishments. These trends are not artifacts of a changing composition of production, since they also appear when the data are recalculated to take this into account.[15]

Nevertheless, we can not draw quick conclusions from these trends because, as noted above, the ratios in the table for the largest enterprises have a downward bias. As I argue below, if foreign establishments of U.S. firms were the same average size as their U.S. counterparts, the ratio of establishments to enterprises would have probably risen for the largest firms over the entire period.

In brief, it appears from these imperfect data that the new information technology may have lowered the internal costs of managing a large corporation, especially in the 1960s and 1970s when mainframe computers were being introduced. Credible empirical evidence pertaining to the other arguments about the impact of information technology are not at hand. Since the three major theories about changing enterprise size do not lead to a consistent conclusion, we cannot make predictions about the future by reference only to theoretical evidence alone. Instead, we must take a more inductive approach which, fortunately, allows us to gain considerable clarity.

B. The Impact of Mergers[16]

All three theories about firm size reviewed above assume that the growth of enterprise size is continuous and is related in some way to technology. But firm size can also be influenced by factors that are quite discontinuous and, moreover, unrelated to technology. Of these, the most important are mergers, which

---

[15] I separated eight sectors (mining; construction; manufacturing; transportation, communications, and public utilities; wholesale trade; retail trade; finance, insurance, and real estate; and services) and recalculated the indices. In these calculations I omit agriculture (which in 1960 accounted for slightly over three percent of the labor force), the government sector, and the rest-of-the-world sector.

[16] In the text in this section I mention studies by Friedheim (1998) and also Scherer and Ravenscraft (1987).

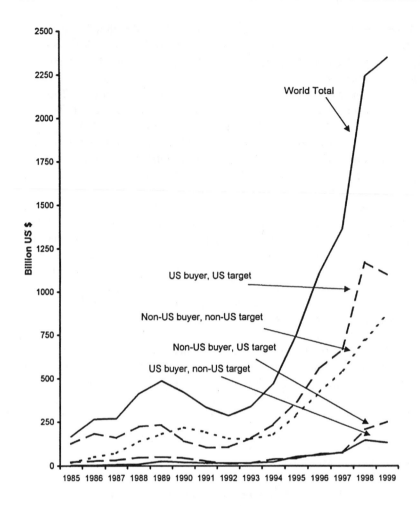

Chart 9.1. Estimated Value of Business Mergers

Note: Description of sources and methods are discussed in Appendix 9.1.

are often carried out for the purpose of gaining market power with suppliers and vendors or, as noted above, gaining an easy foothold in a totally different market. I argue below that mergers have had a crucial impact on firm size, especially in the last decade of the 20th century.

Chart 9.1 shows the dollar value of four types of mergers, defined in terms of the nationality of the buying and the target enterprises. From 1985 through

1999, the dollar value of mergers just within the U.S. increased at an average annual rate of 18 percent; for mergers in the world as a whole, the annual rate was 21 percent; elsewhere I present more detailed data and discussion on these matters.[17] The value of mergers and acquisitions involving just U.S. firms reached slightly more than 1 trillion dollars in 1999; cross-border mergers involving U.S. firms added 0.4 trillion more; and mergers between foreign firms amounted to another 0.9 trillion. A capstone was laid in the first five weeks of 2000 with the announcement of five mega-mergers with a total value of more than 0.5 trillion dollars. (As an anti-climax, however, anti-trust authorities did not allow certain parts of these mega-mergers to be carried out.)

The merger wave in the 1960s featured a large share of conglomerate mergers—the combining of firms in unrelated industries. By way of contrast, roughly three quarters of the mergers in the last decade and a half of the 20th century were between firms with lines of production in the same narrowly defined industry (more specifically, four-digit industries in the standard industrial classification of the early 1990s), as I show in the next chapter. Furthermore, these horizontal combinations characterized not just mergers between U.S. companies, but mergers with foreign firms as well. Although the impact of such horizontal mergers on market concentration is discussed in the next chapter, one implication is worth emphasizing at once.

Although F. M. Scherer and David Ravenscraft show that a large share of mergers are not successful, the conglomerate or vertical mergers can later be undone without enormous difficulties, witness the "back to basics" movement in the U.S. corporate world in the 1960s and 1970s. But dissolving horizontal mergers is not so easy. Where the two merged firms are producing the same product, there is often no obvious way to split the firm, especially if the two parts have been closely integrated before the merged enterprise decided to unbundle.[18] Indeed, in many cases the major purpose of the merger was to gain market share and managers may be unwilling to divest part of the firm which they still hope will eventually pay off in increased market share and greater profits. As a result, the merged firm will not shrink back to its former size and the size of the average enterprise in the economy as a whole will be greater—in this case, it's easier to gain weight than to take it off.

Merger data in isolation tell us little about changes in the size distribution of enterprises. Obviously, if managers are simultaneously buying and selling parts

---

[17] Pryor (2001-a).

[18] How important are troubled mergers? From studies of stock prices it is often claimed that roughly one half of all enterprise mergers fail in the sense that they do not provide additional value for the stockholders. This can, of course, be simply due to an original overvaluation of the stock prices of the two companies or to managerial conflicts between the merging firms that

of enterprises, the size distribution and average size of firms could remain roughly the same. It is certainly possible to imagine that a rising volume of mergers will lead to a radical shift in the size distribution of firms so that most of us would end up working for giant enterprises—the trillion-dollar enterprise, as Cyrus Friedheim discusses in a recent book.[19] We need to look directly at some data on changes in enterprise size.

C. A Brief Foray into Methodology

I have spoken glibly about the "average size" of enterprises and establishments, but some serious problems are involved in determining what this term means, because their size distribution is highly skewed. Some conceptual difficulties need immediate attention. In addition, some serious problems arise in adjusting the data for comparability, a topic which, according to one long-time observer (who wishes to remain anonymous), is a "statistical Vietnam, from which it is impossible to emerge without wounds and to declare an honorable victory." As a result, the estimates must be taken cautiously, especially for the 1958–77 period. I discuss my methods of data adjustment in detail in External Appendix X-9.1 .

As an indicator of enterprise size we can use labor force, value-added, total sales, total assets, or net worth. I have chosen to measure size in terms of labor force, because, for my purposes, sufficiently long time-series to make the proper comparisons cannot be estimated for any other indicator. Further, this measure directly relates to the oft-discussed question of whether most Americans will be working in the future for a giant enterprise. Moreover, using a labor force measure also permits easy and valid comparisons with establishment size.

---

hamper efficiency, even though productivity on the shop-floor increases. The anticipated gain in market share may also not materialize, as shown in a small-scale sample survey of conglomerate mergers (Pryor, 1973, pp. 410-2) where I asked managers about this possibility and found that less than half of them believed that the combined market share of the merged firms had increased. Other studies have approached the matter differently and obtained similar results, for instance, Mueller (1986, pp. 178-9} notes that firms formed as a result of mergers grew more slowly than a control group after the merger took place.

The most rewarding approach for determining the impact of mergers on productivity moves away from stock prices and surveys of managers and focuses on changes in cost and productivity indicators. This is, however, a relatively new research area and, although some fine research has been carried out (for instance, Lichtenberg (1992) or Kaplan (2000)), much remains to be done.

[19]   This possibility is certainly not the only one that can be imagined. For instance, Ijiri and Simon (1971) present a model with the counter-intuitive conclusion that even without divestment,

In measuring enterprise size the arithmetic average is a very imperfect indicator, because it does not take into account the highly asymmetric nature of the distribution. For instance, 90 percent of all enterprises have less than 20 workers (9 percent of all enterprises have no employees at all).[20] As a result, the arithmetic average changes considerably when the small firms under a certain limit are not included in the calculations. In 1992, for instance, the average enterprise had 19 employees. If the enterprises with no employees are excluded (these are often just empty legal entities or companies with only a part-time, sole proprietor), the average rises to 21, if enterprises with less than five workers are excluded, 44; if enterprises with less than 20 are excluded, 144. In brief, the skewness means that a simple arithmetic average has little economic meaning.

Given the type of grouped size data which are available, I have chosen to use six different definitions of size. The first four measure the firm in terms of its absolute size (sometimes called the "centralization of capital"): (1) the arithmetic average of employees in firms with more than 19 workers; (2) and (3) the arithmetic average sizes of the largest 100 and 1000 firms; and (4) the "Florence median," which is calculated in a manner equivalent to arranging in a row all firms in the country by the size of their labor force, then lining up all their workers in front of each of the firms, and finally determining the size of the enterprise in which the employee exactly halfway down this line of workers is employed. This statistic reduces the impact of very small or very large firms on size statistics. The final two statistics deal with size on a relative basis (sometimes called the "concentration of capital"), namely the percentage of the labor force employed in enterprises with more than 999 and 9,999 employees. Although other measures of enterprise size can be employed, they are less intuitively clear.[21]

common dynamic conditions underlying the merger process do not necessarily lead to any significant changes in either the distribution or average size of enterprises. They argue this might explain the roughly stable structure in the size distribution of manufacturing from 1930 to 1960.

[20] All data in this paragraph come from *Enterprise Statistics*. Other publications of the Census Bureau such as *Characteristics of Business Owners* or tax data from the IRS yield even more skewed statistics on this matter.

[21] For instance, Ijiri and Simon (1977, p. 13) argue that the kind of measures of size that I employ are atheoretic and that a more theoretically informed set of measures should be used. On the basis of a stochastic model, they suggest that the Pareto coefficient (α) would be more appropriate. In External Appendix X-9.3 I explore such issues and present calculations using such a measure. It shows the same trends as more conventional measures of size used in this chapter. In addition, the underlying data used in some of these calculations permit the calculation of the Ijiri-Simon statistic of the dynamism of the market, as revealed by the changing size ranks of the largest firms, a topic also explored in the same appendix.

D. The Empirical Results and the Impact of Mergers

1. Enterprises

The time-series data of enterprise size presented below allow us to see what has happened in the last half-century and to begin to get a sense of what might happen in the future. Table 9.2 presents a set of estimated statistics of enterprise size for the entire private sector excluding agriculture. Calculations for just the core sectors, for which comparable data are available for the entire period, reveal the same results.

From 1958 through 1997, five out of the six measures show a growing enterprise size. From this we might quickly infer that the second half of the 20th century represents merely a continuation of the first half, with enterprise size rising because of the growing importance of the economies of large scale production.

Such a conclusion, however, is overhasty, because of the undulating pattern of enterprise size between the end points. Five out of the six measures show an increase from the late 1950s to the early and mid 1970s. Thereafter up to 1992, five of the six series reveal a decrease.[22] Finally, from 1992 to 1997, all measures show an increase in enterprise size. The most telling clues about the causal forces underlying the changing size of enterprises can be gained by focusing on why enterprise size declined in the middle of the half century period. Several explanations come immediately to mind:

• *Back-to-basics:* The years between the mid 1970s and the early 1990s were a time when U.S. managers began to sell off various parts of their companies acquired during the conglomerate merger boom of the 1960s and early 1970s which did not fit well with their main lines of business. This divestment movement appears also to have accounted for the great changes in the size rankings of the largest enterprises.

• *Computerization:* The years between the mid 1970s and the early 1990s were, of course, the years when investment in the new information technology began to take off as American producers of goods and services started to become computerized. This may have led to a reduction in the work force.

• *Change in composition of production:* Much faster growth took place in the service sector, which features smaller firms, than in the manufacturing sector where firms are larger in size. To explore the impact of a changing industrial structure, I recalculated the various measures of enterprise size assuming a

---

[22]   The Pareto coefficients of the size distribution data also reveal the same picture as Table 9.2. Nevertheless, for such data covering each of the top 100 industrial firms, the decline in size appears to have begun somewhat later.

Table 9.2. *Measures of the Size of Non-Agricultural Enterprises by the Number of Employees, 1958–1997*

Year	Number of employees		Average number of		Percent of employees	
	in firms with >19 employees (average)	Florence median	employees in the largest		in firms with more than:	
			100 firms	1000 firms	999 employees	9,999 employees
1958	154.2	286	59829	13288	40.9%	23.6%
1963	150.3	334	67600	14785	42.1	24.9
1967	155.5	443	87441	17894	44.5	28.1
1972	147.2	409	93332	19306	44.1	28.0
1977	148.8	421	98214	20842	44.2	28.0
1982	143.5	346	101695	22085	42.9	26.8
1987	142.5	331	99558	23868	42.1	25.4
1992	144.1	358	84448	23896	42.3	24.4
1997	147.9	430	96973	27644	43.3	25.7

Note: For all years but 1997 these series are based on estimations described in External Appendix X-9.1. The underlying data come from U.S. Department of Commerce, Census Bureau, Enterprise Statistics, various years and, for 1997, from a special tabulation of the Census Bureau. These data include only employment within the U.S.

constant structure of production. The results show what we would expect:[23] Between 1958 and 1992 the various measures of enterprise size reveal a much greater growth than in Table 9.2. Even between 1977 and 1992, many of the measures of firm size in the nation show an increase in the employment size of enterprises. In brief, enterprise size (measured in terms of employment) has been increasing in many sectors, but for all industries considered together, the shift toward the production of services, where firms are smaller, has pulled down the national average size of firms.

Some combination of the back-to-basics movement, computerization, and a shift in the industrial distribution of firms seem to be the key elements for understanding why enterprise size decreased from the mid 1970s to the early 1990s. As noted below, the changing size of establishments also played an important role.[24] After 1992, however, this trend in declining size was reversed, and two explanations appear most plausible:

[23] This estimate appears in Pryor (2001-e).
[24] Two other possible explanations deserve mention. The decline may have been caused by the

• *Mergers*: As shown in Chart 9.1, during the 1990s the merger wave approached tsunami magnitudes. It seems likely that this is the most important single cause for increasing enterprise size in this decade,

• *Attenuation of the employment impact of computerization*: It is also quite possible that although computerization took a somewhat different form in the 1990s—the move away from mainframes and toward desktop computers—the employment impact of the information technology revolution was ebbing. Unfortunately, there is little solid evidence on this matter.

In brief, in the 1990s the impact of the merger wave, and possibly the ebbing of the employment impact of computers, were sufficiently strong to outweigh the shift toward services that leads to a reduction in average enterprise size.

2. Establishments

To what extent is the change in firm size attributable to changing costs of production or coordination? Trends in establishment size, where production is actually carried out, provide some important clues. To carry out this analysis, it is not necessary to worry about the concentration of production into ever fewer establishments, so I have estimated only four measures of establishment size. Table 9.3 presents the results of these calculations, along with some much rougher estimates for the 1953-1959 period.

Between 1953 and 1997, the size of establishments fell, with a particularly marked decline occurring in the share of workers employed in the largest plants. Like the data on enterprise size, the overall patterns undulate and vary in the different subperiods.

Up to the early 1960s, patterns in establishment size are mixed: Some measures of establishment size show a slight increase; others, a slight decrease. From the early 1960s to the early 1990s, establishment size generally fell. After 1992, however, different trends appeared. Between 1992 and 1997, the two absolute measures of establishment size, the arithmetic average and the Florence median, increased. At the same time, the percentage of employees in very small and very large establishments decreased, which means that middle-sized plants were growing in relative importance at their expense.

---

exportation of jobs: the large multinational U.S. firms reduced their domestic production as they placed production facilities abroad. However, the decline in employment is also reflected in a series for the 100 largest U.S. enterprises when employment in their foreign subsidiaries is included, as I show elsewhere in Pryor (2001-e).

Some also argue that in this period technological change with a labor-saving bias was greater for the largest firms, although the evidence to support this conjecture leaves much to be desired.

Table 9.3. *Measures of the Size of Non-Agricultural Private Establishments by Number of Employees, 1953–97*

Year	Number of employees		Percent of total employees in establishments with:		
	establishments with >19 employees (average)	Florence median	< 20 employees	> 500 employees	> 1000 employees
1953*	109.6	113	26.2%	29.6%	n.a.
1956*	105.0	100	27.4	28.0	n.a.
1959*	101.0	91	28.3	26.5	n.a.
1962	101.3	99	27.0	27.6	18.7%
1967	102.7	112	24.7	28.6	19.4
1972	96.7	102	24.4	26.4	17.6
1977	92.2	78	26.9	23.1	15.1
1982	88.4	74	26.6	21.6	14.3
1987	83.6	69	26.8	19.7	12.7
1992	83.8	70	26.7	20.1	13.3
1997	84.3	76	25.3	19.8	12.8

Note: The asterisks mark those years for which the estimates are very approximate since only the number of establishments in each size category were given. Estimation methods and data problems are described in External Appendix X-9.2. The underlying data come from U.S. Department of Commerce, Census Bureau, *County Business Patterns,* various years, and have been adjusted for comparability to cover the entire private sector excluding agriculture. n.a. = not available.

These descriptive results allow us to distinguish four phases in the changing size of enterprises since the 1950s: (a) From the late 1950s to the early 1960s, enterprises increased in size as both establishments and the ratio of establishments to enterprises (Table 9.1) increased. (b) From the mid 1960s to the mid 1970s, enterprises increased in size because the ratio of establishments to enterprises increased faster than the declining size of establishments. (c) From the mid 1970s through 1992, enterprises declined in size because establishments decreased slowly in size, the ratio of establishments to enterprises leveled off, and overall employment turned toward those sectors with smaller enterprises. (d) From 1992 onward, enterprises increased in size because of the merger wave, while the establishment/enterprise ratio and the size of establishments remained roughly constant, at least when only establishments within U.S. borders are taken into account. This complex pattern makes prediction about the future growth of enterprise size more difficult.

3. Some Impacts of Globalization

The census data used up to now in the various tables refer only to enterprises and establishments within the United States, regardless of whether they are U.S. or foreign owned. By comparing statistics of enterprise size with the *Fortune* magazine database of large companies, which includes the worldwide activities of all American firms, we can not only gain some insight on the activities of U.S. companies abroad but also determine some of the bias in previous results on enterprise size. I carry out such an exercise elsewhere and obtain two useful results:[25]

As noted in Chapter 5 in the discussion of globalization, large U.S. firms were increasingly developing foreign production facilities, either by building them or, as shown in Table 9.2, purchasing them. In the 100 largest U.S. industrial enterprises the ratio of foreign employment to total employment rose from 1963 through 1997, so that in the latter year, it amounted to roughly one fourth. If their foreign production units are added into the count of domestic establishments managed by these largest U.S. firms, this means that their ratio of total establishments to an enterprise did not turn down in the 1980s (shown just for domestic production units in Table 9.1), but continued to rise. Further, the dip in average employment size between 1982 and 1992 would be much smaller than in the domestic employment series.

It is also noteworthy that the 100 largest enterprises outside the U.S. are larger than their U.S. counterparts. Although this size difference may be temporary, non-U.S. firms have experienced the same increase in size as the U.S. firms. In brief, the increasing importance of large firms is not a trend that is somehow special to the U.S.

E. The Future[26]

Predictions about the death of the present corporate form of business enterprise seem premature. Given the glacial speed at which many important organizations change, corporations will probably maintain roughly their current form for the coming decades. Moreover, as I argue below, enterprise size will probably continue to increase, even as certain supra-enterprise forms might become relatively much more important. I also briefly discuss some impacts of these developments on other aspects of the economic system.

---

[25] Pryor (2001-e).
[26] In the text of this section I refer to research by Fukuyama (1999) and Scholes (1998).

1. Future Trends in the Size of U.S. Enterprises

It seems likely that as long as the merger wave continues, the average size of enterprises in the U.S. will rise. No one can be sure how long this merger wave will last, but several relevant factors deserve consideration:

• *Globalization*: As long as the global integration of markets continues, many firms will feel compelled to have a production presence in foreign countries to be closer to these markets. Merging with an established firm abroad is considerably easier than starting up afresh, since the purchasing firm can take advantage of a functioning production team with established market expertise. As a result, cross-border mergers should increase in importance in the decades to come, even if mergers within national borders should taper off. Such cross-national mergers represent a consolidation of the world capitalist system that has been brought about by the fall in the costs of transportation and communications, as well as other barriers to trade. In important respects it parallels the merger wave seen in the U.S. in the last few decades of the 19th century, which represented a consolidation of the national capitalist system.

• *Finance*: Further development of global financial markets will make it continually easier for firms to raise the necessary funds to engage in merger activities. Moreover, as long as the U.S. continues to run substantial trade deficits, foreign enterprises will have the dollars to continue their purchase of U.S. companies.

• *Offsetting shifts in production patterns*: A key factor leading to declining average enterprise size will become less important, namely the shift from manufacturing, which features large enterprises, to the service sector, which has smaller enterprises. This is because manufacturing accounts for a much less important share of production and of the labor force. More specifically, the share of the labor force in the manufacturing sector in total non-agricultural employment declined from roughly 34 percent in 1950 to 14 percent in 1999,[27] so that a further halving of this share in the next half century will bring about much less change in the average size of enterprises.

• *Computerization*: Further computerization should have a less important impact in the coming decades than in the second half of the 20th century.

• *Legal barriers*: Although anti-trust authorities in Europe and the U.S. are deepening their cooperation, few laws apply to cross-border mergers where the merging firms do not have a significant presence in the other country. In the next chapter I discuss in greater detail some aspects of how the different national anti-trust authorities work together.

---

[27]   U.S. Council of Economic Advisers (2000), p. 358.

These considerations suggest that the global merger wave may continue for the next few decades, barring, of course, a major war or economic recession. Several objections to this prediction might be raised, and they deserve attention:

• *New entities:* The formal size of business enterprises, as measured by the number of employees, may become an increasingly irrelevant economic indicator, as firms more and more turn to industrial alliances as a source of growth. Strategic alliances, business consortia for particular purposes, and other types of cooperative arrangements between firms create supra-enterprise entities, which might prove an important organizational form for business in the future. This argument is discussed in detail in the next chapter.

• *Internet:* Technological developments have been a crucial factor underlying the growth in the size of enterprises in the past, and the data on corporate size up to the end of the 20th century do not reflect the full impact of the internet. According to this line of argument, the internet should exert a decentralizing pull that will prove stronger than the centralizing tendency of the merger wave. However, as I discuss in the next chapter, the internet can decrease competition and stimulate a consolidation of enterprises, rather than the reverse, depending upon certain underlying conditions. Moreover, many of the aspects of the new information technology leading to smaller firm sizes, reviewed earlier in this chapter, may become less important in the future, for instance, when firms reach a point that further outsourcing of their activities would pose serious risks to quality control and other functions.

• *Corporate divestment:* As enterprises become too large to be effectively managed, some major divisions are often transformed into separate companies. As noted above, this is much easier for firms created from vertical or conglomerate mergers. Merged firms, where both were in the same line of business, account for roughly three quarters of the new mergers, as I show in the next chapter. These firms may find it more difficult to split unless different parts of the firm deal with geographically different markets or with unrelated products.

• *Personnel:* As noted above, some believe that managing knowledge workers requires a much different type of internal organization than the hierarchies to which we are accustomed and that, as a result, firms will become smaller. This proposition is related to empirical findings that after firms reach a certain size, the productivity of their R and D workers, in comparison to those in smaller firms, appears to decline. Although this might be overcome by granting such workers much greater autonomy, it is difficult to envision an extremely large firm with a very flat pyramid of authority, since the coordination problems would be severe and following a unified market strategy might prove difficult. Nevertheless, a pattern seems to be emerging of large firms buying up smaller firms with greater research productivity in order to take advantage of their discoveries, patents, and personnel. Thus, the lower productivity of the acquiring company's knowledge workers can be offset without radical changes in the distribution of authority and the size of enterprises continues to grow.

• *Social factors*: Finally, as noted in Chapter 7, social trust and social capital are declining, at least on a macro-level, and such trends seem to place in doubt whether large firms can be successfully managed. Can employees in giant firms, predisposed to feel suspicious and alienated, be brought to cooperate with each other? Francis Fukuyama argues in a convincing fashion that social solidarity is different on the macro- and micro-levels. More specifically, with proper leadership, orientation, and indoctrination of workers, trust and social capital can be provided on a micro-level, even while the same workers persist in distrusting their fellow citizens, and decline to participate with them in social or political activities or projects of mutual interest.

The five objections raised above do not, I believe, have sufficient weight to invalidate my prediction about enterprises increasing in size in the future, especially if we define any supra-enterprise entities as a single firm. In other words, trends in enterprise size in the 20st century should continue in the next century, even though the underlying causes will be somewhat different. Furthermore, a growing share of the labor force should be employed in giant firms spanning continents. The conclusions of this analysis should also drive one more nail into the coffin of the notion that seems to revive vampire-like every few decades that it is the small firms which have been and will continue to be the most important generators of employment in the U.S.[28]

2. Some Impacts on the Economy and Economic System

If enterprises continue to grow, it seems likely that worker alienation might intensify because, as previously mentioned, such a state of mind appears to be greater among workers in large firms than small. Further, because wage inequalities are also greater in large firms than small, an increase in the relative importance of large firms would lead to wider wage differentials for the industry and, under certain conditions, for the nation as a whole as well. Such a trend toward greater income inequality would be reinforced if corporate financial practices

---

[28]   The hypothesis that small firms have accounted for most employment growth in the past few decades has also been refuted in other ways by others, for instance, Harrison (1994) or Brown, Hamilton, and Medoff (1990). The one part of the phenomenon that is difficult to research is the employment impact of small firms which grow sufficiently rapidly to move out of the "small firm" category.

change in the manner envisioned by Myron Scholes. As noted above, he foresaw that the increasing use of sophisticated financial instruments would result in more concentrated ownership of the large corporations by corporate insiders, who would use such instruments to syphon off more successfully the extra-high profits resulting from their managerial skills, rather than passing them on to either the stockholders, the workers, or other stakeholders.

The growing size of business enterprises also increases the probability of two major changes in the organizations and institutions of the economic system: a change in government-business relations and a change in the degree of market competition. To the extent that the business sector has common interests, a smaller group of larger enterprises can more easily mobilize for political lobbying, although whether they choose to do so is a different matter. Legislators are also more likely to listen to representatives of enterprises employing a significant share of their constituents, and to grant particular favors to such firms, for instance, subsidies or tax breaks to confer advantages over foreign competition. Very large enterprises are also "too big to fail," so that government bailouts and other extraordinary interventions are likely to become more frequent.

In brief, the vision of many small enterprises participating in a relatively perfectly competitive market has become increasingly obsolete. The economic system in the future could become increasingly dominated by a small number of very large firms—or supra-enterprise entities. In an optimistic scenario, a kind of "corporate welfare state" might emerge, with the business sector as primary beneficiaries, not the low-income population. In a pessimistic scenario an oligarchic system might emerge, with a fused corporate/government elite setting economic and social policy for the nation. The two scenarios differ primarily in the degree to which democratic rights for the mass of citizens are preserved.

As enterprises in the same line of business merge more often with each other, market competition will invariably decline. This is the focus of analysis in the next chapter.

CHAPTER 10

Evolution of Market Competition

The increase in wealth and leisure should, by 1984, have forced us to abandon, as a major source of human effort, the one-against-all competitiveness which we have relied on so much hitherto.

—*Geneticist C. H. Waddington, 1964* [1]

Starting in the early 1980s, the share of sales in individual markets of the largest four firms began to increase, and this indicator in market concentration, in turn, points to an ebbing of market competition. I expect two new institutional and organizational developments, namely the rise of e-commerce and industrial alliances to reinforce this trend. Given certain other conditions discussed below, this suggests that markets will operate less competitively in the future than now. These claims are, of course, bold, especially at a time in which markets appear more vigorous and competitive than ever before and when the internet is supposed to liberate markets from lingering forces of monopoly.

To support these assertions, I begin with a brief discussion of counteracting forces on market competition, namely the merger wave and globalization. Although governmental antitrust policies can also influence the structure of markets and reduce merger activity, I argue that the constraints globalization places on the implementation of these policies have hampered the U.S. government's effectiveness in preventing the rise of industrial concentration. But theory alone cannot determine the relative strength of these various forces, and, therefore, a major purpose of discussion in the first part of this chapter is to present the results of an empirical analysis of changes in competition in the last third of the 20th century.

But what of the future? I focus on three issues of particular importance in the coming decades:

---

[1]   Cited by Laura Lee, *Bad Predictions: 2000 Years of the Best Minds Making the Worst Forecasts* (2000).

- The ever increasing "strategic alliances" or "strategic partnerships" between corporations in recent years provides a set of cooperative arrangements that can encourage cartel behavior and reduce competition. I show that these agreements extend not only over the nation but also between large corporations of different nations.

- Mergers in the "new economy industries" are supposed to bring efficiencies because these sectors are based on new technologies with alleged economies of large scale production and network economies. I show that these effects are overrated.

- The rise of the internet and e-commerce is supposed to make entry into new markets easier and, thereby, increase competition. I show, however, that this new technology may have an anti-competitive impact, especially as e-commerce is considerably more concentrated than traditional markets.

A. Two Key Factors Influencing Market Concentration[2]

As background to the empirical analysis of market competition, we need to look briefly at the two most important but counteracting influences—the merger wave and increased globalization.

1. The Role of the Merger Wave

In the previous chapter I present data on the volume of the merger wave in the last 15 years of the 20th century. Although the government can influence the concentration of industry in a variety of ways, its tolerance for various horizontal mergers (i.e., mergers in the same industry) has the most direct impact on competition.

Some idea of the actual, as opposed to potential, impact on market structure of horizontal mergers can be gained from Table 10.1, which presents data on the volume of mergers and acquisitions throughout the world. My measure of a horizontal merger is whether the companies involved are producing goods or services in the same narrowly defined industry, which I define as one of the roughly 930 "four-digit industries" in the U.S. standard industrial classification (SIC) in use up to the late 1990s. The most important product or service of a company is designated as its "primary SIC"; other production of each company is

---

[2]   In the text of this section I mention studies by Drucker (1999-a) and Sorkin and Petersen (2000).

Table 10.1. *Global Data on the Share of Recent Mergers Within the Same Narrowly Defined Industry (Horizontal Mergers)*

(Four-digit codes in the Standard Industrial Classification)

Buyer-target	Ranking of Four-Digit SIC codes			Total horizontal mergers	Total value billion US $
	Primary-primary	Primary-secondary	Secondary-secondary		
Measured in terms of recorded value of deals					
U.S.–U.S.					
1985	24.4%	32.8%	12.6%	69.8%	$105.7
1992	43.9	25.1	3.3	72.3	90.0
1999	47.8	23.2	6.0	77.0	921.6
U.S.–non U.S.					
1985	84.3	3.5	0.0	87.7	3.4
1992	23.0	33.7	20.4	77.1	12.2
1999	43.3	29.5	2.5	75.3	103.4
Non U.S.–U.S.					
1985	42.9	32.5	2.0	77.4	18.0
1992	19.6	16.8	3.7	40.2	10.8
1999	57.3	15.0	4.6	76.9	224.8
Non U.S.–non U.S.					
1985	37.7	12.7	4.8	55.2	15.2
1992	40.5	14.6	5.1	60.2	118.8
1999	34.0	33.3	4.7	72.0	714.2
Total					
1985	29.6	29.9	10.1	69.7	142.4
1992	39.9	19.8	5.1	64.9	231.7
1999	43.7	26.2	5.2	75.1	1964.0
Measured in terms of number of mergers with a recorded deal value					
Total					
1985	28.9%	20.3%	6.5%	55.7%	959
1992	34.9	13.6	3.4	51.9	4,115
1999	32.4	14.6	2.7	49.8	8,560
Measured in terms of total number of all mergers					
Total					
1985	28.7%	19.0%	4.3%	52.0%	1,923
1992	38.0	12.6	2.3	52.9	9,996
1999	34.8	13.6	2.2	50.6	19,946

Note: The sources of the data and how I have adjusted them are discussed in Pryor (2001-a).

aggregated as "secondary SICs." I also divide the data into four categories, depending upon the nationality of the buyer and the target companies, and provide perspective not just on the impact of domestic mergers but also those involving foreign companies.

The most important conclusion to be drawn from these data is that, in value terms, roughly three quarters of the mergers, both in the U.S. and abroad were between companies producing goods or services in the same industry (horizontal mergers). In terms of number, roughly half of the mergers (both where deal values were and were not recorded) fall in this category. This development contrasts with the merger wave in the 1960s, at least in the United States, where vertical or conglomerate combinations seemed to predominate.[3] Many of the mergers in the last decade and a half of the 20th century were, of course, ill-conceived since the process has had much of the same inner momentum found in teen-age dances—to pair up at any cost. For instance, Andrew Sorkin and Melody Petersen report that the $76 billion merger of two U.K. firms, SmithKline Beecham and Glaxo Welcome, to form the world's largest pharmaceutical company in January 2000, was driven in part by Warner-Lambert's announcement several days earlier that it was talking merger plans with Pfizer. The latter deal would have, in turn, resulted in the world's largest drug company. According to one stock analyst at the time, "In this era of merger mania, you don't want to be the last company without a partner."

How permanent are these mergers? As noted in the previous chapter, the "back to basics" movement in the U.S. in the 1960s and 1970s showed that conglomerate or vertical mergers can later be split without enormous difficulties. By way of contrast, dissolving horizontal mergers presents more problems, especially if the merger was undertaken to gain market share. This is because the product lines of the merged companies are more closely integrated, so that unbundling requires the creation of competing firms.

---

[3]   The data provide several other surprises. Contrary to expectations, horizontal mergers comprised a somewhat higher share of total mergers within the U.S. than between firms abroad. This flies in the face of the conventional belief that antitrust enforcement is far more rigorous in the U.S. than in most other countries. Moreover, because firms in many countries abroad face a more regulated business environment, vertical or conglomerate mergers outside of the U.S. require more specialized business expertise and might be considered by some as more risky merger prospects.

In addition, we might expect that most mergers across national lines would tend to occur in the same industry, because this would reduce the risk of entering a new industry in a different nation. Although this seemed to be true for non-U.S. companies buying U.S. firms, this was not the case for U.S. companies buying non-U.S. firms. In this latter instance, the share of horizontal mergers was slightly below that of mergers between U.S. firms—and it was declining over time.

Two long-term factors, however, seem likely to nullify some of the short-term effects of the current merger boom that result in greater market concentration and less market competition.

• Many of the mergers were carried out quickly and for allegedly defensive purposes. As a result, a considerable number of these mergers may founder in the future. Indeed, some of these mergers united enterprises with weak market positions because of their lack of new products. In such cases, it is doubtful whether increased size will solve any of their major problems. For instance, among the world's 18 largest pharmaceutical companies, 11 out of the 12 companies which participated in mergers lost (combined) market share between 1990 and 1998; while all six of the companies which had not merged with another pharmaceutical company gained market share.[4]

• To the extent that smaller firms are more innovative, the long-run market share of these giant firms may also erode.

2. Some Impacts of Globalization

Contrary to popular belief, globalization *per se* does not necessarily increase competition. Of course, under ordinary circumstances, an increase in imports should certainly sharpen competition, because consumers have a greater choice of goods. As Peter Drucker declared, in a burst of enthusiasm, "Distance has been eliminated ... every business must become globally competitive, even if it manufactures or sells in a regional or local market. The competition is not local anymore." As I discuss in Chapter 5, the ratio of imports both to the GDP and to the total production of goods has dramatically increased since the early 1970s.

Nevertheless, if these imports come from foreign companies which are controlled by domestic companies, then globalization may actually reduce, rather than intensify, competition. In 1997, about 30 percent of all U.S. imports were by multinationals importing from their foreign affiliates. Moreover, imports which come from foreign cartels with strong informal ties ("strategic alliances") with domestic firms may also reduce competition. I document below the rise of such informal cross-national ties, which contain the elements of an international cartel.

A major difficulty in assessing quantitatively the impact of the foreign sector on domestic competition is the lack of any adequate measures. Concentration

---

[4] Anon (2000-c). In some cases the firms merged because they were losing market share, but the merger did not seem to change this situation.

ratios—the most common measure of competition—give no indication of the impact of trade. Adjusting these concentration ratios to take account of imports raises difficulties because available statistics do not distinguish the national ownership of companies producing specific goods that are imported into the U.S. In my quantitative analysis of the manufacturing sector, I try to determine the maximum competitive impact of these imports, but my crude adjustments leave much to be desired.

B. The Changing Degree of Market Concentration in the U.S. [5]

Market competition is an abstract phenomenon and difficult to "see." Farmers who pay higher prices for their seed and fertilizer and who receive lower prices for their wheat and cattle (or consumers who pay higher prices for their bread and meat) cannot easily determine to what extent these changes came about because of impersonal shifts in supply and demand or because fewer agro-businesses are vying for their business. We can, however, measure the degree to which sales in narrowly defined industries are dominated by a few large companies, and this indicator of market concentration helps us to assess the state of competition. Moreover, by examining trends in market concentration in the last half of the 20th century, we can begin to assess the relative impact on market structure of the merger boom and globalization.

Some definitions are in order. I measure market concentration by the share of shipments accounted for by the largest 4 or 8 producers in a narrowly defined industry for the nation as a whole (the four-digit SIC industries). An example of such an industry is hog processing, which buys pigs from farmers and sells pork chops and bacon to grocery wholesalers. In 1980, the top four firms controlled 34 percent of the market, but by 2000 that share rose to roughly 56 percent—an increase driven in large measure by the purchase by Smithfield Farms (a very large pork producer) of two large competitors (Carroll's Foods and Murphy Family Farms) in 1998 and 1999. Of course, for industries where the relevant market is local, rather than national (for instance, firms making household repairs), such concentration ratios may overstate the degree of competition; and the same may be true for those industries producing highly heterogeneous goods or services (for instance, many consumer products). Nevertheless, the *time trends* of the concentration ratios are the best indicators we have of *changing* market conditions.

---

[5]   In the text of this section I draw on the research of: Ikeda (1996) Meyer (1998), Rhoades (1996), (1997), Shepherd (1982), and Whalen (1996).

Table 10.2. *Weighted Four-Digit Concentration Ratios in the U.S., 1963 through 1992*

(Percentage of shipments of the largest 4 or 8 firms in 4-digit markets)

Industrial Sectors	Weighted 4 firm ratios				Weighted 8 firm ratios			
	1963	1971	1982	1992	1963	1972	1982	1992
Agriculture, forestry, fishing	—	—	—	—	—	—	—	—
Mining	—	—	—	—	—	—	—	—
Construction	—	—	—	—	—	—	—	—
Manufacturing	40.1%	39.7%	37.7%	39.9%	52.6%	52.1%	50.1%	51.8%
Transportation, communication, public utilities	—	—	—	47.0	—	—	—	68.4
Wholesale trade	—	22.5	20.3	21.2	—	29.3	27.4	28.4
Retail trade	—	13.8	14.4	17.9	—	18.5	20.3	24.9
Finance, insurance, real estate	—	—	—	19.8	—	—	—	28.2
Selected services	—	14.4	14.7	14.2	—	19.7	21.7	19.5
Other services	—	—	—	—	—	—	—	—
Government	—	—	—	—	—	—	—	—
Six sectors: current year weights	—	—	—	47.0	—	—	—	68.4
Four sector: current year weights	—	28.4	26.1	26.5	—	37.4	35.4	35.0
Four sectors: 1972 weights	—	28.4	27.8	29.5	—	37.4	37.4	38.1

Note: the dashes indicate either that such data are not available or, for the government sector, that they are meaningless. These ratios refer only to domestically produced products. Sources and greater details of the estimation procedures, as well as additional data, are provided in Pryor (2001-d). The weights used for the totals are GDP originating from each sector. Estimates for three sectors for 1997 are presented in External Appendix X-10.2 .

1. An Aggregate View

To gain an overview of changing market concentration and to see how market concentration fell and then rose over the second half of the 20th century, the most relevant data are weighted averages of the hundreds of concentration ratios that are available. Table 10.2 shows weighted concentration ratios for six different sectors, which, in 1992, accounted for 80 percent of the GDP originating outside of the government sector.[6] For the period 1972–92 the table shows the weighted concentration ratios for four sectors that cover about half of the GDP originating outside of the government sector. In the bottom part of the table the individual sectors are combined to calculate aggregated series. Developments in market concentration since 1992 cannot be determined to such great detail as in the 1982–1992 comparisons. From the calculations in Table 10.2 and the rough estimates for 1997 that are presented in External Appendix X-10.2, I draw two major conclusions:

  • Market concentration has been relatively high, especially when we take account that markets are local in most service sectors, as well as construction and public utilities, so that the national concentration ratios understate the actual degree of market concentration faced by local consumers.

  • Although it appears that market concentration was lower in 1992 than 1972, this is partly a function of the shift in the structure of production from the production of goods toward the production of services. If we use 1972 industrial weights so as to hold this structural factor constant, then market concentration increased between 1972 and 1992. In the 1990s, this increase in industrial concentration appeared to be accelerating in manufacturing and retail trade (but not wholesale trade).[7]

For the omitted sectors in the table, namely agriculture, construction, and mining, the concentration ratios at any single point in time are scattered and not

---

6.   These data represent a recalculation of the results in an earlier study (Pryor, 1994-b), but they reveal the same trends. I have, however, made two important changes. First, in order to achieve comparability with the 1992 data (which were not available when the previous estimates were made), the data in Table 10.2 are for four digit industries, not products. Second, my procedure for building up comparable weighted averages when the SIC classification changed was somewhat different.

7.   Unfortunately, the Census Bureau has published data on industrial concentration for 1997 using an industrial nomenclature that is quite different than for 1992, so that comparisons could be made for only three sectors. In the five years between 1992 and 1997, the weighted four-firm, four-digit industrial concentration increased in manufacturing by 2.7 percentage points (or 6.8 percent), in retail trade by 5.4 percentage points (or 29.8 percent), and in wholesale trade by 0.2 percentage points (or 1.1 percent). These estimates are discussed in External Appendix X-10.2

very comparable from year to year.[8] Nevertheless, qualitative evidence suggests that the movement of the concentration ratios over time were similar to those sectors of the economy for which data are available.

2. Special Notes on Changes in Market Structure in Particular Sectors

Two decades before the end of the 20th century, William G. Shepherd conducted a broad review of market concentration in the U.S. from 1939 to 1980 and, taking account of a series of other factors as well, concluded that market competition for the entire U.S. increased in the period, with the two decades from 1960 to 1980 showing the most improvement. Shepherd cited various contributing factors including import competition, deregulation, antitrust action, and a possible decline in the minimum efficient scale of production. These four factors, however, do not appear to have had as an important an impact in the last two decades of the century. The discussion below considers the importance of some of the causal factors influencing market structure and competition in particular sectors, especially those that I believe might have an important impact in the future.

• *Manufacturing*: Market concentration in the manufacturing sector fell between 1963 and 1982 and then took a sharp jump upward between 1982 and

---

[8]   Agriculture obviously has a very.low concentration ratio. Nevertheless, concentration of production appears to have increased through the 20th century. For instance, the land in farms with more than 1000 acres rose from 24 percent in 1900 to 43 percent in 1950 to 66 percent in 1997. In this latter year, sales from the 69,000 farms with total sales of more than $500,000 amounted to 42 percent of total farm sales. These data come from Department of Commerce, Bureau of the Census (1975), Series K 162–73 and the 1997 Census of Agriculture (www.nass,usda.gov/census/).

In construction, except for large commercial buildings, the market is primarily local, so national concentration ratios are low. For instance, in 1995 the largest 8 builders of private homes accounted for only 5.1 percent of total sales. In the same year the concentration ratios for the largest 8 commercial construction firms was 22.6 percent. These were calculated from data from the Census Bureau (annual, 1997, p. 715) and Lazich (1997), p. 146.

By way of contrast, much of the domestic mining sector was highly concentrated. For instance, in 1996, domestic copper mining had a four firm concentration ratio of 83.6 and the 1999 purchase by Phelps Dodge of Asarco and Cyprus Amax Minerals made it the largest producer in the world. Although the copper market is really international, as a result of such cross-border mergers copper imports were dominated by the same firms that played a large domestic role in the U.S. For other mining products four-firm concentration ratios are lower, for instance, coal (21.7 percent in 1992) and natural gas (15.7 percent in 1994). For a few mining products such as crude sand and gravel or crushed stone, the markets are strictly local and the national four-firm concentration ratios are below 4 percent. These data come from Census Bureau (annual 1997) and Lazich (1997).

1997. Was such an increase in domestic market concentration offset by an increase in imports?

Assuming, for the moment, that all imports compete against the production of the top four domestic producers, we can easily estimate "trade adjusted concentration ratios" by calculating the ratio of shipments of the top four domestic producers to total domestic production plus imports. This crude adjustment reflects the largest *decrease* in market concentration that imports could effect. If, however, the imports come from foreign affiliates of the top four firms (which we cannot determine), then market concentration would slightly *increase*. In most cases, the actual effect of imports on market concentration lies somewhere in between these extremes.

The most important result drawn from estimation of the trade adjusted concentration ratios, is that effective industrial concentration in manufacturing markets increased from the 1980s to 1992, even if we assume the maximum competitive impact of imports.[9] If we could take into consideration the high share of imports accounted for by foreign affiliates of domestic firms, especially as a result of horizontal mergers between U.S. and foreign firms (shown in Table 10.1), the rise in market concentration would be even greater than suggested by trade adjusted concentration ratios.[10]

To understand what is driving these long-run changes in concentration ratios, we must perform a regression analysis to separate out the various possible underlying causes. Such an exercise, carried out in an earlier study of mine for the period between 1958 and 1982, showed that two offsetting factors were quantitatively the most important during this period:[11] On the one hand, as the size of individual markets increased (measured by growth in production), market concentration fell as new firms entered to enjoy the fruits of increasing sales.

---

[9] The calculations are presented in Pryor (2001-d). Although the data were not available to make a similar calculation for 1997, the same results would undoubtedly be obtained.

[10] The trade-adjusted concentration ratios also do not include the impact of exports, which, if taken in account, would lower the concentration ratio. This is because the largest firms in a given industry tend to export relatively more than the small firms, so that their total shipments in domestic markets are less than their total shipments included as the numerator of the concentration ratio. Only the U.S. government has all the information necessary to calculate proper trade-adjusted concentration ratios, but it has not yet taken this statistical initiative. To my knowledge, only the Swedish government publishes the results of such calculations.

[11] Pryor (1994-b). Quantitative importance was measured by using the calculated coefficients and the values for the various trends. This statistical analysis separated short-term adjustment factors from long-term changes and showed that concentration ratios fall as economies of scale decline, as the capital/labor ratios (and perhaps barriers to entry) fall, and as market size increases. The regression also showed that concentration ratios rise as total factor productivity (TFP) and science-intensity or technological opportunities (imperfectly proxied by the ratio of scientists and engineers to total employment) increases. This empirical analysis also showed

On the other hand, as productivity (more exactly, total factor productivity) increased in a particular industry, market concentration increased as the more productive firms (often the larger firms) were able to knock the less productive firms out of the market. The calculations also showed that two less important factors also led to greater market concentration: a rising level of mechanization (more exactly, a rising capital/output ratio); and a rising "research intensity" (more exactly, the ratio of research and development expenditures to total sales). Both of these factors also widen the competitive differences between stronger and weaker firms.

From this type of abstract approach, coupled with projection of trends in market size and productivity, I concluded in this earlier study that in the future, the domestic concentration ratios would rise—a bold prediction, since in the two decades before I made this analysis, domestic concentration ratios had been falling. In the intervening decade since that research was carried out, I have found no new evidence to change my mind about this trend: market concentration in narrowly defined manufacturing industries will increase in the future. What I did not predict was that the increase in domestic concentration ratios would more than offset the impact of trade, so that the trade-adjusted concentration ratios would begin to increase as well. It seems likely that the impact of trade on effective market concentration in the 21st century will begin to weaken.[12]

To the list of causes underlying an increase in market concentration in manufacturing, two more factors must be added. In the 1970s and 1980s, financial markets and institutions changed, especially the rise of the junk bond market, which facilitated mergers by allowing firms to buy other firms more easily. Further, in 1982 the government changed its criteria for taking antitrust actions and this, in turn, allowed more horizontal buyouts and mergers to occur, a topic taken up later in greater detail.

• *Brief Notes on Industrial Concentration in Other Sectors*: In contrast to most manufacturing industries, the markets for various providers of other goods and services are more often local, so that an increase in concentration ratios can reflect not just the rise of concentration in these local markets but the growth of

---

that such productivity changes set up important first-mover advantages that more than offset the effects of any type of institutional sclerosis.

12 The world-wide horizontal merger wave, especially between U.S. and non-U.S. firms, is expected to continue for at least several years into the 21st century and, as noted above, this reduces the competitive impact of imports. Meanwhile, the growth of the ratio of the imports of goods to the total domestic production, which was rising throughout the last three decades of the 20th century, began to taper off so that the potential impact of increased imports on the effective concentration of industry is moderating.

national chains as well. I discuss certain aspects of the wholesale and retail sector in the following section, but other sectors deserve brief attention now, especially those in which the government has tried to reduce concentration by lifting governmental constraints on entry.

Deregulation of industry has had a particularly important impact in the fields of transportation and communications. As I discuss in greater detail elsewhere,[13] after a flurry of new entrants and increased competition following deregulation, these sectors began to consolidate again as a result of considerable merger activity. In some cases, such as railroads and airlines, the high degree of market concentration prevailing at the end of the 20th century is likely to become greater unless forceful anti-merger actions are taken—which seem unlikely in the short term. The future of market competition in parts of the communications industry is more uncertain. For instance, although the seven Baby Bells created by the breakup of AT&T in 1984 had shrunk to four by 2000, wireless and alternative cable methods of delivering telephone calls were coming into widespread use, so that the state of competition in the coming decades in telephone communications is not clear. Still other parts of the communications industry, such as radio stations, media enterprises (e.g., TimeWarner and America Online), and cable and internet companies also experienced a rash of mergers in the 1990s, and such a trend seems likely to continue in the near future as well, so that the greater market concentration should also be expected.

Mergers in the financial sector during the 1980s and 1990s may possibly have a major impact on U.S. economic growth in the future, especially since this merger wave will undoubtedly continue in the coming decades as well. According to the research of Stephen Rhoades and of Laurence Meyer, the period between 1980 and 1997 witnessed more than 6,300 bank mergers, involving $1.8 trillion dollars of acquired assets. As a result, the number of banks shrank by 27 percent, some banks achieved enormous size, and the share of banking assets accounted for by the 100 largest banking organizations rose from 51 to 75 percent. Bank mergers in the U.S. paralleled similar merger activity in the rest of the world.[14]

Despite such merger activity between banks, local market concentration of banks in the various Metropolitan Statistical Areas (MSAs) declined slightly, according to research of Stephen Rhoades. Nevertheless, Stephen Rhoades

---

[13]   Pryor (2001-d).

[14]   With the completion of pending mergers to create the Dai-Ichi Kangyo/ Fuji/Industrial Bank and also the Sumitomo/Sakura Bank, by 2001 there will be more than a half dozen banks with assets greater than a half trillion dollars (including in the U.S., Citigroup and Bank of America) (*New York Times*, 3/9/2000).

and also Gary Whalen emphasize that in more than one third of the MSAs, bank concentration was very high and that statewide concentration actually increased over the period. Since 1992, when these measures of market concentration were calculated, bank consolidation has proceeded rapidly. For instance, between the middle of 1992 and the middle of 1999, the percentage of assets of very large banks (FDIC-insured commercial banks and savings banks, both with more than $10 billion of assets) rose from 36 percent to 66 percent, as bank mergers became ever larger.[15] In 2000 Chase Manhattan Bank merged with the J.P. Morgan Bank. This means that the 15 largest banks in New York in 1950 merged into just four giant banks in a half century period.

Since 1990 mega-mergers united a variety of financial intermediaries.[16] The 1994 Branch Banking and Efficiency Act and the 1999 law repealing the Glass Steagall Act will only amplify the merger wave, not just within the banking industry but also between banks and other financial intermediaries. Satoshi Ikeda shows that the number of U.S. banks listed among the 50 largest banks in the world has dramatically declined, and this fact provided U.S. banks with the dubious excuse of "meeting foreign competition," when attempting to justify merger plans to antitrust authorities.[17]

The future impact of such consolidation in the financial sector can, of course, be modified by actions of U.S. governmental regulators, although again major changes seem unlikely. If consolidation continues, U.S. financial markets will probably more closely resemble those found in certain European nations, where small enterprises find it much more difficult to obtain loans to finance expansion than do large, relatively less risky enterprises. In many circumstances, such a development could, in turn, have an adverse impact on industrial dynamism in the U.S.

---

[15] In 1984 this percentage was 28 percent. The data come from Holland, et al. (1996), updated with 1999 data from *FDIC Quarterly Banking Profile*, 2nd quarter (1999).

[16] These included the merger between Aetna and Prudential Health, two mammoth health insurance companies which together cover about 22 million Americans; or the 1998 merger of CitiCorp and Travelers Insurance.

[17] Some such as Dymski (1999) have also cast doubt on the claim that such mergers have led to great efficiency gains. I have not, however, found conclusive evidence on this matter, although the reasons given for the Chase Manhattan–J.P. Morgan merger do not encourage much optimism. The management of J.P. Morgan, which sold for $30.9 billion, claimed that it was "too small" to compete (*Financial Times*, September 13, 2000). Although the Chase management claimed that it wanted to be an "end-game winner," analysts asserted that Chase Manhattan bought the bank primarily "for prestige." "No matter how much stock trading or underwriting Chase did, its competitors continued to disparage it as a déclassé commercial bank." (*New York Times*, September 13, 2000).

3. Antitrust Actions

The quantitative and qualitative information provided above shows that from 1982 onward, concentration in narrowly defined markets increased. Moreover, the rate of merger and acquisition activities accelerated when the Clinton administration took over from the Reagan and Bush administrations. What happened?

One argument is that many of the horizontal mergers occurring in the U.S. are not really anti-competitive, since they are between firms in different markets. These include, for instance, banks dealing with distinct geographical regions, or between firms producing different products classified under the same industrial code. Unfortunately, it is impossible to obtain quantitative evidence distinguishing these from mergers that have an anti-competitive impact.

A more common explanation is that antitrust authorities are no longer relying on simple considerations of market share and structure to guide its actions toward mergers, but are taking into account a more sophisticated variety of criteria. These include, for instance, the actual ability of the merged firms to raise prices and act as a monopoly; the cost savings resulting from the merger; and greater ability to compete effectively on a world market.

The antitrust authorities during the Clinton administration, especially in the Justice Department, were much more vigilant than they had been in the previous decade, and the number of antitrust filings more than doubled (but mergers, of course, rose even more rapidly). It stopped or reshaped certain large mergers (for instance; BP-Amoco was allowed to purchase Atlantic Richfield (ARCO), but had to sell off ARCO's Alaskan properties to Phillips Petroleum). Even so, the number of mergers increased more rapidly than before, and most were permitted.

Governmental authorities face several major problems in deciding whether to prevent or reshape a proposed merger. They often have a difficult time in judging the validity of the evidence the companies provide about their alleged cost savings, their inability to influence market prices, or enhanced ability to compete on the world market. Moreover, such data are often very difficult for the antitrust authorities to generate from their own investigations. The problem is compounded by the growing volume of cases that must be reviewed. Finally, the changing link between market structure and market competition raises a number of theoretical questions that have not yet been satisfactorily resolved. I discuss some of these below.

At the cusp of the 21st century, a limited restraint on mergers in the U.S. came from an unlikely source, namely the European Commission's Competition Office, which blocked or modified a number of well-publicized mergers. These included not just mergers between European firms, but also those between European and

U.S. firms (e.g., Time Warner and EMI or Microsoft and Telewest) and between U.S. firms with branches in Europe (e.g., MCIWorldCom and Sprint or G.E. and Honeywell). Nevertheless, the European antitrust authorities have primarily focused on mega-deals and have allowed almost all other mergers to go through, although they have also taken aim at dubious business practices of U.S. based firms in Europe. In this globalizing economy, collaboration between national antitrust authorities seems essential. The European Commission's Competition Office is considerably more powerful than U.S. antitrust authorities, since it serves as prosecutor, judge, and jury; and, as a result, it can more easily stop or modify cross-border mergers or megers between non-European companies with branches or significant sales in Europe.[18]

During the Clinton administration, antitrust authorities also took actions against a number of companies, such as Microsoft, which it believed to be violating laws against anti-competitive behavior, even though no mergers were involved. Unfortunately, as companies become larger and have more resources available for lobbying purposes, antitrust prosecutions get more and more politicized. For instance, as noted in Chapter 8, Microsoft lobbied to reduce the budget of the Antitrust Division of the Department of Justice while the company had an important case pending before the Division

U.S. and European antitrust authorities have begun to work together on certain actions (e.g., the Microsoft case and certain merger cases). At a summit conference of social democratic and progressive heads of government in Berlin in June 2000, attempts were made to discuss the formation of an international antitrust agency that would have authority to stop mergers or break up companies in any industrialized nation. Because of its radical nature, especially regarding tricky issues of national sovereignty, the proposal went nowhere. It does, however, indicate an important global problem that must be addressed more forcefully as market concentration continues its upward trend.

The evidence presented above suggests that in the U.S. narrowly defined markets began to become more concentrated in the early 1980s in most sectors and that this trend will continue in the coming years. The major underlying cause for this rising market concentration was the merger boom, both at home and abroad; and this was not offset by the competitive impact of rising imports. Moreover, the growing volume of cross-national horizontal mergers will further reduce the competitive role of foreign trade, since imports are more likely to come from companies that are already producing in the U.S.

---

[18] Although some have seen in their actions a conspiracy of the Commission to stymie the globalization efforts of U.S. firms, this is far from proven.

C. The Increasing Importance of Informal Cooperation Between Competitors[19]

The merger wave has been supplemented by a growing and implicit market concentration in the form of "strategic alliances," "strategic partnerships," or "business consortia," many of which are cross-border. These are agreements between firms, very often competitors, to collaborate on a particular project for a specified purpose and time period. Such arrangements are not new, but they are growing in importance and offer the potential for anti-competitive activities by price setting, division of markets, and other cartel behaviors.

Such alliances exist, for instance, between Shell and Texaco, AT&T and British Telecom, or Dell and Cisco.[20] Such arrangements take a variety of forms and often start in a seemingly innocent manner. For example, according to a report from Sematech, representatives from all major microchip manufacturers and equipment suppliers in the world attended a meeting in June 1999 to develop an "international technology road map for semiconductors." Although these kinds of meetings, as well as trade association conventions, are legal, they can easily provide many informal opportunities for manufacturers to set prices, which is clearly proscribed by U.S. law. It is unknown, however, if such meetings are increasing in frequency and scope and, since they are usually not publicly announced, what exactly takes place.

The interaction of domestic and foreign competition is particularly disturbing in the airline industry. After its partial deregulation in 1978 (many safety and the environment regulations remained), the airline industry in the U.S. first became more competitive and then began to consolidate. Moreover, the major U.S. companies also formed strategic alliances with many foreign partners so that six large alliances accounted for roughly over half of all passenger revenues in 2000.[21] These alliances have aimed at the close cooperation obtained in a merger, while skirting national rules against foreign ownership. In addition to

---

[19] In the text of this section I mention studies by: Friedheim (1998), Halal (1999), and Sematech (1999).

[20] It should be noted that such alliances are formed not just between companies with global markets but between small entities as well, like St. Francis Hospital and Vassar Brothers Hospitals in Poughkeepsie, NY, both of whom ended up raising prices 40 percent and later facing antitrust charges (Anon, 1999-b). This incident also suggests that the difference between non-profit and profit oriented institutions is eroding.

[21] The Oneworld Alliance included American Airways, British Airways, Canadian Airways, Cathay Pacific, Iberia, JAI, Quantas, and US Airways and in 2000 accounted for 16 percent of all revenue passenger kilometers (RPKs). The Star Alliance consisted of Air Canada, ANA, ANZ, Ansett, Australia Airways, Lufthansa, South African Airline, SAS, Singapore Airlines, Thai Airways, United Airways, and Varig and accounted for 21 percent of all RPKs. The other

these formal alliances, individual airlines have forged special joint- or cross-ownership arrangements for particular purposes.[22]

Unfortunately, most discussions in the economics literature of these alliances are through anecdotes, because we have relatively little quantitative information about them. Nevertheless, Cyrus Friedheim presents evidence that about 1 percent of the revenues of the top 1000 public U.S. corporations in 1980 came from alliance activities; in 1990, this had risen to about 8 percent; and he projected such revenues to be roughly 20 percent in 2000, an estimate that seems high to me.[23] His view of this development receives support, however, from an estimate by Andersen Consulting that in 2004, companies in such alliances will have about $25 to $40 trillion in assets.[24] Governmental concentration ratios do not include the impact of these informal arrangements—in part because the government does not systematically track them or, in most cases, require that they be reported.

In the case of enterprises producing the same products or services, many of these strategic alliances amount to a cartel, albeit sanitized by a trendy description. Up to the end of the 20th century, however, they do not seem to have been vigorously attacked by antitrust or other governmental regulatory authorities.[25] The international dimension of these strategic alliances also presented particular difficulties of regulation. Although the Federal Trade Commission issued guidelines about such alliances in 1999, it remains to be seen how much teeth these guidelines will have.

Business consortia, in which ostensible business rivals work together on common research, are another manifestation of the same trend. According to William Halal, about 250 research consortia (such as Sematech) and 1600 business research agreements were in operation in the U.S. at the end of the 20th

---

three alliances (Skyteam, Wings, and Qualiflyer) were much smaller. (Anon 1998-b, 2001). In 1999 in just the U.S., the top five airlines accounted for slightly more than 70 percent of all RPKs.

[22] For instance, American Airways had a "close cooperation" with Swissair; and Delta had similar arrangements with Air France and Aer Lingus. Cross-ownership is illustrated by the 1999 deal in which Virgin Airways, which competed with British Airways for transatlantic flights, sold 49 percent of itself to Singapore Airlines, although it initially announced that it would not join the Star Alliance.

[23] Freidheim does not specify his exact sources (some of the data come from internal memoranda from Booz-Allen Hamilton) nor explain how he adjusted the data, so such figures must be taken with caution.

[24] Cited by Anon (1999-b).

[25] For instance, News Corp. and Viacom, which owned rival children's cable channels in the U.S., jointly own the British version of Viacom's Nickelodeon channel. At the time this deal was signed, the former president at Viacom placed the following bizarre spin on this incipient cartel (undoubtedly for the benefit of antitrust authorities): "Sometimes you have to grit your teeth and treat your enemy as your partner ... No one ever said this business was all fun" (cited by Anon, 1999-b).

century. In the auto industry, for instance, the three major car makers worked together in 12 consortia to develop a range of products from new fuels to electric cars (and, in the 1960s, to delay introduction of antipollution equipment). Other consortia that set industry standards may also have a potential anti-competitive impact.

The falling costs of communications make the establishment and maintenance of such strategic alliances—or, in many cases, informal cartels—easier. Unfortunately, this development in the organization of industry has not received due attention, so that their exact impact on competition is not known. Nevertheless, if such arrangements continue to grow in the future, they may possibly have an important anti-competitive influence.

D. Novel Elements in Market Competition: New Economy Industries and E-commerce[26]

Industries introducing dramatically new products or using totally new technologies generally have a fluid structure, with many startups, many mergers, and many failures. If these new technologies feature considerable economies of large scale production, the efficiency gains achieved through mergers might offset any loss in consumer welfare occurring because of a more concentrated industrial structure which would allow the firms surveyed to raise prices over the previous level.

To the extent that the new information technology (IT) leads to a reduction of average firm size and opens up new niches of competition in various industries, it should enhance market competition by creating a market with a larger number of small companies competing against each other. In the previous chapter I present evidence that IT has not had such an effect and, as argued below, e-commerce will prove a similar disappointment for those wishing to see more competitive markets.

1. Mergers in the New Economy Industries (NEIs)

NEIs comprise those narrowly defined industries utilizing very new technologies usually featuring considerable economies of large scale production

---

[26] In the text of this section I cite studies by: Adamic and Huberman (2000), Brown and Goolsbee (2000), eMarketer (1999), Evans and Wurster (2000), OECD (1999-a), Rosen and Howard (2000), Simon (1997), Smith, Bailey, and Brynjolfsson (2000), U.S. Department of Commerce (1999), and Varian (2000).

and/or network economies (where the value of the good or service increases with the number of users, such as a telephone network). Since the application of these criteria is somewhat subjective, I define these industries both narrowly and broadly, and use both definitions in the empirical analysis (for more details, see External Appendix X-10.1). In the U.S. in 1997, according to the two definitions, the NEIs employed respectively 4.3 to 8.2 percent of the labor force in the private sector.

In 1999, these NEI firms accounted for roughly 40 to 50 percent (by value) of all horizontal mergers between U.S. firms, depending on the definition of NEI employed. In comparison to their share of the total labor force, they accounted for a disproportionate share of total horizontal mergers. Given the newness of many of these industries, this result accords with our intuition.

It is noteworthy that the share of total horizontal mergers of NEI firms is much lower between firms located outside the U.S. than between those located in the U.S. By way of contrast, the share of horizontal mergers is highest between NEI firms where the buying company is located outside the U.S. and the purchased firm is located within the U.S. This seems to reflect the desire of non-U.S. NEI enterprises to purchase new U.S. technologies.

Although the share of NEIs involved in mergers was high, the volume of mergers involving "old economy industries" was even higher, and, as noted above, industrial concentration rose in most narrowly defined industries. Although the mergers involving NEIs might have some economic benefit to the nation as a whole, mergers in the more traditional industries merely lead to higher industrial concentration with the potential for monopoly behavior and few offsetting benefits. As noted above in the brief discussion of the hog processing market, both farmers selling their pigs and consumers buying pork now face a more concentrated market and, under reasonable assumptions, the farmers will receive lower prices, the consumers will pay higher prices, and the hog processors will have higher profits.

2. The Growth of E-commerce and Its Possible Impacts on the Trade Sector

Given the relative novelty of e-commerce, it is important to review some critical facts about it. At the end of the 20th century, the volume of e-commerce was still small, amounting in 1999 to less than 1 percent of the GDP, according to an estimate of the U.S. Department of Commerce. Before the dot.com crash in late 2000, predictions for the future volume of e-commerce were dazzling and, moreover, varied by several orders of magnitude. A low estimate came from the staid OECD, which expected e-commerce to grow more than 50 percent a year in the early years of the 21st century. Even though business-to-consumer (B2C) e-commerce has received the most publicity, the volume of business-to-business (B2B) sales accounted for roughly three quarters of all e-commerce at the end of the 20th century and, despite the shakeout in the early years of the 21st century, is expected to constitute the largest share of all e-commerce in that century as well.

Although the reported growth of B2B e-commerce may be staggering, much of this rise represents merely a substitution of the internet for the previously employed EDI (electronic data interchange), which is a cumbersome method of linking the computers of various companies together as a communications network. It is worth noting that in 1999 e-commerce represented somewhat less than 2 percent of the volume of EDI. Although new technologies and computers will allow the shift from EDI to the internet to be accelerated, the growth of B2B e-commerce may be less of a significant change in the way that business is conducted than the volume of such commerce, current or predicted, might suggest.

Since EDI is expensive and limited primarily to large firms, substitution of the internet will certainly allow more suppliers to come into contact with more buyers. In an interesting analysis Philip Evans and Thomas Wurster note that there has always been a tradeoff between the number of trading partners that a business can reach and the richness of the information transmitted (including the amount, customization, and security of information and the interactivity between partners). Although the internet does not eliminate this tradeoff, it is less painful, since businesses can now reach more potential customers or suppliers and, at the same time, provide them with richer information about their products at lower costs.

E-commerce can have several direct effects on the structure of the trade sector: Retailers can now easily deal directly with producers, which is leading to a shakeout in wholesaling. It is argued that only the largest venders—those who have the financial resources to maintain an active web presence—will survive. The jump in market concentration in the retail sector between 1992 and 1997 (noted above) probably arose more as a result of mergers than e-commerce. Certainly e-commerce will reduce catalogue sales, and in certain branches of the retail sector, e-tailers may wipe out local retail selling. Amazon.com, for instance, with its three million books on call, has been driving many local bookstores out of business.

It is noteworthy, however, that much more important factors were affecting the retail sector in the 1990s than e-commerce, given the sharp jump in the percentage of sales accounted for by the largest outlets that I have previously noted.

Clearly, e-commerce will transform, but not eliminate, wholesaling, since smaller retailers have good reasons for dealing with a few distributors, rather than with a large number of manufacturing companies. Manufacturers may also not wish to focus their efforts on servicing orders of individual customers for single units of their product. Indeed, some manufacturers, who have experimented with internet sales, have abandoned these efforts and relied again on wholesalers. E-commerce will certainly provide low-cost contacts between retailers and wholesalers in the same way that EDI facilitated (at high cost) contacts between large businesses, and thus expand the role of wholesalers as information providers to retailers.

The final outcome, however, is far from clear; but at the turn of the millennium B2B appeared to be dominated by a few large companies. If, however, the role of wholesalers as suppliers of information becomes increasingly important, then economies of scale in wholesaling will become more decisive, smaller wholesalers will get knocked out of the market, and the wholesale market will become more concentrated. This had not happened by the end of the century.

In retailing several additional factors come into play as well. For many types of retail sales, the customer trust of the company is vitally important. To a certain extent, those being first into a new market, and who have been able to gain such trust, have a distinct advantage over latecomers to the market. Acting on this idea, various major e-tailers have rushed into new e-markets and invested enormous amounts on advertising to build up the requisite trust and good will. Amazon.com's belief that they can dominate e-markets by establishing such trust, even if their prices are higher than other e-commerce sites selling the same goods, was to some extent vindicated when the company became the largest e-tailer of CDs only three months after entering the market,[27] even though its prices were approximately $1.00 more than prices at other on-line CD vendors. The company's first-place position in the sale of on-line movie videos was achieved even more rapidly. Maintaining market dominance to sustain first-mover advantages is not cheap: e-tailers must continue to invest heavily in the newest technologies to accommodate customers, for instance, making it possible to deal with the company by cellular phone as well as by computer. First mover strategies are also of little use if, in the process, the company cannot obtain additional financing and goes bankrupt. It should be noted that for all of its high volume of sales, Amazon.com never had a profitable year (at the time of writing, six years after the company started), and had lost over $1.5 billion. After a certain point, lenders may wish to see some profits before they risk any more to the company.

B2C commerce was changing rapidly around the turn of the millennium, as established large chain stores, such as Wal-Mart, Borders Books, and Barnes and Noble, set up e-commerce outlets to meet the new competition of the upstart

[27]   Anon. (1998-a), (2000-a)

e-tailers. Of particular interest to the future of e-tailing, they began to explore ways to combine both their conventional and their virtual transactions for greater customer convenience. The older retailers are trying to capitalize on the consumer trust and knowledge built up in traditional ways in order to attract those consumers who might be able to purchase the goods at a lower price from some no-name e-tailer whose honesty and expedient deliveries are not broadly known or advertised.

Finally, it should be noted that the competition between traditional retailers and e-tailers will also, of course, be affected by governmental tax policies. At the turn of the millennium, e-tailers did not need to charge sales taxes. State governments fought this policy, both to prevent state sales tax revenues from falling and to keep e-tailers from gaining an unfair advantage over brick-and-mortar stores within their state. Although serious technical issues arise in implementing e-commerce taxation, the political opposition seemed even more insurmountable. As a result of this stalemate, e-tailing has received an important impetus.[28]

3. E-commerce, E-markets, and Competition

It is alleged that the ability of the internet easily to reach a vast number of potential buyers will encourage an upsurge in market competition, especially as the number of participating buyers and sellers becomes greater. Of particular importance, small firms are now able to capture profitable slivers of the information-intensive business of large firms, and developments along these lines can be easily seen in the financial sector. For instance, eSchwab, a no-frills, discount on-line brokerage firm, has been able to capture considerable business from established brokerage firms, which use the profits gained from a wider spread between buying and selling prices of stock to offer full-scale advisory and research services. More examples in the field of finance are easy to find.[29]

---

[28] Internet companies and other "new economy" industries are not only tax-shy but labor-union shy as well, which may point toward an important future development in the economy as a whole.
    An interesting parallel to this taxation problem arises in the case of Indian reservations, whose sales are not subject to federal or state taxes. At the end of the 1990s they began internet sales of cigarettes, which have a high "sin tax." Some have forecast that in the early years of the 21st century their sales will account for 20 percent of the cigarette market. As discussed in the next chapter, a similar situation on the international market arose at the end of the 20th century in the form of off- shore, on-line firms located in various tax havens.

[29] In the late 1990s, people began surfing the web to find the lowest mortgage rates and to locate internet banks paying the highest interest rates on deposits. With the widespread introduction of ATM machines, people were no longer tied to their local banks to obtain cash, although

In various other lines of business, firms have been using the large reach and information richness of the internet to capture the highly profitable classified advertising business from established newspapers. Such developments have given rise to enormous optimism about the competitive impact of the internet.

Several counter-arguments to these sanguine projections of a less concentrated market structure emerging from e-commerce need emphasis.

• E-business sites are expensive to build, maintain and secure. According to some available projections from eMarketer, 1999, only about one fifth of the B2B websites would turn a net profit in 2000. Small firms cannot afford a long-term financial hemorrhage, so only large firms with deep pockets may survive the e-commerce race. These remarks are even more pertinent to B2C sites. In B2C retailing, Kenneth Rosen and Amanda Howard emphasize that costs are extremely high, averaging in the late 1990s over $26 per order generated, compared with an average of $2.50 for physical retailers; and return rates of merchandise are also apparently high (drawing from the experience of catalogue sales). Furthermore, according to the same source, the costs of constructing a successful site averages between $1 and $1.5 million and maintenance costs also run high.

• E-business features considerable economies of large scale production, often arising from network economies. Moreover, the production and transmission of information features considerable economies of scale as well. The likely result in the future is both a rise in concentration of e-business in particular, and higher market concentration in general. In this regard it is worth noting that

it must also be noted that consolidation of ATM networks has proceeded rapidly, with some regional monopolies emerging (Baker, 1996).The e-bond market, which short-circuits the New York dealers and underwriting firms, began to take off in the late 1990s.

According to some e-commerce experts, such as Evans and Wurster (2000, p. 50), retail banking is a profitable sliver of the banking industry that is bound to be swept away by internet banking. Evans and Wurster pose, however, the embarrassing question of why, if this is true, banks are wasting so much money on mergers. Their answers (p. 236) are unconvincing: "One, traditional distribution-centered economics still count for a lot, and mergers are a means of shrinking capacity and wringing out the last increment of physical scale economies. Two, even in a deconstructed industry, large corporations may survive, provided that they are run as loose federations of largely autonomous business units (this is the structure of much of wholesale banking today); size may not do much good, but neither need it do any harm. Three, as the swamp dries up, the biggest dinosaurs stay alive longest; size is a smart strategy, if it is a given that you are a dinosaur."

This puzzle raises the possibility that internet banking is so new that few accurate predictions can be made about it. Certainly, past predictions have foundered, for instance, the expected boom in on-line sales of mutual funds, a major investment vehicle for many Americans, has not materialized.

between 1992 and 1997, the four-firm concentration ratio of "electronic shopping and mail-order houses" rose from 15.8 to 24.4 percent.[30]

• The reverse side of the increased reach and richness of e-commerce is that potential consumers are inundated with too much data to process. Philip Evans and Thomas Wurster use the analogy of a consumer facing an infinite choice of breakfast cereals in the supermarket. Since most consumers have no interest in wrestling with all the alternatives, they fall back on a few high-profile brands, which enjoy a high measure of loyalty and insensitivity to price changes, and buy Kellogg's Corn Flakes, a company that is already one of the largest companies in its industry. Although Evans and Wurster argue that this Corn-Flakes-phenomenon is a consequence of the underdeveloped state of internet navigators (discussed in greater detail below), it is also a function of the fact that our purchasing choice depends not just on price, but on quality of product or service, reliability, promptness of delivery, post-sale support and other characteristics which search engines or navigators cannot easily track. The willingness of buyers to process enormous amounts of new information is also a factor: as noted by Nobel Prize laureate Herbert Simon, "A wealth of information creates a poverty of attention."

• E-commerce faces some finite limits. According to the evaluation of Kenneth Rosen and Amanda Howard, B2C sales of travel, entertainment, and financial services are likely to dominate total sales up to 2005. Goods and services that are highly heterogeneous, or that have high transport costs, (e.g., refrigerators), or that require special servicing, or that are difficult to sell through catalogues seem better suited for brick-and-mortar retailers. Many e-commerce sites are also much too complicated for general use. According to one authority, a site must be "brain-dead simple" to attract a customer base.

The hype about e-commerce promoting more competition and lower prices by creating more perfect markets with uniform prices is also flimsy, at least if we can judge from the evidence available at the dawn of the new millennium. Several studies comparing prices offered by e-tailers and conventional stores reveal that goods bought over the internet are more expensive, while one careful study shows the reverse.[31] Unfortunately, the available studies cover only a limited array of products, and they deal with an immature market that is under-

---

[30]   The sources of these data come from the sources discussed in External Appendix X-10.2. This particular industry is 5961 in the SIC nomenclature used in 1992 and 45411 in the NAICS nomenclature used in 1997.

[31]   Most of the studies carried out on these matters were not yet widely circulated when this chapter was written, so I have had to rely on secondary sources. In 1997 Goldman Sachs (cited by OECD, 1999-a, p. 70) surveyed the price of a market basket of 30 products sold by Wal-Mart both online and offline and found that, even after the value of shopping time were added , the goods were less expensive in conventional stores. In a 1996-97 survey Joseph Bailey (cited by

going rapid changes. They also do not take into account the value of the time saved by shopping on the internet, rather than in visiting a brick-and-mortar store.

Frictionless markets with few price divergences for a given product have not yet been realized, and probably never will be, even with e-commerce. Three early studies, analyzed by Michael Smith and his coauthors, reveal substantial price variations over the internet, some of which are roughly of the same magnitude as such price dispersions in more conventional markets.[32] These studies also do not take into account that some well-known e-tailers are alleged to have begun "dynamic pricing," which is varying the price of a good offered to individual customers on the basis of information in the company's files that allows an assessment of this particular buyer's willingness to pay a higher price. Such practices appear illegal under current regulations against price discrimination, but they are difficult to detect and, at the time of writing, were not yet tested in court.

Any price dispersion is particularly surprising in view of the availability of internet navigational aids that allow price comparisons to be quickly made. These include shop-bots (shopping robots), which scan a variety of on-line sites to report the range of prices at various e-tailer sites, or meta-sites, which take this approach one step further by searching the results returned by a number of shop-bots.[33]

Few studies of the impact of the internet on competition in particular markets were carried out by the end of the 20th century, but one quantitative analysis of

---

Smith, Bailey, and Brynjolfsson, 2000) also found that prices for matched sets of books, CDs, and software were higher on the internet. By way of contrast in a 1998-99 survey Brynjolfsson and Smith (1999) found that prices for matched sets of books and CDs were lower on the internet than in conventional stores. A 1999 Lehman Brothers study by Ethan S. Harris and Joseph T. Abate (cited by Koretz, 1999) found that for a set of common consumer items including drugs, apparel, groceries, toys, and hardware, internet prices after shipping costs were 13 percent lower than in conventional stores. Ho Guen Lee (1997) found that internet prices for used cars were higher than prices in conventional dealers, but he was unable to control completely the quality of the cars.

[32] In one important respect, e-commerce markets are more competitive than conventional markets. The studies quoted above found that in B2C commerce, e-tailers change their prices more often than traditional stores and, moreover, in smaller increments. Their costs of changing prices are lower, especially since they don't need to change price stickers or publish new catalogues.

[33] E-tailers dislike shop-bots for several major reasons. They allow the surfer to avoid seeing the advertisements serving as an important source of revenue to them and, therefore, reduce their revenues from this source (DeLong and Froomkin, 1999). They bog down the computers of the e-tailers. And, in many cases, the shop-bots deliver incomplete information, for instance, omitting special bargains. Shop-bots, however, have their own problems with meta-sites: in 1999 MySimon.com sued Priceman.com for copyright infringement since the latter uses the former as one of its sources (France,1999). The question of who "owns" a price has yet to be decided by the courts.

the life insurance industry deserves mention. Jeffrey Brown and Austan Goolsbee present evidence that the ability to compare insurance costs using the internet led to a decrease in insurance prices in the 1990s, especially after the development of programs that could easily collect price information of different companies. They also argue that price dispersion increased and then decreased as the percentage of people buying insurance engage in comparative shopping (for instance, with shop-bots) over the internet. Both conclusions are, however, tentative.[34]

One problem, as noted above, is that consumers buy from certain suppliers on the basis of criteria other than price and, up to now, trustworthy navigational aids that can judge these various characteristics of the seller and the product are in their infancy. Indeed, in light of the type of information need-ed to make such judgements, adequate navigational aids may never be fully developed, especially for B2B transactions that involve a complex array of such criteria.

4. The Current Market Concentration of E-commerce

At the turn of the millennium, e-commerce was highly concentrated. In 1998, for instance, eMarketer reports that the top five e-commerce sellers (both B2B and B2C) in the U.S. accounted for more than two-thirds of all U.S. e-commerce sales. In retailing alone, internet web sites feature a higher con-centration of visits than the concentration of sales in brick-and-mortar stores. For instance, according to an analysis by Lada Adamic and Bernardo Huberman of records of AOL users in December 1997, the top 5 percent of all sites accounted for 75 percent of all visits. At first glance, this does not seem out of line, since data from the *1992 Census of Retail Trade* shows that the top 5 percent of all retailers account for roughly 72 percent of all sales. Nevertheless, if pornographic and educational sites are eliminated from the sample, both of which feature a much lower concentration of hits than the total universe of sites, then the concentration of hits in the remaining sites is considerably higher than 75 percent.[35] Moreover, this concentration is likely to continue, in part because common internet search engines list the most popu-

---

[34] It is unclear whether Brown and Goolsbee have included in their regression analysis all factors that might account for the fall in insurance costs. Their results for price dispersion also raise dif-ficult problems of interpretation, because the final degree of price dispersion depends on whether one includes a constant and also a cubed term in their formulae (their Table 6, substi-tuting various assumptions about the share of buyers using the internet to compare prices).

[35] Equity trading provides a more specific example. In 2000 the market share of the top four and eight online traders were 58 and 86 percent (Anon., 2000-d). According to 1992 Enterprise Sta-

lar sites first and thereby reinforce the popularity of an established site that already has many hits.

On-line markets have an indeterminate impact on retail prices. If there are many e-tailers for a particular product, buyers can quite easily search for the lowest price. But if there are relatively few such sites, the sellers can more easily learn the prices offered by competitors and informally coordinate them. Hal Varian argues that this is exactly what happened in the airline industry in the 1990s. He also notes that when Toys "R" Us and Amazon.com announced a joint venture, this prospect of implicit collusion must have been in the back of the mind of the chief executive of a rival company, eToys, who made a peculiar statement, "This is great news for us. Last year we had half a dozen competitors. Now our two remaining competitors are merging into one."

For B2B sales, the exchange sites jointly set up by a group of competing companies create biased markets which have a high potential for the exercise of anti-competitive market power. In 2000, for instance, Ford, G.M., Daimler/Chrysler, Renault, and Nissan began setting up a joint website (Covisint.com) to be used by each company for purchasing parts from suppliers. The car makers, by forcing suppliers to do all their selling through the site, could compare prices offered by suppliers (even though this is against rules promulgated by the Federal Trade Commission) and use this information to force supply prices down. This possibility drew the attention of antitrust authorities, but they nevertheless gave their tentative approval to the site, subject to good behavior on the part of the car makers. How the antitrust authorities will set and enforce the standards for acceptable business behavior were unresolved issues at the start of the new millennium. To what extent the car makers can force suppliers to do business through the web where the prices of auto parts will be hammered down also remains to be seen. In the 21st century, however, these policy issues will become increasingly salient, since a number of similar joint websites of ostensibly competing firms were set up at the same time as well. Some of these, such as the planned joint website that includes Sears of the U.S. and Carrefour of France, cross national boundaries. At the time of writing, it was too early to determine the actual impact of these biased markets.

Although e-commerce has been hailed as a new competitive element, the evidence above suggests that such claims are overstated and that the e-commerce may act to lessen, rather than to increase, overall market concentration.

---

tistics, the four largest security and commodity brokers accounted for 42 percent of all sales, and the top eight, about 52 percent. Although these data are not quite comparable, they give some idea of the orders of magnitudes involved.

E. Competition and Market Structure[36]

Up to now I have focused almost exclusively on market structure as an indicator of competition. Now it is necessary to explore the possibility that both competition and market concentration could increase together. In other words, as Geoffrey Shepherd has argued, market structure is only one of several factors underlying the degree of market competition and we need a broader perspective.

What factors might counteract the anti-competitive impact of the growing concentration of industry?

• *Government action*: Although, as noted above, antitrust authorities face a series of constraints that will probably prevent a vigorous attack on new mergers, other governmental actions may favor increased competition. In particular, as I discuss in considerable detail in the next chapter, various levels of government deregulated many different branches of industry during the last quarter of the 20th century. In the coming decades, however, the impact on competition of more deregulation will be limited because the regulated industries are now fewer in number. Indeed, in certain cases previous deregulation may have to be reversed to correct mistakes, for instance, in the electricity industry in California.

• *Foreign trade*: The impact of imports on the effective market structure has been overwhelmed in recent years by the impact of mergers, at least in manufacturing. The future competitive impact of globalization on market competition also does not seem very promising for three reasons: (i) The volume of mergers between U.S. and non-U.S. firms is rising, fueled in part by the persistent trade deficit. This means that the "competitive imports" from abroad are coming from companies that are merged with U.S. firms so that the imports are not really competitive. (ii) Market concentration in the largest trade partners of the U.S. also seems to be on the upswing, so that competition between foreign suppliers may be less in the future. (iii) The volume of cross-border strategic partnerships and other arrangements with the potential to facilitate cartel activity also has an upward trend. Some economists, for instance, Lester Thurow, argue that increasing growth of the giant-multinationals will actually increase competition in the United States as an unintended effect of the long-term struggle between the U.S., Japan, and Europe for economic hegemony. Given the evidence presented above, such an argument rings hollow.

• *Non-internet technology*: As argued in the previous chapters, inventions in certain sectors, particularly communications, might reduce the minimum efficient size of producers, especially at the plant level. The total impact of the

---

[36]   In the text of this section I cite studies by: Darnay and Reddy (1997) Shepherd (1982), and Thurow (1992). Results of the Millennium Survey are presented in Pryor (2000-b).

information-technology revolution, however, seems to increase enterprise size, as argued in the previous chapter. Still other new technologies might have different effects on plant and firm sizes as well and their impact is difficult to predict with any confidence.

• *E-commerce*: The most convincing argument for a future intensification of market competition rests on the development of e-commerce, the availability of more market information, and greater transparency of markets. Unfortunately, as indicated above, the available evidence does not suggest that e-commerce will bring about more perfect competition, with myriads of buyers and sellers competing so that the market will rapidly converge to a single price. Instead, several factors about e-commerce act to reduce market competition. These include: (i) The currently high state of concentration in e-commerce and the great importance of first-mover advantages in creating consumer trust; (ii) The economies of large scale production in e-commerce, so that large, low-cost sellers can drive small, high-cost sellers out of business; (iii) The high costs of creating and maintaining a good site and of keeping up with ever-changing technology; and, finally, (iv) Other barriers to entry arising from the years of monetary losses necessary to achieve market dominance.

But three counter-arguments of e-commerce optimists deserve our attention:

• *Expanding niche markets*: The internet can serve to exploit competitive slivers of established businesses in highly concentrated industries. That is, if large online or offline firms become too greedy (or too inefficient) and raise their prices sufficiently high, it may be profitable for someone to offer the same goods or services at a lower price. Such entrepreneurs must, of course, figure out a way to get noticed by buyers—a serious challenge. Some envision a website serving as a hub of these business rebels, where the primary criterion for membership is that the prices offered are at least 20 percent below the prices offered by the established e-tailers. The various sellers on such a site must, of course, still overcome problems of trust by the potential buyers and their sales volume may be low. Nevertheless, the very existence of a well-known discount site might force the large sellers to lower their prices.

• *More information*: The development of the internet may increase competition by giving potential buyers access to more information about alternative sources of supply. Many markets that were previously local, because of the high costs of obtaining information about distant producers, suddenly become national with the advent of internet. Even though measures of market concentration may not greatly change, actual competition is greater, because local markets have become more contestable.

• *Countervailing consumer power:* The net may allow consumers more easily to band together into groups ("buyer clubs") that can bargain with suppliers for lower prices.

At this point it becomes difficult to forecast whether the pro-competitive effects of the internet will outweigh the anti-competitive effects. To me, it seems likely that overall e-market concentration will continue to increase in most lines of business, in major part because the first mover advantages, network economies, other economies of scale, and financial constraints that led to high market concentration in e-commerce at the end of the 20th century will probably continue to be dominant. Thus, increasing market concentration in both traditional markets and e-commerce seem likely to lead to less market competition. This prediction runs against the results of the Millennium Survey of the economics profession, showing that a majority of professional economists see little change in the state of competition in the next half century.

One intriguing possibility has yet to be explored, namely that markets will become both more concentrated and more competitive. The reigning companies in highly concentrated industries might keep prices down for fear of attracting new challengers into their markets, who would undercut them. A number of economists have pointed out, for instance, that Microsoft does not charge a monopoly price for its operating systems (in part, because they wish to compete against the earlier versions of their product; in part, because of fear of possible new entrants). I see few signs that this will happen on a broad scale, but if it does, then we will have to scrap the conventional belief that measures of market concentration also reflect the degree of competition in the relevant market and, in addition, that concentration leads to higher profits.

While these theoretical possibilities deserve attention, they make prediction difficult. Nevertheless, without any compelling counter-evidence on hand about current trends, it seems likely that market structure will continue to be a useful indicator of the degree of market competition for a number of years in the future. That is, in most cases, increasing market concentration will have an anti-competitive impact, despite any positive impacts that might result from e-commerce. If I am correct, we will experience higher prices for consumers, higher profits for producers, and possibly slower innovation and lower productivity. Such changes will, of course, occur slowly and will first be noticed in dry statistical analyses that will not engender much political ferment. Although these changes will certainly not be immediately visible to the eye, they will have an effect in the future on our quality of life, which will be noticed. But by that time, it may be too late for effective government actions to turn back the trend.

CHAPTER 11

Evolution of Government Regulation and Ownership

Laws will be simplified [over the next century]. Lawyers will
have diminished and their fees will have been vastly curtailed.
—Journalist Junius Henri Browne, 1893 [1].

Like the private sector, the government sector will also experience some important changes in institutions and organization. In this chapter I argue that both government regulation and public ownership are likely to decrease in the coming decades. In the next chapter, by way of contrast, I show how government expenditures as a share of GDP will probably increase in the coming decades.

The government can influence and structure the production and distribution of goods and services directly, through the ownership of the means of production, or indirectly, through an infinite variety of regulations and interventions. If the government wishes to modify the impact of market breakdowns and other imperfections in the system, some economics textbooks claim that either of these two policy approaches can be used—that regulation and public ownership are, in effect, substitutes for each other. I show below that among the OECD nations, this argument does not hold.

Governmental regulation and other forms of indirect participation in the economy are extremely difficult to measure, and the judgements of respected economists vary widely about their magnitude, and whether such market interventions will increase or decrease in the future. Given the difficulty in evaluating the impact of any particular government regulation, it should not be surprising that there is little agreement about their success. Even in measuring the extent of public ownership, serious problems arise and for many countries estimates vary considerably.

---

[1]   Cited by Laura Lee, *Bad Predictions: 2000 Years of the Best Minds Making the Worst Forecasts* (2000).

I turn first to U. S. governmental regulation and distinguish between three types:

• *Legal-framework regulations* act through civil and criminal law: to define and limit property rights (for instance, zoning restrictions); to specify contractual obligations; to set quality standards for goods and services through tort law; and to establish conditions defining fraud, discrimination, and improper or incompetent behavior by market participants.

• *Industry-specific regulations* focus on particular industries: to set prices (such as, for electricity); to determine eligibility for entering a market (for example, occupational licenses); to specify users of a particular resource (for instance, public lands or frequencies in the electromagnetic spectrum); to provide special subsidies or taxes for particular industries; and to promulgate certain rules of operations for specific types of businesses such as banks and other financial intermediaries (for instance, bank reserve ratios).

• *General economic regulations* act on the economy as a whole: to restrict pollution; to establish health and safety standards for workplaces; to limit the content of advertising; to set antitrust policies; to determine general business practices; and to formulate the rules for economic transactions with the rest of the world. Although the boundaries between these three types of regulation are fuzzy, these distinctions help us to limit the analysis to avoid discussing the entire legal system.

The first three sections of this chapter deal primarily with general economic regulation, although I examine certain special issues concerning the other two types of regulation as well. I also focus primary attention on two key questions: How has government regulation of the U.S. economy changed in past decades? What changes in regulation are to be expected in the future?

To attack such broad issues, I start by placing the U.S. system of governmental regulation in perspective by using other large industrialized nations in the OECD as a basis for quantitative comparisons. This type of cross-national approach permits several important hypotheses to be formulated that illuminate the behavior of government regulation of the U.S. economy over time. It also provides the quantitative basis for the overall evaluation of the role of government in the last chapter. Employing more detailed but qualitative indicators of U.S. government regulations and interventions into the economy over the second half of the 20th century, I argue that, in general, government regulation has diminished and that such a trend will continue in the coming decades. I also deal with three crucial side issues: the relation between the extent and effectiveness of government regulation; the increasingly important limitations which globalization places on the regulatory process; and the degree to which deregulation of industry and the fall of the welfare state are tied.

My discussion of public ownership is brief because it represents only a small share of total wealth in the U.S. and this portion will probably decrease even more in the future. Patterns of property holdings in the private sector are more important and a crucial trend in the last half of the 20th century, which will become even more significant in the future, is the "socialization of ownership." This signifies that an increasing share of assets are owned or held by financial intermediaries, rather than directly by individuals.

A. An International Perspective on General Economic Regulation[2]

Few credible objective indicators are readily available for measuring the extent of government regulation. Nevertheless, we can utilize the results of two large-scale international comparisons analyzing the "international competitiveness" of various nations. These are surveys of the opinions of business executives who must daily deal with governmental regulations and who are asked, among other things, to assess the extent of regulation in their own nations along many different dimensions.[3] For instance, each year the International Institute of Management Development (IMD) asks about 100 business people in each country to rate the extent to which government price controls in their own nation affect the pricing of goods and services, the degree to which labor legislation affects the hiring and firing of workers, and so forth. The World Economic Forum carries out a similar type of survey.

I combine these assessments for 32 different areas into six broad categories of general economic regulation, which, in turn, are merged into one overall index.[4] To carry out this task, all answers are transformed on a scale running from 1 (highly regulated) to 10 (no regulation). A high score reflects a governmental policy of laissez faire, while a low score reflects a high degree of governmental intervention into the economy.

The most relevant countries with which to compare U.S. governmental regulation are the leading OECD nations. Table 11.1 presents the results of such an

---

[2]   In the text of this section, I cite studies by: International Institute of Management Development (IMD) (1999), Kagan *et al.* (2000-a), (2000-b), OECD (1998-a), World Economic Forum (1999)

[3]   Appendix A11.1 describes in detail how my index was constructed, the exact questions composing the index, the weights placed on each, and the source. Two other estimates of the extent of governmental regulation are also available: Nicoletti, Scarpetta, and Boylaud (2000) and Kaufmann, Kraay, and Zoido-Lobatón (1999-a; 1999-b; 2000). These studies, which are compared with my results in Pryor (2001-c) and Nicoletti and Pryor (2002), reveal roughly the same picture as my data.

[4]   Although factor analysis provides another way of handling the data, for my purposes it seems more revealing to look at the regulations in specific areas so that progress in different but distinct spheres of economic activity can be more easily compared.

Table 11.1. *Indices of Laissez Faire Micro-Economic Policies for OECD Nations in the Late 1990s*

Panel A: Index and its components

Weights	Foreign sector 20%	Labor markets 20%	Product markets 20%	Financial affairs 15%	Environment 5%	General economic/ administrative 20%	Total index Score	Rank in sample
Australia	8.32	4.99	8.05	4.19	6.20	6.09	6.43	11
Austria	8.70	4.78	8.12	4.49	5.45	5.65	6.40	12
Belgium	8.23	3.97	7.47	4.08	5.10	5.29	5.86	20
Canada	8.36	6.22	8.53	4.18	6.46	6.25	6.82	5
Denmark	8.78	5.83	8.08	4.43	5.98	5.68	6.64	7
Finland	8.41	5.04	8.31	4.73	7.10	7.46	6.91	4
France	8.03	3.64	8.01	4.19	6.09	4.79	5.83	21
Germany	8.64	3.95	8.30	4.33	5.13	5.91	6.27	5
Greece	8.25	5.23	6.78	3.69	5.87	4.82	5.86	19
Ireland	8.57	5.94	7.73	4.80	6.31	6.48	6.78	6
Italy	8.23	4.16	7.20	4.71	5.08	4.99	5.88	18
Japan	7.88	6.36	7.81	4.69	6.13	5.84	6.59	9
Netherlands	8.91	4.81	8.03	4.37	5.82	6.60	6.62	8
New Zealand	8.63	6.83	8.38	4.78	5.26	6.59	7.07	2
Norway	8.20	4.91	7.62	4.20	5.81	5.77	6.22	17
Portugal	8.53	5.42	7.40	4.84	5.74	5.42	6.37	13
Spain	7.99	5.22	7.66	4.25	6.25	6.03	6.33	14
Sweden	8.63	4.01	7.96	4.17	6.04	5.98	6.24	16
Switzerland	8.63	7.25	8.55	4.84	6.11	6.95	7.31	1
UK	8.60	6.80	8.03	4.01	6.18	6.87	6.97	3
USA	7.99	6.86	7.36	4.00	5.56	6.15	6.55	10

	Foreign	Labor	Product	Financial	Environment	General	Total
Average	8.41	5.34	7.88	4.38	5.89	5.98	6.47
Coef. Variation.	3.5%	20.3%	5.8%	7.5%	8.5%	11.7%	6.5%
US Rank	19	2	18	20	16	8	10

Panel B: Matrix of correlation coefficients

	Foreign	Labor	Product	Financial	Environment	General	Total
Foreign		0.06	0.46*	0.28	-0.08	0.38	0.43*
Labor			0.23	0.22	0.26	0.55*	0.80*
Product				0.35	0.31	0.64*	0.67*
Financial					0.05	0.33	0.46*
Environment						0.51*	0.43*
General							0.88*
Total							

Note: In Panel A, a low score designates a high degree of general-economic-regulation; a high score designates a low degree of regulations (or a high degree of laissez faire). All scores range from 1 through 10. The coefficient of variation is the standard deviation divided by the mean. In Panel B the asterisks designate statistical significance at the .05 level.

Appendix A11.1 presents the 32 questions aggregated in these indices, the weights placed on each question, and other details of the estimation.

exercise in the form of a laissez faire index. Panel A shows the numerical scores and Panel B presents the correlation of the six components of the index with each other and with the total index.

Several noteworthy features emerge. The components of the index show quite different degrees of government intervention: the financial sector is the most regulated; and the foreign sector, the least. The latter result is surely an outcome of globalization and the international liberalization of foreign trade. Further, the six components of the index are significantly related to each other in only a few cases (they are significantly correlated in only 4 out of 15 cases, as shown in Panel B); but all are significantly correlated with the combined index. This result provides some confidence that government regulation in the six different areas of the economy has at least one common underlying element. Finally, the spread in the values in each of the six components, as measured by the coefficients of variation, are quite different, being least in the foreign sector (where international agreements are most binding) and most for labor markets. All of these results make intuitive sense.

Of the 21 nations in the comparison, the United States ranks 10th from the top along the laissez faire scale, which may come as a surprise to many who view the U.S. as the standard bearer for free market government policies. Similarly, the conventional wisdom might also place Switzerland somewhat lower on the laissez faire scale. In interpreting my results for the U.S., however, three obvious factors must be taken into account. First, my estimates cover only general economic regulation, not industry-specific regulation, which focuses on particular industries, or legal-framework regulations. Second, these responses cover regulation by all levels of government, not just by the central government. As a result, respondents were also taking into account state and local zoning regulations, business permit requirements, and so forth. Third, many OECD nations made considerable (but quiet) progress toward liberalizing their economies in the last few decades of the 20th century in order to increase their competitiveness in world markets.

The most important consideration in assessing the individual rankings is that the questions focused on the entire regulatory process, and not just the laws themselves. In an extremely useful set of essays, Robert A. Kagan and his collaborators interviewed corporate executives of multinational enterprises on their experience in dealing with the entire regulatory process of various nations and reach some startling conclusions.

In comparison to other industrialized nations, Kagan characterizes the U.S. regulatory process as: (1) more complex and with a more detailed body of rules; (2) requiring more frequent recourse to formal legal methods; (3) more adversarial and requiring more expensive forms of legal contestation; (4) more punitive in its legal sanctions (including larger civil damage awards); (5) subject to more frequent judicial review, revision, and delay of administrative decision-making; and (6) plagued by more legal uncertainty, malleability, and unpredictability. Such features of the system tend to override substantive differences in law. For instance, the Canadian law against arbitrary discharge of employees is more comprehensive in coverage than the patchwork of U.S. laws, yet costly post-dismissal legal conflicts are much more frequent in the U.S., so that employers in the U.S. are more constrained in a crucial sense than in Canada. Similarly, a detailed OECD study of its member nations showed that the U.S. ranks among the highest in the administrative burdens of its business license and permit requirements.

In brief, the U.S. suffers from much more "adversarial legalism" in its regulatory system and from more fragmentation of the regulatory process among competing governmental authorities than most other industrialized nations. This appears to be the underlying reason why relative expenditures on lawyers, investigative studies, litigation, liability insurance, and legally imposed delays seem to be considerably larger in the U.S. than in other OECD nations. Thus, the evaluations revealed in the table seem to reflect not merely the number or even the stringency of government regulation, but their impact on the conduct of business.

Certain obvious objections can be raised against using the opinions of business executives to compare regulatory systems.[5] Nevertheless, these rough results allow us to begin investigating why governments in industrialized nations intervene to quite different degrees in the conduct of business.

Since there is no generally accepted economic theory about the determinants of government regulation among nations, we must approach the problem more inductively. Several plausible factors warrant investigation:

• *Size of economy:* This factor influences the extent of regulation in two ways which work against each other. Because production in large countries is more difficult to regulate, governments may give up on it, in which case laissez faire and national size would be positively correlated. Nevertheless, in a large country, enterprises are also larger (measured in an absolute sense such as labor force) and, some argue, regulation becomes more necessary. This, in turn, suggests that size of the economy and laissez faire would be inversely related. From a different perspective, the voters might also feel a greater need for protection

---

[5] For instance, U.S. business people who rated their own country's regulatory system severely in isolation might have evaluated it more favorably if asked to make comparison with that of other nations. Unfortunately, there is no way to test this conjecture. Nevertheless, since most of the respondents for the two surveys had considerable international experience, they might have had some implicit basis of comparison. Moreover, since most respondents also had previous contact with the two business groups sponsoring the surveys and presumably understood their approaches, they might have had an important common basis of evaluation.

against the possible excesses of large firms than against smaller, more local industries, which would tend to be more amenable to social, in contrast to legal pressures. I measure size of a nation by the logarithm of the population in 1995 and find that the latter influence of size predominates: larger nations have more governmental regulation, other factors held constant.

• *Level of economic development:* This factor also influences regulation in two conflicting ways. It is commonly believed that governmental regulation increases as per capita income increases, because the government has more resources with which to carry out regulatory activities. Moreover, some goals of such regulatory activity, such as a clean environment, are luxury goods and services and are more highly prized in high income nations. But it is also possible that as the level of development rises, the economy becomes more complex; and governmental regulation, more counterproductive. I measure the level of economic development by the per capita GDP in 1995, calculated according to its purchasing power in a common currency. As it turns out, these counteracting forces seem roughly equal in strength so that the laissez faire index cannot be correlated with the level of economic development.

• *Income inequality:* It can be cynically argued that when the income gap between the rich and the poor is wide, the high income population has relatively more political power and, as a result, fewer regulations are imposed on their economic activities.[6] In measuring income inequality I use statistics adjusted for the size of the household. For 18 of the 21 countries in Table 11.1 for which comparable income inequality data are available, the results confirm the hypothesis, namely that as income inequality increases, the laissez faire index is higher.

In brief, the degree of economic laissez faire is inversely related to economic size and directly related to income inequality, other factors held constant.[7] The predicted degree of laissez faire for the United States is quite close to its actual

---

[6]   Some might argue that with widening inequality, more regulation would be needed—and provided—to prevent economic disaster among the low income population. This conjecture is based on an excessively sanguine view of politics and is not confirmed by the data.

[7]   The statistic measuring income inequality is the Gini coefficient which indicates the percentage of total income that must be redistributed for all household incomes (adjusted for size) to be equal. I obtain the following regression results (the standard errors are placed below the calculated coefficients):

$$LF = 7.529^* + 0.014 \text{ GDP/capita} - 0.281^* \ln \text{pop} - 0.387 \text{ trade/GDP} + 6.068^* \text{ Gini} \quad R^2 = 0.4814$$
$$\quad (1.199) \quad (0.032) \quad\quad (0.102) \quad\quad (0.375) \quad\quad (2.556) \quad\quad n = 18$$

where LF = laissez faire index (Table 11.1), the GDP/capita is measured in terms of 1000 dollars in 1995, ln pop is the logarithm of the population in 1995, and trade/GDP is the ratio of exports plus imports to the GDP in 1995. An asterisk designates statistical significance at the degree, so in this respect the country does not appear anomalous. Other possible variables influencing the extent of regulation come to mind, but experiments along these lines proved fruitless.[8]

The direct relation between income inequality and laissez faire (or the direct relation between income equality and considerable general economic regulation) has some important implications. It suggests that power relations between income groups are crucial in determining the extent of the regulatory regime. Of the two factors that seem to determine the extent of laissez faire, the inequality of income dominates the results. If my calculation is accurate, an increase in the laissez faire index resulting from a small increase in the index of inequality (more exactly, a 1 percent increase in the Gini index) would swamp any reasonable estimate of the increase in population.

Moreover, since income differences widened in the last quarter of the century and are likely to become even greater in coming decades (Chapter 4), we can expect the drive toward deregulation to continue, other things being equal. We must be careful, however, in generalizing about changes over time from cross-section evidence; the future direction of government regulation within the U.S. is discussed in much greater detail below.

0.05 level. The regression is the same as the results reported in Table 7.1 except that I am using as a variable income inequality, rather than equality (1–Gini coefficient).

In some of these experiments I found a statistically significant relation between higher social capital and greater regulation. Since social capital in the U.S. is declining (Chapter 7), this suggests that the importance of government regulation will become weaker in the future.

The population and per capita GDP data (PPP method of calculation) for these regressions come from OECD (1998-b). The data on income distribution come from Gottschalk and Smeeding (1999). For New Zealand, I estimated the Gini from data on decile shares. The data on trust and social capital, based on membership in various groups, comes from Inglehart, et al. (1999). For social capital I added the percentage of the population belonging to the following types of groups: social welfare, cultural, community action, conservation, youth work, professional associations, and political groups or parties.

[8] It can be argued that the more open the economy, the less able or willing is the government to regulate domestic economic activity. I measured trade openness by the ratio of exports plus imports to the GNP. This hypothesis received no statistical confirmation.

Chapter 7 discusses social capital and social trust, which have important influences on a number of economic variables. From a theoretical standpoint, they both have an ambiguous impact on the laissez faire index. On the one hand, it can be argued that if they are high, businesses would need less regulation because they can be counted upon to follow the public interest. On the other hand, it also seems likely that if they are high, the public is more willing to place restrictions on the exercise of undue power by business enterprises. As it turns out, neither social capital nor social trust have a statistically significant relationship with laissez faire.

One last question needs to be asked of the data in Table 11.1: Is there any relationship between the level of general economic regulation and various measures of success, either of the economy as a whole or of the general operations of the government? Two such indicators immediately come to mind:

• *Economic growth*. In the sample of OECD nations, I could find no statistically significant relationship between my particular measure of laissez faire and the average annual per capita GDP growth between 1985 and 1995 (two mid-business-cycle years), either alone or when other possible causal factors are held constant.[9]

• *Governmental effectiveness*. To measure such effectiveness I use an index employed in the discussion in Chapter 7 and derived from the answers given by business executives to fifty different questions to survey data.[10]

The results of a regression analysis show quite clearly a significantly positive relation between laissez faire and governmental effectiveness (or an inverse relationship between the extent of regulation and governmental effectiveness), both with and without other factors held constant.[11]

Given the important issues involved—many of which are subject to fierce ideological debate- several interpretations of these results can be offered. We might take the results at face value: Governments govern the economy best when they govern least; or, less tendentiously, that it is easier for governments to fulfill a few goals than many. These statistical results, however, may also be due to three types of biases in the data:

• *Perception*. The respondents may perceive that government regulations are more extensive than they actually are if the government administers them arbitrarily and general governmental effectiveness is low.[12]

• *Ideology*. The respondents to the surveys on which both the laissez faire and governmental effectiveness indices are constructed are all business

---

9   For my experiments I used a simple OLS linear equation and held constant per capita GDP, the trade/GDP ratio, and the logarithm of the population size. Because the degree of government regulation changes considerably over time, it does not seem useful to carry out such calculations for a longer time period.

10 Sources and methods are discussed in detail in Pryor (2001-c).

11 Using the same procedures and abbreviations as in the previous footnote, the relationship is:

$$GE = -0.768 + 1.25^* \ LF + 0.0487 \ Y/cap - 0.145 \ \ln pop - 0.169 \ \ Trade/GDP \quad R^2 = .6508$$
$$\quad\ \ (2.573) \ (0.29) \quad\ \ (0.0350) \quad\ \ (0.127) \quad\quad\ \ (0.498) \quad\quad\quad\quad n = 21$$

where GE = governmental effectiveness (Table A7.3). None of the three social variables is significantly related to governmental effectiveness, once the laissez faire variable is included.

12 Of course, if the government does not seriously administer them, business people may perceive the extent of governmental regulation as less than it actually is (at least , in a formal sense).

executives, who may be ideologically predisposed to believe that governmental ineffectiveness and the extent of governmental regulation are directly related. Experiments with the other measures of the extent of government regulation that are less subject to this criticism, however, yielded the same results.

• *Culture.* The executives from nations with a great deal of regulation may be culturally conditioned to believe that the regulations in their country are particularly ineffective.

Unfortunately, we have no way of knowing which interpretation is most reasonable. It seems to me, however, that all three explanations probably contain a certain grain of truth. The results obtained in the above discussion still seem usable, however, if they are employed in a cautious manner.

It is unfortunate that a similar type of analysis cannot be carried out with either legal-framework regulations or industry-specific regulations, since we do not have the appropriate measures of their extent in the OECD nations. Nevertheless, two components of the index of governmental effectiveness shed light on legal-framework regulation. The first reflects the effectiveness of the judicial system and includes evaluations of such phenomena as the extent of corruption or bribes, tax evasion, and the lack of protection of physical and intellectual property; the second reflects the lack of personal security, the crime rate, and the costs of organized crime to business.

We can calculate regressions for the leading OECD nations to determine the extent to which the effectiveness of the judicial system is significantly related to the various hypothesized determinants of general economic regulation. The results show that such judicial effectiveness is significantly and positively correlated only with the level of social capital, measured in terms of share of the adult population that participate in certain group activities. It is also positively related to the level of social trust, measured from survey data, at a slightly less rigorous level of statistical significance than the .05 level. None of these conjectured determinants seem to explain some of the particular components of my measure of governmental effectiveness, for instance, the police system. It might be added that neither the judicial nor the police effectiveness seem related to growth of per capita GDP.

Aside from providing perspective on the relative extent of general economic regulation in the U.S., these results also provide a basis for several hypotheses about the future of the U.S. regulatory environment. In particular, we can conjecture that both the growing population and the widening income differentials (Chapter 4) will strengthen the deregulation movement. At this point, it is useful now to turn to a direct examination of changes in U.S. governmental regulations of the economy.

B. Regulation Trends in the U.S.[13]

Devising indicators to view trends in regulation within the U.S. raises many of the same problems as making cross-section comparisons.[14] Although all jurisdictions regulate economic activity, the lack of readily available and comparable information on state and local governments regulation makes it impossible to gain a quantitative overview at this level. As a result, I concentrate only of federal regulation of the economy, and, for this, the most promising approach is to examine data on various "regulation inputs," that is, the resources used by the government to promulgate and enforce the various regulations and the costs to the private sector of complying with them. Some recent calculations presented in Table 11.2 provide a useful overview of changes over time on the government side.

On the federal level, the ratio of expenditures on regulatory activities to the GDP rose from about 0.084 percent in the 1960s to a peak of 0.225 percent in 1980. Annual data show that the greatest increase occurring during the Nixon administration. From the highpoint in 1980, the year Ronald Reagan was elected president, this ratio declined; by 2000 it was down to 0.190 percent.[15] This overall pattern of a rise in the regulatory cost/GDP ratio up to around 1980 and a decline thereafter also holds for both general economic and industry specific regulation. In addition, it is noteworthy that the composition of these expenditures on regulation shifted: Over the period the costs of general economic regulation grew relatively more important than cost of industry specific regulation.

For individual industries, the costs of regulation should be standardized by the size of the industry, as measured, for instance, by the GDP originating from that industry. Calculated in this way, the regulation costs rose in the energy and the finance/banking industries and declined in the securities industry. For other industries, however, the ratios followed the general rise-and-fall pattern shown in the table.[16]

---

[13] In the text of this section I draw on research by: Hopkins (1998), OECD (1997-d), and Viscusi, *et al.* (1995).

[14] The use of certain common indices such as the "economic freedom index" of the Fraser Institute (Gwartney and Lawson, 1997), raises problems of interpretation. In this index, the most important factor underlying the increase in U.S. "economic freedom" for the period between 1975 and 1995 was the reduction in the marginal tax rate for those in the highest bracket. The three factors that are next most important in this index are: a reduction in inflation variability, a decrease in federal governmental consumption expenditures, and the avoidance of negative real interest rates. None of these factors directly captures government regulation or market interventions.

[15] For the 1950s the ratio averaged roughly about 0.074 percent, an estimate obtained by splicing my own regulation-cost calculations (Pryor, 1996, p. 227) to the Warren data presented in Table 10.2.

[16] Table 11.2 shows that costs of general business regulation (those regulations that cannot be eas-

Table 11.2. *Trends in Federal Governmental Expenditures on Regulation (as a Percentage of GDP in current dollars)*

	1960	1970	1980	1990	2000
General economic regulation					
General business practices	0.007%	0.009%	0.010&	0.010%	0.013%
Job safety, work conditions	0.007	0.012	0.027	0.017	0.015
Environment	0.004	0.021	0.059	0.072	0.061
Consumer safety and health	0.031	0.041	0.048	0.036	0.038
Subtotal	0.049	0.083	0.144	0.135	0.126
Specific-industry regulation					
Energy	0.002%	0.006%	0.020%	0.008%	0.005%
Finance/banking	0.006	0.008	0.013	0.019	0.017
Other industry specific	0.026	0.036	0.046	0.035	0.038
Securities	0.002	0.002	0.003	0.003	0.004
Subtotal	0.035	0.052	0.082	0.064	0.063
All regulation	0.084	0.135	0.225	0.199	0.190

Note: These underlying data come from Warren (2000) and were drawn from a careful analysis of the budget of the federal government. I have, however, slightly rearranged their results. More specifically, I reclassified SEC expenditures from their "general business" category to "securities," and I removed transportation from their "consumer safety and health" category and placed it in "other industry specific." As explained in the text, the 1950 ratios were little different from those in 1960. Totals may not add because of rounding.

What underlay such deregulation? Although President Reagan was given considerable credit for initiating the process, most of the groundwork had been laid in the previous administrations, starting roughly in 1975. The first important steps toward deregulation, taken by Presidents Ford and Carter, were not,

ily classified) did not follow the general pattern and from 1960 onward were fueled primarily by antitrust enforcement costs and patent protection. Many of these expenditures are supposed to improve the competitiveness of markets although, as shown in Chapter 10, their effectiveness might be questioned since industrial concentration increased during the last two decades of the century. Of course, it is possible that without such antitrust expenditures, market concentration would have increased even faster.

however, driven by any massive public outcry against regulation.[17] Although political ideologies played a role in the process, many important deregulation advocates were members of the Democratic party. Although for many years business interest groups had generally not welcomed federal regulation in their industry, it was a sea-change in the perceptions of other elites about the effectiveness of regulation that underlay the deregulation movement.

Barring any kind of serious economic downturn, it seems probable that the declining ratio of both general economic and industry specific regulation that has occurred since the 1980s will persist in the coming decades. The shift in emphasis from industry specific to general economic regulation will most probably continue as well, due in considerable measure to the support of an increasingly affluent public for environmental protection and consumer safety and health regulation.

Other kinds of data reflecting governmental intervention into markets do not present a greatly different picture. For instance, direct subsidies, which are aimed at specific industries, doubled from 0.2 percent of the GDP to 0.4 percent by the beginning of the 1960s.[18] Thereafter, the ratio experienced several cycles, but ended up again at 0.4 percent in the late 1990s. In the discussion in the next chapter, I provide a much more thorough discussion of both direct and indirect (the so-called tax-expenditures) subsidies.

Another measure of governmental intervention is the number of pages in the *Federal Register*, which records new governmental rules and regulations.[19] W. Kip Viscusi and his coauthors calculate that this publication rose from roughly 10,000 pages in the early 1950s to 87,000 in 1980, only to decline somewhat

---

[17]   There is, of course, a linkage between certain types of governmental regulation and private expenditures. For instance, environmental protection laws lower the individual costs of finding healthy recreational space, and controls on gun ownership might lower individual costs of protection. This linkage, however, did not play any important role in public opinion about regulation.
       Curiously, religious differences seem to play a more determinant role in public attitudes toward the scope of government, with committed evangelical or mainline Protestants taking a much more conservative stance than Jews or committed Catholics (Kohut, *et al.*, 2000, pp. 41–54), even when other explanatory factors such as education, age, and income are held constant.

[18]   Such data are available in the national accounts (NIPA) only from 1959. They come from U.S. Department of Commerce, Bureau of Economic Analysis (1998-b) and the BEA website at http://www.bea.doc.gov/bea/dn1.htm.
       The distortions in market prices caused by subsidies are paralleled by the other distortions arising from indirect taxes (sales taxes, excise taxes, and customs duties) at all levels of government. In the 1950s these averaged 4.4 percent and, after rising slightly, fell to 4.2 percent in the 1980s and 1990s. These data come from Tables 3.2 and 3.3 of the NIPA. Other distortions, more difficult to measure, arise from import quotas and similar measures.

[19]   Another measure is the number of regulatory agencies or the total regulatory acts, which Gatti (1981, pp. 4–5) showed to have risen dramatically, at least up to 1980.

thereafter. Such a measure of regulatory activity, however, is highly imperfect as a measure of regulatory costs, because some of the new rules merely annul old rules. The *Code of Federal Regulations* summarizes the stock of existing regulations; and the pages of this collection, which were under 10,000 in the early 1950s, rose to 100,000 by 1980, then declined to just over 50,000 pages in 1990. So these input data confirm the general pattern we found in expenditures data.

Alternatively, the extent of federal regulation might be understood in terms of the costs it imposed on the private economy or the benefits it brings to the public. Although various measures of the cost of regulation, including direct costs imposed both on producers and consumers, have been made, I have been able to locate only one time-series that uses a consistent methodology. According to the data of Thomas D. Hopkins, which cover the period from 1977 to the end of the century, regulation costs imposed on private U.S. businesses rose in absolute terms but, as a percent of GDP, steadily declined. More specifically, his calculated costs of regulation amounted to almost 15 percent of the GDP in 1977, but only 8.5 percent by 1998.[20]

The other side of the story—the benefits of regulation—raises extreme difficulties of measurement. Although such calculations have been made for very particular laws, credible time-series data for the entire regulatory system are not available.

Determining trends in regulation by looking at changes in regulatory legislation is a more questionable approach, especially since the rules and standards promulgated by the various regulatory bodies may have a greater impact than the formal laws passed by the legislature. Nevertheless, a sample list of some of the most important legislative acts is presented in Appendix A11.1. To a considerable extent, they reinforce our impressions about the decline in industry specific regulation in the last quarter of the 20th century, particularly in agriculture, transportation, energy, and banking.

Other and more obtrusive types of governmental intervention into markets, such as economic planning and allocation of resources, or wage and price controls, were negligible during most of the second half of the 20th century. The generalization, however, admits of three important exceptions: the temporary measures taken as a result of U.S. participation in the Korean War, the short-lasting wage and price controls instituted by the Nixon administration, and the

---

[20] Hopkins' data are in constant prices and I have used a constant dollar GDP series in the same year prices as the denominator of the ratio. According to a recent government estimate (cited by Executive Office of the President (1999), p. 280), the costs imposed on industry by the regulatory system in 1998 ranged from $170 to $230 billion (in contrast to Hopkins' estimate of $700 billion). Measuring the benefits of regulation is even harder, and estimates in the same government study ranged from $260 to $3500 billion.

oversight over certain energy prices after the energy shocks in the 1970s until 1981, when they were abandoned by the Reagan administration. For the most part these regulatory measures were not successful, and it seems unlikely that such controls will reappear in the 21st century, short of an all-out war or a looming environmental catastrophe.

State and local governments also engage in considerable regulation of markets. On the state level, the most dramatic moves toward deregulation have been driven by changes in technology, rather than changes in ideology. With the advent of new technologies for transmitting long-distance calls, competition became possible in the long distance market, and this part of the telephone industry was considerably deregulated. At the end of the 20th century, cell phone technologies were encouraging deregulation of local phone services as well. Similarly, an OECD report points out that new technologies in electricity generation make small scale production more cost effective than previously. Moreover, such technologies can be combined with new methods of coordinating the generation and transmission of electricity, which means that vertically integrated electricity companies are no longer necessary. By the end of the 1990s many states, such as Pennsylvania and California, had deregulated parts of the electricity industry and allowed certain kinds of competition.[21] Local electricity and telephone lines, however, are still natural monopolies and have remained regulated.

These deregulation measures reinforce the general impression that regulation aimed at specific industries is declining. Of course, state and local governments regulate a variety of other activities, ranging from taxicab rates, licensing of barbers, maximum loan interest rates, and land zoning. Regulatory trends of state and local governments in these areas defy generalization, due to the extreme diversity of such market interventions and the large number of governmental units to take into account.

Despite the difficulties in obtaining an overview of regulation at all levels of government, our general conclusion still appears to hold: The extent of specific industry regulation slowly declined in the second half of the 20th century, while the extent of general economic regulation rose and then fell. The share of GDP

---

[21]   California's deregulation of the electricity industry provides a textbook case on how the process should not be carried out. Demand was underestimated, little new generating capacity was added, and in most areas prices paid by consumers were regulated while wholesale prices electricity distributors had to pay were not. Long-run contracts between electricity producers and distributors were also not allowed in most situations. In 2000, brownouts began to occur and, at the same time, electricity prices soared in cities where they were deregulated. Pennsylvania deregulated later and in a quite different manner; up to 2001, that state did not experience such problems.

devoted to regulation appears to have declined, as have the apparent compliance costs of these regulations. Thus, the time-series data reinforce the rough conclusion based on the cross-section study of the OECD nations: in the coming decades, deregulation in most fields of economic activity will continue to decline.

C. Regulation and the Strength of the State [22]

It is useful to examine governmental regulation from another angle, namely the changing ability of the government to regulate and intervene effectively. This discussion continues a theme introduced in Chapter 5 and carried forward in Chapter 8 on the declining economic powers of the government in a globalizing economy. It is also important to consider briefly whether declining regulation has any impact on other aspects of the economic system, particularly welfare state expenditures.

1. The Government's Diminished Ability to Regulate and Intervene

In the second half of the 20th century, all western governments found themselves less able to intervene into particular industries, in part because of a growing web of trade rules designed to prevent unfair international trade practices. As briefly noted in Chapter 5, certain types of markets—particularly financial—became more difficult to regulate as the speed of communications between nations accelerated and ever larger amounts of money could be instantaneously moved from country to country. The government's ability to regulate economic activities, especially in individual markets, has been further limited by three interrelated factors: the impact of the internet, the rising importance of offshore havens, and competition between nations. Each warrants brief discussion.

• *The internet once again:* The use of the internet allows many types of government regulation to be circumvented. For instance, internet sites located outside the U.S. mail prescription drugs directly to anyone who wishes to avoid either the high drug prices in the U.S. or the necessity of a prescription. Robert Pear reports that a Thai company even offered a refund if their package was confiscated by the U.S. Customs Service. Similarly, those wishing to

---

[22]   In the text of this section I mention studies or reports by: Cowell and Andrews (1999), Hines and Rice (1994), O'Brien (2000), Palan (1998), Pear (2000), and Peel (2000).

avoid anti-gambling or anti-pornography laws can easily indulge their passions over the net, with no restrictions of any kind. Until constrained by a public outcry, Amazon.com was even selling Hitler's *Mein Kampf* to residents in Germany, whose laws forbid the sale of this book in that country.[23]

With the cooperation of foreign governments, the U.S. government has tried to crack down on some of these businesses, since in many cases these sites were violating the laws of their home country. For instance, it successfully urged the Thai government to close down some on-line pharmacies accused of breaking Thai laws about money laundering and trade in prescription drugs. But other countries, less cooperative with the U.S., beckon such internet entrepreneurs whose operations are highly mobile. The U.S. government is said to be exploring measures to prevent many of these illicit international sales by restricting money transfers of credit card companies to foreign firms accused of violating U.S. laws, but such measures also raise enforcement difficulties and, up to the time of writing, these efforts have not borne fruit.

In brief, almost any type of small but illicit transaction requiring merely a buyer, a seller, and an exchange of money can be carried out over the web, in defiance of the laws of the land. Such i-e-commerce (illicit e-commerce) is almost impossible for individual governments to stop, short of introducing a gigantic censorship apparatus and dramatically beefing up personnel in customs and postal inspection to intercept packages from abroad.

• *Offshore Havens:* Globalization has led to the creation of offshore havens that also allow the circumvention of domestic laws. In recent decades these havens were accounting for an increasing volume of economic activity.

One of the oldest offshore-economy gambits is the flag of convenience, whereby a ship owned by a citizen of one country is registered in another country that has less irksome safety, financial, or tax laws. Ronen Palan points out that Panama and Liberia are two of the most notable examples, and boast the largest merchant marine fleets in the world. More than two thirds of all cargo ships sail under such flags of convenience, and by the end of the 20th century, shipping registry companies mushroomed to facilitate such transactions. For instance, International Registries, Inc. runs the registry of the Marshall Islands from Reston, Virginia—allegedly so that they can be close to their customers.

Offshore financial markets (OFMs) are a more recent phenomenon. Palan estimates that somewhere between 65 and 80 percent (in volume) of all international banking transactions involve such markets. OFMs provide deposit secrecy

---

[23]   The French government threatened to fine Yahoo.com for allowing the auctioning of Nazi memorabilia from a site in the U.S. because such sales are illegal in France. The degree to which national law extends to foreign citizens operating in other countries is an unresolved problem.

and tax advantages to the depositors and, at the same time, are free from such banking regulations as interest rate ceilings, reserve requirements, or foreign exchange controls of the home country. Alan Cowell and Edmund Andrews cite a report by Merrill Lynch and Company which estimates that in 1998 roughly $6 trillion was held in these offshore shelters, safe from national regulation and oversight. For those wishing to own an offshore bank, Timothy O'Brien reports that charters from Nauru and Vanuatu are easily available through the internet for a fee of $20,000 (price as of February 2000); that, in the same year, a simple private account in Belize plus a mail-drop address and information on obtaining a second or third diplomatic passport cost $2299; and that a mere $399 provided a private account in "Estonia's largest bank." Of course, all these arrangements are really selling one product—privacy of financial assets from the sharp-sighted eyes of tax authorities, creditors, and ex-spouses.

J. R. Hines and E. M. Rice describe the various forms in which tax havens come: They can be as simple as tax concessions for locating a business in a particular nation or as elaborate as export processing zones (EPZs) in manufacturing, which combine both tax and regulatory advantages. Although the U.S. government taxes net repatriated profits from these tax havens at the domestic rate, total post-tax income of U.S. firms is higher than if they had located in the U.S. The U.S. Treasury is the loser to the extent that these enterprise profits can be disguised or not repatriated or that the firm shifts its investment out of the U.S. to such havens.[24]

The first EPZ was established near the Shannon Airport in Ireland in 1959. By the end of the 20th century EPZs had spread over the planet. For instance, Palan cites OECD data that one-fourth of total manufacturing in developing nations originates from such zones. In the 1990s various telecommunication organizations began to set up operation in one or another tax haven and to invite multinational corporations to locate their headquarters in these countries— where the corporations could be in constant and reliable communications with their branch plants located elsewhere and, at the same time, enjoy lower tax rates and fewer regulations than in their home countries.

---

[24] Hines and Rice (1994) argue that although low tax rates in these tax havens encourage American companies to shift profits out of U.S. and other high-tax countries, it is possible that such tax havens ultimately enhance U.S. tax collections if the companies expand faster in the tax havens than they would have in their original location. This is because the U.S. would have a higher level of repatriated profits (after taxes are paid to the tax haven). This argument seems unrealistic. For instance, if all multi-national enterprises shifted their activities to the Big-7 tax havens (Hong Kong, Ireland, Liberia, Lebanon, Panama, Singapore, and Switzerland), it seems unlikely that world growth would be higher and, as a result, the national governments of all countries not in the Big-7 would be poorer.

• *Competition between nations:* Just as the states within the U.S. compete for the location of business by offering lower tax rates, so also do nations, which means that taxes are shifted from business to the consumer.[25] Moreover, as documented in Chapter 5, certain multinational enterprises (MNE) with sales all over the world have used the threat of relocating their factories and headquarters to obtain tax and other concessions from their home governments. As federalism once strengthened the hand of businesses in their relations with local governments, so globalization strengthens businesses in their dealings with national governments.

In brief, in a world increasingly dominated by e-mail, fax communications, teleconferencing, and the internet, the importance of geography to management declines and the bargaining power of enterprises against the national government increases. It is becoming ever easier for MNEs to play one national government off against another, learning from the experience of U.S. corporations, whose bargaining with individual state and local governments have led to special tax breaks, subsidies, or other concessions, such as a better transportation infrastructure.[26]

2. Discussion of the Government's Ability to Regulate

What do these changes driven by new information technologies portend for the future of governmental regulation of economic activity? Ronen Palan argues an interesting proposition:

> "The state system is not disappearing, but is in the process of creating secondary, relatively unregulated juridical spaces in which economic activities can develop more or less without hindrance. The juridical space of sovereignty, therefore, is bifurcating into two simultaneous domains, one still very much 'on-shore', subject to strict controls, regulations, and taxation ... the other consisting of 'fictitious spaces' ... a new and relatively unregulated realm in which economic transactions take place with minimal intervention by the state."

---

[25] Of course, in a market economy business taxes are ultimately paid by consumers in any case. Nevertheless, using certain reasonable assumptions about the incidence of business taxes, the shift in taxes from businesses to consumers results in a lower share of taxes paid by high-income families (who receive the profits from these companies) and a corresponding increase in the share of taxes paid by low-income families.

[26] Many examples of very large companies can be given. For instance, Tyco International, a company with $22 billion in sales in 1999 (and net profits of about $1 billion), was founded in the U.S. in 1960, has manufacturing plants in most states, but has established its corporate headquarters in Bermuda.

He also suggests that the end result will be an international race to the bottom, with few controls and low taxes on corporations and, in turn, higher direct taxes on individuals. Although I have doubts (see below) about the race to the bottom, I find this proposition about taxation quite plausible.

One offset to the competitive advantage of tax havens deserves comment, namely, the long-run shifting of the costs of regulation. If a particular country places costly regulations on its industries, its exchange rate may depreciate in future years, or its prices and wages may increase less than in other nations. In this case, the real income of the population would rise more slowly than otherwise, but its goods become internationally competitive at these lower relative prices. For instance, as many have noted, the individual U.S. states have quite different regulations on markets, yet an equilibrium has been achieved such that the economy in the regulating state is not destroyed. Nevertheless, other things equal, the regulating states must pay the price in lower personal incomes for their residents.

This brief survey points to one major conclusion: by the end of the 20th century in all industrial nations, the ability of the government to regulate certain parts of their economies, particularly the financial sector and the collection of taxes, was eroding. To some degree, a globalized economy needs global regulation and certain international groups have begun to be set up to combat the dubious practices discussed above. For instance, the Financial Action Task Force focuses on money laundering; and the Financial Stability Forum deals with lax banking rules. Although their published lists of offending nations have goaded some of the offending nations into tightening up their regulatory procedures, the "name and shame" strategy has intrinsic weaknesses. More potent are the actions of the OECD, which, as reported by Michael Peel, published in June 2000 a list of 35 countries as tax havens that lacked transparency and effective rules on exchanging information with overseas tax authorities. The OECD provides powerful incentives for the offending nations to confess their economic sins and change their ways, since, by the summer of 2001, its member nations are given the right to impose sanctions against the unrepentant nations. The efficacy of this action was severely undercut in the spring of 2001 when the administration of George W. Bush pulled out of the agreement, arguing that the U.S. had no right to tell other nations how to structure their tax system.

Nevertheless, in the coming decades the outcome of the race between companies using the new information technology to evade governmental scrutiny and the government's ability to regulate economic and financial transactions is far from certain. At the present time, the supply factors are reinforcing the trend toward deregulation on the national level, even as regulation on the international level is slowly gaining momentum.

3. Regulation and Trade Competitiveness

The deregulation drive in Western nations, combined with the increasing integration of world markets, may, as many claim, create a "race to the bottom" as each nation strives to remain competitive in world markets. Moreover, this process can also lead to a reduced state expenditures for health and welfare. Such arguments, however, do not stand scrutiny.

• *Trade impacts:* From the standpoint of basic economic theory, the proposition about the race-to-the-bottom is wrong: If one country deregulates, thus lowering its production costs and raising exports, the trade effects can be offset by a realignment of currency values. After such a step, the deregulating country may still retain a comparative advantage in the products of the particular industry that is deregulated, but it will then lose a comparative advantage in other products. In time, trade will become balanced again.

• *Relation of regulation to the welfare state:* In a sample of 21 OECD nations in the mid 1990s, the laissez-faire index is not significantly related to the ratio of government expenditures to the GDP, either alone or holding other factors constant.[27] Sweden provides an interesting example, since it began to deregulate in the last quarter of the 20th century, while maintaining its welfare state at the same time. Although this country experienced at the same time some structural difficulties and low economic growth from the 1980s to the early 1990s, it achieved a respectable per capita annual GDP growth rate of 2.33 percent from 1993 through 1998, which also appears to be sustainable into the near future.[28] In Chapter 5 I offer a more theoretical explanation of why increased trade and globalization will not hurt the welfare state. It is based on an argument about the realignment of exchange rates that is essentially the same as my reasoning in the previous paragraph about the impact of deregulation.

D. Changes in Patterns of Ownership, State and Private [29]

Governments can influence production indirectly through regulation, but they can also play a more direct role through the activities of state-owned enter-

---

27 The other factors include per capita GDP, the ratio of trade to the GDP, and the logarithm of the population.

28 This is calculated from data on the Statistika Centralbyrån website (www.scb.se) and is calculated by fitting an exponential curve. It represents an acceleration of per capita GDP growth of 1.70 percent from 1980 through 1992.

29 In the text of this section I utilize studies by: Berle and Means (1932), CEEP (1997), Galambos (2000), Gylfason, *et al.* (2000), and Millward (2000).

prises. As noted above, it has been claimed that government regulation can function as a substitute for government ownership, especially with regard to natural monopolies—those industries, such as electricity transmission, which feature very important economies of large scale production. In the discussion below I present both international and U.S. data to show that this proposition needs revision. I also use the international data to place U.S. governmental ownership in a quantitative perspective. Finally, the data used for this analysis also allow an opportunity for a brief discussion of more important changes in ownership that might affect U.S. capitalism in the future.

1. The Extent of State-Owned Enterprises: An International Perspective

Gaining an international overview of the extent of governmental ownership of the means of production provides many challenges, even for the industrialized nations.[30] Part of the problem lies in separating strictly governmental activities from governmental production of goods and services for the market. For instance, are the post office and the air traffic control board government agencies or state-owned enterprises?[31] In some countries the luxuriant profusion of legal forms in which governmental ownership is manifested on both federal and local levels creates other data difficulties.[32] Definitional problems also arise in situations where the government has only part ownership in an enterprise. Finally, various indicators of the extent of state-owned enterprises—in terms of labor force, value-added, or gross fixed capital formation—yield somewhat

---

[30] The three major sources on the extent of the state-owned enterprises (SOE) are World Bank (1995), the OECD (1997-c), and the Centre européen des entreprises à participation publique et des entreprises d'intérêt économique général (CEEP) (1997). The World Bank does not present labor force data for the industrialized nations, the OECD makes its estimates from the various sources of aggregate statistics, and the CEEP builds up its estimates from micro data. I rely primarily on CEEP data, which, in general, yield larger SOE sectors than the OECD data.

[31] Although in previous decades they were thought to be government agencies, those wishing to privatize them now argue that they are state owned enterprises.

[32] According to Toninelli (2000-a), "At the state level, the term 'state-owned enterprise' provides only an approximate description of the complexity of forms and organization that state companies may assume. This reaches an apogee of fantasy and ingenuity in the terminology and legal forms used in Italy, where state companies, state share-holding companies, state concerns, and so on have coexisted throughout the twentieth century. Finally, considerable differences are to be found in the ways public enterprises are managed, as 'state-owned enterprise' does not automatically mean 'state-managed enterprise'." These data problems are considerably more severe for Italy than for the United States. The CEEP database which I use goes further in overcoming these problems of consistency than other estimates.

Table 11.3. *Employment in State-Owned Enterprises in Key OECD Nations in 1998*

Percent of the total employed labor force

Australia	4.08%	Germany	5.52%	Norway	n.a.
Austria	5.30	Greece	3.89	Portugal	2.48%
Belgium	5.30	Ireland	4.45	Spain	2.27
Canada	2.47	Italy	3.92	Sweden	6.79
Denmark	3.47	Japan	0.50	Switzerland	n.a.
Finland	5.96	Netherlands	1.32	U.K.	1.48
France	5.94	New Zealand	7.84	U.S.	1.40

Note: n.a. = not available. Most data come from a personal communication from CEEP that will be published in 2001. Data for Australia (1995), Canada (1994), Japan (1995) and New Zealand (1995), come from OECD (1997-e). Data for the U.S. come from the national income and product data (Table 6.04) from the website of the Bureau of Economic Analysis (www.bea.doc.got/dn1.htm).

different results. For reasons of data availability, I focus on labor force in state-owned enterprises.

Table 11.3 provides some data for the late 1990s for key OECD nations. It should be clear that the extent of state enterprises was quite limited in most countries by the end of the millennium. Moreover, as shown in the data collected by the Centre européen des entreprises à participation publique et des entreprises d'intérêt économique général (CEEP), in Western Europe their share in the total national capital stock fell slowly in the last two decades of the 20th century, the result of both deliberate privatization and slower growth of such enterprises in comparison to the rest of the economy.

For purposes of the present discussion, the most important conclusion to be drawn from these results is that the United States ranked among those countries with the smallest state enterprise sector. The data in the table do not, however, cover all types of government ownership of the means of production. In the United States, for instance, Louis Galambos points out that the government owns about one third of the land, and in certain European nations the government owns sub-surface mineral rights.

The proposition that government regulation and government ownership are policy substitutes can be easily tested by examining the relationship between the estimates of government ownership and the estimates of the extent of laissez faire (the lack of government regulation) in Table 11.1. The two series are not significantly (at a 95 percent confidence limit) correlated, either when simply examined alone or when other possible causal factors are held constant.[33] At a 90 percent confidence limit, however, it appears that as the state enterprise sector expands, government regulation blossoms (laissez faire fades). This suggests (but does not prove) that government ownership and regulation, which spring from the same urge to control economic activity from the center, are not policy alternatives, but rather are policies that are used together.

From the Reagan-Thatcher era it became a truism that state-owned enterprises are not as well managed as privately owned enterprises and cannot readily compete against them. From this standpoint we would expect to find lower economic growth in nations with extensive state-enterprise sectors. Thorvaldur Gylfason and his coauthors provide some evidence from a worldwide sample of nations to support this proposition. For the OECD nations between 1985 and 1995, however, I could not find any statistically significant relationship between such a success criterion as per capita GDP growth and the public-ownership data in Table 11.3.

My results might be explained in two ways. The public ownership sector in most OECD nations might be too small to have had much impact on the overall growth rate. Or the proposition about the inefficiencies of state-owned enterprises might be wrong, particularly for those SOEs facing considerable international competition. For instance, Robert Millward examines a variety of economic success indicators of certain industrial sectors featuring primarily state-owned enterprises in the U.K. and privately-owned enterprises in the U.S. and finds that in many cases the British public sector performed considerably better than the U.S. private sector, at least according to his criteria.

2. Trends in U.S. Governmental Ownership of Capital

The ownership of the means of production might have an impact on the way in which markets function, since state-owned enterprises (or, for that matter, nonprofit enterprises) might respond differently to particular market signals than for-profit private enterprises. For instance, in the case of an extreme short-

---

[33] Using the laissez faire index (LF) in Table 11.1, the ownership data (SOE) in Table 11.3, the 1995 per capita GDP in thousand dollars (PPP method) (Y/cap), the logarithm of the 1995 population (ln pop) and the 1995 trade/GDP ratio, the following regression can be calculated for the key OECD nations (standard errors are below the calculated coefficients; an asterisk designates statistical significance at the .05 level):

LF = 8.72* - 9.10 SOE + 0.0000174 Y/cap -0.209 ln pop - 0.303 trade/GDP R^2 = .2361
(1.38) (5.43) (0.0000165) (0.114) (0.386) n = 19

age, SOEs might be less inclined to raise prices and more inclined to employ certain rationing devices instead. Nevertheless, in the U.S. the share of public ownership in the total stock of the means of production is so small that this phenomenon should not be readily apparent.

In Appendix A11.2 I present data on the changing share of government ownership in the physical capital stock of the nation—buildings, machines, and inventories. This share appears to have slowly declined throughout the second half of the 20th century. Further, state-owned enterprises do not appear to have a quantitatively significant role in the U.S. economy during this period, although earlier they figured importantly in the economic development of the nation, as documented by Louis Galambos. Moreover, at the end of the century, there was little political support for any significant extension of government ownership, and I see little evidence of a dramatic extension in state ownership in coming decades. Rather, the slow decline in their relative importance will continue.

The pattern of ownership of capital by different levels of government greatly changed over the second half of the 20th century. As shown in Appendix A11.2, the federal government held roughly the same amount of physical capital (and, for that matter, employed roughly the same number of people) in the 1950s as the combined state and local government sector.[34] In the next two decades, the federal government's share of both wealth and employment in the U.S. dramatically declined, so that by the 1970s, according to both indicators, state and local government combined were more than twice the size of the federal government. For the rest of the century, the federal government's capital stock and employment as a share of the U.S. total continued to fall, but that of the combined state and local government remained roughly constant. In short, the criticism of "big government" that has focused on activities of the federal government is misplaced, since the growth of state and local governments has been the primary source of governmental growth in the second half of the 20th century. I can find no reason why these trends will not continue in the next few decades.

3. Changes in the Pattern of Private Ownership

In Chapter 4 I discuss briefly how private wealth became increasingly concentrated in the latter third of the 20th century. But patterns have changed in other important ways as well.[35]

---

[34]   The employment data for the federal government includes the military; for the state and local governments, teachers.

[35]   I do not discuss here the changing boundary between public and private property rights. In

Table 11.4. *Composition of the Wealth Portfolios of Private Individuals and the Nonprofit Sector*

	Tangible assets to total assets (tangible + financial)	Equities to total financial assets	Equities held directly to total equities held either directly or through financial intermediaries
1950s	35.4%	22.8%	96.1%
1960s	33.3	31.2	93.0
1970s	37.4	20.8	78.6
1980s	39.4	15.9	74.7
1990–98	34.1	26.0	66.3

Note: The equities are valued at their current market values. The underlying data come from Table B-100e of the flow-of-funds data of the Board of Governors of the Federal Reserve Bank at their website (http://www.bog.frb.fed.us/releases/z1/Current/data.htm).

A really important change in private sector ownership patterns in the second half of the 20th century can be designated as the "socialization of private ownership." By this I mean that a growing share of wealth is held by financial intermediaries, while individual portfolios are more and more composed of shares in these intermediaries, rather than of tangible assets that are directly held.

Table 11.4 shows trends in the composition of the wealth portfolios of private individuals and nonprofit organizations (unfortunately, the Federal Reserve does not publish separate data for these two sectors). Both the share of financial to total assets and the share of equities to total financial assets remained roughly the same over the period. The share of equities held

External Appendix X-11.1, I look at changes in the meaning of property and contract, pointing out that in the field of property law in the second half of the 20th century, individual ownership rights appear to have strengthened at the expense of the government's power to make public interest decisions about the use of land for zoning or for environmental, recreational, and other purposes. Unfortunately, the future of property rights is difficult to foresee, because much depends on Supreme Court decisions and on the political climate of the nation, both of which are notoriously hard to predict.

In the same appendix I also show that the shares of the capital stock in the U.S. total that were held by nonprofit organizations and by cooperatives in the U.S. were very small in the last half of the 20th century. Moreover, these shares did not greatly change over the period and are unlikely to change greatly for decades to come.

directly, however, declined; and the share held by financial intermediaries, for instance, pension funds, mutual funds, and insurance companies, rose dramatically.

The rising share of equities held by financial intermediaries appears inexorable: In 1952 financial intermediaries held 8.2 percent of the equities in domestic corporations; by 1990 they held 44.7 percent, as I document elsewhere.[36] On the basis of other data, a number of economists, most notably Peter Drucker (1976), have spoken of "pension fund socialism" as the emerging economic system, because corporate equities are less and less directly held by individuals. Although "socialism" may be a witty but somewhat misleading term, present trends suggest that pension and insurance funds will soon hold in their portfolios a majority share in American corporations.

This development is another manifestation of the separation of ownership and control, but in a somewhat different sense than Adolf Berle and Gardiner Means discussed in their path breaking 1932 book, *The Modern Corporation and Private Property*. They focused primarily on the shift in power from the individual stockholders of a corporation to the corporate manager. The data in Table 5.1 suggest a shift in power from individual investors to financial intermediaries. In both cases, however, individual investors have less power over the corporation in which they directly—or indirectly—hold stock.

Although many financial intermediaries are constrained by law from holding more than a certain percentage of any one company's stock, numerous studies show that the representatives from financial groups can be found on the boards of almost all major corporations.[37] The degree of power exercised by such representatives, however, is the subject of fierce debate. In a number of well-documented cases, financial intermediaries have played key roles in removing high executives of corporations in which their institutions held stock; their power in other decisions has not been as well studied. The potential power of these financial intermediaries was strengthened by a 1993 ruling by the SEC eliminating barriers that prevented institutional investors from coordinating their policy positions for the operations or management of particular companies without prior public notification.

Although these developments look like important steps on the road toward some type of "finance capitalism," they are hesitant ones, because financial intermediaries, at the end of the 20th century, were usually unwilling (except episodically) to play aggressive roles in the management of the firms in which

---

[36] Pryor (1996), p. 145.
[37] Evidence for this claim is presented in Pryor (1996), p. 147. The benefits of such bloc ownership by financial intermediaries to the success of company is also an issue that has not received any definitive answer.

they held large ownership interests. Except in unusual circumstances, these institutional investors appear to have chosen to play a more passive role in corporate management, in part because of legal constraints. Despite the presence of outside directors, this meant that corporate decision-making powers devolved back to the managers, whose own power was enhanced by the large block of stock proxies they could count on receiving from financial intermediaries.

Nevertheless, the rapid consolidation of financial institutions documented in Chapter 10, combined with the devolution of power from individual investors, gives rise to concern that the organization of the U.S. financial sector will more closely resemble that found in certain continental European nations.[38] In some of these nations, finance is dominated by several large banks and financial institutions, which are often loath to lend to new entrepreneurs. If private saving as a share of GDP will fall, as I argue in Chapter 2, this will add to the difficulties of new firms in raising capital.

These developments, in turn, point toward ways in which the economy can lose considerable dynamism. Under certain circumstances, concentration of financial power over the firm into the hands of ever fewer financial intermediaries can also intensify the widening income differentials, a worrisome prospect given current trends (Chapter 4).

The degree to which intermediaries would be willing to exercise operational powers over the corporations, even if current legal constraints are removed, is uncertain. Cynics can argue, for instance, that the financial intermediaries really do not wish to exercise their potential power, as they have been unwilling to dampen soaring CEO compensation.

E. Summary

This chapter provides more evidence for two themes introduced in previous chapters—a decline in both the government's degree of economic intervention and, in some cases, the government's strength to make and to implement various economic policies.

[38] The last two decades of the 20th century in the U.S. witnessed an explosion of financial innovations and products; and the functions of different kinds of financial intermediaries have gradually merged. Predictions about the future structure of the financial sector range widely, from relatively innocuous forecasts (the continual growth of derivative contracts) to more radical scenarios (the obsolescence of commercial banking). Although current innovations may have profound implications for the future structure of the financial sector, my argument is based only on the assumption that the consolidation of financial institutions discussed in Chapter 10 will continue.

Government regulations aimed at specific market activities declined over the course of the second half of the 20th century. In some cases, especially long-distance telephones and electricity generation, the underlying cause of the relaxed regulatory regime was a change in technology. In other cases, the underlying cause has been a change in the economic environment or in ideology. It seems likely that more deregulation of specific market activities will continue in the coming decades, although perhaps at a slower pace.

General economic regulation became more relaxed as well, particularly in the last two decades of the 20th century. This trend is consistent with the generalization reached through my statistical analysis of regulation in various OECD nations at a single point in time, namely, that government regulation tends to diminish as income differentials widen. As shown in Chapter 4, income inequality began to rise in the late 1970s and it seems highly likely that rising income inequality played an important role in the deregulation movement occurring at the same time.

These arguments, combined with the lack of any credible evidence that the trend of federal governmental deregulation in the U.S. will reverse, strongly suggest a continued ebbing of general economic regulation as well, and this decline will be manifested both in terms of the various measures of regulatory inputs and also in terms of the cost of compliance to these regulations. Exceptions to this prediction, however, might be found in the areas of consumer health (for instance, HMOs) and amenities such as preservation and increase of park lands and national forests.

General economic and also industry-specific regulations will continue to become weaker. This change will be accelerated by the increasing integration of the world economy, combined with the opportunities of circumventing government regulation through trading via the internet or producing in offshore havens. These changes in the economic environment have already reduced the effectiveness of many types of governmental intervention.

My analysis of governmental ownership in OECD nations suggests that increased government regulation and ownership occur together and are not used as substitutes for each other. The economic role of state-owned enterprises in the U.S. was small in the latter part of the 20th century, and little evidence is at hand that this situation will change in the coming decades. Similarly, I argue that the share of all governmental tangible wealth in total U.S. tangible wealth, as well as the wealth of nonprofit organizations and cooperatives, is small and does not seem likely to increase in the foreseeable future. The most remarkable change in the pattern of governmental wealth holding is the declining share in the hands of the federal government, and the corresponding rising share held by state and local governments—a trend that is likely to continue, barring a major war or economic recession.

It seems to me that the most striking change in the pattern of ownership has taken place in the private, not the public sector, namely the rising share of corporate equities held by financial intermediaries. This indicates a widening gap—not just in physical proximity but also in decision-making power—between individuals who, in a legal sense, are the ultimate owners of such assets and those who manage them. This trend is likely to become even more important in the coming decades and, as I note, can have under certain conditions an adverse impact on economic growth and also the distribution of income.

But all this is not the end of the story of the changing government sector and, at this late stage, several important characters have yet to make their appearance. In the next chapter I focus on government expenditures, a discussion that provides a much different perspective on the evolving government sector than we can gain from examination of regulation and ownership alone.

CHAPTER 12

Evolution of Government Spending

By the end of the Twentieth Century, taxation will be reduced to a minimum ... and there will be no need of a standing army.
—Railroad executive Erastus Wiman, 1893[1]

In previous chapters I provide considerable evidence to support a thesis argued by Martin van Creveld about "the decline of the state." Confidence in the government has been falling; the private sector has begun to supplement certain services previously considered almost exclusively in the realm of the government, such as internal security; governmental monetary and fiscal policies are becoming less effective; deregulation will continue; and many of the remaining governmental regulations will become increasingly difficult to enforce because of greater globalization. But in this chapter I argue that in one critical respect—namely the ratio of taxes or public spending to the GDP—the government sector will expand, primarily as a result of the changing age structure of the population.[2]

In the first section I look briefly at some critical determinants of public expenditures, not just those emphasized by public finance economists, but also less tangible political and demographic factors, which I believe to be more important. To provide perspective, I briefly compare current U.S. public expenditures (current outlays and transfers) with those of other leading OECD nations. I then analyze the changing pattern of U.S. public expenditures over the last half century, an exercise that requires exploration of the "hidden" public expenditures seldom appearing in discussions of governmental budgets and yet

---

[1] Cited in Dave Walter, *Today Then: America's Best Minds Look 100 Years into the Future on the Occasion of the 1893 World's Columbian Exposition* (1992). In the text of this section I mention a book by Creveld (1999).

[2] Throughout this chapter I present ratios of various types of transfers, or current outlays plus transfers, as a ratio of GDP. Although transfers do not represent any production of goods and services, this type of comparison is useful in providing perspective on the relative magnitudes involved.

accounting for an increasing share of spending. This quantitative analysis provides the framework for the final section, where I develop a set of qualitative forecasts for public expenditures in the coming decades.

A. Key Determinants of Public Expenditures[3]

The rich public finance literature on the determinants of governmental expenditures starts on the European continent more than two centuries ago. In the latter part of the 19th century Adolph Wagner, an otherwise obscure German economics professor, seemed to argue (his opaque writings are difficult to decipher) that public expenditures as a percentage of GDP will continually rise in economically developed nations, an hypothesis now called Wagner's law. The history of public expenditures over the long term in most industrialized nations has borne out Wagner's prediction, at least until recent times. He said nothing about the speed of this increase or whether the expenditures ratio would asymptotically approach a limit. Moreover, he never considered how such public expenditures would affect the economy. Furthermore, he did not explain the underlying mechanisms and seemed to assume that some inherent public demand for government spending is gradually revealed as the economy becomes more developed which, in turn, leads to the appropriate increase in public expenditures.

Since that time, a variety of determinants have been proposed and tested on different types of data sets for public expenditures.[4] On the demand side, the effects of urbanization and growing population density, the rising need for higher education, the shift in consumption from goods to services, the ever greater heterogeneity of the population, the rising literacy level, the increasing availability of alternative private services, the changing mix of homes and apartments, and other factors have been offered as determinants. On the supply side, the economic system, the differential growth of productivity in the public and private sectors, bureaucratic inertia, political pandering by legislators, fiscal illusion, and other factors have been argued as playing important causal roles.

Although this list could be considerably extended, I prefer to end this aspect of the discussion with three obvious observations. First, the determinants of public expenditures depend in large measure on what types of spending—education, defense, welfare, national parks—are under consideration. Second, the political process underlying such spending depends a great deal on the level at which it is carried out—federal, state, or local. Third, the demand side appears

---

[3] In the text of this section I cite studies by: Hansen (1998), Lee-Tuljapurkar (1994), and Mueller (1963).

[4] These are summarized by Lybeck and Henrekson (1988) and Pryor (1968).

to be more important in driving the political process underlying changing share of such public spending to the GDP. In particular, I argue below that the change in the age composition of the population and the increasing need for public transfers for pensions and health care to the elderly will be the most important factors underlying the rising share of public expenditures in the GDP in the decades to come. For these reasons I start with a brief discussion about public attitudes toward governmental expenditures and the increasing "need" for public expenditures (current outlays plus transfers) directed at the elderly.

1. Public Opinion toward Public Expenditures

In Chapter 8, I present certain indicators of a decreasing citizen participation in government and the declining trust in it. Many argue that if people do not trust their government, they are less willing to support it with their tax funds and are more likely to vote (if they vote at all) for candidates who favor lower governmental expenditures and taxes. Chart 8.1 provides additional evidence about the resentment of taxes, but it also reveals a curious political situation. Although the fraction of total federal income tax payments to aggregate personal income did not greatly change from 1950 to the end of the century, over this period in any year, roughly two thirds of those paying these income taxes believed that the rates were too high. If such public opinion data have any meaning, and if voters have any influence over the actions of government, this would suggest that governmental taxes (and expenditures) at the federal level should have decreased. As shown in the next section, however, this has not happened, and we must look more carefully at public attitudes toward taxes and public expenditures to understand why.

Most public opinion data reveal that respondents simultaneously favor lower deficits, lower taxes, and higher public expenditures! Despite discontent with taxes, a majority of Americans have a favorable attitude toward government expenditures. For instance, reporting on the results of an exhaustive survey in 1960-61, Eva Mueller noted that a large majority of the American people had favorable attitudes toward a number of major public expenditure programs, especially in the areas of health, education, and welfare, and that a large majority also believed in spending any surplus on other governmental programs, rather than lowering taxes. Nevertheless, they still wanted lower taxes. Since then, most survey data reveal a majority of respondents wishing to spend more money on almost every governmental program. The conflict between attitudes toward public expenditures and taxation was most clearly shown in the 1980 presidential election, when Ronald Reagan obtained votes by supporting lower taxes, higher governmental expenditures for defense (and no apparent change in other expenditures), and an elimination of the government deficit.

As John Hansen argues:

> ...even the best survey instruments have neglected the essential aspect of the public budgetary process: the tradeoffs inherent in establishing public priorities. Typically, survey questions offer respondents unrealistic choices among incomplete sets of options.

Thus, recorded public views on the federal income tax or views about public expenditures in isolation from the rest of the budget, or level of trust in the government appear irrelevant, either to policy making (except as they influence voting patterns) or to prediction.

To probe more deeply into these issues, in the 1995 Pilot Study for the 1996 American National Election Study, Hansen asked a series of questions to force the respondent to make critical tradeoffs, e.g., "Do you favor increases in taxes paid by ordinary Americans in order to cut the federal budget deficit." Later in the survey the same question was asked in the reverse manner "Do you favor an increase in the federal budget deficit in order to cut the taxes of ordinary Americans?" The results show that the respondents had relatively consistent preference orderings and, moreover, overwhelmingly supported the policy *status quo* existing at that time.

In brief, this more careful survey of attitudes toward the federal budget suggests that, in so far as public views influence the governmental spending, no dramatic short-run changes in the size of the government as a fraction of the GDP should be expected in the coming decades. Nevertheless, such a survey has not been conducted over a long time period, so we do not know how actual governmental expenditures are influenced by, or correlated with, public opinion; or how such public opinion correlates with voting patterns. It may turn out that the manifest values revealed by public opinion polling may have little influence on expenditure and tax policies, and that the roles of elite opinion or the sources of campaign financing have much greater weight. Finally, we do not know how critical changes in the economy might alter opinions (or voting patterns) of both the public and political elites, which, in turn, might affect governmental spending. I argue below that the aging of the population, combined with a rising need for financial assistance to a considerable segment of the aged, will prove the critical factor that will change current opinion toward public spending, causing the expenditure/GDP ratio to rise.

2. A Change in the Age-Structure and the Increased Need for Governmental Expenditures

The population estimates of Ronald Lee and Shripad Tuljapukar, which I use in Chapter 2, show considerable change in the elderly-dependency-ratio (the ratio of those over 65 to those between 20 and 64) in the first half of the 21st century. In 1995 it was 21.9 percent, between 2010 and 2030 it will rise dramatically, and by 2050, according to their median estimate, it will hit 39.1 percent. Moreover, their median estimate of the ratio of the old-old (those over 84) to those from 20 up to 65 will rise from 2.4 percent in 1995 to 10.4 percent in 2050.

Changes in government transfers for Social Security and health are tied to changes in life expectancy, in the retirement age, and in the level of health among the elderly. Life expectancy for those 65 and older increased at a relatively constant average annual rate of 0.48 percent between 1950 and 1995. It is worth noting that many nations have considerably longer life expectancies so that this extension of life in the U.S. might continue for some time before the elderly in this nation reach any alleged biological limit. If levels of health and the retirement age do not rise at least as fast as life expectancy, then an ever larger percent of the population will have to rely on transfers (either from the government via Social Security and Medicare, or from various private pension and health insurance plans) or on their own savings to finance their retirement and health care.

The critical policy consideration is that a large share of the population are currently entering old age with very few assets and very little income except from Social Security. Some relevant data presented in Table 12.1 show that a majority of the elderly rely predominantly on Social Security as their source of income (Panel A). Their financial assets are extremely limited and their primary assets, if any, are their homes. This has one immediate implication: any reduction of Social Security benefits and other governmental transfers to the elderly will strongly and adversely affect a considerable share of the elderly population, a lamentable fact that puts certain constraints on reducing benefits in order to achieve long-term balance in the Social Security trust fund. Moreover, as the life expectancy increases, they may need more support, especially if their longer life is accompanied by more years of ill-health. And, of course, even if individual families of the elderly may be receiving no more than today, the population shift will result in higher total government expenditures on, and transfers to, the elderly.

B. An International Perspective on Public Expenditures

Before examining trends in the U.S., it is useful to place U.S. public expenditures in a broader context. Table 12.2 presents data on several different types of government expenditures in various OECD nations.

Table 12.1. *The Economic Status of the Elderly Famillies*

Panel A: Cash Income by Earning Quintiles, 1997

Quintile distribution (from lowest income to highest)

	Earnings	OASDI (Social Security)	Income	Pensions from assets	Other and annuities	Total
First	1.9%	87.9%	5.2%	1.9%	3.1%	100%
Second	1.3	87.1	6.7	3.1	1.7	100
Third	3.3	77.6	9.6	8.0	1.5	100
Fourth	8.0	53.5	15.1	21.1	2.4	100
Fifth	25.2	21.0	27.2	24.7	1.9	100
All	16.6	41.4	20.4	19.6	1.9	100

Panel B. Distribution of Total Net Worth, 1992

Percentile	Total	Non-Financial	Financial
10 (lowest net worth)	$150	$150	$0
20	8,000	8,000	0
30	28,005	27,405	600
50	77,800	69,000	8,000
70	154,000	118,000	36,000
90	384,000	232,000	152,000
95 (highest net worth)	618,999	343,999	275,000

Note: For the income data, the "elderly" include individuals age 65 or older plus married couples in which one spouse is older than 65. This measure of income does not include non-cash income such as housing. "Other" income includes public assistance, Supplemental Social Security income, financial assistance from friends and relatives, and so forth. These data were supplied by the Employee Benefit Research Institute and are based on tabulations from the various March *Current Population Surveys*. The asset data are for households with a household head who is 70 or over. The data come from Smith (1997), p. 77.

From these data one important conclusion is immediately apparent: In comparison to other industrial nations, U.S. public expenditures rank at or close to the bottom for transfers, subsidies, and gross capital formation, and in the bottom half for interest and rents and also for goods and services. The goods and services are heavily influenced by military expenditures, which are relatively

Table 12.2. *Government Expenditures in Leading OECD Nations in 1995 as Percent of GDP*

	Total current expenditures	Current expenditures of which				Gross fixed capital
		Goods, services	Transfers	Interest, rents	Subsidies	
Australia	35.3%	17.0%	13.3%	3.8%	1.3%	1.9%
Austria	48.5	18.9	22.6	4.4	2.7	2.9
Belgium	52.2	14.7	26.1	9.0	2.5	1.4
Canada	46.3	21.7	13.8	9.8	1.1	2.6
Denmark	56.1	23.5	22.6	6.5	3.5	1.9
Finland	56.5	21.8	26.1	5.3	3.3	2.6
France	50.9	19.3	25.9	4.0	1.6	3.2
Germany	46.8	19.8	21.2	3.8	2.1	2.4
Greece	41.4	14.8	13.5	12.4	0.6	3.2
Ireland	58.4	36.3	16.0	5.0	1.1	2.2
Italy	49.3	16.1	20.0	11.7	1.6	1.6
Japan	28.5	9.8	14.1	3.8	0.8	6.4
Netherlands	48.5	14.3	26.3	6.0	1.9	2.7
New Zealand	36.2	14.4	15.6	5.8	0.3	2.4
Norway	45.6	20.9	18.1	2.9	3.6	3.2
Portugal	41.7	17.7	15.9	6.8	1.3	3.6
Spain	41.5	16.7	17.5	5.3	1.9	3.6
Sweden	63.7	25.8	25.7	7.1	5.1	3.2
Switzerland	33.5	14.3	14.9	2.2	2.0	2.0
U.K.	42.4	21.2	16.4	3.7	1.0	1.8
U.S.	34.3	16.0	13.2	4.6	0.5	1.7
Average	46.1%	18.8%	19.0%	6.4%	1.9%	2.7%
Coefficient of variation	21.7%	29.2%	25.9%	52.9%	63.6%	39.8%
U.S. rank (from highest)	19	15	21	13	20	19

Note: the coefficient of variation is the standard deviation divided by the mean. The data come primarily from Table 6 of the various OECD nations in OECD (1998-b). For Portugal the data are for 1993. For New Zealand and Greece I made certain estimates on the basis of data for other years.

high in the U.S. in comparison with most other OECD nations; and the rents and interest are influenced by past deficits. For the other expenditures, the U.S. seems to be fighting for the bottom rank with Japan and Switzerland.

It should also be apparent that variation in these expenditures among the OECD nations is considerable. In most cases this variation can be traced to differences in policy and historical experience. For instance, since the ratio of social security payments to the GDP is, to a certain extent, related to the length of time the system has been in operation, we should expect that the ratio of these transfers to GDP would be higher in Germany and Austria, where the system began over a half century before the Social Security system in the United States.[5]

How are these current government expenditures (current outlays plus transfers) for the various OECD nations related to other economic factors? The first step is to examine the correlation between various types of government expenditures and such economic variables as the per capita GDP, the size of the population, and the ratio of trade to GDP, as well as to three social variables: income inequality, social capital, and social trust.[6]

In these statistical investigations I find that neither social capital nor social trust is related to the ratio of current government expenditures or of government transfers alone to the GDP, when various other causal factors are held constant. Income inequality is also not related to current government expenditures, other causal factors held constant. Nevertheless, it is inversely and significantly related to the ratio of transfer expenditures to the GDP: the greater the inequality of

---

[5] I demonstrate these propositions in Pryor (1968).

[6] For these different variables I used the same 1995 data on Y/cap (GDP/capita), lnPop (logarithm of population), and Tr/Y (exports + imports as a ratio of GDP) as in other regression experiments in this book. For the ratio of current government expenditures (current outlays plus transfers) to GDP (CG/Y) the results are:

$$CG/Y = 0.244 + 0.0000012 \text{ Y/cap} - 0.0075 \text{ lnPop} + 0.247^* \text{ Tr/Y} \qquad n = 21$$
$$\quad\quad (0.244) \quad (0.0000058) \quad\quad (0.0211) \quad\quad (0.086) \qquad\qquad R^2 = 0.4041$$

where the data in parentheses are standard errors; and the asterisks designate statistical significance at the 0.05 level.

For the ratio of transfers alone to GDP (Tran/Y) the results are:

$$Tran/Y = 0.090 + 0.00000031 \text{ Y/cap} + 0.0042 \text{ lnPop} + 0.0803 \text{ Tr/Y} \qquad n = 20$$
$$\quad\quad (0.141) \quad (0.00000369) \quad\quad (0.0120) \quad\quad (0.0492) \qquad\qquad R^2 = 0.1733$$

$$Tran/Y = 0.237 + 0.0000017 \text{ Y/cap} + 0.0216^* \text{ lnPop} + 0.0644 \text{ Trade/Y} - 0.938^* \text{ Gini} \quad n = 18$$
$$\quad\quad (0.127) \quad (0.0000034) \quad\quad (0.0107) \quad\quad (0.0397) \quad\quad (0.271) \quad R^2 = 0.5594$$

where Gini = the gini coefficient of income inequality.

income, the lower the ratio of transfer expenditures to the GDP; conversely, the higher the equality of income, the higher is this transfer ratio.

In part this is to be expected, because if such governmental transfers are administered to reduce income inequality, they should be inversely related to inequality. But another explanation is also available: If income is more equally distributed so that lifestyles of various income groups are not greatly different, voters as a whole might feel a greater social solidarity with the poor in their midst. That is they might consider the poor to be similar to themselves, but having bad luck. If, by way of contrast, incomes are greatly different, those with higher incomes have little in common with the poor and might believe them solely to blame for their poverty. In the former case, the majority of voters might be more willing to approve of governmental transfers to the poor. Time-series evidence presented below for the U.S. provides support for this conjecture.

C. An Historical View on U.S. Public Expenditures

1. Visible Public Expenditures

In the second half of the 20th century, the ratio of current government expenditures (including transfers) to the GDP rose rapidly from the 1950s through the 1970s, and then leveled off so that the differences between the 1980s and 1990s were small.[7] I present data in Table 12.3 to support these claims. As noted in a different context in the previous chapter, the state and local sector also grew much faster than the federal sector during this half-century period.

After the 1950s, health, education, and welfare (HEW) accounted for the largest share of government expenditures. Moreover, as a share of GDP, such expenditures increased considerably faster than those for administration, external and internal security, economic purposes, or interest. The various components of HEW expenditures, however, increased at different rates: health related expenditures as a share of GDP grew the fastest, while spending for

---

[7] Current governmental expenditures include spending for goods and services, subsidies to producers, transfers of funds for which no immediate quid pro quo is expected (for instance, for welfare and health), and depreciation.

Gross investment for buildings and capital equipment by the government is not included in Table 12.3. Nevertheless, trends in such spending, shown in Appendix 12.1, can be quickly summarized. As a share of GDP, government investments fell, particularly those of the federal government. As a share of total gross investment, the federal government's share declined while the share of state and local government rose slightly. Appendix 11.2 provides other indicators of the size of different levels of government.

unemployment insurance, job training, and veterans (again as a percent of GDP) actually decreased.

Of critical importance, two expenditures strongly related to the aging of the population and the savings that the elderly bring to their retirement—namely health care and retirement benefits—rose steadily, from 3.0 percent in the 1950s to 9.7 percent of the GDP in the 1990s. At the same time, the elderly-dependency-ratio rose from 15.7 to 21.7 percent. In brief, the expenditures related to the elderly increased very much faster than my measure of the aging of the population.

The various trends in current expenditures that are shown in the table are well known and it is not necessary to dwell on them. These "visible" expenditures of the government are not, however, the whole story that we must consider.

2. Invisible Expenditures from the Federal Budget

In this discussion I briefly review three types of hidden federal expenditures—the so-called tax-expenditures, off-budget expenditures, and inter-governmental transfers—and demonstrate that for certain functions, they are considerably greater in magnitude than the corresponding items in the visible budget. External Appendix X-12.1 presents the quantitative evidence on which I base my argument.

a. Tax-expenditures: Tax-expenditures are the hidden subsidies given in the form of tax exemptions. Three simple examples will suffice: (i) If the government wishes to encourage private education, it might allow a family to reduce its taxable income by the $5000 spent on a child's school tuition. If the family is wealthy and subject to a marginal tax rate of 39 percent, this exemption is equivalent to a governmental grant of $1950; for a poorer family subject to a marginal tax rate of only 15 percent, the exemption is equivalent to a governmental grant of $750. (ii) Or if an employer gives $1000 of health benefits to a worker, which the U.S. tax code does not consider as part of the employee's income, and if that worker is subject to a 20 percent marginal tax rate, the tax exemption is equivalent to a grant from the government to the employee of $200.[8] (iii) Or if the government wishes to encourage production of alternative fuels and allows an exemption from the profit tax of 50 percent, a business selling such a product and earning a profit of $1000 is essentially given a $500 subsidy. None of these three types of implicit grants shows up in the usual type of

---

[8]   Since both a wage or a health benefit are an expense to the employer, the company tax bill remains the same.

Table 12.3. *Current Public Expenditures (Federal, State, and Local) as a Percentage of GDP*

	1952-1959	1960-1969	1970-1979	1980-1989	1990-1997	*Percentage change in ratios, 1950s to 1990s*
Total current expenditures	22.5%	24.7%	29.2%	31.2%	31.8%	+41.5%
of which direct federal	16.3	16.5	17.9	20.5	19.8	+ 21.9
of which direct state and local	6.2	8.2	11.3	10.8	12.0	+ 92.5
Administrative	0.8	0.8	1.1	1.1	1.1	+45.4
External security	10.0	8.7	6.5	6.3	5.0	- 50.4
Internal security	0.6	0.8	1.0	1.1	1.4	+126.5
Health, education, welfare	7.7	10.8	16.5	17.3	18.9	+144.8
Education	2.4	3.7	5.0	4.8	4.9	+101.3
Hospitals and health	0.6	1.1	2.5	3.4	4.9	+791.3
Retirement pensions	1.7	3.0	4.3	4.8	4.8	+280.4
Disability, workman's compensation	0.2	0.4	0.7	0.8	0.8	+361.2
Unemployment, job training	0.6	0.6	0.8	0.7	0.6	-6.7
General income support	0.8	0.8	1.6	1.6	1.8	+144.9
Veterans	1.3	1.0	1.0	0.7	0.6	-54.3
Housing, community development culture, recreation	0.1	0.2	0.4	0.5	0.5	+386.3

Economic (commercial, support for energy, agriculture, other sectors)	1.9	2.0	2.2	2.1	1.7	- 11.3
Not specified						
(state and local govts.)	0.1	0.2	0.5	0.6	0.6	+522.2
Interest	1.3	1.3	1.5	2.6	3.0	+136.9

Notes: The components may not add up exactly to the totals because of rounding. These data include current consumption, transfers, subsidies, and depreciation. Expenditures are attributed to the governmental level where they are made, so that inter-governmental transfers are excluded from federal expenditures. Economic expenditures include expenditures for energy, agriculture, transportation, communications, public utilities, economic development, plus net expenditures (subsidies) for the post office and commercial activities by state and local governments.

The data come from Tables 3.16 and 3.17 of the national income and product accounts, primarily from U.S. Department of Commerce, Bureau of Economic Analysis (1998-b), but updated with more recent information from various articles in the *Survey of Current Business*. Government expenditures are measured in a somewhat different way from the OECD data in Table 12.2.

data on government spending, and the only impact on the budget is a smaller surplus (or a larger deficit).

The estimates from External Appendix X-12 show that the expenditure equivalent of all major federal tax-expenditures was 5.1 percent of the GDP in 1968 and 6.7 percent in 1997. Although state and local governments also have tax-expenditures, it is difficult to gain an overview of their magnitude since estimates are available for only a few of these jurisdictions. The ratio of invisible tax-expenditures to visible government expenditures (including subsidies) for the same purpose have been highest for housing and community development (for instance, tax breaks on mortgage interest) and second highest for stimulating private productive activities, primarily through various types of tax breaks for businesses.

The magnitude of these tax-expenditures is often difficult to calculate. For this reason it is politically easier to benefit a particular group in this way, rather than giving them a direct subsidy which is more open to political attack. Tax breaks can also be more easily targeted to benefit upper-income groups, who are, of course, the major contributors to political campaigns. It should come as no surprise that, measured as a percentage of their income, the upper income groups benefit disproportionately from such tax-expenditures (External Appendix X-12.1).

There is, however, an upper limit to tax-expenditures, namely, when the tax code becomes so riddled with these exceptions that it becomes totally unfathomable, and the necessity for tax reform becomes apparent and urgent. For instance, between 1967 and 1982 the ratio of tax-expenditures to the GDP almost doubled. The tax reform of 1986 eliminated many of these tax breaks, but since that time the ratio has risen, in large part because the Clinton administration chose to stimulate particular activities through this mechanism, especially in the areas of health, education, and welfare.

It seems likely that the ratio of invisible to visible governmental expenditures should be cyclical, falling after each tax reform and rising thereafter. The politics of tax-expenditures are intricate, however, and party labels seems to mean less than particular political circumstances.[9] It is possible that increasing globalization may lead to some type of supervision of such tax-expenditures so that

---

[9]   In the 2000 presidential election, the Democratic Party favored a series of tax-expenditures for particular purposes such as education, that were designed to aid the middle income groups. In the same election the Republican Party, by way of contrast, stepped away from its traditional support of tax-expenditures (which primarily benefited the wealthy) and advocated an explicit across-the-board income tax cuts (which were also slanted toward the wealthy, but, at least, were more transparent). Nevertheless, within a fortnight of his inauguration, President George W. Bush presented to Congress a new tax-expenditure favoring those paying private school tuition.

a particular nation will not gain an unfair advantage in luring footloose companies to its shores.

   b. *Off-budget expenditures:* Off-budget expenditures include outlays from a variety of federal trust funds and federally-owned entities such as the post office. These units can spend considerable money, but if they are able to offset some or all of these with various types of revenues, such as fees, only the difference between receipts and expenditures may appear as a line in the federal budget.

   In the last half of the 20th century these off-budget expenditures, measured as a percentage of total federal on-budget expenditures, rose rapidly until the 1970s. Thereafter, they leveled off at about 24 percent of on-budget expenditures (or about 4 percent of GDP). Throughout this period most of these off-budget entities also ran a small surplus. An exception was the Social Security system, which ran a very large surplus for many years. This is projected to disappear as the baby-boomers retire unless the system is revamped (see below). External Appendix X-12.1 contains a more extensive discussion of these expenditures.

   c. *Inter-governmental transfers:* Transfers from the federal government to state and local governments allow expenditures to be made by officials closest to the people benefitted and, at the same time, to be financed by the governmental level most easily able to collect revenues. Such transfers can be tailored to encourage state and local governments to carry out particular activities (for instance, specific educational projects). They can also be distributed as general block grants, whose use is left to the discretion of the recipient governments, such as the general revenue sharing program which was initiated by the Nixon administration and lasted from 1972 through 1987.

   Although this type of fiscal federalism found supporters along the entire political spectrum, individual members of both parties of Congress also realized that they might gain votes from taxpayers if they eliminated the program and thereby lowered federal income taxes. Such a step, of course, forced the state and local governments to finance these expenditures from their own resources, usually by raising taxes. It is difficult to find a more glaring example of the loss of common purpose in the nation's political life or an act more specifically designed to reduce trust in government and the legislative process.[10]

---

[10] This type of political nonsense takes place on the state level as well. In New Jersey, Christine Whitman gained a strong political advantage by pledging to reduce the state income tax. After winning the governorship, she and the Republican Party fulfilled this pledge, thereby forcing the local governments to increase local property taxes in order to finance expenditures for which they had previously received state transfers.

The level of government at which a particular expenditure is financed is an important policy concern. Transfers from the federal government to state and local governments allow poorer states to be subsidized by richer ones, thereby reducing real income inequalities in the nation as a whole. Moreover, the federal taxation system is considerably more progressive than the tax systems of most state and local governments, especially since it can collect taxes on high-income individuals or corporations which can threaten to move to another jurisdiction as a bargaining chip in negotiations about state and local taxes. As noted in Chapter 5, with increasing globalization even this tax advantage of the federal government is weakening, since industries are now more internationally foot-loose. In addition, as discussed in Chapter 4, the federal government is less likely to cut back on spending during recessions because it is not constrained by balanced-budget laws, in contrast to most state and local governments. As a result, automatic fiscal stabilizers can operate more effectively when federal transfers to state and local governments are high. Furthermore, costs of tax collection for the government and also for the corporations conducting business in many states, who fill out the forms, are much lower when the federal government collects them. Finally, the judicious structuring of particular types of transfer arrangements allows much greater standardization of these programs across the nation, an important consideration for a highly mobile population.[11]

Although inter-governmental transfers are visible in the budget, they are usually buried so deeply in the fine print that they receive little discussion. The transfers from the federal government to the state and local governments, as a fraction of GDP, rose from the 1950s through the 1970s and leveled off thereafter. They financed about one fifth of state and local governmental expenditures and amounted to about 2.5 percent of the GDP in the 1980s and 1990s. In addition, some inter-governmental transfers occurred in the form of tax-expenditures, for instance, exemption of local taxes from the federal income tax base. These tax-expenditures amounted to about 1 percent of the GDP.

d. A final note: In the short-run, the ratio of tax-expenditures to visible governmental spending had an upward creep because they were a convenient way of subsidizing particular groups, but the resultant complexity of the tax code provides a long-term constraint to their deployment. We can probably expect a cyclical pattern of expansion and retrenchment in the future. Barring some dramatic developments, the ratio of off-budget to on-budget spending does not seem likely to change.

---

[11]   To this list might be added a more technical consideration: The costs to the government of collecting business taxes on enterprises with multi-state activities and the administrative costs to the enterprises in paying these taxes, are less if these are collected at the federal level.

The most disturbing developments may arise in the arcane area of inter-governmental transfers. The federal government retreated from the emphasis on fiscal federalism of the Nixon administration and political support has waned. If this trend continues because the U.S. Congress and President place more weight on obtaining short-run political credit for reducing taxes than on the long-run benefits of maintaining or increasing these inter-governmental transfers, then we can expect to see several adverse effects in the coming decades. The nation's economy will experience more violent business cycles because automatic fiscal stabilizers will be weakened. Moreover, real income differentials will widen, both because taxes will be less progressive and because inter-state transfers from richer to poorer states will be smaller. The future of fiscal federalism is determined by political will and ideology, not by economics.

D. Where are Individual Public Expenditures Heading?[12]

My general conclusion in the discussion below is that in the first half of the 21st century, Wagner's Law will operate, despite anti-governmental ideologies or rational arguments against an expanding government sector. To approach the topic, it is useful to divide the various current public expenditures (including transfers) into four groups: those for which the ratio to GDP should decline or not greatly change, those for which the ratio is likely to increase slowly, those for which the ratio will rise considerably, and those for which responsible predictions are impossible.

1. The Expenditure/GDP Ratio Will Decline or Not Greatly Increase

These expenditures include those for administration, interest, social assistance for the needy, and for general economic purposes. In the 1990s, spending for these purposes amounted to about 10.0 percent of the GDP (Table 12.3). This group as a whole exhibits offsetting trends, so that their share in the GDP should not greatly change and, conceivably, might slightly decline.

a. Administration and interest: Between 1952 and 1997, administrative expenditures rose at about the same rate as total current governmental expenditures. If I am correct that public expenditures will increase faster than GDP, the

---

[12]   In the text of this section I draw on studies by: Baker and Weisbrot (1999), Cutler and Meara (1998), (1999), Fuchs (1998), Lee and Skinner (1999), Lee and Tuljapurkar (1994), (1998), Lindbeck, Nyberg, and Weibull (1999), U.S. Congressional Budget Office (1998), U.S. Council of Economic Advisers (2000) and Wallerstein (2000).

ratio of current administrative expenditures to GDP, should rise as well, but the
ratio is small to start with.

Future interest payments are difficult to predict, since they depend on the
political will of legislatures to increase or reduce government debt. Many state
and local governments are constrained by balanced-budget mandates so their
room for maneuver to increase their debt is small. Although this is not the case
for the federal government, dramatic changes in the federal debt are problematic. It seems unlikely, however, that the federal government's debt will be significantly reduced in the near future for two reasons: as a goal, it is not accepted by respected policy makers, who question the feasibility of rapid debt
reductions; and the short-term political advantages of tax cuts or increased
federal spending seem compelling to many members of Congress. It seems
more likely that over the long run the federal debt will increase. We can hope
that the increase will not be as fast as the growth in GDP so that the debt/GDP
ratio declines. This hope, however, is based on the possibility that future political leaders will learn from the fiscal mistakes of the past, so that government debt will not grow as fast in the future as it did between 1980
and 1992.

In the 1990s, interest payments on the national debt amounted to about 3.0
percent of the GDP. Assuming that the national debt will not grow faster than
the GDP in the foreseeable future, the ratio of interest payments to GDP will
probably fall in the coming decades, at least until the nation encounters a serious economic depression.

b. Social assistance: In this category I include traditional "welfare"
expenditures (general income support for the poor) plus a group of smaller
programs including disability payments, unemployment compensation, job
training costs, and various programs for war veterans. As the distribution of
income becomes more and more unequal, it might be argued that such welfare transfers must inevitably increase to meet the needs of the growing low-
income population. However, as I discuss below, some crucial political/eco-
nomic variables, revolving around voting behavior and the impact of
governmental welfare expenditures on the economy, intervene to counteract
such an effect.

The effects of welfare expenditures on work incentives and voting have been
elegantly modeled by Assar Lindbeck, Sten Nyberg, and Jörgen Weibull (hereafter LNW), who posit a situation where people must make two choices. The
first choice is political and made in the voting booths, where citizens must
decide how much to tax themselves to pay transfer expenditures to those not
working (LNW assume a balanced budget). The second choice is economic and
made in the market, where they must decide whether to work or to be idle and
live on welfare payments from the government (LNW do not consider social

security payments to the elderly in this model). In this decision they must not only compare their possible wages with welfare payments but also take into account the extra utility of more leisure minus the extra disutility arising from the stigma of receiving welfare (a social norm), a stigma that diminishes as those living on welfare increases.

From these assumptions LNW demonstrate that because the volume of transfers is limited by the taxes that the voting population is willing to impose on itself, two stable equilibria emerge. The first is a system of relatively low welfare expenditures and a relatively low share of the population receiving them—the voting results are dominated by the voters who work. The second is a system with a high share of the population receiving these welfare payments—the voting results are dominated by the welfare recipients. These two equilibria are not just theoretical possibilities: In Appendix 12.2 I discuss a particularly dramatic example of the difference between these two equilibria that can be seen in two small island states, Iceland and Greenland.

The two stable equilibrium states have, of course, very different implications for the operation of the rest of the economy. If the norm against living off of governmental social benefits fades, work incentives decrease as well, and a higher percentage of the population will not work, a situation that appears to characterize Sweden and several other West European nations.[13] The high taxes needed to pay such assistance can also have adverse effects on investment and innovative activity.

From the LNW approach and the relatively modest ratio of government welfare expenditures to the GDP (Table 12.2), it appears that the U.S. is in the low-welfare equilibrium posited by LNW. Although the U.S. could break out of this equilibrium, two important social and economic factors intervene to keep the *status quo*: (i) The declining level of social capital, discussed in Chapter 7, suggests that generalized altruism is declining, so that recipients of governmental welfare transfers will be viewed in an increasingly negative light; (ii) Social solidarity also seems likely to decline since empathy with the poor declines as the distribution of income becomes more unequal. That is, the low-income groups

---

[13] In Sweden in the mid 1990s, about 25 percent of the population in the working ages lived exclusively on such social benefits, a population share that was only 8 percent in 1960 (LNW). In this case, the stigma of living off of these social benefits was surely minuscule. A similar situation appears in certain other European nations as well. According to "Down with Disablement" (*The Economist,* May 22, 1999), 13 percent of the working age population in the Netherlands received social benefits as disabled; in Norway 57 percent of those between 55 to 64 registered as disabled, while in the UK, only 25 percent of those between 60 and 65 claimed disability benefits.

come more and more to be seen as "different" to the middle class (or the median voter) and less worthy of social support.[14]

   c. *Economic development expenditures*: This category covers not just traditional economic expenditures (including subsidies and commercial activities), but also those for housing and community development. As shown in Table 12.3, their combined total was roughly constant as a share of GDP over the entire second half of the century, and I could find no credible evidence to suggest that this long-term trend will be different in the coming decades. It is worth noting that tax-expenditures for both types of economic development spending were greater than visible budgetary expenditures for the same purposes (External Appendix X-12.1). Although the combined tax-expenditures for these two purposes as a ratio of GDP declined between 1968 and 1997, this downward trend seems unlikely to continue, given the stress both political parties placed on more tax breaks for business around the turn of the millennium.

2. The Expenditure/GDP Ratio is Likely to Increase Slowly

It seems likely that government expenditures for internal security and education will slowly rise. In the 1990s they amounted to 6.3 percent of the GDP (Table 12.3).

   a. *Internal security expenditures: police, prisons, justice:* Current internal security expenditures, which amounted to 1.4 percent of the GDP in the 1990s, are likely to increase.

Starting from a low base in the 1950s, the ratio of internal security expenditures to the GDP increased annually at about 2.1 percent a year to the 1990s. This upward trend, however, seems unlikely to continue, in major part because the recorded crime rate began to fall in the 1990s. Nevertheless, if my argument in Chapter 6 is correct that the drop in crime rates in the 1990s was due in part to the incarceration of criminals likely to be repeat offenders, then it seems probable that the ratio of internal security expenditures in the GDP will rise because of increasing prison expenditures. As documented in Chapter 6, the

---

[14]   In his historical researches, Peter H. Lindert (1994) has unearthed some interesting evidence on this hypothesis, showing that as the gap between the median income and those in the bottom 20th percentile widened in the U.S., governmental, welfare expenditures that redistributed income to the needy declined as a percent of the GDP.

   A strange confirmation is also found in survey data reviewed by Alesina, Di Tella, and MacCulloch (2001), which show that income inequalities have a large, negative, and significant effect on the self-declared happiness of Europeans, but not Americans. This suggests that support for governmental programs for the redistribution of income in the U.S. is relatively weaker.

number of prisoners has climbed dramatically over the second half of the 20th century and shows no sign of slowing down. To the extent that greater social breakdown is expected in the future because of widening income differentials and a decline in social capital, the crime rate might increase again so that the internal security expenditure ratio will rise even faster.

   b. *Education:* In the 20th century current public expenditures for education were mostly financed by state and local governments and represented a major item in their budgets. One seemingly important influence on these expenditures is the number of school-age children relative to the adult population in the working ages (20 through 64). In the second half of the 20th century this ratio rose from 41.6 percent in the 1950s to 51.2 percent in the 1960s and then fell to 34.9 percent in the 1990s.[15] From the 1960s to the 1990s, two factors explain why education expenditures as a percentage of GDP actually rose (Table 12.3) when the share of children in the population was declining: More educational resources were being allocated to each student; and a higher percentage of students were receiving post-secondary school education and training, which is more costly.

   From the median population estimates of Lee and Tuljapurkar, we can estimate that the ratio of school age children to working age adults should fall to 27.1 percent by 2050.[16] This does not match the decline between the 1960s and the 1990s. This decline will be more than offset if education expenditures per child continue to rise in the future at the same rate as in the past, so that the ratio of governmental education expenditures to the GDP will slowly rise.

   This argument assumes, of course, that state and local government will continue their historic role of financing the bulk of educational expenditures on the primary and secondary level, as well as a large share of the expenses of public universities. In the last fifteen years of the 20th century, presidential candidates from both parties vied for the title of the "education president," so that it seems reasonable to expect that, at least for a while, the government will continue to be heavily involved in the financing of education. If, however, voters become disenchanted with the results of public education and turn either to home schooling or private schools (see Chapter 7), then public expenditures for education as a share of GDP may shrink as Americans become increasingly unwilling to support both public schools for other peo-

---

[15]   U.S. Council of Economic Advisers (2000), p. 345.
[16]   Lee-Tuljapurkar (1994) presented only estimates for those 20 and younger. Over the second half of the 20th century, the ratio of school age children to those 20 and younger did not greatly change, so I used the ratio for the 1990s to make the estimate used above. The .95 confidence limits to the L-T estimates suggest, however, that the ratio of school age children to working-age adults could range from 24.5% to 31.0%.

ple's children and private schools for their own. This scenario assumes, of course, that current legal provisions against using public funds for private schools continue.

3. Considerable Increase in the Expenditure/GDP Ratio: Pensions

The most dramatic changes in public expenditures should take place in spending for Social Security and other retirement pensions and health care, including Medicare, Medicaid, and direct expenditures for hospitals (except VA hospitals). In the 1990s current government expenditures for these purposes amounted to 9.7 percent of the GDP (Table 12.3). In this subsection I discuss pension payments; in the next subsection, I turn to expenditures on health care.

In a strict pay-as-you-go social insurance system, the prominence of pension expenditures in the national economy can be usefully analyzed as the product of two ratios. The first is the retirement ratio, the ratio of retired people to those in the labor force who are producing the goods and services and paying the taxes to finance the retirement pensions.[17] The second is the benefit ratio, the ratio of the average benefits received by social insurance recipients to the average income of those financing such expenditures through their taxes.

The Lee-Tuljapurkar population estimates foresee that the ratio of those 65 and over to those in the working ages between 25 and 65 will increase about 75 percent between 2000 and 2050. If we assume, for a moment, a strict pay-as-you-go system, and a fixed benefit-ratio, then two implications can be immediately drawn. Other things equal, the share of Social Security taxes on the income of those working would have to increase by the same percentage if the financial balance of the system is to be maintained. At the same time, Social Security expenditures as a ratio of the GDP would also rise by about the same percentage. But other things will not remain equal and tax relief—or a decline in the percentage of such Social Security expenditures to the GDP—could come about in two ways:

(i) The age at which such retirement benefits can be received might be raised, which would cause the retirement ratio to fall. For instance, in the U.S. an increase of the Social Security retirement age from 65 to 70 and a five-year extension of the working lifetime in which Social Security taxes are paid would mean that in 2050 the retirement ratio would rise only about 25 percent, instead of 75 percent.

---

[17]   In turn, the retirement ratio is a function of the elderly-dependency ratio, the retirement age, and the eligibility rules for receiving a pension.

(ii) The statutory benefits paid to retired workers might remain fixed while the average incomes of active workers rise. In this case the benefit-ratio would automatically fall, along with both the Social Security tax rate and the ratio of total Social Security expenditures to the GDP. For instance, if a worker's income increases at 1 percent a year but the Social Security benefits per retiree remain fixed, then monetary wages would be 64 percent higher in 2050 and the benefit ratio would fall about 40 percent. It should be noted, however, that under current law, certain automatic increases (for instance, for inflation) are built into Social Security benefits. If, for instance, the Social Security payout rate were increased at one half the wage rate, the benefit ratio would fall about 22 percent.

At the end of the 20th century, outlays for Old Age, Survivors, and Disability Insurance (OASDI, which accounted for most—but not all—of public expenditures for pensions), were about 4.6 percent of the GDP. If prices were fixed, if the retirement age were raised to 70, and if benefits were raised by one half the increase in wages (assumed to be 1 percent a year), then the ratio of OASDI payments to the GDP would be roughly the same in 2050 as it is now. Thus, there is no inherent reason why the ratio of aggregate Social Security expenditures to the GDP should rise, if compensating policy measures are taken. These numerical examples are based, however, on hypothetical situations and two questions immediately arise: Under current legislation, what will really happen to Social Security expenditures? And is it politically possible to take compensating measures that will rein in the projected increase?

Under the laws current in 2000, estimates of the ratio of OASDI expenditures to the GDP by 2050 pointed to an increase of two to four percentage points by 2050, and this is the (deliberately) conservative estimate I use below. Others foresee a higher increase, for instance, the U.S. Congressional Budget Office forecast this ratio to be 6.9 percent of the GDP, while data presented by Ronald Lee and Jonathan Skinner allow rough estimates of 7.8 to 8.5 percent.[18] Nevertheless, the uncertainties surrounding such estimates are considerable, not just because the population estimates have a wide margin of error. The U.S. does not have a pay-as-you-go system and it is uncertain when the Social Security system will run out of funds. If this occurs, the system will have to obtain federal

---

[18] Lee and Skinner focus only on balanced budget tax rates, which are currently 12.4 percent of wages up to a given income limit. If the life expectance at birth in 2070 rises to 87 and a pure pay-as-you-go system of financing is in place (so that yearly receipts and benefits must be in balance), then the tax rate must rise to 21 percent by 2050. Lee and Skinner assume a real productivity growth of 1 percent, an interest on trust fund balances of 2.3 percent, and a total lifetime fertility rate per woman of 1.9 children. If life expectancy in 2070 rises to 90, this tax rate in 2050 must be 23 percent of wages. Since OASDI expenditures were 4.6 percent of the GDP in the middle 1990s, I simply adjusted this ratio by the increase in Social Security taxes to arrive at the estimates in the text.

financing to meet its obligations, a circumstance that may affect benefit payouts. For instance, Lee and Tuljapurkar calculate that if no changes are made to the current system, the trust fund of Social Security System has a 95 percent probability of being exhausted between 2014 to 2037. If the system is allowed to borrow to avoid bankruptcy, their estimates show huge accumulated deficits in later years.[19] At the same time, real consumption of those in the labor force must decline to finance these higher Social Security paymenst.

Reducing benefits to stave off bankruptcy of the Social Security system raises some serious political problems. As shown in Table 12.1, half of elderly households in the U.S. depend on Social Security benefits to supply five-sixths or more of their retirement income. A large share of these families had low incomes during their working lifetimes, and the health status of the elderly poor is considerably lower than that of the more affluent elderly. If the retirement age were raised by five years, it is problematic how many could work the additional years before receiving their pensions. Finally, it seems likely that in the future, the elderly will receive less financial support from other family members than currently. This is because, as Judith Wallerstein points out, people with a history of divorce receive less care and support from their children during their years of retirement than people who have never been divorced. Given high level of divorce in the last quarter of the 20th century (see Chapter 7), this means that a higher share of the elderly will have to turn to the government, rather than their families, to survive.

At the turn of the millennium, average Social Security benefits amounted to roughly 30 percent of the average annual pay of U.S. workers and employees.[20] A considerably slower increase of such benefits would widen the income gap between retirees and workers to a degree that would probably result in successful political action to redress this situation. The likelihood of this scenario seems high, given the fact that those over 64 have higher rates of voting than other age groups and will account for over a quarter of those eligible to vote. For this reason, it is probable that Social Security pension payments as a share of GDP will rise considerably in the first half of the 21st century.

---

[19]   Using their stochastic forecasting technique for various mortality and natality assumptions and setting a tax rate that the system is financially balanced in the long run (so that the discounted stream of benefit payments is equal to the discounted stream of tax revenues), they calculate 750 possible paths the Social Security system might take. Three quarters of the paths show the system ending up with large deficits by 2070, with a mean accumulated in that year of $26 trillion. The margin of error is wide, however, and taking a 95 percent confidence limit, the range of accumulated debt could be anywhere from $6 to $60 trillion. Setting the tax rate so that the system would always have at least enough funds for the following year would require gradual tax increases so that the median estimated tax rate would be roughly double the current rate by 2070.

[20]   *Statistical Abstract* 1999, pp. 391, 444.

This discussion is based on the assumption that the Social Security system will remain relatively intact. Dean Baker and Mark Weisbrot provide (controversial) evidence that the alleged crisis in Social Security is due in part to the highly conservative assumptions used in the projections—particularly concerning the growth of the economy and wages—and, moreover, that the pending deficit can be closed by relatively small increases in Social Security taxes. But much greater attention has been given to more radical solutions, particularly partial or full privatization. While it is certainly possible that the system will be slowly privatized in the next half century, three serious problems, nevertheless, will remain and these undoubtedly require government expenditures.

• *Past commitments:* Over the second half of the 20th century the Congress raised the Social Security benefits, in part so that they would not decrease in real value, given the average annual inflation rate over the period of roughly 3.8 percent. As a result, they obligated future generations to pay the difference between what the earlier generations paid in and what they will receive from the system. If the Social Security system is privatized, such commitments must still be met, presumably out of some type of funds financed by taxes, but no one has explained from what part of the federal budget these will come.

• *Private profligacy:* If a system of private provident funds is set up as a substitute for Social Security and if current experience (Table 12.1) is any guide, many people may not pay into such funds unless required by law. In their old-age, such profligates will have to be supported by public funds unless the public is willing to stand by without taking action and witness a high increase in the number of destitute elderly. Such moral blindness is, unfortunately, quite possible.

• *Declining value of provident funds:* As argued in Chapter 2, the aging of the population will change the balance between saving and dissaving, the relative demand and supply of assets will shift accordingly, and asset prices will fall. This, in turn, will bring about a decline in the real value of private wealth and a corresponding decline in the income obtained by liquidating such assets. Again, the government will be faced with a large population of indigent retirees.

4. Considerable Increase in the Expenditure/GDP Ratio: Health

In the future governmental expenditures for health care will increase much more dramatically than for pensions. This follows the trend already apparent in the second half of the 20th century, as shown in Table 12.3. In order to make any kind of credible projections, however, several difficult questions need to be addressed.

What will happen to the health of the elderly as life expectancy increases? Perhaps the young-old (65–84) will enjoy better health, which will partly offset the much higher health expenditures of the rapidly growing population of old-old (those over 84), who require greater health care. Ronald Lee and Jonathan Skinner claim that the general health of the young-old is actually improving. As evidence, they cite a downward trend in measures of disability among the elderly, defined as an inability to carry out ADLs (activities of daily living such as eating, dressing, or bathing) and IADLs (instrumental activities of daily living such as light housework, meal preparation, or money management).

But optimism about health expenditures that is based on such indicators is unwarranted, because such improved health seems to have come about because of much higher expenditures on health care. In an analysis focusing on age-specific health expenditures, David Cutler and Ellen Meara show that relative health expenditures per person have increased most dramatically among those over 64. Between 1953 and 1987 real per capita income rose annually at 2.0 percent, but real medical expenditures rose at roughly 2.9 percent a year for those under 65, and at roughly 4.8 percent a year for those over.[21] So total health expenditures climbed considerably, both because there were more elderly and because the elderly were, individually, spending more on health care. Victor Fuchs demonstrates this graphically through data on seven frequently used surgical procedures. As such operations become safer, utilization rates rose sharply, and, in many cases, especially among the aged. This, of course, does not necessarily represent waste, because such operations save lives or, in the case of hip or knee replacements, alleviate pain that the elderly had suffered for years. Finally, according to Cutler and Meara, it is the post-acute medical services that increased the fastest among the elderly, particularly home health and nursing care for the old-old.

The explosion in health expenditures has another dimension, one that raises some disturbing moral issues: The percentage of total health expenditures accounted for by the 10 percent of the population who are the most sick increased about 30 percentage points and now accounts for more than 70 percent of all health expenditures. In an earlier era, of course, the very ill would have died early. Nowadays, we are seeing the growth of a special group, the high-medical-cost elderly, whose survival comes at a steep price. As a result,

---

[21] Cutler and Meara (1998, 1999) provide the basic data for the age specific health expenditures. They use, however, a GDP price index to deflate medical care expenditures for the various age groups and this seems inappropriate. Using a medical care price index derived from Tables 2.2 and 2.3 in the NIPA, I recalculated their series to derive my estimates. If their deflator is used, the average growth rates of per-person health care expenditures for those under 65 and those over 64 rose at 4.0 and 6.7 percent per year respectively.

health costs for the entire elderly population will require more resources as a share of the GDP each succeeding year.

Will medical technology change in a direction toward more and more expensive procedures and medical interventions, both curative and preventive? For example, Lee and Skinner describe a new technique for heart surgery which employs small localized entry points, so that there is no need to break ribs or subject the patient to as high a degree of postoperative risk. One result, however, is that a large group of patients who once wouldn't have risked this operation now demand it. They also mention a newly developed technique of implanted defribrillators which delivers shocks as needed to restore rhythmic heartbeats. While this is apparently a highly effective method for reducing sudden cardiac death among high-risk patients, each implant operation costs $88,000.

Or will medical technology move toward methods that lower medical costs, such as inexpensive drugs which lessen the need for surgery? One example is "simvastatin," a cholesterol-lowering drug that allegedly reduces incidence of mortality among many with preexisting heart disease and decreases both hospital costs and the loss of income of patients who would otherwise be unable to work.

I have found little agreement in the literature about which of these two roads medical technology will take, and, as a result, I cannot easily factor technology into my estimate of future health expenditures. But since a great deal of medical research is funded by the government, public policy has some—perhaps limited—influence on the direction technological change in medicine will take.

Because of such imponderables, we can estimate future health expenditures only in a crude fashion, starting from an aggregative perspective by using the Cutler-Meara approach and some additional assumptions. More specifically, let us assume that inflation-adjusted total medical expenditures per capita of those under 65 will rise at 1.25 percent a year, while such per capita expenditures of those 65 and older will rise at 1.75 percent a year. Both of these assumptions are, in fact, considerably lower than trends during the past half century. Such a conservative approach allows us to calculate the rising share of medical expenditures in the GDP.[22]

My estimate of rising real health care costs, when combined with an assumption of real per capita GDP growing at 1.0 percent a year, means that as a share of GDP, medical expenditures would be 25 percent in 2050—roughly 9 percentage points above the 1995 level. Because this type of estimation technique

---

[22] I have calculated medical care expenditures from NIPA accounts by adding private out-of-pocket expenditures for health care (NIPA Table 2-2) to government expenditures taken from the data underlying Table 12.3. The price deflator of medical care expenditures is described in the previous footnote. Considerable controversy has raged around the proper price index, but for the purposes of this argument, only rough orders of magnitude are important. Of crucial impor-

is transparent, alternative estimates can be easily made. This projection, which I use in the discussion below, is also very much in line with recent U.S. government estimates made by a blue-ribbon committee of experts, who used a different (and more sophisticated, but less transparent) estimation technique.[23]

Although such forecasts provide some idea about the orders of magnitude involved, they do not take into account changes in health technology or any changes in health care prices in comparisons to that of other goods and services. If health care prices rise faster than other prices, which has been the situation over the last half century, the ratio of health care costs to the GDP would, of course, be higher than my forecast.

For the purposes of this chapter, the key questions are: Who will pay for this staggering bill? And what impact will it have on government expenditures for medical care? For answers, we need to take into account that the share of total health expenditures financed by the government has risen from about one sixth in 1950 to about one third in 1990.[24] Given that a considerable segment of the elderly enters retirement with few financial resources (Table 12.1), the nation faces a moral choice: either the government finances a very large share of the rising health-care expenditures for the elderly in the future, or else the distribution of health may become considerably more unequal than it is today. The latter situation would mean that the wealthy elderly, who could afford these extra health care expenditures, would enjoy better health in their retirement years than previous generations. At the same time, the indigent elderly, who would be unable to finance such additional expenditures from their own savings, would have much worse health and would die much earlier than their affluent neighbors. So far, the nation has leaned toward subsidization and equalization of health care, which is one important reason why the government has assumed an ever larger share of total health care costs and why governmental health care spending has risen much faster than other types of expenditure listed in Table 12.3.

The U.S. Congressional Budget Office foresees federal governmental expenditures for Medicare and Medicaid increasing to 12.2 percent of the GDP over the first half of the 21st century, about 8 percentage points higher than in 1995.

tance, between 1950 and 1997 current expenditures for health care, as a share of GDP, rose from 3.1 percent in 1950 to 15.6 percent (current prices).

[23] In a report to the Secretary of Health and Human Services in December 2000, the Technical Review Panel on the Medicare Trustees Report (2000, p. 39) provides assumptions from which we can calculate that total expenditures for health in the U.S. would amount to roughly 26 percent of the GDP in 2050, if changes in the age distribution are taken into account.

[24] These percentages are derived from my health care estimates, discussed in the previous footnote. The U.S. Health Care Financing Agency defines total health care expenditures somewhat differently and, according to estimates from their web-site (www.hcfa.gov/stats/), the share of governmental expenditures rose from 25 percent in 1960 to 46 percent in 1997.

The CBO assumes that present disbursement rules for these two programs are maintained. Using a much cruder method than the CBO's model, I arrive at a similar forecast. More specifically, if total medical expenditures rise to 25 percent of the GDP (see above) and if the share of these costs covered by the government rises from one-third to one-half, then government expenditures on medical care will amount to 12.5 percent of the GDP in 2050.

5. Public Expenditures Impossible to Predict

Certain public expenditures are inherently impossible to predict, at least with a straight face, because they are subject to so many unknown exogenous pressures from political and social spheres. These include current defense expenditures and "unspecified state and local expenditures," which, in the 1990s, amounted respectively to 5.0 and 0.6 percent of the GDP (Table 12.3).

As indicated in Chapter 8, it seems likely that wars will continue in the future. The underlying causes will range from purely economic reasons involving access to vital resources to ethnic self-determination. It is difficult to predict whether or not the U.S. will allow itself to be drawn into such wars. Although I do not believe it likely that the share of U.S. defense expenditures in the GDP will greatly rise by 2050, it also does not seem likely that it will dramatically fall. At this point my crystal ball becomes cloudy.

6. The Scope of Policy Choices

I argue above that pension expenditures financed by the government as a share of the GDP might rise 2 to 4 percentage points by 2050; and health expenditures, 8 to 9 percentage points. If other governmental expenditures as a share of the GDP move up several percentage points, then by 2050 total current government expenditures might amount to 45 to 50 percent of the GDP. This would bring the size of the U.S. governmental expenditures in 2050 close to that of a number of West European nations such as Germany, Netherlands, or Norway at the end of the 20th century (Table 12.2).

Such an argument assumes, however, a certain passivity in the face of the aging of the population. Although it can be argued that policy options are available that could limit such an expansion of the government sector, it is important to explore briefly how realistic are these options.

In the discussion above about the possibilities of raising the retirement age or reducing the benefits-ratio, I note the increasing share of the elderly population in the total pool of voters. Given that their rate of voting is higher than other age groups, their political impact is magnified. Moreover, if any cuts in Social Security or Medicare benefits are made, special care will have to be taken so that their impact does not fall most heavily on the poorer half of the elderly population, whose primary means of support come from these governmental health and income support programs. Given that these governmental programs have been sold to the public as insurance, not income redistribution, the political feasibility of such tailored cuts seems dubious.

E. Summary and Conclusions

As shown in Table 12.2, the ratio of public expenditures in the U.S. to the GDP ranks quite low in comparison to other industrialized nations. Furthermore, despite discontent with the rate of taxes, this ratio does not seem likely to greatly change in the near future, because the public, having weighed the pain of taxes and the benefits of public expenditures, is relatively satisfied with the *status quo*.

In the long run, however, I argue that the share of public expenditures to the GDP will rise. This will not be due to the emergence of a more socialist ideology—indeed, as I suggest in Chapter 7, social capital and trust in the government will decline. Rather, it is due to the aging of the population and the relatively meager assets that a large segment of the population bring into their retirement years, combined with their rising need for medical coverage and for income supplements. Unable to depend on their families for support during their declining years, many must rely on government transfers.

Given the growing distrust of government and the move toward deregulation in other areas, several possibilities are open in the future. Major parts of the Social Security and Medicare program could be privatized, which would probably mean that the high-medical-cost elderly and other elderly whose health status is perceived as too risky might have to rely on the Social Security system, at least if the government were unable to force private insurance or pension plans to accept them. Moreover, if asset prices fall, as I predict in Chapter 2, those pensioners in defined contribution plans would see their pension income and health payments shrink and would undoubtedly turn to the government for help. Those pensioners in defined benefit plans might also receive much less than they anticipated, as a large number of pension and insurance plans would face bankruptcy at the same time, unless certain government guarantees, such as those under ERISA (Employee Retirement Income Security Act), will be paid. This will, of course, increase government expenditures.

One last scenario deserves brief attention. Whether or not Social Security and Medicare are privatized, the U.S. government might sit back and refuse to raise the percentage of its expenditures directed toward the elderly as a percentage of GDP. Although I do not believe such a course of action to be politically feasible, given the demographic changes in the first half of the 21st century, such a policy would give rise to an widening inequality of income among the population as a whole, as well as health among the elderly. The clash between an ideology of rugged individualism and the necessity for higher taxes and greater governmental transfer expenditures to the elderly will be the defining political conflict in the coming decades.

F. Institutional and Organization Changes in the U.S. Economic System: A Wrap-up

The last four chapters focus on important institutional and organizational developments in the U.S. economic system. I make the following major arguments:

• Other things equal, the average size of firms will increase and large firms will account for a larger share of production and employment of the labor force. A key causal factor is the merger wave, with firm consolidations occurring at high frequency both between domestic firms and also between domestic and foreign firms (Chapter 9).

• Other things equal, market structure will become more concentrated, fed by a high volume of mergers between firms in the same industries. Although certain offsets to the impact of higher market concentration can be envisioned—especially the rise of the commerce over the internet—it does not seem likely that these will be sufficient to counterbalance a trend toward a decline in market competition (Chapter 10).

• Other things equal, government regulation of the economy will diminish. In part, this trend is driven by the decreasing effectiveness of regulation, which is due to growing complexity of the economy and rising globalization (Chapter 11).

• Other things equal, government expenditures should become an ever growing part of the GDP. Expenditures on the aged will be driving these changes (Chapter 12).

These structural trends point toward a greater dominance in the economic system of a small elite, whose power base will be in large, oligopolistic firms. This trend, in turn, will reinforce the trend toward decreased governmental regulation of the economy, increased expenditures on internal security, and greater income inequality. To preserve domestic tranquility, however, it seems unlikely that such an elite will prevent the growing importance of transfers to the aged.

CHAPTER 13

Whither U.S. Capitalism?

*The year 1999, seven months, from the sky will come a great
King of Terror: to bring back to life the great King of the
Mongols, before and after Mars to reign by good luck.*

—*Astrologer Michel Nostradamos, 16th century*[1]

In the preceding pages I look at many different building blocks of
the future economic system. Now is the time to put them together into a single
edifice. The scaffolding of the building already stands—the economic, political,
and social factors discussed in Chapter 1 and diagrammed on page 9—so that
most of the individual pieces can be easily fitted within it. But once the edifice
is complete, it is necessary to stand back and to gain a broader perspective of
the completed structure.

A. The Economic Dimensions and the State of Competition

1. A Stormy Economic Atmosphere

Four aspects of the atmosphere of the future capitalist system of the U.S.
deserve note: declining economic growth, increasing volatility, widening
income differentials, and unsteadily rising globalization.

• *Declining economic growth:* A number of developments point towards
lower growth of the U.S. economy in the first half of the 21st century than in
the last half of the 20th century. Of greatest importance, demographic changes
will lead to lower rates of saving and investment, a change that can be foreseen
by looking at the changing age structure of the population in terms of those in
the working ages and those who are retired. As a group, the former save and the
latter draw down their savings (Chapter 2). Thus the aging of the population

---

[1] Cited by Laura Lee, *Bad Predictions: 2000 Years of the Best Minds Making the Worst Forecasts*
(2000). Some might claim that this prediction has been realized, but they have a difficult case
to argue.

will lead to a lower rate of saving for the country as a whole which, in turn, points to a lower rate of capital formation and, under defensible assumptions, a slower rate of economic growth.

The growth rate will also be adversely influenced by other future developments of the economy. Any growing shortages of food and natural resources might divert funds away from investment (Chapter 6). The decline in social capital and trust in government will lead to greater difficulties in formulating and implementing governmental policies that could provide a more favorable economic environment for growth and that could take effectively steps against economic recessions (Chapter 7). Mergers in the financial sector might also lead to lower growth if giant banks would be less willing to finance new business ventures than they would be in a more competitive banking environment (Chapter 10).

• *Increasing volatility:* The business cycle is far from tamed and macroeconomic fluctuations will accompany this slower growth. It appears that the economy will become more fragile (Chapters 3 and 5). In part this is because deepening globalization will gradually enfeeble national monetary and fiscal policies to stabilize the economy. Such globalization will also intensify the vulnerability of the U.S. system to external shocks arising from the global economy, particularly in the monetary sector as the foreign funds entering and leaving the U.S. increase in volume and become more difficult to control. If the imbalance in the current accounts of the U.S. balance of payments continues in the future so that the net flow of foreign capital into the U.S. continues, the share of foreign ownership of enterprises will proceed to rise and problems faced by the U.S. government to control the domestic economy will become more difficult. Both the growing indebtedness of individuals and firms, in comparison to their incomes (Chapter 3) and the creation of giant dysfunctional firms in the ongoing merger boom (Chapter 10) can, under plausible economic circumstances, also destabilize the financial system. Finally, the fall in asset prices and the rise in interest rates occasioned by the reduced rate of saving could also lead to a fall in aggregate demand and, possibly, to a serious economic downturn (Chapters 2 and 3).

• *Widening income differentials:* In the long run, income inequalities will probably increase. Differences in incomes between high and low income families, both in an absolute sense and in relation to the median income, rose considerably in the last quarter of the 20th century (Chapter 4). Although this widening of income differentials was briefly halted in the late 1990s and, in certain ways, reversed, I argue that this trend reversal was temporary and due in major part to an unparalleled prosperity, accompanied by a decline in the rate of joblessness. Although proponents of the "new economy" argue that such prosperity will continue into the far future, so that income inequality will decrease, the sources of growth underlying such prosperity were narrow, and I find little credible evidence to support such optimism (Chapter 2).

Instead, a number of causal forces are still at work that should lead to increasing income inequality. The poverty trap brought about by neighborhood effects will, I suggest in Chapter 4, become stronger and will continue to lower the relative (to the median) incomes of those at the bottom end of the income distribution. The rising concentration of wealth, combined with higher profits arising from higher industrial concentration and less market competition (Chapters 9 and 10), will act to raise relative (to the median) incomes of those at the upper end of the income distribution. If governmental expenditure for pensions and health do not increase considerably, a new class of indigent aged will be created. Other factors may also reinforce trends toward greater income inequality. Under certain circumstances, the growth of ever larger enterprises will lead to greater inequalities in wages (Chapter 9). Adverse ecological considerations may also reinforce trends toward greater inequality. In particular, since low-income families spend proportionately more on food and resource intensive products than do high income families, any rise in the prices of food and raw materials brought about by environmental factors will fall more heavily on the poor (Chapter 6).

Looking at income inequality for the world as a whole, for a moment, per capita incomes of the nations of the world will probably diverge as well. In major part this is because many third world nations will probably prove unequal to the task of escaping from the trap of poverty, poor health, corrupt government, and low investment, all of which lead to economic stagnation (Chapter 4).

• *Unsteadily rising globalization:* Although the world economic integration that gathered speed in the last quarter of the 20th century will undoubtedly continue in the short run in the 21st century, important political factors might place limits on the process (Chapter 5). As it proceeds, the globalization process leads to a diminished ability of national governments to regulate business within their own borders and to protect particular segments of the economy that are considered politically important to protect. The ability of groups of citizens of any country to influence international economic arrangements becomes, of course, much more limited than their power to effect political changes on a national or subnational level. Thus, globalization acts in important respects to reduce the political impact of the voters and this, in turn, might lead to a serious nationalist backlash. At this point, however, prediction becomes difficult for two reasons. First, although public opinion data suggest a growing unease about globalization, it is unclear how the public could mount an effective political opposition to stop globalization. Second, although the economic crises in Asia, Russia, and Latin America during the 1990s laid bare the inadequacies of the international financial architecture, it is not certain at the turn of the millennium what, if anything, will finally be introduced to replace it.

In brief, the economic atmosphere of the U.S. capitalist system in the future has many storm clouds looming on the horizon.

2. Declining Economic Competition

The economic system consists of the structures that allocate goods, services, and the inputs to produce them within any particular economic atmosphere. Since the market is the main allocation mechanism, I focus considerable attention in this book on the changing state of market competition. Such behavior of markets depends considerably on the size of the enterprises within the system and the degree to which production in narrowly defined markets becomes ever more concentrated. The average size of U.S. enterprises rose until the mid 1970s, declined somewhat until the early 1990s, and then began to rise again (Chapter 9). The immediate cause of the rise in enterprise size in the 1990s was a merger wave whose endpoint appears to lie far in the future. Unlike the mergers in the 1960s and 1970s, most of which were primarily vertical and conglomerate, those in the 1980s and 1990s were horizontal (Chapter 10). This qualitative change means that, short of bankruptcy, the newly merged firms are more difficult to unbundle if they run into financial difficulties.

The merger boom in the late 1980s and 1990s is open to three quite different interpretations. It could be a relatively short-lived phenomenon that will taper off after large firms become better positioned to deal with increasingly globalized markets. In that case, there is little cause for alarm. Alternatively, the new information technology might lead to increased economies of large scale production and enterprise administration despite all the rosy predictions of a "new era" of the small firm. In that case, the world of the future would be dominated by giant firms, a development that gives rise to grave concern. Or finally, the current merger boom might be spawning large and dysfunctional firms, whose eventual disintegration could initiate, as noted above, extreme financial disorder.

In the final quarter of the 20th century, increasing enterprise size was accompanied by a rising concentration of industry in narrowly defined markets for particular goods and services (Chapter 10). Moreover, such market concentration was taking place not just within the U.S., but also on a global level, as shown by the rising number of cross-border mergers in the same industries. In so far as mergers combine firms in different nations, they are also difficult for national antitrust authorities to control. Although the Competition Office of the European Commission has achieved some successes in stopping some mergers between giant firms, it seems unlikely to me that any international antitrust authority will arise, at least in the next few decades, that would include both the United States, Japan, and other industrialized nations, given the current political circumstances. As a result, the international concentration of industry will continue. This trend toward concentration is reinforced by the rising number of strategic partnerships and alliances, both between U.S. firms and between U.S.

and foreign firms. The exact nature of the various individual business arrangements is far from clear, but in many cases these inter-firm agreements appear to represent important steps toward international cartelization.

In the face of a greater concentration of industry, could competitive markets flourish in the future? I discuss a number of possible offsets (Chapter 10), of which the growth of internet commerce seems the most promising because it allows buyers and sellers to seek alternative buyers and sellers at relatively low costs. Unfortunately, this optimistic scenario does not take into consideration that e-commerce already exhibits a high concentration and that the established e-companies can offer more reliability to compensate for the higher price that they may charge (Chapter 10) in comparison to new entrants. It takes a new firm entering e-commerce considerable resources to gain trust of customers over the internet. Unfortunately, new firms may not have the necessary funds to make the large investment in advertising and other measures, especially when consumers are already inundated with a rising volume of (conflicting) messages. As a result, e-commerce may be unable to provide the competition necessary to offset the increasing concentration of individual markets.

Because e-business is so new, it is impossible to foresee clearly what the future of competition will be. Current signs, however, point toward a lower level of competition, both nationally and internationally. In such a case, world economic integration would unexpectedly lead to less, not more, market competition.

B. The Political Dimension and the Role of the Government[2]

In many parts of this study I look at the changing roles of the U.S. government in the economy. Such changes do not necessarily mean that governmental institutions will become weaker in some overall sense. Three developments deserve note: a changing participation of the government in the economy, declining effectiveness of many economic policies, and greater tension between rich and poor nations.

1. Changing Participation of the Government in the Economy

a. *An international perspective:* Before turning to the role of the government in the economy, it is useful to examine briefly the relative magnitude of U.S. governmental participation in the economy from an international perspec-

---

[2]   In the text of this section, I cite Block (1990).

Table 13.1. *A Classification of the Role of Government in Leading OECD Nations in the 1990s*

Government expenditures	Government regulation	Government ownership	
Low	Low	Low	Japan, Switzerland, U.K., U.S.
High	Low	Low	Canada, Denmark, Ireland, Netherlands
Low	High	Low	Australia, Greece, Portugal, Spain
Low	Low	High	New Zealand
High	High	Low	Italy
High	Low	High	Finland
Low	High	High	—
High	High	High	Austria, Belgium, France, Germany, Norway, Sweden

Note: The countries are arranged so that the first and last group of countries contain those where the three ratings are all either "low" or "high." Comparisons are made on a relative, not an absolute scale because I classified the countries by whether they fall above or below the average for the entire group. The data come from Tables 11.1, 11.3, and 12.2. For ownership I supplement the data presented in Table 11.3 by estimating in a rough fashion that public ownership was relatively low in Switzerland and relatively high in Norway.

tive. Given the quantitative comparisons made in previous chapters, we can easily gain an overview of the role of government in various industrial nations along three dimensions: expenditures, regulation, and ownership. Table 13.1 provides the requisite information and several conclusions can be quickly drawn.

Almost half of the 21 countries fall in two groups, placing either low or high in all three dimensions. The U.S. is among the four nations that rank low on all three criteria. The weak correlation between government regulation and ownership previously shown in a regression equation (Chapter 11) is evident here: two thirds of the nations in the sample are either relatively high or relatively low in both these dimensions.

If we compare these results with those from a similar analysis of 12 OECD nations in an earlier period,[3] we see that of the six nations scoring either high or low on all three criteria in the early 1960s, five (Switzerland and the U.S. at the low end, France, Sweden, and Norway at the high end) were in the same place in the mid 1990s. Among the other seven nations, the most extreme shift in position occurred in the U.K. which moved from "low government expenditures, high regulation, and high government ownership" category in the early 1960s to the "low expenditures, low regulations, low ownership" category in the mid 1990s. These changes in the U.K. reflect, of course, Margaret Thatcher's legacy. The other countries either did not change their relative position (Canada) or else changed along only one dimension (Austria, Belgium, Germany, Greece, and Netherlands).

These results have important implications: Any alleged mechanism that is leading to a convergence of different national capitalist systems is weak—the roles of the government sector in various advanced capitalist nations do not seem to be moving toward a similar configuration over time. Furthermore, the advantages of the Anglo-American type of capitalist system are far from evident. Some nations, for instance, give much greater importance in their economic systems to the participation of workers in the management of the enterprises in which they work (e.g., Germany) or to the role of government in promoting economic and social equality (e.g., Sweden).[4] The correlation between the degree of government ownership and important performance indicators, such as economic growth, is not statistically significant (Chapter 11), and similar experiments with government ownership and government regulation variables also do not yield any significant correlations. This seems to be the crucial reason why many key institutions and organizations in various advanced capitalist economies have not converged. Over the years, as economic integration within the European Union proceeds, we will undoubtedly learn more about the forces of systemic convergence.

b. Mixed trends of governmental participation in the U.S. economy: In the past half century, most types of governmental participation in the U.S. economy rose and then fell. For government ownership (as a percent of the total capital

---

[3]   Pryor (1973), p. 23. The results for the 1960s were also based on relative, not absolute, standards. Both the calculations for the 1960s and 1990s measure government expenditures and ownership, but they are not quite comparable, because in the earlier analysis the third criterion was government planning, rather than regulation as in Table 13.1. Nevertheless, for this discussion, such a difference is not important.

[4]   This argument is made with considerable vigor by Esping-Anderson (1990). The lack of convergence is also made in a different but forceful manner by Groenewegen (1997) and, with regard to labor market institutions, by Freeman (2000).

stock), the inflection point was in the 1960s, for federal regulation, in the 1980s, and for current federal expenditures (as a percent of GDP), in the 1970s. Only state and local governmental expenditures (as a percent of GDP) increased over the entire period. The future governmental participation in the economy will not, however, be as straightforward, and the various types of government activity need a brief review.

The small share of governmental ownership in the national capital stock seems likely to continue in the coming decades (Chapter 11). I foresee no political forces on the horizon that would result in a dramatic shift of current trends.

The future path of governmental regulation is more difficult to discern. Certain developments in the economy, particularly globalization, point toward less regulation of industry by federal, state, and local governments at home and, to a certain extent, more regulation by international bodies. The deregulation trend on the national level is reinforced by the growing inequality of income, since the business elite will have more economic power to block and/or weaken unwelcomed restraints placed on their activities (Chapter 11). But several forces pointing toward more governmental regulation also deserve mention. If business cycles become more severe, financial regulations might become more extensive in order to reduce shocks to the economy that arise from this sector. Similarly, if Americans save less (Chapter 2), the government might have to play a more active role in investment, either directly or through various indirect incentives, if economic growth is to be maintained. Finally, if environmental conditions dramatically deteriorate, which I doubt will happen (Chapter 7), governmental regulation in this area might become considerably more stringent. My subjective impression is that the forces pointing toward a reduced regulatory role will prevail.

The current trend toward a rising ratio of state and local governmental expenditures to the GDP seem likely to continue, perhaps at a slower rate. Of particular importance, the ever greater income inequalities, abetted by the declining degree of social capital and trust (Chapter 7), can lead to greater social unrest and crime, unless expenditures for internal security are considerably increased. On the federal level, the ratio of expenditures on pensions and health care will also increase, due to the aging of the population. In particular, with the rising ratio of total health expenditures to the GDP, it seems likely that a higher percent will be financed through the government. This is because a growing segment of the population will be unable to meet their rising health care costs, either directly or through their private insurance (Chapter 12). It should be emphasized, however, that this argument rests on the assumption that beyond a certain point, increasing inequality in the area of health becomes politically unsustainable. This supposition can certainly be challenged, especially since, in the past few decades, the social and political acceptance of economic inequalities has increased, as evidenced by a reduced willingness to redistribute income from the rich to the poor through governmental transfers and private charity (Chapters 7 and 12). If, however, the income differentials continue to widen, greater social unrest may force a rise in government transfers in addition to those for internal security. As a result of these various considerations, public expenditures as a share of GDP will slowly increase in the coming decades, a prediction in sharp contrast not just to the belief of many conservative politicians but also to the implicit assumption of many leading politicians and policy makers that the share of federal governmental expenditures (excepting defense) in the GDP can be considerably reduced.

c. *Declining policy effectiveness:* I emphasize (Chapters 3 and 5) that a globalized economy means that governmental monetary and fiscal policies will be less effective on the national level. The nation's ever more porous borders also give rise to greater difficulties in implementing various kinds of micro-economic policies, such as the regulation, encouragement, or restructuring of industry.

I also provide evidence (Chapters 3, 7 and 8) that greater income inequalities and, in some cases, lower social capital and lower social trust, make it more difficult for the government to formulate and implement economic policies. The lower rate of economic growth will also make legislative action to ameliorate some problems more contentious, because the impacts on the income distribution of such measures becomes more important (Chapter 2). Obviously, all of these developments will also reduce the effectiveness of government participation in the economy.

• *Public attitudes toward government:* Another consideration in forecasting the future participation of government in the economic system needs brief attention, namely the attitude of the U.S. public about the government's ability to solve our social and economic problems. This is not just an "ideological issue" but also a matter of experience. As Fred Block has noted:

> Structural-functionalism in sociology, pluralism in political science, and liberal Keynesianism in economics shared in common an evolutionary triumphalism that saw American society as having evolved new institutional arrangements that provided solutions to such historic problems of industrialism as class conflict, economic crises, and exploitation. All three approaches proclaimed the arrival of a new stage in history in which enlightened state action and the spirit of consensus would make possible the gradual solution of the remaining social problems ... These optimistic visions of American society were shattered by the political and social developments of the 1960s and 1970s.

From evidence about the inverse relation between social solidarity and the effectiveness of government action (Chapters 7 and 8) , it seems unlikely that such optimism about the efficacy of government will be regained in the coming decades. Quite the reverse, the "new pessimism" will further erode the role of government in most aspects of the U.S. economic system.

Public attitudes toward government are also related to participation in political activities and trust in government, both of which have declined over the second half of the 20th century (Chapter 8). Under circumstances that might possibly arise in future decades, greater political apathy on the part of ordinary citizens, combined with their increasing alienation reflecting the decline in social capital, could lead either to a rise in governmental despotism and/or the fusion of political and economic elites into a more oligarchic regime.

2. The Changing Context of International Politics: Rising North-South Tensions

International politics also has an important influence on the government's participation in the domestic economy. Although I do not foresee warfare between industrial nations (the "north"), the situation in the developing nations (the "south") is more troublesome. At the turn of the millennium, a number of states in the south were gradually collapsing, and in the future, more seem likely to fail as well. Such difficulties will be exacerbated by greater scarcities of water for irrigation, which will reduce per capita food supply (Chapter 6), and by high death rates from AIDS. Because AIDS will fall most heavily on the productive members of the society, relatively fewer of the population will be available to support the rest.

I also provide some evidence (Chapter 8) that ethnic tensions in the south are rising. Added to this boiling cauldron of problems the rising income inequalities between rich and poor nations (Chapter 4) will probably lead to greater north-south tensions.

The extent to which the U.S. can avoid being sucked into armed conflicts, either between nations in the south or between these nations and nations in the north is difficult to predict, because it depends in considerable measure on the degree to which perceived vital interests of the U.S. are at stake. Any war requiring a massive use of resources by the U.S. will, however, lead to a strengthening of governmental participation in the economy.

C. The Social Dimension and the Decline of Social Solidarity [5]

Five facets of social solidarity that influence the economic system receive attention in this study: economic inequalities, social cleavages, social capital,

---

[5]   In the text of this section I draw on studies by: Fukuyama (1999) and Putnam (2000).

social trust, and crime. Most social cleavages in the U.S. are tied in some manner to income disparities, which I discuss above. Both are manifestations of social heterogeneity, which, as I show elsewhere, is also becoming greater in the U.S.[6] The other three indicators of social solidarity also raise some important issues.

• *Social capital and social trust:* To a certain extent, social capital and social trust are correlated with each other. I show that both have waned in the U.S. since the mid 1970s (Chapter 7). Although the causes are not entirely clear, three culprits can be identified: growing social heterogeneity; television watching, which leads to a reduction in social contact between people; and globalization, which focuses our attention on a larger sphere of activity at the cost of participation in local community life. The decline in these facets of social solidarity is associated with a fall in political participation (Chapter 8) and trust in government.

It seems highly likely that social capital and social trust will continue to decline in the coming decades (Chapter 7), especially since most of the indicators reflecting these trends show no sign of deceleration. Others, however, dispute this prediction. For instance, Francis Fukuyama argues that the "great [social] disruption" has already occurred, and the U.S. is now busily engaged in reconstructing the social order on a new basis, from which we can infer that the downward trend in social capital and social trust will be reversed. At the turn of the millennium, for instance, divorce rates had begun slowly to fall and crime rates were plunging. But other indicators point in the opposite direction: marriage rates, for instance, were still declining, and the percentage of children born out of wedlock and/or living with one parent was climbing. Furthermore, as Robert Putnam argues, the decline in social capital (and implicitly, social trust) is the result of a replacement of generations, and not a change within particular generations. Although it is very difficult to determine exactly how the youngsters of today will turn out, I find no credible evidence that present trends in social capital and social trust will not continue in the future.

• *Crime:* The crime rate began a dramatic fall in the 1990s, but this seemed due in part to a shift in the age composition of the population, to soaring rates of incarceration, and to a rise in abortions two decades previously which reduced the number of "unwanted children" who are responsible for a certain amount of crime. I present evidence, however, that this welcomed decline in crime may be reversed (Chapter 8). Moreover, the nature of crime appears also to have shifted—from visible assaults, robberies, and murders to less detectable white-collar crimes, so that our indicators of crime have become ever more faulty.

---

[6]   Pryor (1996).

If I am correct about an adverse trend in social solidarity, as manifested in rising income inequalities, greater social cleavages, and falling social capital and social trust, the economic system will face some severe problems. Many aspects of social solidarity appear to be positively correlated with higher governmental efficiency and the absence of governmental corruption (Chapter 7 and 8). Social capital and social trust are also correlated with entrepreneurship, technological cooperation between companies, and the degree to which managers take their social responsibilities seriously. In addition, the decline of social trust and capital should lead to a rise in transaction costs, as managers place greater weight on formal legal arrangements to enforce contracts, rather than on more informal agreements.

D. The Economic System in 2050[7]

As emphasized in different ways throughout this book, I expect slow, not rapid, evolution of U.S. capitalism in the first half of the 21st century. The shrill claims that we will face sharp discontinuities in the future should be given little credence. Neither the causal forces leading to such significant breaks, nor the nature of the system thereafter, are specified in sufficient detail to gain understanding into the various causes and effects.

Although there are limits to our prescience, it is also important to determine where creditworthy forecasts are possible and what are the limits of responsible prediction. Difficulties in forecasting arise for several reasons: In many cases we cannot determine from currently available information exactly what is occurring *now* or which of several factors influencing the direction of change is strongest. Moreover, the direction of change is often affected by policy steps taken either by governments or by other collective bodies, as shown dramatically by the change in course of the U.K. economic system between the early 1960s and the middle 1990s. Finally, the economic system is affected by large historical events, such as the outbreak of war or a severe depression, which do not lend themselves to easy prediction.

Despite these difficulties, I try to sketch the most probable future of the economic system, barring cataclysmic events such as war and economic depressions. More perspective can be gained by comparing my vision of the future with those of others.

---

[7]   In the text in this section I mention studies by: Bell (1960), Brown, *et al.* (1998), Ehrlich (1968), Fukuyama (1992), Gallopin *et al.* (1997), Hammond (1998), Kahn *et al.* (1976), Macrae (1984), (1994), Meadows, *et al.* (1972), and Simon (1996).

1. The Future of U.S. Capitalism: My Views

From the evidence presented in this book, I do not see sunny skies for the future of U.S. capitalism. Its emerging configuration can be located in the three-dimensional diagram in Chapter 1. Along the *political* dimension, the overall level of governmental intervention will be roughly the same, but with a different composition: public expenditures will be higher, regulation of industry will be lower, government intervention into the economy will be less effective, and repression of the population will be harsher. Along the *economic* dimension, markets will be less competitive. And along the *social* dimension, solidarity will probably be less, and, despite increased affluence, the quality of our lives will deteriorate and economic life will be more pitiless.

These results, combined with the ever larger size of enterprises, point toward a greater oligarchical control of both the state and the economy. That is, economic and political elites will continue to fuse, government intervention in the economy will be less aimed at raising the general welfare of the population than at ameliorating certain economic problems faced by particular segments of the elite. The decreasing progressivity of the tax structure and rising income inequalities will be telling indicators of these developments. These trends will be reinforced by declining political participation and mounting distrust toward the government, in major part because more people will feel powerless to influence policies and events. Expenditures on internal security, pensions, and health will increase, primarily to palliate political discontent that might erupt into serious domestic strife.

I also look at alternative scenarios. One optimistic scenario foresees the emergence of a "corporate welfare state" (Chapter 9). Most of the other alternative scenarios are more pessimistic. If, for instance, the social glue holding together the economy, society, and the political system dissolves more quickly than I anticipate, liberal capitalism might be slowly replaced, at least for a period, by Hobbesian anarchy or mafia capitalism. Or if widening income inequalities lead to heightened social tensions, the fear of anarchy might lead toward more extensive governmental security measures so that the U.S. might arrive at a rotating authoritarian, interventionalist economy (Chapter 1). Or, in the case of a serious ecological crisis that cannot be mastered by market incentives, U.S. capitalism might evolve toward a centrally planned economy. If the country is buffeted by serious war or economic depression, the governmental role in the economy might also greatly expand. Although none of these scenarios seems likely, they remain within the realm of possibility.

The analysis in Table 13.1 of various dimensions of governmental participation in the economy in different OECD nations reveals in a stark fashion some important economic aspects of "American exceptionalism." Although I do not examine changes in the economic systems of these other OECD nations, I expect these differences in economic systems to continue, primarily because of lack of compelling evidence that one particular configuration of capitalism produces more favorable long-term economic outcomes than others. This prediction flies in the face of those who, pointing to a certain homogenization of world cultures (manifested by the ubiquity of Hollywood movies or coca-colonization), foresee the predominance of U.S. economic and political power leading to a replication of the U.S. economic system in other nations.

2. The Futures of U.S. Capitalism: Other Views

My vision of the future of U.S. capitalism is quite different from others that have received considerable attention. Let me note briefly some of these dissimilarities I consider most telling:

• Unlike Karl Marx, I do not believe that capitalism will collapse, at least from economic causes. Although some of my predictions about the future of the U.S. economy are similar to his—for instance, widening inequality of income, considerable financial volatility, and greater concentration of production—I do not foresee a growing discipline and power of the proletariat that he believed so important in forging the ideological orientation needed for a revolution. Nor do I foresee the future dysfunctionalities of the economic system to be sufficiently severe that they would lead to very rapid and dramatic changes in U.S. capitalism carried out by disadvantaged social groups.[8]

• Unlike Daniel Bell, I do not believe that we have reached the "end of ideology," even though the traditional capitalism versus socialism argument may appear to be dead. In general, ideological discourse in the U.S. about economic policy was relatively quiescent at the turn of the millennium, and political debate focused primarily on minor differences in policies.[9] It is not difficult, however, to imagine a different type of ideological struggle emerging in the

---

[8]   Economic systems can collapse not just because of dysfunctionalities of the system, but also because of serious policy traps. In order to show more concretely some of the ways in which these two factors operate to undermine an economic system, I discuss in External Appendix X-1.4 their respective roles in the collapse of Soviet communism.

Examples of policy traps that could seriously undermine U.S. capitalism can easily be provided, for instance, dramatic tax cuts that would make it impossible to finance highly popular governmental expenditures in the future. Given the requisite political will, however, the situation is correctible in many of these cases.

[9]   The ideological furor surrounding globalization, the IMF, and the WTO seemed limited to a small group of people, although, as noted in Chapter 5, such issues may become more politically salient in the future. The discussion in the text does not take into account ideological dis-

future, a debate not only about the path that U.S. capitalism should take, such as the degree of globalization we should embrace, but also about more intractable issues, such as the redistribution of income or the degree of control we, as employees, should have over our working conditions.

• Unlike Francis Fukuyama, I do not believe that we have reached the "end of history." Rather, as argued throughout this book, the U.S. economic system will evolve considerably in ways which I try to forecast. Given the contingent nature of the future, I also indicate alternative paths. The key point is that liberal capitalism in the U.S. will not remain static.

• Unlike ecological Jeremiahs (doomsters) such as Lester Brown, Paul Ehrlich, or Donella and Dennis Meadows, I am skeptical that the problems due to overpopulation, pollution, global warming, resource scarcity, or other damages to our physical environment will lead *directly* to significant changes in the economic system. On the other hand, unlike cornucopians (boomsters) such as Herman Kahn and Julian Simon, I believe that ecological damages might possibly have an important impact on the economy and, therefore, we need to make an effort to analyze the possible consequences of these developments, for instance, on the distribution of real income, that might have *indirect* effects on the economic system.

• Unlike Norman Macrae, I do not believe in strict technological determinism. He argues that because of the fall in communication costs and the rise of the World Wide Web, factories and enterprises will shrink, formal organizations will yield to direct person-to-person online communication, governments will largely wither away because their functions can be carried out more efficiently by private contractors; and citizens will vote on the macro-economic policies to be followed by the government, basing their choices on highly accurate computer-based forecasts of the different alternatives. As a result of such a technological revolution, he argues, world production will increase at 5 percent annually; and the rising level of productivity will narrow the economic gap between nations and solve the looming food shortage in the world. I share neither his belief that technology can unambiguously point toward one efficient structure of the economic system nor his optimism about future growth that somehow will occur without investment or saving.

• Finally, unlike many, I believe that certain key institutions such as the national state and the large corporation will endure through the next half century or so, albeit, perhaps, in somewhat different forms. Idle chatter about a post-modern, post-industrial, "post-fordist," and post-national world does little to advance our understanding of what the future really holds.

---

course about social issues such as abortion or school prayer that have little impact on the economic system.

In scanning the literature of futurology, I find a family resemblance between my picture of U.S. capitalism in the 21st century and several of the scenarios of Gilberto Gallopin and his colleagues, which have been popularized by Allen Hammond—in particular, their scenarios of crumbling social solidarity and declining governmental effectiveness in solving emerging economic problems.[10] They argue that such changes raise the specter either of unbridled conflict and institutional disintegration of a fortress world, an authoritarian response to the threat of breakdown. Given the events in Russia in the 1990s, this latter scenario points toward the stunning irony that the Soviet communists might have been right after all, when they proclaimed that Russia would provide the future model of the U.S. economic system.

3. Coda

Fortunately, the future depends on many factors, of which deliberate human intervention is one of the most important. Many of the dangers that I foresee are based on the hidden assumption that the policy steps necessary to alleviate emerging economic problems will either not be taken or will prove ineffective, either in design or implementation. I believe this assumption to be realistic: In part, this is because the complexity of these emerging economic problems does not permit them to be explained in a manner simple enough to become vital political issues, as shown in the 2000 presidential campaign about budgetary forecasts and privatization of Social Security. In part, this is because well-funded interests will fight vigorously to prevent those solutions that will have adverse effects on them, while the public interest is less well financed. As a result, the U.S. economic system will evolve in many different ways toward a capitalism with an inhuman face. I hope I'm wrong.

[10] By way of contrast, I find some of their scenarios highly unlikely, for instance, their "conventional world," which features little institutional change, and their "transformed world," which has a more optimistic view of human nature and the political will to share power and resources by various interest groups than most people would accept.

Appendices*

Appendix 2.1. ECONOMIC GROWTH RATES, 1950–2000

Table A2.1 summarizes some relevant data on economic performance of the U.S. economy over the last half of the 20th century. The changes in growth rates between the third and fourth quarter of the century and the upsurge in the last five years of the 1990s were particularly dramatic for the measure of productivity which takes into account both labor and capital inputs (total factor productivity, hereafter, TFP). More refined estimates of both inputs and outputs for this period by Jorgenson and Stiroh (2000) or Oliner and Sichel (2000) show an even greater late-century acceleration of TFP than do my calculations, which are based on official statistics. In other words, the surge in productivity in the last five years of the 20th century was real.

Appendix 2.2. DETAILS ABOUT THE SIMULATION MODEL

The simulation model was carried out on one spreadsheet and had five modules, four of which featured lookup-tables that were calculated on auxiliary spreadsheets.

A. Module for Population and Labor Force

1. The lookup-table contained the three Lee-Tuljapurkar (hereafter L-T) (1994) population projections for selected years between 2000 and 2050 for four different age cohorts: 1–19, 20–64, over 64, and over 85. For the years between the benchmark years, I assumed a constant growth rate of each population group. From these data I estimated the population within two special age groups (20–24 and 65–69) by multiplying the relevant L-T age-groupings by the fixed ratios representing the share of these groups in the total cohort in 1998. This allowed the working age in the simulations to start at 25 and the retirement age to be changed from 65 to 70. Such demographic approximations had little impact on the final results.

---

* The "External Appendices" can be viewed at website: http://www.swarthmore.edu/socsci/economics/fpryor1/. A compact disk of these appendices is also in the collection of the Swarthmore College McCabe Library.

Table A2.1. *Average Annual Growth Rates of GDP, GDP per Capita, and Productivity*

	GDP	GDP per capita	GDP per labor hour	GDP per unit of all inputs (labor hours and capital)
1950-1974	3.8%	2.4%	2.6%	2.2%
1975-1999	3.0	2.0	1.4	1.1
1995-1999	4.0	3.1	1.9	1.7

Note: These growth rates were calculated by fitting exponential curves to annual data. Because a production function linking real GDP to labor hours and capital stock did not yield stable coefficients, the input index used for the calculations in the last column was a geometrical index of labor hours and the net capital stock, with the former weighted by 0.75 and the latter weighted by 0.25. These data approximated the growth of total factor productivity.

Data on GDP and labor hours came from national account data from the U.S. Department of Commerce, Bureau of Economic Analysis Web Site: (http://www.bea.doc.gov/bea/dn1.htm). The labor hours were the total hours of the employed (NIPA 6.9) plus an estimate of the labor hours of the self employed (NIPA 6.7), assuming they worked the same number of hours per day as the employed (derived from NIPA 6.5 and 6.9). The capital stock data came from *Survey of Current Business*, 9/2000.

The labor supply was calculated separately for the 25–64 and the 65–69 age groups. For the former, I simply multiplied the population in that age group by a participation ratio, which was usually fixed but which could be changed at specified increments over time. Workers in the 65–69 age group were estimated in two steps. If the retirement age remained at 65, obviously the number of workers from 65 through 69 was zero; if the retirement age was chosen to be 70 in 2050, I multiplied the population in the 65–69 age group by a fraction rising from 0 to 1 in regular increments over the half century period from 2000 to 2050 and then by the same labor force participation ratio used for the 25–64 age group.

B. Module for Saving Rate

This calculation centered around a lookup-table of the consumption level of workers that had to be maintained throughout their working lifetime in order to accumulate the necessary savings to finance their annual retirement consumption at some designated fraction of their consumption during their working life (consumption replacement ratio). The consumption level depended on the growth of a worker's annual income, the interest rate, the year of retirement, and the year of death. These consumption levels were determined iteratively on an auxiliary spreadsheet, and the solution required the worker to have exhausted all saving at the time of death.

From the data on the pattern of consumption and income of a single worker over a working lifetime, I calculated the ratio of the chosen consumption level to the average aggregate total income over the working life. Within each of the four age groupings, I assumed that each age cohort had the same number of people; and, using this assumption, I could easily calculate the saving rate for the cohort of all workers in each year.

A problem arose when it was assumed that the life expectancy between 2000 and 2050 increased from 80 to 85 and that the age of retirement rose from 65 to 70 in the same period. To take these changes into account, I calculated two sets of optimal saving rates, one assuming a life expectancy of 80 years and a retirement age of 65 and another assuming a life expectancy of 85 years, and a retirement age of either 65 or 70. These defined, respectively, the initial and endpoint saving rates, with the saving rate in the other years rising over the 50-year period at even increments between these endpoint values.

C. Income Module

The net income of workers on which they base their saving decisions was equal to their work income (which increased at a constant annual rate) plus their interest income (or minus their interest payments, if they were in debt). As noted in the text, the interest income on savings or interest payments on loans came from a source outside the model, but this did not amount to very much and is simply a bookkeeping device.

When calculating the saving rate, I also determined the ratio of total aggregate income over the working lifetime to total work income over the same period. This varied according to the interest rate, growth rate, income replacement rate, age of retirement, and age of death, and the information was contained in a lookup-table. To calculate the income of the average worker, I multiplied the work income in a given year by this ratio. Total savings of workers was equal to the saving rate times this adjusted income times the number of workers.

D. Module for Consumption (Dissaving) Rates by Retired Workers

This calculation centered around a lookup-table providing levels of consumption of retired workers. This was merely the level of annual consumption maintained through the working lifetime multiplied by the consumption replacement ratio and was part of the calculations used to determine the optimum consumption level during a worker's lifetime.

This needed, however, to be related to the current level of income of active workers, which was easily determined by calculating the ratio of consumption of a retired worker to the average income of a current worker. For simplicity, I made three calculations to find the ratio of the consumption of a worker who just retired to the average income of workers 1 to 5 years in the past; 6 to 20 years in the past, and 21 to 30 years in the past. From the results of such a procedure I then calculated the total consumption level of all retired workers by taking account of the total number of retirees in the three age brackets and the average current wage.

Because life expectancy and, for some simulations, the age of retirement were rising, I followed the same procedure as for saving. That is, I based the initial consumption ratio on one set of assumptions about age and retirement and the consumption ratio at the end of the period on another set of assumptions, and then created a weighted average that increased in regular increments over the 50-year period.

E. The Main Simulation

Since most of the calculations were carried out in the saving, income, and dissaving modules, the aggregate results were simple to make and consisted of the calculations for income, average consumption of workers, aggregate saving of active workers, aggregate dissaving of retired workers, and, finally, net saving.

Table A2.2. *Changes in the Saving Ratio When Other Parameter Values are Varied*

Consumption replacement ratios (r)	0.8	1.0	1.2
Median population growth, annual per capita income growth = 1.8%, retirement age = 70			
1. Interest = 3 %	+0.4%	-4.8%	-9.9%
2. Interest = 7 %	-0.1	-4.3	-8.5
Median population growth, annual per capita income growth = 1.8%, retirement age = 65			
3. Interest = 3 %	-2.4	-3.0	-3.5
4. Interest = 7 %	-4.6	-5.7	-6.8
Low population growth, annual per capita income growth = 1.8%, retirement age = 70			
5. Interest = 3 %	-2.6	-8.4	-14.2
6. Interest = 7 %	-3.1	-8.0	-12.9
High population growth, annual per capita income growth = 1.8%, retirement age = 70			
7. Interest = 3 %	+2.5	-2.0	-6.5
8. Interest = 7 %	+2.0	-1.6	-5.2
Median population growth, annual per capita income growth = 0.9%, retirement age = 70			
9. Interest = 3 %	-0.3	-6.0	-11.6
10. Interest = 7 %	-0.9	-5.7	-10.6
Median population growth, annual per capita income growth = 2.4%, retirement age = 70			
11. Interest = 3 %	+0.6	-4.2	-8.9
12. Interest = 7 %	+0.1	-3.8	-7.6

I assumed that average income increases at a constant annual rate. Average consumption could be calculated by multiplying the income by the saving rate, determined in the saving module. Total saving was calculated by multiplying the average saving by the number of active workers. Total dissaving was determined by multiplying the number of retired workers by the average current consumption of workers. The result was multiplied by the consumption replacement rate and the ratio of consumption of retired to active workers that was calculated in the dissaving module. Net saving was simply the sum of aggregate saving of active workers and aggregate dissaving of retired workers.

Appendix 2.3. THE IMPACT OF THE INTEREST RATE ON THE SAVING RATE

Table A2.2 presents some simulation results with two different interest rates, when the consumption replacement ratio, the population growth rate, per capita income growth, and the retirement age are varied.

Table A2.3. *Changes in Net Saving Between 2000 and 2050 with Different Consumption Replacement Ratios and Different Population and Income Growth Rates*

Consumption replacement ratios (ρ) =	0.8	1.0	1.2
Median population growth, annual per capita income growth = 1.8%, interest = 3%			
1. Retirement in 2050 at 70	+0.4%	-4.8%	-9.8%
2. Retirement in 2050 at 65	-2.4	-3.0	-3.5
Median population growth, annual per capita income growth = 1.8%, interest = 7%			
3. Retirement in 2050 at 70	-0.1	-4.3	-8.5
4. Retirement in 2050 at 65	-4.6	-5.7	-6.8
Low population growth, annual per capita income growth = 1.8%, interest = 3%			
5. Retirement in 2050 at 70	-2.6	-8.4	-14.2
6. Retirement in 2050 at 65	-7.6	-9.3	-10.9
High population growth, annual per capita income growth = 1.8%, interest = 3%			
7. Retirement in 2050 at 70	+2.5	-2.0	-6.5
8. Retirement in 2050 at 65	+1.2	+1.4	+1.6
Median population growth, annual per capita income growth = 0.9%, interest = 3%			
9. Retirement in 2050 at 70	-0.3	-6.0	-11.6
10. Retirement in 2050 at 65	-4.8	-5.9	-6.9
Median population growth, annual per capita income growth = 2.4%, interest = 3%			
11. Retirement in 2050 at 70	+0.6	-4.2	-8.4
12. Retirement in 2050 at 65	-1.2	-1.6	-1.9

Appendix 2.4. NOTES ON THE CONSUMPTION REPLACEMENT RATIO

In the text I refer to simulations using different consumption replacement ratios, and population and income growth rates. The results are contained in Table A2.3.

The magnitude of the consumption replacement ratio is controversial. Most of the literature focuses only on the decisions of individual savers and does not take into account the other factors outlined in the text. Three main approaches to this problem can be distinguished.

Engen, *et al.* (1999) present a sophisticated stochastic, dynamic programming model, taking into account, among other things, random shocks to income during the working lifetime, the time-preference rate, the interest rate, and the growth rate of income. They end up with median replacement rates of 80 percent or 72 percent if the time preference rates are, respectively, 0 and 3 percent. Comparing the results of this theoretical model to actual data of income and assets from several surveys, they draw a startling conclusion: Although the national saving rate may be low, U.S. individuals may still be saving at their optimal rate. Nevertheless, as Christopher D. Carroll (1999) has noted:

> [T]he 'dirty little secret' of the modern dynamic stochastic optimization model
> [is that] with multiple realistic kinds of uncertainty, and with plausible assumptions
> about other parameters, the model can predict a very wide range of behavior, depend-
> ing on the precise configuration of parameter values.

A second approach looks at the popular financial literature to see what financial gurus are advising the general public. In a brief review Engen *et al.* note that most advocate saving so that the replacement of consumption is roughly between 65 and 85 percent.

A third approach is to look at budgetary needs at different ages. Engen *et al.* (1999, p. 1121) point out that retired workers have no commuting expenses and lower mortgage expenses (since mortgages are usually paid off by the time of retirement). Further, their families are smaller (the number of "equivalent adults" in the family falls from 1.68 to 1.30).[1] On the other hand, the Consumer Expenditure Survey for 1998 shows that the increase in average out-of-pocket medical expenses on an equivalent-adult basis represents roughly 4 percent of consumption expenditures of a family headed by a person between 25 and 65. Moreover, per capita income in kind for the elderly through Medicare and Medicaid (calculated from data from *Statistical Abstract* (1999) amounted in 1998 to about 35 percent of the consumption (on an equivalent-adult basis) of a family headed by a person between 25 and 65. Added to the amount of saving advocated by personal finance experts, the true consumption needs of the retired range from 85 to 125 percent of those in the working ages.

Gokhale *et al.* (1996) approach budget needs from a different angle and divide governmental expenditures on those at different ages in a more precise manner. They argue that the ratio of nonmedical expenditures of those who were 70 and 80 years old to those who were 30 and 40 ranged between 0.63 and 0.91 in 1987–90, but they also point out that much of this higher expenditure by the elderly can be traded to a redistribution of income to them through the Social Security system.

The range of consumption replacement ratios that I have used in these simulations takes into account in a rough way the results of these various approaches.

Appendix 3.1. SOURCES OF DATA FOR TABLES AND CHARTS IN CHAPTER 3

A. Chart 3.1

1. Interest Rates: Data on three-year government bonds came from Moody's Investor's Service, updated by the "Fred" data-file of the St. Louis Federal Reserve (http://www.stls.frb.org/fred/)

---

[1]   I follow a common approach and assume that the "equivalent adults" in a family with N people is $N^{0.5}$. In 1998 the average family with household heads between 25 and 65 had 2.8 people; for those over 64, 1.7 people. The ratio of the average post-tax income of those over 64 to those between 25 and 65 was about half, but if we take into account the equivalent adults, then the ratio was 62.4 percent. These data, as well as those for out-of-pocket medical expenditures, came from the Consumer Expenditure Survey (http://stats.bls.gov/csxstn.htm). The data on government in-kind health expenditures for those over 64 covered only Medicare and 1/3 of Medicaid spending. Other governmental health programs for the aged, such as veteran's expenditures, were not included. These data for 1998 came from *Statistical Abstract of the United States* 1999, p. 120.

2. S & P 500 Stock Index: The data came from various issues of U.S. Department of Commerce, Bureau of Economic Analysis, *Business Statistics*, supplemented by data from various issues of U.S. Council of Economic Advisers, *Economic Report of the President* (annual). In earlier years this index included the stocks of only 400 companies.

3. Exchange rate: The data for G-10 nations from 1967 up to 1997 came from the website of the Board of Governors of the Federal Reserve (http://www.bog.frb.fed.us/releases/H10/Summary/). I calculated this index from the bilateral exchange rates of each of the individual currencies with the U.S. dollar from 1947 to 1967, as recorded in the Federal Reserve data bank. With the introduction of the Euro in January 1999 the G-10 series was discontinued, so I spliced onto the G-10 index an exchange rate index for "industrialized nations."

B. Chart 3.2

The data on the foreign exchange turnover in the New York money market came from a letter from the New York Federal Reserve and the "Foreign Exchange and Interest Rate Derivatives Markets Survey" (www.ny.frb.org). Similar data for other nations came from Bank of International Settlements (1996), Table 2-E. Data on the monetary base came from U.S. Council of Economic Advisers .(2000, p. 388). Data on the market value of sale of all securities came from Census Bureau (annual, various issues).

C. Table 3.1

1. Debt/GDP ratio: Data on total credit market debt came from Table L-1 of the flow-of- funds tables of the Board of Governors, Federal Reserve Bank (www.bog.frb.fed.us/releases/z1/data.htm).

2. Banking/financial crises: These are listed by name in footnote 7 of Wolfson (1990).

3. Household data: These series include households and nonprofit organizations. Three major liabilities of nonprofit organizations are excluded so that these data more closely match those of households. For commercial banks, liquid assets include vault cash, reserves at the Federal Reserve, checkable deposits and currency, U.S. government securities, and open market paper. Liquid liabilities include net interbank liabilities and checkable deposits. The fragility indicators based on assets and liabilities came from the flow of funds accounts (see above), Tables B-100, L-1, and L-109. Fragility indicators based on flow data came from the NIPA accounts, Tables 1.16 and 8.18.

4. Business failure rate and liabilities data: The series excludes farm bankruptcies. The data came from Dunn and Bradstreet, cited by U.S. Council of Economic Advisers (annual), and *1997 Business Failure Record* (www.dnbeconomics.com). The data before 1984 were adjusted in a crude fashion to reflect a change in methodology for collecting the raw data.

5. Personal bankruptcies: Data for early years were supplied in a letter from the Administrative Office of the United States Court. Later data came from U.S. Department of Commerce, Census Bureau (annual, various editions). Before 1980, personal and business bankruptcies were not separated. Since personal bankruptcies accounted for about 85 percent of total bankruptcies from 1980 to 1984, this fraction was used to estimate personal bankruptcies prior to 1980.

6. Mortgage data: Data for 1990–1997 came from U.S. Department of Commerce, Census Bureau (annual, 1997). Earlier data came from a letter from the Mortgage Bankers Association. In early years the data represent a complete sample; in later years a sampling procedure was used. Data for 1950-52 and 1972-73 are not available.

Appendix 4.1. DATA SOURCES FOR CHARTS IN CHAPTER 4

A. Chart 4.1

For the median family income, as well as for various points along the income distribution, the data came from the Census Bureau web site (http://www.census.gov/hhes/income/histinc/, Table F-5). For family income at the 10th percentile I used data from various issues of the *Current Population Reports*, series P-60, that give the percentage of families with incomes below certain levels. I then interpolated to obtain the numbers in the chart by assuming a log normal distribution of income. For deflating income I used a CPI-U-X1 index, which is also employed by the Census Bureau.

B. Chart 4.2

The wealth data came from Wolff (1995, 1996) and are interpolated for the missing years. For 1992 to 1995 I extrapolated the series using 1992 and 1995 values of percentage of net worth held by top 1 percent from Wolff (1998).

The data on female-headed households came from Table F-7 on the Census Bureau website cited for Chart 4.1. Estimates on the prime-age men (25–50) without employment were calculated from data in the various March editions of the *Current Population Survey* from 1964 through 1994 (Pryor and Schaffer, 2000). These data were extrapolated back to 1950 and from 1994 to 1998 by using another series, based on readily available data showing the ratio of employed men over 20 to the number of men between 20 and 65 excluding those in the armed forces or institutionalized, who are not counted among the employed.

Appendix 5.1. QUANTITATIVE INDICATORS OF GLOBALIZATION

A. Foreign Trade

Chart A5.1a shows that the openness of the economy, as measured by the ratio of exports or imports to the GDP, varied considerably in the U.S. in the 20th century. These measures of openness were very roughly the same in the early 1970s as in 1900. Since then, however, they rose considerably. By the middle of the 1990s the export measure even began to exceed the peaks occasioned by World War I. Campa and Goldberg (1997), Makhija and Williamson (2000), and Bordo, *et al.* (1999) present more disaggregated indicators of the openness of the economy.

Nevertheless, the trade/GDP measure provides a misleading picture of globalization, since most trade consists of manufactured goods, raw materials, and agricultural products, and it is well known that these sectors have greatly declined as a share of total GDP over the century. It seems more appropriate to measure globalization in terms of the ratio of foreign trade to production in those sectors which produce the traded goods and services.

Chart A5.1b presents some rough estimates for the 20th century of the ratio of the trade of goods to the value added in the total production of goods and also the ratio of trade in services to value added in the production of tradable services. For goods, the ratio of trade to domestic production began to exceed the 1990 levels by the 1970s. For tradable services, the trade/production ratios are much lower but have increased slowly over the century—and much faster for exports than for imports.

These ratios of trade to GDP or to tradable production are considerably lower in the United States than in most industrialized nations, a result that can be traced to the much larger internal mar-

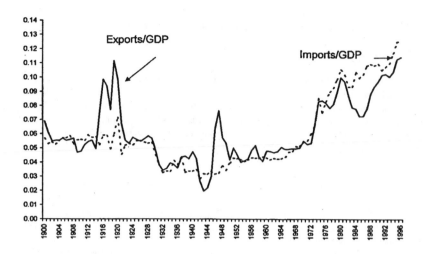

Chart A5.1a: U.S. Exports and Imports as a Percentage of GDP

Chart A5.1b: U.S. Exports and Imports of Goods and Services as a Ratio of Exportable Goods and Services

Note: Exportable or importable goods are agriculture, mining, and manufactured goods; exportable or importable services (ExS or ImS) are transportation, wholesale trade, and finance. S GDP = GDP originating from these service sectors. Notes on sources are presented in Appendix 5.2, p. 381.

ket in the U.S. Just as in the U.S., the trade/production ratios of goods rose considerably in most industrial nations (Japan and the U.K. were exceptions), even if the ratios of such trade to the overall GDP did not (Feenstra, 1998).

Several other major differences in trade between the beginning and the end of the 20th century are useful to note:

• *Composition of trade*. By the end of World War II the U.S. changed from a net exporter of raw materials to a net importer. Over the century the value of such raw materials fell as a percent of total manufacturing production.

• *Increasing vertical specialization (disintegration of the production chain)*. Since the mid-1970s, the vertical chain of production began to disintegrate with the rising importance of the outsourcing abroad ("global sourcing") of intermediate products, especially those which were highly labor intensive. Although amounting to less than 15 percent of total imports in the late 1990s, the imports of intermediate products for further processing in the U.S. rose dramatically in the last quarter of the 20th century. For merchandise exports, the share of vertically specialized trade rose from 6 to 11 percent in the U.S. between 1972 and 1990 (Hummels, *et al.*, 1999). Hanson, Mataloni, and Slaughter (2001) provide some new data suggesting that vertical specialization of production has been underestimated and, moreover, the degree of outsourcing increased considerably during the 1990s.

• *Changing location of trade transactions*. Over the 20th century, foreign trade moved from an activity primarily centered in the coastal states to one that was nationwide. Further, as discussed in Chapter 5, much of this trade was carried out by U.S. and foreign multinational corporations, a phenomenon occurring primarily in the third quarter of the century, since the share of MNEs in foreign trade did not greatly change in the last quarter of the century.

• *Shifting direction of trade*. At the beginning of the 20th century, about two-thirds of U.S. foreign trade was with Europe and another 9 percent was with Canada and Mexico. By the end of the 20th century this pattern was quite different, in part due to the rise of trade blocs. About 30 percent of U.S. trade was with Canada and Mexico, its NAFTA partners; about the same share was with industrialized nations (with Japan accounting for much of this); about 15 percent was with the newly industrialized nations; and the remaining quarter was with non-industrialized nations, many of which shipped not just raw materials but also manufactured items to the U.S.

• *Growth of intra-industry trade*. Intra-industry trade reflects the share of imports that are in the same category of goods that are exported, in contrast to inter-industry trade, where one type of good is exported, and another type is imported. The OECD (1996-a) calculated the Grubel-Lloyd index (1971) (which runs from 0 to 100 percent) for the United States and showed that intra-industry trade only increased from 44.4 percent in 1970 to 46.5 percent in 1980, but then took a leap to 71.8 percent in 1990. Part of this increase represented an increase in the greater variety of goods available to consumers and greater competition in traditional domestic markets.

B. Flows of Labor

Chart 5.2a focuses on the gross flows of immigrants into the United States; comparable data for the period for the subsequent outflow of many of these immigrants or of emigration of U.S. citizens are not available. These data show quite clearly that, as a percent of the population, the legal immigrant flow into the United States was considerably smaller at the end of the 20th century than at the beginning. The spike in the late 1980s represented a legalization of the status of many who had entered the country illegally. The composition of immigrants also changed over the century; for instance, a much higher percentage of legal immigrants were educated and had a professional background and an increasing percentage were from Asia or Latin America.

Chart 5.2b shows the percentage of foreign born in the U.S. These data are from the decennial

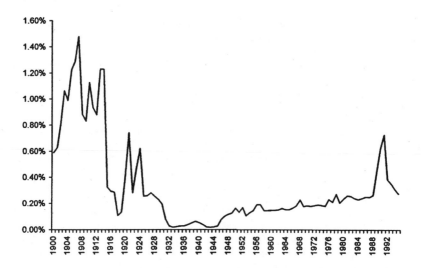

Chart A5.2a. Annual Flow of Legal Immigrants as a Percent of the Total U.S. Population

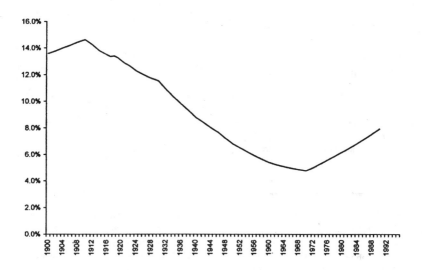

Chart A5.2b. Percent of Foreign Born in the U.S.

Note: Data sources and other notes are given in Appendix 5.2, p. 381.

census and include many, but not all, of the non-documented immigrants. Again, the data show that the percentage of foreign born in the country in 1900 was considerably higher than at the end of the century, but that an upturn occurred around 1970.

C. Flows of Capital

In contrast to the flow of labor into the U.S., the international gross capital flows (combined short and long term) into the country were greater at the end of the 20th century than at the beginning. The solid lines in Chart A5.3a show the outflows of U.S. capital abroad. Aside from a brief period during and after World War I, the outflow of U.S. capital generally amounted to less than 1 percent of the U.S. GDP until the 1970s, when it began to rise dramatically. The broken lines show the inflow of foreign capital to the United States, which was much more volatile. Again, such inflows seldom amounted to more than 1 percent until the late 1960s, when they began to increase dramatically.

This process is also reflected in data on capital stocks, which, it must be emphasized, are very problematic, because of difficulties of measurement and valuation. A rough picture of U.S. long-term investment abroad and foreign long-term investment in the U.S. is shown in Chart A5.3a. Although the data are not very good, they do provide some approximate orders of magnitude.

At the beginning of the century, the stock of foreign investment in the U.S., measured as a percentage of the U.S. GDP, was high. During World War I, considerable disinvestment took place, and the relative amount of such investment remained low until the 1970s, when, with the advent of large U.S. trade deficits, foreign investment in the U.S. soared. U.S. investment abroad reveal some curious zigs and zags; but again such investment took off in the early 1970s. By the end of the century, the previous highs of the early part of the century were exceeded.

The composition of long-term capital flows between direct and portfolio investment fluctuated considerably over the years. From the beginning of the century to the end, however, direct investment appears to account for a very slowly declining share of both U.S. long-term investment abroad and foreign investment in the U.S., a trend that is different from what is happening in many other countries. The geographical composition of foreign investment had not greatly changed: from 1929 to the late 1990s, somewhat more than half of U. S. foreign investment went either to Canada or to Western Europe.

Appendix 5.2. SOURCES OF DATA ON GLOBALIZATION

This Appendix contains the sources of data both in Chapter 5 and Appendix 5.1.

A. Chart 5.1 in the Text

The index has four components: international mail flows, international telephone calls, international travel, and international fax messages.

Per capita international mail flows, it should be noted, were roughly the same at the two ends of the century. The data came from U.S. Department of Commerce, Census Bureau (annual, various issues). For much of the early period, the data are in terms of weight, rather than actual letters; so a conversion had to be made from data in the overlap years. Moreover, the data between 1910 and 1915, between 1915 and 1920, and between 1920 and 1922 were interpolated.

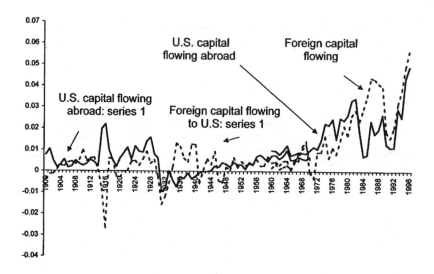

Chart A5.3a. International Capital Flows as Percent of GDP

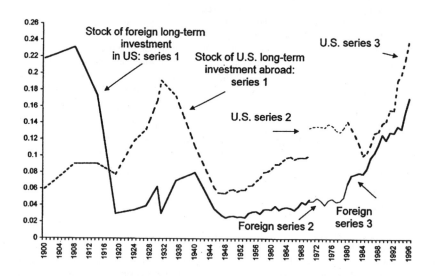

Chart A5.3b. The Stock of Long-Term Foreign Investment as a Percent of GDP

Note: Data sources and other notes are given later in Appendix 5.2.

International telephone calls first became economic in the early 1920s, and from 1921 to 1970 per capita international calls rose at an annual rate of 17 percent, accelerating thereafter to the end of the century at an average annual rate of 22 percent. The time-series data for telephone calls came from Census Bureau (1975, Series R-78) and Census Bureau (annual, various years). I assumed that one telephone call equals one letter, and that the average weight of a letter did not change between 1921 and 1950. I also assumed that communications with Canada and Mexico followed the same trend as with the rest of the world, so that their omission did not greatly affect the trend.

Travel provides an important means of face-to-face communication. The data on international travel came from Census Bureau (1975, Series H-932) and Census Bureau (annual, various years). I arbitrarily assumed that one visit overseas was equal to 10 letters or phone calls.

The final component is an extremely rough estimate of international fax messages and e-mails. I assumed that in 1975 there were one million fax or e-mail messages overseas (since neither method of communication was widespread at that time) and that these increased 20 percent a year thereafter.

My international communications index does not include indirect communications through newspapers, news wire services, or radio and TV broadcasts via satellite technology. These types of communication have, of course, increased considerably, but measurement problems seem insurmountable.

Given the nature of the data and the rough assumptions used in combining the various series, Chart 5.1 can only be viewed as a very rough estimate, indicating only the most basic trends.

B. Charts A5.1a and A5.1b

The GDP data for 1929–1996 came from U.S. Department of Commerce, Bureau of Economic Analysis (1997). For earlier years I spliced onto this data series a series from U.S. Department of Commerce, Census Bureau (1975, Series F-1). Data for GDP originating from individual industrial sectors for 1948–1996 came from Lum and Yusckavage (1997). For 1929–1947 I spliced onto the Lum/Yaskavage series sectoral data of national income without capital consumption adjustments from U.S. Department of Commerce, Bureau of Economic Analysis (1998), Table 6-1A.

For data from 1900–1929 I spliced onto sectoral national income data a series from U.S. Department of Commerce, Census Bureau (1949, Series A154–164). For production of goods I included the agriculture, forestry, and fishing; mining; and manufacturing sectors; for production of exportable services I included transportation, communications, and public utility; wholesaling; and finance, insurance, and real estate sectors.

For trade in goods and services comparable to the GDP data for 1929–1996, the data came from U.S. Department of Commerce, Bureau of Economic Analysis (1997). For 1900 to 1929 I spliced onto this series a data series on merchandise trade and selected services from U.S. Department of Commerce, Census Bureau (1975, Series U-2 to U-11).

C. Charts A5.2a and A5.2b

Data on legal immigrants came from U. S. Department of Justice, Immigration and Naturalization Service (1996). Data on foreign born population came from U.S. Department of Commerce, Census Bureau (1975, Series C-228); and Census Bureau (annual, 1995), p.52. The stock of foreign born is available only in the census years, so interpolations based on the assumption of a constant growth rate were made for the inter-census years.

D. Charts A5.3a and A5.3b

In Chart A5.3a, the data for 1900-1970 came from U.S. Department of Commerce, Census Bureau (1975, Series U19-U23). Data for 1960 through 1996 came from *Survey of Current Business* 78, July 1998, pp. 70-71, and U.S. Council of Economic Advisers (Annual, 1998), p. 399. These two series are not quite comparable, but since they are in the same order of magnitude, no adjustments were made.

In Chart A5.3b data for 1900-1970 came from U.S. Department of Commerce, Census Bureau (1975, Series U26-U39). The data from 1982 (which I extrapolated back to 1980) to 1996 came from *Survey of Current Business* 77, July 1997, p. 39. In order to make these series roughly comparable with the earlier series, it was necessary to estimate that part of "long-term" investment that was not foreign direct-investment, and for this purpose I employed the series on investment in corporate stocks. All other types of foreign investment were considered as "short-term." Moreover, since the comparisons are with the GDP, I believed it useful to use the current, rather than the historic cost estimates. Problems arose, however, for the data between 1970 and 1980, which were based on data from *Survey of Current Business* 64, August 1984. The series on direct investment used historic cost data which, for U.S. investment abroad, were hopelessly out of date. Therefore, I made a rough estimate by taking the ratio of current cost to historic cost estimates in 1980 and adjusting upward the foreign direct investment data for 1970 to 1980.

E. Experiments with International Interest Rate Convergence

A simple trend calculation revealed no statistically significant narrowing of such interest differentials from the mid 1950s to the mid 1990s, either for the short or medium-term nominal or real interest rates. Although the standard deviations of the real interest rates showed no significant trend, both the standard deviations and the coefficient of variation of the nominal rates, both long and medium term, revealed a significant widening, not a narrowing.

The interest rates used to make these comparisons for different countries are: *United States*, 3 month T-bills and 3 year government bond rate; *Belgium*, T-bills and average government bond yield; *Canada*, T-bills and the average rate on 3 to 5 year government bonds; *France*, 3 month lending rate and average yield on government bonds; *Germany*, T-bill rate and average government bond yield. *Italy*, average T-bill rate before taxes and average rate on medium term government bonds; Japan, the government bond yield (no short-term rates comparable to the other countries were available); *Netherlands*, T-bill and average government bond rates; *Switzerland*, T-bills and government bond yields; and *United Kingdom*, T-bills and short-term government bond rate.

The data came from International Monetary Fund (1997). I calculated real interest rates for a given year by subtracting the change in the GDP price deflator from the interest rate. Real interest rates for a given year "for the long-term" were calculated by subtracting the average annual change in the GDP price deflator for that year and the two previous years. Other types of calculations along these lines are carried out by Herring and Litan (1995).

Appendix 6.1. TRENDS: RESOURCE AND ENVIRONMENTAL INDICATORS

Chapter 6 contains a number of generalizations about trends in various resource and environmental indicators. This appendix presents some underlying data to support those judgments.

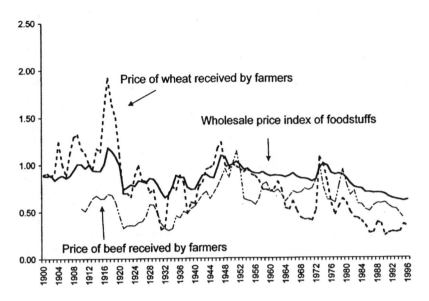

Chart A6.1a. Food Prices Deflated by the Cost of Living, 1950 = 1

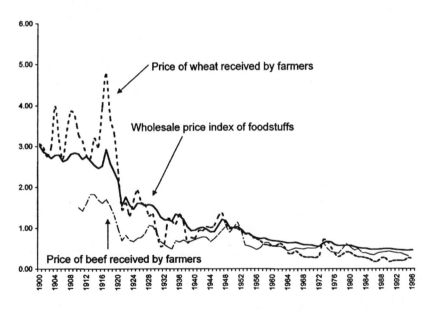

Chart A6.1b. Food Prices Deflated by a Wage Index, 1950 = 1

Note: Data sources and other notes are given in Appendix 6.2, p.387.

A. Changes in the Real Price of Food

1. Changes in the real price of food and natural resources

Charts A6.1a and A6.1b present three series from 1900 to 1995: a wholesale price index of food and also the prices of a bushel of wheat and of 100 pounds of beef received by farmers. In Chart 6.1a, these price series are deflated by the consumer price index in order to determine in rough terms whether the relative price of food has increased or decreased in relation to the prices of all consumer goods. In general, it appears that food prices became relatively cheaper over the 20th century. Even if, as some have argued, the consumer price index overstates the real rise in prices, it does not appear that food prices rose in comparison to other prices faced by consumers. Since food is a major export of the United States and prices of internationally traded foodstuffs in various countries are pulled toward a common level, such data also suggest that, under plausible assumptions, world food prices decreased relative to prices of other traded consumer goods.

Chart A6.1b shows in relative terms how long a laborer in manufacturing had to work in order to pay for food. The results are unambiguous: the price of food in terms of work-time declined over the 20th century. Since the wage data used to deflate the price data do not include fringe benefits and, as a result, understate total worker compensation, the work-time equivalent of food fell even faster than shown in the graph.

2. Changes in the Real Price of Natural Resources

Chart A6.2a shows a wholesale price index of fuels and related products and of metals and metal products, as well as individual prices of crude petroleum and copper, all deflated by an index of prices paid for consumer goods and services. The trends of the four series of raw material prices were relatively flat and reveal no striking increase or decrease over the 20th century.

Chart A6.2b shows the same price series, but this time calculated as a ratio of average hourly wages of production workers in manufacturing. In general, they reveal a declining trend over the century, especially in the first third. Again, diminishing returns in the extraction of raw materials appears to have been offset by other factors and the Malthusian prediction has not yet been realized in the U.S.

C. Environmental Degradation

1. Air Quality

Although estimates of various types of emissions into the air are available for many years, few nationwide data series on the actual concentration of various pollutants were estimated until the middle 1970s. Chart A6.3a presents readily available nationwide data on the concentration of three major types of air pollutants—sulfur dioxide, carbon monoxide, and particulate matter. It also shows an overall indicator that takes into account a variety of different types of pollutants and measures the number of days at various monitoring sites in which the air quality index exceeds a specified level. At least for these three pollutants, Chart A6.3a shows a definite decline in air pollution. As noted in the text, the situation for other air contaminants is mixed.

2. Water Quality

Chart A6.3b presents three series measuring water pollution—DDT residues in fish and the concentrations of fecal coliform and dissolved phosphorus in the U.S. rivers and streams. All three series

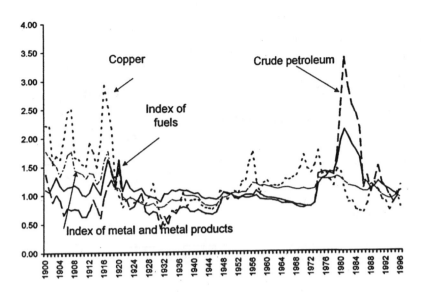

Chart A6.2a. Raw Material Prices Defalted by the Cost of Living, 1950 = 1

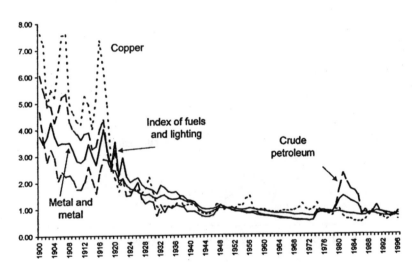

Chart A6.2b. Raw Material Prices Defalted by a Wage Index, 1950 = 1

Note: Notes and sources are presented in Appendix 6.2, p. 387.

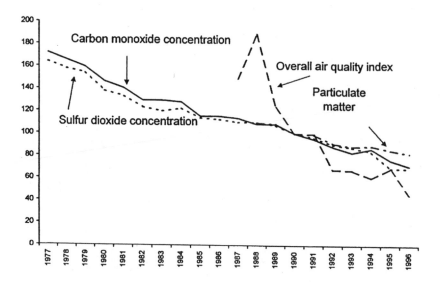

Chart A6.3a. Air Pollution Indicators, 1990 = 100

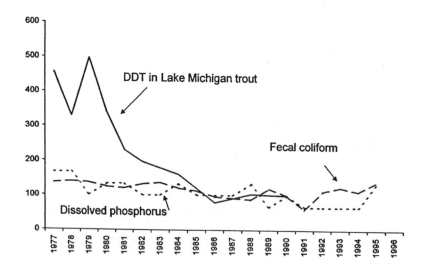

Chart A6.3b. Water Pollution Indicators, 1990 = 100

Note: Sources and explanations are presented in Appendix 6.2, pp. 387-88.

show a statistically significant decline but, as indicated in the text, other indicators of water ecology show mixed trends.

3. Global Warming

Chart A6.4 presents annual average temperature data for the United States after a variety of corrections were made, for instance, to take account of "urban heat islands" (see Appendix 6.2). Although the series is highly irregular, calculation of a simple linear regression reveals a statistically significant upward trend between 1900 and 1990, yielding the result, as others have shown using different data series, that the average annual temperature rose about 0.5 degrees centigrade (0.9 degrees Fahrenheit) over the century.

Appendix 6.2. NOTES AND DATA SOURCES FOR CHARTS AND TABLES

A. Notes on Tables 6.1a and 6.1b in the Text

The sources are cited in the note under the tables. The consumption data shown in Table 6.1a are slightly different from those in Table 6.1b because the expenditures in the former are based on the consumer expenditures survey (CES) or the Department of Labor, while the expenditures in the latter are based on the input-output (I-O) estimates of the Department of Commerce. The two data sets are not completely comparable.

Even though the goods and services from the CES survey can be easily arranged according to the categories of the I-O matrix, the CES estimates include retail and wholesale margins in the value of the final purchase of goods, while the I-O table separates these margins and considers them as a separate service. Nevertheless, average retail and wholesale margins can be calculated for total consumption of goods using data from the I-O table and this percentage can then be applied to the purchase of individual goods in the CES data. The total value of these sale margins was then placed in the appropriate I-O category. Several more minor adjustments for comparability were also made. Although expenditures in one major category—education, social services, and membership organizations—are greatly different in the two data sets, no corrections could be made without changing total consumption expenditures.

B. Sources and Notes for Charts A6.1a and A6.1b

Data for the consumer price index up to 1970 came from Series E-135 of U.S. Department of Commerce, Census Bureau (1975) (hereafter cited as *1975 Historical Statistics*). The remaining data came from U.S. Council of Economic Advisers (annual, 1997, p. 365). The wholesale price of food, as well as the prices of wheat and beef, came from *1975 Historical Statistics*, Series E54, K508, and K585, supplemented by data from U.S. Department of Agriculture (annual, various issues). Data for the hourly wage of production workers in manufacturing came from *1975 Historical Statistics*, Series D802, supplemented by data from *Employment and Earnings*, January 1997, p. 46. Manthy (1978) has a much more extensive study of agricultural prices, but his series go only to 1973.

C. Sources and Notes for Charts A6.2a and A6.2b

The Bureau of Labor Statistics (BLS) wholesale price index of fuels, related products, and power and also of metals and metal products for the period 1926 to 1970 came from *1975 Histori-*

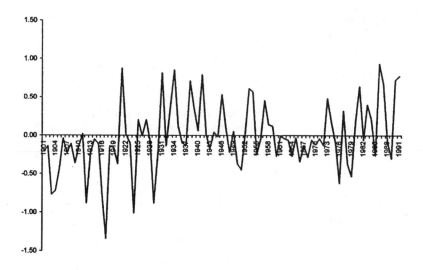

Chart A6.4 Annual Deviations from Average Temperature of the 20th Century in the U.S.

Note: Sources and notes are prsented in Appendix 6.2, p. 389.

cal Statistics, Series E29 and E34. They were extrapolated from 1926 to 1900 with the aid of indices by Warren and Pearson from *1975 Historical Statistics*, Series E57 and E58. They were spliced to BLS series from 1970 to 1996 from U.S. Council of Economic Advisers (annual, 1997), pp. 374-5. The data on crude petroleum and copper prices came from *1975 Historical Statistics*, Series M139 and M241, supplemented for years after 1970 by data from *Statistical Abstract* (various years). Given the heavy weighting placed on raw materials in the wholesale price index, deflating the individual series of raw material prices by the consumer price index, rather than by the wholesale price index, seemed more appropriate. The wage index came from the same sources as data in Chart A6.1b. Earlier data are available in Manthy (1978).

D. Sources and Notes for Appendix Charts A6.3a and A6.3b

Data on air pollution came from the U.S. Council on Environmental Quality (CEQ) (1998), Tables 5.10 and 5.11. All series are scaled so that 1990 = 100 and cover the entire U.S. For carbon monoxide and sulfur dioxide, the measurement is parts to million; for particulate matter, it is PM-10 particulates in grams per cubic meter; for overall air quality, the number of days in which the pollutant standards index is greater than 100. Between 1986 and 1987 the number of sites was increased, a change making no difference in the trends in any series except carbon monoxide. In this case, I assumed that no change occurred between 1986 and 1987 and rescaled the series from 1977 through 1986.

Data on water pollution came from CEQ (1998), Table 6.6 and CEQ (1997), Table 82. All series are scaled so that 1990 = 100 and cover the entire U.S. The DDT contamination of Lake Michigan trout is measured in micrograms per gram wet weight of fish; the fecal coliform bacteria and dissolved phosphorus are measured in terms of percent of all readings exceeding national water quality criteria in U.S. rivers and streams.

E. Sources and Notes for Chart A6.4

Data on deviation of average annual temperature came from T. R. Karl, *et al.* (1994-a). They have adjusted the data to account for the "time-of-observation bias," non-climatic biases, such as changes in instrumentation or station location, and potential heat-island biases. The authors divided the country into 23 regions, averaged the data for 1221 stations for each region, and then calculated a composite value for the contiguous U.S. states by weighting the regional averages by the area of the region. The data are calculated in terms of degrees centigrade deviation from the 1961–90 mean for each station.

Appendix 7.1. SOURCES OF DATA USED IN REGRESSIONS IN TABLE 7.1

In the correlations reported in the text, the data on the per capita GDP (PPP method), population; and the ratio of exports and imports to GDP came from OECD (1998-b).

The Gini coefficients to measure income inequality are for family income data before taxes and are adjusted for family size. These are the most comparable international data available and came from the files of the Luxembourg Income Study (http://lissy/ceps.lu/ineq.htm). For the regressions with social capital and social trust, I used income equality (1– Gini coefficient) for 1990 or for the closest year to that date in the 1980s; for the other regressions, the income equality data were for 1994 or 1995.

For data on social trust in the 1990-93 period, I used Variable V-94 from Inglehart, *et al.* (1998). For group membership I used the percentage of the population belonging to groups with the following purposes: social welfare for elderly, handicapped, and deprived (V-19); education, art, music, and culture (V-21); community action (V-23); youth work (V-28); professional associations (V-27); and political parties and groups (V-23).

The sources and methods by which the index of government effectiveness was calculated are discussed in Pryor (2001-c).

The data on per capita GDP growth from 1985 through 1995 came from OECD (1998-b). The index on governmental effectiveness is discussed in Appendix A7.5. The data on various social indicators are presented in Table A7.1 on the next page.

Appendix 8.1. DATA SOURCES FOR CHAPTER 8

A. Chart 8.1

The voter participation data came from Census Bureau, *Statistical Abstract of the United States 1997* (Washington, D.C.: GPO, 1997), p. 289. The sample survey data came from the National Election Studies website (www.umich.edu/~nes/). The percentage decline in voter participation cited in the text was determined by a simple linear regression. Roughly the same results are obtained for elections to the House of Representatives. Data on voter participation between 1824 and 1969 are found in U.S. Department of Commerce, Census Bureau (1975, series Y-27). This series is, however, slightly different from that found in *Statistical Abstract*.

Table A7.1. *Sources of Data for Social Indicators*

Area		
Subarea	*Source*	
Objective variables		
Number of murders, violent crimes,		
or armed robberies per 100,000 inhabitants, 1996	IMD	#3.48
Workdays lost to labor disputes per 1000 employees, 1996: log (strikes+1)	WEF	#7.16
Other variables: Survey of business executives		
A. Society and government		
Social cohesion is a priority for the government (survey)	IMD	#3.46
Corruption index (survey of surveys)	TI	
Discrimination (race, gender, family background)		
does not pose a handicap in the society (survey)	MD	#8.43
Values of the society (hard work, innovation)		
support competitiveness (survey)	IMD	#8.44
B. Managers		
Managers do not neglect their responsibility		
toward society (survey)	IMD	#6.36
Managers generally have a sense of entrepreneurship (survey)	IMD	#6.35
Globalization is not threatening to your economy (survey)	IMD	#2.41
Technological cooperation is common between companies (survey)	IMD	#7.12
C. Labor		
People in your country are flexible enough to adapt to new challenges	IMD	#8.42
The average worker is among the world's most hard-working (survey)	WEF	#7.02
Labor relations are generally productive (survey)	IMD	#6.29
Alcohol and drug abuse do not pose a serious		
problem in the work place (survey)	IMD	#8.40
Harassment and violence do not seriously		
destabilize the workplace (survey)	IMD	#8.41

Note: The data came from World Economic Forum (WEF, 1999); International Institute for Management Development (IMD, 1999); and Transparency International (TI) (www.transparency.de). The # in the last column designates the number of the variable.

B. Chart 8.2

The public opinion data came from the archives of the Roper Center: (http://www.roper-center.uconn.edu/). The tax data came from the national income and product accounts, Tables 1.9 and 3.2.

C. Chart 8.3

Data on the FBI crime index came from Census Bureau (1975, series H952 and H962); various issues of FBI (annual-a and annual-b); and the FBI website (http://www.fbi.gov/ucr.htm). This series was revised a number of times and I spliced the various series to each other to create one covering the entire period.

Data on crime victimization came from U.S. Department of Justice (1994), (Annual), and data on their website (http://www.ojp.usdoj.gov/bjs/cvict.htm#top). Since the series was revised in the early 1990s, the two parts of the series were chained to create a time-series for the entire period.

Data on inmates in federal and state prisons came from U.S. Department of Justice (1998). The series on inmates in local prisons came from the same source and various issues of Census Bureau (annual); it is, however, much less reliable. Data for those in local prisons from 1950 to 1981 were based primarily on interpolations of data in scattered years and can only be considered as approximate. The total series excludes those in youth detention facilities, but does include youth who were serving time in prison.

Data on population over 15 came from Council of Economic Advisers (annual, 1999).

Appendix 8.2. TWO POSSIBLE POLITICAL OUTCOMES OF DECLINING SOCIAL SOLIDARITY

In this section I look at two possible outcomes of declining social solidarity in the U.S., both of which could have important impacts on the economic system, namely, tyranny and social revolution. Although I believe that neither outcome is likely, each deserves brief consideration.

1. Tyranny

The most alarmist view is that a decline in social capital will force the government to assume despotic power. Such a conjecture occurred to Alexis de Tocqueville more than 175 years ago, anticipating the ideas of those interested in social capital (1969 (1835), pp. 691-2):

> I am trying to imagine under what novel features despotisms may appear in the world. In the first place I see an innumerable multitude of men, alike and equal, constantly circling around in pursuit of the petty and banal pleasures with which they glut their souls. Each one of them, withdrawn into himself, is almost unaware of the fate of the rest. Mankind, for him, consists in his children and his personal friends. As for the rest of his fellow citizens, they are near enough, but he does not notice them. He touches them but feels nothing.

The path to such an all-powerful state would, we can infer, about through an expanding system of internal security, which, although justified in terms of fighting crime, would gradually assume more political powers.[2] I find this scenario unlikely, not just because it violates all of the country's

---

[2] At another place in his discussion, he foresees an all-smothering welfare state also arising from the lack of social capital (pp. 672): "When no man is obliged to put his powers at the disposal of another, and no one has any claim of right to substantial support from his fellow man, each is both independent and weak ... his weakness makes him feel the need for some outside help which he

historical traditions, but also because the tie between social capital and democracy may not be as strong as such an argument assumes. For instance, using survey data from the World Value Study on membership in voluntary associations as a measure of social capital, Curtis, Baer and Grabb (1992) show that America ranks at the top of a sample of 15 industrialized nations, but the nations far below the U.S. are not noticeably deficient in comparison to the U.S. in either economic performance or, for that matter, democracy.[3] According to this line of argument, a decline in social capital in the U.S. would have little impact on the political system.

2. Class Struggle and Social Revolution

Another possible political consequence of the declining degree of social solidarity is increasing class struggle and, eventually, a social revolution. Certain evidence both for and against this Marxist-type deserve brief note.

Some economic trends might possibly point toward increasing class warfare and social unrest. These include the increasing inequality of income discussed in Chapter 4 and the rising number of prime-age men who were jobless—about 10 percent at the end of the century.[4]

As noted in Chapter 1, however, blue-collar workers who would allegedly form the vanguard in any sharpening class struggle have become an ever smaller share of the labor force. Nevertheless, in the 1990s considerable political discontent could be found in the U.S. For instance, according to the data collected by the World Value Study (Inglehart, et al., 1997, pp. 359-61; and 1998, V-249) roughly three quarters of the population thought that "reforms" were desirable, and 7 percent

---

cannot expect from any of his fellows, for they are both impotent and cold. In this extremity he naturally turns his eyes toward that huge entity which alone stands out above the universal level of abasement. His needs, and even more his longing, continually put him in mind of that entity, and he ends by regarding it as the sole and necessary support of his individual weakness."

[3] Measuring social capital by membership in formal organizations raises some obvious problems. When the authors of this study exclude union membership (mandatory in some nations) and church membership (which may depend on social pressure) from the list of organizations, four nations are not significantly different from the U.S. in terms of this measure of social capital. When only active membership (defined in terms of doing some unpaid voluntary work for the organization) is considered, six nations equal or surpass the U.S. If six different determinants of associational membership are held constant, then ten nations surpass the U.S. Such a reformulation suggests that because the social capital in the U.S. and these other nations is not greatly different, we should not expect much difference in macro-performance of the polity or economy.

My own estimates of social capital, based on newer data from the World Value Study, are used in Table 8.1. They show the U.S. ranking 2nd out of 18 nations with regard to the level of social capital, as measured by group membership. In the same 18 nation sample, the U.S. ties for 6th (with Canada) on degree of social trust. A somewhat different set of measurements by Inglehart (1997) shows that around 1990 the U.S. ranked 5th out of 18 OECD nations in the degree of social trust and 4th out of 18 in the level of social capital (he included more organizations in his count than I).

[4] These include both the unemployed and those who have left the labor force. As shown in Pryor and Schaffer (1999), this percentage was steadily rising in the last third of the 20th century.

thought that "revolution" was necessary. Although it is unclear what the respondents meant by revolution, it is worth noting that the U.S. tied with Italy for having the highest percentage of such responses among the OECD nations.

To me, this unexpected survey result suggests considerable latent political discontent (or political posturing), rather than revolutionary potential, especially since other conditions favorable to such a dramatic change were not present.[5] For instance, labor union membership steadily declining, from 30.3 percent of the non-agricultural civilian labor force in the first half of the 1950s to 13.3 in the mid 1990s. The union membership in the private sector alone in the mid-1990s was even smaller, 9.2 percent.[6] Furthermore, open manifestations of the class struggle, for instance, strike days lost per worker, have declined, not increased, over the same period (Jacobs, 1998, p. 316), and the data in Table 8.1 show no statistically significant relation between days lost in strikes and the variables reflecting social trends.

Finally, a revolutionary cadre has not arisen among those who were involuntarily without work for a long period or those new workers who poured into the labor market and who because of family breakdown (discussed in Chapter 7) or lack of skills could not easily find employment. As Marx pointed out over a century ago, the Lumpenproletariat are politically inactive, and voting studies show that in the U.S., the proportion of the underclass who vote is low. Moreover, white-collar workers, at least in the past century, have shown little revolutionary potential. If a class struggle develops, it will be quite different from what was imagined by socialists in bygone eras. Such a struggle may manifest itself in passive obstruction—workers withdrawing their energy and creativity from their jobs, so that their companies slowly stagnate—rather than in any open conflict. Given the conclusions reached in the discussion in Chapter 7 about the work ethic, however, even such a "passive revolution" does not seem very likely, at least in the coming few decades.

Appendix 11.1. A FORMAL VIEW OF CHANGES IN U.S. GOVERNMENTAL REGULATION

A qualitative and formal approach to the problem of determining trends in regulation focuses attention on various acts of the federal government which influence the market environment. These include legislation both to change the powers of certain regulatory bodies or to change the degree of enforcement of existing regulations. Table A11.1 lists some important regulatory actions taken by the federal government during the latter half of the 20th century.

Table A11.1 shows legislation both increasing and decreasing the range of federal regulation. Nevertheless, the data reinforce the general impression gained from the input data on regulation presented in Chapter 11 that market regulation in specific sectors—agriculture, transportation, energy, or banking—became less important, while general economic regulations became more important over the second half of the 20th century.

---

[5]   If revolutions have anything to do with general unhappiness, then an empirical study of survey data by Alesina, Di Tella, and MacCulloch (2001) provides some useful insights. The amount of self-declared happiness among those in the lowest quartile of the income distribution in the U.S. was somewhat higher than in Europe and, moreover, differences in happiness between the rich and the poor were less in the U.S.

[6]   The estimate for the 1950s came from Pryor (1996), p. 88; the estimates for the mid 1990s are calculated from U.S. Department of Commerce, Census Bureau (annual, 1997).

Table A11.1: *Selected Federal Actions Directly Affecting the Regulation of Markets*

	Impact + = more regulation − = less regulation
General economic regulations	
Antitrust: 1950, Celler-Kefauver Act, closed loopholes to previous antitrust legislation	+
Antitrust: 1952, McGuire Act permitted manufacturers to set "fair trade" prices in certain circumstances	+
Safety and health: 1970, Clean Air Act; 1972/4, strengthened by Clean Water and Safe Drinking Water Acts; 1976, Toxic Substances Control Act; 1990, Clean Air Act (allowed free market in pollution rights)	+
Safety and health: 1971, Occupational Safety and Health administration set up	+
Safety and health: 1972, Consumer Product Safety Commission set up	+
Environment: 1969, National Environmental Policy Act empowers courts to review agency actions with an impact on the environment; 1972, Environmental Protection Agency set up	+
Labor market: various years, minimum wages raised; additional labor market standards set	+/−
Prices: 1974, Council of Wage and Price Stability set up; 1981, eliminated	+/−
Investment: late 1970s, loosening of prudent investor standards for pension funds	+
Overall: 1970s, 1980s, OMB began oversight of regulations to take economic effects into account	−
Specific industry regulation	
Agriculture: 1996, Federal Agricultural Improvement and Reform Act lifted production controls and gradually phased out price supports	−
Mining: 1973, Mine Enforcement Safety Administration set up	+
Energy: 1973, Federal Energy Administration set up to administer petroleum prices and allocation; 1974, Energy Regulation Administration set up; 1981,decontrol of petroleum and oil prices; 1989, decontrol of natural gas	+/−
Energy: 1975, Nuclear Regulatory Commission to regulate nuclear materials and commercial reactors	+
Energy: 1978, Public Utilities Regulatory Policy Act promoted competition; 1992, Energy Policy Act lifted most restrictions on independent power producers	−
Transportation: 1970, National Highway Traffic Safety Administration set up to regulate automobile safety and, at a later date, fuel consumption	+

Transportation: 1976, Railroad Revitalization and Regulatory Reform Act partially deregulates railroads; 1980, strengthened with Staggers Rail Act; 1987, sale of Conrail	–
Transportation: 1977, Deregulation of air freight; 1978, Airline Deregulation Act; 1984, Civil Aeronautics Board eliminated	–
Transportation: 1980, Motor Carrier Act eliminated barriers to entry in trucking, 1982 Bus Regulatory Reform Act gave greater flexibility to bus lines	–
Communications: late 1960s, a series of decisions by FCC to loosen regulations	+
Communications: early 1980s, FCC started auctions of auctions of frequency spectrum for radio, TV	+/–
Communications: 1984, breakup of AT&T into 7 Baby Bells	–
Communications: 1993, Bill to auction frequency spectrum for new personal communication services	–
Communications: 1996, Telecommunications Act permitting increased competition	–
Public utilities: 1978, Public Utility Regulatory Power Act loosened restrictions on producing electric power	–
Banking: 1980, Depository Institutions Deregulation Act; 1982, Garn-St Germain Depository Act; 1989, Financial Institutions Reform, Recovery, and Enforcement Act; 1994, Branch Banking and Efficiency Act; 1999, revocation of major elements of Glass-Steagall Act Securities: 1975.	–
Securities: 1975, SEC ends fixed brokerage fees	–

Note: Information drawn from Carlton and Perloff (1999); Viscusi *et al.* (1995); and Feldstein (1994).

Table A11.2. *Trends in the Size of the U.S. Governmental and Nonprofit Sectors*

Panel A: Capital Stock Indicators: Ratios of Fixed Reproducible Tangible Wealth Excluding Consumer Durables

A = total governmental wealth including government enterprises to total wealth
B = residential wealth to total wealth
C = government residential wealth to total residential wealth
D = government non-residential wealth to total non-residentail wealth:
D1 = total
D2 = government enterprises alone

	A	B	C	D1	D2
1950s	25.5%	37.8%	1.9%	39.8%	5.9%
1960s	26.8	36.9	2.1	41.3	6.7
1970s	26.3	36.5	2.2	40.1	7.7
1980s	23.3	37.9	2.3	36.1	8.0
1990-97	22.9	38.8	2.3	35.7	8.5

Note: The current cost data came from the website of the U.S. Department of Commerce, Bureau of Economic Analysis, http://www.bea.doc.gov/ bea/dn2.htm, Tables KCU-1 and KCU-11. These data represent averages of annual data.

Panel B: Labor and GDP Indicators

A = Ratio of full-time equivalent workers to total in labor force:
A1 = government enterprises;
A2 = general government
B Percentage of GDP originating in the sector:
B1 = government enterprises;
B2 = general government;
B3 = total nonprofit sector;
B4 = membership organizations;
B5 = other nonprofit organizations

	A1	A2	B1	B2	B3	B4	B5
1950s	1.7%	16.3%	1.2%	11.1%	1.4%	0.6%	0.8%
1960s	1.9	18.0	1.4	12.3	2.1	0.7	1.4
1970s	1.9	18.0	1.4	13.4	2.8	0.7	2.1
1980s	1.7	16.3	1.4	12.5	3.2	0.6	2.6
1990–97	1.6	15.4	1.5	12.1	4.2	0.6	3.8

Note: General government includes civilian and military government services and administration. These data came from the website of the U.S. Department of Commerce, Bureau of Economic Analysis http://www.bea.doc.gov/bea/dn1.htm, Tables 1.7 and 6.5; and http://www.bea.doc.gov/bea/dn2.htm.

Table A11.3. *The Size of the Different Levels of Government: Capital Stock and Employment Measures*

A. Fixed, reproducible, tangible wealth excluding consumer durables: Government ownership as a percent of the national total

	1950 1959	1960- 1969	1970- 1979	1980- 1989	1990 1997
Total	25.5%	26.8%	26.3%	23.3%	22.8%
Federal	12.1	11.3	8.8	7.0	6.5
State and local	13.4	15.5	17.5	16.3	16.3

B. Government employees as percent of total employees (full time equivalents)

Total	18.0%	19.9%	19.8%	18.0%	17.0%
Federal of which	9.9	9.1	6.9	5.6	4.5
Civilian	3.1	2.9	2.6	2.2	1.9
Military	5.7	5.0	3.2	2.5	1.8
Government enterprises	1.1	1.2	1.1	0.9	0.8
State and local of which	8.1	10.8	12.9	12.4	12.5
Education	3.4	5.2	6.4	5.9	6.1
Other	4.2	5.0	5.8	5.7	5.6
Government enterprises	0.5	0.7	0.8	0.8	0.8

Note: The data represent averages for each year in the specified period. Totals may not add, because of rounding. The underlying data came from the same sources cited in Table A11.4, supplemented by Department of Commerce, Bureau of Economic Analysis (1998), Table 6.5C and data for more recent years from Survey of Current Business, August 1978.

Appendix 11.2. CHANGES IN PATTERNS OF U.S. GOVERNMENTAL OWNERSHIP

Table A11.2 summarizes some crucial aspects of the changing size of government ownership from 1950 through 1997. The first and fourth columns show that the share of the government's fixed, reproducible, tangible wealth increased in the 1950s (the Eisenhower years) and then slowly declined each decade thereafter. Such wealth includes both government buildings and equipment and various types of economic infrastructure, such as roads, bridges, dams, and airports, as well as government enterprises.

The different series on the importance of government enterprises are, unfortunately, contradictory. Panel A shows the government's rapidly rising share of wealth; Panel B, however, shows its declining share of the labor force; and its slightly rising share of the GDP. Given that the official statistics from which these data are drawn provide no explanation for these ostensibly conflicting results, several interpretations are possible. Perhaps the capital/labor ratio of these government enterprises increased much faster than that of enterprises in other sectors. Or perhaps an increasing share of the highly capital intensive processes of the general government was transferred to the government enterprise sector, so that the definition of "government enterprises" has changed. Or perhaps the official statistics on these matters are in need of revision. I have no evidence to support any of these views, and replies to my letter of enquiry to the governmental authorities responsible for these statistics provided little enlightenment.

To gain perspective on the size of the government sector, one must take into account the rising importance of state and local governments relative to the federal government. Table 11.3 shows clearly that in the 1950s, the relative size of these two parts of the government sector were roughly equal, when measured either by ownership of fixed capital or employment. By the 1990s, however, both measures showed that the state and local governments were more than twice as large as the federal government.

Appendix 12.1. GROSS INVESTMENT BY THE PUBLIC SECTOR

See table next page)

Appendix 12.2. TWO ISLANDS: A PARABLE ABOUT WELFARE EXPENDITURES[7]

The welfare states in Iceland (1995 population, 268,000) and Greenland (1995 population, 55,000) serve as useful guideposts for delineating possible futures of the welfare expenditures in the U.S. At the end of the 20th century, both island nations had highly developed welfare-state legislation, but actual behavior of expenditures diverged significantly because of different attitudes toward work and welfare.

In Iceland, the welfare state was instituted through national legislative action that resulted in a full panoply of pensions, health insurance, children's allowances, unemployment payment, and disability insurance programs that were considerably more developed than in the U.S.A. or England but are somewhat less generous than in other Nordic countries. Unlike Greenland, Iceland also had a private pension system. In Greenland the public welfare system was introduced by its Danish colonizer and, with certain modifications, was similar to that found in the mother country. In major part it was financed by subsidies from Denmark which, in 1993, amounted to about 50 percent of Greenland's GDP.

One important difference in 1993 between these two nations can be found in governmental transfer expenditures to households (which include welfare payments, pensions, and other types of social support). In Greenland and Iceland, these amounted respectively to 14.9 and 8.3 percent of the factor price GDP. In the same year private pension payments in Iceland amounted to 2.3 percent of the factor price GDP. Total governmental expenditures for social security, welfare, housing and

---

[7]   For this discussion I have relied on Iceland, Hagstofa Íslands/Statistics Island (1996), Greenland, Kalaallit Nunaanni Naatsorsueqqissaartarfik/Statistics Greenland (1997), the Nordic Social Statistical Committee (1996), and the *Annual Report of the Central Bank of Iceland* (www.sedlabanki.is). Although considerable materials about the Icelandic economy are readily available, this is not the case for Greenland. The most extensive treatment of Greenland is a controversial but fascinating book by Martin Paldam (1994); an English language source summarizing his argument is Paldam (1997). I have also greatly benefitted from a discussion of these matters with Bjorn Matthiasson.

Table A12.1. *Gross Investment by the Public Sector in the U.S.*

	1950-1959	1960-1969	1970-1979	1980-1989	1990-1997	Change in ratios: 1950s to 1990s
As a percent of GDP						
Total	5.3%	5.2%	3.6%	3.4%	3.1%	-41.1%
Federal	3.0	2.3	1.2	1.4	1.1	-64.3
State and local	2.4	2.9	2.4	2.0	2.1	-12.6
As a percent of total gross investment						
Total	25.4	25.3	18.1	17.4	18.5	-27.1
Federal	14.0	11.4	5.9	7.2	6.2	-55.5
State and local	11.4	13.8	12.2	10.2	12.3	+7.9

Note: These underlying data came from the national income and product accounts (U.S. Department of Commerce, Bureau of Economic Analysis (1998), supplemented for more recent years by data from *Survey of Current Business,* August 1998), Tables 1.1 3.16 and 3.17.

community development, and culture as a percent of the factor price GDP in the same year were 29.3 and 15.3 percent in Greenland and Iceland respectively.[8] In brief, Iceland spent much less on both transfers and total welfare expenditures, even though it had considerable welfare state legislation.

The crucial difference between the two islands lay, I believe, in attitudes toward work and welfare. Icelanders put considerable emphasis on the work ethic. More specifically, in the World Value Study (Inglehart, *et al.*, 1998) Iceland placed quite high among OECD nations for motivation for high achievement (V-110), pride in work (V-115), and work satisfaction (V-116), and Icelanders laid great importance on teaching their children to be independent, thrifty, and determined (V-227 to 230). They also scored high on the emphasis they put on personal development (V-267). Such values also received concrete implementation. Children of 12 and 13 have been encouraged to obtain jobs during the summer. All children of 14 must work at least one summer month in the labor force; and with each additional year of age, this work requirement is increased. Most municipalities run summer job programs for teenagers, and farm work is also available.

In brief, the national view has been that hard work, even for young children, is both educational and a contributor to maturity of the children. As a result, Icelandic youth not only have had experience in a variety of jobs but a certain realization that work is an integral part of their lives. This seems reflected in the ratio of the employed labor force to the population from 16 through 64, which was about 80 percent in 1993. The share of long-term unemployment in total employment was also lower, than in other Nordic nations—unemployment appears to be an undesirable state for Icelanders. Another aspect of the Icelandic work ethic can be seen in statistics on absences for at least

[8]   If we add the Danish subsidy to Greenland to its GDP this "welfare percentage" falls to 19.5 percent of the GDP.

one week due to illness. Although all of the Nordic nations have high quality public health services, Iceland has a considerably smaller percentage of workers claiming sick leave (NOSOSCO, 1996).

In Greenland, attitudes appeared different. Why work if you can receive welfare from Denmark, the colonizing country? In 1993 the labor force participation ratio was about 62.5 percent and, furthermore, unemployment was much higher than in Iceland.[9] Data on sick leaves or other objective indicators of the work ethic are not, unfortunately, readily available. On a more subjective basis, a visitor to Greenland does not see during the summer, as in Iceland, groups of young people working either in stores or in various public works projects.

The moral of this parable is that social factors have an important impact not just on work and productivity, but also on governmental expenditures for social support. In Iceland, welfare expenditures might be much higher (as in Greenland) if they had different attitudes toward work. If the declining social capital in the U.S. (discussed in Chapter 7) begins to influence attitudes toward work, then governmental welfare expenditures might increase, assuming, of course, that the rules for receiving such social support will not be greatly changed.

[9]   Given the dispersed population and the nature of hunting/fishing work, which is not steady employment, we should not place too much weight on the exactness of this datum.

Bibliography*

Abowd, John M., and Michael L. Bognanno. 1995. "International Differences· in Executive and Managerial Compensation." In Freeman and Katz (1995), 67–103.

Abramson, Alan J., Mitchell S. Tobin, and Matthew R. VanderGood. 1995. "The Changing Geography of Metropolitan Opportunity: The Segregation of the Poor in U.S. Metropolitan Areas, 1970 to 1990." *Housing Policy Debate* 6, No. 1, 45–72.

Acs, Zoltan J., and David B. Audretsch. 1990. *Innovation and Small Firms*. Cambridge, Massachusetts: MIT Press.

———. 1991-a. "Innovation and Size at the Firm Level." *Southern Economic Journal* 57, No. 3 (January), 739–45.

———. 1991-b. "R&D, Firm Size, and Innovative Activity." In Zoltan J. Acs and David Audretsch, editors. *Innovation and Technological Change: An International Comparison*. Ann Arbor: University of Michigan Press, 39–59.

Adamic, Lada A., and Bernardo A. Huberman. 2000. "The Nature of Markets in the World Wide Web." *Journal of eCommerce and Psychology* 1, No. 1 (April).

Adams, Henry Carter. 1887. "The Relation of the State to Industrial Action." *Publications of the American Economic Association* 1, No. 6 (January), 471–549.

Aghion, Philippe, Eve Caroli, and Cecilia García-Peñalosa. 1999. "Inequality and Economic Growth: The Perspective of the New Growth Theories." *Journal of Economic Literature* 37, No. 4 (December), 1615–1660.

Albert, Michael. 1993. *Capitalism versus Capitalism: How America's Obsession with Individual Achievement and Short-Term Profit has Led it to the Brink of Collapse*. New York: Four Wall Eight Windows.

Alesina, Alberto and Eliana Là Ferrara. 2000. "The Determinants of Trust." National Bureau of Economic Research, *NBER Working Paper* 7621. Cambridge, Massachusetts.

---

*   This bibliography contains not just the sources listed in this book, but also in the External Appendices, which can be found at website: http://www.swarthmore.edu/socsci/economics/fpryor1.

Alesina, Alberto, Rafael Di Tella, and Robert MacCulloch. 2001. "Inequality and Happiness: Are Europeans and Americans Different." National Bureau of Economic Research, *NBER Working Paper* 8198. Cambridge, Massachusetts.

Alesina, Alberto, and Enrico Spolaore. 1997. "On the Number and Size of Nations." *Quarterly Journal of Economics* 112, No. 4 (November), 1027–56.

Alexander, John B. 1999. *Future War: Non-Lethal Weapons in the Twenty-First-Century Warfare.* New York: St. Martins Press.

Alpay, Savas. 2000. "Does Trade Always Harm the Global Environment? A Case for Positive Interaction." *Oxford Economic Papers* 52, No. 2 (April), 272–89.

Alvarez, A. 1996. "Learning from Las Vegas." *New York Review of Books*, 43, No. 1 (January 11), 15–19.

American Association of Fund-Raising Counsel. Annual. *Giving USA.* New York: AAFRC.

Anderson, Benedict. 1983. *Imagined Communities: Reflections on the Origin and Spread of Nationalism.* London: Verso.

Anderson, David A. 1999. "The Aggregative Burden of Crime." *Journal of Law and Economics* 42, No. 2 (October), 611–43.

Anderson, James E., and Eric van Wincoop. 2001-a. "Borders, Trade and Welfare." In Collins and Rodrik (2001).

———. 2001-b. "Gravity with Gravitas: A Solution to the Border Puzzle." National Bureau of Economic Research, *NBER Working Paper* 8079. Cambridge, Massachusetts.

Anderton, Bob, and Paul Brenton. 1999. "Outsourcing and Low-Skilled Workers in the UK." In Paul Brenton and Jacques Pelkmans, editors. 1999. *Global Trade and European Workers.* New York: St. Martin's Press.

Andreas, Peter. 1999. *Sovereigns and Smugglers: Enforcing the U.S.-Mexico Border in the Age of Economic Integration.* Ph. D. dissertation, Cornell University.

Andreoni, James, Brian Erard and Jonathan Feinstein. 1998. "Tax Compliance." *Journal of Economic Literature* 35, No. 2 (June), 818–60.

Angel, J. K. 1994. "Global, Hemispheric, and Zonal Temperature Anomalies Derived from Radiosonde Records." In Boden (1994), 636–48.

Anon. 1920. "The Future as Suggested by Developments of the Past Seventy-five Years." *Scientific American* 123, No. 14 (October 2, 1920), 320-1.

———. 1968. "Opinion Poll Results: Future Advances–Readers Tell When They Should be Expected." *Industrial Research* 10, May: p. 45.

———. 1998-a. "Amazon.com: The Wild World of E-commerce." *Business Week*, December 14: 108–9.

———. 1998-b, "Airline Alliances: Mergers in Mind." *Economist*, September 26, 68.

———. 1999-a. "Crunch Time–DaimlerChrysler." *Economist*, September 25, 73–4.

———. 1999-b. "Partners: Special Report." *Business Week*, October 25, 106–5.

———. 1999-c. "Riding the Storm." *Economist*, November 6, 634.

———. 2000-a. "Amazon's Amazing Ambition." *Economist*, February 26, 24.

———. 2000-b. "Lawyers go Global." *Economist*, February 16, 79–81.

———. 2000-c. "The New Alchemy." *Economist*, January 22, 61–2.

———. 2000-d. "On-Line Finance Survey: Going for Brokers." *Economist*, May 20, 15.

———. 2000-e. "What's An Old-Line CEO to Do?" *Business Week*, March 27, 38–9.

———. 2001. "Huddling Together." *Economist*, March 10, 8–9 (Air Travel Survey).

Atiyah, P. S. 1979. *The Rise and Fall of Freedom of Contract.* Oxford: Clarendon Press.

Atkinson, Anthony B. 1999. "The Distribution of Income in Industrialized Nations." In Federal Reserve Bank of Kansas City (1999), 11–33.

———. 2000. "The Tall Story of Widening Inequality." *Financial Times*, August 16, 11.

Audretsch, David. Forthcoming. "The Growth of Enterprises from a Theoretical and Historical Perspective."

Auerbach, Alan J., and Kevin Hassett. 1991. "Corporate Saving and Shareholder Consumption." In B. Douglas Bernheim and John B. Shoven, editors. *National Saving and Economic Performance*. Chicago: University of Chicago Press for National Bureau of Economic Research, 75–98.

Auerbach, Alan J., and Laurence J. Kotlikoff. 1990. "Demographics, Fiscal Policy, and U.S. Saving in the 1980s and Beyond." In Lawrence Summers, editor. *Tax Policy and the Economy 4*. Cambridge, Massachusetts: MIT Press, 73–103.

Auerbach, James A., and Richard S. Belous, editors. 1998. "The Inequality Paradox: Growth of Income Disparity." *NPA Publication* 228. Washington, D.C.: National Policy Association.

Baier, Scott, and Jeffrey H. Bergstrand. 1998. "The Growth of World Trade." unpublished paper, Notre Dame University.

Baker, Dean, and Mark Weisbrot 2000. *Social Security: The Phony Crisis*. Chicago: University of Chicago Press. 2000.

Baker, Donald I. 1996. "Shared ATM Networks–The Dimension." *Bulletin* 41, No. 2 (Summer), 399–425.

Balling, Robert C. 1992. *The Heated Debate: Greenhouse Predictions Versus Climate Realists*. San Francisco: Pacific Research Institute for Public Policy.

Banerjee, Abhijit, and Esther Duflo. 2000. "Inequality and Growth: What Can the Data Say?" National Bureau of Economic Research, *NBER Working Paper* 7793. Cambridge, Massachusetts.

Bank of International Settlements, Monetary and Economics Department. 1996. *Central Bank Survey of Foreign Exchange and Derivatives Market Activity*. Basel.

Banuri, Tariq, and Juliet B. Schor, editors. 1992. *Financial Openness and National Autonomy: Opportunities and Constraints*. Oxford: Clarendon Press.

Barro, Robert. 1999. "Inequality, Growth and Investment." National Bureau of Economic Research, *NBER Working Paper* 7038. Cambridge, Massachusetts.

Bell, Daniel. 1960. *The End of Ideology: On the Exhaustion of Political Ideas in the Fifties*. Glencoe, Illinois: Free Press.

———. 1973. *The Coming of Post-Industrial Society*. New York: Basic Books.

———. 1976. *The Cultural Contradictions of Capitalism*. New York: Basic Books.

———. 1987. "The World and the United States in 2013." *Daedalus* 116, No. 3 (Summer), 1–33.

———. 1996. "Afterwords." In 1996 reprint of Bell (1973).

Bénabou, Roland. 1996. "Inequality and Growth." In Ben S. Bernanke and Julio J. Totemberg, editors, *NBER Macroeconomics Annual 1996*. Cambridge, Massachusetts: MIT Press.

Benen, Steve. 1999. "Evolution Evasion." *Church and State* 53, No. 9 (October), 4–8.

Bennett, William J. 1994. *The Index of Leading Cultural Indicators: Facts and Figures on the State of American Society*. New York: Touchstone.

———. 1999. *The Index of Leading Cultural Indicators: American Society at the End of the Twentieth Century*, updated edition. New York: Broadway Books.

Berg, Andrew, and Jeffrey Sachs. 1988. "The Debt Crisis: Structural Explanations of Country Performance." *Journal of Development Economics* 29, 271–306.

Berle, Adolf A., Jr., and Gardiner C. Means. 1933. *The Modern Corporation and Private Property*. New York: The Macmillan Company.

Bernstein, Jared, and Ellen Houston. 2000. *Crime and Work: What We Can Learn from the Low-Wage Labor Market*? Washington, D.C.: Economic Policy Institute.

Bhagwati, Jagdish. 1958. "Immiserizing Growth: A Geometric Note." *Review of Economic Studies* 68, No. 3 (June), 201–6.

Bishop, John A., John P. Formby, and Ryoichi Sakano. 1994. "Estimating Changes in the Distribution of Income in the United States." *Journal of Income Distribution* 4, No. 1: 79–105.

Blakely, Edward J., and Mary Gail Snyder. 1997. *Fortress America: Gated Communities in the United States.* Cambridge, Massachusetts: Lincoln Institute of Land Policy.

Blank, Rebecca M. 1997. *It Takes a Nation: A New Agenda for Fighting Poverty.* New York: Russell Sage.

Blank, Rebecca M., and Alan S. Blinder. 1986. "Macroeconomics, Income Distribution, and Poverty." In Danziger and Weinberg (1986), 180–209.

Blendon, John M., Richard Morin Benson, *et al.* 1997. "Changing Attitudes in America." In Nye, Zelikow, and King (1997), 205–17.

Block, Fred. 1990. *Postindustrial Possibilities: A Critique of Economic Discourse.* Berkeley: University of Chicago Press.

Bloom, David E., and Jeffrey D. Sachs. 1988. "Geography, Demography, and Economic Growth in Africa." *Brookings Papers on Economic Activity,* No. 2, 207–297.

Blough, Stephen. 1992. "The Relationship between Power and Level for Generic Unit Root Tests in Finite Samples." *Journal of Applied Econometrics* 7, No. 3 (July-September), 295–308.

Blumstein, Alfred. 2000. "Disaggregating the Violence Trends." In Blumstein and Wallman (2000), 13–45.

Blumstein, Alfred, and Joel Wallman, editors. 2000. *The Crime Drop in America.* New York: Cambridge University Press.

Bock, Betty, Harvey J. Goldschmid, Ira M. Millstein, and F. M. Scherer, editors. 1984. *The Impact of the Modern Corporation.* New York: Columbia University Press.

Boden, Thomas A., editor. 1994. *Trends '93: A Compendium of Data on Global Change.* Oak Ridge Tennessee: Oak Ridge National Laboratory..

Bok, Derek. 1997. "Measuring the Performance of Government." In Nye, Zelikow, and King (1997), 55–75.

Bolton, Patrick and Gerard Roland. 1997. "The Breakup of Nations: A Political Economy Analysis." *Quarterly Journal of Economics* 112, No. 4 (November), 1057–89.

Bookman, Milica Zarkovic. 1993. *The Economics of Secession.* New York : St. Martin's Press.

Bordo, Michael D., Barry Eichengreen, and Douglas A. Irwin. 1998. "Was There Really and Earlier Period of International Financial Integration Comparable to Today?" National Bureau of Economic Research, *NBER Working Papers* 6738. Cambridge, Massachusetts.

———. 1999. "Is Globalization Today Really Different than Globalization A Hundred Years Ago?" National Bureau of Economic Research, *NBER Working Paper* 7195. Cambridge, Massachusetts.

Bosworth, Barry, and Gary Burtless. 1998. *Aging Societies: The Global Dimension.* Washington, D.C.: Brookings.

Bosworth, Barry, Gary Burtless, and John Sabelhaus. 1991. "The Decline in Saving: Evidence from Household Surveys." *Brookings Papers on Economic Activity,* No. 1, 183–241.

Bowles, Samuel, David M. Gordon, and Thomas E. Weisskoff. 1990. *After the Waste Land: A Democratic Economics for the Year 2000.* Armonk: M.E. Sharpe.

Bowman, Karlyn H. 1996. "A Reaffirmation of Self-Reliance? A New Ethic of Self-Sufficiency?" *Public Perspective* 7, No. 2 (February), 5–9.

Bracken, Paul. 1999. *Fire in the East: Asian Military Power and the Second Nuclear Age.* New York: HarperCollins.

Braudel, Fernand. 1982. *The Perspective of the World,* Vol. 3, *Civilization and Capitalism: 15th–18th Century.* New York: Harper and Row.

Breen, Richard, and Cecilia Garcia-Peñalosa. 1999. "Income Inequality and Macroeconomic Volatility: An Empirical Investigation." unpublished paper.

Bregger, John E. 1996. "Measuring Self-Employment in the United States." *Monthly Labor Review* 119, No. 1–2 (January/February), 3–10.

Brewer, Thomas L., and Gavin Boyd. 2000. *Globalizing America: The USA in World Integration*. Northhampton, Massachusetts: Elgar.

Bright, Chris. 2000. "Anticipating Environmental 'Surprises' ." In Worldwatch Institute, *State of the World 2000*. New York: Norton, 20–39.

Brimelow, Peter. 1995. *Alien Nation: Common Sense about America's Immigration Disaster*. New York: Random House.

Brooks, David. 2000. *Bobos (Bourgeois Bohemians) in Paradise: The New Upper Class and How They Got There*. New York: Simon and Schuster.

Brown, Charles, James Hamilton, and James Medoff. 1990. *Employers: Large and Small*. Cambridge, Massachusetts: Harvard University Press.

Brown, Eleanor. 1999. "Patterns and Purposes of Philanthropic Giving." In Clotfelter and Ehrlich (1999), 212–31.

Brown, Jeffrey and Austan Goolsbee. 2000. "Does the Internet Make Markets More Competitive? Evidence from the Life Insurance Industry." National Bureau of Economic Research, *NBER Working Paper* 7996. Cambridge, Massachusetts.

Brown, Lester R., Gary Gardner, and Brian Halweil. 1998. *Beyond Malthus: Sixteen Dimensions of the Population Problem*. Washington, D.C.: Worldwatch Institute.

Bryant, Ralph. Forthcoming. *Turbulent Waters: Cross-Border Finance and International Governance*. Washington, D.C.: Brookings Institution Press.

Brynjolfsson, Erik, and Brian Kahin, editors. 2000. *Understanding the Digital Economy: Data, Tools, and Research*. Cambridge, Massachusetts: MIT Press.

Brynjolfsson, Erik, Thomas W. Malone, Vijay Gurbaxani, and Ajit Kambil. 1994. "Does Information Technology Lead to Smaller Firms?" *Management Science* 40, No. 12 (December), 1628–45.

Brynjolfsson, Erik, and Michael D. Smith. 1999. "Frictionless Commerce: A Comparison of Internet and Conventional Retailers." http://ecommerce.mit.edu/erik/index.html.

Brzezinski, Zbigniew. 1993. *Out of Control: Global Turmoil on the Eve of the Twenty-First Century*. New York: Charles Scribner's Sons.

Buchanan, Patrick J. 1998. *The Great Betrayal: How American Sovereignty and Social Justice are Being Sacrificed to the Gods of a Global Economy*. Boston: Little, Brown and Company.

Burtless, Gary. 1998. "Technological Change and International Trade: How Well Do They Explain the Rise in U.S. Income Inequality." In Auerbach and Belous {1998}: 66–91.

Burtless, Gary, Robert Z. Lawrence, Robert E. Litan, and Robert J. Shapiro. 1998. *Globaphobia: Confronting Fears about Open Trade*, Washington, D.C.: Brookings Institution, The Progressive Policy Institute, and The Twentieth Century Fund.

Byrne, John A. 1999. "The Global Corporation Becomes the Leaderless Corporation." *Business Week*, August 30, 88–90.

Calvin, William H. 2000. "The Great Climate Flip-Flop." *Atlantic Monthly* 281, No. 1 (January), 47–64.

Campa, José, and Linda S. Goldberg. 1997. "The Evolving External Orientation of Manufacturing: A Profile of Four Countries." Federal Reserve Bank of New York, *Economic Policy Review*, 3, No. 2 (July), 53–81.

Campbell, John Y., Martin Lettau, Burton G. Malkiel, and Yexiao Xu. 2000. "Have Individual Stocks Become More Volatile? An Empirical Exploration of Idiosyncratic Risk." National Bureau of Economic Research, *NBER Working Paper* 7590. Cambridge, Massachusetts.

Campbell, John Y., and Pierre Perron. 1991. "Pitfalls and Opportunities: What Macroeconomists Should Know about Unit Roots." In Olivier Jean Blanchard and Stanley Fisher, editors. *NBER Macroeconomics Annual 1991*. Cambridge, Massachusetts: MIT Press, 141–201.

Cancian, Maria, and Deborah Reed. 1999. "The Impact of Wives' Earnings on Income Inequality: Issues and Estimates." *Demography* 36, No. 2 (May), 173–64.

Cantwell, John. 1995, "Multinational Corporations and Innovation Activities: Toward a New, Evolutionary Approach." In José Molero, editor, *Technological Innovation, Multinational Corporations and New International Competitiveness.* Australia, United States: Harwood Academic Publisher.

Cantwell, John, and Christian Bellak. 1998. "How Important Is Foreign Direct Investment? *Oxford Bulletin of Economics and Statistics* 60, No. 1 (February), 99–106.

Card, David, and Richard B. Freeman, editors. 1993. *Small Differences That Matter: Labor Markets and Income Maintenance in Canada and the United States.* Chicago: University of Chicago Press.

Carlsson, Bo, David B. Audretsch, and Zoltan J. Acs. 1994. "Flexible Technology and Plant Size: U. S, Manufacturing and Metalworking Industries." *International Journal of Industrial Organization* 12, No. 10 (September), 359–372.

Carlton, Dennis W., and Jeffrey M. Perloff. 1999. *Modern Industrial Organization,* Third edition. Reading, Massachusetts: Addison Wesley Longman.

Carroll, Christopher D. "Comments and Discussion." *Brookings Papers on Economic Activity,* No. 1, 1999: 166–74.

Carter, Susan B., *et al.*, editors. Forthcoming 2002. *Historical Statistics of the United States, Earliest Times to the Present, Millennial Edition.* New York: Cambridge University Press.

Case, Anne, I-Fen Lin, and Sara McLanahan. 2000, "Educational Attachment in Blended Families." National Bureau of Economic Research, *NBER Working Paper* 7874. Cambridge, Massachusetts.

Case, Anne, and Christina Paxson. 2000. "Mothers and Others: Who Invests in Children's Health?" National Bureau of Economic Research, *NBER Working Paper* 7691. Cambridge, Massachusetts.

Ceglowski, Janet. 1994. "The Law of One Price Revisited: New Evidence on the Behavior of International Prices." *Economic Inquiry* 32, No. 3 (July), 407–19.

———. 1998. "Has Globalization Created a Borderless World?" Federal Reserve Bank of Philadelphia, *Business Review.* March/April, 17–27.

———. 1999. "Regionalization and Home Bias: The Case of Canada." Unpublished manuscript.

Centre européen des entreprises à participation publique et des entreprises d'intérêt économique général (CEEP). 1997. *Mutations in the European Public Sector since 1992: CEEP Statistical Survey.* Brussels.

Chakrabarti, Avik. 2000. "Do Nations that Trade Have a More Unequal Distribution of Income?" University of Wisconsin, Unpublished paper.

Cicero, Marcus Tullius. 1923. *De divinatione, Latin and English,* translated by William Armstrong Falconer. New York: G.P. Putnam Sons, Loeb Classical Library.

Citrin, Jack. 1974. "Comment on Political Issues and Trust in Government." *American Political Science Review* 68, No. 3 (September), 973–89.

Clark, Colin. 1940. *The Conditions of Economic Progress.* London: Macmillan.

———. 1950. "The Danger Point in Taxes." *Harper's Magazine,* No. 1207 (December), 67–9.

Cline, William R. 1992. *The Economics of Global Warming.* Washington, D.C.: Institute for International Economics.

Clotfelter, Charles T., and Thomas Ehrlich, editors. 1999. *Philanthropy and the Nonprofit Sector in a Changing America.* Bloomington: Indiana University Press.

Cochrane, John H. 1991. "A Critique of the Application of Unit Root Tests." *Journal of Economic Dynamics and Control* 15, No. 2 (April), 285–84.

Cohany, Sharon R., Steven F. Hipple, Thomas J. Nardone, Anne E. Polivka, and Jay C. Stewart. 1998. "Counting the Workers: Results of a First Survey." In Kathleen Barker and Kathleen Christensen, editors. 1998. *Contingent Work: American Employment Relations in Transition.* Ithaca: ILR Press, 41–51.

Cohen, Benjamin J. 1998. *The Geography of Money*, Ithaca: Cornell University Press.

Cole, H. S. D., Christopher Freeman, Marie Jahoda and K. L. R. Pavitt, editors. 1973. *Models of Doom: A Critique of the Limits of Growth*. New York: Universe Book.

Coleman, William D., and Geoffrey R. D. Underhill, editors. 1998. *Regionalism and Global Integration: Europe, Asia and the Americas*, New York: Routledge.

Colimore, Edward. 1998. "Getting into the Spirit of Millennium Change." *Philadelphia Inquirer*, March 22.

Collins, Susan, and Dani Rodrik, editors. 2001. *Brookings Trade Forum 2001*. Washington, D.C.: Brookings Institution.

Cooper, Richard N. 1986. "The United States as an Open Economy." In Hafer (1986), 1–25.

———. 1999. "Should Capital Controls be Banished? *Brookings Papers on Economic Activity*, No. 1, 89–143.

Costa, Dora L. and Matthew E. Kahn. 2001. "Understanding the Decline in Social Capital, 1952–1998." National Bureau of Economic Research, *NBER Working Papers* 8295. Cambridge, Massachusetts.

Cowell, Alan and Edmund L. Andrews. 1999. "Undercurrents at a Safe Harbor." *New York Times*, September 24, 1999, C1.

Creveld, Martin van. 1991. *The Transformation of War*. New York: Free Press.

———. 1999. *The Rise and Decline of the State*. New York: Cambridge University Press.

Crockett, Andrew. 1997. "Global Capital Markets and the Stability of Banking and Financial Systems." In Enoch and Green (1997).

Crosson, Pierre. 1983. "Impact of Erosion on Land Productivity and Water Quality in the United States." In S. A. El-Swaify, *et al.*, editors. *Soil Erosion and Conservation*. Ankeng, Iowa: Soil Conservation Society of America, 217–36.

Crowther, Samuel. 1933. *America Self-Contained*. Garden City, N.Y.: Doubleday, Doran & Company.

Curtis, James E., Douglas E. Baer, and Edward G. Grabb. 1992. "Voluntary Association Membership in Fifteen Countries: A Comparative Analysis." *American Sociological Review* 57, No. 2 (April), 139–52.

Cutler, David M., and Ellen Meara. 1998. "The Medical Costs of the Young and Old: A Forty-Year Perspective." In Wise (1998), 215–74.

———. 1999. "The Concentration of Medical Spending: An Update." National Bureau of Economic Research, *NBER Working Papers* 7279. Cambridge, Massachusetts.

Cutler, David M., James M. Poterba, Louise M. Sheiner, and Lawrence H. Summers. 1990. "An Aging Society: Opportunity or Challenge?" *Brookings Papers on Economic Activity*, No. 1, 1–75.

CyberSource. 1999. "CyberSource Fraud Research." www.cybersource.com/fraud_survey/ .

Daniels, Arlene Kaplan. 1985. *Invisible Careers: Women Civic Leaders from the Volunteer World*. Chicago: University of Chicago Press.

Danziger, Sheldon H., and Daniel H. Weinberg. 1986. *Fighting Poverty: What Works and What Doesn't*. Cambridge, Massachusetts: Harvard University Press.

Danziger, Sheldon H., and Peter Gottschalk, editors. 1993. *Uneven Tides: Rising Inequality in America*. New York: Russell Sage Foundation.

Darmstadter, Joel, and Michael A. Toman, editors. 1993. *Assessing Surprises and Non linearities in Greenhouse Warming*. Washington, D.C.: Resources for the Future.

Darnay, Arsen J. 1992. *Statistical Record of the Environment*. Detroit: Gale Research.

Darnay, Arsen J., and Marlita A. Reddy. 1995. *Market Share Reporter*. Detroit: Gale Research.

Davis, Steven J., and John Haltiwanger. 1995. "Employer Size and the Wage Structure in U.S. Manufacturing." National Bureau of Economic Research, *NBER Working Paper* 5393. Cambridge, Massachusetts.

Davis, Steven J., John Haltiwanger, and Stephen Schuh. 1996. *Job Creation and Destruction*. Cambridge, Massachusetts: MIT Press.

Dean, Jodi. 1998. *Aliens in America: Conspiracy Cultures from Outerspace to Cyberspace*. Ithaca, New York: Cornell University Press.

Dean, Judith M. 2000. "Does Trade Liberalization Harm the Environment? A New Test." Center for International Economic Studies, University of Adelaide, *Policy Discussion Paper* 15.

Delli-Carpini, Michael X., and Scott Keeter. 1997. *What Americans Know about Politics and Why It Matters*. New Haven: Yale University Press.

DeLong, J. Bradford, and A. Michael Froomkin. 1999. "Speculative Microeconomics for Tomorrow's Economy." Unpublished paper.

Derdak, Thomas, editor. Various years. *International Directory of Company Histories*. Chicago: St. James Press.

Derlugian, Georgi. 1996. "The Social Cohesion of the States." In Terence K. Hopkins and Immanuel Wallerstein, editors. 1996. *The Age of Transition: Trajectory of the World-System, 1945–2025*. London: Zed Books, 148–78.

Devroye, Dan, and Richard B. Freeman. 2001. "Does Inequality in Skills Explain Inequality in Earnings Across Advanced Countries?" National Bureau of Economic Research, *NBER Working Paper* 9140. Cambridge, Massachusetts.

Diamond, Sara. 1997. "Political Millennialism within the Evangelical Subculture." In Charles B. Strozier and Michael Flynn, editors. *The Year 2000: Essays on the End*. New York: New York University Press, 206–16.

Dionne, E. J. Jr. 1991. *Why Americans Hate Politics*. New York: Simon and Schuster.

Dixon, Huw. 1999. "Controversy: On the Use of the 'Hidden Economy Estimates'." *Economic Journal* 109, No. 456 (June), F-335–7.

Dolan, Kerry, *et. al.* 1999. "200 Global Billionaires." *Forbes*, July 5.

Dollar, David, and Aart Kraay. 2000. "Growth is Good for the Poor." *World Bank Research Paper* (www.worldbank.org/research).

Donahue, John J., III, and Steven D. Levitt. 2001. "Legalized Abortion and Crime." *Quarterly Journal of Economics* 116, No. 2 (May), 279–420.

Doremus, Paul N., William W. Keller, Louis W. Pauly, and Simon Reich. 1998. *The Myth of the Global Corporation*. Princeton: Princeton University Press.

Dosi, Giovanni. 1988. "Sources, Procedures, and Macroeconomic Effects of Innovations." *Journal of Economic Literature* 26, No. 3 (September), 1120–71.

Dosi, Giovanni, *et al.*, editors. 1988. *Technical Change and Economic Theory*. New York: Pinter.

Drucker, Peter F. 1969. *The Age of Discontinuity; Guidelines to our Changing Society*. New York: Harper & Row.

———. 1976. *The Unseen Revolution: How Pension Fund Socialism Came to America*. New York: Harper and Row.

———. 1999-a. "Beyond the Information Revolution." *The Atlantic Monthly*, October, 47–57.

———. 1999-b. *Management Challenges for the 21st Century*. New York: HarperBusiness.

DuBoff, Richard B. 1989. *Accumulation & Power: An Economic History of the United States*. Armonk, New York: M.E. Sharpe.

Duncan, Greg J., and Jeanne Brooks-Gunn. 1997. *Consequences of Growing Up Poor*. New York: Russell Sage.

Dunn, Lucia F. 1982. "The Effects of Firm Size on Wages, Fringe Benefits, and Work Disutility." In Bock *et al.* (1984), 5–59.

Durham, William. 1979. *Scarcity and Survival in Central America: The Ecological Origins of the Soccer War*. Stanford, California: Stanford University Press.

Durlauf, Steven N. 1996. "A Theory of Persistent Income Inequality." *Journal of Economic Growth* 1, No. 1 (March), 75–93.

Dymski, Gary A. 1999. *The Bank Merger Wave: The Economic Causes and Social Consequences of Financial Consolidation.* Armonk, New York: M.E. Sharpe.

Dyson, Freeman. 1997. *Imagined World.* Cambridge, Massachusetts: Harvard University Press.

Easterly, William, and Ross Levine. 1997. "Africa's Growth Tragedy: Policies and Ethnic Divisions." *Quarterly Journal of Economics* 112, No. 4 (November), 1203–49.

Ehrenberg, Ronald G. 1994. *Labor Markets and Integrating National Economies,* Washington, D.C.: Brookings.

Ehrenfeld, David. 1999. "The Coming Collapse of the Age of Technology." *Tikkun* 14, No. 1 (January/February), 33–8.

Ehrlich, Paul R. 1968. *The Population Bomb.* New York: Ballantine Books.

———. 1988. "The Loss of Diversity: Causes and Consequences." In Wilson and Peter (1988), 21–28.

Eichengreen, Barry. 1990. "Currency Union." *Economic Policy,* No. 10, April, 118–66.

Eisner, Robert. 1989. *The Total Incomes System of Accounts.* Chicago: University of Chicago Press.

Ellin, Nan, editor. 1997. *Architecture of Fear.* New York: Princeton Architectural Press.

Ellwood, David T., and Lawrence H. Summers. 1986. "Poverty in America: Is Welfare the Answer or the Problem?" in Danziger and Weinberg (1986), 78–105.

eMarketer. 1999. *eBusiness Report,* 2, (December), (www.eMarketer.com).

Engel, Charles, and John H. Rogers. 1998. "Regional Patters in the Law of One Price: The Roles of Geography versus Currencies." In Frankel (1998), 153–183.

Engen, Eric M., William G. Gale, and Cori E. Uccello. 1999. "The Adequacy of Household Saving." *Brookings Papers on Economic Activity,* No. 2, 65–187.

Enoch, Charles, and John H. Green, editors. 1997. *Banking Soundness and Monetary Policy: Issues and Experiences in the Global Economy.* Washington, D.C.: IMF Institute.

Epstein, Gerald A., and Juliet B. Schor. 1992. "Structural Determinants and Economic Effects of Capital Controls in OECD Countries." In Banuri and Schor (1992), 136–63.

Epstein, Richard A. 1995. *Simple Rules for a Complex World.* Cambridge, Massachusetts: Harvard University Press.

Erdos, Richard. 1988. *A.D. 1000: Living on the Brink of Apocalypse.* San Francisco: Harper and Row.

Esping-Andersen, Gøsta. 1990. *The Three Worlds of Welfare Capitalism.* Princeton, N.J. : Princeton University Press.

Evans, Philip, and Thomas S. Wurster. 2000. *Blown to Bits: How the Economics of Information Transforms Strategy.* Cambridge, Massachusetts: Harvard Business School Press.

Executive Office of the President, Office of Management and Budget (previously Budget Bureau). Annual. *Budget of the United States Government.* Washington D.C.: G.P.O.

———. 1998. *Budget of the United States Government, Analytical Perspectives.* Washington D.C.: G.P.O.

———. 1999. *Budget of the Unite States Government, Fiscal Year 2000.* Washington, D.C.: G.P.O.

Falk, Irving A., editor. 1970. *Prophecy for the Year 2000.* New York: Julian Messner.

Fallick, Bruce C. 1999. "Part-Time Work and Industry Growth." *Monthly Labor Review.*122, No. 3 (March), 22–30.

Federal Bureau of Investigation (FBI). Annual. *Uniform Crime Statistics.* Washington, D.C.

———. Annual-b. *Crime in the United States.* Washington, D.C.

Federal Deposit Insurance Corporation. 1998. *1996 Annual Report.* Washington, D.C.: G.P.O.

Federal Reserve Bank of Kansas City, editor. 1999. *Income Inequality: Issues and Policy Options.* Kansas City.

Federman, Maya, *et al.* 1996. "What Does it Mean to be Poor in America?" *Monthly Labor Review* 199, No. 5 (May), 3–18.

Feenstra, Robert C. 1998. "Integration of Trade and Disintegration of Production in the Global Economy." *Journal of Economic Perspectives* 12, No. 3 (Fall), 31–51

Feenstra, Robert C., and Gordon H. Hanson. 1995. "Globalization, Outsourcing, and Wage Inequality." National Bureau of Economic Research, *NBER Working Paper* 5424. Cambridge, Massachusetts.

———. 1996-a. "Foreign Investment, Outsourcing and Relative Wages." In Robert C. Feenstra, Gene M. Grossman and Douglas A. Irwin, editors, *The Political Economy of Trade Policy: Papers in Honour of Jagdish Bhagwati*, Cambridge, Massachusetts: MIT Press, 89–127.

———. 1996-b. "Globalization, Outsourcing, and Wage Inequality." *American Economic Review* 86, No. 2 (May), 240–45.

Fehr, Hans, and Laurence J. Kotlikoff. 1996. "Generational Accounting in General Equilibrium." *Finanz Archiv* 53, Heft 1, 1–27.

Feige, Edgar L. 1989-a. "The Meaning and Measurement of the Underground Economy." In Feige (1989-b), 13–57.

———. editor. 1989-b. *The Underground Economy: Tax Evasion and Information Distortion.* Cambridge: Cambridge University Press.

———. 1994. "The Underground Economy and the Currency Enigma." *Public Finance/Finances publiques*, Supplement, S119–36.

———. 1996. "Overseas Holdings of U.S. Currency and the Underground Economy." In Suzan Pozo, editor. *Exploring the Underground Economy.* Kalamazoo, Michigan: Upjohn, 5–63.

Feldstein, Martin, editor. 1994. *American Economic Policy in the 1980s.* Chicago: University of Chicago Press.

———. 1999. "Overview." In Federal Reserve Bank of Kansas City (1999), 357–67.

Feshbach, Murray and Albert Friendly, Jr. 1992. *Ecocide in the USSR: Health and Nature under Siege.* New York: Basic Books.

Fields, Jason, and Kristin Smith. 1998. "Poverty, Family Structure, and Child Well-Being Indicators from the SIPP." Census Bureau *Population Division Working Paper*, http://www.census.gov/population/www/documentation/twps0023.html.

Flusty, Steven. 1997. "Building Paranoia." In Ellin (1997), 47–69.

Fogel, Robert William. 2000. *The Fourth Great Awakening and the Future of Egalitarianism.* Chicago: University of Chicago Press.

Foote, Nelson N., and Paul K. Hatt, 1953. "Social Mobility and Economic Advancement." *American Economic Review* 43, No. 2 (May), 364–79.

Forbes, Kristin J. 2000. "A Reassessment of the Relationship Between Inequality and Growth." *American Economic Review* 90, No. 4 (September), 869–87.

Forman, Jonathan Barry. 1986. "Origins of the Tax Expenditure Budget." *Tax Notes* 30, No. 6 (February 10), 537–45.

Fox, Alan. 2000. "Demographics and U.S. Homicide." In Blumstein and Wallman (2000), 288–317.

France, Mike. 1999. "Copyright on the Net: Who "Owns" a Price." *Business Week*, December 13, 1999, EB-14.

Frankel, Jeffrey A. 1985. "International Capital Mobility and Crowding-out in the U.S. Economy: Imperfect Integration of Financial Markets or of Goods Markets?" In Hafer (1985), 33–69.

———. editor. 1998. *The Regionalization of the World Economy.* Chicago: University of Chicago Press for National Bureau of Economic Research.

Frankel, Jeffrey A., and David Romer. 2000. "Does Trade Cause Growth?" *American Economic Review* 89, No. 3 (June), 379–400.

Freeman, Richard B. 1993. "How Much Has De-Unionization Contributed to the Rise in Male Earnings Inequality?" In Danziger and Gottschalk (1993), 133–63.

———. 1998-a. "The Facts about Rising Economic Disparities." In Auerbach and Belous (1998), 19–34.

———. 1998-b. "Is the New Income Inequality the Achilles' Heel of the American Economy." Auerbach and Belous (1998), 219–233.

———. 2000. "Single Peaked Vs. Diversified Capitalism: The Relation Between Economic Institutions and Outcomes." National Bureau of Economic Research, *NBER Working Paper* 7556. Cambridge, Massachusetts.

Freeman, Richard B., and Lawrence F. Katz, editors. 1995. *Differences and Changes in Wage Structures*. Chicago: University of Chicago Press.

Freeman, Richard B., and William M. Rodgers III. 1999. "Area Economic Conditions and the Labor Market Outcomes of Young Men in the 1990s Expansions." National Bureau of Economic Research, *NBER Working Paper* 7073. Cambridge, Massachusetts.

Frey, Bruno S., and Werner W. Pommerehne. 1982. "Measuring the Hidden Economy." In Vito Tanzi, editor. *The Underground Economy in the U.S. and Abroad*. Lexington, Massachusetts: D.C. Heath, 3–27.

Friedheim, Cyrus. 1998. *The Trillion Dollar Enterprise: How the Alliance Revolution Will Transform Global Business*. Reading, Massachusetts: Perseus Books.

Friedman, Thomas L. 2000. "Corporations on Steroids." *New York Times*, February 4.

Friman, H. Richard, and Peter Andreas, editors. 1999. *The Illicit Global Economy and State Power*. New York: Rowman and Littlefield.

Fuchs, Dieter, and Hans-Dieter Klingemann. 2000. "Eastern Enlargement of the European Union and the Identity of Europe." Research Unit: Institutions and Social Change, Wissenschaftszentrum Berlin für Sozialforschung, *Working Paper* FS-III-00-206. Berlin.

Fuchs, Victor R. 1998. "Health Care for the Elderly: How Much? Who Will Pay for It?" National Bureau of Economic Research, *NBER Working Paper* 6755. Cambridge, Massachusetts.

Fukuyama, Francis. 1992. *The End of History and the Last Man*. New York: Free Press.

———. 1999. *The Great Disruption: Human Nature and the Reconstitution of Social Order*. New York: Free Press.

Furman, Jason, and Joseph E. Stiglitz. 1999. "Economic Consequences of Rising Income Inequality." In Federal Reserve Bank of Kansas City (1999), 221–65.

Galambos, Louis. 2000. "State-Owned Enterprises in a Hostile Environment: The U.S. Experience." In Toninelli (2000-b), Chapter 12.

Gale, William G. and John Sabelhaus. 1999. "Perspectives on the Household Saving Rate." *Brookings Papers on Economic Activity*, No. 1, 181–225.

Gallopin, Gilberto, Al Hammond, Paul Raskin, and Rob Swart. 1997. *Branch Points: Global Scenarios and Human Choice*. Stockholm: Stockholm Environmental Institute.

Gatti, James F. 1981. "An Overview of the Problem of Government Regulation." In James F. Gatti, editor. *The Limits of Government Regulation*. New York: Academic Press, 1–11.

Ger, Güliz and Russell W. Belk. 1996. "Cross-cultural Differences in Materialism." *Journal of Economic Psychology* 17, No. 7 (February), 55–77.

Gilpin, Robert. 2000. *The Challenge of Global Capitalism: The World Economy in the 21st Century*. Princeton: Princeton University Press.

Glaeser, Edward L., David Laibson, Jose A. Scheinkman, and Christine L. Soutter. 1999. "What is Social Capital? The Determinants of Trust and Trustworthiness." National Bureau of Economic Research, *NBER Working Paper* 7216. Cambridge, Massachusetts.

Gleick, Peter H. 1993. "Water and Conflict: Fresh Water Resources and International Security." *International Security* 18, No. 1 (Summer), 79–113.

Goel, Rajeene K., and Michael A. Nelson. 1998. "Corruption and Government Size: A Disaggregated Analysis." *Public Choice* 97, No. 1–2, 107–20.

Goethe, Johann Wolfgang. 1988 (1825?). "Den Vereinigten Staaten." *Goethe Sämtliche Werke, Gedichte 1800–1832*, edited by Karl Eibl. Frankfurt am Main: Deutscher Klassiker Verlag, Vol. 2, 739.

Gokhale, Jagadeesh, Laurence J. Kotlikoff and John Sabelhaus. 1996. "Understanding the Postwar

Decline in U.S. Saving: A Cohort Analysis." National Bureau of Economic Research, *NBER Working Paper* 5571. Cambridge, Massachusetts.

Gokhale, Jagadeesh, Laurence Kotlikoff, James Sefton, and Martin Weale. 1999. "Simulating the Transmission of Wealth Inequality Via Bequests." National Bureau of Economic Research, *NBER Working Paper* 7183. Cambridge, Massachusetts.

Goklany, Indur. 2001. "Applying the Precautionary Principle to Global Warming." Center for the Study of American Business, *Policy Study* 158, St. Louis.

Goldman, Marshall. 1972. *The Spoils of Progress: Environmental Pollution in the Soviet Union* Cambridge, Massachusetts: MIT Press.

Golub, Stephen S. 1990. "International Capital Mobility: Net versus Gross Stocks and Flows." *Journal of International Money and Finance* 9, No. 4 (December), 424–39.

Goodman, Robert.1995. *The Luck Business: The Devastating Consequences and Broken Promises of America's Gambling Explosion.* New York: Free Press.

Gordon, David M. 1996. *Fat and Mean: The Corporate Squeeze of Working Americans and the Myth of Managerial Downsizing.* New York: Free Press.

Gordon, Robert J. 2000. "Does the 'New Economy' Measure up to the Great Inventions of the Past? *Journal of Economic Perspectives* 14, No. 4 (Fall), 49–75.

Gordon, T. J., and Olaf Helmer. 1964. *Report on a Long-Range Forecasting Study.* Rand Corporation Report P-2982. Santa Monica, California: September 1964.

Gottschalk, Peter, and Sheldon Danziger. 1998. "Family Income Mobility–How Much Is There, and Has It Changed?" in Auerbach and Belous (1998), 92–112.

Gottschalk, Peter. and Timothy M. Smeeding. 1997. "Cross-National Comparisons of Earnings and Income Inequality." *Journal of Economic Literature* 35, No. 2 (June), 633–687.

———. 1999 "Empirical Evidence on Income Inequality in Industrialized Countries." Luxembourg Income Study, *Working Paper* 154. Luxembourg.

Graham, Fred P. 1969. "A Contemporary History of American Crime." In Hugh Davis Graham and Ted Robert Gurr, editors. 1969. *The History of Violence in America: Historical and Comparative Perspectives.* New York: Praeger.

Gramsci, Antonio. 1977 (1916). "Indifference." In *Selected from Political Writings, 1910–1920.* Edited by Quintin Hoare. New York: International Publishers: 17–19, 687.

Granger, Clive.W. J., and Paul Newbold. 1974. "Spurious Regressions in Econometrics." *Journal of Econometrics* 2, No. 2 (July), 111–20.

Gray, John. 1998. *False Dawn: The Delusions of Global Capitalism.* New York: The New Press.

Greenland, Kalaallit Nunaanni Naatsorsueqqissaartarfik/Statistics Greenland. 1997. *Kaalaallit Nunaat 1997, Statistical Yearbook.* Nuuk: Greenland Home Rule Government.

Greenwood, Jeremy. 1999. "The Third Industrial Revolution": Technology, Productivity, and Income Equality." Federal Reserve Bank of Cleveland, *Economic Review* 35, No. 2, 2–13.

Grilli, Enzo, and Maw-Chen Yang. 1988. "Primary Commodity Prices, Manufactured Goods Prices, and the Terms of Trade of Developing Countries: What the Long Run Shows." World Bank *Economic Review* 2, No. 1 (January), 1–47.

Grimmett, Richard F. 1996. "Instances of the United States Armed Forces Abroad, 1798–1995." *Congressional Research Service Report* 96–119F. Washington, D.C.

Groenewegen, John. 1997. "Institutions of Capitalisms: American, European, and Japanese Systems Compared." *Journal of Economic Issues* 31, No. 2 (June), 333–47.

Grogger, Jeff. 1998. "Market Wage and Youth Crime." *Journal of Labor Economics* 16, No. 4 (October), 756–92.

Grubel, Herbert G., and P. J. Lloyd. 1971. "The Empirical Measurement of Intra-Industry Trade." *Economic Record* 47, No. 120 (December), 494–517.

Gruber, Jonathan. 2000. "Is Making Divorce Easier Bad for Children?" National Bureau of Economic Research, *NBER Working Paper* 7968. Cambridge, Massachusetts.

Gunther, Gerald, and Kathleen M. Sullivan. 1997. *Constitutional Law*, 13th edition. Westbury, New York: The Foundation Press.

Gurr, Ted Robert, and Barbara Harff. 1994. *Ethnic Conflict in World Politics*. Boulder, Colorado: Westview Press.

Gwartney, James D., and Robert A. Lawson. 1997. *Economic Freedom of the World: 1997 Annual Report*. Vancouver: Fraser Institute.

Gwartney, James D. *et al.* 2000. *Economic Freedom of the World: 2000 Annual Report*. (www.freetheworld.com).

Gylfason, Thorvaldur, Tryggvi Thor Herbertsson, and Gylfi Zoega. 1998. "Ownership and Growth." University of Iceland, Centre for Economic Policy Research, *Discussion Paper:* 1900. Reykjavik.

Hafer, R. W., editor. 1986. *How Open Is the U.S. Economy?* Lexington, Massachusetts: D.C. Heath.

Halal, William E. 1986. *The New Capitalism*. New York: Wiley and Son.

———. 1999. "The Infinite Resource: Mastering the Boundless Power of Knowledge." In William E. Halal, and Kenneth B. Taylor editors. *Twenty-First Century Economics: Perspectives of Socioeconomics for a Changing World*. New York: St. Martin's Press: 53–75.

Hall, John A., and Charles Lindholm. 1999. *Is America Breaking Apart?* Princeton: Princeton University Press.

Hammermesh, Daniel S. 2000. "12 Million Salaried Workers are Missing." National Bureau of Economic Research, *NBER Working Paper* 8016. Cambridge, Massachusetts.

Hammond, Allen. 1998. *Which World? Scenarios for the 21st Century: Global Destinies, Regional Choices*. Washington, D.C.: Island Press.

Hampden-Turner, Charles, and Alfons Trompenaars.1993. *The Seven Cultures of Capitalism*. New York: Doubleday.

Hansen, John Mark. 1998. "Individuals, Institutions, and Public Preferences over Public." *American Political Science Review* 92, No. 3 (September), 513–33.

Hanson, Gordon H., Raymond J. Mataloni, Jr., and Matthew J. Slaughter. 2001. "Expansion Strategies of U.S. Multinational Firms." In Collins and Rodrik (2001).

Harrigan, James. 1993. "OECD Imports and Trade Barriers in 1983." *Journal of International Economics* 35, No. 1, 91–111.

Harrison, Bennett.1994. *Lean and Mean: The Changing Landscape of Corporate Power in the Age of Flexibility*. New York: Basic Books.

Harrison, Lawrence E., and Samuel P. Huntington, editors. 2000. *Culture Matters: How Values Shape Human Progress*. New York: Basic Books.

Hartz, Louis. 1955. *The Liberal Tradition in America: An Interpretation of American Political Thought Since the Revolution*. New York: Harcourt, Brace.

Helliwell, John F. 1996. "Do Borders Matter for Social Capital? Economic Growth and Civic Culture in U.S. States and Canadian Provinces." National Bureau of Economic Research, *NBER Working Paper* 5863. Cambridge, Massachusetts.

Helliwell, John F., and Robert D. Putnam. 1995. "Economic Growth and Social Capital in Italy." *Eastern Economic Journal* 21, No. 3, 293–307.

Herring, Richard J., and Robert E. Litan. 1995. *Financial Regulation in the Global Economy*. Washington, D.C.: Brookings.

Higgins, Matthew, and Jeffrey G. Williamson. 1999. "Explaining Inequality the World Round: Cohort Size, Kuznets Curves, and Openness." Federal Reserve Bank of New York, *Staff Report* 79: New York.

Hines, J.R, and E.M. Rice. 1994. "Fiscal Paradise: Foreign Tax Havens and American Business." *Quarterly Journal of Economics* 109, No. 1, 149–82.

Hipple, Steven. 1998. "Contingent Work: Results from the Second Survey." *Monthly Labor Review* 121, No. 11 (November), 22–36.

Hirschman, Charles, Philip Kasinitz, and Josh DeWind, editors. *The Handbook of International Migration: The American Experience*. New York: Russell Sage Foundation.

Hobsbawm, Eric. 1994. *The Age of Extremes: The Short Twentieth Century, 1914–1991*. London: Michael Joseph Ltd.

Hodgkinson, Virginia, and Murray S. Weitzman. 1984. *Dimensions of the Independent Sector: A Statistical Profile*, 1st Edition. Washington D.C. Independent Sector.

———. 1986. *Dimensions of the Independent Sector: A Statistical Profile*, 2nd edition. Washington, D.C.: Independent Sector.

———. 1992. *Giving and Volunteering in the United States, 1992*. Washington, D.C.: Independent Sector.

———. 1996. *Dimensions of the Independent Sector: A Statistical Profile*. Washington, D.C.: Independent Sector.

———. 1998. "Responding to Factual Errors Present in the Schervish and Havens Article." *Nonprofit and Voluntary Sector Quarterly* 27, No. 2 (December), 522–8.

———. 1999. *Giving and Volunteering in the United States: Executive Summary*. Washington, D.C.: Independent Sector.

Holland, David, Don Inscoe, Ross Waldrop and William Kuta. 1996. "Interstate Banking: The Past, Present, and Future." *FDIC Banking Review* 9, No. 1 (Fall), 1–18.

Homer-Dixon, Thomas F. 1991. "On the Threshold: Environmental Changes as Causes of Acute Conflict." *International Security* 10, No. 1 (Fall), 76–117.

Hopkins, Thomas D. 1998. "Regulatory Costs in Profile." *Policy Sciences* 31, No. 4: 301–20.

Horrigan, Michael W., and Ronald B. Mincy. 1999. "The Minimum Wage and Earnings and Income Inequality." In Danziger and Gottschalk (1993), 251–272.

Howard, Christopher.1997. *The Hidden Welfare State: Tax-Expenditures and Social Policy in the United States*. Princeton: Princeton University Press.

Howell, David R. and Friedrich Huebler. 2001. "Trends in Earnings Inequality and Unemployment Across the OECD: Labor Market Institutions and Simple Supply-Demand Stories." Center for Economic Policy Analysis, *CEPA Working Paper* 23. New York: New School University.

Hummels, David, Jun Ishii, and Kei-Mu Yi. 1999. "The Nature and Growth of Vertical Specialization in World Trade." *Staff Reports of the New York Federal Reserve*, No. 72, March.

Huntington, Samuel P. 1996. *The Clash of Civilizations and the Remaking of World Order*. New York: Simon & Schuster.

Hurd, Michael D., and Naohiro Yashiro, editors. 1997. *The Economics Effects of Aging in the United States and Japan*. Chicago: University of Chicago Press.

Huxley, Aldous. 1958. *Brave New World Revisited*. New York: Harper and Row.

Hyams, Edward. 1952. *Soil and Civilization*. New York: Thames and Hudson.

Hyclak, Thomas. 2000. *Rising Wage Inequality: The 1980s Experience in Urban Labor Markets*. Kalamazoo, Michigan: Upjohn Institute.

Iceland, Hagstofa Íslands/Statistics Island. 1996. *Landshagir, Statistical Yearbook of Iceland, 1996*. Reykjavik.

Ijiri, Yuji, and Herbert A. Simon. 1971. "Effects of Mergers and Acquisitions on Business Firm Concentration." *Journal of Political Economy* 79, No. 2 (March), 314–22.

———. 1977. *Skew Distributions and the Sizes of Business Firms*. Amsterdam: North-Holland Publishing Company.

Ikeda, Satoshi. 1996. "World Production." In Terence K. Hopkins and Immanuel Wallerstein, editors. *The Age of Transition: Trajectory of the World-System, 1945–2025*. London: Zed Books, 38–87.

Inglehart, Ronald. 1990. *Culture Shift in Advanced Industrial Society*. Princeton, New Jersey: Princeton University Press.

———. 1997. *Modernization and Postmodernization: Cultural, Economic, and Political Change in 43 Societies*. Princeton: Princeton U. Press.

Inglehart, Ronald, Miguel Basañez and Alejandro Moreno. 1998. *Human Values and Beliefs; A Cross-Cultural Sourcebook*. Ann Arbor: University of Michigan Press.

Ingraham, Patricia W., and Donald F. Kettl, editors. 2000. *Agency for Excellence: Public Service in America*. Chatham, New Jersey: Chatham House Publishers.

Ingraham, Patricia W., and David H. Rosenbloom. 2000. "The State of Merit in the Federal Government." In Ingraham and Kettl (2000): 274–97.

International Institute for Management Development (IMD). 1999. *The World Competitive Yearbook*. Lausanne: IMD.

International Labour Office (ILO). Annual. *Year Book of Labour Statistics*. Geneva.

——— 1990. *Retrospective Edition on Population Censuses, 1945–1989*. Geneva.

International Monetary Fund. 1997. *International Financial Statistics CD Data Diskette*. Washington, D.C.: June.

Jacobs, Eva E., editor. Annual. *Handbook of U.S. Labor Statistics*. Lanham, Maryland: Bernan Press.

James, Harold. 2001. *The End of Globalization?* Cambridge, Massachusetts: Harvard University Press.

Jäntti, Markus, and Sheldon Danziger. 2000. "Income Poverty in Advanced Countries." In Anthony B. Atkinson and François Bourguignon, editors. *Handbook of Income Distribution*, Vol. 1. Amsterdam: Elsevier, 309–373.

Jargowsky, Paul A. 1997. *Poverty and Place: Ghettos, Barrios, and the American City*. New York: Russell Sage.

Jefferson, Philip N. 1998. "Seigniorage Payments for Use of the Dollar: 1977–1995." *Economic Letters* 58, 225–230.

Jefferson, Philip N., and Frederic L. Pryor. 2001. "Rich versus Poor? An Econometric Analysis of Relative Income Extremes." *Eastern Economic Journal*, 27, No. 1 (Winter), 1–17.

Johansen, Søren. 1991. "Estimation and Hypothesis Testing of Cointegration Vectors in Gaussian Vector Autoregressive Models." *Econometrica* 59, No. 6, 1551–80.

Johnson, Bryan T., Kim R. Holmes, and Melanie Kirkpatrick. 1999. *1999 Index of Economic Freedom*. Washington, D.C. and New York: Heritage foundation and the Wall Street Journal.

Jones, Charles I. 1997. "On the Evolution of the World Income Distribution." *Journal of Economic Perspectives* 11, No. 3 (Summer), 19–36.

Jorgenson, Dale, and Kevin J. Stiroh. 2000. "Raising the Speed Limit: U.S. Economic Growth in the Information Age." *Brookings Papers on Economic Activity*, No. 1, 125–237.

Joyce, Ted. 2001. "Did Legalized Abortion Lower Crime?" National Bureau of Economic Research, *NBER Working Paper* 8319. Cambridge, Massachusetts.

Kagan, Robert A. 2000-a. "How Much do National Styles of Law Matter?" Chapter 1 in Kagan (2000-b).

———. editor. 2000-b. *Regulatory Encounters. Multinational Corporations and American Adversarial Legalism*. Berkeley: University of California Press.

Kagen, Robert A., and Lee Axelrod. 2000. "Adversarial Legalism: An International Perspective." In Pietro S. Nivola, editor. 1997. *Comparative Disadvantages? Social Regulations and the Global Economy*. Washington, D.C.: Brookings Institution Press, 146–203.

Kahn, Herman. 1979. *World Economic Development: 1979 and Beyond*. Boulder, Colorado: Westview Press.

Kahn, Herman, William Brown, and Leon Martel. 1976. *The Next 200 Years: A Scenario for America and the World*. New York: Marrow.

Kahn, Herman, and Anthony J. Wiener. 1967. *The Year 2000: A Framework for Speculation on the Next Thirty-Three Years*. Toronto: Macmillan.

Kant, Immanuel. 1795 (1957). *Perpetual Peace*, edited by Lewis White Beck. Indianapolis: Bobbs-Merrill.

Kaplan, Robert D. 1994. "The Coming Anarchy: How Scarcity, Crime, Overpopulation, Tribalism, and Disease are Destroying the Social Fabric of Our Planet." *The Atlantic Monthly* 273 (February), 44–65.

———. 1998. *An Empire Wilderness: Travels into America's Future*. New York: Random House.

Kaplan, Steven N., editor. 2000. *Mergers and Productivity*. Chicago: University of Chicago Press.

Kappell, Jonathan. 2000. "Big Government." *The Standard*, February 7 (also www.thestandard.com).

Karl, Thomas R., *et al.* 1993 "A New Perspective on Recent Global Warming: Asymmetric Trends of Daily Maximum and Minimum Temperature." *Bulletin of the American Meteorological Society* 74, 1007–23.

Karl, Thomas R., *et al.* 1994-a. "U.S. National and Regional Temperature Anomalies." In Boden (1994), 686–736.

Karl, Thomas R., *et al.* 1994-b. "United States Historical Climatology Network–National and Regional Estimates of Monthly and Annual Precipitation." In Boden (1994), 830–905.

Karl, Thomas R., *et al.* 1995. "Trends in U.S. Climate During the Twentieth Century." *Consequences: The Nature and Implications of Environmental Change*, Vol. 1, No. 1, 2–13.

Karoly, Lynn. 1993. "The Trend in Inequality Among Families, Individuals, and Workers." In Danziger and Gottschalk (1993), 19–99.

Karoly, Lynn A., and Gary Burtless. 1995. "Demographic change, Rising Earnings Inequality, and the Distribution of Personal Well-Being, 1959–1989." *Demography* 32, No. 3 (August), 379–405.

Katz, Lawrence F. 1999. "Commentary: The Distribution of Income in Industrialized Countries." In Federal Reserve Bank of Kansas City (1999), 33–48.

Katz, Lawrence F., Gary W. Loveman, and David G. Blanchflower. 1995. "A Comparison of Changes in the Structure of Wages in Four OECD Countries." In Freeman and Katz (1995), 25–67.

Kaufmann, Daniel, Aart Kraay, and Pablo Zoido-Lobatón. 1999-a. "Aggregating Governance Indicators." www.worldbank.org/wbi/governance/.

———. 1999-b. "Governance Matters." www.worldbank.org/wbi/governance/.

———. 2000. "Governance Matters: From Measurement to Action." *Finance and Development* 37, No. 2 (June).

Keeling, C. D. 1994. "Global Historical CO_2 Emissions." In Boden (1994), 501–504.

Keeling, C. D., and T. P. Whorf. 1994. "Atmospheric CO_2 Records from Sites in the SIO Air Sampling Network." In Boden (1994), 16–26.

Kennickell, Arthur B. 2000-a. "An Examination of Changes in the Distribution of Wealth from 1989 to 1998: Evidence from the Survey of Consumer Finances." Levy Institute, *Working Paper 307*, www.levy.org.

Kennickell, Arthur B., Martha Starr-McCluer, and Brian J. Surette. 2000-b. "Recent Changes in U.S. Family Finances: Results from the 1998 Survey of Consumer Finances." *Federal Reserve Bulletin* 86, No. 1 (January), 1–30.

Keynes, John Maynard. 1971 (1919). *The Economic Consequences of the Peace*, Vol. 11, *The Collected Writings of John Maynard Keynes*. London: Macmillan.

King, David C. 1997. "The Polarization of American Parties and Mistrust of Government." In Nye, Zelikow, and King (1997), 155–78.

Kitshelt, Herbert, *et al.*, editors. 1999. *Continuity and Change in Contemporary Capitalism*. New York: Cambridge University Press.

Klingemann. Hans-Dieter. 1999. "Mapping Political Support in the 1990s: A Global Analysis." In Pippa Norris, editor. *Critical Citizens: Global Support for Democratic Government*. New York: Oxford University Press, 31–56.

Knack, Stephen, and Phillip Keefer. 1997. "Does Social Capital Have an Economic Payoff? A Cross Country Investigation." *Quarterly Journal of Economics* 112, No. 4 (November), 1251–1288.

Kohut, Andrew, John C. Green, Scott Keeter, and Robert C. Toth. 2000. *The Diminishing Divide: Religion's Changing Role in American Politics*. Washington, D.C.: Brookings.

Komninos, Nicholas. 1994. *The Effect of Information Technology on Average Firm Size and the Degree of Vertical Integration in the Manufacturing Sector*. Washington, D.C.: The American University, unpublished Ph. D. dissertation.

Koretz, Gene. 1999. "Inflation's New Adversary: The Web is only Starting to Bite." *Business Week*, October 4, 30.

Kraut, Robert, *et al.* 1998-a. "Internet Paradox: A Social Technology That Reduces Social Involvement and Psychological Well-Being?" *American Psychologist* 53, No. 9 (September), 1017–31.

———. 1998-b. "Implications of the Internet Paradox Research." Communications of the ACM 41, No 12 (December), 21–22.

Kull, Steven. 2000. *Americans on Globalization: A Study of U.S. Public Attitudes, Summary of Findings*. Program on International Policy Attitudes, University of Maryland, March.

Kurth, James.1994. "The *Real Clash*." *The National Interest* 17, No. 3 (Fall), 3–15.

———. 1999. "Religion and Globalization: The 1998 Templeton Lecture on Religion and World Affairs." *Foreign Policy Research Institute Wire* 7, No. 7 (May), 1–4.

Kuszczak, John, and John D. Murray. 1985. "A VAR Analysis of Economic Interdependence: Canada, the United States, and the Rest of the World." in Hafer (1985), 77–131.

Laband, David N., and John P. Sophocleus. 1992. "The Estimate of Resource Expenditures on Transfer Activity in the United States." *Quarterly Journal of Economics* 107, No. 3 (August), 959–85.

Ladd, Everett Carl. 1999. *The Ladd Report*. New York: Free Press.

Ladurie, Emmanuel Le Roy. *1971. Times of Feast, Times of Famine: A History of Climate since the Year 1000*. Garden City, New York: Doubleday and Company.

Laird, Sam, and Alexander Yeats. 1990. *Quantitative Methods for Trade-Barrier Analysis*. New York: New York University Press.

Lamb, Hubert H. 1982. *Climate, History and the Modern World*. New York: Methuen.

Landa, Janet Tai. 1984. *Trust, Ethnicity, and Identity: Beyond the New Institutional Economics of Ethnic Trading Networks, Contract Law, and Gift-Exchange*. Ann Arbor: University of Michigan Press.

Lang, James R., and Nancy B. Johnson. 1994. "Job Satisfaction and Firm Size: An Interactionist Perspective." *Journal of Socio-Economics* 23, No. 4 (Winter), 405–25.

La Porta, Rafael, Florencio Lopez-de-Silanes and Andrei Shleifer. 1998. "Corporate Ownership around the World." National Bureau of Economic Research, *NBER Working Paper* 6625. Cambridge, Massachusetts.

La Porta, Rafael *et al.* 1999. "The Quality of Government." *Journal of Law, Economics, and Organization* 15, No. 1 (April), 222–79.

Lasch, Christopher. 1995. *The Revolt of the Elites and the Betrayal of Democracy*. New York: W.W. Norton.

Lawrence, Robert Z. 1996. *Regionalism, Multilateralism, and Deeper Integration*. Washington, D.C.: Brookings.

Lawrence, Robert Z., and Matthew J. Slaughter. 1993." International Trade and American Wages in the 1980s: Giant Sucking Sound or Small Hiccup?" *Brookings Papers on Economic Activity: Microeconomics*, 161–210.

Lazich, Robert S. 1997. *Market Share Reporter, 1997*. Detroit: Gale Research.

Lebergott, Stanley. 1996. *Consumer Expenditures: New Measures and Old Motives*. Princeton, N.J.: Princeton University Press.

Lee, Ho Geun. 1999. "Do Electronic Marketplaces Lower the Price of Goods?" *Communications of the ACM* 41, No. 12 (January).

Lee, Jong-Wha, and Phillip Swagel. 1997. "Trade Barriers and Trade Flows across Countries and Industries." *Review of Economics and Statistics* 79, No. 3 (August), 372–82.

Lee, Laura. 2000. *Bad Predictions: 2000 Years of the Best Minds Making the Worst Forecasts*. Rochester, Michigan: Elsewhere Press.

Lee, Ronald, D., Andrew Mason, and Timothy Miller. Forthcoming-a. "Life Cycle Saving and the Demographic Transition in East Asia, *Population and Demographic Review*.

———. Forthcoming-b. "Saving, Wealth and the Demographic Transition in East Asia."

Lee, Ronald, D., and Jonathan Skinner. 1999. "Will Aging Baby Boomers Bust the Federal Budget?" *Journal of Economic Perspectives* 13, No. 1 (Winter), 118–140.

Lee, Ronald D., and Shripad Tuljapurkar. 1994. "Stochastic Population Forecasts for the United States: Beyond High, Medium, and Low." *Journal of the American Statistical Association* 89, No. 428 (December), 1175–90.

———. 1998. "Stochastic Forecasts for Social Security." In David A. Wise, editor. 1998. *Frontiers in the Economics of Aging*. Chicago: University of Chicago Press for National Bureau of Economic Research, 393–428.

Levine, Charles H., and Rosslyn S. Kleeman. 1992. "The Quiet Crisis in the American Public Service." In Ingraham and Kettl (1992), 208–74.

Levy, Frank. 1998. *The New Dollars and Dreams: American Incomes and Economic Change*. New York: Russell Sage Foundation.

Lichtenberg, Frank R. 1992. *Corporate Takeovers and Productivity*. Cambridge, Massachusetts: MIT Press.

Liebman, Jeffrey. Forthcoming. "Redistribution in the Current U.S. Social Security System." In Martin Feldstein and Jeffrey Liebman, editors. *The Distributional Effects of Social Security Reform*, National Bureau of Economic Research.

Lindbeck, Assar, Sten Nyberg, and Jörgen W. Weibull. 1999. "Social Norms and Economic Incentives in the Welfare State." *The Quarterly Journal of Economics* 114, No. 1 (February), 1–35.

Lindert, Peter H. 1994. "The Rise of Social Spending, 1880–1930." *Explorations in Economic History* 31, No. 1 (January), 1–37.

———. "Three Centuries of Inequality in Britain and America." In Anthony B. Atkinson and François Bourguignon, editors. *Handbook of Income Distribution*, Vol. 1. New York: Elsevier.

Lipset, Seymour Martin. 1996. *American Exceptionalism: A Double -Edged Sword*. New York: Norton.

Lipset, Seymour Martin, and Gabriel Salman Lenz. 2000. "Corruption, Culture, and Markets." In Harrison and Huntington (2000), 112–26.

Locke, John L. 1998. *The De-Voicing of Society: Why We Don't Talk to Each Other Anymore*. New York: Simon and Schuster.

Lovell, Michael C. 1998. "Inequality Within and Among Nations." *Journal of Income Distribution* 8, No. 1, 5–44.

Lovelock, James. 1998. "A Book for All Seasons." *Science* 280, May 8, 832–3.

Ludwig, Jens, *et al.* 2001-a, forthcoming. "The Effects of Urban Poverty on Educational Outcomes, Evidence from a Randomized Experiment." *Brookings-Wharton Papers on Urban Affairs*, 2.

———. 2001-b, forthcoming. "Urban Poverty and Juvenile Crime: Evidence from a Randomized Housing-Mobility Experiment." *Quarterly Journal of Economics*.

Lum, Sherlene K. S., and Robert E. Yuskavage. 1997. "Gross Product by Industry, 1947–1996." *Survey of Current Business* 77, No. 11 (November), 30–36.

Lundberg, Mattias, and Lyn Squire. 1999. "The Simultaneous Evolution of Growth and Inequality." unpublished World Bank research paper.

Lutz, Matthias, and H. W. Singer. 1994. "The Link between Trade Openness and the Terms of Trade." *World Development* 22, No. 11 (November), 1697–1709.

Lybeck, J. A., and M. Henrekson, editors. 1988. *Explaining the Growth of Government.* New York: North-Holland Publishing.

MacKinnon, James G. 1991. "Critical Values for Cointegration Tests." In Robert. F. Engel and Clive W.J. Granger, editors. *Long-Term Economic Relationships: Readings in Cointegration, Advanced Texts in Econometrics.* New York: Oxford University Press, 267–76.

Macrae, Norman. 1984. *The 2025 Report: A Concise History of the Future, 1975–2025.* New York: Macmillan.

——— 1994. "The Next Forty Years." *Futures* (London) 26, May.

Mahoney, Richard J. 1999. "The Composition of Boards of Directors in the New World Economy: Globalization or Globaloney?" Center for the Study of American Business, *CEO Series* 36.

McCallum, John. 1996. "National Borders Matter: Canada-U.S. Regional Trade Patterns." *American Economic Review* 85, No. 4 (June), 615–23.

McConnaughey, James W., and Wendy Lader, editors. 1999. "Falling Through the Net II: New Data on the Digital Divide." http://www.ntia.doc.gov/ntiahome/net2/falling,html.

McConnell, Margaret, and Gabriel Perez Quiros. 1997. "Output Fluctuations in the United States: What Has Changed Since the Early 1980s." Federal Reserve Bank of New York, *Research Paper* No. 9735. New York.

McKenzie, Evan. 1994. *Privatopia: Homeowner Associations and the Rise of Residential Private Government.* New Haven: Yale University Press.

Makhija, Mona, and Sandra Williamson. 2000. "The Globalization of U.S. Industries." In Brewer and Boyd (2000).

Malkiel, Burton G., and Yexiao Xu. 1995. "The Structure of Stock Market Volatility." Princeton University Financial Research Center, *Memorandum* 154. Princeton, N.J., December.

Mandelbaum, Michael. 1998–99. "Is Major War Obsolete?" *Survival* 40, No. 4 (Winter), 20–38.

Mann, Charles C. 1999. "Money Hunger." *The New Republic*, August 16, 16–18.

Mannusson, Paul. 2000. "Burned by the WTO, Corporate America is Scrambling." *Business Week*, March 20, 118.

Manthy, Robert S. 1978. *Natural Resource Commodities–A Century of Statistics, Resources for the Future.* Baltimore: Johns Hopkins University Press, 1978.

Marland, C. *et al.* 1994. "Global, Regional, and National CO_2 Emission." In Boden (1994), 505–84.

Marx, Karl. 1906. *Capital*, Vol. 1. New York: Kerr (Modern Library reprint).

Mason, Andrew. 1990. "National Saving Rates and Population Growth: A New Model and New Evidence." In Gale D. Johnson and Ronald D. Lee, editors. *Population Growth and Economic Development: Issues and Evidence.* Madison: University of Wisconsin Press, 523–59.

Massey, Douglas S. 1996. "The Age of Extremes: Concentrated Affluence and Poverty in the Twenty-First Century." *Demography* 33, No. 4 (November), 395–412.

Massey, Douglas S., and Nancy A. Denton. 1993. *American Apartheid: Segregation and the Making of the Underclass.* Cambridge, Massachusetts: Harvard University Press.

Mataloni, Raymon J., Jr. 1999. "U.S. Multinational Companies: Operations in 1997." *Survey of Current Business* 79, No. 7 (July), 8–35.

Mattera, Philip. 1985. *Off the Books: The Rise of the Underground Economy.* New York: St. Martin's Press.

Mauro, Paolo. 1995. "Corruption and Growth." *Quarterly Journal of Economics* 110, No. 3 (August), 681–712.

Mayer, Martin. 2001. *The Fed.* New York: The Free Press.

Meadows, Dennis, *et al.* 1974. *Dynamics of Growth in a Finite World.* Cambridge, Massachusetts: Write-Allen Press.

Meadows, Donella H., Dennis L. Meadows, Jørgen Randers, and William W. Behrens III. 1972. *The Limits to Growth: A Report for the Club of Rome's Project on the Predicament of Mankind.* New York: Universe Books.

Meadows, Donella H., Dennis L. Meadows, and Jørgen Randers. 1992. *Beyond the Limits: Confronting Global Collapse: Envisioning a Sustainable Future.* Post Mills, Vermont: Chelsea Green Publishing Company.

Mendelsohn, Robert, and Jaime E. Newman. 1999. "Summary and Conclusions." In Mendelsohn and Newman, editors. *The Impact of Climate Change on the U.S. Economy.* New York: Cambridge U. Press.

Mesa-Lago, Carmelo. 2000. *Market, Socialist, and Mixed Economies: Comparative Policy and Performance–Chile, Cuba, and Costa Rica.* Baltimore, Maryland: Johns Hopkins University Press.

Mesarovic, Mihajlo, and Eduard Pestel. 1974. *Mankind at the Turning Point.* New York: E. P. Dutton.

Meyer, Laurence H. 1998. "Mergers and Acquisitions in Banking and Other Financial Services." Testimony Before the Committee on the Judiciary, U.S. House of Representatives June 3, 1998, http://www.federalreserve.gov/boarddocs/testimony/1998/19980603.htm.

Michaels, Patrick J., and Robert C. Balling, Jr. 2000. *The Satanic Gases: Clearing the Air about Global Warming.* Washington, D.C.: Cato Institute.

Milanovic, Branko. 1999. "True World Income Distribution, 1988 and 1993: First Calculations Based on Household Surveys Alone." World Bank, Development Research Group, unpublished *Discussion Paper.*

Millward, Robert. 2000. "State Enterprise in Britain in the Twentieth Century." In Toninelli (2000-b), Chapter 7.

Minsky, Hyman P. 1982. *Can "It" Happen Again? Essays on Instability and Finance.* Armonk, New York: M.E. Sharpe.

Miringoff, Marc, and Marque-Luisa Miringoff. 1999. *The Social Health of the Nation: How America is Really Doing.* New York: Oxford.

Mishel, Lawrence, Jared Bernstein, and John Schmitt. 1999. *The State of Working America, 1998-99.* Ithaca: Cornell University Press for Economic Policy Institute.

Mishkin, Frederic S. 1994. "Preventing Financial Crises: An International Perspective." *The Manchester School, Supplement, Papers in Money, Macroeconomics and Finance,* 1–40.

Moody's Investors Service. 1992. *Moody's Municipal and Government Manual.* New York.

Morrison, Catherine J., and Ernst R. Berndt. 1991. "Assessing the Productivity of Information Technology Equipment in U.S. Manufacturing Industries." National Bureau of Economic Research, *NBER Working Paper* 3582. Cambridge, Massachusetts.

———. 1992. "High-Tech Capital Formation, and Labor Composition in U.S. Manufacturing Industries: An Exploratory Analysis." National Bureau of Economic Research, *NBER Working Paper* 4010. Cambridge, Massachusetts.

Mueller, Dennis. 1986. *The Modern Corporation: Profits, Power, Growth, and Performance.* Lincoln: University of Nebraska Press.

Mueller, Eva. 1963. "Public Attitudes toward Fiscal Programs." *Quarterly Journal of Economics* 77, No. 2 (May), 210–35.

Myers, David G. 2000. *The American Paradox: Spiritual Hunger in an Age of Plenty.* New Haven: Yale University Press.

National Research Council. 1986. *Soil Conservation: Assessing the National Resources Inventory.* Washington, D.C.: National Academy Press.

Neftel, A. *et al.* 1994. "Historical CO_2 Record from the Siple Station Ice Corp." In Boden (1994), 11–14.

Negroponte, Nicholas. 1995. *Being Digital.* New York : Knopf.

Nelson, Richard R. 1988. "Institutions Supporting Technical Change in the United States." In Dosi, *et al.* (1988), 312–29.

Nickell, Stephen. 1997. "Unemployment, and Labor Market Rigidities: Europe versus North America." *Journal of Economic Perspectives*, 11, No. 3 (Summer), 55–75.

Nicoletti, Giuseppe, and Frederic L. Pryor. 2002 forthcoming. "Subjective and Objective Measures of the Extent of Governmental Regulation: A Note."

Nicoletti, Giuseppe, Stefano Scarpetta, and Olivier Boylaud. 2000. "Summary Indicators of Product Market Regulation with an Extension to Employment Protection Legislation." OECD Economics Department, *Working Papers* 237. Paris: OECD.

Nie, Nortman H., and Lutz Erbring. 2000. *Internet and Society: A Preliminary Report.* Stanford Institute for the Quantitative Study of Society, www.stanford.edu/group/siqss.

Nordhaus, William D. 2001. "Productivity Growth and the New Economy." National Bureau of Economic Research, *NBER Working Paper* 8096. Cambridge, Massachusetts.

Nordhaus, William D., and Joseph Boyer. 2000. *Warming the World: Economic Models of Global Warming.* Cambridge, Massachusetts: MIT Press.

Nordic Social Statistical Committee (NOSOSCO). 1996. *Social Security in the Nordic Countries: Scope, Expenditure and Financing 1994.* Copenhagen.

Norton, Bryon. 1998. "Commodity, Amenity, and Morality: The Limits of Quantification in Valuing Biodiversity." In Wilson and Peter (1988), 200–5.

Nye, Joseph S., Jr., Philip D. Zelikow, and David C. King. 1997. *Why People Don't Trust Government.* Cambridge, Massachusetts: Harvard University Press.

O'Brien, Timothy. 2000. "That's Laird to You, Mister." *New York Times*, February 27, p. 2, Section 4.

Obstfeld, Maurice. 1988. "The Global Capital Market: Benefactor or Menace?" *Journal of Economic Perspectives* 12, No. 4 (Fall), 9–31.

Ohmae, Ken'ichi. 1995. *The End of the Nation State: The Rise of Regional Economies.* New York: Free Press.

Oliner, Stephen, and Daniel E. Sichel. 2000. "The Resurgence of Growth in the Late 1990s" Is Information Technology the Story." *Journal of Economic Perspectives* 14, No. 4 (Fall), 3–23.

Olson, Mancur. 1982. *The Rise and Decline of Nations: Economic Growth, Stagflation, and Social Rigidities.* New Haven, Connecticut: Yale University Press.

Olson, Walter K. 1997. *The Excuse Factor: How Employment Law is Paralyzing the American Workplace.* New York: Free Press.

Orfield, Gary, and John T. Yun. 1999. "Resegregation in American Schools." Harvard University, Civil Rights Project, http://www.law.harvard.edu/groups/civilrights/publications/ .

Organization of Economic Cooperation and Development (OECD). 1965. *Manpower Statistics 1954–1964.* Paris.

———. 1984. *Tax-expenditures: A Review of the Issues and Country Practices.* Paris.

———. 1996-a. *Globalisation of Industry: Overview and Sector Reports.* Paris.

———. 1996-b. *Tax-expenditures: Recent Experiences.* Paris.

———. 1997-a. *Employment Outlook.* Paris. July 1997.

———. 1997-b. *Labour Force Statistics, 1976–1996.* Paris.

———. 1997-c. *La mesure de l'emploi public dans les pays de l'OCDE: Sources, méthodes et résultats.* Paris.

———. 1997-d. *OECD Report on Regulatory Reform*, Vol. I: *Sectoral Studies.* Paris.

———. 1998-a. "Indicators of Regulatory Capacities in OECD Countries: Preliminary Analysis." *OECD Working Papers* 6, No. 44. Paris.

———. 1998-b. *OECD National Accounts*, Vols. 1 and 2. Paris.

———. 1999-a. *The Economic and Social Impact of Electronic Commerce: Preliminary Findings and Research Agenda.* Paris.

———. 1999-b. *National Accounts, Main Aggregates, 1960–1997*, Vol. 1. Paris. 1999.

———. 1999-c. *OECD Environmental Data: Compendium* 1999. Paris.

O'Rourke, Kevin, and Jeffrey Williamson. 1999. *Globalization and History: The Evolution of a Nineteenth-Century Atlantic Economy.* Cambridge, Massachusetts: MIT Press.

Orren, Gary. 1997. "Fall from Grace: The Public's Loss of Faith in Government." In Nye, Zelikow, and King (1997), 77–107.

Ostrower, Francie. 1995. *Why the Wealthy Give: The Culture of Elite Philanthropy.* Princeton: Princeton University Press.

Paglin, Martin. 1994. "The Underground Economy: New Estimates from the Household Income and Expenditure Survey." *Yale Law Journal* 103, No. 8 (June), 2239–59.

Palan, Ronen. 1998. "The Emergence of an Offshore Economy." *Futures* (Guild, England) 30, No. 1, 63–73.

Paldam, Martin. 1994. *Grønlands økonomiske udvikling.* Aarhus, Denmark: Aarhus Universitets forlag.

———. 1997. "Dutch Disease and Rent Seeking: the Greenland Model." *European Journal of Political Economy* 13, No. 3 (September), 591–614.

Park, Donghyun. 1999. "Intercountry Income Inequality: An Expansion and an Update." *Comparative Economic Studies* 41, No. 4 (Winter), 103–9.

Park, Thae S. 1998. "Comparison of BEA Estimates of Personal Income and IRS Estimates of Adjusted Gross Income." *Survey of Current Business* 78, No. 11 (November), 13–19.

Parker, Jonathan A. 1999. "Spendthrift in America? On Two Decades of Decline in the U.S. Saving Rate." National Bureau of Economic Research, *NBER Working Paper* 7238. Cambridge, Massachusetts.

Paxson, Christina. 1996. "Saving and Growth: Evidence from Micro Data." *European Economic Review* 40 (February), 255–88.

Peacock, Alan T., and Jack Wiseman. 1961. *The Growth of Public Expenditures in the United Kingdom.* Princeton: Princeton University Press for National Bureau of Economic Research.

Pear, Robert. 2000. "Online Sales Spur Illegal Importing of Medicine to U.S.: Seizures of Drugs Soar." *New York Times*, January 10, p. 1.

Peel, Michael. 2000. "Tax Havens' Promise May End Dispute with OECD." *Financial Times*, August 5–6.

Perkins, John A. 1997. "The Changing Foundations of International Law: From State Consent to State Responsibility." *Boston University International Law Journal* 15, No. 2 (Fall), 434–509.

Pew Research Center for the People and the Press. 1998. *Deconstructing Distrust: How Americans View Government.* Washington, D.C.

———. 1999. *Americans Look to the 21st Century: Optimism Reigns, Technology Plays Key Role.* http://www.people-press.org/mill2que.htm.

Pfaller, Alfred, Ian Gough, and Göran Therborn, editors. 1991. *Can the Welfare State Compete? A Comparative Study of Five Advanced Capitalist Countries.* London: Macmillan.

Pithart, Petr. 1996. "Rival Visions, Václav Havel and Václav Klaus." *Journal of Democracy* 7, No. 1 (January), 12–23.

Platteau, Jean-Philippe. 1994-a. "Behind the Market Stage Where Real Societies Exist: Part I, The Role of Public and Private Order Institutions." *Journal of Development Studies* 30, No. 3 (April), 533–77.

———. 1994-b. "Behind the Market Stage Where Real Societies Exist: Part II, The Role of Moral Norms." *Journal of Development Studies* 30, No. 4 (July), 753–817.

Polanyi, Karl. 1944. *The Great Transformation.* New York: Farrar and Rinehart.

Polivka, Anne E. 1998. "A Profile of Contingent Workers." *Monthly Labor Review* 119, No. 10 (October), 10–25.

Popenoe, David. 1996. *Life Without Father: Compelling New Evidence that Fatherhood and Marriage are Indispensable for the Good of Children and Society.* New York: Martin Kessler Books.

Popenoe, David, and Barbara Dafoe Whitehead. 1999. *The State of Our Union: The Social Health of Marriage in America*. *National Marriage Project*, Rutgers University. http://marriage.rutgers.edu/cpubstat.htm.23.

Porter, Richard D., and Amanda S. Bayer. 1989. "Monetary Perspective on Underground Economic Activity in the United States." In Feige (1989-b),129–57.

Poterba, James M. 1996. "Demographic Structure and the Political Economy of Public Education." National Bureau of Economic Research, *NBER Working Paper* 5677. Cambridge, Massachusetts.

Prigogine, Ilya. 1997. *The End of Certainty: Time, Chaos, and the New Laws of Nature*. New York: Free Press.

Pritchett, Lant. 1997. "Divergence, Big Time." *Journal of Economic Perspectives* 11, No. 3 (Summer), 3–17

Pryor, Frederic L. 1968. *Public Expenditures in Communist and Capitalist Nations*. Homewood, Illinois: Irwin.

———. 1972. "An International Comparison of Concentration Ratios." *Review of Economics and Statistics* 54, No. 2 (May), 130–40.

———. 1973. *Property and Industrial Organization in Communist and Capitalist Nations*. Bloomington, Indiana: Indiana University Press.

———. 1977. "Some Costs of Markets: An Empirical Study." *Quarterly Journal of Economic*, 91, No. 1 (February 1977), 81–102

———. 1983. "Some Economics of Sloth." *The Social Science Review* 5, No. 1 (Fall), 82–192.

———. 1994-a. "Growth Deceleration and Transaction Costs." *Journal of Economic Behavior and Organization*, 25, No. 3 (1994), 121–33.

———. 1994-b. "The Evolution of Competition in U.S. Manufacturing." *Review of Industrial Organization* 9, No. 6 (December), 695–714.

———. 1995-a. "Behavior of Retail Prices: A Note on Market Integration in the U.S." *Eastern Economic Journal* 21, No. 1 (Winter), 83–97.

———. 1996. *Economic Evolution and Structure: The Impact of Complexity on the U.S. Economic System*. New York: Cambridge University Press.

———. 1999. "The Impact of Foreign Trade on the Employment of Unskilled U.S. Workers: Some New Evidence." *Southern Economic Journal*, 65, No. 3 (January), 472–93.

———. 2000-a. "Internationalization and Globalization of the American Economy." In Brewer and Boyd (2000), 1–40.

———. 2000-b. "The Millennium Survey: How Economists View the U.S. Economy in the 21st Century." *American Journal of Economics and Sociology* 59, No. 1 (January), 3–33.

———. 2001-a. A Note on the Dimensions of the World-Wide Merger Wave." *Journal of Social Issues*, forthcoming.

———. 2001-b, forthcoming. "U.S. Demographic Change and Economic Growth in the First Half of the 20th Century."

———. 2001-c, forthcoming. "Quantitative Notes on the Extent of Governmental Regulation in Various OECD Nations," *International Journal of Industrial Organization*.

———. 2001-d. "New Trends in U.S. Industrial Concentration." *Review of Industrial Organization*. 18, 301–326.

———. 2001-e. "Will Most of Us Be Working for Giant Enterprises by 2028?" *Journal of Economic Behavior and Organization* 44, No. 4 (April), 363–382.

Pryor, Frederic L., and David Schaffer. 2000. *Who's Not Working and Why*, 2nd printing. New York: Cambridge University Press.

Pryor, Frederic L., and Elliott Sulcove. 1995. "A Note on Volatility." *Journal of Post Keynesian Economics* 17, No. 4 (Summer), 525–545.

Putnam, Robert. 2000. *Bowling Alone: The Collapse and Revival of American Community*. New York: Simon & Schuster.

Quandt, Richard E. 1966. "On the Size Distribution of Firms." *American Economic Review* 56, No. 3 (June), 416–33.

Quinn, Joseph F. "Retirement Patterns and Bridge Jobs in the 1990s." Employment Benefit Research Institute *Issue Brief*. Washington, D.C.: February, 1999.

Raphael, Steven, and Rudolf Winter-Ebmer. 1999. "Identifying the Effect of Unemployment on Crime." University of California at San Diego, Center for Economic Policy Research *Discussion Paper* 2129.

Raspail, Jean. 1975. *The Camp of the Saints*, translated by Norman Shapiro. New York: Charles Scribner's Sons.

Republic of China. 1996. *Statistical Yearbook of the Republic of China, 1996*. Taipei.

Reynolds, Paul D., Michael Hay, and S. Michael Camp. 1999. *Global Entrepreneurship Monitor: 1999 Executive Report*. Babson Park, Massachusetts: Babson College, Kauffman Center for Entrepreneurial Leadership.

Reynolds, Paul D., et al. 2000. *Global Entrepreneurship Monitor: 1999 Research Report*. Babson Park, Massachusetts: Babson College, Kauffman Center for Entrepreneurial Leadership.

Rhoades, Stephen A. 1996. "Competition and Bank Mergers: Directions for Analysis from Available Evidence." *Bulletin* 41, No. 2 (Summer), 339–365.

———. 1997. "Research on IO Topics in Banking: An Introduction and Overview." *Review of Industrial Organization* 12, No. 1 (February), 1–8.

Rhodes, Martin. 1998. "'Subversive Liberalism': Market Integration, Globalization and West European Welfare States." In Coleman and Underhill (1998), 99–121.

Riesman, David. 1950. *The Lonely Crowd: A Study of the Changing American Character*. New Haven: Yale University Press.

Rifkin, Jeremy. 2000. *The Age of Access: The New Culture of Hypercapitalism, Where All of Life is a Paid-for Experience*. New York: Putnam.

Robinson, John P. 1994. "The Over-Estimated Workweek? What Time Diary Measures Suggest." *Monthly Labor Review* 117, No. 8 (August), 11–23.

Robinson, John P., and Geoffrey Godbey. 1997. *Time for Life: The Surprising Ways Americans Use Their Time*. University Park, Pennsylvania: The Pennsylvania State University Press.

Rodrik, Dani. 1997. *Has Globalization Gone Too Far?* Washington: Institute for International Economics.

———. 1998. "Where Did All the Growth Go? External Shocks, Social Conflict and Growth Collapses." National Bureau of Economic Research, *NBER Working Paper* 6350. Cambridge, Massachusetts.

———. 2000. "How Far Will International Economic Integration Go?" *Journal of Economic Perspectives*, 14, No. 1 (Winter), 177–87.

Röller, Lars-Hendrik, and Christian Wey, editors. "Einleitung–die Makrotrends in der New Economy, " in Röller and Wey, editors. *Die soziale Marktwirtschaft in der New Economy: Jahrbuch 2001 des Wissenschaftszentrum Berlin*. Berlin: WZB.

Romer, Christine D. 1999. "Changes in the Business Cycle: Evidence and Explanations." *Journal of Economic Perspectives* 13, No. 2 (Spring), 23–45.

Roncaglia, Alessandro. 1988. "William Petty and the Conceptual Framework for the Analysis of Economic Development." In Kenneth J. Arrow, editor. *The Balance between Industry and Agriculture in Economic Development*. Vol. 1. Basic Issues. New York: St. Martin's Press: 157–74.

Rosen, Kenneth T., and Amanda L. Howard. 2000. "E-Retail: Gold Rush or Fool's Gold?" *California Management Review* 42, No. 1 (Spring), 72–100.

Rosenfeld, Richard. "Patterns in Adult Homicide: 1980–1995." In Blumstein and Wallman (2000), 130–164.

Ryscavage, Paul, Gordon Green, Edward Welniak, and John Coder. 1995. "Studies in the Distribution of Income." U.S. Department of Commerce, Bureau of the Census. *Current Population Reports* P60–183. Washington, D.C.: G.P.O.

Sachs, Jeffrey, and Xavier Sala-i-Martín. 1992. "Fiscal Federalism and Optimum Currency Areas, Evidence for Europe from the United States." In Matthew B. Canzoneri, Vittorio Grilli, and Paul R. Masson, editors. *Establishing a Central Bank: Issues in Europe and Lessons from the U.S.*. New York: Cambridge University Press, 195–219.

Sadowski, Yahya.1998. *The Myth of Global Chaos.* Washington, D.C.: Brookings Institution.

Salamon, Lester M., and Helmut K. Anheier. 1996. *The Emerging Nonprofit Sector: An Overview.* New York: Manchester University Press.

Samuelson, Robert J. 1995. *The Good Life and its Discontents: The American Dream in the Age of Entitlement.* New York: Random House (Times Books).

Sassen, Saskia. 1996. *Losing Control? Sovereignty in an Age of Globalization.* New York: Columbia U. Press.

Scherer, F. M. 1965. "Firm Size, Market Structure, Opportunity, and the Output of Patented Inventions." *American Economic Review* 53, No. 5 (December), 1097–1125.

———. 1976. "Industrial Structure, Scale Economies, and Worker Alienation." In Robert T. Masson and P. David Qualls, editors. *Essays on Industrial Organization, in Honor of Joe S. Bain.* Cambridge, Massachusetts: Ballinger Publishing Co., 105–20.

———. 1991. "Changing Perspectives on the Firm Size Problem." In Acs and Audretch (1991), 24–38.

Scherer, F. M., and David J. Ravenscraft. 1987. *Mergers, Sell-offs, and Economic Efficiency.* Washington, D.C.: Brookings.

Schieber, Sylvester J., and John B. Shoven. 1997. "The Consequences of Population Aging for Private Pension Fund Saving and Asset Markets." In Hurd and Yashiro (1997), 111–30.

Schiff, Maurice. 2000. "Labor Market Integration and Social Capital Disintegration." World Bank, unpublished paper.

Schiller, Nina Glick. 1999. "Transmigrants and Nation States: Something Old and Something New in the U.S. Immigrant Experience." In Hirschman *et al.* (1999), 94–119.

Schmidt, Christoph M., and Klaus F. Zimmermann. 1991. "Work Characteristics, Firm Size, and Wages." *Review of Economics and Statistics* 73, No. 4 (November), 705–10.

Schnaars, Steven P. 1989. *Megamistakes: Forecasting and the Myth of Rapid Technological Change.* New York: Free Press.

Scholes, Myron S. 1998. "Derivatives in a Dynamic Environment." In Tore Frängsmyr, editor. *Les Prix Nobel.* Stockholm: Norstedts Tryckeri, 468–502.

Schor, Juliet B. 1991. *The Overworked American: The Unexpected Decline of Leisure.* New York: Basic Books.

Schumpeter, Joseph A. 1950. *Capitalism, Socialism, and Democracy,* 3d edition. New York: Harper.

Schwert, G. William. 1989. "Why Does Stock Market Volatility Change Over Time?" *Journal of Finance* 44, No. 5 (December), 1115–1153.

Scott, Alan, editor. 1997. *The Limits of Globalization: Cases and Arguments.* New York: Routledge.

Segal, Lewis M., and Daniel G. Sullivan. 1997. "The Growth of Temporary Services." *Journal of Economic Perspectives* 11, No. 2 (Spring), 117–36.

Sematech. 1999. "Worldwide Chipmakers and Equipment Supplier Executives Meet to Discuss Industry Issues." www.sematech.org/public/news/releases/wcesemdi.htm.

Sennett, Richard. 1998. *The Corrosion of Character: The Personal Consequences of Work in the New Capitalism.* New York: W. W. Norton.

Shepard, Jon M., and James G. Hougland, Jr. 1982. "Organizational Size and Worker Satisfaction." In Bock, *et al.* (1984), 59–79.

Shepherd, William G. 1982. "Causes of Increased Competition in the U.S. Economy, 1939–1980." *Review of Economics and Statistics* 64, No. 4 (November), 613–26.

Siebert, Horst. 1999. "Commentary: Economic Consequences of Income Inequality." In Federal Reserve Bank of Kansas City (1999), 265–83.

Simon, Herbert. 1997. "Designing Organizations for an Information-Rich World." In Donald M. Lamberton, editor. *The Economics of Communication and Information. Cheltenham,* U.K.: Elgar.

Simon, Julian L. 1996. *The Ultimate Resource 2.* Princeton: Princeton U. Press.

Singer, S. Fred. 1997. *Hot Talk, Cold Science: Global Warming's Unfinished Debate.* Oakland, Calif. : The Independent Institute.

Sivard, Ruth Leger. 1996. *World Military and Social Expenditures, 1996.* Washington: World Priorities.

Slaughter, Matthew J., and Phillip Swagel. 1997. "The Effects of Globalization on Wages in the Advanced Economies." In International Monetary Fund, Research Department. *Staff Studies for the World Economic Outlook.* Washington, D.C.: 78–93.

Smeeding, Timothy M. 1998. "U.S. Income Inequality in a Cross-National Perspective: Why Are We So Different." In Auerbach and Belous (1998), 194–217.

Smith, James P. 1997. "Wealth Inequality Among Older Americans." *Journal of Gerontology* 52, Series B (Special Issue), (May), 74–81.

Smith, Michael D., Joseph Bailey, and Erik Brynjolfsson. 2000. "Understanding Digital Markets: Review and Assessment." In Brynjolfsson and Kahin (2000), 99–107.

Sobol, Dorothy Meadow. 1998. "Foreign Ownership of US Treasury Securities: What the Data Show and Do Not Show." Federal Reserve Bank of New York. *Current Issues in Economics and Finance* 4, No. 3 (May), 1–6.

Social Security Administration. 2000. *Social Security Bulletin, Annual Statistical Supplement.* Washington, D.C.: G.P.O.

Sorkin, Andrew Ross, and Melody Petersen. 2000. "Glaxo and SmithKline Agree to Form Largest Drugmaker." *New York Times,* January 17, p. 1.

Soskice, David. 1999. "Divergent Production Regimes: Coordinated and Uncoordinated Market Economies in the 1980s and 1990s." In Kitschelt (1999), 101–34.

Spellman, William. 2000. "The Limited Importance of Prison Expansion." In Blumstein and Wallman (2000), 97–130.

Spencer, R. W., and J. R. Christy. 1994. "Global and Hemispheric Tropospheric and Stratospheric Temperature Anomalies from Satellite Records." In Boden (1994), 615–29.

Stevens, William K. 1999. "Lessons from Ancient Heat Surge." *New York Times,* November 23, p. F3.

Stock, James H., and Mark W. Watson. 1993. "A Simple Estimator of Cointegrating Vectors in Higher Order Integrated Systems." *Econometrica* 61., No. 4 (July), 783–820.

Stockman, David A. 1986. *The Triumph of Politics–How the Reagan Revolution Failed.* New York: Harper and Row.

Storey, D. J. 1994. *Understanding the Small Business Sector.* New York: Routledge.

Strong, Maurice. 2001. *Where on Earth Are We Going?* New York: Knopf.

Summers. Lawrence H. "Distinguished Lecture on Economics in Government: Reflections on Managing Global Integration." *Journal of Economic Perspectives* 13; No. 2 (Spring), 3–19.

Summers, Robert, and Alan Heston. 1988. "A New Set of International Comparisons of Real Product and Price Levels: Estimates for 130 Countries." *Review of Income and Wealth* 34, No. 1 (March), 1–25.

Sunstein, Cass. 2001. *Republic.com.* Princeton, New Jersey: Princeton University Press.

Surrey, Stanley. 1969. "Remarks." *Annual Report of the Secretary of the Treasury for the Fiscal Year Ended June 30, 1968.* Washington, D.C.: GPO, 322–40.

Surrey, Stanley S., and Paul R. McDaniel. 1985. *Tax Expenditures.* Cambridge, Massachusetts: Harvard University Press.

Sutton, John. 1997. "Gibrat's Legacy." *Journal of Economic Literature* 35, No. 1 (March), 40–59.

———. 1998. *Technology and Market Structure: Theory and History.* Cambridge: MIT Press.

Sykes, Alan O. 1995. *Product Standards for Internationally Integrated Goods Markets.* Washington, D.C.: Brookings.

Tanzi, Vito. 1998. "Corruption Around the World: Causes, Consequences, Scope, and Cures." International Monetary Fund, *Staff Papers* 45, No. 4 (December), 559–95.

Tashakori, Ahmad, James H. Barnes, Jr., and George E. Lyne. 1988."The Future of U.S. Free Enterprise: A Delphi Study." *Futures Research Quarterly* 4, No. 1 (Spring), 29–43.

Technical Review Panel on the Medicare Trustees Report. 2000. *Review of the Medicare Trustees' Financial Projections,* www.hcfa.gov/pubforms/actuary/TechnicalPanel/default.htm.

Thurow, Lester C. 1992. *Head to Head: The Coming Economic Battle among Japan, Europe, and America.* New York: Morrow.

Tierney, John. 1990. "Betting the Planet." *New York Times Magazine,* December 2, 52 ff.

Tilgher, Adriano. 1931. *Work: What It has Meant to Men Through the Ages,* translated. by Dorothy C. Fisher. New York: Harcourt, Brace, and Company.

Tobin, James, and Dan Sommers. 2000. "Explanation of Revised Estimates of Tobin's 'q' Ratio, 1950–1997." unpublished paper.

Tocqueville, Alexis de. 1969 (1835). *Democracy in America,* edited by J. P. Mayer. New York : Harper and Row (Anchor Books).

Toninelli, Pier Angelo. 2000-a. "The Rise and Fall of Public Enterprise: The Framework." Chapter 1 in Toninelli (2000-b)

Toninelli, Pier Angelo, editor. 2000-b. *The Rise and Fall of State-Owned Enterprise in the Western World.* New York: Cambridge University Press.

Turow, Joseph. 1997. *Breaking Up America: Advertisers and the New Media World.* Chicago: University of Chicago Press.

Union of International Organizations. 1998. *Yearbook of International Organizations, 1998/99.* 35th edition. Munich: Ö K. G. Saur.

United Nations. Annual. *Demographic Yearbook.* New York.

———.1995. *World Population Prospects, the 1994 Revision.* New York.

United Nations Development Programme (UNDP). 1999. *Human Development Report 1999.* New York: Oxford.

U.S. Commission on National Security/21st Century. 1999. *New World Coming: American Security in the 21st Century, Supporting Research and Analysis.* Washington, D.C.

U.S. Congress, Congressional Budget Office. 1998. *Long-Term Budgetary Pressures and Policy Options.* CBO website. www.cbo.gov/

U.S. Congress, Committee on the Budget of the House of Representative. 1996. *The Economic and Budget Outlook: Fiscal Years 1996-2006.* Washington, D.C.: G.P.O.

U.S. Council of Economic Advisers. Annual. *Economic Report of the President.* Washington, D.C.: G.P.O.

U.S. Council on Environmental Quality (CEQ).1997. *25th Anniversary Report.* Washington, D.C.: G.P.O.

———. 1998. *Along the American River: The 1996 Report of the Council on Environmental Quality.* Washington, D.C.: G.P.O.

U.S. Department of Agriculture. Annual. *Agricultural Statistics.* Washington, D.C.: G.P.O.

U.S. Department of Commerce. 1999. *The Emerging Digital Economy II.* June. http://www.ecommerce.gov/ede/.

U.S. Department of Commerce, Bureau of Economic Analysis. Biennial. *Business Statistics.* Washington, D.C. G.P.O.

———. 1997. *U.S. National Income and Product Accounts.* diskette BE-54 (September).

———. 1998-a. *Benchmark Input-Output Accounts of the United States, 1992.* Washington, D.C.: G.P.O.

———. 1998-b. *National Income and Product Accounts of the United States, 1929–94.* Washington, D.C.: G.P.O.

U.S. Department of Commerce, Census Bureau. Annual. *Statistical Abstract of the United States.* Washington, D.C.: G.P.O.

———. Various years. *County Business Patterns.* Washington, D.C.: G.P.O.

———. Various years. *Enterprise Statistics.* Washington, D.C.: G.P.O.

———. 1949. *Historical Statistics of the United States, 1979–1945.* Washington, D.C.: G.P.O.

———. 1964. *1960 Census of Population,* Vol. 1. Washington, D.C.: G.P.O.

———. 1965. *Historical Statistics of the United States, Continuation to 1962 and Revisions.* Washington, D.C.: G.P.O.

———. 1975. *Historical Statistics of the United States: Colonial Times to 1970.* Washington, D.C.: G.P.O.

———. 1987. *Fixed Reproducible Tangible Wealth in the United States, 1925–85.* Washington, D.C.: G.P.O.

———. 1993-a. *1990 Census of Population,* Vol. CP-3-1. *The Foreign-Born Population in the United States.* Washington, D.C.: G.P.O.

———. 1993-b. *1990 Census of the Population,* Vol. CP-2-1, *Social and Economic Characteristics: United States.* Washington, D.C.·G.P.O.

———. 1996. "Population Projections of the United States by Age, Sex, Race, and Hispanic Origin, 1995–2050." *Current Population Reports* P25-1130. Washington, D.C.: G.P.O.

———. 1999. Poverty in the United States. *Current Population Reports* P60–207. Washington, D.C.:G.P.O.

U.S. Department of Commerce, Office of Business Economics. Biennial. *Business Statistics.* Washington, D.C.: G.P.O.

———. 1979. *The Detailed Input-Output Structure of the U.S. Economy: 1972,* Vol. 1. *The Use and Make of Commodities by Industries.* Washington, D.C.: G.P.O.

U.S. Department of Education, National Center for Education Statistics. 1999. *Digest of Education Statistics 1998.* Washington, D.C.: G.P.O.

U.S. Department of Justice. Annual. *Criminal Victimization in the United States.* Washington: G.P.O.

———. 1994. *Criminal Victimization in the United States, 1973-92 Trends.* Washington, D.C.: G.P.O.

U.S. Department of Justice. Bureau of Justice Statistics. 1998. *Sourcebook of Criminal Justice Statistics–1997.* Washington D.C.: G.P.O.

U.S. Department of Justice, Immigration and Naturalization Service. *1996. Statistical Yearbook* Washington, D.C.: G.P.O.

U.S. Department of Labor, Bureau of Labor Statistics. 1983. "Handbook of Labor Statistics," *Bulletin* 2175. Washington, D.C.: G.P.O.

———. 1995. "Consumer Expenditures Survey, 1992-93." *Bulletin* 2462. Washington, D.C.: G.P.O.

———. 1996. "Productivity Measures for Selected Industries and Government Services." *Bulletin* 2480. Washington, D.C.: G.P.O.

———. Monthly. *Employment and Earnings.* Washington, D.C.: G.P.O.

U.S. Geological Survey. 1995. *Yearbook 1994.* Washington, D.C.: G.P.O.

U.S. Social Security Administration. 1999. *1999 OASDI Trustee Report.* www.ssa.gov/OACT. (publications).

Varian, Hal. 2000. "Economic Scene." *New York Times*, August 24.

Venti, Steven F., and David A. Wise. 1996. "The Wealth of Cohorts: Retirement Saving and the Changing Assets of Older Americans." National Bureau of Economic Research, *NBER Working Paper* 5609. Cambridge, Massachusetts.

Verba, Sidney, Kay Lehman Schlozman, and Henry E. Brady. 1995. *Voice and Equality: Civic Volunteerism in American Politics*. Cambridge, Massachusetts: Harvard University Press.

———. 1997. "The Big Tilt: Participatory Inequality in America." *The American Prospect*, No. 32 (May-June), 74–81.

Viscusi, W. Kip, John M. Vernon, and Joseph E. Harrington, Jr. 1995. *Economics of Regulation and Antitrust*, Second edition. Cambridge, Massachusetts: MIT Press.

Vogel, David. 1982. "A Case Study of Clean Air Legislation 1967–1981." In Bock *et al.* (1984), 309–87.

Wade, Richard. 2001. "Winners and Losers." *The Economist*, April 28, 72–74.

Wallensteen, Peter, and Margareta Sollenberg. 1999. "Armed Conflict, 1989–98." *Journal of Peace Research* 36, No. 5 (September), 593–606. G.P.O.

Wallerstein, Immanuel. 1999. *The End of the World as We Know It*. Minneapolis: University of Minnesota Press.

Wallerstein, Judith S., *et al.* 2000. *The Unexpected Legacy of Divorce*. New York: Hyperion.

Walter, Dave, editor. 1992. *Today Then: America's Best Minds Look 100 Years Into the Future on the Occasion of the 1893 World's Columbian Exposition*. Helena, Montana: American & World Geographic Publishers.

Warren, Melinda. 2000. "Federal Regulatory Spending Reaches a New Height: An Analysis of the Budget of the U.S. Government for the Year 2001." Center for the Study of American Business, *Regulatory Budget Report* 23, http://csab.wustl.edu/home.asp.

Wattenberg, Ben. 1991. *The First Universal Nation: Leading Indicators and Ideas about the Surge of America in the 1990s*. New York: Free Press.

Weber, Max. 1958 (1904). *The Protestant Ethic and the Spirit of Capitalism*, translated by Talcott Parsons. New York: Scribners.

Wei, Shang-Jin. 1996. "Intranational Versus International Trade: How Stubborn Are Nations in Global Integration." National Bureau of Economic Research, *NBER Working Paper* 5531. Cambridge, Massachusetts.

Whalen, Gary W. 1996. "Nonlocal Concentration, Multimarket Linkages, and Interstate Banking." *Antitrust Bulletin* 41, No. 2 (Summer), 365–99.

White, Michael J. 1987. *American Neighborhoods and Residential Differentiation*. New York: Russell Sage Foundation.

Williamson, Jeffrey G. 1995. "Globalization, Convergence, and History." National Bureau of Economic Research, *NBER Working Paper* 5259. Cambridge, Massachusetts.

———. 1996. "Globalization and Inequality Then and Now: The Late 19th and Late 20th Centuries Compared." National Bureau of Economic Research, *NBER Working Paper* 5491. Cambridge, Massachusetts.

———. 1998. "Globalization, Labor Markets and Policy Backlash in the Past." *Journal of Economic Perspectives* 12, No. 4 (Fall), 61–73.

Wilson, Edward O. 1988. "The Current State of Biological Diversity." In Wilson and Peter (1988), 3–18.

Wilson, Edward O., and Frances M. Peter, editors. 1988. *Biodiversity*. Washington, D.C.: National Academy Press.

Wilson, James Q. 1975. *Thinking About Crime*. New York: Vintage Books.

Wise, David A., editor. 1998. *Frontiers in the Economics of Aging*. Chicago: University of Chicago Press for National Bureau of Economic Research.

Wise, George. 1976. "The Accuracy of Technological forecasts: 1890–1940." *Futures* (Guilford, England) 8, No. 5 (October), 410–29.

Wojcik, Daniel. 1997. *The End of the World As We Know It: Faith, Fatalism, and Apocalypse in America*. New York: New York University Press.

Wolfe, Alan. 1998. *One Nation, After All: What Middle-Class Americans Really Think About*. New York: Viking.

Wolff, Edward N. 1995. *Top Heavy: A Study of the Increasing Inequality of Wealth in America*. New York: 20th Century Fund.

———. 1996. "International Comparisons of Wealth Inequality." *Review of Income and Wealth* 42, No. 4 (December), 433–51.

———. 1998. "Recent Trends in the Size Distribution of Household Wealth." *Journal of Economic Perspectives* 12, No. 3 (Summer), 131–50.

———. 1999-a."The Economy and Philanthropy." In Charles T. Clotfelter and Thomas Ehrlich, editors. *Philanthropy and the Nonprofit Sector in a Changing America*. Bloomington: Indiana University Press: 73–99.

———. 1999-b. "Recent Trends in Wealth Ownership, 1983–1998." Levy Institute *Working Paper* 300, http://www.levy.org/docs/wrkpap/papers/300.html.

Wolfson, Martin H. 1986. *Financial Crises: Understanding the Postwar U.S. Experience*. Armonk, New York: M.E. Sharpe.

———. 1990. "The Causes of Financial Instability." *Journal of Post Keynesian Economics* 12, No. 3 (Spring), 333–55.

Womack, James P., and Daniel T. Jones. 1996. *Lean Thinking: Banish Waste and Create Wealth in Your Corporation*. New York: Simon and Schuster.

Wood, Adrian. 1994. *North-South Trade, Employment and Inequality*. Oxford: Clarendon Press.

World Bank. 1995. *Bureaucrats in Business: The Economics and Politics of Government Ownership*. New York: Oxford University Press.

———. 2000. *2000 World Development Indicators*, CD-Rom. Washington, D.C.: World Bank.

World Economic Forum (WEF). 1999. *The Global Competitiveness Report*. Geneva.

Yankelovich, Daniel. 1994. "How Changes in the Economy are Reshaping American Values." In Henry J. Aaron, *et al. Values and Public Policy*. Washington, D.C.: Brookings, 16–54.

Zarnowitz, Victor. 1999. "Theory and History Behind Business Cycles: Are the 1990s the Onset of a Golden Age?" *Journal of Economic Perspectives* 13, No. 2 (Spring), 89–91.

Zeile, William J. 1997. "U.S. Intrafirm Trade in Goods." *Survey of Current Business* 77, No. 2 (February), 23–38.

———. 1999. "Foreign Direct Investment in the United States." *Survey of Current Business* 79, No. 8 (August), 21–53.

Zevin, Robert. 1992. "Are World Financial Markets More Open? If so, Why and with What Effect?" In Banuri and Schor (1992), 43–85.

Name Index*

Abate, James, 285
Abowd, John M., 87, 88, 401
Abramson, Alan J., 97, 103, 401
Acs, Zoltan J., 239, 241–2, 401, 406, 425
Adamic, Lada A., 278, 286, 401
Adams, Henry Carter, 401
Aghion, Philippe, X-4.3 , 401
Albert, Michael, 14, 199, 202, 401
Alesina, Alberto, 176, 180, 211, 340, 392, 401, 402
Alexander, John B., 225, 230, 402
Alpay, Savas, 168, 402
Alvarez, A., 402, X-7.1
Anderson, Benedict, 402, X-7.1
Anderson, David A., 209, 218, 402
Anderson, James E., 122, 402
Anderton, Bob, 87, 95, 119, 122, 402
Andreas, Peter, 209, 222–4, 402, 411
Andreoni, James, 217, 402
Andrews, Edmund L., 307, 309, 407
Andropov, Yuri, X-1.3
Angel, J. K., 155, 402
Anheier, Helmut K., 425, X-11.1
Annan, Kofi, 138
Arrow, Kenneth, 424
Åslund, Anders, X-1.3
Atiyah, P. S., 402, X-11.1
Atkinson, Anthony B., 82, 83, 87, 94, 402, 418

Audretsch, David B., 239, 241–2, 244, 401, 403, 425, X-9.4
Auerbach, Alan, 31, 34, 46, 47, 403
Auerbach, James A., 403, 405, 410, 412, 426
Axelrod, Lee, 415
Baer, Douglas E., 391, 407
Baier, Scott, 119, 120, 403
Bailey, Joseph, 278, 284–5, 426
Baker, Dean, 46, 50, 337, 344, 403
Baker, Donald I., 283, 403
Balling, Robert C., 147, 155, 157, 403, 420
Banerjee, Abhijit, 403, X-4.3
Banuri, Tariq, 403, 409, 430
Barker, Kathleen, 401
Barnes, James H., Jr., 427
Barro, Robert, 403, X-4.3
Basañez, Miguel, 13, 415
Bauer, Gary, 197
Bayer, Amanda S., 222, 423
Behrens, William W., 420
Belk, Russell W., 193, 196, 411
Bell, Daniel, 5,6, 17, 19, 20, 192–3, 196, 209, 211, 363, 365, 403
Bellak, Christian, 406
Belous, Richard S., 403, 405, 410, 412, 426
Bénabou, Roland, 403, X-4.1
Benen, Steve, 197, 403
Bennett, William J., 178–9, 209, 403

* External Appendices can be viewed at my website: http://www.swarthmore.edu/socsci/ economics/fpryor1/. In addition, a compact disk with these appendices is also in the collection of the McCabe Library of Swarthmore College.

431

Benson, Richard Morin, 404
Berg, Andrew, 106, 108, 181, 183, 403, X-4.3
Bergstrand, Jeffrey H., 119, 120, 403
Berle, Adolf A., Jr., 312, 318, 403
Berndt, Ernst R., 245, 420
Bernheim, B. Douglas, 403
Bernstein, Jared, 90, 91, 92, 97. 209, 221, 403, 420
Bhagwati, Jagdish, 403, X-5.2
Bishop, John A., 403, X-4.1
Blakely, Edward J., 404, X-7.1
Blanchflower, David G., 416
Blank, Rebecca M., 103, 404, X-4.1
Blendon, John M., 215, 404
Blinder, Alan S., 404, X-4.1
Block, Fred, 356, 360, 404
Bloom, David E., 34, 404
Blough, Stephen, 404, X-4.1
Blumstein, Alfred, 209, 219, 404, 425, 426
Bock, Betty, 404, 408
Boden, Thomas A., 404, 416, 426
Bognanno, Michael L., 87, 88, 401
Bohr, Neils, 1
Bok, Derek., 192, 198, 404
Bolton, Patrick, 211, 404
Bookman, Milica Zarkovic, 211, 404
Bordo, Michael D., 65, 119, 125, 127, 375, 404, X-5.2
Bosworth, Barry, 27, 30, 46, 47, 404
Bourguinon, François, 415, 418
Bowles, Samuel, 106, 110, 404, X-4.1
Bowman, Karyln H., 192, 196, 199, 404
Boyd, Gavin, 405
Boyer, Joseph, 421
Boylaud, Olivier, 293, 421
Bracken, Paul, 225, 231, 404
Brady, Henry E., 209, 214, 429
Braudel, Fernand, 175, 404
Breen, Richard, 404, X-4.3
Bregger, John E., 404, X-7.3
Brenton, Paul, 87, 95, 402
Brewer, Thomas, 405
Breznev, Leonid, X-1.3
Bright, Chris, 156, 405
Brimelow, Peter, 133, 142, 405
Brock, Sydney, 175
Brooks, David, 199, 202-3, 405
Brooks-Gunn, Jeanne, 106, 107, 408
Brown, Charles, 259, 405

Brown, Eleanor, 405, X-7.1
Brown, Jeffrey, 278, 286, 405
Brown, Lester R., 157, 162, 363, 366, 405
Brown, William, 167, 415
Browne, Junius Henri, 291
Bryant, Ralph, 133, 134, 405
Bryne, John, 238, 286, 405
Brynjolfsson, Erik, 241, 245-6, 278, 285, 405, 426
Brzezinski, Zbigniew, 228, 405
Buchanan, Patrick J., 138, 405
Burrough, Bryan, 193
Burtless, Gary, 27, 30, 46, 47, 87, 90, 91, 93, 96, 404, 405, 416, X-4.1
Bush, George H. W., 274, 334
Bush, George W., 140, 195, 197, 214, 311, X-7.1
Calvin, William H., 156, 405
Camp, S. Michael, 199, 424
Campa, José, 175, 405
Campbell, John Y., 55, 57, 405, X-4.1
Cancian, Maria, 90, 91, 406
Cantwell, John, 113, 115, 406
Canzoneri, Matthew, 425
Card, David, 14, 406
Carlsson, Bo, 241, 244, 406
Carlton, Dennis W., 395, 406
Caroli, Eve, 401, X-4.3
Carroll, Christopher D., 372-3, 406
Carter, Jimmy, 303
Carter, Susan B., 406, X-7.2
Case, Anne, 189-90, 406
Catlin, Aaron, X-7.2
Cato the Elder, 19
Ceglowski, Janet, 119, 121, 122, 406
Chakrabati, Avik, 406, X-5.2
Cheney, Richard, 173
Cherneno, Konstatin, X-1.3
Christensen, Kathleen, 406
Christy, J. R., 155, 426
Cicero, Marcus Tullius, 19, 406
Citrin, Jack, 216, 406
Clark, Colin, 406, X-1.1
Cline, William R., 165, 169-70, 406
Clinton, William J., 274-5, 334, X-7.1
Clotfelter, Charles T., 406, X-4.1
Cochrane, John H., 406, X-4.1
Coder, John, 425
Cohany, Sharon R., 406, X-7.3

Cohen, Benjamin J., 65, 73, 407
Cole, H. S. D., 172, 407
Cole, Troy, 246
Coleman, William D., 407
Colimore, Edward, 192, 197, 407
Collins, Susan, 402, 407
Cooper, Richard N., 119, 127, 130, 407
Costa, Dora L., 176, 178, 407
Cowell, Alan, 307, 309, 407
Creveld, Martin van, 223, 225, 322, 407
Crockett, Andrew, 119, 125, 407
Crosson, Pierre, 147, 153, 407
Crowther, Samuel, 138, 407
Curtis, James E., 391, 407
Cutler, David M., 34, 42, 337, 346–7, 407
Daniels, Arlene Kaplan, 407, X-7.1
Danziger, Sheldon H., 83, 86, 97, 102, 407,
    409, 410, 412, 414, 416, X-4.1
Darmstadter, Joel, 165, 169, 407
Darnay, Arsen J.,147, 150, 288, 407
Davis, Steven J., 239, 241, 243, 407, 408
Dean, Jodi, 193, 198, 408
Dean, Judith M., 408, X-5.2
Delli-Carpini, Michael X., 209, 214, 408
DeLong, J. Bradford, 285, 408
Denton, Nancy A., 419, X-7.3
Derdak, Thomas, 408, X-9.3
Derlugian, Georgi, 209–10, 408
Devroye, Dan, 87, 96, 408
DeWind, Josh, 414
Diamond, Sara, 197, 408
Dionne, E. J. Jr., 209, 215, 408
Di Tella, Rafael, 340, 392, 402
Dixon, Huw., 221, 408
Dolan, Kerry, 408, X-5.2
Dollar, David, 408, X-5.3
Donahue, John J. III, 209, 220, 408
Doremus, Paul N., 113, 115, 408
Dosi, Giovanni, 241, 244, 408, 421
Drucker, Peter F., 238, 262, 265, 408, X-1.2
DuBoff, Richard B., 241–2, 408
Duflo, Esther, 403, X-4.3
Duncan, Greg J., 106, 107, 408
Dunn, Lucia F., 239, 408
Durham, William, 231, 408
Durlauf, Steven N., 97, 103, 409
Dymski, Gary A., 273, 409
Dyson, Freeman, 97, 104, 409
Easterly, William, 181, 183, 409

Ehrenberg, Ronald G., 133, 134, 409
Ehrenfeld, David, 409, X-1.2
Ehrlich, Paul R., 147–9, 154, 157, 164, 363,
    366, 409
Ehrlich, Thomas, 406, 430
Eichengreen, Barry, 65, 69, 404, 409, X-5.3
Eisenhower, Dwight D., 393
Eisner, Robert, 192, 409
Ellin, Nan, 181, 409, 410
Ellman, Michael, X-1.3
Ellwood, David T., 87, 94, 409
El-Swaify, S. A., 407
Engel, Charles, 119, 121, 409, 419
Engen, Eric M., 372–3, 409
Enoch, Charles, 409
Epstein, Gerald A., 55, 58, 409
Epstein, Richard A., 409
Erard, Brian, 217, 402
Erbring, Lutz, 421, X-7.1
Erdos, Richard, 26, 409
Esping-Andersen, Gøsta, 5, 12, 358, 409
Evans, Philip, 278, 280, 283–4, 409
Falk, Irving A., 17, 409
Fallick, Bruce C., 409, X-7.3
Federman, Maya, 97, 106, 107, 409
Feenstra, Robert C., 87, 95, 133, 141, 410
Fehr, Hans, 34, 410
Feige, Edgar L., 217, 221, 410, 423
Feinstein, Jonathan, 217, 402
Feldstein, Martin, 82, 87, 395, 410, 418
Feshbach, Murray, 150, 410
Fields, Jason, 190. 410
Flusty, Steven, 181, 410
Flynn, Michael, 408
Fogel, Robert William, 193–4, 410
Foote, Nelson N., 410, X-1.1
Forbes, Kristin J., 410, X-4.3
Forbes, Steve, 197
Ford, Gerald, 303
Forman, Jonathan Barry, 410, X-12.1
Formby, John P., 403, X-4.1
Fox, Alan, 209, 221, 410
France, Mike, 285, 410
Frängsmyr, Tore, 425
Frankel, Jeffrey A., 127, 410, X-5.3
Freeman, Christopher, 407
Freeman, Richard B., 13, 14, 87, 93, 96, 209,
    221, 358, 403, 406, 408, 410, 411 X-1.2
Frey, Bruno S., 222, 411

Friedheim, Cyrus, 247, 250, 276–7, 411
Friedman, Thomas L., 233, 411
Friendly, Albert, Jr., 150, 410
Friman, H. Richard, 209, 222, 411
Froomkin, A. Michael, 285, 408
Fuchs, Dieter, 176, 411
Fuchs, Victor R., 337, 411
Fukuyama, Francis, 256, 259, 361–3, 366, 411, X-1.2, X-7.1
Fuller, R. Buckminster, 112, 207
Furman, Jason, 106, 107, 411, X-4.3
Galambos, Louis, 312, 314, 411
Gale, William G., 30, 409, 411
Gallopin, Gilberto, 3, 4, 363, 367, 411
García-Peñalosa, Cecilia, 401, 404, X-4.3
Gardner, Gary, 157, 405
Gatti, James F., 304, 411
Ger, Güliz, 193, 196, 411
Gibrat, Robert, 243
Gilpin, Robert, 133, 135, 136, 411
Glaeser, Edward L., 191, 411
Gleick, Peter H., 231, 411
Godbey, Geoffrey, 176, 178–9, 199, 200, 424
Goel, Rajeene K., 233–4, 411
Goethe, Johann Wolfgang, 14, 411
Gokhale, Jagadeesh, 27, 30, 34, 373, 411, 412
Goklany, Indur, 147, 156, 412
Goldberg, Linda S., 375, 405
Goldman, Marshall, 150, 412
Goldschmid, Harvey J., 404
Golub, Stephen S., 127, 412
Gonzales, Elián, 142, 222
Goodman, Robert, 412, X-7.1
Goolsby, Austan, 278, 286, 405
Gorbachev, Mikhail, X-1.3
Gordon, David M., 106, 404, 412, X-1.1, X-4.1
Gordon, Robert J., 27, 28, 412
Gordon, T. J., 17, 412
Gore, Al, 195, 197, 214
Gottschalk, Peter, 82, 83, 86, 299, 407, 410, 412, 414, 416, X-4.1
Gough, Ian, 133, 422
Grabb, Edward G., 391, 407
Graham, Fred P., 218, 412
Graham, Hugh Davis, 412
Gramsci, Antonoio, 233–4, 412
Granger, Clive.W. J., 412, 419, X-4.1
Gray, John, 133, 136, 412
Green, Gordon, 425

Green, John C., 417
Green, John H., 409
Greenwood, Jeremy, 92, 412
Grilli, Enzo, 412, X-5.3
Grilli, Vittorio, 425
Grimmett, Richard F., 412
Groenewegen, John, 358, 412
Grogger, Jeff, 221, 412
Grossman, Gene, 410
Grubel, Herbert G., 377, 412
Gruber, Jonathan, 189–90, 413
Gunther, Gerald, 413, X-11.1
Gurbaxani, Vijay, 246, 405
Gurr, Ted Robert, 225, 228, 412, 413
Gwartney, James D., 302, 413
Gylfason, Thorvaldur, 312, 315, 413
Hafer, R. W., 413
Halal, William E., 3, 4, 276–7, 413
Hall, John A., 211, 413
Haltiwanger, John, 239, 241, 407, 408
Halweil, Brian, 157, 405
Hamilton, James, 259, 405
Hammermesh, Daniel S., 201–2, 413
Hammond, Allen, 363, 367, 411, 413
Hampden-Turner, Charles, 14, 413
Hansen, J., 154
Hansen, John, 323, 325, 413
Hanson, Gordon H., 87, 95, 377, 410, 413
Harff, Barbara Harff, 225, 228, 413
Harrigan, James, 122, 413
Harrington, Joseph E., Jr., 429
Harris, Ethan, 285
Harrison, Bennett, 259, 413
Harrison, Lawrence E., 199, 413
Hartz, Louis, 14, 413
Hashimoto, Ryutaro, 64
Hassett, Kevin, 46, 47, 403
Hatt, Paul K., 410, X-1.1
Havel, Václav, 212
Hay, Michael, 199, 424
Helliwell, John F., 413, X-7.1
Helmer, Olaf, 17, 412
Henrekson, M., 323, 419
Herbertsson, Tryggvi Thor, 413
Herring, Richard J., 119, 122, 413
Heston, Alan, 123, 426
Higgins, Matthew, 413, X-5.3
Hines, J.R., 307, 309, 413
Hipple, Steven F., 406, 414, X-7.3

Hirschman, Charles, 142, 413, 425
Hitler, Adolf, 308
Hobbes, Thomas, 8
Hobsbawm, Eric, 193, 414
Hodgkinson, Virginia, 414, X-7.1, X-7.2
Holdren, John, 164
Holland, David, 273, 414
Holmes, Kim R., 415
Homer-Dixon, Thomas F., 231, 414
Hopkins, Terrence, 408, 414
Hopkins, Thomas D., 302, 305, 414
Horrigan, Michael W., 93, 414
Hougland, James G., Jr., 239, 426
Houston, Ellen, 209, 221, 403
Howard, Amanda L., 278, 283–4, 424
Howard, Christopher, 414, X-12.1
Howell, David, 87, 93, 414
Huberman, Bernardo A., 278, 286, 401
Huebler, Friedrich, 87, 93, 414
Hummels, David, 377, 414
Humphrey, Hubert, 17
Huntington, Samuel P., 199, 225, 229, 413, 414
Hurd, Michael D., 414, 425
Huxley, Aldous, 191, 238, 414
Hyams, Edward, 146, 414, X-1.3
Hyclak, Thomas, 87, 93, 94, 414
Ijiri, Yuji, 241, 243, 250-1, 414, X-9.3
Ikeda, Satoshi, 266, 414
Indrapala, K., X-1.3
Inglehart, Ronald, 13, 176–7, 193, 195, 199, 202, 209, 216, 225–6, 389, 398, 415
Ingraham, Patricia W., 209, 215, 415
Inscoe, Don, 414
Irwin, Douglas A., 65, 404, 410, X-5.3
Ishii, Jun, 414
Jacobs, Eva E., 415, X-1.1, X-7.3
Jahoda, Marie, 407
James, Harold, 133, 138, 415
Jäntti, Markus, 97, 102, 415
Jargowsky, Paul A., 97, 103, 415, X-7.1
Jefferson, Philip N., 65, 73, 87, 415, X-4.1
Johansen, Søren, 415, X-4.1
Johnson, Bryan T., 415
Johnson, Gale, 419
Johnson, Nancy B., 239, 417
Jones, Charles I., 119, 129, 415
Jones, Daniel T., 27, 430
Jones, P.D., 154

Jorgenson, Dale, 27, 28, 368, 415
Joyce, Ted, 209, 220, 415
Kagan, Robert A., 293, 296, 415
Kahin, Brian, 405, 426
Kahn, Herman, 3, 4, 17, 19, 167, 363, 366, 415, 416
Kahn, Matthew, 176, 178, 407
Kambil, Ajit, 246, 405
Kant, Immanuel, 228, 416
Kaplan, Ann, X-7.2
Kaplan, Robert D., 119, 209–10, 231, 416
Kaplan, Steven N., 250, 416
Kappell, Jonathan, 209–10, 416
Karl, Thomas R., 147, 157, 389, 416
Karoly, Lynn, 87, 90, 91, 416, X-4.1
Kasinitz, Philip, 414
Katz, Lawrence F., 83, 87, 403, 411, 416
Kaufmann, Daniel, 188, 293, 416
Keefer, Phillip, 180, 181, 184, 417
Keeling, C. D., 153, 416
Keeter, Scott, 209, 214, 408, 417
Keller, William W., 408
Kennickell, Arthur B., 98, 416
Kettl, Donald F., 415
Keynes, John Maynard, 112, 113, 416
King, David C., 209, 416, 421, 422, X-7.1
Kirkpatrick, Melanie, 415
Kitshelt, Herbert, 416, 426
Kleeman, Rosslyn S., 209, 215, 418
Klingemann, Hans-Dieter, 176–7, 411, 416
Knack, Stephen, 180–1, 184, 417
Kohn, C. Harry, X-7.2
Kohut, Andrew, 158, 178, 193–4, 304, 417
Komninos, Nicholas, 246, 417
Kontorovich, Vladimir, X-1.3
Koretz, Gene, 285, 417
Kotlikoff, Laurence J., 27, 30, 39, 403, 410, 411, 412
Kraay, Aart, 293, 408, 416, X-5.1
Kraut, Robert, 417, X-7.1
Krugman, Paul, 58
Kull, Steven, 417, X-5.1
Kurth, James, 193–4, 225, 229, 417
Kuszczak, John, 133, 417
Kuta, William, 414
Laband, David N., 106, 110, 218, 417
Ladd, Everett Carl, 178, 209, 214, 216, 417, X-7.1
Lader, Wendy, 419

Ladurie, Emmanuel Le Roy, 156, 417
La Ferrara, Eliana, 176, 180, 401
Laibson, David, 411
Laird, Sam, 122, 417
Lamb, Hubert H., 156, 417
Lamberton, Donald M., 426
Landa, Janet Tai, 181, 417
Lang, James R., 239, 417
La Porta, Rafael, 113, 115, 181, 183–4, 417
Lasch, Christopher, 417, X-7.1
Lawrence Robert Z, 87, 96, 117, 405, 417
Lawson, Robert A., 302, 413
Lazich, Robert S., 269, 418
Lebergott, Stanley, 418, X-7.1, X-7.2
Lee, Ho Geun, 285, 418
Lee, Jong-Wha, 122, 418
Lee, Laura, 1, 26, 54, 112, 146, 175, 207, 291, 352, 418
Lee, Ronald, 27, 334, 46, 51, 147, 261, 323, 326, 337, 341–2, 346–7, 368, 418, 419
Lenz, Gabriel Salman, 181, 183, 418
Lerner, Abba, 71
Lettau, Martin, 405
Levine, Charles H., 209, 215, 418
Levine, Ross, 181, 183, 409
Levitt, Steven D., 209, 220, 408
Levy, Frank, 91, 418
Lichtenberg, Frank R., 250, 418
Liebman, Jeffrey, 105, 418
Lin, I-Fen, 406
Lincoln, Abraham, 140
Lindbeck, Assar, 337–9, 418
Lindert, Peter, 97, 106, 340, 418
Lindholm, Charles, 211, 413
Lipset, Seymour Martin, 14, 181, 183, 193, 196, 418
List, Friedrich, X-5.3
Litan, Robert E., 119, 122, 405, 413
Lloyd, P. J., 377, 412
Locke, John L., 418, X-7.1
Lopez-de-Silanes, Florencio, 417
Lovell, Michael C., 418, X-5.3
Lovelock, James, 418, X-1.2
Loveman, Gary W., 416
Lubbers, Rund, 184
Ludwig, Jens, 104, 418
Lum, Sherlene K. S., 381, 418
Lundberg, Mattias, 419, X-4.3, X-5.3
Lutz, Matthias, 419, X-5.3

Lybeck, J. A., 323, 419
Lyne, George E., 427
MacCulloch, Robert, 340, 392, 402
MacKinnon, James G., 419, X-4.1
Macrae, Norman, 130, 132, 238, 363, 366, 419
McCallum, John, 122, 419
McConnaughey, James W., 419
McConnell, Margaret, 65, 66, 419
McDaniel, Paul R., 427, X-12.1
McKenzie, Evan, 419, X-7.1
McKitrick, Ross, 155
McLanahan, Sara, 406
Mahoney, Richard J., 113, 114, 419
Makhija, Mona, 375, 419
Malkiel, Burton G., 55, 58, 419
Malone, Thomas W., 245–6, 405
Malthus, Thomas, 148
Mandelbaum, Michael, 225, 228–9, 419
Mann, Charles C., 157, 419
Mannusson, Paul, 234, 419
Manthy, Robert S., 385, 388, 419
Marland, C., 155, 419
Marshall, Alfred, 14, 71
Martel, Leon, 167, 167, 416
Marx, Karl, 54, 66, 89, 101, 241–3, 365, 392–3, 419, X-1.3
Mason, Andrew, 34, 418, 419
Massey, Douglas S., 102, 419, X-7.1
Masson, Paul R., 425
Masson, Robert T., 425
Mataloni, Raymond J., 114, 377, 413, 419
Mattera, Philip, 221, 419
Matthiasson, Bjorn, 398
Mauro, Paolo, 181, 183, 234, 419
Mayer, Martin, 65, 75, 419
Meadows, Dennis, 172, 363, 366, 420
Meadows, Donella H., 151, 170, 172, 363, 366, 420
Means, Gardiner C., 312, 318, 403
Meara, Ellen, 42, 337, 346–7, 407
Medoff, James, 259, 405
Mendelsohn, Robert, 165, 169, 420
Mesa-Lago, Carmelo, 207, 420
Mesarovic, Mihajlo, 172–3, 420
Meyer, Laurence H., 266, 272, 420
Michaels, Patrick J., 157, 420
Milanovic, Branko, 420, X-5.3
Miller, Timothy, 34, 418
Millstein, Ira M., 404

Millward, Robert, 312, 315, 420
Mincy, Ronald B., 93, 414
Minsky, Hyman P., 55, 420
Miringoff, Marque-Luisa, 176, 420
Miringoff, Marc, 176, 420
Mishel, Lawrence, 86, 90, 91, 92, 97, 420
Mishkin, Frederic S., 420, X-5.3
Molero, José, 406
Moreno, Alejandro, 13, 415
Morrison, Catherine J., 245, 420
Mueller, Eva, 323–4, 420
Mueller, Dennis, 250, 420
Murray, John D., 133, 417
Myers, David G., 193, 196, 420
Nardone, Thomas J., 406
Neftel, A., 155, 420
Negroponte, Nicholas, 420, X-7.1
Nelson, Michael A., 233–4, 411
Nelson, Ralph, X-7.2
Nelson, Richard R., 421, X-7.4
Neuman, Alfred E., 437
Newbold, Paul, 412, X-4.1
Newman, Jaime E., 165, 170, 420
Nickell, Stephen, 421, X-11.1
Nicoletti, Giuseppe, 293, 421
Nie, Nortman H., 421, X-7.1
Nietzsche, Friedrich, 194
Nivola, Pietro S., 415
Nixon, Richard M., 305
Nordhaus, William D,, 27, 28, 165, 169, 421
Norris, Pippa, 417
Norton, Bryon, 154, 421
Nostrodamos, Michel, 352
Novak, Michael, 195
Nyberg, Sten, 337–9, 418
Nye, Bill, 238
Nye, Joseph S., Jr., 209, 215, 421, 422
O'Brien, Timothy, 307, 309, 421
Obstfeld, Maurice, 119, 125, 127, 421
Ohmae, Ken'ichi, 209–10, 421
Oliner, Stephen, 27, 28, 368, 421
Olson, Mancur, 180–1, 184, 421
Olson, Walter K., 421, X-11.1
Orfield, Gary, 421, X-7.1
O'Rourke, Kevin, 133, 422
Orren, Gary, 193, 198, 422
Orwell, George, 238
Ostrower, Francie, 422, X-7.1
Paglin, Martin, 222, 422

Palan, Ronen, 307–8, 422
Paldam, Martin, 398, 422
Park, Donghyun, 422, X-5.3
Park, Thae S., 209, 216, 422
Parker, Jonathan A., 27, 30, 31, 422
Pauly, Louis W., 408
Pavitt, K. L. R., 407
Paxson, Christina, 34, 189, 406, 422
Peacock, Alan T., 227, 422
Pear, Robert, 307, 422
Peel, Michael, 307, 422
Pelkmans, Jacques, 402
Perkins, John A., 113, 118, 422
Perloff, Jeffrey M., 395, 406
Perot, H. Ross, 134, 135
Perron, Pierre, 405, X-4.1
Pestel, Eduard, 172–3, 420
Peter, Frances M., 429
Petersen, Melody, 262, 264, 426
Petty, William, 5, 6, X-1.1
Pfaller, Alfred, 133, 139, 422
Pinochet, Augusto, 10, 138, 207
Pithart, Petr, 209, 212, 422
Platteau, Jean-Philippe, 182, 422
Polanyi, Karl, 133, 141, 422
Polivka, Anne E., 406, 422, X-7.3
Pommerehne, Werner W., 222, 411
Popenoe, David, 190, 422, 423, X-7.1
Porter, Richard D., 222, 423
Poterba, James M., 34, 181, 183, 407, 423
Powderly, T. V. , 82
Prigogine, Ilya, 119, 124, 197, 423
Pritchett, Lant, 119, 124, 177–9, 423, X-5.3
Putnam, Robert D., 176–80, 188, 191, 209,
    213–4, 222, 361–2, 413, 424, X-7.1
Qualls, David, 425
Quandt, Richard E., 241, 243, 424
Quinn, Joseph F., 27, 33, 424
Quiros, Gabriel Perez, 65, 66, 419
Randers, Jørgen, 420
Raphael, Steven, 209, 221, 424
Raskin, Paul, 411
Raspail, Jean, 225, 230, 424
Ravenscraft, David J., 247, 249, 425
Reagan, Ronald, 274, 303, 306, 315, 324
Reddy, Marlita A., 288, 407
Reed, Deborah, 90, 91, 406
Reich, Robert, X-7.1
Reich, Simon, 408

Reynolds, Paul D., 199, 204, 424
Rhoades, Stephen A., 266, 272, 424
Rhodes, Martin, 133, 139, 424
Rice, E.M., 307, 309, 413
Riesman, David, 176–7, 424
Rifkin, Jeremy, 3, 4, 424
Robinson, John P., 176, 178–9, 199, 200, 424
Rodgers, William M., III, 209, 221, 411
Rodrik, Dani, 87, 95, 106, 107, 130, 132, 133, 137, 141, 184, 187, 402, 407, 424, X-4.3, X-5.3
Rogers, John H., 119, 121, 209, 221, 409
Roland, Gerard, 211, 404
Röller, Lars-Hendrik, 424, X-10.1
Romer, Christine D., 66, 424, X-5.3
Romer, David, 410
Roncaglia, Alessandro, 424, X-1.1
Rosen, Kenneth T., 278, 424
Rosenbloom, David H., 209, 215, 415
Rosenfeld, Richard, 209, 221, 425
Ruste, R. G., 26
Ryscavage, Paul, 90, 425
Sabelhouse, John, 27, 30, 404, 411
Sachs, Jeffrey, 34, 72, 106, 108, 181, 183, 403, 404, 425, X-4.3
Sadowski, Yahya, 225, 229, 425
Sakano, Ryoichi, 403, X-4.1
Sala-i-Martín, Xavier, 72, 425
Salamon, Lester M., 425, X-11.1
Samuelson, Robert J., 20, 425
Sassen, Saskia, 113, 114, 425
Scarpetta, Stefano, 293, 421
Schaffer, David, 65, 67, 87, 91, 92, 93, 96, 97, 100, 101, 110, 135, 202, 224, 375, 392, 423, X-4.1
Scheinkman, Jose A., 411
Scherer, F. M., 239, 241–3, 247, 249, 404, 425
Schieber, Sylvester J., 46, 425
Schiff, Maurice, 133, 142, 180, 425, X-7.1
Schiller, Nina Glick, 142, 425
Schlozman, Kay Lehman, 209, 214, 429
Schmidt, Christoph M., 234 , 425
Schmitt, John, 90, 91, 92, 97, 420
Schnaars, Steven P., 17, 18, 425
Scholes, Myron S., 238–9, 256, 260, 425
Schor, Juliet B., 55, 58, 179, 403, 409, 425, 430
Schuh, Stephen, 241, 408
Schumpeter, Joseph A., 193, 199, 241–2, 425

Schwert, G. William, 55, 57, 425
Scott, Alan, 425
Sefton, James, 412
Segal, Lewis M., 425, X-7.3
Sennett, Richard, 181, 184, 203, 425, X-7.1
Shapiro, Robert J., 405
Sheiner, Louise M., 34, 407
Shepard, Jon M., 239, 426
Shepherd, William G., 266, 269, 288, 427
Shleifer, Andrei, 417
Shoven, John B., 46, 403, 425
Sichel, Daniel E., 27, 28, 368, 421
Siebert, Horst, 83, 426, X-4.3
Simon, Herbert A., 241, 243, 250–1, 278, 284, 363, 366, 414, 426, X-7.3
Simon, Julian L., 147–9, 153, 166, 426
Singer, H. W., 419, X-5.3
Singer, S. Fred, 147, 155, 169, 426
Sivard, Ruth Leger, 225, 227, 426
Skinner, Jonathan, 337, 343, 346–7, 418
Slaughter, Matthew J., 87, 95, 377, 413, 417, 426
Smeeding, Timothy M., 83, 105, 106, 299, 412, 426
Smith, James P., 327, 426
Smith, Kristin, 190, 410
Smith, Michael D., 278, 285, 405, 426
Snyder, Mary Gail, 404, X-7.1
Sobol, Dorothy Meadow, 55, 64, 426
Sollenberg, Margareta, 225, 227, 429
Sommers, Dan, 27, 427
Sophocleus, John P., 106, 110, 218, 417
Sorkin, Andrew Ross, 262, 264, 426
Sorokin, Pitirim, 194
Soskice, David, 5, 11, 12, 426, X-1.2
Soutter, Christine L., 411
Spellman, William, 209, 220–1, 426
Spencer, R. W., 155, 426
Spolaore, Enrico, 211, 402
Squire, Lyn, 419, X-4.3, X-5.3
Starr-McCluer, Martha, 416
Stevens, William K., 156, 426
Stewart, Jay C., 406
Stiglitz, Joseph E., 106, 107, 411, X-4.3
Stiroh, Kevin J., 27, 28, 368, 415
Stock, James H., 426, X-4.1
Stockman, David A., 193, 426
Storey, D. J., 426, X-9.4
Strong, Maurice, 157, 165, 426

Strozier, Charles B., 408
Sulcove, Elliott, 55, 65, 66, 423
Sullivan, Daniel G., 425, X-7.3
Sullivan, Kathleen M., 413, X-11.1
Summers, Lawrence H., 34, 87, 94, 137, 407, 409, 426
Summers, Robert, 123, 426
Sunstein, Cass, 230, 225, 426, X-7.1
Surette, Brian J., 416
Surrey, Stanley S., 426, 427, X-12.1
Sutton, John, 241, 243, 427
Swagel, Phillip, 87, 96, 122, 418, 426
Swart, Rob, 411
Sykes, Alan O., 113, 427
Tanzi, Vito, 234, 427
Tashakori, Ahmad, 18, 427
Taylor, Kenneth B., 413
Thatcher, Margaret, 315, 358
Therborn, Göran, 133, 422
Thurow, Lester C., 288, 427
Tierney, John, 147, 427
Tilgher, Adriano, 199, 201, 427
Tito, Josef Broz, 229
Tobin, James, 27, 427
Tobin, Mitchell S., 401
Tocqueville, Alexis de, 14, 176–7, 391, 427
Toman, Michael A., 165, 169, 407
Toninelli, Pier Angelo, 313, 411, 420, 427
Toth, Robert C., 417
Trompenaars, Alfons, 14, 413
Tuljapurkar, Shripad, 27, 46, 51, 147, 323, 326, 337, 341–2. 363, 418
Turow, Joseph, 427, X-7.1
Uccello, Cori E., 409
Underhill, Geoffrey R. D., 407
Vandemia, Mark, X-7.2
VanderGood, Matthew R., 401
Varian, Hal, 278, 287, 429
Venti, Steven F., 30, 429
Verba, Sidney, 209, 214, 429
Vernon, John M., 429
Vinikov, K. Ya., 155
Viscusi, W. Kip, 395, 302, 304, 429
Vogel, David, 240, 429
Waddington, C. H., 261
Wade, Richard, 124, 429
Wagner, Adolf, 323, 337
Waldrop, Ross, 414
Wallensteen, Peter, 225, 227, 429

Wallerstein, Immanuel, 3, 408, 414, 429
Wallerstein, Judith S., 189, 191, 337, 344, 429, X-7.1
Wallman, Joel, 404, 425, 426
Walter, Dave, 17, 82, 238, 352, 429
Warren, Melinda, 303, 429
Watson, Mark W., 426, X-4.1
Watt, James, 158
Wattenberg, Ben, 97, 429
Weale, Sefton, 412
Weber, Max, 193, 195, 200, 429
Wei, Shang-Jin, 122, 429
Weibull, Jörgen W., 337–9, 418
Weinberg, Daniel H., 407, 409
Weisbrot, Mark, 46, 50, 337, 345, 403
Weisskoff, Thomas, 106, 404, X-4.1
Weitzman, Murray S., 414, X-7.1, X-7.2
Welniak, Edward, 425
Wey, Christian, 119, 424, X-10.1
Whalen, Gary W., 266, 273, 429
White, Michael J., 429, X-7.1
Whitehead, Barbara Dafoe, 423, X-7.1
Whitman, Christine Todd, 335
Whorf, T.P., 155, 416
Wiener, Anthony J., 17, 19, 416
Williamson, Jeffrey G., 133, 134, 413, 429, X-5.3
Williamson, Sandra, 375, 419
Wilson, Edward O.,154, 429
Wilson, James Q., 429, X-7.1
Wiman, Erastus, 322
Wincoop, Eric van, 122, 402
Winter-Ebmer, Rudolf, 209, 221, 424
Wise, David A., 30, 429
Wise, George, 17–8, 429
Wiseman, Jack, 227, 422
Wojcik, Daniel, 197, 430
Wolfe, Alan, 430, X-7.1
Wolff, Edward N., 98, 106, 109, 375, 430
Wolfson, Martin H., 55, 60, 374, 430
Womack, James P., 27, 430
Wood, Adrian, 87, 95, 430
Wurster, Thomas S., 278, 280, 283–4, 409
Wuthnow, Robert, X-7.1
Xu, Yexiao, 55, 58, 405, 419
Yang, Maw-Chen, 412, X-5.3
Yankelovich, Daniel, 195, 199, 203, 430
Yashiro, Naohiro, 414, 425
Yates, Alexander, 122, 417

Yeltsin, Boris, 207
Yi, Kei-Mu, 414
Yun, John T., 421, X-7.1
Yuskavage, Robert E., 381, 418
Zarnowitz, Victor., 54, 70, 430
Zeile, William J., 114, 430
Zelikow, Philip D., 209, 421, 422
Zevin, Robert, 119, 127, 430
Zimmermann, Klaus F., 239, 425
Zoega, Gylfi, 413
Zoido-Lobatón, Pablo, 293, 416

Subject Index*

Adversarial legalism, *see* regulation
American exceptionalism, 13, 357, 364,
    see also values
Anti-trust, *see* industrial concentration
Assets, 31
    of retirees, 327
    prices, 48, 51–2, 62, 65, 76
Australia, 12, 294, 314, 328, 357
Austria, 12, 294, 314, 328, 357, 358
Automatic stabilizers, *see* fiscal policy, gross
    domestic product, taxes
Banks, *see* finance
Bankruptcies, 61–2
Belgium, 12, 294, 314, 328, 357, 358
Business-to-business (B2B), *see* e-business
Business-to-consumer (B2C), *see* e-business
Canada, 12 , 14, 83, 294, 314, 328, 357
Capital flows, 29, 33, 125–8, 380, *see also*
    investment
    financial market integration, 126–7, 132
Capital gains, 31, 48
Capitalism, 7–16, *see also* economic system,
    welfare state
    definition, 7
    changes, 2,3, 8, 9
    Fascism, X-1.3
    finance capitalism, 318

    political dimension, 7, 8
    social dimension, 8
    types of capitalism, 8, 9, 13
    U. S. future, 352–67
Cartels, *see* industrial concentration
Charity, 179, X-7.2, *see also* nonprofit sector
Chile, 207
China, X-1.3
Class struggle, *see* revolution
Communications, 128–9, 379–81, *see also*
    information
    costs, 128–9
    volume, 128–9
Competition, 2, 355–6, 388–9, *see also*
    industrial concentration
    competitive dynamics, X-9.3
Complexity, 6, 16, 75
Consumption-replacement ratio, 35, 39–41,
    43–44, 371–2, *see also* population, saving
    definition, 35
    impact, 371
Cooperative sector, *see* nonprofit sector
Computers, 27, 28, *see also* information
    technology
Corruption, *see* crime
Crime, 185, 219, *see also* underground economy
    cheating on taxes, 216

---

*   References to external appendices are designated by an X, followed by the appendix number,
rather than the page number. The External Appendices can be viewed at my website:
http://www.swarthmore.edu/socsci/ economics/fpryor1/. In addition, a compact disk with these
appendices is also in the collection of the McCabe Library of Swarthmore College.

corruption, 183, 234
impact of social capital, 187
lawlessness, 185, 218–22
prisons, 219–21
Crises, *see* finance
Cultural trends, 192–215, *see also* values
impact, 199–205
Czechoslovakia, X-1.3
Demography, *see* population
Denmark, 12, 294, 314, 328, 357
Depression, *see* gross domestic product
Deregulation, see regulation
Diminishing returns, 148
Disconnected labor, 180, X-7.3
Earnings, *see* wages
e-business, 279–87, *see also* information
    technology
B2B (business-to-business), 280–2
B2C (business-to-consumer), 280–2
concentration, 282–6
impact on regulation, 307–8
impact on trade sector, 280–1
volume, 279–80
Economic growth, 22–29, 39, 40, 49–50,
    308–9, 352–3, *see also* gross domestic
    product, technical change
Economic oligarchy, *see* oligarchy
Economic system, 7–17, *see also* capitalism,
    nonprofit sector, underground economy
centralization, 163
collapse, 163, X-1.3
contrasted with economy, 2, 5
convergence, 358, X-1.2
definition, 2–3, 7
direction and forces of change, X-1.2, X-1.3
dysfunctions, 16, X-1.3
economic performance, 352–6
future, 363–7, X-1.2
policy traps, X-1.3
Economy, *see also* economic system
contrasted with economic system, 2, 5
performance, 12, 13, 352–56
Education, *see* public expenditures
Elderly-dependency ratio, 32, 39, X-2.1, *see
    also* population
definition, 32
Enterprises (firms), 238–260, *see also*
    establishments, industrial concentration,
    multinational enterprises, e-business
corporate form, 238–9, 256–9

establishments per enterprise, 246–7
Gibrat's law, 243
impact of globalism, 256
impact of information technology, 243–7,
    252, 257
impact of returns to scale, 241–3
impact of size, 239–44, 259–60
large enterprises, X-9.4
measuring size, 250–1
mergers, 247–50
new economy industries, 278–9, X-10.1
size, 252–4, X-9.1
strategic alliances, 276–8
Entrepreneurship, 203–4
Environment, 150–7, 168, 382–9
air pollution, 150–1, 384, 386
biodiversity, 154
floods and hurricanes, 156
global warming, 154–7, 164–5, 168–70,
    173–4, 388
impact on economic system, 146, X-1.3
impact of globalization, X-5.2
impact on political situation, 163
land degradation, 153–4
solid wastes, 153–4
water quality, 151–3, 384–6
water quantity, 152–3, 162, 387
Establishments (plants), 254–5, X-9.2, *see also*
    enterprises
Exchange rate, 62–4, 119–24, *see also* finance,
    foreign trade
rate regime, 71–2, 74
volatility, 56, 58–9
Exports, *see* foreign trade
Family, *see also* social capital
breakup of traditional family, 176, X-7.1
female-headed households, 88, 90–1, 101–2,
    X-4.1
illegitimate children, 176
impact of divorce or illegitimacy, 182,
    190–1
Finance, *see also* foreign exchange rate
banks, 60–1
crises, 55–65
data, 373–4
distress, 60–62
enterprise finance, 239, 257
finance capital, 318
financial fluctuations, 55–65
financial institutions, 60–1

financial leverage, 60–62
foreign investment, 64
fragility, 59–62
interest rates, 35. 40–42, 48–49, 51–2,
        55–65, 73–5, 382
international financial market, 125–8
markets, 74, 126–7
merger of financial institutions, 272–3
shocks, 62–65
stock prices, 48–9, 52
volatility, 55–56, 76
Finland, 12, 294, 314, 328, 357
Firms, *see* enterprises
Fiscal policy, 67–72, 77–8
    Automatic stabilizers, 76
    Effectiveness, 67–72
    Lags, 71
Foreign exchange rate, *see* exchange rate
Foreign trade, 119–24, 375–7, *see also*
        exchange rate, globalization
    by multinational enterprises, 114
    exports, 119
    export processing zone (EPZ), 309
    home bias, 121–2
    impact on competition, 265–6, 288
    impact on employment, 134–5
    impact on wages, 94–6, 134–5
    imports, 75–6, 119
    intra-industry and inter-industry trade, 120
    international market integration, 121–3
    marginal propensity to import, 69–70
    outsourcing, 120
    protectionist sentiments, 135–7, X-5.1
    services, 119
    shocks, 62–3, 75–6
    volume, 119–24, 375–7
France, 12, 83, 294, 314, 328, 357, 358
Germany, 12, 83, 51, 294, 314, 328, 357, 358,
        X-1.3
Gibrat's law, *see* enterprise
Global warming, *see* environment
Globalization, 80, 112–44, 354, 375–82, *see*
        also foreign trade
    backlash against, 80, 133–42, X-5.2
    definition, 112
    hidden, 117–9
    impact on competition, 265–6, 288
    impact on enterprise size, 356
    impact on environment, X-5.2
    impact on fiscal policy, 69–70

impact on GDP fluctuations, 75–6, X-5.2
impact on GDP growth, X-5.2
impact on governmental microeconomic
        policies, 131–3
impact on income distribution, X-5.2
impact on monetary policy, 73–4
impact on personal insecurity, 141
institutional/organizational aspects, 113–9
multinational corporations, 114–6
objections against, X-5.2
quantitative indicators, 119–130
standardization, 117–8
Government, *see also* fiscal policy, monetary
        policy, public expenditures, political
        forces, regulation, saving, taxes
    centrifugal forces, 210–11
    determinants of economic interventions,
        227–32
    effectiveness, 67–72, 359–60, X-7.4
    functions, 223–5, 310, 357–60
    ideologies about role, 226
    internal security, 223–4
    intervention into the economy, 11, 12, 16,
        225–33
    investment, 399–400
    monopoly of force, 224–5
    ownership, 312–19, 373, 396–7
    relation to social capital, 211–3
    relation to social trust, 211–3
    sovereignty, 137–41
    strength, 204–22, 307–12
    treaties, 117
Greece, 294, 314, 328, 357, 358
Greenland, 398–400, X-1.3
Gross domestic product (GDP), *see also*
        economic growth, home production,
        technical change
    automatic stabilizers, 76
    fluctuations and volatility, 54–81, 65–77,
        353, X-5.2
    growth, X-5.2
    performance, 66–71
    Petty's law, 5, 6, X-1.1
    recession or depression, 48, 66–66, 79, 208
    shocks, 75–7, 78–9
    structural change, X-1.1
Health expenditures, 345–9, *see also* public
        expenditures, welfare state
    impact of age structure, 346–7
    private, 348–9

public, 348–9
Heckscher-Ohlin theorem, 95
Hong Kong, 309
Home production, 22, 191–2
Iceland, 398–400
Immigration, 124–5, 134–5, 141, 377–9
    impact on social capital, 142, 180, X-7.1
Import, *see* foreign trade
Income distribution, 82–111, 353–4, *see*
        also wages
    data for U.S., 83–7, 375
    determinants or causes, 87–106
    future income inequality, 97–106
    impact of female labor force participation,
    impact of foreign trade, 94–6
    impact of raw material prices, 107,
    impact of wages of females, 91–2
    impact of welfare system, 94
    impact on economic policy, 52, 107–9
    impact on economic system, 109–11
    impact on economic variables, 186–9
    impact on government sector, 189
    impact on health, 106
    impact on industrial concentration, 100
    impact on political variables, 186–9
    impact on social variables, 186–9
    income extremes, 83–6, X-4.1
    income mobility, 86–7
    income shares, 161, X-4.2
    inheritance tax, 99
    international, 82–3
    of retirees, 327
    poverty, 102–3, 106–7
    poverty trap, 102–4
    regressions of determinants, X-4.1
    relation to economic growth, 107–9, X-4.3
    relation to government efficiency, 108–9
Industrial concentration, 261–90, *see also*
        competition, e-business
    anti-trust, 274–6
    impact of foreign trade, 265–6
    competition, 288–9, X-9.3
    concentration ratios, 266–9, X10.2
    impact of e-business, 279–87
    impact of mergers, 262–5
    new economy industries, 278–9
    particular industries, 269–76
    strategic alliances, 276–8
    trends in U.S., 266–8
Information technology, *see also*

communications, enterprise
    impact on enterprise size, 243–7, 252, 257
    volume of communications, 128–30
Institution, definition of, 7
Interest rate, *see* finance
Internal security, *see* crime, government,
        public expenditures
International organizations, 113–9, *see also*
        globalization, multinational enterprises
Internet, *see* e-business
Ireland, 83, 294, 314, 328, 357
Italy, 12, 83, 294, 314, 328, 357
Investment, 29, 30–53, 399–400, *see also*
        capital flows, finance, interest rate
Iraq, 231
Japan, 83, 294, 314, 328, 357
    yen/dollar exchange rate, 59
Korea, South, 18
L-T (Lee-Tuljapurkar) population estimates,
        see population
Labor force, *see also* migration, retirement,
unemployment, wages
    absenteeism, 201
    distribution, X-1.1
    female participation, 88, X-4.1
Labor unions, 93
Lawlessness, *see* crime
Lean production, 21
Lebanon, 309
Liberia, 308–9
Life expectancy, *see* population
Macroeconomic policies, *see* automatic
        stabilizer, fiscal policy, gross domestic
        product, monetary policy
Manufacturing, 21, 267, 269–71
Markets, *see also* competition, finance,
        industrial concentration, regulation
    capital, 126–7
    goods and services, 112–9, 121–4
    impact of e-business, 287–90
    labor, 124–5, 134–7
Medical expenditures, 45, 345–90, *see also*
        Social Security
Medicare, *see* Social Security
Mergers, *see* enterprise
Migration, *see* immigration
Millennium survey, 26, 54, 82, 106, 112–3,
        165, 168, 290
Money, 73, *see also* finance, monetary policy
Monetary policy, 60, 72–5, 78, *see also*

finance, fiscal policy
    effectiveness, 72–5
    impact of complexity, 75
Multinational enterprise (MNE), 114–6
Multiplier, Keynesian, 68
Natural resources, *see also* scarcity
    price, 149–50, 158–62, 166–8, 171–3
    reserves, 166–7
Netherlands, 12, 294, 314, 328, 357
New economy, 26, 27–29, 278–9
    new economy industries, 27–29, 278–9,
        X-10.1
New Zealand, 12, 294, 314, 328, 357
Nonprofit and cooperative sector, 22
    assets, X-11.1
    international connections, 116
Norway, 12, 83, 294, 314, 328, 357, 358
OECD (Organization of Economic
        Cooperation and Development), *see
        also* individual countries
    income distribution, 83
    determinants of economic variables, 186–7
    determinants of political variables, 186–7
    determinants of social variables, 186–7
    government sector, 12, 357
    ownership, 314
    public expenditures, 328
    regulation, 294
Occupational structure, X-1.1, *see also* labor
        force
Oligarchy, 9, 233–5
    Fascism, X-1.3
    rotating, authoritarian, interventionalist
        economy, 9, 10
    tyranny, 391–2,
Organization, definition of, 7
Ownership
    private, 313–6, 343, 396, X-11.1
    public, 313–6, 343, 396–7, X-11.1
Panama, 308–9
Pensions, 52, 327, 342–5, *see also* Social
        Security
Perestroika, X-1.3
Petty's law, *see* gross domestic product
Plants, see establishments
Police, *see* crime, government, political forces
Political forces, *see also* government, war
    attitudes or ideology, 226, 324–5, 360
    centrifugal forces, 210–11
    centripetal forces, 163

dimensions in economy, 7, 8
functions of state, 223–5
internal security, 110, 223–5
impact of social class, 214
knowledge of political issues, 213–4
participation, 212
political dimension of capitalism, 8, 356–61
trust in government, 213, 215–6
Pollution, see environment
Population, 147, X-2.1, X-2.2 *see also*
        consumption-replacement ratio,
        elderly-dependency ratio, retirement
        ratio, simulation model
    age structure, 32, 33
    family size, 45
    forecasts, 32, 40, X-2.1
    growth, 39
    level, 32
    life expectancy, 33
Portugal, 294, 314, 328, 357
Prediction, 17–21
Prices and price changes, *see also* natural
        resources, scarcity
    food, 83–4, 148–9, 162–3, 165–6, 171,
        383–4
    impact on consumption, 158–61
    impact on GDP aggregates, 160–1, X-6.1
    metals, 147–8
    natural resources, 147–50, 385
    political response, 162–3
Prisons, *see* crime
Production, *see* gross national product,
        technical change
Profits, 88, *see also* income distribution
Protectionism, 135–7, X-5.1, X-5.2,
Protestant ethic, *see* values
Public expenditures, 80, 322–51, X-12.1, *see
        also* government, health expenditures,
        pensions, Social Security
    determinants, 323–4, 329–30
    education, 341–2
    fiscal federalism, 335–6
    health, 345–9
    internal security expenditures, 110, 340–2
    inter-governmental expenditures, 335–6,
        X-12.1
    international comparisons, 326–30
    investment, 399
    Medicaid, 86
    off-budget expenditures, 335, X-12.1

pension expenditures, 342–45
public opinion, 324–5
social assistance, 338–40
tax expenditures, 331, 333-4, X-12.2
transfers, 86, 91, 94, 105, 109–10, X-4.1
trends in U.S., 330–7
welfare state, 11, 12, 94
Raw materials, *see* natural resources
Recession, *see* gross national product
Regulation, 80–1, 291–312, 393–5, *see also*
     government
   adversarial legalism, 297
   cost, 303
   deregulation, 303–4, 393–5
   determinants, 297–9
   general economic regulations, 292
   impact of e-business, 307–8
   impact on economy, 297
   international comparisons, 293–301
   industry-specific regulations, 292
   laws, 393–5
   legal-framework regulations, 292
   measurement, 293, 300–5
   off-shore havens, 308
   trends, 302–7, 393–5
Religion, role in economy, 158, 178, 193–4, 304
Rent seeking, 233
Retirement, 33 *see also* saving
   age, 33, 34, 39–41, 342–3
   retirement-ratio definition, 33
Revolution, 88–90, 208
   class struggle, 88–90, 392–3
Russia, 8, X-1.3, *see also* Soviet Union
Saving, 29, 30–53, 200, 207, 369–70, X-2.2,
     see also investment, simulation
     model
   aggregate, 46–47
   bequest motive, 36, 46
   business, 29, 30, 47
   definition, 30
   demographic influence, 34–42
   family size impact, 45
   forced saving, 44, 47
   governmental, 29, 47
   lifetime income approach, 35, 43
   impact of interest rate, 371–2
   impact of consumption-replacement ratio,
     372–3
   marginal propensity to save, 69

personal, 29, 30–53
   precautionary motive, 30–1, 46
   rationality, 35–6, 42–4
Scarcity, 158–64, *see also* prices
   foodstuffs, 165–6, 148–9, 171
   natural resources, 149–50, 166–8, 172–3
   water, 162
Scenario analysis, 4
Services, 5, 6, 119, X-1.1
Simulation model, 34–42, 368–73, X-2.2, *see
     also* saving
   mathematical properties, X-2.2
Singapore, 309
Social assistance, see public expenditures
Social capital, 177–9, 361–3, X-7.1. *see also*
     crime, family, social cleavages, income
     inequality, social trust, values
   definition, 177
   impact of foreign trade,
   impact of migration, 162, 180
   impact on economic performance, 188–90
   impact on governmental effectiveness, 182–4
   impact on markets, 181
   impacts on various economic, political,
     social variables, 185–9
   self reliance, 117
Social cleavages, *see* social trust
Social dimension of capitalism, 8, 361–3
Social indicators, 389–90
Social market economy, 9, 10
Social Security, 37, 44, 47, 51, 198, 342–5, *see
     also* welfare state
   health expenditures, 45
   Medicare, 45
Social solidarity, 8, *see also* social capital,
     social trust
Social tensions, *see* crime, social capital
Social trends, 89–91, 176–81, X-7.1
Social trust, 180–1, 361–3, *see also* social
     capital, social cleaves
   impact on economic performance, 188–90
   impact on government effectiveness, 182–4
   impact on globalization, 141–2
   impact on economic, political, social
     variables, 184–92
Socialism, 9, 10
Sovereignty, 137–41, *see also* government
Soviet Union, 150, X-1.3
Spain, 294, 314, 328, 357

Standardization, 117–8
State, *see* government, political forces
State enterprises, *see* government ownership
Stock prices, 56–8, 60, 65
Stolper-Samuelson theorem, 95
Strategic Partnership, *see* industrial
    concerntration, cartel
Supra-enterprise coordination, 11, 12, 276–7
Sweden, 12, 139, 294, 314, 328, 357, 358
Switzerland, 12, 13, 294, 314, 328, 357, 358
Taiwan, 18
Tariffs, *see* foreign trade
Taxes, *see also* foreign trade
    attitudes, 217
    cheating on taxes, 216
    public opinion, 324–5
    tax havens, 308–10
Tax expenditures, X-12.2
Technical change, 27, 49–50, 96–7, *see also*
    economic growth
    agriculture, 157
    productivity, 27–8, 165–6
Time budgets, 178–9
Tobin's q, 31
Transfers, *see* public expenditures
Transportation, costs, 121–2
Trust, *see* political forces, social trust
Tyranny, *see* oligarchy
Underground economy, 22, 218, 221–2, *see*
    also crime
United Kingdom (U.K.), 12, 13, 16, 83, 294,
    314, 328, 357, 358
United Nations, 116
Unemployment, 66–7, 92–3, 100–1, X-4.1
Values, 193–9, *see also* American
    exceptionalism, taxes
    entrepreneurship, 203–4
    hedonism, 199–200
    post-materialist values, 195–6
    Protestant ethic, 13, 200
    revolt against rationalism, 196–8
    work ethic, 193–4, 200–3
Volunteering, *see* charity
Wages, 92–7
    female, 91–2
    impact of cognitive skills, 66
    impact of foreign trade, 94–6
    impact of labor unions, 93
    impact of migration, 234–5
    impact of new information technology, 96

    impact of minimum wage, 91–1, 105
    impact of skill-biased technical change,
      96–7
    industrial norms, 94
    minimum wage. 105
War, 227–37
    allies, 232
    clash of civilizations, 229–30
    ethnic wars, 228
    general influences, 208
    influence of foreign trade, 208
Water, *see* environment
Wealth, 98–9, *see also* assets
    inheritance tax, 99
    of retirees, 327, 326–7
Welfare state, 11, 12, 338–9, 364, 398–400,
    see also public expenditures, Social
    Security
Work ethic, *see* values